GENERAL MOTORS | S10/S15/SONOMA/PICK-UPS
1982-93 REPAIR MANUAL

CHILTON'S

Covers all U.S. and Canadian models of Chevrolet S10 and GMC S15, Sonoma and Syclone Pick-Ups; 2 and 4 wheel, drive

by Kevin M. G. Maher, A.S.E.

CHILTON *Automotive Books*

PUBLISHED BY **HAYNES NORTH AMERICA, Inc.**

Manufactured in USA
© 1996 Haynes North America, Inc.
ISBN 0-8019-8844-6
Library of Congress Catalog Card No. 96-84546
8901234567 9876543210

Haynes Publishing Group
Sparkford Nr Yeovil
Somerset BA22 7JJ England

Haynes North America, Inc
861 Lawrence Drive
Newbury Park
California 91320 USA

ABCDE
FGHIJ
KLMNO
PQR 2

7E1

Contents

Contents

SAFETY NOTICE

Proper service and repair procedures are vital to the safe, reliable operation of all motor vehicles, as well as the personal safety of those performing repairs. This manual outlines procedures for servicing and repairing vehicles using safe, effective methods. The procedures contain many NOTES, CAUTIONS and WARNINGS which should be followed, along with standard procedures to eliminate the possibility of personal injury or improper service which could damage the vehicle or compromise its safety.

It is important to note that repair procedures and techniques, tools and parts for servicing motor vehicles, as well as the skill and experience of the individual performing the work vary widely. It is not possible to anticipate all of the conceivable ways or conditions under which vehicles may be serviced, or to provide cautions as to all possible hazards that may result. Standard and accepted safety precautions and equipment should be used when handling toxic or flammable fluids, and safety goggles or other protection should be used during cutting, grinding, chiseling, prying, or any other process that can cause material removal or projectiles.

Some procedures require the use of tools specially designed for a specific purpose. Before substituting another tool or procedure, you must be completely satisfied that neither your personal safety, nor the performance of the vehicle will be endangered.

Although information in this manual is based on industry sources and is complete as possible at the time of publication, the possibility exists that some car manufacturers made later changes which could not be included here. While striving for total accuracy, the authors or publishers cannot assume responsibility for any errors, changes or omissions that may occur in the compilation of this data.

PART NUMBERS

Part numbers listed in this reference are not recommendations by Haynes North America, Inc. for any product brand name. They are references that can be used with interchange manuals and aftermarket supplier catalogs to locate each brand supplier's discrete part number.

SPECIAL TOOLS

Special tools are recommended by the vehicle manufacturer to perform their specific job. Use has been kept to a minimum, but where absolutely necessary, they are referred to in the text by the part number of the tool manufacturer. These tools can be purchased, under the appropriate part number, from your local dealer or regional distributor, or an equivalent tool can be purchased locally from a tool supplier or parts outlet. Before substituting any tool for the one recommended, read the SAFETY NOTICE at the top of this page.

ACKNOWLEDGMENTS

Portions of materials contained herein have been reprinted with the permission of General Motors Corporation, Service Technology Group.

1

GENERAL INFORMATION AND MAINTENANCE

HOW TO USE THIS BOOK

Chilton's Total Car Care Manual for Chevrolet S-10/S-15 Pick-Ups is intended to help you learn more about the inner workings of your truck and save you money on its upkeep and operation.

The beginning of the book will likely be referred to the most, since that is where you will find information for maintenance and tune-up. The other sections deal with the more complex systems of your vehicle. Systems (from engine through brakes) are covered to the extent that the average do-it-yourselfer can attempt. This book will not explain such things as rebuilding a differential because the expertise required and the special tools necessary make this uneconomical. It will, however, give you detailed instructions to help you change your own brake pads and shoes, replace spark plugs, and perform many more jobs that can save you money and help avoid expensive problems.

A secondary purpose of this book is a reference for owners who want to understand their vehicle and/or their mechanics better.

Where to Begin

Before removing any bolts, read through the entire procedure. This will give you the overall view of what tools and supplies will be required. So read ahead and plan ahead. Each operation should be approached logically and all procedures thoroughly understood before attempting any work.

If repair of a component is not considered practical, we tell you how to remove the part and then how to install the new or rebuilt replacement. In this way, you at least save labor costs.

Avoiding Trouble

Many procedures in this book require you to "label and disconnect . . . " a group of lines, hoses or wires. Don't be think you can remember where everything goes—you won't. If you hook up vacuum or fuel lines incorrectly, the vehicle may run poorly, if at all. If you hook up electrical wiring incorrectly, you may instantly learn a very expensive lesson.

You don't need to know the proper name for each hose or line. A piece of masking tape on the hose and a piece on its fitting will allow you to assign your own label. As long as you remember your own code, the lines can be reconnected by matching your tags. Remember that tape will dissolve in gasoline or solvents; if a part is to be washed or cleaned, use another method of identification. A permanent felt-tipped marker or a metal scribe can be very handy for marking metal parts. Remove any tape or paper labels after assembly.

Maintenance or Repair?

Maintenance includes routine inspections, adjustments, and replacement of parts which show signs of normal wear. Maintenance compensates for wear or deterioration. Repair implies that something has broken or is not working. A need for a repair is often caused by lack of maintenance. for example: draining and refilling automatic transmission fluid is maintenance recommended at specific intervals. Failure to do this can shorten the life of the transmission/transaxle, requiring very expensive repairs. While no maintenance program can prevent items from eventually breaking or wearing out, a general rule is true: MAINTENANCE IS CHEAPER THAN REPAIR.

Two basic mechanic's rules should be mentioned here. First, whenever the left side of the vehicle or engine is referred to, it means the driver's side. Conversely, the right side of the vehicle means the passenger's side. Second, screws and bolts are removed by turning counterclockwise, and tightened by turning clockwise unless specifically noted.

Safety is always the most important rule. Constantly be aware of the dangers involved in working on an automobile and take the proper precautions. Please refer to the information in this section regarding SERVICING YOUR VEHICLE SAFELY and the SAFETY NOTICE on the acknowledgment page.

Avoiding the Most Common Mistakes

Pay attention to the instructions provided. There are 3 common mistakes in mechanical work:

1. Incorrect order of assembly, disassembly or adjustment. When taking something apart or putting it together, performing steps in the wrong order usually just costs you extra time; however, it CAN break something. Read the entire procedure before beginning. Perform everything in the order in which the instructions say you should, even if you can't see a reason for it. When you're taking apart something that is very intricate, you might want to draw a picture of how it looks when assembled in order to make sure you get everything back in its proper position. When making adjustments, perform them in the proper order. One adjustment possibly will affect another.

2. Overtorquing (or undertorquing). While it is more common for overtorquing to cause damage, undertorquing may allow a fastener to vibrate loose causing serious damage. Especially when dealing with aluminum parts, pay attention to torque specifications and utilize a torque wrench in assembly. If a torque figure is not available, remember that if you are using the right tool to perform the job, you will probably not have to strain yourself to get a fastener tight enough. The pitch of most threads is so slight that the tension you put on the wrench will be multiplied many times in actual force on what you are tightening.

There are many commercial products available for ensuring that fasteners won't come loose, even if they are not torqued just right (a very common brand is Loctite®). If you're worried about getting something together tight enough to hold, but loose enough to avoid mechanical damage during assembly, one of these products might offer substantial insurance. Before choosing a threadlocking compound, read the label on the package and make sure the product is compatible with the materials, fluids, etc. involved.

3. Crossthreading. This occurs when a part such as a bolt is screwed into a nut or casting at the wrong angle and forced. Crossthreading is more likely to occur if access is difficult. It helps to clean and lubricate fasteners, then to start threading the bolt, spark plug, etc. with your fingers. If you encounter resistance, unscrew the part and start over again at a different angle until it can be inserted and turned several times without much effort. Keep in mind that many parts have tapered threads, so that gentle turning will automatically bring the part you're threading to the proper angle. Don't put a wrench on the part until it's been tightened a couple of turns by hand. If you suddenly encounter resistance, and the part has not seated fully, don't force it. Pull it back out to make sure it's clean and threading properly.

Be sure to take your time and be patient, and always plan ahead. Allow yourself ample time to perform repairs and maintenance.

TOOLS AND EQUIPMENT

▶ **See Figures 1 thru 15**

Without the proper tools and equipment it is impossible to properly service your vehicle. It would be virtually impossible to catalog every tool that you would need to perform all of the operations in this book. It would be unwise for the amateur to rush out and buy an expensive set of tools on the theory that he/she may need one or more of them at some time.

The best approach is to proceed slowly, gathering a good quality set of those tools that are used most frequently. Don't be misled by the low cost of bargain tools. It is far better to spend a little more for better quality. Forged wrenches, 6 or 12-point sockets and fine tooth ratchets are by far preferable to their less expensive counterparts. As any good mechanic can tell you, there are few worse experiences than trying to work on a vehicle with bad tools. Your monetary savings will be far outweighed by frustration and mangled knuckles.

Begin accumulating those tools that are used most frequently: those associated with routine maintenance and tune-up. In addition to the normal assortment of screwdrivers and pliers, you should have the following tools:

• Wrenches/sockets and combination open end/box end wrenches in sizes 1/8–3/4 in. and/or 3mm–19mm 13/16 in. or 5/8 in. spark plug socket (depending on plug type).

➡**If possible, buy various length socket drive extensions. Universal-joint and wobble extensions can be extremely useful, but be careful when using them, as they can change the amount of torque applied to the socket.**

• Jackstands for support.
• Oil filter wrench.
• Spout or funnel for pouring fluids.

• Grease gun for chassis lubrication (unless your vehicle is not equipped with any grease fittings)

• Hydrometer for checking the battery (unless equipped with a sealed, maintenance-free battery).

• A container for draining oil and other fluids.

• Rags for wiping up the inevitable mess.

In addition to the above items there are several others that are not absolutely necessary, but handy to have around. These include an equivalent oil absorbent gravel, like cat litter, and the usual supply of lubricants, antifreeze and fluids. This is a basic list for routine maintenance, but only your personal needs and desire can accurately determine your list of tools.

After performing a few projects on the vehicle, you'll be amazed at the other tools and non-tools on your workbench. Some useful household items are: a large turkey baster or siphon, empty coffee cans and ice trays (to store parts), a ball of twine, electrical tape for wiring, small rolls of colored tape for tagging lines or hoses, markers and pens, a note pad, golf tees (for plugging vacuum lines), metal coat hangers or a roll of mechanic's wire (to hold things out of the way), dental pick or similar long, pointed probe, a strong magnet, and a small mirror (to see into recesses and under manifolds).

A more advanced set of tools, suitable for tune-up work, can be drawn up easily. While the tools are slightly more sophisticated, they need not be outrageously expensive. There are several inexpensive tach/dwell meters on the market that are every bit as good for the average mechanic as a professional model. Just be sure that it goes to a least 1200–1500 rpm on the tach scale and that it works on 4, 6 and 8-cylinder engines. The key to these purchases is to make them with an eye towards adaptability and wide range. A basic list of tune-up tools could include:

• Tach/dwell meter.

• Spark plug wrench and gapping tool.

• Feeler gauges for valve adjustment.

• Timing light.

The choice of a timing light should be made carefully. A light which works on the DC current supplied by the vehicle's battery is the best choice; it should have a xenon tube for brightness. On any vehicle with an electronic ignition sys-

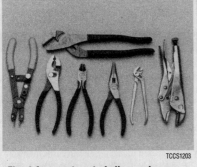

Fig. 1 All but the most basic procedures will require an assortment of ratchets and sockets

Fig. 2 In addition to ratchets, a good set of wrenches and hex keys will be necessary

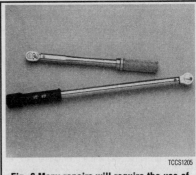

Fig. 3 A hydraulic floor jack and a set of jackstands are essential for lifting and supporting the vehicle

Fig. 4 An assortment of pliers, grippers and cutters will be handy for old rusted parts and stripped bolt heads

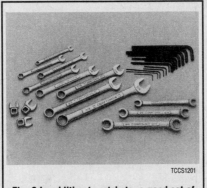

Fig. 5 Various drivers, chisels and prybars are great tools to have in your toolbox

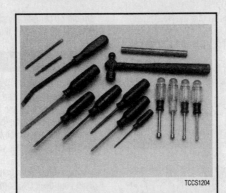

Fig. 6 Many repairs will require the use of a torque wrench to assure the components are properly fastened

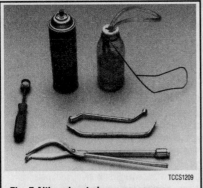

Fig. 7 Although not always necessary, using specialized brake tools will save time

Fig. 8 A few inexpensive lubrication tools will make maintenance easier

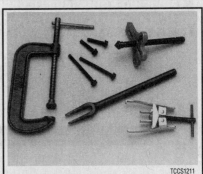

Fig. 9 Various pullers, clamps and separator tools are needed for many larger, more complicated repairs

Fig. 10 A variety of tools and gauges should be used for spark plug gapping and installation

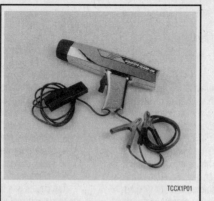

Fig. 11 Inductive type timing light

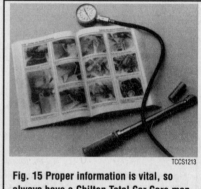

Fig. 12 A screw-in type compression gauge is recommended for compression testing

Fig. 13 A vacuum/pressure tester is necessary for many testing procedures

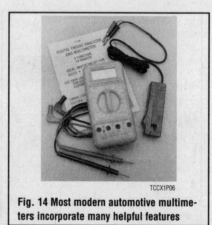

Fig. 14 Most modern automotive multimeters incorporate many helpful features

Fig. 15 Proper information is vital, so always have a Chilton Total Car Care manual handy

tem, a timing light with an inductive pickup that clamps around the No. 1 spark plug cable is preferred.

In addition to these basic tools, there are several other tools and gauges you may find useful. These include:

• Compression gauge. The screw-in type is slower to use, but eliminates the possibility of a faulty reading due to escaping pressure.
• Manifold vacuum gauge.
• 12V test light.
• A combination volt/ohmmeter
• Induction Ammeter. This is used for determining whether or not there is current in a wire. These are handy for use if a wire is broken somewhere in a wiring harness.

As a final note, you will probably find a torque wrench necessary for all but the most basic work. The beam type models are perfectly adequate, although the newer click types (breakaway) are easier to use. The click type torque wrenches tend to be more expensive. Also keep in mind that all types of torque wrenches should be periodically checked and/or recalibrated. You will have to decide for yourself which better fits your pocketbook, and purpose.

Special Tools

Normally, the use of special factory tools is avoided for repair procedures, since these are not readily available for the do-it-yourself mechanic. When it is possible to perform the job with more commonly available tools, it will be pointed out, but occasionally, a special tool was designed to perform a specific function and should be used. Before substituting another tool, you should be convinced that neither your safety nor the performance of the vehicle will be compromised.

Special tools can usually be purchased from an automotive parts store or from your dealer. In some cases special tools may be available directly from the tool manufacturer.

SERVICING YOUR VEHICLE SAFELY

▶ **See Figures 16, 17 and 18**

It is virtually impossible to anticipate all of the hazards involved with automotive maintenance and service, but care and common sense will prevent most accidents.

The rules of safety for mechanics range from "don't smoke around gasoline," to "use the proper tool(s) for the job." The trick to avoiding injuries is to develop safe work habits and to take every possible precaution.

Do's

• Do keep a fire extinguisher and first aid kit handy.
• Do wear safety glasses or goggles when cutting, drilling, grinding or prying, even if you have 20–20 vision. If you wear glasses for the sake of vision, wear safety goggles over your regular glasses.

• Do shield your eyes whenever you work around the battery. Batteries contain sulfuric acid. In case of contact with, flush the area with water or a mixture of water and baking soda, then seek immediate medical attention.
• Do use safety stands (jackstands) for any undervehicle service. Jacks are for raising vehicles; jackstands are for making sure the vehicle stays raised until you want it to come down.
• Do use adequate ventilation when working with any chemicals or hazardous materials. Like carbon monoxide, the asbestos dust resulting from some brake lining wear can be hazardous in sufficient quantities.
• Do disconnect the negative battery cable when working on the electrical system. The secondary ignition system contains EXTREMELY HIGH VOLTAGE. In some cases it can even exceed 50,000 volts.
• Do follow manufacturer's directions whenever working with potentially hazardous materials. Most chemicals and fluids are poisonous.

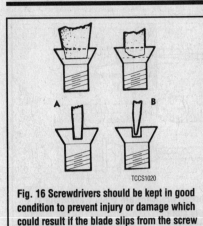

Fig. 16 Screwdrivers should be kept in good condition to prevent injury or damage which could result if the blade slips from the screw

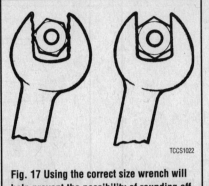

Fig. 17 Using the correct size wrench will help prevent the possibility of rounding off a nut

Fig. 18 NEVER work under a vehicle unless it is supported using safety stands (jackstands)

- Do properly maintain your tools. Loose hammerheads, mushroomed punches and chisels, frayed or poorly grounded electrical cords, excessively worn screwdrivers, spread wrenches (open end), cracked sockets, slipping ratchets, or faulty droplight sockets can cause accidents.
- Likewise, keep your tools clean; a greasy wrench can slip off a bolt head, ruining the bolt and often harming your knuckles in the process.
- Do use the proper size and type of tool for the job at hand. Do select a wrench or socket that fits the nut or bolt. The wrench or socket should sit straight, not cocked.
- Do, when possible, pull on a wrench handle rather than push on it, and adjust your stance to prevent a fall.
- Do be sure that adjustable wrenches are tightly closed on the nut or bolt and pulled so that the force is on the side of the fixed jaw.
- Do strike squarely with a hammer; avoid glancing blows.
- Do set the parking brake and block the drive wheels if the work requires a running engine.

Don'ts

- Don't run the engine in a garage or anywhere else without proper ventilation—EVER! Carbon monoxide is poisonous; it takes a long time to leave the human body and you can build up a deadly supply of it in your system by simply breathing in a little at a time. You may not realize you are slowly poisoning yourself. Always use power vents, windows, fans and/or open the garage door.
- Don't work around moving parts while wearing loose clothing. Short sleeves are much safer than long, loose sleeves. Hard-toed shoes with neoprene soles protect your toes and give a better grip on slippery surfaces. Watches and jewelry is not safe working around a vehicle. Long hair should be tied back under a hat or cap.
- Don't use pockets for toolboxes. A fall or bump can drive a screwdriver deep into your body. Even a rag hanging from your back pocket can wrap around a spinning shaft or fan.
- Don't smoke when working around gasoline, cleaning solvent or other flammable material.
- Don't smoke when working around the battery. When the battery is being charged, it gives off explosive hydrogen gas.
- Don't use gasoline to wash your hands; there are excellent soaps available. Gasoline contains dangerous additives which can enter the body through a cut or through your pores. Gasoline also removes all the natural oils from the skin so that bone dry hands will suck up oil and grease.
- Don't service the air conditioning system unless you are equipped with the necessary tools and training. When liquid or compressed gas refrigerant is released to atmospheric pressure it will absorb heat from whatever it contacts. This will chill or freeze anything it touches.
- Don't use screwdrivers for anything other than driving screws! A screwdriver used as an prying tool can snap when you least expect it, causing injuries. At the very least, you'll ruin a good screwdriver.
- Don't use an emergency jack (that little ratchet, scissors, or pantograph jack supplied with the vehicle) for anything other than changing a flat! These jacks are only intended for emergency use out on the road; they are NOT designed as a maintenance tool. If you are serious about maintaining your vehicle yourself, invest in a hydraulic floor jack of at least a 1½ ton capacity, and at least two sturdy jackstands.

FASTENERS, MEASUREMENTS AND CONVERSIONS

Bolts, Nuts and Other Threaded Retainers

▶ See Figures 19 and 20

Although there are a great variety of fasteners found in the modern car or truck, the most commonly used retainer is the threaded fastener (nuts, bolts, screws, studs, etc.). Most threaded retainers may be reused, provided that they are not damaged in use or during the repair. Some retainers (such as stretch bolts or torque prevailing nuts) are designed to deform when tightened or in use and should not be reinstalled.

Whenever possible, we will note any special retainers which should be replaced during a procedure. But you should always inspect the condition of a retainer when it is removed and replace any that show signs of damage. Check all threads for rust or corrosion which can increase the torque necessary to achieve the desired clamp load for which that fastener was originally selected. Additionally, be sure that the driver surface of the fastener has not been compromised by rounding or other damage. In some cases a driver surface may become only partially rounded, allowing the driver to catch in only one direction. In many of these occurrences, a fastener may be installed and tightened, but the driver would not be able to grip and loosen the fastener again.

If you must replace a fastener, whether due to design or damage, you must ALWAYS be sure to use the proper replacement. In all cases, a retainer of the

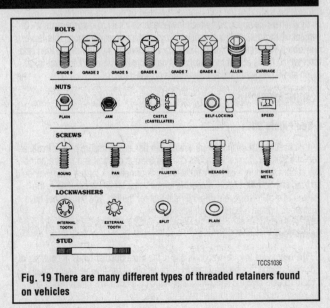

Fig. 19 There are many different types of threaded retainers found on vehicles

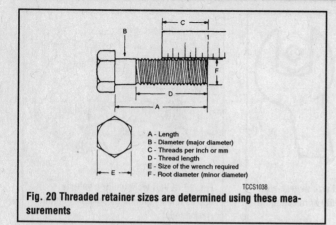

A - Length
B - Diameter (major diameter)
C - Threads per inch or mm
D - Thread length
E - Size of the wrench required
F - Root diameter (minor diameter)

TCCS1038

Fig. 20 Threaded retainer sizes are determined using these measurements

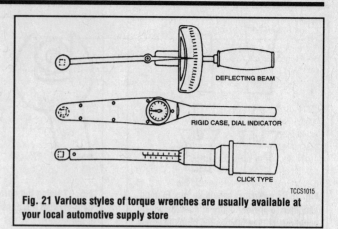

DEFLECTING BEAM

RIGID CASE, DIAL INDICATOR

CLICK TYPE

TCCS1015

Fig. 21 Various styles of torque wrenches are usually available at your local automotive supply store

same design, material and strength should be used. Markings on the heads of most bolts will help determine the proper strength of the fastener. The same material, thread and pitch must be selected to assure proper installation and safe operation of the vehicle afterwards.

Thread gauges are available to help measure a bolt or stud's thread. Most automotive and hardware stores keep gauges available to help you select the proper size. In a pinch, you can use another nut or bolt for a thread gauge. If the bolt you are replacing is not too badly damaged, you can select a match by finding another bolt which will thread in its place. If you find a nut which threads properly onto the damaged bolt, then use that nut to help select the replacement bolt.

✳✳ WARNING

Be aware that when you find a bolt with damaged threads, you may also find the nut or drilled hole it was threaded into has also been damaged. If this is the case, you may have to drill and tap the hole, replace the nut or otherwise repair the threads. NEVER try to force a replacement bolt to fit into the damaged threads.

Torque

Torque is defined as the measurement of resistance to turning or rotating. It tends to twist a body about an axis of rotation. A common example of this would be tightening a threaded retainer such as a nut, bolt or screw. Measuring torque is one of the most common ways to help assure that a threaded retainer has been properly fastened.

When tightening a threaded fastener, torque is applied in three distinct areas, the head, the bearing surface and the clamp load. About 50 percent of the measured torque is used in overcoming bearing friction. This is the friction between the bearing surface of the bolt head, screw head or nut face and the base material or washer (the surface on which the fastener is rotating). Approximately 40 percent of the applied torque is used in overcoming thread friction. This leaves only about 10 percent of the applied torque to develop a useful clamp load (the force which holds a joint together). This means that friction can account for as much as 90 percent of the applied torque on a fastener.

TORQUE WRENCHES

▶ **See Figure 21**

In most applications, a torque wrench can be used to assure proper installation of a fastener. Torque wrenches come in various designs and most automotive supply stores will carry a variety to suit your needs. A torque wrench should be used any time we supply a specific torque value for a fastener. Again, the general rule of "if you are using the right tool for the job, you should not have to strain to tighten a fastener" applies here.

Beam Type

The beam type torque wrench is one of the most popular types. It consists of a pointer attached to the head that runs the length of the flexible beam (shaft) to a scale located near the handle. As the wrench is pulled, the beam bends and the pointer indicates the torque using the scale.

Click (Breakaway) Type

Another popular design of torque wrench is the click type. To use the click type wrench you pre-adjust it to a torque setting. Once the torque is reached, the wrench has a reflex signaling feature that causes a momentary breakaway of the torque wrench body, sending an impulse to the operator's hand.

Pivot Head Type

▶ **See Figure 22**

Some torque wrenches (usually of the click type) may be equipped with a pivot head which can allow it to be used in areas of limited access. BUT, it must be used properly. To hold a pivot head wrench, grasp the handle lightly, and as you pull on the handle, it should be floated on the pivot point. If the handle comes in contact with the yoke extension during the process of pulling, there is a very good chance the torque readings will be inaccurate because this could alter the wrench loading point. The design of the handle is usually such as to make it inconvenient to deliberately misuse the wrench.

➡️**It should be mentioned that the use of any U-joint, wobble or extension will have an effect on the torque readings, no matter what type of wrench you are using. For the most accurate readings, install the socket directly on the wrench driver. If necessary, straight extensions (which hold a socket directly under the wrench driver) will have the least effect on the torque reading. Avoid any extension that alters the length of the wrench from the handle to the head/driving point (such as a crow's foot). U-joint or wobble extensions can greatly affect the readings; avoid their use at all times.**

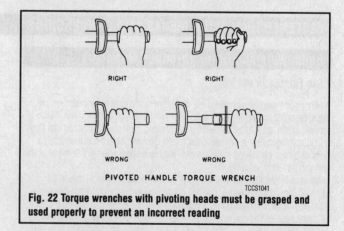

RIGHT

RIGHT

WRONG

WRONG

PIVOTED HANDLE TORQUE WRENCH

TCCS1041

Fig. 22 Torque wrenches with pivoting heads must be grasped and used properly to prevent an incorrect reading

Rigid Case (Direct Reading)

A rigid case or direct reading torque wrench is equipped with a dial indicator to show torque values. One advantage of these wrenches is that they can be held at any position on the wrench without affecting accuracy. These wrenches are often preferred because they tend to be compact, easy to read and have a great degree of accuracy.

TORQUE ANGLE METERS

Because the frictional characteristics of each fastener or threaded hole will vary, clamp loads which are based strictly on torque will vary as well. In most applications, this variance is not significant enough to cause worry. But, in certain applications, a manufacturer's engineers may determine that more precise clamp loads are necessary (such is the case with many aluminum cylinder heads). In these cases, a torque angle method of installation would be specified. When installing fasteners which are torque angle tightened, a predetermined seating torque and standard torque wrench are usually used first to remove any compliance from the joint. The fastener is then tightened the specified additional portion of a turn measured in degrees. A torque angle gauge (mechanical protractor) is used for these applications.

Standard and Metric Measurements

▶ See Figure 23

Throughout this manual, specifications are given to help you determine the condition of various components on your vehicle, or to assist you in their installation. Some of the most common measurements include length (in. or cm/mm), torque (ft. lbs., inch lbs. or Nm) and pressure (psi, in. Hg, kPa or mm Hg). In most cases, we strive to provide the proper measurement as determined by the manufacturer's engineers.

Though, in some cases, that value may not be conveniently measured with what is available in your toolbox. Luckily, many of the measuring devices which are available today will have two scales so the Standard or Metric measurements may easily be taken. If any of the various measuring tools which are available to you do not contain the same scale as listed in the specifications, use the accompanying conversion factors to determine the proper value.

The conversion factor chart is used by taking the given specification and multiplying it by the necessary conversion factor. For instance, looking at the first line, if you have a measurement in inches such as "free-play should be 2 in." but your ruler reads only in millimeters, multiply 2 in. by the conversion factor of 25.4 to get the metric equivalent of 50.8mm. Likewise, if the specification was given only in a Metric measurement, for example in Newton Meters (Nm), then look at the center column first. If the measurement is 100 Nm, multiply it by the conversion factor of 0.738 to get 73.8 ft. lbs.

CONVERSION FACTORS

LENGTH–DISTANCE

Inches (in.)	x 25.4	= Millimeters (mm)	x .0394	= Inches
Feet (ft.)	x .305	= Meters (m)	x 3.281	= Feet
Miles	x 1.609	= Kilometers (km)	x .0621	= Miles

VOLUME

Cubic Inches (in3)	x 16.387	= Cubic Centimeters	x .061	= in3
IMP Pints (IMP pt.)	x .568	= Liters (L)	x 1.76	= IMP pt.
IMP Quarts (IMP qt.)	x 1.137	= Liters (L)	x .88	= IMP qt.
IMP Gallons (IMP gal.)	x 4.546	= Liters (L)	x .22	= IMP gal.
IMP Quarts (IMP qt.)	x 1.201	= US Quarts (US qt.)	x .833	= IMP qt.
IMP Gallons (IMP gal.)	x 1.201	= US Gallons (US gal.)	x .833	= IMP gal.
Fl. Ounces	x 29.573	= Milliliters	x .034	= Ounces
US Pints (US pt.)	x .473	= Liters (L)	x 2.113	= Pints
US Quarts (US qt.)	x .946	= Liters (L)	x 1.057	= Quarts
US Gallons (US gal.)	x 3.785	= Liters (L)	x .264	= Gallons

MASS–WEIGHT

Ounces (oz.)	x 28.35	= Grams (g)	x .035	= Ounces
Pounds (lb.)	x .454	= Kilograms (kg)	x 2.205	= Pounds

PRESSURE

Pounds Per Sq. In. (psi)	x 6.895	= Kilopascals (kPa)	x .145	= psi
Inches of Mercury (Hg)	x .4912	= psi	x 2.036	= Hg
Inches of Mercury (Hg)	x 3.377	= Kilopascals (kPa)	x .2961	= Hg
Inches of Water (H2O)	x .07355	= Inches of Mercury	x 13.783	= H2O
Inches of Water (H2O)	x .03613	= psi	x 27.684	= H2O
Inches of Water (H2O)	x .248	= Kilopascals (kPa)	x 4.026	= H2O

TORQUE

Pounds–Force Inches (in-lb)	x .113	= Newton Meters (N·m)	x 8.85	= in-lb
Pounds–Force Feet (ft-lb)	x 1.356	= Newton Meters (N·m)	x .738	= ft-lb

VELOCITY

Miles Per Hour (MPH)	x 1.609	= Kilometers Per Hour (KPH)	x .621	= MPH

POWER

Horsepower (Hp)	x .745	= Kilowatts	x 1.34	= Horsepower

FUEL CONSUMPTION*

Miles Per Gallon IMP (MPG)	x .354	= Kilometers Per Liter (Km/L)	
Kilometers Per Liter (Km/L)	x 2.352	= IMP MPG	
Miles Per Gallon US (MPG)	x .425	= Kilometers Per Liter (Km/L)	
Kilometers Per Liter (Km/L)	x 2.352	= US MPG	

*It is common to covert from miles per gallon (mpg) to liters/100 kilometers (1/100 km), where mpg (IMP) x 1/100 km = 282 and mpg (US) x 1/100 km = 235.

TEMPERATURE

Degree Fahrenheit (°F)	= (°C x 1.8) + 32
Degree Celsius (°C)	= (°F – 32) x .56

TCCS1044

Fig. 23 Standard and metric conversion factors chart

MODEL IDENTIFICATION

Three separate models of the S10/S15 pick-up are offered—the regular cab, the extended cab, and the chassis cab. The chassis cab comes without a cargo bed so that a specialized aftermarket bed may be added after purchase.

Four wheel drive versions of the S-10/S-15 were introduced in 1983. Model reference (5th digit of the VIN number) indicates "S" as a two wheel drive vehicle, and "T" as a four wheel drive vehicle.

SERIAL NUMBER IDENTIFICATION

Vehicle

VEHICLE IDENTIFICATION PLATE

▶ See Figures 24, 25 and 26

The Vehicle Identification Number (VIN) is stamped on a plate located on the top left hand side of the instrument panel, so it can be seen by looking through the windshield. It is also found on various other anti-theft labels found throughout the vehicle. The VIN is a seventeen digit sequence of numbers and letters which can be important for ordering parts and for servicing. The VIN plate is part of the Federal Vehicle Theft Prevention Standard and cannot be removed or altered in anyway. The 8th digit of the VIN identifies the factory equipped engine while the 10th digit will give the vehicle model year.

SERVICE PARTS IDENTIFICATION LABEL

▶ See Figure 27

The service parts identification label has been developed and placed on the vehicle to aid in identifying parts and options which were originally installed on the vehicle. The service parts identification label is located on the inside of the

glove box door. In most cases, the label lists the VIN, wheelbase, paint information and all production options or special equipment on the truck when it was shipped from the factory. Always refer to this information when ordering parts.

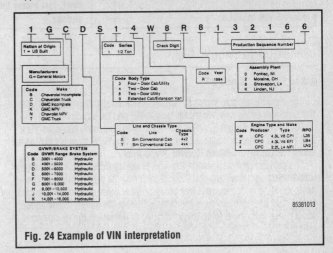

Fig. 24 Example of VIN interpretation

VEHICLE IDENTIFICATION CHART

It is important for servicing and ordering parts to be certain of the vehicle and engine identification. The VIN (vehicle identification number) is a 17 digit number visible through the windshield on the driver's side of the dash and contains the vehicle and engine identification codes. The tenth digit indicates model year and the eighth digit indicates engine code. It can be interpreted as follows:

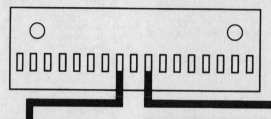

Engine Code						Model Year	
Code	Liters	Cu. In. (cc)	Cyl.	Fuel Sys.	Eng. Mfg.	Code	Year
A	1.9	119 (1949)	4	2 bbl	Isuzu	C	1982
Y	2.0	121 (1990)	4	2 bbl	Chevrolet	D	1983
A	2.5	151 (2474)	4	TBI	CPC	E	1984
E	2.5	151 (2474)	4	TBI	Pontiac/CPC-North	F	1985
B	2.8	173 (2835)	6	2 bbl	Chevrolet	G	1986
R	2.8	173 (2835)	6	TBI	CPC	H	1987
W	4.3	262 (4293)	6	CMFI	CPC	J	1988
Z	4.3	262 (4293)	6	TBI	CPC	K	1989
Z	4.3	262 (4293)	6	MFI-Turbo	CPC	L	1990
						M	1991
						N	1992
						P	1993

2 bbl—2 barrel carburetor
CMFI—Central Multi-Port Fuel Injection
CPC—Chevrolet/Pontiac/Canada
MFI—Multi-Port Fuel Injection
TBI—Throttle Body Fuel Injection

8844R030

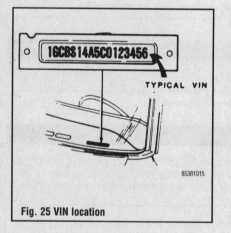

Fig. 25 VIN location

Fig. 26 The VIN plate is secured to the cowl, just above the windshield mating surface

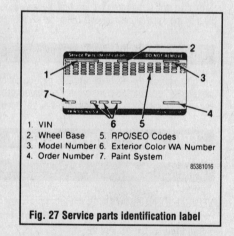

1. VIN
2. Wheel Base
3. Model Number
4. Order Number
5. RPO/SEO Codes
6. Exterior Color WA Number
7. Paint System

85381016

Fig. 27 Service parts identification label

VEHICLE CERTIFICATION LABEL

▶ See Figures 28 and 29

The certification label shows the Gross Vehicle Weight Rating (GVWR), the front and rear Gross Axle Weight Rating (GAWR) and the payload rating.

Gross Vehicle Weight (GVW) is the weight of the originally equipped truck and all items added to it after leaving the factory. The GVW must not exceed the Gross Vehicle Weight Rating (GVWR) of your truck.

The payload rating shown on the label is the maximum allowable cargo load (including the weight of the occupants) that the truck can carry. The payload rating is decreased if any accessories or other equipment is added to the truck after delivery from the factory. Deduct the weight of any added accessories from the original payload rating to determine the new payload rating.

Certification label

85381017

Fig. 28 Vehicle certification label

Fig. 29 This vehicle certification label is affixed to the driver's door jamb

Engine

Engine identification can take place using various methods. The VIN, described earlier in this section contains a code identifying the engine which was originally installed in the vehicle. In most cases, this should be sufficient for determining the engine with which your truck is currently equipped. But, some older vehicles may have had the engine replaced or changed by a previous owner. If this is the case, the first step in identification is to locate an engine serial number and code which is stamped on the block or located on adhesive labels that may be present on valve covers or other engine components. The next step would be to discuss the codes on that label with your local parts dealer.

1.9L ENGINE

▶ See Figure 30

The engine identification number is on a machined flat surface, on the lower left-side of the block, near the flywheel.

ENGINE IDENTIFICATION

Year	Engine Displacement Liters (cc)	Engine Series (ID/VIN)	Fuel System	No. of Cylinders	Engine Type
1982	1.9 (1949)	A	2 bbl	4	OHV
	2.8 (2835)	B	2 bbl	6	OHV
1983	1.9 (1949)	A	2 bbl	4	OHV
	2.0 (1990)	Y	2 bbl	4	OHV
	2.8 (2835)	B	2 bbl	6	OHV
1984	1.9 (1949)	A	2 bbl	4	OHV
	2.0 (1990)	Y	2 bbl	4	OHV
	2.8 (2835)	B	2 bbl	6	OHV
1985	1.9 (1949)	A	2 bbl	4	OHV
	2.5 (2474)	E	TBI	4	OHV
	2.8 (2835)	B	2 bbl	6	OHV
1986	2.5 (2474)	E	TBI	4	OHV
	2.8 (2835)	R	TBI	6	OHV
1987	2.5 (2474)	E	TBI	4	OHV
	2.8 (2835)	R	TBI	6	OHV
1988	2.5 (2474)	E	TBI	4	OHV
	2.8 (2835)	R	TBI	6	OHV
	4.3 (4293)	Z	TBI	6	OHV
1989	2.5 (2474)	E	TBI	4	OHV
	2.8 (2835)	R	TBI	6	OHV
	4.3 (4293)	Z	TBI	6	OHV
1990	2.5 (2474)	E	TBI	4	OHV
	2.8 (2835)	R	TBI	6	OHV
	4.3 (4293)	Z	TBI	6	OHV
1991	2.5 (2474)	A	TBI	4	OHV
	2.5 (2474)	E	TBI	4	OHV
	2.8 (2835)	R	TBI	6	OHV
	4.3 (4293)	Z	TBI	6	OHV
	4.3 (4293)	Z	MFI-Turbo	6	OHV
1992	2.5 (2474)	A	TBI	4	OHV
	2.8 (2835)	R	TBI	6	OHV
	4.3 (4293)	W	CMFI	6	OHV
	4.3 (4293)	Z	TBI	6	OHV
	4.3 (4293)	Z	MFI-Turbo	6	OHV
1993	2.5 (2474)	A	TBI	4	OHV
	2.8 (2835)	R	TBI	6	OHV
	4.3 (4293)	W	CMFI	6	OHV
	4.3 (4293)	Z	TBI	6	OHV

2 bbl—2 barrel carburetor
CMFI—Central Multi-Port Fuel Injection
MFI—Multi-Port Fuel Injection

TBI—Throttle Body Fuel Injection
OHV—Overhead Valves

8844R031

2.0L ENGINE

♦ See Figure 31

The engine identification number is stamped on a flat, machined surface, facing forward, on the front of the engine block, just below the head.

2.5L ENGINE

♦ See Figure 32

The engine identification number is stamped on a flat, machined surface, on the left rear-side of the engine block, near the flywheel.

2.8L ENGINE

The engine identification code is stamped either on an upward facing, machined surface on the right-front of the block, just below the head, or on the left front of the block just above the water pump.

4.3L ENGINE

♦ See Figure 33

The engine identification number is stamped either on a flat, machined surface, on the right-front of the engine block, just above the water pump (on some earlier model engines), or on the left-rear side of the engine block, where the transmission is joined to the engine.

Transmission

MANUAL

♦ See Figure 34

A transmission serial number is stamped on each transmission case or to a plate which is welded to the case. Location of the ID number will vary with the transmission manufacturer. On many of the transmissions covered by this manual the ID number is located on a metal plate which is attached to the extension housing case bolt, on the left-side. Some later model vehicles, such as those equipped with the Borg Warner T-5 transmission locate the transmission ID number on the front right of the housing.

AUTOMATIC

♦ See Figures 35, 36 and 37

• The identification number for the 180C is located on a metal tag attached to the left-front of the transmission case.
• The identification numbers for the 200C (3-spd) are stamped on the right rear-side of the transmission case, behind the modulator on the left rear of the case and on the right front of the case, on or near the bellhousing.
• The identification number for the 700-R4 is stamped on the right or left rear-side of the transmission pan rail.
• The identification number for the 4L60 and 4L60-E is stamped on the right rear of the housing just above the pan rail.

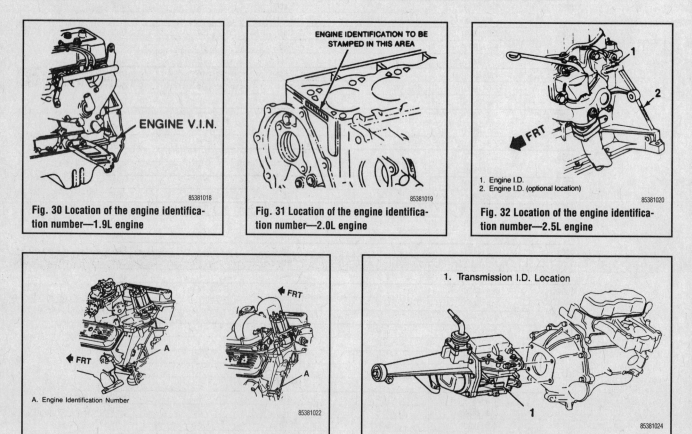

Fig. 30 Location of the engine identification number—1.9L engine

Fig. 31 Location of the engine identification number—2.0L engine

Fig. 32 Location of the engine identification number—2.5L engine

Fig. 33 Late model location of the engine identification number—4.3L engine

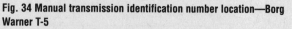

Fig. 34 Manual transmission identification number location—Borg Warner T-5

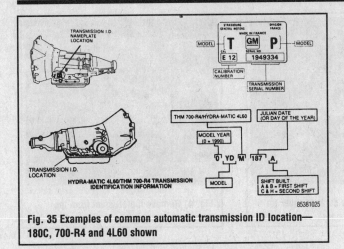

Fig. 35 Examples of common automatic transmission ID location—180C, 700-R4 and 4L60 shown

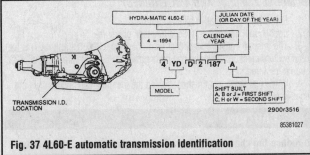

Fig. 36 Location of the 220C automatic transmission identification numbers

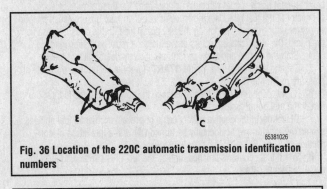

Fig. 37 4L60-E automatic transmission identification

Drive Axle

▶ See Figure 38

On most rear axles, the identification number is stamped on the right-front side of the axle tube, next to the differential. On front axles, the ID number is stamped on a tag, attached to the differential cover by a cover bolt.

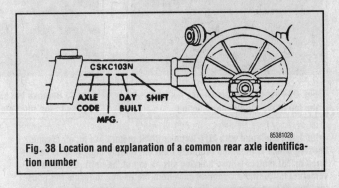

Fig. 38 Location and explanation of a common rear axle identification number

Transfer Case

The model 207 (early vehicles) and 231 (late vehicles) transfer cases are equipped with an identification tag which is attached to the rear half of the case; the tag gives the model number, the low range reduction ratio and the assembly part number. If for some reason it becomes dislodged or removed, reattach it with an adhesive sealant. Late model vehicles may be equipped with an electronic shift transfer case, the 233 model. The MFI-Turbo is equipped with the Borg Warner 4472 transfer case.

Vehicle Emission Control Information Label

The Vehicle Emission Control Information (VECI) label is located in the engine compartment (fan shroud, radiator support, hood underside, etc) of every vehicle produced by General Motors. The label contains important emission specifications and setting procedures, as well as a vacuum hose schematic with various emissions components identified.

Because the label will often contain information regarding mid-production updates or changes, you should always differ to the information or procedures located on the label when servicing your vehicle.

➡️**Always follow the timing procedures on this label when adjusting ignition timing.**

ROUTINE MAINTENANCE

Proper maintenance and tune-up is the key to long and trouble-free vehicle life, and the work can yield its own rewards. Studies have shown that a properly tuned and maintained vehicle can achieve better gas mileage than an out-of-tune vehicle. As a conscientious owner and driver, set aside a Saturday morning, say once a month, to check or replace items which could cause major problems later. Keep your own personal log to jot down which services you performed, how much the parts cost you, the date, and the exact odometer reading at the time. Keep all receipts for such items as engine oil and filters, so that they may be referred to in case of related problems or to determine operating expenses. As a do-it-yourselfer, these receipts are the only proof you have that the required maintenance was performed. In the event of a warranty problem, these receipts will be invaluable.

The literature provided with your vehicle when it was originally delivered includes the factory recommended maintenance schedule. If you no longer have this literature, replacement copies are usually available from the dealer. A maintenance schedule is provided later in this section, in case you do not have the factory literature.

Air Cleaner

The air cleaner has a dual purpose. It not only filters the air going to the carburetor or throttle body (as equipped), but also acts as a flame arrester if the engine should backfire. The engine should never be run without the air cleaner installed unless an engine maintenance procedure specifically requires the temporary removal of the air cleaner. Operating a vehicle without its air cleaner results in some throaty sounds from the engine giving the impression of increased power but will only cause trouble. Unfiltered air to the carburetor will eventually result in a dirty, inefficient carburetor and engine. A dirty carburetor increases the chances of carburetor backfire and, without the protection of an air cleaner, an underhood fire becomes a very real danger.

Your truck is equipped with an air cleaner element of the paper cartridge type. The element should be replaced every year or 30,000 miles, whichever comes first. If the truck is operated in heavy traffic or under dusty conditions, replace the element at more frequent intervals.

REMOVAL & INSTALLATION

▶ See Figures 39, 40 and 41

For most vehicles, the filter element is easily accessible by removing the cover from the air cleaner assembly.

1. Loosen the wing nut(s) at the center of the air cleaner cover, and/or release all of the clamp fasteners along the cover's edge.

Fig. 39 Loosen and remove the nut from the top of the air cleaner housing

Fig. 40 Remove the air cleaner cover for access to the filter element

Fig. 41 Remove the element from the housing

➡**Vehicles equipped with MFI-Turbo or CMFI motors use an air cleaner housing which is mounted remotely from the throttle body (unlike carbureted or TBI motors whose housing sits on top of the unit). On these vehicles, follow the air snorkel back from the engine to locate the housing. It may be necessary to disconnect one or more of the air hoses from the housing before removing the filter.**

2. Remove the cover from the air cleaner assembly, then remove the air cleaner element from the housing.

3. If necessary, disconnect the air intake hose, and, if applicable, the heat stove and/or vacuum line(s), from the air cleaner housing, then remove the housing from the vehicle.

To install:

4. If removed, position the air cleaner housing, then connect the air intake hose and, if applicable, the heat stove and/or vacuum line(s).

5. Install the air cleaner element to the housing, then position the cover onto the assembly.

6. Secure the cover using the clamp fasteners and/or wing nut(s).

Fuel Filter

The fuel filter should be serviced every 15,000 miles on most carbureted vehicles, while most fuel injected vehicles have a suggested interval of 30,000 miles. If the truck is operated under severe conditions, change it more often. Three types of fuel filters are used, an internal pleated-paper element type (located in the carburetor fuel fitting), an inline filter (located in the fuel feed line) and an in-tank type (the "sock" on the fuel pickup tube).

➡**If an inline fuel filter is used on an engine which has a filter installed in the carburetor body, be sure to change both at the same time.**

✴✴ CAUTION

Before removing any fuel system component, always relieve pressure from the system.

FUEL PRESSURE RELEASE

Carbureted

To release the fuel pressure on the carbureted system, remove the fuel filler cap from the fuel tank in order to allow the expanded vapor to escape, then reinstall the cap. A rag should be placed around a fuel fitting before it is disconnected in order to catch any remaining fuel which may escape.

Throttle Body Injection (TBI)

TBI MODEL 300 OR 700 (2.5L ENGINE)

1. Place the transmission selector in PARK (automatic transmissions) or NEUTRAL (manual transmissions), then set the parking brake and block the drive wheels.

2. Loosen the fuel filler cap to relieve tank pressure.

3. Either remove the FUEL PUMP fuse from the fuse block in the passenger compartment (early model vehicles) or disengage the three terminal electrical connector at the fuel tank (late model vehicles). If you are unsure which method works for your truck, try removing the fuel pump fuse. If this does not disable the pump, the electrical connectors at the fuel tank must be disengaged.

4. Start the engine and allow to run until it stops due to lack of fuel.

5. Engage the starter (turn key to **START**) for three seconds to dissipate all pressure in the fuel lines.

6. Turn the ignition **OFF**, then re-engage the connector at the fuel tank or install the fuel pump fuse.

7. Disconnect the negative battery cable to prevent accidental fuel spillage should the ignition key accidentally be turned **ON** with a fuel fitting disconnected.

8. When fuel service is finished, tighten the fuel filler cap and connect the negative battery cable.

TBI MODEL 220 (2.8L AND 4.3L ENGINES)

1. Disconnect the negative battery cable.

2. Loosen fuel filler cap to relieve fuel tank pressure.

3. The internal constant bleed feature of the Model 220 TBI unit relieves fuel pump system pressure when the engine is turned **OFF**. Therefore, no further action is required.

4. When fuel service is finished, tighten the fuel filler cap and connect the negative battery cable.

✴✴ CAUTION

To reduce the chance of personal injury when disconnecting a fuel line, always cover the fuel line with cloth to collect escaping fuel, then place the cloth in an approved container.

Multi-Port Fuel Injection (MFI)/Central Multi-Port Fuel Injection (CMFI)

A schrader valve is provided on components of these fuel systems in order to conveniently test or release the fuel system pressure. A fuel pressure gauge and adapter will be necessary to connect to the fitting. The MFI system covered by this manual uses a pressure fitting located on the fuel rail assembly or at the fuel inlet pipe junction. The CMFI system covered here uses a valve located on the inlet pipe fitting, immediately before it enters the CMFI assembly (towards the rear of the engine).

1. Disconnect the negative battery cable to assure the prevention of fuel spillage if the ignition switch is accidentally turned **ON** while a fitting is still disconnected.

2. Loosen the fuel filter cap to release the fuel tank pressure.

3. Make sure the release valve on the fuel gauge is closed, then connect the fuel gauge to the pressure fitting located on the fuel rail, pipe or fitting, as applicable.

4. Install the bleed hose portion of the fuel gauge assembly into an approved container, then open the gauge release valve and bleed the fuel pressure from the system.

5. When the gauge is removed, be sure to open the bleed valve and drain all fuel from the gauge assembly.

REMOVAL & INSTALLATION

✳✳ CAUTION

Filter replacement should not be attempted when the engine is HOT. Additionally, it is a good idea to place some absorbent rags under the fuel fittings to absorb any gasoline which will spill out when the lines are loosened.

Internal Filter

▶ **See Figures 42, 43 and 44**

The carburetor inlet fuel filter should be replaced every 15,000 miles, or more often if necessary.

1. Disconnect the fuel line connection at the fuel inlet filter nut on the carburetor. A backup wrench should be used to prevent the fuel filter nut from loosening while trying to remove the line.
2. Carefully loosen and remove the fuel inlet filter nut from the carburetor.
3. Remove the filter and spring.

To install:

➡️ **If a check valve is not present with the filter, one must be installed when the filter is replaced. The check valve is necessary in order to meet Motor Vehicle Safety Standards (MVSS) for roll-over.**

4. Install the spring, filter and check valve making sure the valve end of the filter is facing the fuel line. Ribs on the fuel filter will prevent it from being installed incorrectly, unless it is forced into position.
5. Torque the filter nut-to-carburetor fitting to 25 ft. lbs. (34 Nm).

➡️ **When working on fuel line fittings, take care not to overtighten the fittings. A crow's foot will be necessary to use the torque wrench to tighten fuel fittings.**

6. Connect the fuel line to the filter inlet nut and tighten the fuel line to 18 ft. lbs. (24 Nm). Be sure to use a backup wrench to prevent the filter nut from tightening.
7. Start the engine and check for leaks.

Inline Filter

▶ **See Figures 45, 46 and 47**

To locate the inline filter, follow the fuel line back from the carburetor or throttle body. Inline filters are often mounted to the frame rail underneath the vehicle. It may be necessary to raise and safely support the vehicle using jackstands in order to access the filter.

✳✳ CAUTION

Before disconnecting any component of the fuel system, refer to the fuel pressure release procedures found earlier in this section.

1. Properly relieve the fuel system pressure.

➡️ **Some late model vehicles are equipped with "quick-connect" fittings. A special tool must be used to release the locking tangs on these fittings.**

2. Using a backup wrench (on threaded fittings) to prevent overtorquing the lines or fittings, loosen and disconnect the fuel lines from the filter. Be sure to position a rag in order to catch any remaining fuel which may escape when the fittings are loosened.
3. Remove the fuel filter from the retainer or mounting bolt. For most filters which are retained by band clamps, loosen the fastener(s) and remove the filter. For some filters it may be necessary to completely remove the clamp and filter assembly.

To install:

4. Position the filter and retaining bracket with the directional arrow facing away from the fuel tank, towards to carburetor or throttle body.

Fig. 42 If necessary, disengage any wiring which is in the way of the fuel inlet filter nut

Fig. 43 Once the fuel line is disconnected, the filter nut may be unthreaded from the carburetor

Fig. 44 Remove the filter and spring from the nut

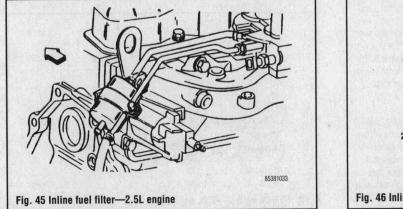

Fig. 45 Inline fuel filter—2.5L engine

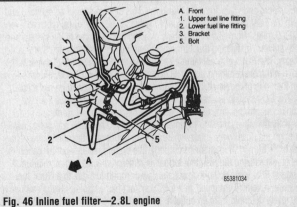

A. Front
1. Upper fuel line fitting
2. Lower fuel line fitting
3. Bracket
5. Bolt

Fig. 46 Inline fuel filter—2.8L engine

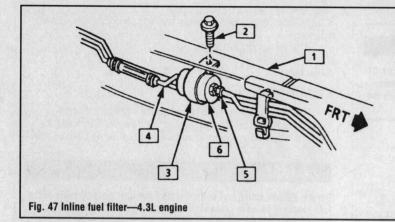

1	LEFT FRAME SIDE MEMBER
2	BOLT – TIGHTEN 16 N·m (24 lb. ft.)
3	CLAMP
4	REAR FUEL FEED PIPE TIGHTEN 26 N·m (20 lb. ft.)
5	INTERMEDIATE FUEL FEED PIPE TIGHTEN 26 N·m (20 lb. ft.)
6	IN – LINE FUEL FILTER

85381035

Fig. 47 Inline fuel filter—4.3L engine

➡The filter has an arrow (fuel flow direction) on the side of the case, be sure to install it correctly in the system, the with arrow facing away from the fuel tank.

5. Install and tighten the filter/bracket retainer(s), as applicable.
6. Connect the fuel lines to the filter and tighten using a backup wrench to prevent damage.
7. Connect the negative battery cable and tighten the fuel filler cap, then start the engine and check for leaks.

In-Tank Filter

▶ See Figure 48

To service the in-tank fuel filter, please refer to the electric fuel pump procedures found in Section 5 of this manual.

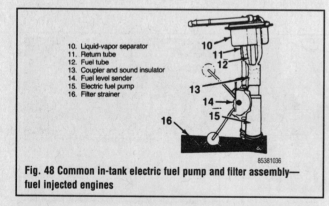

10. Liquid-vapor separator
11. Return tube
12. Fuel tube
13. Coupler and sound insulator
14. Fuel level sender
15. Electric fuel pump
16. Filter strainer

85381036

Fig. 48 Common in-tank electric fuel pump and filter assembly— fuel injected engines

Positive Crankcase Ventilation (PCV) Valve

▶ See Figure 49

The PCV system must be operating properly in order to allow evaporation of fuel vapors and water from the crankcase. This system should be serviced and both the PCV valve and filter (usually located in the air cleaner) replaced every 30,000 miles. Normal service entails cleaning the passages of the system hoses with solvent, inspecting them for cracks and breaks, and replacing them as necessary. The PCV valve contains a check valve and, when working properly, this valve will make a rattling sound when the outside case is tapped. If it fails to rattle, then it is probably stuck in a closed position and needs to be replaced.

The PCV system is designed to prevent the emission of gases from the crankcase into the atmosphere. It does this by connecting a crankcase outlet (usually the valve cover) to the intake with a hose. The crankcase gases travel through the hose to the intake where they are returned to the combustion chamber to be burned. If maintained properly, this system reduces condensation in the crankcase and the resultant formation of harmful acids and oil dilution. A clogged PCV valve will often cause a slow or rough idle due to a richer fuel mixture. A vehicle equipped with a PCV system has air going through a hose to the intake manifold from an outlet at the valve cover. To compensate for this

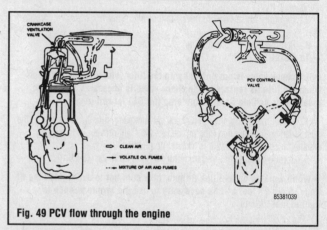

CLEAN AIR
VOLATILE OIL FUMES
MIXTURE OF AIR AND FUMES

85381039

Fig. 49 PCV flow through the engine

extra air going to the manifold, carburetor specifications require a richer (more gas) mixture at the carburetor. If the PCV valve or hose is clogged, this air doesn't go to the intake manifold and the fuel mixture is too rich. A rough, slow idle results. The valve should be checked before making any carburetor adjustments. Disconnect the valve from the engine or merely clamp the hose shut. If the engine speed decreases less than 50 rpm, the valve is clogged and should be replaced. If the engine speed decreases much more than 50 rpm, then the valve is good. The PCV valve is an inexpensive item and it is suggested that it be replaced, if suspected. If the new valve doesn't noticeably improve engine idle, the problem might be a restriction in the PCV hose. For further details on PCV valve operation please refer to Section 4 of this manual.

FUNCTIONAL CHECK

▶ See Figures 50, 51 and 52

If the engine is idling rough, check for a clogged PCV valve, dirty vent filter or air cleaner element, or plugged hose. Test the system using the following procedure and replace components as necessary.

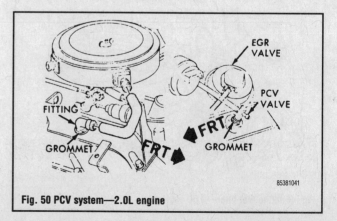

EGR VALVE
PCV VALVE
FITTING
GROMMET
GROMMET

85381041

Fig. 50 PCV system—2.0L engine

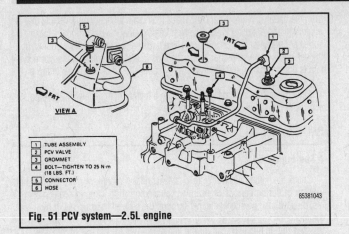

1 TUBE ASSEMBLY
2 PCV VALVE
3 GROMMET
4 BOLT—TIGHTEN TO 25 N·m
  (18 LBS. FT.)
5 CONNECTOR
6 HOSE

85381043

Fig. 51 PCV system—2.5L engine

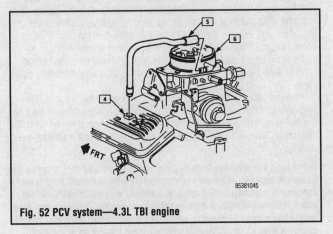

85381045

Fig. 52 PCV system—4.3L TBI engine

1. Remove the PCV valve from the rocker cover.
2. Run the engine at idle and place your thumb over the end of the valve to check for vacuum.
3. If no vacuum exists, check for plugged hoses, manifold port vacuum at the carburetor or TBI unit, or a defective PCV valve.
4. To check the PCV valve, remove the valve from the hose and shake it. If a rattling noise is heard, the valve is good. If no noise is heard, the valve is plugged and replacement is necessary.

REMOVAL & INSTALLATION

▶ **See Figures 53 and 54**

1. Grasp the valve and withdraw it from the valve cover.
2. Holding the valve in one hand and the hose in the other, carefully pull the valve from the hose and remove from the vehicle.

➡**Some PCV valve hoses will be retained to the valve using a clamp. If so, use a pair of pliers to slide the clamp back on the hose until it is clear of the bulged area on the end of PCV valve nipple. With the clamp in this position, the hose should be free to slip from the valve.**

To install:
3. Check the PCV valve for deposits and clogging: (1) Shake it to see if the valve is free; (2) Blow through it (air will pass in one direction only). The valve should rattle when shaken. If the valve does not rattle, clean the valve with solvent until the plunger is free or replace the valve.
4. Install the PCV hose to the grommet in the valve cover.
5. Connect the PCV hose to the valve.

Evaporative Canister

▶ **See Figure 55**

This system is designed to limit gasoline vapor, which normally escapes from the fuel tank and the intake manifold, from discharging into the atmo-

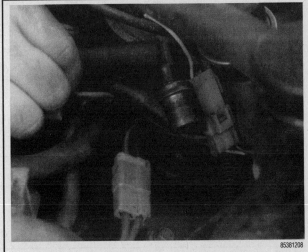

85381208

Fig. 53 Withdraw the PCV valve from the grommet located in the valve cover

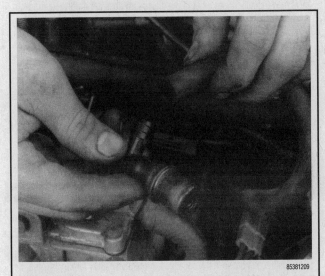

85381209

Fig. 54 Grasp and pull the valve from the end of the hose

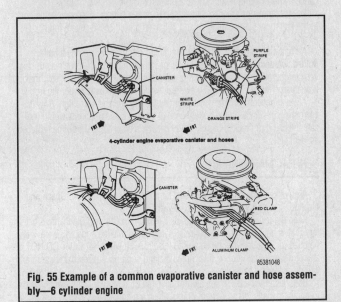

PURPLE STRIPE
CANISTER
WHITE STRIPE
ORANGE STRIPE
FRT
4-cylinder engine evaporative canister and hoses

CANISTER
RED CLAMP
FRT
ALUMINUM CLAMP
FRT

85381048

Fig. 55 Example of a common evaporative canister and hose assembly—6 cylinder engine

sphere. Vapor absorption is accomplished through the use of the charcoal canister. The canister absorbs fuel vapors and stores them until they can be removed and burned in the combustion process. Removal of the vapors from the canister to the engine is accomplished through: a canister mounted purge valve, the throttle valve position, a Thermostatic Vacuum Switch (TVS) or a computer controlled canister purge solenoid.

In addition to the canister, the fuel tank requires a non-vented gas cap. This cap does not allow fuel vapor to discharge into the atmosphere. All fuel vapor travels through a vent line (inserted high into the domed fuel tank) directly to the canister.

SERVICING

Every 30,000 miles or 24 months, check all fuel, vapor lines and hoses for proper hookup, routing and condition. If equipped, check that the bowl vent and purge valves work properly. Remove the canister and check for cracks or damage and replace, if necessary.

FUNCTIONAL TEST

1. Apply a short length of hose to the lower tube of the purge valve and attempt to blow through it. Little or no air should pass into the canister.
2. With a hand vacuum pump, apply a vacuum of 15 in. Hg to the control valve tube (usually upper tube). If the diaphragm does not hold vacuum for at least 20 seconds, the diaphragm is leaking and the canister must be replaced.
3. If the diaphragm holds vacuum, again try to blow through the hose connected to the lower tube while vacuum is still being applied. An increased flow of air should be observed. If not, the canister must be replaced.

REMOVAL & INSTALLATION

1. Label and disconnect the charcoal canister vent hoses.
2. Remove the canister-to-bracket bolt(s).
3. Lift the canister from the bracket.
4. To install, reverse the removal procedures. It is essential that the vent hoses be properly connected as noted during removal.

Battery

PRECAUTIONS

Always use caution when working on or near the battery. Never allow a tool to bridge the gap between the negative and positive battery terminals. Also, be careful not to allow a tool to provide a ground between the positive cable/terminal and any metal component on the vehicle. Either of these conditions will cause a short circuit, leading to sparks and possible personal injury.

Do not smoke or all open flames/sparks near a battery; the gases contained in the battery are very explosive and, if ignited, could cause severe injury or death.

All batteries, regardless of type, should be carefully secured by a battery hold-down device. If not, the terminals or casing may crack from stress during vehicle operation. A battery which is not secured may allow acid to leak, making it discharge faster. The acid can also eat away at components under the hood.

Always inspect the battery case for cracks, leakage and corrosion. A white corrosive substance on the battery case or on nearby components would indicate a leaking or cracked battery. If the battery is cracked, it should be replaced immediately.

GENERAL MAINTENANCE

Always keep the battery cables and terminals free of corrosion. Check and clean these components about once a year.

Keep the top of the battery clean, as a film of dirt can help discharge a battery that is not used for long periods. A solution of baking soda and water may be used for cleaning, but be careful to flush this off with clear water. DO NOT let any of the solution into the filler holes. Baking soda neutralizes battery acid and will de-activate a battery cell.

Batteries in vehicles which are not operated on a regular basis can fall victim to parasitic loads (small current drains which are constantly drawing current

from the battery). Normal parasitic loads may drain a battery on a vehicle that is in storage and not used for 6–8 weeks. Vehicles that have additional accessories such as a phone or an alarm system may discharge a battery sooner. If the vehicle is to be stored for longer periods in a secure area and the alarm system is not necessary, the negative battery cable should be disconnected to protect the battery.

Remember that constantly deep cycling a battery (completely discharging and recharging it) will shorten battery life.

BATTERY FLUID

▶ **See Figure 56**

Check the battery electrolyte level at least once a month, or more often in hot weather or during periods of extended vehicle operation. On non-sealed batteries, the level can be checked either through the case (if translucent) or by removing the cell caps. The electrolyte level in each cell should be kept filled to the split ring inside each cell, or the line marked on the outside of the case.

If the level is low, add only distilled water through the opening until the level is correct. Each cell must be checked and filled individually. Distilled water should be used, because the chemicals and minerals found in most drinking water are harmful to the battery and could significantly shorten its life.

If water is added in freezing weather, the vehicle should be driven several miles to allow the water to mix with the electrolyte. Otherwise, the battery could freeze.

Although some maintenance-free batteries have removable cell caps, the electrolyte condition and level on all sealed maintenance-free batteries must be checked using the built-in hydrometer "eye." The exact type of eye will vary. But, most battery manufacturers, apply a sticker to the battery itself explaining the readings.

➡ **Although the readings from built-in hydrometers will vary, a green eye usually indicates a properly charged battery with sufficient fluid level. A dark eye is normally an indicator of a battery with sufficient fluid, but which is low in charge. A light or yellow eye usually indicates that electrolyte has dropped below the necessary level. In this last case, sealed batteries with an insufficient electrolyte must usually be discarded.**

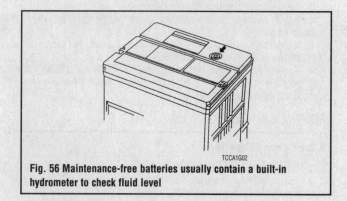

TCCA1G02

Fig. 56 Maintenance-free batteries usually contain a built-in hydrometer to check fluid level

Checking the Specific Gravity

▶ **See Figures 57, 58 and 59**

A hydrometer is required to check the specific gravity on all batteries that are not maintenance-free. On batteries that are maintenance-free, the specific gravity is checked by observing the built-in hydrometer "eye" on the top of the battery case.

✲✲ CAUTION

Battery electrolyte contains sulfuric acid. If you should splash any on your skin or in your eyes, flush the affected area with plenty of clear water. If it lands in your eyes, get medical help immediately.

The fluid (sulfuric acid solution) contained in the battery cells will tell you many things about the condition of the battery. Because the cell plates must be kept submerged below the fluid level in order to operate, the fluid level is extremely important. And, because the specific gravity of the acid is an indica-

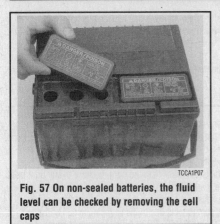

Fig. 57 On non-sealed batteries, the fluid level can be checked by removing the cell caps

Fig. 58 If the fluid level is low, add only distilled water until the level is correct

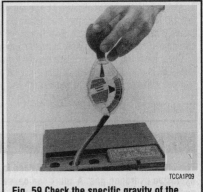

Fig. 59 Check the specific gravity of the battery's electrolyte with a hydrometer

tion of electrical charge, testing the fluid can be an aid in determining if the battery must be replaced. A battery in a vehicle with a properly operating charging system should require little maintenance, but careful, periodic inspection should reveal problems before they leave you stranded.

At least once a year, check the specific gravity of the battery. It should be between 1.20 and 1.26 on the gravity scale. Most auto stores carry a variety of inexpensive battery hydrometers. These can be used on any non-sealed battery to test the specific gravity in each cell.

The battery testing hydrometer has a squeeze bulb at one end and a nozzle at the other. Battery electrolyte is sucked into the hydrometer until the float is lifted from its seat. The specific gravity is then read by noting the position of the float. If gravity is low in one or more cells, the battery should be slowly charged and checked again to see if the gravity has come up. Generally, if after charging, the specific gravity between any two cells varies more than 50 points (0.50), the battery should be replaced, as it can no longer produce sufficient voltage to guarantee proper operation.

CABLES

▶ See Figures 60 thru 65

Once a year (or as necessary), the battery terminals and the cable clamps should be cleaned. Loosen the clamps and remove the cables, negative cable first. On top post batteries, the use of a puller specially made for this purpose is recommended. These are inexpensive and available in most parts stores. Side terminal battery cables are secured with a small bolt.

Clean the cable clamps and the battery terminal with a wire brush, until all corrosion, grease, etc., is removed and the metal is shiny. It is especially important to clean the inside of the clamp thoroughly (an old knife is useful here), since a small deposit of oxidation there will prevent a sound connection and inhibit starting or charging. Special tools are available for cleaning these parts, one type for conventional top post batteries and another type for side terminal batteries. It is also a good idea to apply some dielectric grease to the terminal, as this will aid in the prevention of corrosion.

Fig. 60 Loosen the battery cable retaining nut . . .

Fig. 61 . . . then disconnect the cable from the battery

Fig. 62 A wire brush may be used to clean any corrosion or foreign material from the cable

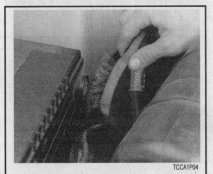

Fig. 63 The wire brush can also be used to remove any corrosion or dirt from the battery terminal

Fig. 64 The battery terminal can also be cleaned using a solution of baking soda and water

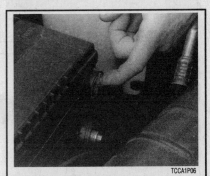

Fig. 65 Before connecting the cables, it's a good idea to coat the terminals with a small amount of dielectric grease

After the clamps and terminals are clean, reinstall the cables, negative cable last; DO NOT hammer the clamps onto battery posts. Tighten the clamps securely, but do not distort them. Give the clamps and terminals a thin external coating of grease after installation, to retard corrosion.

Check the cables at the same time that the terminals are cleaned. If the cable insulation is cracked or broken, or if the ends are frayed, the cable should be replaced with a new cable of the same length and gauge.

CHARGING

✷ CAUTION

The chemical reaction which takes place in all batteries generates explosive hydrogen gas. A spark can cause the battery to explode and splash acid. To avoid personal injury, be sure there is proper ventilation and take appropriate fire safety precautions when working with or near a battery.

A battery should be charged at a slow rate to keep the plates inside from getting too hot. However, if some maintenance-free batteries are allowed to discharge until they are almost "dead," they may have to be charged at a high rate to bring them back to "life." Always follow the charger manufacturer's instructions on charging the battery.

REPLACEMENT

When it becomes necessary to replace the battery, select one with an amperage rating equal to or greater than the battery originally installed. Deterioration and just plain aging of the battery cables, starter motor, and associated wires makes the battery's job harder in successive years. This makes it prudent to install a new battery with a greater capacity than the old.

Drive Belts

INSPECTION

▶ **See Figures 66, 67, 68, 69 and 70**

Check the drive belt(s) every 15,000 miles/12 months (heavy usage) or 30,000 miles/24 months (light usage) for evidence of wear such as cracking, fraying and incorrect tension. Determine the belt tension at a point halfway between the pulleys by pressing on the belt with moderate thumb pressure. The belt should deflect about ¼ in. (6mm) over a 7–10 in. (178–254mm) span, or ½ in. (12.7mm) over a 13–16 in. (330–406mm) span. If the deflection is found to be too much or too little, refer to the tension adjustments.

ADJUSTING TENSION

When adjusting belt tension note the following:
- A used belt is one that has been rotated at least one complete revolution on the pulleys. This begins the belt seating process and it must never be tensioned to the new belt specifications again.
- It is better to have belts too loose than too tight, because overly tight belts will lead to bearing failure, particularly in the water pump and alternator. However, loose belts can also cause problems, as they place an extremely high impact load on the driven components due to the whipping action of the belt.
- A GM Belt Tension Gauge No. BT-33-95-ACBN (regular V-belts), BT-33-97M (poly V-belts) or an equivalent tool is required for tensioning accessory drive belts on most 1982–86 trucks.

V-Belt Tensioning (1982–86)

▶ **See Figures 71 and 72**

1. If the belt is cold, operate the engine (at idle speed) for 15 minutes; the belt will seat itself in the pulleys allowing the belt fibers to relax or stretch. If the belt is hot, allow it to cool, until it is warm to the touch.
2. Loosen the component mounting bracket/pivot bolts.
3. Place GM Belt Tension Gauge No. BT-33-95-ACBN (standard V-belts), BT-33-97M (poly V-belts) or equivalent at the center of the belt between the longest span.
4. Pivot the component in order to apply more/less belt tension, as needed. Adjust the drive belt tension to the correct specifications.
5. While holding the component in a position resulting in the correct tension, tighten the component-to-mounting bracket bolt and pivot bolts.
6. Double check tension was not lost during tightening, then remove the tension gauge.

Serpentine Belt Tensioning (1987–93)

Most 1987–93 trucks are equipped with a single serpentine drive belt and an automatic tensioner. No belt adjustment is necessary as the tensioner adjusts by spring action. If a problem with the belt is suspected (it squeals often during

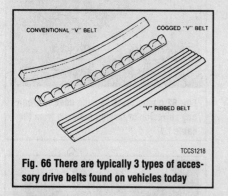

TCCS1218

Fig. 66 There are typically 3 types of accessory drive belts found on vehicles today

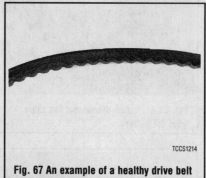

TCCS1214

Fig. 67 An example of a healthy drive belt

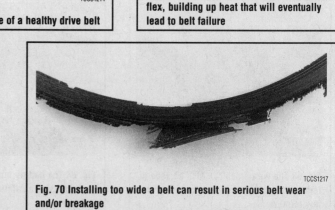

TCCS1215

Fig. 68 Deep cracks in this belt will cause flex, building up heat that will eventually lead to belt failure

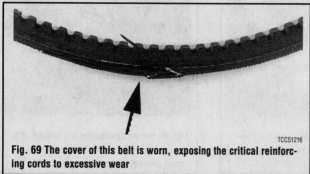

TCCS1216

Fig. 69 The cover of this belt is worn, exposing the critical reinforcing cords to excessive wear

TCCS1217

Fig. 70 Installing too wide a belt can result in serious belt wear and/or breakage

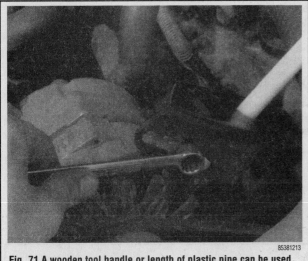

Fig. 71 A wooden tool handle or length of plastic pipe can be used to pivot the alternator outward

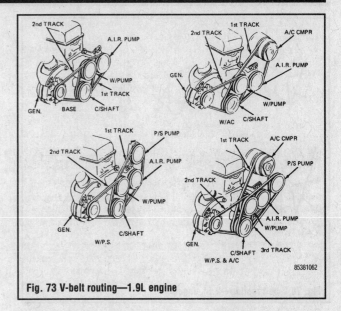

Fig. 73 V-belt routing—1.9L engine

Fig. 72 A prybar can be used on some brackets (a power steering pump bracket in this case)

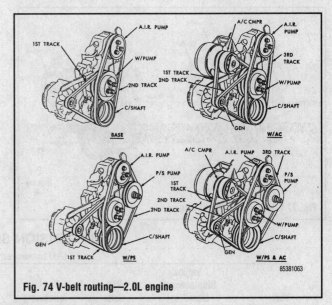

Fig. 74 V-belt routing—2.0L engine

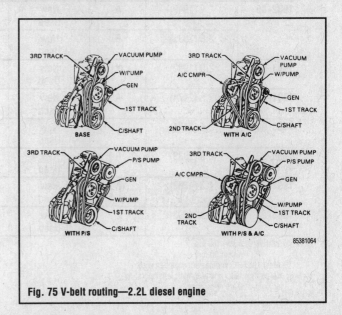

Fig. 75 V-belt routing—2.2L diesel engine

operation or appears too loose), check the belt length scale on the tensioner. If outside the acceptable range, check for improper belt routing, belt damage or wear. Most multiple ribbed belts stretch very little. If you are still unsure, compare the belt to a new one at your local parts store. If the belt length is the same, the tension may need to be replaced.

➡On multiple ribbed serpentine drive belts, cracks across the rib material are a normal part of belt aging process. These cracks do not affect belt operation and do not indicate a need to replace it.

REMOVAL & INSTALLATION

V-Belt

▶ See Figures 73, 74, 75, 76 and 77

1. Loosen the component mounting bracket/pivot bolts.
2. Rotate the component to relieve belt tension.
3. Slip the drive belt from the component pulley and remove it from the engine. If the engine uses more than one belt, iot may be necessary to remove outer belts first.
4. To install, slip the belt into position over the pulleys. Pivot the component to properly adjust the belt tension, then secure the fasteners. For details, please refer to the tension adjustment procedure earlier in this section.

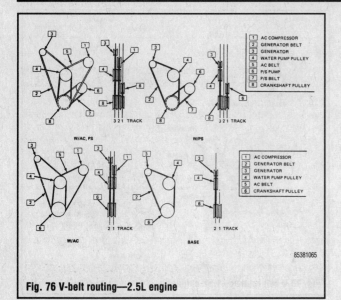

Fig. 76 V-belt routing—2.5L engine

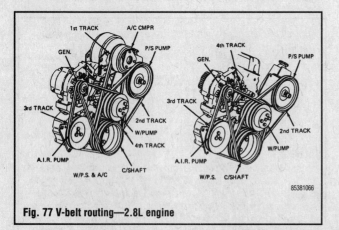

Fig. 77 V-belt routing—2.8L engine

Serpentine Belt

▶ **See Figures 78 and 79**

1. Place a large box wrench or ½ in. breaker bar and socket over the tensioner pulley axis bolt and rotate the tensioner counterclockwise loosen the belt.

2. While holding the tensioner in this position, remove the accessory drive belt and gently release the tensioner.

➡️ **Never allow the tension to snap back into position with or without the belt installed. Allowing the sudden release of tension could result in damage to the tensioner assembly.**

To install:

3. Begin to position the belt over the pulleys making sure the routing is correct.

4. Use the box wrench or breaker bar to pivot and hold the tensioner, then slip the belt fully into position.

5. Slowly ease the tensioner into contact with the belt.

6. No belt tensioning is necessary as the automatic tensioner is spring loaded.

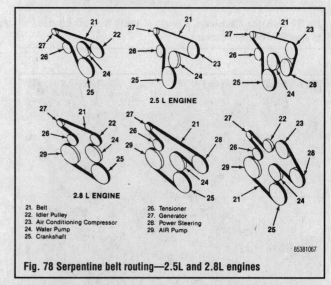

Fig. 78 Serpentine belt routing—2.5L and 2.8L engines

BELT TENSION SPECIFICATIONS
(All measurements in lbs.)

Year	Engine Displacement Liters (cc)	VIN Code	Tensioning	Alternator	Power Steering	Air Conditioning	Air Pump
1982–85	1.9 (1949)	A	New Used	135 67	135 78	157 90	135 67
	2.8 (2835)	B	New Used	146 67	135 67	146 67	135 67
1983–84	2.0 (1990)	Y	New Used	146 67	146 67	169 90	146 67
1991–93	2.5 (2474)	A	New Used	② 	② 	② 	②
1985–91	2.5 (2474)	E	New Used	146 67①②	146 67①②	169 90②	— —②
1986–93	2.8 (2835)	R	New Used	135 67②	135 67②	146 67②	146 67②
1992–93	4.3 (4293)	W	New Used	② 	② 	② 	②
1988–93	4.3 (4293)	Z	New Used	② 	② 	② 	②

① With A/C: (new) 169 lbs.
       (used) 90 lbs.
② Most 1987–93 engines are equipped with serpentine belts and automatic tensioners; no adjustments are necessary.

8844RA61

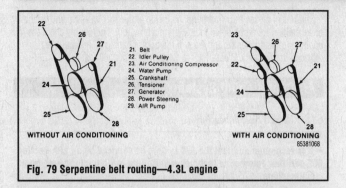

21. Belt
22. Idler Pulley
23. Air Conditioning Compressor
24. Water Pump
25. Crankshaft
26. Tensioner
27. Generator
28. Power Steering
29. AIR Pump

WITHOUT AIR CONDITIONING

WITH AIR CONDITIONING

85381068

Fig. 79 Serpentine belt routing—4.3L engine

Hoses

INSPECTION

▶ **See Figures 80, 81, 82 and 83**

Upper and lower radiator hoses, along with the heater hoses, should be checked for deterioration, leaks and loose hose clamps at least every 15,000 miles. It is also wise to check the hoses periodically in early spring and at the beginning of the fall or winter when you are performing other maintenance. A quick visual inspection could discover a weakened hose which might have left you stranded if it had remained unrepaired.

Whenever you are checking the hoses, make sure the engine and cooling system are cold. Visually inspect for cracking, rotting or collapsed hoses, and replace as necessary. Run your hand along the length of the hose. If a weak or swollen spot is noted when squeezing the hose wall, the hose should be replaced.

TCCS1219

Fig. 80 The cracks developing along this hose are a result of age-related hardening

REMOVAL & INSTALLATION

1. Remove the radiator pressure cap.

> ✳✳ **CAUTION**
>
> **Never remove the pressure cap while the engine is running, or personal injury from scalding hot coolant or steam may result. If possible, wait until the engine has cooled to remove the pressure cap. If this is not possible, wrap a thick cloth around the pressure cap and turn it slowly to the stop. Step back while the pressure is released from the cooling system. When you are sure all the pressure has been released, use the cloth to turn and remove the cap.**

2. Position a clean container under the radiator and/or engine draincock or plug, then open the drain and allow the cooling system to drain to an appropriate level. For some upper hoses, only a little coolant must be drained. To remove hoses positioned lower on the engine, such as a lower radiator hose, the entire cooling system must be emptied.

> ✳✳ **CAUTION**
>
> **When draining coolant, keep in mind that cats and dogs are attracted by ethylene glycol antifreeze, and are quite likely to drink any that is left in an uncovered container or in puddles on the ground. This will prove fatal in sufficient quantity. Always drain coolant into a sealable container.**

3. Loosen the hose clamps at each end of the hose requiring replacement. Clamps are usually either of the spring tension type (which require pliers to squeeze the tabs and loosen) or of the screw tension type (which require screw or hex drivers to loosen). Pull the clamps back on the hose away from the connection.

4. Twist, pull and slide the hose off the fitting, taking care not to damage the neck of the component from which the hose is being removed.

➡If the hose is stuck at the connection, do not try to insert a screwdriver or other sharp tool under the hose end in an effort to free it, as the connection and/or hose may become damaged. Heater connections especially may be easily damaged by such a procedure. If the hose is to be replaced, use a single-edged razor blade to make a slice along the portion of the hose which is stuck on the connection, perpendicular to the end of the hose. Do not cut too deep so as to prevent damaging the connection. The hose can then be peeled from the connection and discarded.

5. Clean both hose mounting connections. Inspect the condition of the hose clamps and replace them, if necessary.

To install:

6. Dip the ends of the new hose into clean engine coolant to ease installation.

7. Slide the clamps over the replacement hose, then slide the hose ends over the connections into position.

8. Position and secure the clamps at least ¼ in. (6.35mm) from the ends of the hose. Make sure they are located beyond the raised bead of the connector.

TCCS1220

Fig. 81 A hose clamp that is too tight can cause older hoses to separate and tear on either side of the clamp

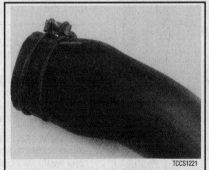

TCCS1221

Fig. 82 A soft spongy hose (identifiable by the swollen section) will eventually burst and should be replaced

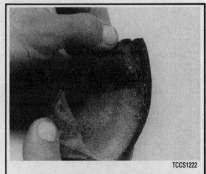

TCCS1222

Fig. 83 Hoses are likely to deteriorate from the inside if the cooling system is not periodically flushed

9. Close the radiator or engine drains and properly refill the cooling system with the clean drained engine coolant or a suitable mixture of coolant and water.

10. If available, install a pressure tester and check for leaks. If a pressure tester is not available, run the engine until normal operating temperature is reached (allowing the system to naturally pressurize), then check for leaks.

❄❄ CAUTION

If you are checking for leaks with the system at normal operating temperature, BE EXTREMELY CAREFUL not to touch any moving or hot engine parts. Once temperature has been reached, shut the engine OFF, and check for leaks around the hose fittings and connections which were removed earlier.

CV-Boots

INSPECTION

▶ See Figures 84 and 85

The CV (Constant Velocity) boots should be checked for damage each time the oil is changed and any other time the vehicle is raised for service. These boots keep water, grime, dirt and other damaging matter from entering the CV-joints. Any of these could cause early CV-joint failure which can be expensive to

Fig. 84 CV-boots must be inspected periodically for damage

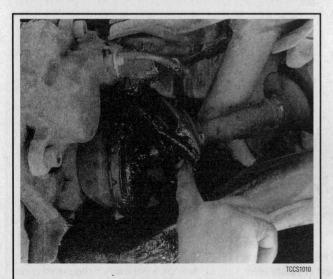
Fig. 85 A torn boot should be replaced immediately

repair. Heavy grease thrown around the inside of the front wheel(s) and on the brake caliper/drum can be an indication of a torn boot. Thoroughly check the boots for missing clamps and tears. If the boot is damaged, it should be replaced immediately. Please refer to Section 7 for procedures.

Air Conditioning System

SYSTEM SERVICE & REPAIR

➡ **It is recommended that the A/C system be serviced by an EPA Section 609 certified automotive technician utilizing a refrigerant recovery/recycling machine.**

The do-it-yourselfer should not service his/her own vehicle's A/C system for many reasons, including legal concerns, personal injury, environmental damage and cost.

According to the U.S. Clean Air Act, it is a federal crime to service or repair (involving the refrigerant) a Motor Vehicle Air Conditioning (MVAC) system for money without being EPA certified. It is also illegal to vent R-12 and R-134a refrigerants into the atmosphere. State and/or local laws may be more strict than the federal regulations, so be sure to check with your state and/or local authorities for further information.

➡ **Federal law dictates that a fine of up to $25,000 may be levied on people convicted of venting refrigerant into the atmosphere.**

When servicing an A/C system you run the risk of handling or coming in contact with refrigerant, which may result in skin or eye irritation or frostbite. Although low in toxicity (due to chemical stability), inhalation of concentrated refrigerant fumes is dangerous and can result in death; cases of fatal cardiac arrhythmia have been reported in people accidentally subjected to high levels of refrigerant. Some early symptoms include loss of concentration and drowsiness.

➡ **Generally, the limit for exposure is lower for R-134a than it is for R-12. Exceptional care must be practiced when handling R-134a.**

Also, some refrigerants can decompose at high temperatures (near gas heaters or open flame), which may result in hydrofluoric acid, hydrochloric acid and phosgene (a fatal nerve gas).

It is usually more economically feasible to have a certified MVAC automotive technician perform A/C system service on your vehicle.

R-12 Refrigerant Conversion

If your vehicle still uses R-12 refrigerant, one way to save A/C system costs down the road is to investigate the possibility of having your system converted to R-134a. The older R-12 systems can be easily converted to R-134a refrigerant by a certified automotive technician by installing a few new components and changing the system oil.

The cost of R-12 is steadily rising and will continue to increase, because it is no longer imported or manufactured in the United States. Therefore, it is often possible to have an R-12 system converted to R-134a and recharged for less than it would cost to just charge the system with R-12.

If you are interested in having your system converted, contact local automotive service stations for more details and information.

PREVENTIVE MAINTENANCE

Although the A/C system should not be serviced by the do-it-yourselfer, preventive maintenance should be practiced to help maintain the efficiency of the vehicle's A/C system. Be sure to perform the following:

• The easiest and most important preventive maintenance for your A/C system is to be sure that it is used on a regular basis. Running the system for five minutes each month (no matter what the season) will help ensure that the seals and all internal components remain lubricated.

➡ **Some vehicles automatically operate the A/C system compressor whenever the windshield defroster is activated. Therefore, the A/C system would not need to be operated each month if the defroster was used.**

• In order to prevent heater core freeze-up during A/C operation, it is necessary to maintain proper antifreeze protection. Be sure to properly maintain the engine cooling system.

• Any obstruction of or damage to the condenser configuration will restrict air flow which is essential to its efficient operation. Keep this unit clean and in proper physical shape.

➡**Bug screens which are mounted in front of the condenser (unless they are original equipment) are regarded as obstructions.**

• The condensation drain tube expels any water which accumulates on the bottom of the evaporator housing into the engine compartment. If this tube is obstructed, the air conditioning performance can be restricted and condensation buildup can spill over onto the vehicle's floor.

SYSTEM INSPECTION

Although the A/C system should not be serviced by the do-it-yourselfer, system inspections should be performed to help maintain the efficiency of the vehicle's A/C system. Be sure to perform the following:

The easiest and often most important check for the air conditioning system consists of a visual inspection of the system components. Visually inspect the system for refrigerant leaks, damaged compressor clutch, abnormal compressor drive belt tension and/or condition, plugged evaporator drain tube, blocked condenser fins, disconnected or broken wires, blown fuses, corroded connections and poor insulation.

A refrigerant leak will usually appear as an oily residue at the leakage point in the system. The oily residue soon picks up dust or dirt particles from the surrounding air and appears greasy. Through time, this will build up and appear to be a heavy dirt impregnated grease.

For a thorough visual and operational inspection, check the following:
• Check the surface of the radiator and condenser for dirt, leaves or other material which might block air flow.
• Check for kinks in hoses and lines. Check the system for leaks.
• Make sure the drive belt is properly tensioned. During operation, make sure the belt is free of noise or slippage.
• Make sure the blower motor operates at all appropriate positions, then check for distribution of the air from all outlets.

➡**Remember that in high humidity, air discharged from the vents may not feel as cold as expected, even if the system is working properly. This is because moisture in humid air retains heat more effectively than dry air, thereby making humid air more difficult to cool.**

Windshield Wipers

ELEMENT (REFILL) CARE & REPLACEMENT

▶ **See Figures 86, 87 and 88**

For maximum effectiveness and longest element life, the windshield and wiper blades should be kept clean. Dirt, tree sap, road tar and so on will cause streaking, smearing and blade deterioration if left on the glass. It is advisable to wash the windshield carefully with a commercial glass cleaner at least once a month. Wipe off the rubber blades with the wet rag afterwards. Do not attempt to move wipers across the windshield by hand; damage to the motor and drive mechanism will result.

To inspect and/or replace the wiper blade elements, place the wiper switch in the **LOW** speed position and the ignition switch in the **ACC** position. When the wiper blades are approximately vertical on the windshield, turn the ignition switch to **OFF**.

Examine the wiper blade elements. If they are found to be cracked, broken or torn, they should be replaced immediately. Replacement intervals will vary with usage, although ozone deterioration usually limits element life to about one year. If the wiper pattern is smeared or streaked, or if the blade chatters across the glass, the elements should be replaced. It is easiest and most sensible to replace the elements in pairs.

If your vehicle is equipped with aftermarket blades, there are several different types of refills and your vehicle might have any kind. Aftermarket blades and arms rarely use the exact same type blade or refill as the original equipment.

Regardless of the type of refill used, be sure to follow the part manufacturer's instructions closely. Make sure that all of the frame jaws are engaged as the refill is pushed into place and locked. If the metal blade holder and frame are allowed to touch the glass during wiper operation, the glass will be scratched.

Tires and Wheels

Common sense and good driving habits will afford maximum tire life. Make sure that you don't overload the vehicle or run with incorrect pressure in the tires. Either of these will increase tread wear. Fast starts, sudden stops and sharp cornering are hard on tires and will shorten their useful life span.

➡**For optimum tire life, keep the tires properly inflated, rotate them often and have the wheel alignment checked periodically.**

Inspect your tires frequently. Be especially careful to watch for bubbles in the tread or sidewall, deep cuts or underinflation. Replace any tires with bubbles in the sidewall. If cuts are so deep that they penetrate to the cords, discard the tire. Any cut in the sidewall of a radial tire renders it unsafe. Also look for uneven tread wear patterns that may indicate the front end is out of alignment or that the tires are out of balance.

TIRE ROTATION

▶ **See Figure 89**

Tires must be rotated periodically to equalize wear patterns that vary with a tire's position on the vehicle. Tires will also wear in an uneven way as the front steering/suspension system wears to the point where the alignment should be reset.

Rotating the tires will ensure maximum life for the tires as a set, so you will not have to discard a tire early due to wear on only part of the tread. Regular rotation is required to equalize wear.

When rotating "unidirectional tires," make sure that they always roll in the same direction. This means that a tire used on the left side of the vehicle must not be switched to the right side and vice-versa. Such tires should only be rotated front-to-rear or rear-to-front, while always remaining on the same side of the vehicle. These tires are marked on the sidewall as to the direction of rotation; observe the marks when reinstalling the tire(s).

Some styled or "mag" wheels may have different offsets front to rear. In these cases, the rear wheels must not be used up front and vice-versa. Furthermore, if

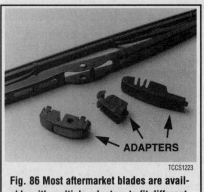

TCCS1223

Fig. 86 Most aftermarket blades are available with multiple adapters to fit different vehicles

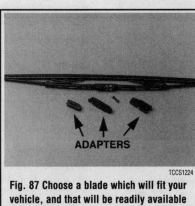

TCCS1224

Fig. 87 Choose a blade which will fit your vehicle, and that will be readily available next time you need blades

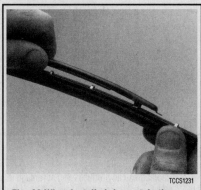

TCCS1231

Fig. 88 When installed, be certain the blade is fully inserted into the backing

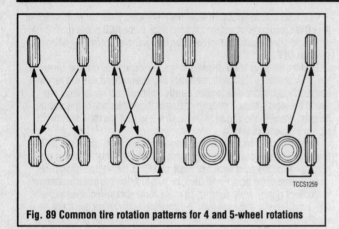

Fig. 89 Common tire rotation patterns for 4 and 5-wheel rotations

these wheels are equipped with unidirectional tires, they cannot be rotated unless the tire is remounted for the proper direction of rotation.

➡The compact or space-saver spare is strictly for emergency use. It must never be included in the tire rotation or placed on the vehicle for everyday use.

TIRE DESIGN

⬥ **See Figure 90**

For maximum satisfaction, tires should be used in sets of four. Mixing of different brands or types (radial, bias-belted, fiberglass belted) should be avoided. In most cases, the vehicle manufacturer has designated a type of tire on which the vehicle will perform best. Your first choice when replacing tires should be to use the same type of tire that the manufacturer recommends.

When radial tires are used, tire sizes and wheel diameters should be selected to maintain ground clearance and tire load capacity equivalent to the original specified tire. Radial tires should always be used in sets of four.

✳✳ CAUTION

Radial tires should never be used on only the front axle.

When selecting tires, pay attention to the original size as marked on the tire. Most tires are described using an industry size code sometimes referred to as P-Metric. This allows the exact identification of the tire specifications, regardless of the manufacturer. If selecting a different tire size or brand, remember to check the installed tire for any sign of interference with the body or suspension while the vehicle is stopping, turning sharply or heavily loaded.

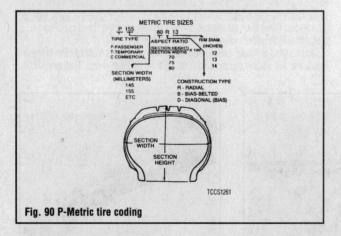

Fig. 90 P-Metric tire coding

Snow Tires

Good radial tires can produce a big advantage in slippery weather, but in snow, a street radial tire does not have sufficient tread to provide traction and control. The small grooves of a street tire quickly pack with snow and the tire behaves like a billiard ball on a marble floor. The more open, chunky tread of a

snow tire will self-clean as the tire turns, providing much better grip on snowy surfaces.

To satisfy municipalities requiring snow tires during weather emergencies, most snow tires carry either an M + S designation after the tire size stamped on the sidewall, or the designation "all-season." In general, no change in tire size is necessary when buying snow tires.

Most manufacturers strongly recommend the use of 4 snow tires on their vehicles for reasons of stability. If snow tires are fitted only to the drive wheels, the opposite end of the vehicle may become very unstable when braking or turning on slippery surfaces. This instability can lead to unpleasant endings if the driver can't counteract the slide in time.

Note that snow tires, whether 2 or 4, will affect vehicle handling in all non-snow situations. The stiffer, heavier snow tires will noticeably change the turning and braking characteristics of the vehicle. Once the snow tires are installed, you must re-learn the behavior of the vehicle and drive accordingly.

➡Consider buying extra wheels on which to mount the snow tires. Once done, the "snow wheels" can be installed and removed as needed. This eliminates the potential damage to tires or wheels from seasonal removal and installation. Even if your vehicle has styled wheels, see if inexpensive steel wheels are available. Although the look of the vehicle will change, the expensive wheels will be protected from salt, curb hits and pothole damage.

TIRE STORAGE

If they are mounted on wheels, store the tires at proper inflation pressure. All tires should be kept in a cool, dry place. If they are stored in the garage or basement, do not let them stand on a concrete floor; set them on strips of wood, a mat or a large stack of newspaper. Keeping them away from direct moisture is of paramount importance. Tires should not be stored upright, but in a flat position.

INFLATION & INSPECTION

⬥ **See Figures 91 thru 96**

The importance of proper tire inflation cannot be overemphasized. A tire employs air as part of its structure. It is designed around the supporting strength of the air at a specified pressure. For this reason, improper inflation drastically reduces the tire's ability to perform as intended. A tire will lose some air in day-to-day use; having to add a few pounds of air periodically is not necessarily a sign of a leaking tire.

Two items should be a permanent fixture in every glove compartment: an accurate tire pressure gauge and a tread depth gauge. Check the tire pressure (including the spare) regularly with a pocket type gauge. Too often, the gauge on the end of the air hose at your corner garage is not accurate because it suffers too much abuse. Always check tire pressure when the tires are cold, as pressure increases with temperature. If you must move the vehicle to check the tire inflation, do not drive more than a mile before checking. A cold tire is generally one that has not been driven for more than three hours.

A plate or sticker is normally provided somewhere in the vehicle (door post, hood, tailgate or trunk lid) which shows the proper pressure for the tires. Never counteract excessive pressure build-up by bleeding off air pressure (letting some air out). This will cause the tire to run hotter and wear quicker.

✳✳ CAUTION

Never exceed the maximum tire pressure embossed on the tire! This is the pressure to be used when the tire is at maximum loading, but it is rarely the correct pressure for everyday driving. Consult the owner's manual or the tire pressure sticker for the correct tire pressure.

Once you've maintained the correct tire pressures for several weeks, you'll be familiar with the vehicle's braking and handling personality. Slight adjustments in tire pressures can fine-tune these characteristics, but never change the cold pressure specification by more than 2 psi. A slightly softer tire pressure will give a softer ride but also yield lower fuel mileage. A slightly harder tire will give crisper dry road handling but can cause skidding on wet surfaces. Unless you're fully attuned to the vehicle, stick to the recommended inflation pressures.

All automotive tires have built-in tread wear indicator bars that show up as ½ in. (13mm) wide smooth bands across the tire when $\frac{1}{16}$ in. (1.5mm) of tread

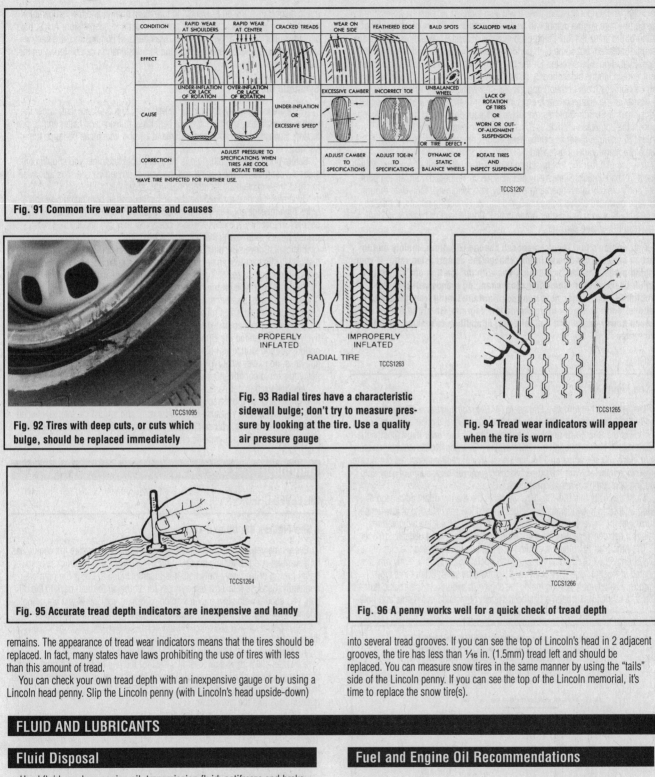

Fig. 91 Common tire wear patterns and causes

Fig. 92 Tires with deep cuts, or cuts which bulge, should be replaced immediately

Fig. 93 Radial tires have a characteristic sidewall bulge; don't try to measure pressure by looking at the tire. Use a quality air pressure gauge

Fig. 94 Tread wear indicators will appear when the tire is worn

Fig. 95 Accurate tread depth indicators are inexpensive and handy

Fig. 96 A penny works well for a quick check of tread depth

remains. The appearance of tread wear indicators means that the tires should be replaced. In fact, many states have laws prohibiting the use of tires with less than this amount of tread.

You can check your own tread depth with an inexpensive gauge or by using a Lincoln head penny. Slip the Lincoln penny (with Lincoln's head upside-down) into several tread grooves. If you can see the top of Lincoln's head in 2 adjacent grooves, the tire has less than 1/16 in. (1.5mm) tread left and should be replaced. You can measure snow tires in the same manner by using the "tails" side of the Lincoln penny. If you can see the top of the Lincoln memorial, it's time to replace the snow tire(s).

FLUID AND LUBRICANTS

Fluid Disposal

Used fluids such as engine oil, transmission fluid, antifreeze and brake fluid are hazardous wastes and must be disposed of properly. Before draining any fluids, consult with the local authorities; in many areas, waste oil, etc. is being accepted as a part of recycling programs. A number of service stations and auto parts stores are also accepting waste fluids for recycling.

Be sure of the recycling center's policies before draining any fluids, as many will not accept different fluids that have been mixed together, such as oil and antifreeze.

Fuel and Engine Oil Recommendations

FUEL

➡**Some fuel additives contain chemicals that can damage the catalytic converter and/or oxygen sensor. Read all of the labels carefully before using any additive in the engine or fuel system.**

All vehicles covered by this manual are designed to run on unleaded fuel. The use of a leaded fuel in a truck requiring unleaded fuel will plug the catalytic converter and render it inoperative. It will also increase exhaust backpressure to the point where engine output will be severely reduced. The minimum octane rating of the unleaded fuel being used must be at least 87, which usually means regular unleaded, but some high performance engines may require higher ratings. Fuel should be selected for the brand and octane which performs best with your engine. Judge a gasoline by its ability to prevent pinging, it's engine starting capabilities (cold and hot) and general all weather performance.

As far as the octane rating is concerned, refer to the general engine specifications chart in Section 3 of this manual to find your engine and its compression ratio. If the compression ratio is 9.0:1 or lower, in most cases a regular unleaded grade of gasoline can be used. If the compression ratio is 9.0:1–9.3:1, use a premium grade of unleaded fuel.

The use of a fuel too low in octane (a measurement of anti-knock quality) will result in spark knock. Since many factors such as altitude, terrain, air temperature and humidity affect operating efficiency, knocking may result even though the recommended fuel is being used. If persistent knocking occurs, it may be necessary to switch to a higher grade of fuel. Continuous or heavy knocking may result in engine damage.

➡️**Your engine's fuel requirement can change with time, mainly due to carbon buildup, which will in turn change the compression ratio. If your engine pings, knocks, or diesels (runs with the ignition off) switch to a higher grade of fuel. Sometimes just changing brands will cure the problem. If it becomes necessary to retard the timing from the specifications, don't change it more than a few degrees. Retarded timing will reduce power output and fuel mileage, in addition to making the engine run hotter.**

ENGINE OIL

▶ **See Figure 97**

The Society of Automotive Engineers (SAE) grade number indicates the viscosity of the engine oil and thus its ability to lubricate at a given temperature. The lower the SAE grade number, the lighter the oil; the lower the viscosity, the easier it is to crank the engine in cold weather. Oil viscosities should be chosen from those oils recommended for the lowest anticipated temperatures during the oil change interval. With the proper viscosity, you will be assured of easy cold starting and sufficient engine protection.

Multi-viscosity oils (5W-30, 10W-30 etc.) offer the important advantage of being adaptable to temperature extremes. They allow easy starting at low temperatures, yet they give good protection at high speeds and engine temperatures. This is a decided advantage in changeable climates or in long distance driving.

The American Petroleum Institute (API) designation indicates the classification of engine oil used under certain given operating conditions. Only oils designated at least for use Service SG or SH should be used. Oils of this type perform a variety of functions inside the engine in addition to their basic function as a lubricant. Through a balanced system of metallic detergents and poly-

meric dispersants, the oil prevents the formation of high and low temperature deposits and also keeps sludge and particles of dirt in suspension. Acids, particularly sulfuric acid, as well as other byproducts of combustion, are neutralized. Both the SAE grade number and the API designation can be found on the side of the oil bottle.

Synthetic Oil

There are excellent synthetic and fuel-efficient oils available that, under the right circumstances, can help provide better fuel mileage and better engine protection. However, these advantages come at a price, which can be much more per quart of conventional motor oils.

Before pouring any synthetic oils into your truck's engine, you should consider the condition of the engine and the type of driving you do. It is also wise to check the vehicle manufacturer's position on synthetic oils.

Generally, it is best to avoid the use of synthetic oil in both brand new and older, high mileage engines. New engines require a proper break-in, and some people feel that the synthetics are so slippery that they can impede this; most manufacturers recommend that you wait at least 5000 miles before switching to a synthetic oil. Conversely, older engines are looser and tend to loose more oil; synthetics will slip past worn parts more readily than regular oil. If your truck already leaks oil (due to bad seals or gaskets), it may leak more with a synthetic inside.

Consider your type of driving. If most of your accumulated mileage is on the highway at higher, steadier speed, a synthetic oil will reduce friction and probably help deliver better fuel mileage. Under such ideal highway conditions, the oil change interval can be extended, as long as the oil filter will operate effectively for the extended life of the oil. If the filter can't do its job for this extended period, dirt and sludge will build up in your engine's crankcase, sump, oil pump and lines, no matter what type of oil is used. If using synthetic oil in this manner, you should continue to change the oil filter at the recommended intervals.

Vehicles used under harder, stop-and-go, short hop circumstances should always be serviced more frequently, and for these trucks synthetic oil may not be a wise investment. Because of the necessary shorter change interval needed for this type of driving, you cannot take advantage of the long recommended change interval of most synthetic oils.

Engine

OIL LEVEL CHECK

▶ **See Figures 98, 99 and 100**

Every time you stop for fuel, check the engine oil making sure the engine has fully warmed and the vehicle is parked on a level surface. If the truck is used for trailer towing or for heavy-duty use, it is recommended to check the oil more frequently. Because it takes a few minutes for all the oil to drain back to the oil pan, you should wait a few minutes before checking your oil. If you are doing this at a fuel stop, first fill the fuel tank, then open the hood and check the oil, but don't get so carried away as to forget to pay for the fuel. Most station attendants won't believe that you forgot.

1. Make sure the truck is parked on level ground.
2. When checking the oil level it is best for the engine to be a normal operating temperature, although checking the oil immediately after stopping will lead to a false reading. Wait a few minutes after turning off the engine to allow the oil to drain back into the crankcase.
3. Open the hood and locate the dipstick which will be in a guide tube mounted in the upper engine block, just below the cylinder head mating surface. The dipstick may be located on the right or left side of the vehicle depending upon your particular engine, but on most of these pick-ups, it will be toward the driver's side of the engine. Pull the dipstick from its tube, wipe it clean (using a clean, lint free rag) and then reinsert it.
4. Pull the dipstick out again and, holding it horizontally, read the oil level. The oil should be between the FULL and ADD marks on the dipstick. If the oil is below the ADD mark, add oil of the proper viscosity through the capped opening in the top of the cylinder head cover or filler tube, as applicable. See the oil and fuel recommendations listed earlier in this section for the proper viscosity and rating of oil to use.
5. Replace the dipstick and check the oil level again after adding any oil. Approximately one quart of oil will raise the level from the ADD mark to the FULL mark. Be sure not to overfill the crankcase and waste the oil. Excess oil will generally be consumed at an accelerated rate.

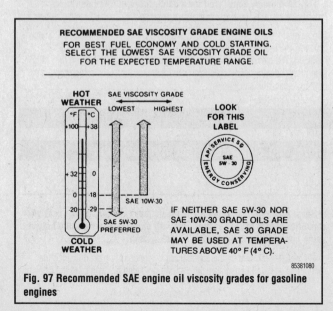

RECOMMENDED SAE VISCOSITY GRADE ENGINE OILS

FOR BEST FUEL ECONOMY AND COLD STARTING, SELECT THE LOWEST SAE VISCOSITY GRADE OIL FOR THE EXPECTED TEMPERATURE RANGE.

HOT WEATHER — SAE VISCOSITY GRADE — LOWEST — HIGHEST

LOOK FOR THIS LABEL — API SERVICE SG — SAE 5W-30 — ENERGY CONSERVING

SAE 10W-30
SAE 5W-30 PREFERRED
COLD WEATHER

IF NEITHER SAE 5W-30 NOR SAE 10W-30 GRADE OILS ARE AVAILABLE, SAE 30 GRADE MAY BE USED AT TEMPERATURES ABOVE 40° F (4° C).

85381080

Fig. 97 Recommended SAE engine oil viscosity grades for gasoline engines

Fig. 98 Withdraw the oil dipstick and wipe it clean with a lint free cloth

Fig. 99 Fully reinsert the oil dipstick into the guide tube

Fig. 100 Withdraw the dipstick again and read the oil level while holding the stick horizontally

OIL AND FILTER CHANGE

▶ **See Figures 101, 102, 103, 104 and 105**

If the vehicle is operated on a daily or semi-daily basis and most trips are for several miles (allowing the engine to properly warm-up), the oil should be changed a minimum of every 12 months or 7500 miles, whichever comes first.

If however, the vehicle is used to tow a trailer, is made to idle for extended periods of time such as in heavy daily traffic or if used as a service vehicle (delivery) or the vehicle is used for only short trips in below freezing temperature, the oil change interval should be shortened. Likewise, if your vehicle is used under dusty, polluted or off-road conditions, the oil should be changed more frequently. Under these circumstances oil has a greater chance of building up sludge and contaminants which could damage your engine. If your vehicle use fits into this circumstance, as most do, it is suggested that the oil and filter be changed every 3000 miles or 3 months, whichever comes first.

Under certain circumstances, Chevrolet and GMC recommend changing both the oil and filter during the first oil change and then only replacing the filter every other oil change thereafter. For the small price of an oil filter, it's cheap insurance to replace the filter at every oil change. One of the larger filter manufacturers points out in its advertisements that not changing the filter leaves one quart of dirty oil in the engine. This claim is true and should be kept in mind when changing your oil.

Oil should always be changed after the engine has been running long enough to bring it to normal operating temperature. Hot oil will flow easier and, more contaminants will be removed along with the oil than if it were drained cold. The oil drain plug is located on the bottom of the oil pan (bottom of the engine, underneath the truck). The filter is usually located on the left side of the engine and in some cases may be easier to reach through the plastic access flap in the wheel well.

You should have available a container that will hold a minimum of 6 quarts of liquid (to help prevent spilling the oil even after it is drained), a wrench to fit the drain plug, a spout for pouring in new oil and a rag or two, which you will

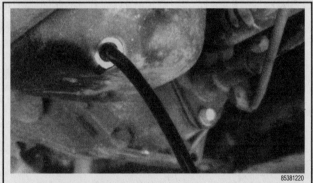
Fig. 101 Drain the old engine oil from the pan by removing the drain plug

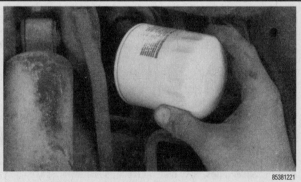
Fig. 102 Oil filter removal and installation may be accomplished through the wheel well on some vehicles

Fig. 103 Before installing a new oil filter, coat the rubber gasket with clean oil

Fig. 104 Remove the oil filler cap from the valve cover or filler spout

Fig. 105 Using a funnel will help prevent unnecessary mess while refilling the crankcase with fresh oil

always need. If the filter is being replaced, you will also need a band wrench or a filter wrench that fits the end of the filter.

➡️If the engine is equipped with an oil cooler, this will also have to be drained, using the drain plug. Be sure to add enough oil to fill the cooler in addition to the engine.

1. Run the engine until it reaches normal operating temperature, then shut the engine **OFF**, make sure the parking brake is firmly set and block the drive wheels.

2. Clearance may be sufficient to access the drain plug without raising the vehicle. If the truck must be lifted, be sure to support it safely with jackstands and be sure to position the drain plug at a low point under the vehicle.

3. Slide a drain pan of a least 6 quarts capacity under the oil pan. Wipe the drain plug and surrounding area clean using an old rag.

✳✳ CAUTION

The EPA warns that prolonged contact with used engine oil may cause a number of skin disorders, including cancer! You should make every effort to minimize your exposure to used engine oil. Protective gloves should be worn when changing the oil. Wash your hands and any other exposed skin areas as soon as possible after exposure to used engine oil. Soap and water, or waterless hand cleaner should be used.

4. Loosen the drain plug using a ratchet, short extension and socket or a box-wrench. Turn the plug out by hand, using a rag to shield your fingers from the hot oil. By keeping inward pressure on the plug as you unscrew it, oil won't escape past the threads and you can remove it without being burned by hot oil.

5. Quickly withdraw the plug and move your hands out of the way, but be careful not to drop the plug into the drain pan as fishing it out can be an unpleasant mess. Allow the oil to drain completely in the pan, then install and carefully tighten the drain plug. Be careful not to overtighten the drain plug, otherwise you'll be buying a new pan or a trick replacement plug for stripped threads.

➡️Although some manufacturers have at times recommended changing the oil filter every other oil change, we recommend the filter be changed each time you change your oil. The added benefit of clean oil is quickly lost if the old filter is clogged and the added protection to the heart of your engine far outweighs the few dollars saved by using a old filter.

6. Move the drain pan under the oil filter. Use a strap-type or cap-type filter wrench to loosen the oil filter. Cover your hand with a rag and spin the filter off by hand; turn it slowly. Keep in mind that it's holding about one quart of dirty, hot oil.

✳✳ CAUTION

On most Chevrolet engines, especially the V6s, the oil filter is next to the exhaust pipes. Stay clear of these, since even a passing contact can result in a painful burn. ALSO, on trucks equipped with catalytic converters, stay clear of the converter. The outside temperature of a hot catalytic converter can approach 1200°F.

7. Empty the old filter into the drain pan and properly dispose of the filter.

8. Using a clean rag, wipe off the filter adapter on the engine block. Be sure that the rag doesn't leave any lint which could clog an oil passage.

9. Coat the rubber gasket on the filter with fresh oil, then spin it onto the engine by hand; when the gasket touches the adapter surface, give it another ½–1 turn. No more, or you'll squash the gasket and it will leak.

10. Refill the engine with the correct amount of fresh oil. Please refer to the Capacities chart at the end of this section.

➡️Remember that any capacity is just a guide and you should always refill a component gradually, checking the level often. When refilling the engine crankcase, you may wish to leave it just a little below the full mark, then run the engine and top off the oil when it is at normal operating temperature.

11. Check the oil level on the dipstick. It is normal for the level to be a bit above the full mark until the engine is run and the new filter is filled with oil. Start the engine and allow it to idle for a few minutes.

✳✳ CAUTION

Do not run the engine above idle speed until it has built up oil pressure, as indicated when the oil light goes out.

12. Shut off the engine and allow the oil to flow back to the crankcase for a minute, then recheck the oil level. Check around the filter and drain plug for any leaks, and correct as necessary.

When you have finished this job, you will notice that you now possess four or five quarts of dirty oil. The best thing to do with it is to pour it into plastic jugs, such as milk containers. Then, locate a service station or automotive parts store where you can pour it into their used oil tank for recycling.

Manual Transmission

FLUID RECOMMENDATIONS

Most of the S-10/S-15 trucks equipped with manual transmissions use Dexron II® automatic transmission fluid, which is a thin, reddish fluid. However, certain models may be equipped with transmissions which MUST use manual transmission fluid, SAE 80W-90 gear oil, or in some cases, Synchromesh® transmission fluid. Be absolutely sure what type of fluid your transmission requires before changing or adding fluid to the manual transmission. Check your owner's manual for the proper recommended fluid for your transmission. If necessary, copy down the transmission codes stamped on the housing and speak with your local parts supplier to verify the type of transmission and the necessary fluid.

➡️Using the incorrect lubricant in your transmission can lead to significant transmission damage and a costly overhaul.

LEVEL CHECK

◆ **See Figure 106**

Remove the filler plug from the side of the transmission (usually located on the passenger's-side of the housing). If the transmission housing contains 2 plugs, the lower is a drain plug, while the upper plug is the filler. The oil should be level with the bottom edge of the filler hole. This should be checked at least once every 6,000 miles or more often if any leakage or seepage is observed.

➡️When checking the fluid, the vehicle must be level. If it was necessary to raise and support the vehicle to access the filler plug, the vehicle must be supported at sufficient points (all wheels or 4 points on the frame) so it is sitting level and is not tilted forward/backward or to one side.

DRAIN AND REFILL

◆ **See Figure 107**

Under normal conditions, the manual transmission fluid should not need to be changed. However, if the truck is driven in deep water (as high as the transmission casing) it is a good idea to replace the fluid. Little harm can come from a fluid change when you have just purchased a used vehicle, especially since the condition of the transmission fluid is usually not known.

If the fluid is to be drained, it is a good idea to warm the fluid first so it will flow better. This can be accomplished by 15–20 miles of highway driving. Fluid which is warmed to normal operating temperature will flow faster, drain more completely and remove more contaminants from the housing.

1. Raise and support the vehicle safely using jackstands.
2. Place a fluid catch pan under the transmission.
3. Remove the bottom transmission housing plug and allow the fluid to drain.
4. Install the bottom plug and refill the transmission housing.

Automatic Transmission

FLUID RECOMMENDATIONS

When adding fluid or refilling the transmission, always use Dexron II® automatic transmission fluid or the latest superceding Dexron® fluid.

Fig. 106 Remove the filler plug; NOTE the preferred method is to use an inexpensive tool designed for this

Fig. 107 Remove the drain plug (lower of the 2 plugs); be careful not to strip the plug if you use a wrench

Fig. 108 Automatic transmission dipstick marks; the proper level for a hot transmission is within the shaded area

LEVEL CHECK

♦ See Figure 108

Check the automatic transmission fluid level at least every 7500 miles. The dipstick can be found in the rear of the engine compartment. The fluid level should be checked only when the transmission is hot (normal operating temperature). The transmission is considered hot after about 15–20 miles of highway driving.

➡ **Although the transmission should be checked while the fluid is at normal operating temperature, do not check it if it is at the extreme high end of the operating temperature range. Wait at least 30 minutes if you have just be driving the vehicle in ambient temperatures in excess of 90°F (32°C), at highway speeds for a long time, in heavy traffic (especially in hot weather) or have been pulling a trailer.**

1. Park the truck on a level surface with the engine idling, then shift the transmission into Park and firmly set the parking brake.
2. With your foot on the brake pedal, move the selector through each gear range (pausing for about 3 seconds in each gear), then place it in Park. Allow the engine to run at idle about 3 more minutes.

➡ **When moving the selector through each range, DO NOT race the engine.**

3. With the engine running at a low idle, remove the dipstick, wipe it clean and then reinsert it firmly. Be sure that it has been pushed all the way in, then pause 3 seconds. Remove the dipstick again and check the fluid level while holding it horizontally. The fluid level should be between the upper notch and the FULL HOT line. If the fluid must be checked when it is cool, the level should be between the lower 2 notches.

➡ **Most of the transmissions for the 4.3L engine are equipped with a flip-top handle on the dipstick. To withdraw these, flip the handle upward, then pull the dipstick from the guide.**

4. If the fluid level is low add DEXRON II® automatic transmission fluid. The fluid must be added through the transmission dipstick tube, which is easily accomplished using a funnel. Add fluid gradually, checking the level often as you are filling the transmission. Be extremely careful not to overfill the transmission, as this will cause slippage, seal damage and overheating. Approximately one pint of ATF will raise the fluid level from one notch/line to the other.

➡ **Always use DEXRON II® or the latest superceding Dexron® ATF. The use of ATF Type F or any other fluid will cause severe damage to the transmission.**

The fluid on the dipstick should always be a bright red color. If it is discolored (brown or black), or smells burnt, serious transmission troubles, probably due to overheating, should be suspected. The transmission should be inspected by a qualified technician to locate the cause of the burnt fluid.

DRAIN AND REFILL

♦ See Figure 109

The truck should be driven 15–20 miles to warm the transmission fluid before the pan is removed.

➡ **The fluid should be drained while the transmission is warm.**

1. Raise and support the front of vehicle safely using jackstands.
2. Place a drain pan or under the transmission housing a fluid pan.
3. Remove the pan bolts from the front and the sides, then loosen the rear bolts 4 turns.

➡ **On some vehicles, it may be necessary to support the transmission tailshaft and remove the crossmember just behind the transmission for pan clearance or access to the pan bolts.**

4. Using a small prybar, carefully pry the pan downward at the front of the transmission. This will allow the pan to partially drain. Remove the remaining pan bolts and lower the pan from the transmission.

➡ **If the transmission fluid is dark or has a burnt smell, transmission damage is indicated. Have the transmission checked professionally.**

5. Empty the transmission pan of the remaining fluid, then remove the gasket material and clean with a solvent.
6. Using a putty knife, carefully clean the gasket mounting surfaces.

To install:

7. Use a new gasket and sealant and install the transmission pan. Install and tighten the retaining bolts to 8 ft. lbs. (11 Nm) using a criss-cross pattern.
8. Remove the jackstands and carefully lower the vehicle.
9. Immediately refill the transmission housing using Dexron II® automatic transmission fluid. Add the fluid through the filler tube. Please refer to the capacities chart found later in this section to determine the proper amount of fluid to be added.

✳ CAUTION

DO NOT OVERFILL the transmission. Foaming of the fluid and subsequent transmission damage due to slippage can result.

10. With the gearshift lever in PARK, start the engine and let it idle. DO NOT race the engine.

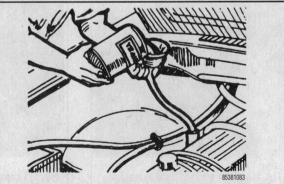

Fig. 109 Fluid may be easily added through the automatic transmission dipstick guide using a funnel with a flexible hose

11. Apply the parking brake and move the gearshift lever through each position. Return the lever to Park and check the fluid level with the engine idling. The level should be between the two dimples on the dipstick, about ¼ in. (6mm) below the ADD mark. Add fluid, if necessary.

12. Check the fluid level after the truck has been driven enough to thoroughly warm the transmission.

PAN AND FILTER SERVICE

1. Remove the transmission oil pan and drain the fluid. For details, please refer to the procedure located earlier in this section.

2. Remove the screen and the filter from the valve body. Most screens are retained using a bolt fastener, though some may use an interference fit between the screen tube and valve body.

To install:

3. Install a new filter using a new gasket or O-ring.

➡**If the transmission uses a filter equipped with a fully exposed screen, it may be cleaned and reused.**

4. Install the transmission oil pan and properly refill the transmission.

Transfer Case

FLUID RECOMMENDATIONS

When adding fluid or refilling the transfer case, use Dexron II® or the latest superceding Dexron® automatic transmission fluid for most vehicles covered by this manual. However, there are indications that some models may have been designed to run with SAE 80W or SAE 80W-90 GL5, so check your owners manual to be sure.

LEVEL CHECK

▶ **See Figure 110**

➡**When checking the fluid, the vehicle must be level. If it was necessary to raise and support the vehicle to access the filler plug, the vehicle must be supported at sufficient points (all wheels or 4 points on the frame) so it is sitting level and is not tilted forward/backward or to one side.**

1. If necessary for access to the filler plug, raise and support the vehicle safely using jackstands, but make sure the vehicle is level.

2. Remove the filler plug (upper plug of 2) from the rear-side of the transfer case.

3. Using your finger, check the fluid level, it should be level with the bottom of the filler hole.

4. If the fluid level is low, use the proper type of fluid to bring the fluid up to the proper level. Most parts stores will carry a small, hand operated pump which will greatly ease the task of adding fluid to the transfer case.

5. Install and tighten the filler plug.

DRAIN AND REFILL

▶ **See Figure 111**

1. Operate the vehicle in four wheel drive in order to warm the fluid to normal operating temperature.

2. If necessary for access to the drain and filler plugs, raise and support the vehicle safely using jackstands. Support the truck so it is level; this is necessary to assure the proper fluid level is maintained when the case is refilled.

3. Position drain pan under transfer case.

4. Remove drain and fill plugs, then drain the lubricant into the drain pan.

5. Install and tighten the drain plug.

6. Remove the drain pan and dump the fluid into a used transmission fluid storage tank, for recycling purposes.

7. Using Dexron II® automatic transmission fluid, fill transfer case to edge of fill plug opening.

8. Install and tighten the fill plug.

9. Remove the jackstands and carefully lower the vehicle, then check for proper operation of the transfer case.

Drive Axles

The fluid in both the rear axle and, if equipped, the front drive axle should be checked at each oil change. The fluid in the rear axle should be changed at the truck's first engine oil change and thereafter at intervals of 7500 miles (vehicles through 1986) or 15,000 miles (1987 and later vehicles). Changing the front drive axle fluid on these vehicles usually requires it's removal and partial disassembly. The fluid in the front drive axle should not need to be changed unless the axle is removed for repair.

The fluid is checked by removing the filler plug, but keep in mind the the truck must be sitting level or an incorrect fluid level will be indicated. Maintain the fluid at a level ⅜ in. below the filler plug hole.

FLUID RECOMMENDATIONS

Always use SAE 80W-90 GL5 gear lubricant, part number 1052271, or equivalent.

LEVEL CHECK

▶ **See Figures 112 and 113**

➡**When checking the fluid, the vehicle must be level. If it was necessary to raise and support the vehicle to access the filler plug, the vehicle must be supported at sufficient points (all wheels or 4 points on the frame) so it is sitting level and is not tilted forward/backward or to one side.**

1. If necessary for access to the filler plug, raise and support the vehicle safely using jackstands, but make sure the vehicle is level.

2. Remove the filler plug, located at the side of the differential carrier.

3. Check the fluid level, it should be ⅜ in. below the bottom of the filler plug hole.

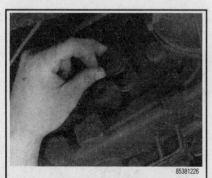

85381226

Fig. 110 Check the fluid level by removing the upper of the 2 plugs from the side of the transfer case

85381227

Fig. 111 Loosen and remove the lower plug (drain plug) in order to drain the fluid from the transfer case

85381229

Fig. 112 Fluid level may be checked on front drive axles using the filler plug

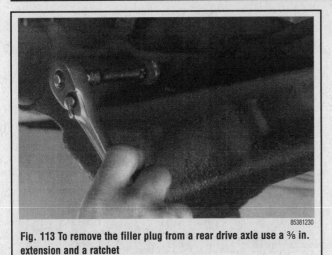

Fig. 113 To remove the filler plug from a rear drive axle use a ⅜ in. extension and a ratchet

4. If necessary add fluid through the filler plug opening. A suction gun or a squeeze bulb may be used to add fluid. Most parts stores will carry a small, hand operated pump which will greatly ease the task of adding fluid.

5. Install and tighten the filler plug.

6. Remove the jackstands and carefully lower the vehicle.

DRAIN AND REFILL

▶ **See Figures 114, 115, 116 and 117**

1. Run the vehicle until the lubricant reaches operating temperature.

2. If necessary for access, raise and support the vehicle safely using jackstands; but make sure that the vehicle is level.

3. Use a wire brush to clean the area around the differential. This will help prevent dirt from contaminating the differential housing while the cover is removed.

4. Position a drain pan under the rear axle.

5. Unscrew the retaining bolts and remove the rear cover. When removing the cover, a small prytool may be used at the base of the cover to gently pry it back from the axle housing, breaking the gasket seal and allowing the lubricant to drain out into the container. Be careful not to use excessive force and damage the cover or housing.

To install:

6. Carefully clean the gasket mating surfaces of the cover and axle housing of any remaining gasket or sealer. A putty knife is a good tool to use for this.

7. Install the rear cover using a new gasket and sealant. Tighten the retaining bolts using a crosswise pattern to 20 ft. lbs. (27 Nm).

➡ **Make sure the vehicle is level before attempting to add fluid to the rear axle or an incorrect fluid level will result.**

8. Refill the rear axle housing using the proper grade and quantity of lubricant as detailed earlier in this section. Install the filler plug, operate the vehicle and check for any leaks.

Cooling System

▶ **See Figures 118 and 119**

❋ CAUTION

Never remove the radiator cap under any conditions while the engine is hot! Failure to follow these instructions could result in damage to the cooling system, engine and/or personal injury. To avoid having scalding hot coolant or steam blow out of the radiator, use extreme care whenever you are removing the radiator cap. Wait until the engine has cooled, then wrap a thick cloth around the radiator cap and turn it slowly to the first stop. Step back while the pressure is released from the cooling system. When you are sure the pressure has been released, press down on the radiator cap (still have the cloth in position) turn and remove the radiator cap.

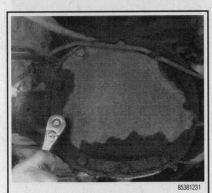

Fig. 114 Loosen and remove the bolts retaining the rear axle housing cover

Fig. 115 Before it is removed, use a wire brush to clean dirt from the outside of the cover

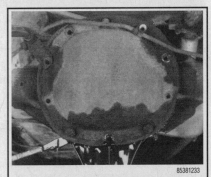

Fig. 116 When all of the bolts are loosened or removed, carefully pry outward allowing the fluid to drain

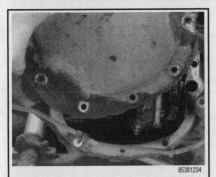

Fig. 117 Once the fluid has drained, remove the cover from the housing so the gasket may be replaced

Fig. 118 Coolant protection can be easily checked using a float-type hydrometer tester

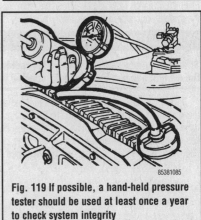

Fig. 119 If possible, a hand-held pressure tester should be used at least once a year to check system integrity

Dealing with the cooling system can be a dangerous matter unless the proper precautions are observed. It is best to check the coolant level in the radiator when the engine is cold. All vehicles covered by this manual should be equipped with a coolant recovery tank. If the coolant level is at or near the ADD/FULL COLD line (engine cold) or the FULL HOT line (engine hot), the level is satisfactory. Always be certain that the filler caps on both the radiator and the recovery tank are closed tightly.

In the event that the coolant level must be checked when the engine is hot and the vehicle is not equipped with a coolant recovery tank, place a thick rag over the radiator cap and slowly turn the cap counterclockwise until it reaches the first detent. Allow all hot steam to escape. This will allow the pressure in the system to drop gradually, preventing an explosion of hot coolant. When the hissing noise stops, carefully remove the cap the rest of the way.

If the coolant level is found to be low, add a 50/50 mixture of ethylene glycol-based antifreeze and clean water. If not equipped with a recovery tank, coolant must be added through the radiator filler neck. On most models, which are equipped with a recovery tank, coolant may be added either through the filler neck on the radiator or directly into the recovery tank.

✳ CAUTION

Never add coolant to a hot engine unless it is running. If it is not running you run the risk of cracking the engine block.

It is wise to pressure check the cooling system at least once per year. If the coolant level is chronically low or rusty, the system should be thoroughly checked for leaks.

At least once every 2 years or 30,000 miles, the engine cooling system should be inspected, flushed and refilled with fresh coolant. If the coolant is left in the system too long, it loses its ability to prevent rust and corrosion. If the coolant has too much water, it won't protect against freezing.

The pressure cap should be examined for signs of age or deterioration. Fan belt and other drive belts should be inspected and adjusted to the proper tension. (See checking belt tension).

Hose clamps should be tightened, and soft or cracked hoses replaced. Damp spots, or accumulations of rust or dye near hoses, water pump or other areas, indicate possible leakage, which must be corrected before filling the system with fresh coolant.

FLUID RECOMMENDATIONS

Whenever adding or changing fluid, use a good quality of ethylene glycol antifreeze (one that will not effect aluminum), mix it with water until a 50–50 antifreeze solution is attained.

LEVEL CHECK

▶ **See Figures 120 and 121**

On most late model vehicles, the fluid level may be checked by observing the fluid level marks of the recovery tank (see through plastic bottle). The level should be near the ADD or FULL COLD mark, as applicable, when the system is cold. At normal operating temperatures, the level should be above the ADD/FULL COLD mark or, if applicable, between the ADD/FULL COLD and the FULL HOT marks. Only add coolant to the recovery tank as necessary to bring the system up to a proper level.

✳ CAUTION

Should it be necessary to remove the radiator cap, make sure that the system has had time to cool, reducing the internal pressure.

On any vehicle that is not equipped with a coolant recovery or overflow tank, the level must be checked by removing the radiator cap. This should only be done when the cooling system has had time to sufficiently cool after the engine has been run. The coolant level should be within 2 in. of the base of the radiator filler neck. If necessary, coolant can then be added directly to the radiator.

Fig. 120 A see-through coolant recovery/overflow tank is usually mounted to the left fender

Fig. 121 When equipped, the cooling system should be topped off using the recovery tank

COOLING SYSTEM INSPECTION

Checking the Radiator Cap Seal

While you are checking the coolant level, check the radiator cap for a worn or cracked gasket. It the cap doesn't seal properly, fluid will be lost and the engine will overheat.

Worn caps should be replaced with a new one.

Checking the Radiator for Debris

Periodically clean any debris—leaves, paper, insects, etc.—from the radiator fins. Pick the large pieces off by hand. The smaller pieces can be washed away with water pressure from a hose.

Carefully straighten any bent radiator fins with a pair of needle nose pliers. Be careful—the fins are very soft. Don't wiggle the fins back and forth too much. Straighten them once and try not to move them again.

DRAINING AND REFILLING THE SYSTEM

♦ **See Figures 122, 123 and 124**

> ❄❄ **CAUTION**
>
> **To avoid injuries from scalding fluid and steam, DO NOT remove the radiator cap while the engine and radiator are still HOT.**

1. Make sure the engine is cool and the vehicle is parked on a level surface, then remove the radiator neck cap and, if equipped, the recovery tank cap in order to relieve system pressure.

2. Position a large drain pan under the vehicle, then drain the existing antifreeze (coolant) by opening the radiator petcock and, if necessary, by removing the engine block drain plug(s). It its also possible to drain the system by disconnecting the lower radiator hose from the bottom radiator outlet.

> ❄❄ **CAUTION**
>
> **When draining the coolant, keep in mind that cats and dogs are attracted by ethylene glycol antifreeze, and are quite likely to drink any that is left in an uncovered container or in puddles on the ground. This will prove fatal in sufficient quantity. Always drain the coolant into a sealable container. Coolant should be reused unless it is contaminated or several years old at which point it should be returned to a coolant recycling or hazardous waste disposal sight. Check your local laws for proper disposal methods.**

3. Close the radiator/engine drains or reconnect the lower hose.

4. If necessary, empty the coolant reservoir and flush it. This is most easily done by removing the reservoir tank from the vehicle.

5. Determine the capacity of your coolant system (see capacities specifications). Through the radiator filler neck, add a 50/50 mix of quality antifreeze (ethylene glycol) and water to provide the desired protection.

6. Leave the radiator pressure cap off, then start and run the engine until the thermostat heats up and opens, this will allow air to bleed from the system and provide room for additional coolant to be added to the radiator.

7. Add additional coolant to the radiator, as necessary, until the level is within 2 in. of the radiator's filler neck base.

8. Stop the engine and check the coolant level.

9. Check the level of protection with an antifreeze tester, then install the radiator pressure cap.

10. If equipped with a coolant recovery/overflow tank, add coolant to the tank, as necessary, to achieve the proper level.

11. Start and run the engine to normal operating temperature, then check the system for leaks.

FLUSHING AND CLEANING THE SYSTEM

The cooling system should be drained, thoroughly flushed and refilled at least every 30,000 miles or 24 months. These operations should be done with the engine cold, especially if a backpressure flushing kit is being used. Completely draining, flushing and refilling the cooling system at least every two years will remove accumulated rust, scale and other deposits. Coolant in late model vehicles is a 50/50 mixture of ethylene glycol and water for year round use. Use a good quality antifreeze with water pump lubricants, rust inhibitors and other corrosion inhibitors along with acid neutralizers.

There are many products available for cooling system flushing. If a backpressure flushing kit is used, it is recommended that the thermostat be temporarily removed in order to allow free flow to the system with cold water. Always follow the kit or cleaner manufacturer's instructions and make sure the product is compatible with your vehicle.

1. Make sure the engine is cool and the vehicle is parked on a level surface, then remove the radiator neck cap and, if equipped the recovery tank cap in order to relieve system pressure.

2. Position a large drain pan under the vehicle, then drain the existing antifreeze and coolant by opening the radiator petcock and/or engine drains. It is also possible to drain the system by disconnecting the lower radiator hose, from the bottom radiator outlet.

> ❄❄ **CAUTION**
>
> **When draining the coolant, keep in mind that cats and dogs are attracted by ethylene glycol antifreeze, and are quite likely to drink any that is left in an uncovered container or in puddles on the ground. This will prove fatal in sufficient quantity. Always drain the coolant into a sealable container. Coolant should be reused unless it is contaminated or several years old at which point it should be returned to a coolant recycling or hazardous waste disposal sight. Check your local laws for proper disposal methods.**

3. Close the radiator/engine drains or reconnect the lower hose, as applicable and fill the system with water.

4. Add a can of quality radiator flush.

5. Idle the engine until the upper radiator hose gets hot and the thermostat has opened. This will allow the solution to fully circulate through the system.

6. Drain the system again.

7. Repeat this process until the drained water is clear and free of scale.

8. Close all drains and connect all the hoses.

9. If equipped with a coolant recovery system, flush the reservoir with water and leave empty.

10. Determine the capacity of your coolant system (see capacities specifications). Through the radiator filler neck, add a 50/50 mix of quality antifreeze (ethylene glycol) and water to provide the desired protection.

11. Leave the radiator pressure cap off, then start and run the engine until the thermostat heats up and opens, this will allow air to bleed from the system and provide room for additional coolant to be added to the radiator.

12. Add additional coolant to the radiator, as necessary, until the level is within 2 in. of the radiator's filler neck base.

13. Stop the engine and check the coolant level.

14. Check the level of protection with an antifreeze tester, then install the radiator pressure cap.

15. If equipped with a coolant recovery/overflow tank, add coolant to the tank, as necessary to achieve the proper level.

16. Start and run the engine to normal operating temperature, then check the system for leaks.

Fig. 122 ONLY remove the cap from the radiator filler neck when the engine is COLD

Fig. 123 Some drains are positioned so coolant will pour on the rad-support (dripping from various points)

Fig. 124 One solution is to use a funnel such as this one made from a plastic milk jug (recycling at its best)

Brake Master Cylinder

▶ **See Figure 125**

Chevrolet and GMC trucks are equipped with a dual braking system, allowing a truck to be brought to a safe stop in the event of failure in either the front or rear brakes. The dual master cylinder has two separate reservoirs, one connected to the front brakes and the other connected to the rear brakes. In the event of failure in either portion, the remaining portion is unaffected.

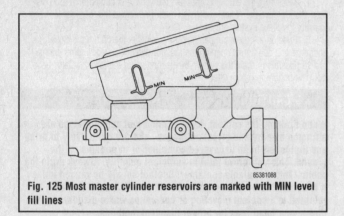

85381088

Fig. 125 Most master cylinder reservoirs are marked with MIN level fill lines

FLUID RECOMMENDATIONS

Use only heavy-duty Delco Supreme 11 or DOT 3 brake fluid.

❊❊ WARNING

Brake fluid damages paint. It also absorbs moisture from the air; never leave a container or the master cylinder uncovered any longer than necessary. All parts in contact with the brake fluid (master cylinder, hoses, plunger assemblies and etc.) must be kept clean, since any contamination of the brake fluid will adversely affect braking performance.

LEVEL CHECK

▶ **See Figure 126**

It should be obvious how important the brake system is to safe operation of your vehicle. The brake fluid is key to the proper operation of the brake system.

85381240

Fig. 126 When adding brake fluid to the master cylinder use only clean, fresh fluid from a sealed container

Low levels of fluid indicate a need for service (there may be a leak in the system or the brake pads may just be worn and in need of replacement). In any case, the brake fluid level should be inspected at least during every oil change, but more often is desirable. Every time you open the hood is a good time to glance at the master cylinder reservoir.

To check the fluid level on most vehicles covered by this manual, you may peer through the side wall of the reservoir and observe the level in relation to the markings. If the reservoir is opaque, simply unsnap and lift off the reservoir cover, to check the fluid level; it should be within ¼ of the tops of the reservoir walls. When making additions of brake fluid, use only fresh, uncontaminated brake fluid which meets or exceeds DOT 3 standards. Be careful not to spill any brake fluid on painted surfaces, as it will quickly eat the paint. Do not allow the brake fluid container or the master cylinder reservoir to remain open any longer than necessary; brake fluid absorbs moisture from the air, reducing its effectiveness and causing corrosion in the lines.

Hydraulic Clutch

➡ **The clutch master cylinder is mounted on the firewall next to the brake master cylinder.**

FLUID RECOMMENDATIONS

Use only heavy duty Delco Supreme 11 or DOT 3 brake fluid.

LEVEL CHECK

The hydraulic clutch reservoir should be checked at least every 6 months. Fill to the line on the reservoir.

Power Steering Pump

The power steering pump reservoir is located at the front left-side of the engine.

FLUID RECOMMENDATIONS

Use GM Power Steering Fluid No. 1050017 or equivalent. On some vehicles, access is difficult without using a flexible funnel.

➡ **Avoid using automatic transmission fluid in the power steering unit.**

LEVEL CHECK

▶ **See Figures 127, 128 and 129**

The power steering fluid should be checked at least every 6 months. There is a Cold and a Hot mark on the dipstick. To prevent possible overfilling, check the fluid level only when the fluid has warmed to operating temperatures and the engine is shut **OFF**. If necessary, add fluid to the power steering pump reservoir.

➡ **On models equipped with a remote reservoir, the fluid level should be ½–1 in. (13–25mm) from the top when the wheels are turned to the extreme left position.**

Manual Steering Gear

The steering gear is factory-filled with a lubricant which does not require seasonal change. The housing should not be drained; no lubrication is required for the life of the gear.

FLUID RECOMMENDATIONS

Use GM steering gear lubricant No. 1052182 or equivalent.

LEVEL CHECK

The steering lubricant should be checked every 6 months or 7500 miles. The gear should be inspected for seal leakage when checking the lubricant. Look for solid grease, not an oily film. If a seal is replaced or the gear overhauled, it should be refilled with lubricant.

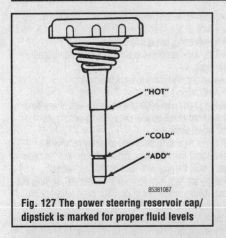

Fig. 127 The power steering reservoir cap/dipstick is marked for proper fluid levels

Fig. 128 Make sure the cap is clean before removing it; this will prevent dirt from contaminating the system

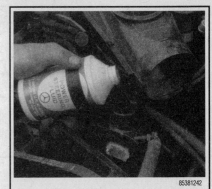

Fig. 129 Add power steering fluid through the opening while the cap is removed

Windshield Washer Pump

FLUID RECOMMENDATIONS AND LEVEL CHECK

▶ See Figure 130

The windshield washer pump fluid reservoir is a plastic container usually found on the side of the engine compartment, near the wiper motor. The reservoir should be filled to the top of the container using a wiper fluid solution which can be found at most automotive stores. Do not further dilute the solution (unless it is sold in concentrate, then follow the manufacturer's instructions), as this will adversely affect its ability to keep from freezing at low temperatures. Also, never place another fluid, such as ethylene glycol antifreeze in the reservoir as other fluids could damage pump seals.

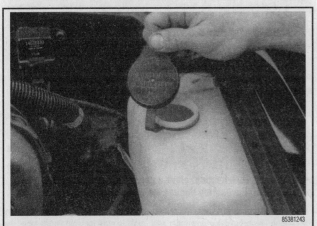

Fig. 130 ONLY add washer fluid to you reservoir; other fluids may freeze or damage the pump/lines

Chassis Greasing

Chassis greasing should be performed every 6 months or 7500 miles for trucks used in normal/light service. More frequent greasing is recommended for trucks in heavy/severe usage; about every 3 months or 3000 miles. Greasing can be performed with a commercial pressurized grease gun or at home by using a hand-operated grease gun. Wipe the grease fittings clean before greasing in order to prevent the possibility of forcing any dirt into the component.

The four wheel drive front driveshaft requires special attention for lubrication. The large constant velocity joint at the front of the transfer case has a special grease fitting in the centering ball. A special needle nose adapter for a flush type fitting is required, as well as a special lubricant (GM part No. 1052497). You can only get at this fitting when it is facing up toward the floorboard, so you need a flexible hose, too.

Water resistant EP chassis lubricant (grease) conforming to GM specification 6031-M (GM part No. 1052497) should be used for all chassis grease points.

Body Lubrication

HOOD LATCH AND HINGES

Clean the latch surfaces and apply white grease to the latch pilot bolts and the spring anchor. Use the engine oil to lubricate the hood hinges as well. Use a chassis grease to lubricate all the pivot points in the latch release mechanism.

DOOR HINGES

The gas tank filler door, truck doors should be wiped clean and lubricated with clean engine oil. Silicone spray also works well on these parts, but must be applied more often. The door lock cylinders can be lubricated easily with a shot of silicone spray or one of the many dry penetrating lubricants commercially available.

PARKING BRAKE LINKAGE

Use chassis grease on the parking brake cable where it contacts the guides, links, levers and pulleys. The grease should be a water resistant for durability under the truck.

ACCELERATOR LINKAGE

Lubricate the throttle body lever, the cable and the accelerator pedal lever (at the support inside the truck) with white grease or a small amount of clean engine oil.

TRANSMISSION SHIFT LINKAGE

Lubricate the manual transmission shift linkage contact points with the EP grease used for chassis greasing, which should meet GM specification 6031-M. The automatic transmission linkage should be lubricated with clean engine oil.

Front Wheel Bearings—2WD Only

▶ See Figure 131

Once every 30,000 miles, clean and repack wheel bearings with a GM Wheel Bearing Grease No. 1051344, No. 1052497, or equivalent. It is wise to perform this service more often if the vehicle is subject to heavy use such as towing a trailer. Use only enough grease to completely coat the rollers. Remove any excess grease from the exposed surface of the hub and seal.

It is important that wheel bearings be properly adjusted after installation. Improperly adjusted wheel bearings can cause steering instability, front-end shimmy and wander, and increased tire wear. Properly adjusted bearings have a slightly loose feeling. Wheel bearings must never be preloaded in service. Preloading will damage the bearings and eventually the spindles. If the bearings are too loose, they should be cleaned, inspected and then adjusted.

Hold the tire at the top and bottom and move the wheel in and out of the spindle. If the movement is greater than 0.005 in. (0.127mm), the bearings are too loose and must be adjusted.

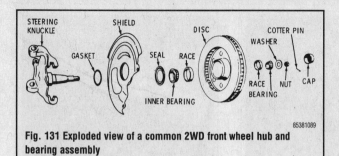

Fig. 131 Exploded view of a common 2WD front wheel hub and bearing assembly

ADJUSTMENT

1. Raise and support the vehicle safely using a jackstand under the lower control arm.
2. If equipped, remove the wheel/hub cover for access, then remove the dust cap from the hub.
3. Remove the cotter pin and loosen the spindle nut.
4. Spin the wheel forward by hand and tighten the nut to 12 ft. lbs. (16 Nm) in order to fully seat the bearings and remove any burrs from the threads.
5. Back off the nut until it is just loose, then finger-tighten the nut.
6. Loosen the nut ¼-½ turn until either hole in the spindle lines up with a slot in the nut, then install a new cotter pin. This may appear to be too loose, but it is the correct adjustment.
7. Proper adjustment creates 0.001–0.005 in. (0.025–0.127mm) end-play.

REMOVAL & INSTALLATION

▶ **See Figures 132 thru 146**

➡**If the bearings are to be replaced, the following procedure recommends the use of GM tools No. J-29117, J-8092, J-8850, J-8457, J-9746-02 or equivalent.**

Before handling the bearings, there are a few things that you should remember to do and and few things you should not. **Always remember to DO the following:**

- Remove all outside dirt from the housing before exposing the bearing.
- Treat a used bearing as gently as you would a new one.
- Work with clean tools in clean surroundings.
- Use clean, dry canvas gloves, or at least clean, dry hands.
- Clean solvents and flushing fluids are a must.
- Use clean paper when laying out the bearings to dry.
- Protect disassembled bearings from rust and dirt. Cover them up.
- Use clean rags to wipe bearings.
- Keep the bearings in oil-proof paper when they are to be stored or are not in use.
- Clean the inside of the housing before replacing the bearing.

There are also a few things NOT to do:

- Don't work in dirty surroundings.
- Don't use dirty, chipped or damaged tools.

- Try not to work on wooden work benches or use wooden mallets.
- Don't handle bearings with dirty or moist hands.
- Do not use gasoline for cleaning; use a safe solvent.
- Do not spin-dry bearings with compressed air. They will be damaged.
- Do not spin dirty bearings.
- Avoid using cotton waste or dirty cloths to wipe bearings.
- Try not to scratch or nick bearing surfaces.
- Do not allow the bearing to come in contact with dirt or rust at any time.

1. Raise and support the front of the vehicle safely using jackstands.
2. Remove the tire and wheel assembly.
3. Remove the brake caliper mounting bolts and carefully remove the caliper (along with the brake pads) from the rotor. Do not disconnect the brake line; instead wire the caliper out of the way with the line still connected.
4. Carefully pry out the grease cap, then remove the cotter pin, spindle nut, and washer. Remove the hub, being careful not to drop the outer wheel bearings. As the hub is pulled forward, the outer wheel bearings will often fall forward and they may easily be removed at this time.
5. If not done already, remove the outer roller bearing assembly from the hub. The inner bearing assembly will remain in the hub and may be removed from the rear of the hub after prying out the inner seal with a small prybar. Discard the seal after removal.

To install:

6. Clean all parts in solvent and allow to air dry, then check for excessive wear or damage. Inspect all of the parts for scoring, pitting or cracking and replace if necessary.

➡**DO NOT remove the bearing races from the hub, unless they show signs of damage.**

7. If it is necessary to remove the wheel bearing races, use the GM front bearing race removal tool No. J-29117 or equivalent, to drive the races from the hub/disc assembly. A hammer and drift may be used to drive the races from the hub, but the race removal tool is quicker.
8. If the bearing races were removed, place the replacement races in the freezer for a few minutes and then install them to the hub:
   a. Lightly lubricate the inside of the hub/disc assembly using wheel bearing grease.
   b. Using the GM seal installation tools No. J-8092 and J-8850 or equivalent, drive the inner bearing race into the hub/disc assembly until it seats. Make sure the race is properly seated against the hub shoulder and is not cocked.

➡**When installing the bearing races, be sure to support the hub/disc assembly with GM tool No. J-9746-02 or equivalent.**

   c. Using the GM seal installation tools No. J-8092 and J-8457 or equivalent, drive the outer race into the hub/disc assembly until it seats.
9. Using a suitable high melting point wheel bearing grease, lubricate the bearings, the races and the spindle; be sure to place a gob of grease (inside the hub/disc assembly) between the races to provide an ample supply of lubricant.

➡**To lubricate each bearing, place a gob of grease in the palm of the hand, then roll the bearing through the grease until it is well lubricated.**

10. Place the inner bearing in the hub, then apply a thin coating of grease to the sealing lip and install a new inner seal, making sure the seal flange faces the bearing cup.

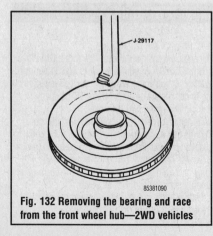

Fig. 132 Removing the bearing and race from the front wheel hub—2WD vehicles

Fig. 133 Pry the dust cap from the hub taking care not to distort or damage its flange

Fig. 134 Once the bent ends are cut, grasp the cotter pin and pull or pry it free of the spindle

TCCS8026

Fig. 135 If difficulty is encountered, gently tap on the pliers with a hammer to help free the cotter pin

TCCS8027

Fig. 136 Loosen and remove the castellated nut from the spindle

TCCS8028

Fig. 137 Remove the washer from the spindle

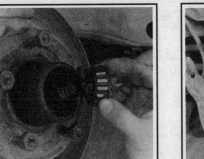

TCCS8029

Fig. 138 With the nut and washer out of the way, the outer bearings may be removed from the hub

TCCS8030

Fig. 139 Pull the hub and inner bearing assembly from the spindle

TCCS8031

Fig. 140 Use a small prytool to remove the old inner bearing seal

TCCS8032

Fig. 141 With the seal removed, the inner bearing may be withdrawn from the hub

TCCS8033

Fig. 142 Thoroughly pack the bearing with fresh, high temperature wheel-bearing grease before installation

TCCS8034

Fig. 143 Apply a thin coat of fresh grease to the new inner bearing seal lip

TCCS8035

Fig. 144 Use a suitably sized driver to install the inner bearing seal to the hub

TCCS8036

Fig. 145 With new or freshly packed bearings, tighten the nut while gently spinning the wheel, then adjust

TCCS8037

Fig. 146 After adjustment, install the cap gently tapping on the flange—DO NOT hammer on the center

➡Although a seal installation tool is preferable, a section of pipe with a smooth edge or a suitably sized socket may be used to drive the seal into position. Make sure the seal is flush with the outer surface of the hub assembly.

11. Carefully install the wheel hub over the spindle.
12. Using your hands, firmly press the outer bearing into the hub.
13. Loosely install the spindle washer and nut, but do not install the cotter pin or dust cap at this time.
14. Install the brake caliper.
15. Install the tire and wheel assembly.
16. Properly adjust the wheel bearings, then install a new cotter pin and the dust cap.
17. Install the wheel/hub cover, then remove the supports and carefully lower the vehicle.

TRAILER TOWING

General Recommendations

Your vehicle was primarily designed to carry passengers and cargo. It is important to remember that towing a trailer will place additional loads on your vehicles engine, drive train, steering, braking and other systems. However, if you decide to tow a trailer, using the prior equipment is a must.

Local laws may require specific equipment such as trailer brakes or fender mounted mirrors. Check your local laws.

Trailer Weight

The weight of the trailer is the most important factor. A good weight-to-horsepower ratio is about 35:1, 35 lbs. of Gross Combined Weight (GCW) for every horsepower your engine develops. Multiply the engine's rated horsepower by 35 and subtract the weight of the vehicle passengers and luggage. The number remaining is the approximate ideal maximum weight you should tow, although a numerically higher axle ratio can help compensate for heavier weight.

Hitch (Tongue) Weight

▶ See Figure 147

Calculate the hitch weight in order to select a proper hitch. The weight of the hitch is usually 9–11% of the trailer gross weight and should be measured with the trailer loaded. Hitches fall into various categories: those that mount on the frame and rear bumper, the bolt-on type, or the weld-on distribution type used for larger trailers. Axle mounted or clamp-on bumper hitches should never be used.

Check the gross weight rating of your trailer. Tongue weight is usually figured as 10% of gross trailer weight. Therefore, a trailer with a maximum gross weight of 2000 lbs. will have a maximum tongue weight of 200 lbs. Class I trailers fall into this category. Class II trailers are those with a gross weight rating of 2000–3000 lbs., while Class III trailers fall into the 3500–6000 lbs. category. Class IV trailers are those over 6000 lbs. and are for use with fifth wheel trucks, only.

When you've determined the hitch that you'll need, follow the manufacturer's installation instructions, exactly, especially when it comes to fastener torques. The hitch will subjected to a lot of stress and good hitches come with hardened bolts. Never substitute an inferior bolt for a hardened bolt.

UMP STARTING A DEAD BATTERY

▶ See Figure 148

Whenever a vehicle is jump started, precautions must be followed in order to prevent the possibility of personal injury. Remember that batteries contain a small amount of explosive hydrogen gas which is a by-product of battery charging. Sparks should always be avoided when working around batteries, especially when attaching jumper cables. To minimize the possibility of accidental sparks, follow the procedure carefully.

PACKING

Clean the wheel bearings thoroughly with solvent and check their condition before installation.

✳✳ WARNING

Do not blow the bearing dry with compressed air as this would allow the bearing to turn without lubrication.

Apply a sizable dab of lubricant to the palm of one hand. Using your other hand, work the bearing into the lubricant so that the grease is pushed through the rollers and out the other side. Keep rotating the bearing while continuing to push the lubricant through it.

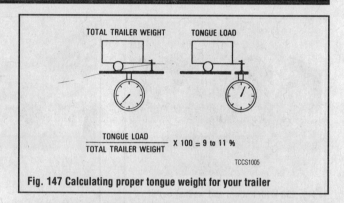

Fig. 147 Calculating proper tongue weight for your trailer

Cooling

ENGINE

Aftermarket engine oil coolers are helpful for prolonging engine oil life and reducing overall engine temperatures. Both of these factors increase engine life. While not absolutely necessary in towing Class I and some Class II trailers, they are recommended for heavier Class II and all Class III towing. Engine oil cooler systems usually consist of an adapter, screwed on in place of the oil filter, a remote filter mounting and a multi-tube, finned heat exchanger, which is mounted in front of the radiator or air conditioning condenser.

Transmission

An automatic transmission is usually recommended for trailer towing. Modern automatics have proven reliable and, of course, easy to operate, in trailer towing. The increased load of a trailer, however, causes an increase in the temperature of the transmission fluid. Heat is the worst enemy of an automatic transmission. As the temperature of the fluid increases, the life of the fluid decreases.

It is essential, therefore, that you install an automatic transmission cooler and that you pay close attention to transmission fluid changes. The cooler, which consists of a multi-tube, finned heat exchanger, is usually installed in front of the radiator or air conditioning compressor, and hooked in-line with the transmission cooler tank inlet line. Follow the cooler manufacturer's installation instructions.

✳✳ CAUTION

NEVER hook the batteries up in a series circuit or the entire electrical system will go up in smoke, including the starter!

Vehicles equipped with a diesel engine may utilize two 12 volt batteries. If so, the batteries are connected in a parallel circuit (positive terminal to positive

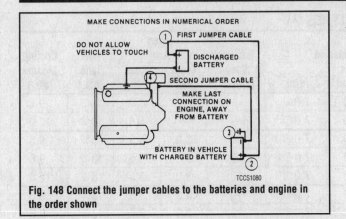

Fig. 148 Connect the jumper cables to the batteries and engine in the order shown

terminal, negative terminal to negative terminal). Hooking the batteries up in parallel circuit increases battery cranking power without increasing total battery voltage output. Output remains at 12 volts. On the other hand, hooking two 12 volt batteries up in a series circuit (positive terminal to negative terminal, positive terminal to negative terminal) increases total battery output to 24 volts (12 volts plus 12 volts).

Jump Starting Precautions

- Be sure that both batteries are of the same polarity (have the same terminal, in most cases NEGATIVE grounded).
- Be sure that the vehicles are not touching or a short could occur.
- On non-sealed batteries, be sure the vent cap holes are not obstructed.
- Do not smoke or allow sparks anywhere near the batteries.
- In cold weather, make sure the battery electrolyte is not frozen. This can occur more readily in a battery that has been in a state of discharge.
- Do not allow electrolyte to contact your skin or clothing.

Jump Starting Procedure

1. Make sure that the voltages of the 2 batteries are the same. Most batteries and charging systems are of the 12 volt variety.
2. Pull the jumping vehicle (with the good battery) into a position so the jumper cables can reach the dead battery and that vehicle's engine. Make sure that the vehicles do NOT touch.
3. Place the transmissions/transaxles of both vehicles in **Neutral** (MT) or **P** (AT), as applicable, then firmly set their parking brakes.

ACKING

Your vehicle was supplied with a jack for emergency road repairs. This jack is fine for changing a flat tire or other short term procedures not requiring you to go beneath the vehicle. If it is used in an emergency situation, carefully follow the instructions provided either with the jack or in your owner's manual. Do not attempt to use the jack on any portions of the vehicle other than specified by the vehicle manufacturer. Always block the diagonally opposite wheel when using a jack.

A more convenient way of jacking is the use of a garage or floor jack. The front and rear crossmembers and the side frame rails and generally safe areas by which to support these vehicles.

Never place the jack under the radiator, engine or transmission components. Severe and expensive damage will result when the jack is raised. Additionally, never jack under the floorpan or bodywork; the metal will deform.

Whenever you plan to work under the vehicle, you must support it on jackstands or ramps. Never use cinder blocks or stacks of wood to support the vehicle, even if you're only going to be under it for a few minutes. Never crawl under the vehicle when it is supported only by the tire-changing jack or other floor jack.

➡**Always position a block of wood or small rubber pad on top of the jack or jackstand to protect the lifting point's finish when lifting or supporting the vehicle.**

➡**If necessary for safety reasons, the hazard lights on both vehicles may be operated throughout the entire procedure without significantly increasing the difficulty of jumping the dead battery.**

4. Turn all lights and accessories OFF on both vehicles. Make sure the ignition switches on both vehicles are turned to the **OFF** position.
5. Cover the battery cell caps with a rag, but do not cover the terminals.
6. Make sure the terminals on both batteries are clean and free of corrosion for good electrical contact.
7. Identify the positive (+) and negative (−) terminals on both batteries.
8. Connect the first jumper cable to the positive (+) terminal of the dead battery, then connect the other end of that cable to the positive (+) terminal of the booster (good) battery.
9. Connect one end of the other jumper cable to the negative (−) terminal on the booster battery and the final cable clamp to an engine bolt head, alternator bracket or other solid, metallic point on the engine with the dead battery. Try to pick a ground on the engine that is positioned away from the battery in order to minimize the possibility of the 2 clamps touching should one loosen during the procedure. DO NOT connect this clamp to the negative (−) terminal of the bad battery.

✳✳ CAUTION

Be very careful to keep the jumper cables away from moving parts (cooling fan, belts, etc.) on both engines.

10. Check to make sure that the cables are routed away from any moving parts, then start the donor vehicle's engine. Run the engine at moderate speed for several minutes to allow the dead battery a chance to receive some initial charge.
11. With the donor vehicle's engine still running slightly above idle, try to start the vehicle with the dead battery. Crank the engine for no more than 10 seconds at a time and let the starter cool for at least 20 seconds between tries. If the vehicle does not start in 3 tries, it is likely that something else is also wrong or that the battery needs additional time to charge.
12. Once the vehicle is started, allow it to run at idle for a few seconds to make sure that it is operating properly.
13. Turn ON the headlights, heater blower and, if equipped, the rear defroster of both vehicles in order to reduce the severity of voltage spikes and subsequent risk of damage to the vehicles' electrical systems when the cables are disconnected. This step is especially important to any vehicle equipped with computer control modules.
14. Carefully disconnect the cables in the reverse order of connection. Start with the negative cable that is attached to the engine ground, then the negative cable on the donor battery. Disconnect the positive cable from the donor battery and finally, disconnect the positive cable from the formerly dead battery. Be careful when disconnecting the cables from the positive terminals not to allow the alligator clips to touch any metal on either vehicle or a short and sparks will occur.

Small hydraulic, screw, or scissors jacks are satisfactory for raising the vehicle. Drive-on trestles or ramps are also a handy and safe way to both raise and support the vehicle. Be careful though, some ramps may be too steep to drive your vehicle onto without scraping the front bottom panels. Never support the vehicle on any suspension member (unless specifically instructed to do so by a repair manual) or by an underbody panel.

Jacking Precautions

The following safety points cannot be overemphasized:
- Always block the opposite wheel or wheels to keep the vehicle from rolling off the jack.
- When raising the front of the vehicle, firmly apply the parking brake.
- When the drive wheels are to remain on the ground, leave the vehicle in gear to help prevent it from rolling.
- Always use jackstands to support the vehicle when you are working underneath. Place the stands beneath the vehicle's jacking brackets. Before climbing underneath, rock the vehicle a bit to make sure it is firmly supported.

CAPACITIES①

Year	Engine ID/VIN	Engine Displacement Liters (cc)	Engine Crankcase with Filter	Transmission (pts.)			Transfer Case (pts.)	Drive Axle		Fuel Tank (gal.)	Cooling System (qts.)
				4-Spd	5-Spd	Auto.		Front (pts.)	Rear (pts.)		
1982	A	1.9 (1949)	4.0	3.0	3.0	7.0④	—	—	3.5	13②	9.5
	B	2.8 (2835)	4.0	3.0	3.0	7.0④	—	—	3.5	13②	12.0
1983	A	1.9 (1949)	4.0	3.0	3.0	7.0④③	10	3.0	3.5	13②	9.5
	Y	2.0 (1990)	4.0	3.0	3.0	7.0④③	10	3.0	3.5	13②	9.6
	B	2.8 (2835)	4.0	3.0	3.0	7.0④③	10	3.0	3.5	13②	12.0
1984	A	1.9 (1949)	4.0	3.0	3.0	7.0④③	10	3.0	3.5	13②	9.5
	Y	2.0 (1990)	4.0	3.0	3.0	7.0④③	10	3.0	3.5	13②	9.6
	B	2.8 (2835)	4.5	3.0	3.0	7.0④③	10	3.0	3.5	13②	12.0
1985	A	1.9 (1949)	4.0	4.0⑤	4.0	7.0④③	4.6	2.6	3.5	13②	9.5
	E	2.5 (2474)	3.5	4.0⑤	4.0	7.0④③	4.6	2.6	3.5	13②	12.0
	B	2.8 (2835)	4.0	4.0⑤	4.0	7.0④③	4.6	2.6	3.5	13②	12.0
1986	E	2.5 (2474)	3.5	4.0⑤	4.0	10.0⑥	4.6	2.6	3.5	13②	11.5
	R	2.8 (2835)	4.0	4.0⑤	4.0	10.0⑥	4.6	2.6	3.5	13②	10.5
1987	E	2.5 (2474)	3.5	4.0⑤	4.0	10.0⑥	4.6	2.6	3.5	13②	11.5
	R	2.8 (2835)	4.0	4.0⑤	4.0	10.0⑥	4.6	2.6	3.5	13②	10.5
1988	E	2.5 (2474)	3.5	—	4.4	10.0⑦	2.2	2.6	3.9	13②	11.5
	R	2.8 (2835)	4.5	—	4.4	10.0⑦	2.2	2.6	3.9	13②	10.5
	Z	4.3 (4293)	5.0	—	4.4	10.0⑦	2.2	2.6	3.9	20	13.5
1989	E	2.5 (2474)	3.5	—	4.4	10.0⑦	—	—	3.9	13②	11.5
	R	2.8 (2835)	4.5	—	4.4	10.0⑦	2.2	2.6	3.9	13②	10.5
	Z	4.3 (4293)	5.0	—	4.4	10.0⑦	2.2	2.6	3.9	20	13.5
1990	E	2.5 (2474)	3.5	—	4.4	10.0⑦	—	—	3.9	13②	11.5
	R	2.8 (2835)	4.5	—	4.4	10.0⑦	2.2	2.6	3.9	13②	10.5
	Z	4.3 (4293)	4.5	—	4.4	10.0⑦	2.2	2.6	3.9	20	13.5
1991	A	2.5 (2474)	3.5	—	4.4	3.0⑧③	2.2	2.6	3.9	13②	11.5
	E	2.5 (2474)	3.5	—	4.4	3.0⑧③	2.2	2.6	3.9	13②	11.5
	R	2.8 (2835)	4.5	—	4.4	3.0⑧③	2.2	2.6	3.9	13②	10.5
	Z	4.3 (4293)	4.5	—	4.4	3.0⑧③	2.2	2.6	3.9	20	12.1
1992	A	2.5 (2474)	3.5	—	4.4	10.0⑨	2.2	2.6	3.9	13②	11.5
	R	2.8 (2835)	4.5	—	4.4	10.0⑨	2.2	2.6	3.9	13②	10.5
	W	4.3 (4293)	4.5	—	4.4	10.0⑨	—	—	4.0	20	12.1
	Z	4.3 (4293)	4.5	—	4.4	10.0⑨	2.2	2.6	3.9	20	12.1
1993	A	2.5 (2474)	4.0	—	4.4	10.0⑨	—	—	3.9	13②	11.5
	R	2.8 (2835)	4.5	—	4.4	—	—	—	3.9	13②	10.5
	W	4.3 (4293)	4.5	—	4.4	10.0⑨	—	—	4.0	20	12.1
	Z	4.3 (4293)	4.5	—	4.4	10.0⑨	2.2	2.6	3.9	20	12.1

① All capacities are approximate. Add fluid gradually and check to be sure a proper fluid level is obtained.
② Optional 20 gal. tank.
③ If equipped w/700-R4:   Pan—10 pts.
                                         Overhaul—23 pts.

④ Specification is for Pan Removal, Overhaul—19 pts.
⑤ Specification is for 77 mm trans., 77.5mm—5.0 pts.
⑥ Overhaul—23 pts.

⑦ Overhaul—21 pts.
⑧ Specification is for Pan Removal on THM 180C, Overhaul—4.6 pts.
⑨ Specification is for Pan Removal on 4L60 or 4L60-E, Overhaul—22 pts.

8844R112

1982-86 MAINTENANCE INTERVAL SCHEDULE I

The services shown in this schedule up to 60,000 miles are to be performed after 60,000 miles at the same intervals

Item No.	To Be Serviced	Minimum Time Interval	3	6	9	12	15	18	21	24	27	30	33	36	39	42	45	48	51	54	57	60
1	Every Oil and Filter Change*	Every 3 months	■	■	■	■	■	■	■	■	■	■	■	■	■	■	■	■	■	■	■	■
2	Chassis Lubrication*	Every 6 months	■	■	■	■	■	■	■	■	■	■	■	■	■	■	■	■	■	■	■	■
3	Engine Idle Speed Adjustment*			■								■										
4	Cooling System Service*	Every 24 months										■										■
5	Air Cleaner & PCV Replacement*											■										■
6	Front Wheel Bearing Repack (2WD)						■					■					■					■
7	PCV System Inspection*											■										■
8	Fuel Filter Replacement*						■					■					■					■
9	Carburetor Choke & Hoses Check*	Every 6 months		■								■					■					
10	Carburetor Bolt Torque Check*	Every 6 months		■								■										
11	TBI Unit Bolt Torque Check*	Every 6 months		■								■										
12	Vacuum Advance System Inspection*	Every 6 months		■								■					■					
13	Spark Plug Replacement*											■										■
14	Spark Plug Wire Service*											■										■
15	EGR System Check*											■										■
16	Engine Timing Check*											■										■
17	Fuel Tank, Cap & lines Inspection*						■					■					■					■
18	Early Fuel Evaporation System Inspection*			■								■										■
19	Thermac Air Cleaner Inspection*											■										■
20	Engine Accessory Drive Belts Inspection*						■					■					■					■
21	Evaporative Control System Inspection*											■										■
22	Valve Lash Adjustment*						■					■					■					■
23	Automatic Transmission Fluid Level Check			■		■		■		■		■		■		■		■		■		■
24	Idle Stop Solenoid*											■										■

FOOTNOTES: * An Emission Control Service

Follow Schedule I if any of the following conditions apply: most trips are less than 4 miles, outside temperatures remain below freezing and most trips are less than 10 miles, when towing a trailer, or when operating the vehicle in dusty conditions.

88441C01

1982-86 MAINTENANCE INTERVAL SCHEDULE II

The services shown in this schedule up to 60,000 miles are to be performed after 60,000 miles at same intervals

Item No.	To Be Serviced	7.5	15	22.5	30	37.5	45	52.5	60
1	Every Oil and Filter Change*	■	■	■	■	■	■	■	■
2	Chassis Lubrication*	■	■	■	■	■	■	■	■
3	Engine Idle Speed Adjustment*	■							■
4	Cooling System Service*				■				■
5	Air Cleaner & PCV Replacement*				■				■
6	Front Wheel Bearing Repack (2WD)				■				■
7	PCV System Inspection*				■				■
8	Fuel Filter Replacement*				■				■
9	Carburetor Choke & Hoses Check*	■			■				■
10	Carburetor Bolt Torque Check*	■							■
11	TBI Unit Bolt Torque Check*	■							■
12	Vacuum Advance System Inspection*	■			■		■		■
13	Spark Plug Replacement*				■				■
14	Spark Plug Wire Service*				■				■
15	EGR System Check*				■				■
16	Engine Timing Check*				■				■
17	Fuel Tank, Cap & lines Inspection*				■				■
18	Early Fuel Evaporation System Inspection*	■			■				■
19	Thermac Air Cleaner Inspection*				■				■
20	Engine Accessory Drive Belts Inspection*				■				■
21	Evaporative Control System Inspection*				■				■
22	Valve Lash Adjustment*		■		■		■		■
23	Automatic Transmission Fluid Level Check	■	■	■	■	■	■	■	■
24	Idle Stop Solenoid*				■				■

FOOTNOTES: * An Emission Control Service

Follow Schedule II if none of the conditions in Schedule 1 apply.

88441C02

1987-93 MAINTENANCE INTERVAL SCHEDULE I

Item No.	To Be Serviced	Minimum Time Interval	3	6	9	12	15	18	21	24	27	30	33	36	39	42	45	48	51	54	57	60
			The services shown in this schedule up to 60,000 miles are to be performed after 60,000 miles at the same intervals																			
1	Every Oil and Filter Change*	Every 3 months	■	■	■	■	■	■	■	■	■	■	■	■	■	■	■	■	■	■	■	■
2	Chassis Lubrication	Every 12 months	■	■	■	■	■	■	■	■	■	■	■	■	■	■	■	■	■	■	■	■
3	Clutch Fork Ball Stud Lubrication											■										■
4	Cooling System Service*	Every 24 months										■										■
5	Air Cleaner Element Replacement*											■										■
6	Front Wheel Bearing Repack (2WD)						■					■					■					■
7	Automatic Transmission Fluid Level Check			■		■		■		■		■		■		■		■		■		■
8	PCV System Inspection											■										■
9	Fuel Filter Replacement*											■										■
10	Spark Plug Replacement*											■										■
11	Spark Plug Wire Service*											■										■
12	EVRV Inspection*																					■
13	Engine Timing Check*																					■
14	Fuel Tank, Cap & lines Inspection*																					■
15	Engine Accessory Drive Belts Inspection*																					■
16	Tire & Wheel Rotation			■				■					■						■			■
17	Drive Axle Service		■	■	■	■	■	■	■	■	■	■	■	■	■	■	■	■	■	■	■	■
18	Brake System Inspection											■										■

FOOTNOTES: * An Emission Control Service

Follow Schedule I if any of the following conditions apply: most trips are less than 4 miles, outside temperatures remain below freezing, and most trips are less than 10 miles, when towing a trailer, or when operating the vehicle in dusty conditions.

88441C03

1987-93 MAINTENANCE INTERVAL SCHEDULE II

Item No.	To Be Serviced	7.5	15	22.5	30	37.5	45	52.5	60
		The services shown in this schedule up to 60,000 miles are to be performed after 60,000 miles at same intervals							
1	Every Oil and Filter Change*	■	■	■	■	■	■	■	■
2	Chassis Lubrication	■	■	■	■	■	■	■	■
3	Clutch Fork Ball Stud Lubrication								
4	Cooling System Service*				■				■
5	Air Cleaner Element Replacement*				■				■
6	Front Wheel Bearing Repack (2WD)				■				■
7	Transmission Service								
8	PCV System Inspection				■				■
9	Fuel Filter Replacement*				■				■
10	Spark Plug Replacement*				■				■
11	Spark Plug Wire Service*								■
12	EVRV Inspection*								■
13	Engine Timing Check*								■
14	Fuel Tank, Cap & lines Inspection*								■
15	Engine Accessory Drive Belts Inspection*								■
16	Tire & Wheel Rotation	■		■		■		■	
17	Drive Axle Service	■	■	■	■	■	■	■	■
18	Brake System Inspection				■				■

FOOTNOTES: * An Emission Control Service

Follow Schedule II if none of the conditions in Schedule I apply.

88441C04

2

ENGINE
PERFORMANCE
AND
TUNE-UP

TUNE-UP PROCEDURES

In order to extract the full measure of performance and economy from your engine it is essential that it is properly tuned at regular intervals. A regular tune-up will keep your truck's engine running smoothly and will prevent the annoying breakdowns and poor performance associated with an untuned engine.

➥**All gasoline models covered in this manual are equipped with an electronic distributor ignition system known as High Energy Ignition (HEI) or more recently as Distributor Ignition (DI).**

A complete tune-up should be performed at least every 30,000 miles. This interval should be halved if the truck is operated under severe conditions such as trailer towing, prolonged idling, start-and-stop driving, or if a driveability problem such as hard starting or poor running is noticed. It is assumed that the routine maintenance described in Section 1 has been kept up, as this will have a decided effect on the results of a tune-up. All of the applicable steps of a tune-up should be followed in order, as the result is a cumulative one. Any adjustment made to the engine is normally performed only when it will not be affected by other adjustments that are yet to be made during the tune-up.

➥**Diesel engines do not require tune-ups per se, as they do not have spark plug ignition systems.**

If the specifications on the underhood tune-up sticker (located in the engine compartment of your truck) disagree with the tune-up specifications chart in this Section, the figures on the sticker must be used. The sticker often reflects changes made during the production run or revised information that apply to the particular systems in that vehicle.

Spark Plugs

▶ **See Figures 1 and 2**

A typical spark plug consists of a metal shell surrounding a ceramic insulator. A metal electrode extends downward through the center of the insulator and protrudes a small distance. Located at the end of the plug and attached to the side of the outer metal shell is the side electrode. The side electrode bends in at a 90° angle so that its tip is just past and parallel to the tip of the center electrode. The distance between these two electrodes (measured in thousandths of an inch or hundredths of a millimeter) is called the spark plug gap. The spark plug does not produce a spark but instead provides a gap across which the current can arc. The HEI ignition coil produces considerably more voltage than the standard type, as much as approximately 50,000 volts, which travels through the wires to the spark plugs. The current passes along the center electrode and jumps the gap to the side electrode, and in doing so, ignites the fuel/air mixture in the combustion chamber. All plugs should have a resistor built into the center electrode to reduce interference to any nearby radio and television receivers. The resistor also cuts down on erosion of plug electrodes caused by excessively long sparking. Resistor spark plug wiring is original equipment on all models.

Spark plug life and efficiency depend upon condition of the engine and the temperatures to which the plug is exposed. Combustion chamber temperatures are affected by many factors such as compression ratio of the engine, fuel/air mixtures, exhaust emission equipment, and your style of driving. Spark plugs are designed and classified by number according to the heat range at which they will operate most efficiently. The amount of heat that the plug absorbs is determined by the length of the lower insulator. The longer the insulator (it extends farther into the engine), the hotter the plug will operate; the shorter it is, the cooler it will operate. A plug that has a short path for heat transfer and remains too cool will quickly accumulate deposits of oil and carbon since it is not hot enough to burn them off. This leads to plug fouling and consequently to misfiring. A plug that has a long path of heat transfer will have no deposits but, due to the excessive heat, the electrodes will burn away quickly and, in some instances, pre-ignition may result. Pre-ignition takes place when plug tips get so hot that they glow sufficiently to ignite the fuel/air mixture before the spark does. This early ignition will usually cause a pinging during low speeds and heavy loads. In severe cases, the heat may become hot enough to start the fuel/air mixture burning throughout the combustion chamber rather than just to the front of the plug as in normal operation. At this time, the piston is rising in the cylinder making its compression stroke. The burning mass is compressed and an explosion results producing tremendous pressure. Something has to give, and it does; pistons are often damaged. Obviously, this detonation (explo-

sion) is a destructive condition that can be avoided by installing a spark plug designed and specified for your particular engine.

A set of spark plugs usually requires replacement after about 20,000–30,000 miles, this is 1½ to 2 times as long as plugs would usually last in a conventional point-type ignition system. Of course, any vehicle which is subjected to severe conditions will need more frequent plug replacement. The electrode on a new spark plug has a sharp edge but, with use, this edge becomes rounded by erosion causing the plug gap to increase. During normal operation, plug gap increases about 0.001 in. (0.0254mm) for every 1000–2000 miles. As the gap increases, the plug's voltage requirement also increases. It requires a greater voltage to jump the wider gap and about 2–4 times as much voltage to fire a plug at high speed and acceleration than at idle.

The higher voltage produced by the HEI ignition coil is one of the primary reasons for the prolonged replacement interval for spark plugs in late model trucks. A consistently hotter spark prevents the fouling of plugs for much longer than could normally be expected; this spark is also able to jump across a larger gap more efficiently than a spark from a conventional system. However, even plugs used with the HEI system wear after time in the engine.

Worn plugs become obvious during acceleration. Voltage requirement is

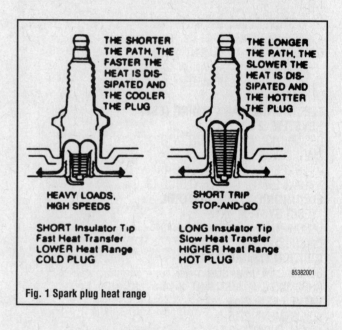

Fig. 1 Spark plug heat range

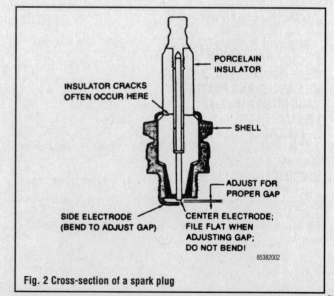

Fig. 2 Cross-section of a spark plug

greatest during acceleration and a plug with an enlarged gap may require more voltage than the coil is able to produce. As a result, the engine misses and sputters until acceleration is reduced. Reducing acceleration reduces the plug's voltage requirement and the engine runs smoother. Slow, city driving is hard on plugs. The long periods of idle experienced in traffic creates an overly rich gas mixture. The engine does not run fast enough to completely burn the gas and, consequently, the plugs become fouled with gas deposits and engine idle becomes rough. In many cases, driving under the right conditions can effectively clean these fouled plugs.

To help clean fouled plugs in a running engine, first accelerate you truck to the speed where the engine begins to miss and then slow down to the point where the engine smooths out. Run at this speed for a few minutes and then accelerate again to the point of engine miss. With each repetition this engine miss should occur at increasingly higher speeds and then disappear altogether. Do not attempt to shortcut this procedure by hard acceleration. This approach will compound problems by fusing deposits into a hard permanent glaze. Dirty, fouled plugs may be cleaned by sandblasting. Many shops have a spark plug sandblaster and there are a few inexpensive models that are designed for home use and available from aftermarket sources. After sandblasting, the electrode should be filed to a sharp, square shape and then gapped to specifications. Gapping a plug too close will produce a rough idle while gapping it too wide will increase its voltage requirement and cause missing at high speed and during acceleration.

→There are several reasons why a spark plug will foul and you can usually learn what is at fault by just looking at the plug. Refer to the spark plug diagnosis figure in this section for some of the most common reasons for plug fouling.

The type of driving you do may require a change in spark plug heat range. If the majority of your driving is done in the city and rarely at high speeds, plug fouling may necessitate changing to a plug with a heat range one number higher than that specified by the car manufacturer. For example, an engine might normally require an R44 plug. Frequent city driving may foul these plugs making engine operation rough. An R45 is the next hottest plug in the AC heat range (the higher the AC number, the hotter the plug) and its insulator is longer than the R44 so that it can absorb and retain more heat than the shorter R44. This hotter R45 burns off deposits even at low city speeds but would be too hot for prolonged turnpike driving. Using this plug at high speed would create dangerous pre-ignition. On the other hand, if the aforementioned engine were used almost exclusively for long distance high speed driving, the specified R44 might be too hot resulting in rapid electrode wear and dangerous pre-ignition. In this case, it might be wise to change to a colder R43. If the truck is used for abnormal driving (as in the examples above), or the engine has been modified for higher performance, then a change to a plug with a different heat range may be necessary. For a modified truck it is always wise to go to a colder plug as a protection against pre-ignition. It will require more frequent plug cleaning, but destructive detonation during acceleration will be avoided.

REMOVAL

♦ **See Figures 5 and 6**

When you're removing spark plugs, you should work on one at a time. Don't start by removing the plug wires all at once because unless you number them, they are going to get mixed up. On some models though, it will be more convenient for you to remove all the wires before you start to work on the plugs. If this is necessary, take a minute before you begin and number the wires with tape before you take them off. The time you spend doing this will pay off later when it comes time to reconnect the wires to the plugs.

→Do not remove spark plugs from a warm engine or damage to the threads may occur. Wait until the engine has sufficiently cooled before attempting to remove the plugs.

1. Disconnect the negative battery cable from the negative battery terminal.

→On some vehicles covered by this manual, spark plug access will be easier through the wheel well panels. If so, raise and support the vehicle on jackstands, then remove the front wheels, followed by the well panels.

2. Twist the spark plug boot slightly in either direction to break loose the seal, then remove the boot from the plug. You may also use a plug wire removal tool designed especially for this purpose. Do not pull on the wire itself or you may separate the plug connector from the end of the wire. When the wire has been removed, take a wire brush and clean the area around the plug. An evaporative spray cleaner such as those designed for brake applications will also work well. Make sure that all the foreign material is removed so that none will enter the cylinder after the plug has been removed.

→If you have access to a compressor, use the air hose to blow all material away from the spark plug bores before loosening the plug. Always protect your eyes with safety glasses when using compressed air.

3. Remove the plug using the proper size socket, extensions, and universals as necessary. Hold the socket or the extension close to the plug with your free hand as this will help lessen the possibility of applying a shear force which might snap the spark plug in half.

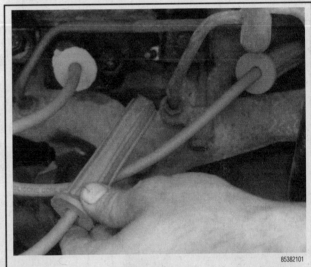

Fig. 5 When disconnecting the spark plug wire, ALWAYS grasp the boot, never pull on the wire itself

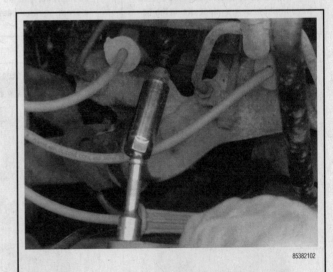

Fig. 6 Use a spark plug socket with the necessary extension(s) to loosen and remove the plug

4. If removing the plug is difficult, drip some penetrating oil (Liquid Wrench®, WD-40®) on the plug threads, allow it to work, then remove the plug. Also, be sure that the socket is straight on the plug, especially on those hard to reach plugs. Again, if the socket is cocked to 1 side a shear force may be applied to the plug and could snap the plug in half.

INSPECTION

▶ **See Figures 7 thru 16**

Check the plugs for deposits and wear. If they are not going to be replaced, clean the plugs thoroughly. Remember that any kind of deposit will decrease the efficiency of the plug. Plugs can be cleaned on a spark plug cleaning machine, which can sometimes be found in service stations, or you can do an acceptable job of cleaning with a stiff brush. If the plugs are cleaned, the electrodes must be filed flat. Use an ignition points file, not an emery board or the like, which will leave deposits. The electrodes must be filed perfectly flat with sharp edges; rounded edges reduce the spark plug voltage by as much as 50%.

Check and adjust the spark plug gap immediately before installation. The ground electrode (the L-shaped one connected to the body of the plug) must be parallel to the center electrode and the specified size gauge (see your under-hood label first, but if one is not present, check the tune-up specifications chart) should pass through the gap with a slight drag. Always check the gap on new plugs, too; since they are not always set correctly at the factory.

Do not use a flat feeler gauge when measuring the gap on used plugs, because the reading may be inaccurate. The ground electrode on a used plug is often rounded on the face closest to the center electrode. A flat gauge will not be able to accurately measure this distance as well as a wire gauge. Most gapping tools usually have a bending tool attached. This tool may be used to adjust the side electrode until the proper distance is obtained. Never attempt to move or bend the center electrode or spark plug damage will likely occur. Also, be careful not to bend the side electrode too far or too often; if it is overstressed it may weaken and break off within the engine, requiring removal of the cylinder head to retrieve it.

TCCS2135

Fig. 7 A normally worn spark plug should have light tan or gray deposits on the firing tip

TCCS2136

Fig. 8 A carbon fouled plug, identified by soft, sooty, black deposits, may indicate an improperly tuned vehicle. Check the air cleaner, ignition components and engine control system

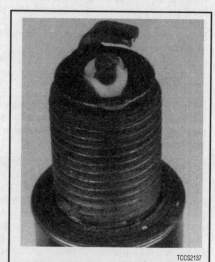

TCCS2137

Fig. 9 A physically damaged spark plug may be evidence of severe detonation in that cylinder. Watch that cylinder carefully between services, as a continued detonation will not only damage the plug, but could also damage the engine

TCCS2138

Fig. 10 An oil fouled spark plug indicates an engine with worn piston rings and/or bad valve seals allowing excessive oil to enter the chamber

TCCS2139

Fig. 11 This spark plug has been left in the engine too long, as evidenced by the extreme gap—Plugs with such an extreme gap can cause misfiring and stumbling accompanied by a noticeable lack of power

TCCS2140

Fig. 12 A bridged or almost bridged spark plug, identified by a build-up between the electrodes caused by excessive carbon or oil build-up on the plug

Fig. 13 A variety of tools and gauges are needed for spark plug service

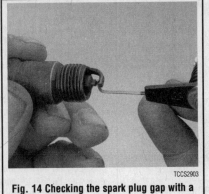

Fig. 14 Checking the spark plug gap with a feeler gauge

Fig. 15 Adjusting the spark plug gap

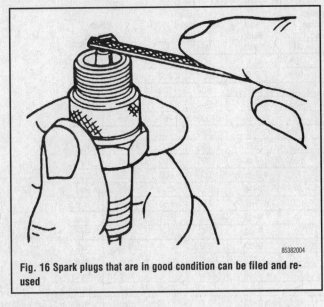

Fig. 16 Spark plugs that are in good condition can be filed and reused

INSTALLATION

1. Inspect the spark plugs and clean or replace, as necessary. Inspect the spark plug boot for tears or damage. If a damaged boot is found, the spark plug wire must be replaced.

➡️**Although an effort has been made to supply you with representative gap specifications, the spark plug gap will vary based on the engine and emission package with which your vehicle is equipped. Most vehicles covered by this manual use a 0.040 or 0.035 in. gap. Refer to the underhood emission control label to determine the proper specification for your vehicle.**

2. Using a feeler gauge, check and adjust the spark plug gap to specification. When using a gauge, the proper size should pass between the electrodes with a slight drag. The next larger size should not be able to pass while the next smaller size should pass freely.

❖❖ CAUTION

Do not use the spark plug socket to thread the plugs. Always thread the plug by hand to prevent the possibility of cross-threading and damaging the cylinder head bore.

3. Lubricate the spark plug threads with a drop of clean engine oil, then carefully start the spark plugs by hand and tighten a few turns until a socket is needed to continue tightening the spark plug. Do not apply the same amount of force you would use for a bolt; just snug them in. If a torque wrench is available, tighten the plugs to 11–15 ft. lbs. (15–20 Nm).

➡️**A spark plug threading tool may be made using the end of an old spark plug wire. Cut the wire a few inches from the top of the spark plug boot. The boot may be used to hold the plug while the wire is turned to thread it. Because the wire is so flexible, it may be turned to bend around difficult angles and, should the plug begin to crossthread, the resistance should be sufficient to bend the wire instead of forcing the plug into the cylinder head, preventing serious thread damage.**

4. Apply a small amount of silicone dielectric compound to the end of the spark plug lead or inside the spark plug boot to prevent sticking, then install the boot to the spark plug and push until it clicks into place. The click may be felt or heard, then gently pull back on the boot to assure proper contact.

5. Connect the negative battery cable.

CHECKING AND REPLACING SPARK PLUG WIRES

▶ **See Figures 17 and 18**

Every 15,000 miles, visually inspect the spark plug wires for burns, cuts, or breaks in the insulation. Check the boots and the distributor cap tower connectors. Replace any damaged wiring.

Every 30,000–45,000 miles, the resistance of the wires should be checked using an ohmmeter. Wires with excessive resistance will cause misfiring and may make the engine difficult to start in damp weather. Generally, the useful life of the cables is 30,000–45,000 miles.

To check resistance, remove the distributor cap, leaving the wires in place. Connect one lead of an ohmmeter to an electrode within the cap; connect the other lead to the corresponding spark plug terminal (remove it from the spark plug for this test). Replace any wire which shows a resistance over 30,000 ohms. Generally speaking, it is preferable that resistance be below 25,000 ohms, but 30,000 ohms; must be considered the outer limit of acceptability. It should be remembered that resistance is also a function of length; the longer the wire, the greater the resistance. Thus, if the wires on your car are longer than the factory originals, resistance will be higher, quite possibly outside these limits.

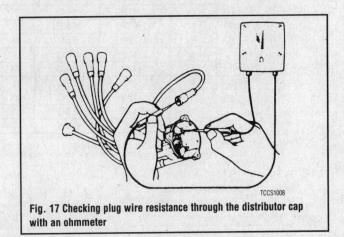

Fig. 17 Checking plug wire resistance through the distributor cap with an ohmmeter

TCCS1009

Fig. 18 Checking individual plug wire resistance with an digital ohmmeter

Wire length can therefore be used to determine appropriate resistance values:

- 0–15 in.—3000–10,000 ohms
- 15–25 in.—4000–15,000 ohms
- 25–35 in.—6000–20,000 ohms
- Wire over 35 in.—6000–25,000 ohms

➡**If all of the wires must be disconnected from the spark plugs or from the distributor at the same time, be sure to tag the wires to assure proper reconnection.**

When installing a new set of spark plug wires, replace the wires one at a time so there will be no mix-up. Start by replacing the longest cable first. Install the boot firmly over the spark plug. Route the wire exactly the same as the original. Connect the wire tower connector to the distributor. Repeat the process for each wire. Be sure to apply silicone dielectric compound to the spark plug wire boots and tower connectors prior to installation.

GASOLINE ENGINE TUNE-UP SPECIFICATIONS

Year	Engine ID/VIN	Displacement Liter (cc)	Spark Plugs Gap (In.)	Ignition Timing (deg.) MT	AT	Fuel Pump (psi)	Idle Speed (rpm) MT	AT	Valve Clearance In.	Ex.
1982	A	1.9 (1949)	0.040	6B	6B	3.0	800	900	0.006	0.010
	B	2.8 (2835)	0.040	6B	10B	7.0	1000	750	Hyd.	Hyd.
1983	A	1.9 (1949)	0.040	6B	6B	3.0	800	900	0.006	0.010
	Y	2.0 (1990)	0.035	12B	12B	5.0	750	700	Hyd.	Hyd.
	B	2.8 (2835)	0.040	6B	10B	7.0	1000	750	Hyd.	Hyd.
1984	A	1.9 (1949)	0.040	6B	6B	3.0	800	900	0.006	0.010
	Y	2.0 (1990)	0.035	12B	12B	5.0	750	700	Hyd.	Hyd.
	B	2.8 (2835)	0.040	6B	10B	7.0	1000	750	Hyd.	Hyd.
1985	A	1.9 (1949)	0.040	6B	6B	4.0–6.5	800	900	0.006	0.010
	E	2.5 (2474)	0.060	①	①	9–13	①②	①②	Hyd.	Hyd.
	B	2.8 (2835)	0.045	6B	10B	4.0–6.5	750	650	Hyd.	Hyd.
1986	E	2.5 (2474)	0.060	①	①	9–13	①②	①②	Hyd.	Hyd.
	R	2.8 (2835)	0.045	①	①	9–13	①②	①②	Hyd.	Hyd.
1987	E	2.5 (2474)	0.060	①	①	9–13	①②	①②	Hyd.	Hyd.
	R	2.8 (2835)	0.045	①	①	9–13	①②	①②	Hyd.	Hyd.
1988	E	2.5 (2474)	0.060	①	①	9–13	①②	①②	Hyd.	Hyd.
	R	2.8 (2835)	0.045	①	①	9–13	①②	①②	Hyd.	Hyd.
	Z	4.3 (4293)	0.045	①	①	9–13	①②	①②	Hyd.	Hyd.
1989	E	2.5 (2474)	0.060	①	①	9–13	①②	①②	Hyd.	Hyd.
	R	2.8 (2835)	0.045	①	①	9–13	①②	①②	Hyd.	Hyd.
	Z	4.3 (4293)	0.045	①	①	9–13	①②	①②	Hyd.	Hyd.
1990	E	2.5 (2474)	0.060	①	①	9–13	①②	①②	Hyd.	Hyd.
	R	2.8 (2835)	0.045	①	①	9–13	①②	①②	Hyd.	Hyd.
	Z	4.3 (4293)	0.045	①	①	9–13	①②	①②	Hyd.	Hyd.
1991	A	2.5 (2474)	0.060	①	①	9–13	①②	①②	Hyd.	Hyd.
	E	2.5 (2474)	0.060	①	①	9–13	①②	①②	Hyd.	Hyd.
	R	2.8 (2835)	0.045	①	①	9–13	①②	①②	Hyd.	Hyd.
	Z	4.3 (4293)	0.045	①	①	9–13	①②	①②	Hyd.	Hyd.
1992	A	2.5 (2474)	0.060	①	①	9–13	①②	①②	Hyd.	Hyd.
	R	2.8 (2835)	0.045	①	①	9–13	①②	①②	Hyd.	Hyd.
	W	4.3 (4293)	0.045	①	①	55–61	①②	①②	Hyd.	Hyd.
	Z	4.3 (4293)	0.035	①	①	9–13	①②	①②	Hyd.	Hyd.
1993	A	2.5 (2474)	0.060	①	①	9–13	①②	①②	Hyd.	Hyd.
	R	2.8 (2835)	0.045	①	①	9–13	①②	①②	Hyd.	Hyd.
	W	4.3 (4293)	0.045	①	①	55–61	①②	①②	Hyd.	Hyd.
	Z	4.3 (4293)	0.045	①	①	9–13	①②	①②	Hyd.	Hyd.

NOTE: The Vehicle Emission Control Information label often reflects specification changes made during production. The label figures must be used if they differ from those in this chart.

B—Before TDC

Hyd.—Hydraulic

① Refer to underhood label

② Idle speed on these engines is computer controlled. No periodic adjustments are necessary or possible

88844R007

FIRING ORDERS

▶ **See Figures 19, 20, 21, 22 and 23**

➡ **To avoid confusion, remove and tag the spark plug wires one at a time, for replacement.**

If a distributor is not keyed for installation with only one orientation, it could have been removed previously and rewired. The resultant wiring would hold the correct firing order, but could change the relative placement of the plug towers in relation to the engine. For this reason it is imperative that you label all wires before disconnecting any of them. Also, before removal, compare the current wiring with the accompanying illustrations. If the current wiring does not match, make notes in your book to reflect how your engine is wired.

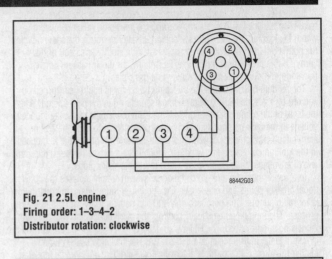

Fig. 21 2.5L engine
Firing order: 1–3–4–2
Distributor rotation: clockwise

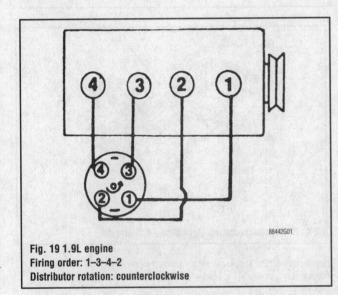

Fig. 19 1.9L engine
Firing order: 1–3–4–2
Distributor rotation: counterclockwise

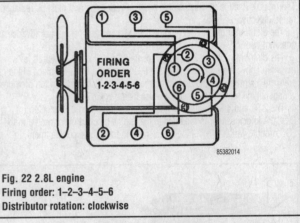

Fig. 22 2.8L engine
Firing order: 1–2–3–4–5–6
Distributor rotation: clockwise

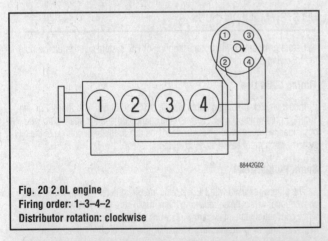

Fig. 20 2.0L engine
Firing order: 1–3–4–2
Distributor rotation: clockwise

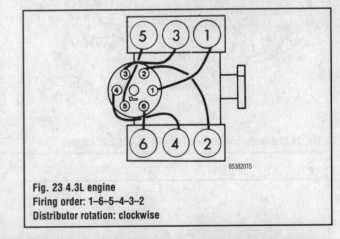

Fig. 23 4.3L engine
Firing order: 1–6–5–4–3–2
Distributor rotation: clockwise

HIGH ENERGY IGNITION SYSTEM

Description & Operation

▶ **See Figures 24, 25, 26 and 27**

The General Motors/Delco-Remy High Energy Ignition (HEI) system is breakerless, pulse-triggered, transistor-controlled, inductive discharge ignition system. It is used on all gasoline engine vehicles covered by this manual. The external ignition coil is normally mounted on the side of the engine, using a secondary circuit high tension wire to connect the coil to the cap. Interconnecting primary wiring is routed through the engine harness.

The distributor, in addition to housing the advance mechanisms, contains the electronic ignition module, and the magnetic pick-up assembly which contains a permanent magnet, a pole piece with internal teeth, and a pick-up coil (not to be confused with the ignition coil).

The HEI distributor is equipped to aid in spark timing changes, necessary for emissions, economy and performance. On some of the early model trucks covered by this manual, these timing changes are accomplished through vacuum and mechanical advance mechanisms. However, most of the models covered by this manual achieve timing changes through the Electronic Spark Timing (EST) control system. On these vehicles, timing changes are electronically controlled through the Engine Control Module (ECM).

In the HEI system, as in other electronic ignition systems, the breaker points have been replaced with an electronic switch, a transistor, which is located within the ignition module. This switching transistor performs the same function the points did in a conventional ignition system; it simply turns coil primary current on and off at the correct time. Essentially, the electronic and conventional ignition systems operate on the same principle.

The module which houses the switching transistor is controlled (turned on and off) by a magnetically generated impulse induced in the pick-up coil. When the teeth of the rotating timer align with the teeth of the pole piece, the induced voltage in the pick-up coil signals the electronic module to open the coil primary circuit. The primary current then decreases and a high voltage is induced in the ignition coil secondary windings which is then directed through the rotor and high voltage leads (spark plug wires) to fire the spark plugs.

In essence then, the pick-up coil module system simply replaces the conventional breaker points and condenser. The condenser found within the distributor is for radio suppression purposes only and has nothing to do with the ignition process. The module automatically controls the dwell period, increasing it with increasing engine speed. The HEI system features a longer spark duration which is instrumental in firing lean and Exhaust Gas Recirculation (EGR) diluted fuel/air mixtures. Since dwell is automatically controlled, it cannot be adjusted. The module itself is non-adjustable and non-repairable and must be replaced if found defective.

The distributor on the 1.9L engine uses vacuum and centrifugal advance and does not use EST.

The distributor on the 2.5L engine contains a Hall Effect Switch. It is mounted above the pick-up coil in the distributor and takes the place of the reference (R) terminal on the distributor module. The Hall Effect Switch provides a voltage signal to the ECM to tell it which cylinder will fire next.

The 2.8L and 4.3L engines are equipped with Electronic Spark Control (ESC). A knock sensor is mounted in the engine block. It is connected to the ESC module which is mounted on the cowl in the engine compartment. In

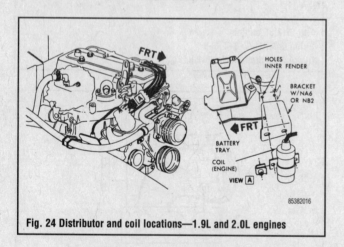

Fig. 24 Distributor and coil locations—1.9L and 2.0L engines

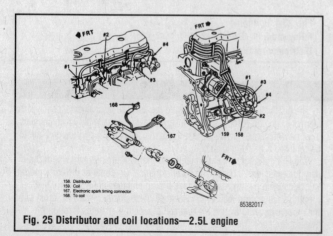

Fig. 25 Distributor and coil locations—2.5L engine

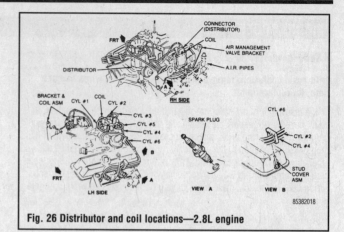

Fig. 26 Distributor and coil locations—2.8L engine

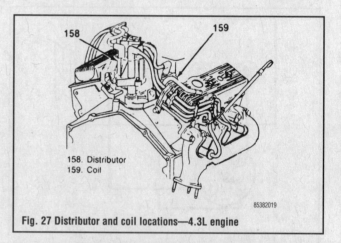

158. Distributor
159. Coil

Fig. 27 Distributor and coil locations—4.3L engine

response to engine knock, the sensor sends a signal to the ESC module. The module will then signal the ECM which will retard the spark timing in the distributor.

HEI SYSTEM PRECAUTIONS

Before proceeding with troubleshooting or HEI system service, please note the following precautions:

Timing Light Use

Inductive pick-up timing lights are the best kind of use with the HEI system. Timing lights which connect between the spark plug and the spark plug wire occasionally (not always) give false readings due to the high voltage of the HEI system which more easily leads to arcing.

Spark Plug Wires

The plug wires used with HEI systems are of a different construction than conventional wires. When replacing them, make sure you get the correct wires, since conventional point system wires won't carry the voltage. Also, handle them carefully to avoid cracking or splitting them and never pierce them.

Tachometer Use

Not all tachometers will operate or indicate correctly when used on a HEI system. While some tachometers may give a reading, this does not necessarily mean the reading is correct. In addition, some tachometers hook up differently from others. If you can't figure out whether or not your tachometer will work on your car, check with the tachometer manufacturer.

HEI System Testers

Instruments designed specifically for testing HEI systems are available from several tool manufacturers. Some of these will even test the module itself. However, most of the tests given in the following section will require only ohmmeter and a voltmeter.

Troubleshooting the HEI System

Diagnosis and testing procedures in this section should be used in conjunction with those in Section 4 (Emission Controls) and Section 5 (Fuel System) of this manual. This will enable you to diagnose problems involving all components controlled by the Electronic Control Module (ECM).

➡An accurate diagnosis is the first step to problem solution and repair. Most of the troubleshooting covered here can be performed using a voltmeter/ohmmeter and a spark tester. Although an old spark plug may be used as a spark tester, the use of an inexpensive tester tool such as ST-125 is highly recommended. The tester tool is similar in appearance to a spark plug, with a spring clip to attach to ground. Because of the high voltage of the HEI system, the tester should be used instead of an old spark plug unless absolutely necessary. If a plug must be used, do not touch the plug or wiring directly in order to minimize the chance of injury from electric shock.

The symptoms of a defective component within the HEI system are exactly the same as those you would encounter in a conventional system. Some of these symptoms are:

- Hard or no starting
- Rough idle
- Poor fuel economy
- Engine misses under load or while accelerating

If you suspect a problem in your ignition system, there are certain preliminary checks which you should carry out before you begin to check the electronic portions of the system. First, it is extremely important to make sure the vehicle battery is in a good state of charge. A defective or poorly charged battery will cause the various components of the ignition system to read incorrectly when they are being tested. Second, make sure all wiring connections are clean and tight, not only at the battery, but also at the distributor cap, ignition coil, and at the electronic control module.

The quickest and easiest test of the ignition system is to check the secondary ignition circuit first (check for spark). If the secondary circuit checks out properly, then the engine condition is probably not the fault of the ignition system. To check the secondary ignition circuit, perform a simple spark test. Remove one of the plug wires and insert a spark tester or some sort of extension in the plug socket. An old spark plug with the ground electrode removed makes a good extension. If using an old plug, hold the wire with an insulated tool so the extension is positioned about ¼ in. away from the block, then crank the engine. If a normal spark occurs, then the problem is most likely not in the ignition system. Check for fuel system problems, or fouled spark plugs.

If, however, there is no spark or a weak spark, then further ignition system testing will have to be performed. Troubleshooting techniques fall into two categories, depending on the nature of the problem. The categories are (1) Engine cranks, but won't start or (2) Engine runs, but runs rough or cuts out. To begin with, let's consider the first case.

ENGINE FAILS TO START

If the engine won't start, perform a spark test as described earlier. This will narrow the problem area down considerably. If no spark occurs, check for the presence of normal battery voltage of the battery (BAT) terminal in the distributor cap. The ignition switch must be in the **ON** position for this test. Either a voltmeter or a test light may be used for this test. Connect the test light wire to ground and probe end to the BAT terminal at the distributor. If the light comes on, you have voltage on the distributor. If the light fails to come on, this indicates an open circuit in the ignition primary wiring leading to the distributor. In this case, you will have to check wiring continuity back to the ignition switch using a test light. If there is battery voltage at the BAT terminal, but no spark at the plugs, then the problem lies within the distributor assembly. Go on to the distributor components test section.

ENGINE RUNS, BUT RUNS ROUGH OR CUTS OUT

1. Make sure the plug wires are in good shape first. There should be no obvious cracks or breaks. You can check the plug wires with an ohmmeter, but do not pierce the wires with a probe. Check the plug wire for a proper resistance using the values listed earlier in this section under spark plug wiring.

2. If the plug wires are OK, remove the cap assembly and check for moisture, cracks, chips, carbon tracks, or any other high voltage leaks or failures. Replace the cap if any defects are found. Make sure the timer wheel rotates when the engine is cranked. If everything is all right so far, go on to the distributor components test section following.

Distributor Component Testing

If the trouble has been narrowed down to the units within the distributor, the following tests can help pinpoint the defective component. An ohmmeter with both high and low ranges should be used. These tests are made with the battery wire disconnected. If a tachometer is connected to the TACH terminal, disconnect it before making these tests.

IGNITION COIL

Except 1.9L Engine

▶ See Figure 28

1. Disconnect the distributor lead and wiring from the coil.
2. Set the ohmmeter to the HIGH scale, then connect it to the coil as shown in Step 1 of the illustration. The reading should be infinite. If not, verify a proper test connection to be assured of a true test result and if still not infinite, replace the coil.
3. Set the ohmmeter to the LOW scale, then connect it as shown in Step 2 of the illustration. The reading should be very low or zero. If not, verify a proper test connection and replace the coil.
4. Set the ohmmeter on the HIGH scale, then connect it to the coil as shown in Step 3 of the illustration. The ohmmeter should NOT read infinite. If it does, verify the connection and replace the coil.
5. Reconnect the distributor lead and wiring to the coil.

1.9L Engine

▶ See Figure 29

1. Check the outer face of the ignition coil for cracking, rust or other visible signs of damage.
2. Check the resistance of the primary and secondary coils as shown in the illustration. If the resistance is not within specification, verify the proper test connections and replace the coil.
- Primary coil resistance—0.090–1.400 ohms
- Secondary coil resistance—7.3–11.1 K ohms
3. If testing the insulation resistance, any reading less than 10 Megohms indicates a need to replace the coil. Since most ohmmeters will not read resistance higher than 10 megohms, any continuity will probably indicate a need to replace the component.

PICK-UP COIL

Except 1.9L Engine

▶ See Figure 30

1. Disconnect the negative battery cable.
2. Remove the distributor cap and disconnect the pick-up coil connector from the module.
3. Connect an ohmmeter to either pick-up coil lead and the housing as shown in Step 1 of the illustration. The reading should NOT be infinite. If the reading is infinite, replace the coil.
4. Connect an ohmmeter to both pick-up coil leads as shown in step 2 of the illustration. Flex the wires by hand at the coil and the connector to locate an intermittent opens.
5. The ohmmeter should read a constant number in the 500–1500 ohm; range. If not, replace the pick-up coil.

1.9L Engine

The pick-up coil and ignition module on the 1.9L engine must be tested as a unit. The use of an ignition module tester to perform this function is highly recommended.

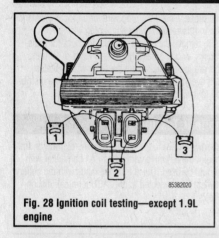

Fig. 28 Ignition coil testing—except 1.9L engine

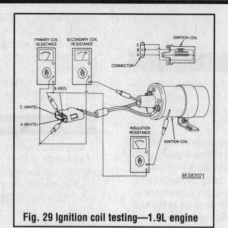

Fig. 29 Ignition coil testing—1.9L engine

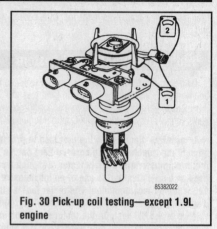

Fig. 30 Pick-up coil testing—except 1.9L engine

Component Replacement

REMOVAL & INSTALLATION

Ignition Coil

♦ See Figures 31, 32 and 33

1. Disconnect the negative battery cable.
2. Disengage the primary electrical wiring connector and the coil-to-distributor high tension cable from the ignition coil.
3. Remove the coil attaching bolts, then remove the coil from the engine.

To install:
4. Position the coil to the engine and secure using the retainers.

5. Engage the primary electrical wiring connector and the coil-to-distributor high tension cable to the ignition coil.
6. Connect the negative battery cable.

Distributor Cap

♦ See Figures 34, 35 and 36

1. Disconnect the negative battery cable and if necessary for access, remove the air cleaner assembly.
2. Remove the retainer and spark plug wires from the cap. If there is no wire retainer, be sure to tag all wires before disconnecting them from the distributor cap. Tagging wires will help preserve the proper firing order and greatly ease cap installation.
3. If retained by spring loaded lock tabs, depress, twist and release the distributor cap-to-housing lock tabs, then lift off the cap assembly. Most integral

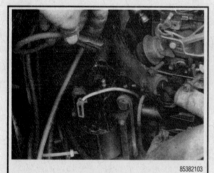

Fig. 31 Disconnect the coil-to-distributor high tension cable from the top of the ignition coil

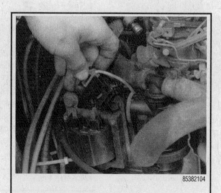

Fig. 32 Disengage any electrical wiring connectors from the coil

Fig. 33 Loosen and remove the retaining bolts, then remove the coil from the bracket

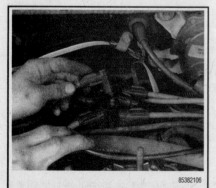

Fig. 34 Disconnect the coil wire from the center of the distributor cap

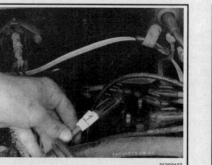

Fig. 35 If there is no wire retainer, tag and disconnect the spark plug wires from the top of the cap

Fig. 36 Release the spring-loaded lock tabs, then remove the cap from the distributor

coil distributor caps will be retained by 2 spring loaded lock tabs, though some models may use more.

4. If retained by mounting screws, loosen the screws, then remove the cap from the distributor assembly.

To install:

5. Install the cap to the distributor assembly and secure using the housing retainers.

6. Install the spark plug wires and retainer to the cap. If no wire retainer is used, carefully connect the wires to the cap as tagged during removal.

7. Connect the negative battery cable.

Rotor

▶ **See Figures 37 and 38**

1. Disconnect the negative battery cable and if necessary for access, remove the air cleaner assembly.

2. Remove the distributor cap from the housing assembly.

➡**Although most rotors can only be installed in one direction, it is still wise to note the position of the rotor before removal to assure proper installation and ignition timing.**

3. Remove the rotor attaching screw(s), if equipped, and note the position of the rotor, then remove the rotor from the distributor.

To install:

4. Install the rotor facing in the direction noted earlier, then if applicable, secure the rotor using the attaching screw(s).

5. Install the distributor cap to the housing assembly.

6. Connect the negative battery cable.

Ignition Module

▶ **See Figures 39 thru 44**

NON-EST DISTRIBUTOR

▶ **See Figures 45 and 46**

➡**Some non-EST distributors may require a partial disassembly of the distributor in order to remove and replace the ignition module. Though most modules are replaceable without disassembling the distributor, removing the distributor assembly from the engine will make access to the components easier. If you wish to avoid removing the distributor from the engine, remove the cap and rotor to see if access to the module retainers and connectors is possible with the distributor installed, then decide if you want to remove the distributor.**

1. Disconnect the negative battery cable.

2. Remove the distributor cap and position it aside with the wiring still attached. If necessary, tag and disconnect all or some of the wiring in order to position the cap out of the way.

3. If necessary to access the module or if distributor disassembly is necessary, remove the distributor from the engine and place it on a work bench. Be sure to matchmark the rotor and housing before and after removal.

4. If necessary, remove the rotor from the distributor assembly. If applicable, remove the packing ring and the cover.

5. If applicable, remove the electrical harness-to-distributor screw.

6. Disengage the electrical harness connectors from the ignition module.

7. If the distributor is being disassembled, use two medium prybars to carefully pry the pole piece from the distributor shaft, then remove the roll pin.

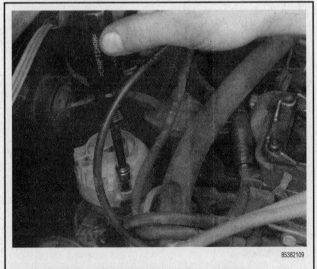
85382109
Fig. 37 Loosen and remove the rotor retaining screws

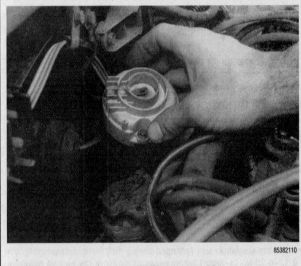
85382110
Fig. 38 Lift the rotor from the distributor assembly

85382111
Fig. 39 Disengage one or both of the module wiring connectors. The coil wiring may be left connected to the module until it is removed from the distributor

85382112
Fig. 40 Loosen and remove the module retainers

85382113
Fig. 41 Remove the module from the distributor; in this case the coil wiring is still attached

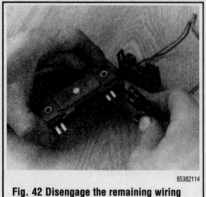

Fig. 42 Disengage the remaining wiring from the module

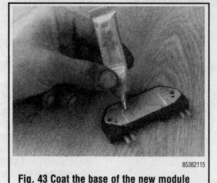

Fig. 43 Coat the base of the new module with silicone lubricant to aid in heat dissipation

Fig. 44 Position the new module to the distributor assembly and engage the wiring

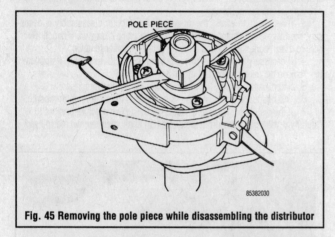

Fig. 45 Removing the pole piece while disassembling the distributor

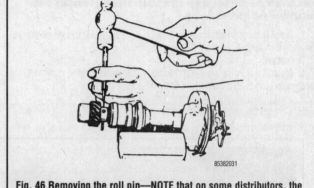

Fig. 46 Removing the roll pin—NOTE that on some distributors, the roll pin is mounted much higher on the shaft

8. Remove the ignition module retaining screws, then lift the module from the distributor. If equipped, be sure to remove the spacers from the module.

9. If the module is suspected as being defective, take it to a module testing machine and have it tested.

To install:

10. Apply a coat of silicone lubricant to the base of the ignition module to aid in heat dissipation.

11. Install the ignition module to the distributor assembly and secure using the retainers. If equipped, be sure to properly position the spacers during installation.

12. If removed, install the pole piece onto the distributor shaft, followed by a new roll pin.

➡**If the breaker plate was loosened during distributor disassembly, use a 0.12–0.20 in. (3–5mm) feeler gauge to measure the air gap between the pole piece and the breaker plate stator.**

13. Engage the electrical harness connectors to the ignition module, then if equipped, install the harness retaining screw.

14. If applicable, install the packing ring and cover.

15. Install the rotor to the distributor assembly.

16. If removed, align the matchmarks made earlier and install the distributor to the engine. Be sure the rotor is facing the proper direction and marks once the distributor is fully installed.

17. Install the cap to the distributor assembly. If any wiring was disconnected, be sure to engage it as tagged or noted during removal.

18. Connect the negative battery cable.

EST DISTRIBUTOR

The ignition modules are located inside the distributor; they may be replaced without removing the distributor from the engine.

1. Disconnect the negative battery terminal.

2. Remove the distributor cap and the rotor.

➡**Although most rotors can only be installed in one direction, it is still wise to note the position of the rotor before removal to assure proper installation and ignition timing.**

3. If the flange of the distributor shaft, is positioned above the module, place a socket on the crankshaft pulley bolt and rotate the crankshaft (turning the distributor shaft) to provide clearance to the ignition module. Since this will alter rotor position it may be wise to reinstall the rotor in order to make new alignment marks.

4. Remove the ignition module-to-distributor screws, lift the module and disengage the electrical connectors from it.

5. If the module is suspected as being defective, take it to a module testing machine and have it tested.

To install:

6. Apply a coat of silicone lubricant to the base of the ignition module (along the module-to-distributor mounting surface) to aid in heat dissipation.

7. Engage the module electrical wiring and install the ignition module to the distributor assembly, then secure using the retaining screws.

8. Install the rotor to the distributor assembly as noted during removal.

9. Install the cap to the distributor assembly.

10. Connect the negative battery cable.

HEI SYSTEM TACHOMETER HOOKUP

These vehicles are equipped with externally mounted ignition coils. Connect one tachometer lead to the TACH terminal on the ignition coil and connect the other one to a suitable ground.

✳✳ CAUTION

Never ground the TACH terminal; serious ignition module and coil damage will result. If there is any doubt as to the correct tachometer hookup, check with the tachometer manufacturer.

ELECTRONIC SPARK TIMING (EST) SYSTEM

The High Energy Ignition (HEI) system controls fuel combustion by providing the spark to ignite the compressed air/fuel mixture in the combustion chamber at the correct time. To provide improved engine performance, fuel economy and control of the exhaust emissions, the ECM controls distributor spark advance (timing) using the Electronic Spark Timing (EST) system.

Description & Operation

The HEI (EST) distributor uses a modified ignition module. The module has seven or eight terminals instead of the four used without EST. Different terminal arrangements are used, depending upon engine application.

To properly control ignition/combustion timing, the ECM needs to know the following information:

- Crankshaft position
- Engine speed (rpm)
- Engine load (manifold pressure or vacuum)
- Atmospheric (barometric) pressure
- Engine temperature
- Transmission gear position (certain models)

The ECM uses information from the MAP and coolant sensors in addition to rpm to calculate spark advance as follows:

- Low MAP output voltage would require MORE spark advance.
- Cold engine would require MORE spark advance.
- High MAP output voltage would require LESS spark advance.
- Hot engine would require LESS spark advance.

Incorrect operation of the EST system can cause the following:

- Detonation—low MAP output or high resistance in the coolant sensor circuit.
- Poor performance—high MAP output or low resistance in the coolant sensor circuit.

The EST system consists of the distributor module, ECM and its connecting wires.

Diagnosis & Testing

➡**Perform the following EST performance check and the ignition system check (earlier in this section) before attempting to diagnose EST system failures.**

ELECTRONIC SPARK CONTROL (ESC) SYSTEM

Because varying octane levels in gasoline can cause detonation (spark knock) in any engine, some of the fuel injected engines covered by this manual which are equipped with HEI (EST) are also equipped with an Electronic Spark Control (ESC) system. The ESC is designed to detect detonation and retard spark timing up to 20° to reduce or eliminate detonation in the engine. This allows the engine to use maximum spark advance to improve driveability and fuel economy.

Description & Operation

The ESC system has three components:
- ESC Module
- ESC Knock Sensor
- ECM (some later models may use a PCM or VCM depending upon application)

The knock sensor detects abnormal vibration in the engine. The sensor is mounted in the engine block near the cylinders. The ESC module receives the knock sensor information and sends a signal to the ECM. The ECM then adjusts the ignition timing to reduce spark knocking.

EST PERFORMANCE TEST

The EST system will usually set a Code 42 when a fault is detected in the system. Please refer to the ECM self-diagnostic information in section 4 of this manual for further information on how to retrieve diagnostic codes from the ECM memory.

Except 2.5L Engine

The ignition timing should change if the Set Timing connector is disengaged. To check EST operation, check and record the engine timing at 2000 rpm with Set Timing connector engaged as normal. Then, disengage the Set Timing connector and recheck the engine timing at 2000 rpm. If the EST system is operating, the timing should be different at the same rpm when checked with and without the timing connector engaged.

2.5L Engine

The ECM will set a specified timing valve when the ALDL diagnostic terminal is grounded. To check EST operation, first check and record ignition timing at 2000 rpm and the diagnostic terminal NOT grounded. Ground the diagnostic terminal of the ALDL connector (refer to self-diagnostics in Section 4 for more information on the ALDL) using a jumper wire and recheck the ignition timing. If the EST system is operating, ignition timing should be different at the same rpm when checked with and without the ALDL diagnostic connector grounded.

HALL EFFECT SWITCH TEST

The 2.5L distributor is equipped with a Hall Effect switch which provides a voltage signal to the ECM to tell it which cylinder will fire next

1. Disconnect and remove the Hall Effect switch from the distributor assembly.
2. Noting the polarity marked on the switch, connect a 12 volt battery and a voltmeter as shown in the illustration.
3. Insert a thin bladed tool against the magnet as shown.
4. The voltmeter reading should be less than 0.5 volts WITHOUT the blade against the magnet. Replace the switch if readings are above 0.5 volts.
5. With the blade against magnet, voltage readings should be within 0.5 volts of battery voltage. Replace the switch if not within specification.

The ESC module sends a voltage signal to the ECM when no spark knocking is detected by the ESC knock sensor, and the ECM provides normal spark advance. When the knock sensor detects spark knock, the module turns off the circuit to the ECM. The ECM then retards EST to reduce spark knock.

Diagnosis

Loss of the ESC knock sensor signal or loss of ground at the ESC module would cause the signal to the ECM to remain high. This condition would cause the ECM to control EST as if there was no spark knock. No retard would occur and spark knocking could become severe under heavy engine load.

Spark retard without the knock sensor connected could indicate a noise signal on the wire to the ECM or a malfunctioning ESC module.

Loss of the ESC signal to the ECM would cause the ECM to constantly retard the EST. This could result in sluggish performance and cause a Code 43 to set. Code 43 indicates that the ECM is receiving less than 6 volts for a 4 second period with the engine running. For more information concerning codes and the self-diagnostic system, please refer to Section 4 of this manual.

IGNITION TIMING

General Information

Ignition timing is the measurement, in degrees of crankshaft rotation, of the point at which the spark plugs fire in each of the cylinders. It is measured in degrees before or after Top Dead Center (TDC) of the compression stroke.

Because it takes a fraction of a second for the spark plug to ignite the mixture in the cylinder, the spark plug must fire a little before the piston reaches TDC. Otherwise, the mixture will not be completely ignited as the piston passes TDC and the full power of the explosion will not be used by the engine.

The timing measurement is given in degrees of crankshaft rotation before the piston reaches TDC (BTDC). If the setting for the ignition timing is 5° BTDC, the spark plug must fire 5° before each piston reaches TDC. This only holds true, however, when the engine is at idle speed.

As the engine speed increases, the pistons go faster. The spark plugs have to ignite the fuel even sooner if it is to be completely ignited when the piston reaches TDC. To do this, distributors have various means of advancing the spark timing as the engine speed increases. On some earlier model vehicles, this is accomplished by centrifugal weights within the distributor along with a vacuum diaphragm mounted on the side of the distributor. Later model vehicles are equipped with Electronic Spark Timing (EST) in which no vacuum or mechanical advance is used. Instead, the EST system makes all timing changes electronically based on signals from various sensors.

If the ignition is set too far advanced (BTDC), the ignition and expansion of the fuel in the cylinder will occur too soon and tend to force the piston down while it is still traveling up. This causes engine ping. If the ignition spark is set too far retarded, after TDC (ATDC), the piston will have already passed TDC and started on its way down when the fuel is ignited. This will cause the piston to be forced down for only a portion of its travel. This will result in poor engine performance and lack of power.

Timing marks consist of a notch on the rim of the crankshaft pulley and a scale of degrees attached to the front of the engine (often on the engine front cover). The notch corresponds to the position of the piston in the number 1 cylinder. A stroboscopic (dynamic) timing light is used, which is hooked into the circuit of the No. 1 cylinder spark plug. Every time the spark plug fires, the timing light flashes. By aiming the timing light at the timing marks while the engine is running, the exact position of the piston within the cylinder can be easily read since the stroboscopic flash makes the mark on the pulley appear to be standing still. Proper timing is indicated when the notch is aligned with the correct number on the scale.

There are three basic types of timing lights available. The first is a simple neon bulb with two wire connections (one for the spark plug and one for the plug wire, connecting the light in series). This type of light is quite dim, and must be held closely to the marks to be seen, but it is quite inexpensive. The second type of light is powered by the car's battery. Two alligator clips connect to the battery terminals, while a third wire connects to the spark plug with an adapter. This type of light is more expensive, but the xenon bulb provides a nice bright flash which can even be seen in sunlight. The third type replaces the battery source with 110 volt house current, but still attaches to the No. 1 spark plug wire in order to determine when the plug is fired. Some timing lights have other functions built into them, such as dwell meters, tachometers, or remote starting switches. These are convenient, in that they reduce the tangle of wires under the hood, but may duplicate the functions of tools you already have.

➡**Never pierce a spark plug wire in order to attach a timing light or perform tests. The pierced insulation will eventually lead to an electrical arc and related ignition troubles.**

Since your truck has electronic ignition, you should use a timing light with an inductive pickup. This pickup simply clamps onto the No. 1 spark plug wire, eliminating the adapter. It is not susceptible to cross-firing or false triggering, which may occur with a conventional light, due to the greater voltages produced by electronic ignition.

Checking & Adjustment

▶ **See Figures 47, 48 and 49**

The following procedure requires the use of a distributor wrench and a timing light. When using a timing light, be sure to consult the manufacturer's recommendations for installation and usage.

The vehicle emission control information label, which is found underhood, will often contain specifications or procedures for checking and adjusting timing that have been updated during production. The information contained on the label should always be used if it differs from these instructions.

On most HEI systems, the tachometer connects to the TACH terminal on the coil and to a ground. Some tachometers must connect to the TACH terminal and to the positive battery terminal. Also, note that some tachometers won't work at all with an HEI system. Consult the tachometer manufacturer if the instructions supplied with the unit do not give the proper connection.

✳✳ WARNING

Never ground the HEI TACH terminal; serious system damage will result, including ignition module burnout.

1. Set the parking brake and block the drive wheels, warm the engine to normal operating temperature.
2. Shut the engine **OFF** and connect the a timing light to the No. 1 spark plug (right front 2.8L engine, left front 4.3L engine or front plug on in-line engines):

   a. If using a non-inductive type, connect an adapter between the No. 1 spark plug and the spark plug wire; DO NOT puncture the spark plug wire, for this will cause a voltage leak.

   b. If using an inductive type, clamp it around the No. 1 spark plug wire.

   c. If using a magnetic type, place the probe in the connector located near the damper pulley; this type must be used with special electronic timing equipment.

➡**Do not under any circumstances pierce the insulation of a spark plug wire in order to connect the timing light.**

3. Clean off the timing marks, then label the pulley or damper notch and the timing scale with white chalk or paint for better visibility. If the timing notch

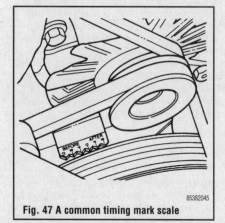

Fig. 47 A common timing mark scale

Fig. 48 Aim the timing light and the mark and scale, but be careful not to contact the fan or drive belts

Fig. 49 Timing marks are often difficult to see; this engine is equipped with a magnetic probe holder which may be used with special equipment

on the damper or pulley is not visible from the top, the crankshaft should be bumped around using the starter or turned using a wrench on the front pulley bolt, in order to bring the mark to an accessible position.

4. On early model vehicles not equipped with EST, disconnect and plug the vacuum advance hose at the distributor to prevent any distributor vacuum advance. The vacuum line is the rubber hose connected to the metal cone-shaped canister on the side of the distributor. A short screw, pencil, or a golf tee can be used to plug the hose.

5. On later model vehicles equipped with EST, the electronic spark timing must be disabled or bypassed to prevent the control module from advancing timing while you are attempting to set it. This would obviously lead to an incorrect base timing setting. There are 2 possible methods of disabling the EST system, depending on the type of engine:

• On 2.5L engines, ground the "A" and "B" terminals on the ALDL connector under the dash before adjusting the timing.

• On all other engines using the EST distributor, disengage the timing connector wire. On a few of the earlier model vehicles, the 4-terminal EST connector must be disengaged from the distributor. Most later model vehicles are equipped with a single wire timing bypass connector. On these later model vehicles the bypass wire is usually a tan wire with a black stripe. The wire usually breaks out of the wiring harness conduit adjacent to the distributor, but on some vehicles it may break out of a taped section just below the heater case in the passenger compartment.

6. Start the engine, then check and adjust the idle speed, as necessary. The idle speed must be properly set to prevent any centrifugal advance of timing in the distributor.

7. Aim the timing light at the timing marks. Be careful not to touch the fan, which may appear to be standing still. Keep your clothes and hair along with the timing light's wires clear of the fan, belts and pulleys. If the pulley or damper notch isn't aligned with the proper timing mark, the timing will have to be adjusted.

➡TDC or Top Dead Center corresponds to 0° mark on the scale. Either B, BTDC, or Before Top Dead Center, may be shown as BEFORE on the scale, while A, ATDC or After Top Dead Center, may be shown as AFTER.

8. Loosen the distributor base clamp locknut. You can buy special wrenches which make this task a lot easier on certain models. Turn the distributor slowly to adjust the timing, holding it by the body and not the cap. Turn the distributor in the direction of rotor rotation (found in the firing order illustrations earlier in this Section) to retard, and against the direction to advance.

9. Once the timing is properly set, hold the distributor to keep it from the turning and tighten the locknut. Check the timing again after finishing with the nut in case the distributor moved as you tightened it.

10. If applicable, remove the plug and connect the distributor vacuum hose.

11. If necessary check and/or adjust the idle speed.

12. Shut off the engine and reconnect the EST wire (if equipped), then disconnect the timing light and tachometer.

VALVE LASH

Valve lash adjustment determines how far the valves enter the cylinder and how long they stay open and/or closed.

➡While all valve adjustments must be made as accurately as possible, it is better to have the valve adjustment slightly loose than slightly tight, as a burned valve may result from overly tight adjustments.

Most of the engines covered by this manual (with the exception of the 1.9L gasoline and the 2.2L diesel) utilize hydraulic valve lifters. The purpose of hydraulic lifters is to automatically maintain zero valve lash, therefore no periodic adjustments are required on engines equipped with them. However, most of the vehicles utilize rocker arms which are retained by adjusting nuts. If the rocker arms and nuts are loosened or removed, they must be properly adjusted upon installation in order for the lifters to work.

Adjustment

1.9L ENGINES

▶ See Figure 50

➡The valves are adjusted with the engine Cold.

1. Remove the rocker arm cover. For details, please refer to Section 3 of this manual.

2. Verify that the rocker arm shaft nuts/bolts are properly torqued to 16 ft. lbs. (22 Nm).

3. Using a wrench on the damper pulley bolt or using a remote starter button, turn the crankshaft until the No. 1 piston is at TDC of the compression stroke. You will know when the No. 1 piston is on it's compression stroke because both the intake and exhaust valves will remain closed as the crankshaft damper mark approaches the timing scale.

➡Another method to tell when the piston is coming up on the compression stroke is by removing the spark plug and placing your thumb over the hole, you will feel the air being forced out of the spark plug hole. Stop turning the crankshaft when the TDC timing mark on the crankshaft pulley is directly aligned with the timing mark pointer or the zero mark on the scale.

4. With the No. 1 piston at TDC of the compression stroke, perform the following valve setting procedures:

    a. Use a 0.006 in. (0.152mm) feeler gauge, to set intake valves of cylinders No. 1 & 2. Using a 0.010 in. (0.254mm) feeler gauge, set the exhaust valves of cylinders No. 1 & 3.

➡When adjusting the valve clearance, loosen the locknut with an open-end wrench, then turn the adjuster screw with a screwdriver and retighten the locknut. The proper thickness feeler gauge should pass between the camshaft and the rocker with a slight drag when the clearance is correct.

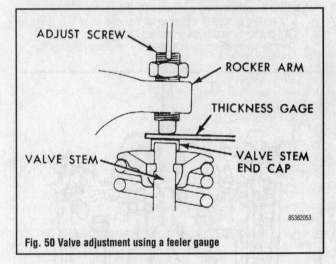

Fig. 50 Valve adjustment using a feeler gauge

5. Rotate the engine one complete revolution, so that cylinder No. 4 is on the TDC of its compression stroke and the timing marks are aligned. This time the No. 4 cylinder valves remain closed as the timing mark approaches the scale.

6. With cylinder No. 4 on the TDC of the compression stroke, perform the following valve setting procedures:

    a. Use a 0.006 in. (0.152mm) feeler gauge, to set intake valves of cylinders No. 3 & 4. Using a 0.010 in. (0.254mm) feeler gauge, set the exhaust valves of cylinders No. 2 & 4.

2.0L AND 2.8L ENGINES

▶ See Figure 51

➡These engines utilize hydraulic valve lifters which means that a valve adjustment is NOT a regular maintenance item. The valves must only be adjusted if the rockers arms have been disturbed for any reason such as cylinder head, camshaft, pushrod or lifter removal.

1. Remove the air cleaner and the rocker arm cover(s). For details, please refer to

2. Rotate the crankshaft until the mark on the crankshaft pulley aligns with the **0** mark on the timing plate. Make sure that the No. 1 cylinder is positioned on the compression stroke. You will know when the No. 1 piston is on it's compression stroke because both the intake and exhaust valves will remain closed as the crankshaft damper mark approaches the timing scale.

➡️**Another method to tell when the piston is coming up on the compression stroke is by removing the spark plug and placing your thumb over the hole, you will feel the air being forced out of the spark plug hole. Stop turning the crankshaft when the TDC timing mark on the crankshaft pulley is directly aligned with the timing mark pointer or the zero mark on the scale.**

3. With the engine in the No. 1 firing position, perform the following adjustments:

    a. If working on the 2.0L engine, adjust the intake valves of cylinders No. 1 & 2 and the exhaust valves of cylinders No. 1 & 3.

    b. If working on the 2.8L engine, adjust the intake valves of cylinders No. 1, 5 & 6 and the exhaust valves of cylinders No. 1, 2 & 3.

4. To adjust the valves, back-out the adjusting nut until lash can be felt at the push rod, then turn the nut until all of the lash is removed.

➡️**To determine if all of the lash is removed, turn the push rod with your fingers until the movement is removed.**

5. When all of the lash has been removed, turn the adjuster an additional 1½ turns; this will center the lifter plunger.

6. Rotate the crankshaft one complete revolution and realign the timing marks; the engine is now positioned on the No. 4 firing position. This time the No. 4 cylinder valves remain closed as the timing mark approaches the scale.

7. With the engine in the No. 4 firing position, perform the following procedures:

    a. If working on the 2.0L engine, adjust the intake valves of cylinders No. 3 & 4 and the exhaust valves of cylinders No. 2 & 4.

    b. If working on the 2.8L engine, adjust the intake valves of cylinders No. 2, 3 & 4 and the exhaust valves of cylinders No. 4, 5 & 6.

8. Once the valves are properly set, install the remaining components.

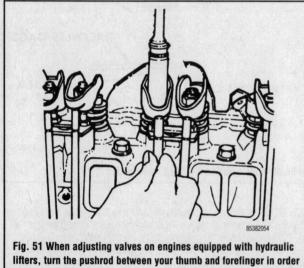

Fig. 51 When adjusting valves on engines equipped with hydraulic lifters, turn the pushrod between your thumb and forefinger in order to determine lash

2.5L ENGINE

Because the rocker arm fasteners are secured and torqued, valve lash is NOT adjustable on the 2.5L engine. If a valve train problem is suspected, check that the rocker arm bolts are tightened to 22 ft. lbs. (30 Nm). Be sure to only tighten the rocker arm bolts when the hydraulic lifter for that rocker arm is on the base circle of the camshaft and NOT when it is held upward on the lobe. When valve lash falls out of specification (valve tap is heard), replace the rocker arm, pushrod and hydraulic lifter on the offending cylinder.

4.3L (VIN Z) ENGINE

▶ **See Figure 51**

➡️**This engine utilizes hydraulic valve lifters which means that a valve adjustment is NOT a regular maintenance item. The valves must only be adjusted if the rockers arms have been disturbed for any reason such as cylinder head, camshaft, pushrod or lifter removal.**

For 1993, the 4.3L (VIN Z) engine may be equipped with either or 2 rocker arm retaining systems. If your engine utilizes screw-in type rocker arm studs with positive stop shoulders, no valve lash adjustment is necessary or possible. If so equipped, please refer to the 4.3L (VIN W) valve lash information, found later in this section. If however, you engine utilizes the pressed-in rocker arm studs, use the following procedure to tighten the rocker arm nuts and properly center the pushrod on the hydraulic lifter:

1. To prepare the engine for valve adjustment, rotate the crankshaft until the mark on the damper pulley aligns with the 0° mark on the timing plate and the No. 1 cylinder is on the compression stroke. You will know when the No. 1 piston is on it's compression stroke because both the intake and exhaust valves will remain closed as the crankshaft damper mark approaches the timing scale.

➡️**Another method to tell when the piston is coming up on the compression stroke is by removing the spark plug and placing your thumb over the hole, you will feel the air being forced out of the spark plug hole. Stop turning the crankshaft when the TDC timing mark on the crankshaft pulley is directly aligned with the timing mark pointer or the zero mark on the scale.**

2. With the engine on the compression stroke, adjust the exhaust valves of cylinders No. 1, 5 & 6 and the intake valves of cylinders No. 1, 2 & 3 by performing the following procedures:

    a. Back out the adjusting nut until lash can be felt at the pushrod.

    b. While rotating the pushrod, turn the adjusting nut inward until all of the lash is removed.

    c. When the play has disappeared, turn the adjusting nut inward 1 additional turn.

3. Rotate the crankshaft one complete revolution and align the mark on the damper pulley with the 0° mark on the timing plate; the engine is now positioned on the No. 4 firing position. This time the No. 4 cylinder valves remain closed as the timing mark approaches the scale. Adjust the exhaust valves of cylinders No. 2, 3 & 4 and the intake valves of cylinders No. 4, 5 & 6, by performing the following procedures:

    a. Back out the adjusting nut until lash can be felt at the pushrod.

    b. While rotating the pushrod, turn the adjusting nut inward until all of the lash is removed.

    c. When the play has disappeared, turn the adjusting nut inward 1 additional turn.

4. Install the remaining components, then start the engine and check for oil leaks.

4.3L (VIN W) Engine

The 4.3L (VIN W) engine and some of the 4.3L (VIN Z) engines are equipped with screw-in type rocker arm studs with positive stop shoulders. Because the shoulders allow the rocker arms to be torqued into proper position, no adjustments are necessary or possible. If a valve train problem is suspected, check that the rocker arm nuts are tightened to 20 ft. lbs. (27 Nm). When valve lash falls out of specification (valve tap is heard), replace the rocker arm, pushrod and hydraulic lifter on the offending cylinder.

Valve Arrangement

1.9L Engine
- E—I—I—E—E—I—I—E (front-to-rear)

2.0L Engine
- E—I—I—E—E—I—I—E (front-to-rear)

2.5L Engine
- I—E—I—E—E—I—E—I (front-to-rear)

2.8L Engine
- E—I—I—E—I—E (right bank—front-to-rear)
- E—I—E—I—I—E (left bank—front-to-rear)

4.3L Engine
- E—I—I—E—I—E (right bank—front-to-rear)
- E—I—E—I—I—E (left bank—front-to-rear)

IDLE SPEED AND MIXTURE ADJUSTMENTS

Carbureted Engines

Idle mixture and speed adjustments are critical aspects of exhaust emission control. It is important that all tune-up instructions be followed carefully to ensure satisfactory engine performance and minimum exhaust pollution. The different combinations of emission systems application on the various available engines have resulted in a great variety of tune-up specifications. All vehicles covered by this manual should have a decal conspicuously placed in the engine compartment giving tune-up specifications.

1.9L ENGINE

▶ See Figures 52 and 53

In order to adjust the idle mixture you must first remove the plug that covers the mixture screw.

1. Set the parking brake, block the drive wheels and place the transmission in Neutral.

2. Remove the carburetor from the engine, place it on a work bench and turn it upside down. For details, please refer to the carburetor procedures located in

3. Using a small prytool and a hammer, carefully drive the idle mixture screw metal plug from the base of the carburetor.

4. Reinstall the carburetor onto the engine. Start the engine and adjust the idle speed.

5. Allow the engine to reach normal operating temperatures, the choke must be Open and the A/C (if equipped) turned Off. Disconnect and plug the distributor vacuum line, the EGR vacuum line and the idle compensator vacuum lines.

6. Turn the mixture screw all the way in, then back it out 1½ turns.

➡ After adjustment, reconnect the vacuum lines.

7. Adjust the throttle speed screw to 850 rpm (MT) or 950 rpm (AT).

8. Adjust the idle mixture screw to achieve the maximum speed.

9. Reset the throttle adjusting screw to 850 rpm (MT) or 950 rpm (AT).

10. Turn the idle mixture screw (clockwise) until the engine speed is reduced to 800 rpm (MT) or 900 rpm (AT).

11. If equipped with A/C, perform the following procedures:

   a. Turn the A/C to Max. Cold and the blower to High.

   b. Open the throttle to ⅓ and allow it to close; this allows the speed-up solenoid to reach full travel.

   c. Adjust the speed-up controller adjusting screw to set the idle to 900 rpm.

2.0L AND 2.8L ENGINES

➡ **The idle mixture adjustments are factory set and sealed; no adjustment attempt should be made, except by an authorized GM dealer.**

Base Idle Adjustment

WITHOUT A/C

▶ See Figures 54 and 55

1. Refer to the emission control label on the vehicle and prepare the engine for adjustments.

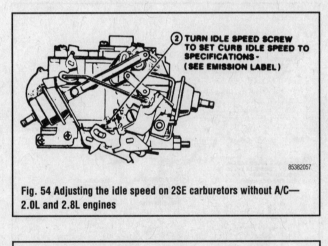

Fig. 54 Adjusting the idle speed on 2SE carburetors without A/C—2.0L and 2.8L engines

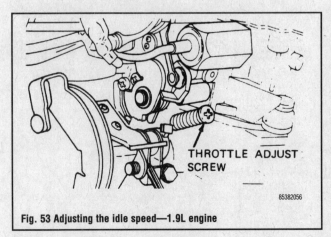

Fig. 52 Removing the idle mixture screw plug—1.9L engine

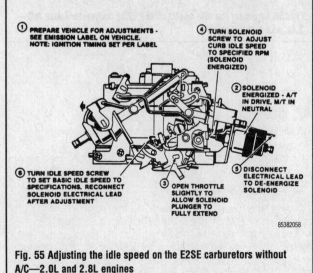

Fig. 55 Adjusting the idle speed on the E2SE carburetors without A/C—2.0L and 2.8L engines

Fig. 53 Adjusting the idle speed—1.9L engine

2. Remove the air cleaner, set the parking brake and block the drive wheels.

3. Connect a tachometer to the distributor connector.

4. Place the transmission in Drive (AT) or Neutral (MT); make sure that the solenoid is energized.

5. Open the throttle slightly to allow the solenoid plunger to extend. Adjust the curb idle speed to the specified rpm by turning the solenoid screw.

6. De-energize the solenoid by disconnecting the electrical lead.

7. Set the base idle speed rpm by turning the idle speed screw. After adjustment, reconnect the solenoid electrical lead.

8. Remove the tachometer and install the air cleaner.

WITH A/C

▶ See Figure 56

1. Refer to the emission label on the vehicle and prepare the engine for adjustments.

2. Remove the air cleaner, set the parking brake and block the drive wheels.

3. Connect a tachometer to the distributor connector.

4. Place the transmission in Drive (AT) or Neutral (MT); make sure that the solenoid is energized.

5. Turn the A/C Off and set the curb idle speed by turning the idle speed screw.

6. Disconnect the A/C lead from the A/C compressor; make sure the solenoid is energized. Open the throttle slightly to allow the solenoid plunger to extend.

7. Turn the solenoid screw to adjust to the specified rpm. After adjustment, reconnect the A/C compressor lead, remove the tachometer and install the air cleaner.

Fast Idle Adjustment

▶ See Figure 57

➡ Following the adjustment of the base idle speed, the fast idle speed may be adjusted.

1. Place the transmission in Park (AT) or Neutral (MT) and refer to the recommendation on the emission label.

2. Place the fast idle screw on the highest step of the fast idle cam.

3. Turn the fast idle screw to obtain the specified fast idle rpm.

Fuel Injected Engines

Beginning in 1985, some engines were available with a throttle body fuel injection system and all engines were fuel injected starting in the 1986 model year. By 1992 a central multi-port fuel injected engine became available as well. All fuel injected engines are controlled by a computer which regulates idle speeds and supplies the correct amount of fuel during all engine operating conditions. No periodic adjustments are necessary or possible. If the engine is suspected of maintaining an incorrect idle speed, refer to Section 4 of this manual for information regarding the self-diagnostic features of the computer engine and emission control systems.

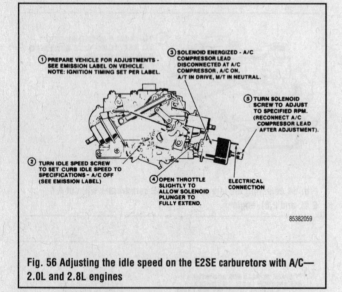

Fig. 56 Adjusting the idle speed on the E2SE carburetors with A/C—2.0L and 2.8L engines

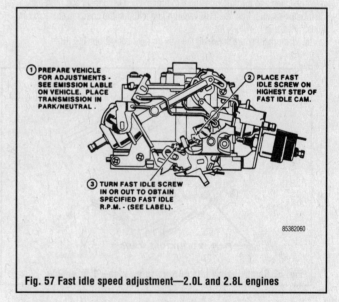

Fig. 57 Fast idle speed adjustment—2.0L and 2.8L engines

3

ENGINE AND ENGINE OVERHAUL

ENGINE ELECTRICAL

The engine electrical system can be broken down into three distinct sub-systems:

1. The starting system
2. The charging system
3. The ignition system.

Battery and Starting System

The battery is the first link in the chain of mechanisms which work together to provide cranking of the engine. In most modern trucks, the battery is a lead-acid electrochemical device consisting of six 2 volt (2V) subsections connected in series so the unit is capable of producing approximately 12V of electrical current. Each subsection, or cell, consists of a series of positive and negative plates held a short distance apart in a solution of sulfuric acid and water. The two types of plates are of dissimilar metals. This causes a chemical reaction to be set up, and it is this reaction which produces current flow from the battery when its positive and negative terminals are connected to an electrical appliance such as a lamp or motor. The continued transfer of electrons would eventually convert the sulfuric acid in the electrolyte to water, and make the two plates identical in chemical composition. As electrical energy is removed from the battery, its voltage output tends to drop. Thus, measuring battery voltage and battery electrolyte composition are two ways of checking the ability of the unit to supply power. During engine starting, electrical energy is removed from the battery. However, if the charging circuit is in good condition and the operating conditions are normal, the power removed from the battery will soon be replaced by the alternator which will force electrons back through the battery, reversing the normal flow, and restoring the battery to its original chemical state.

The battery and starting motor are linked by very heavy electrical cables designed to minimize resistance to the flow of current. Generally, the major power supply cable that leaves the battery goes directly to the starter, while other electrical system needs are supplied by a smaller cable. During starter operation, power flows from the battery to the starter and is grounded through the truck's frame and the battery's negative ground strap.

The starting motor is a specially designed, direct current electric motor capable of producing a large amount of power for its size. One thing that allows the motor to produce a great deal of power is its tremendous rotating speed. It drives the engine through a tiny pinion gear (attached to the starter's armature), which drives the very large flywheel ring gear at a greatly reduced speed. Another factor allowing it to produce so much power is that only intermittent operation is required of it. Thus, little allowance for air circulation is required, and the windings can be built into a very small space.

The starter solenoid is a magnetic device which employs the small current supplied by the starting switch circuit of the ignition switch. This magnetic action moves a plunger which mechanically engages the starter and electrically closes the heavy switch which connects it to the battery. The starting switch circuit commonly consists of the starting switch contained within the ignition switch, a transmission neutral or clutch safety switch and the wiring necessary to connect these with the starter solenoid or relay.

A pinion, which is a small gear, is mounted to a one-way drive clutch. This clutch is splined to the starter armature shaft. When the ignition switch is moved to the start position, the solenoid plunger slides the pinion toward the flywheel ring gear via a collar and spring. If the teeth on the pinion and flywheel match properly, the pinion will engage the flywheel immediately. If the gear teeth butt one another, the spring will be compressed and will force the gears to mesh as soon as the starter turns far enough to allow them to do so. As the solenoid plunger reaches the end of its travel, it closes the contacts that connect the battery and starter, then the engine is cranked.

As soon as the engine starts, the flywheel ring gear begins turning fast enough to drive the pinion at an extremely high rate of speed. At this point, the one-way clutch begins allowing the pinion to spin faster that the starter shaft so that the starter will not operate at excessive speed. When the ignition switch is released from the starter position, the solenoid is de-energized, and a spring contained within the solenoid assembly pulls the gear out of mesh and interrupts the current flow to the starter.

Many late model starters employ a separate relay, mounted away from the starter, to switch the motor and solenoid current on and off. The relay thus replaces the solenoid electrical switch, but does not eliminate the need for a solenoid mounted on the starter used to mechanically engage the starter drive gears. The relay is used to reduce the amount of current the starting switch must carry.

The Charging System

The automobile charging system provides electrical power for operation of the vehicle's ignition system, starting system and all the electrical accessories. The battery serves as an electrical surge or storage tank, storing (in chemical form) the energy originally produced by the belt driven alternator. The system also provides a means of regulating alternator output to protect the battery from being overcharged and to avoid excessive voltage to the accessories.

The storage battery is a chemical device incorporating parallel lead plates in a tank containing a sulfuric acid-water solution. Adjacent plates are slightly dissimilar, and the chemical reaction of the two dissimilar plates produces electrical energy when the battery is connected to a load such as the starter motor. The chemical reaction is reversible, so that when the alternator is producing a voltage greater than that produced by the battery, electricity is forced into the battery, and the battery is returned to its fully charged state.

The vehicle's alternator is driven mechanically, through a belt, by the engine crankshaft. The alternator consists of two coils of fine wire, one stationary (the stator), and one movable (the rotor). The rotor may also be known as the armature and consists of fine wire wrapped around an iron core which is mounted on a shaft. The electricity which flows through the two coils of wire (provided initially by the battery) creates an intense magnetic field around both rotor and stator, and the interaction between the two fields creates voltage, allowing the alternator to power the accessories and charge the battery.

All vehicles covered in this manual will be equipped with an alternating current generators or alternators because they are more efficient than the generators used in older vehicles, can be rotated at higher speeds, and have fewer brush problems. In an alternator, the field rotates while all the current produced passes only through the stator windings. The brushes bear against continuous slip rings rather than a commutator. This causes the current produced to periodically reverse the direction of its flow. Diodes (electrical one-way switches) block the flow of current from traveling in the wrong direction. A series of diodes is wired together to permit the alternating flow of the stator to be converted to a pulsating, but unidirectional flow at the alternator output. The alternator's field is wired in series with the voltage regulator.

The regulator consist of several circuits. Each circuit has a core, or magnetic coil of wire, which operates a switch. Each switch is connected to ground through one or more resistors. The coil of wire responds directly to system voltage. When the voltage reaches the required level, the magnetic field created by the winding of wire closes the switch and inserts a resistance into the generator field circuit, thus reducing the output. The contacts of the switch cycle open and close many times each second to precisely control voltage. Alternators are self-limiting as far as maximum current is concerned,

Ignition System

Most of the S/T trucks utilize an HEI distributor ignition system. On earlier models, this distributor is equipped with mechanical and vacuum timing advance devices to adjust the ignition spark advance curve. Most later model distributors are equipped with Electronic Spark Timing (EST) and ignition spark advance is electronically controlled through a computer module.

➡**For more information on these ignition systems, please refer to Section 2 of this manual.**

Safety Precautions

Observing these precautions will help avoid damage to the vehicle's electrical system and ensure safe handling of the system components:

• Be absolutely sure of the polarity of a booster battery before making connections. Connect the cables positive-to-positive, and negative-to-a good ground. Connect positive cables first and then make the last connection to an engine ground on the booster vehicle so that arcing cannot ignite hydrogen gas that may have accumulated near the battery. Even momentary connection of a booster battery with the polarity reversed will damage alternator diodes.

• Disconnect both vehicle battery cables before attempting to charge a battery.

• Never ground the alternator output or battery terminal. Be cautious when using metal tools around a battery to avoid creating a short circuit between the terminals.

• Never run an alternator without load unless the field circuit is disconnected.

• Never attempt to polarize an alternator.

Distributor

➡ **For ignition system service not found below, please refer to Section 2 of this manual.**

REMOVAL

♦ **See Figures 1, 2, 3, 4 and 5**

Except MFI-Turbo

1. Disconnect the negative battery cable. For the 4.3L (VIN Z) engine, remove the air cleaner and hoses.

2. Tag and disengage the electrical wiring connectors either from the distributor or from the ignition coil, whichever is applicable or easier.

3. Remove the distributor cap (If possible, DO NOT remove the coil or spark plug wires) from the distributor and position it aside. On most 4.3L (VIN Z) engines, it will be necessary to tag and disconnect the coil wire along with the spark plug wires from 1 side (either left or right) of the engine.

➡ **On non-EST equipped vehicles, disconnect the vacuum hose from the distributor vacuum advance module.**

4. Using a crayon, chalk or a marker, make locating marks (for installation purposes) on the rotor, the distributor housing and the engine. Scribe a mark on the distributor body and the engine block showing their relationship. Mark the distributor housing to show the direction in which the rotor is pointing or otherwise matchmark the rotor with the housing.

5. Loosen and remove the distributor hold-down bolt and clamp, then carefully lift the distributor out of the engine. Note the position of the rotor alignment mark on the housing and make a second mark on the housing to align with the rotor.

4.3L MFI-Turbo

1. Disconnect the negative battery cable.
2. Properly drain the charge air cooler radiator.
3. Loosen the charge air cooler clamps, then remove the ducts and hoses.
4. Remove the charge air cooler.
5. Detach the upper intake manifold connectors and hoses.
6. Unfasten the bolts from the upper intake manifold, then remove the manifold.
7. Disconnect the two screws on the sides of the distributor cap.
8. Tag and disconnect the coil wire along with the spark plug wires from 1 side (either left or right) of the engine.
9. Remove the distributor cap and position it aside.
10. Using a crayon, chalk or a marker, make locating marks (for installation purposes) on the rotor, the distributor housing and the engine. Scribe a mark on the distributor body and the engine block showing their relationship. Mark the distributor housing to show the direction in which the rotor is pointing or otherwise matchmark the rotor with the housing.
11. Loosen the remove the distributor hold-down bolt, washer and clamp, then carefully lift the distributor out of the housing and make a second mark on the housing to align with the rotor.

Fig. 1 Disengage the ignition module wiring

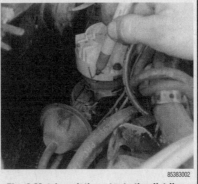

Fig. 2 Matchmark the rotor to the distributor housing

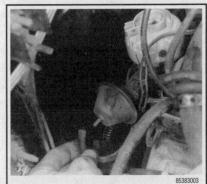

Fig. 3 On non-EST distributors, disengage the vacuum hose from the distributor

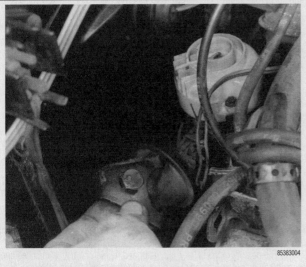

Fig. 4 Remove the distributor hold-down bolt and clamp

Fig. 5 Remove the distributor by lifting and tilting until there is sufficient clearance

INSTALLATION

Undisturbed Engine

EXCEPT MFI-TURBO

This condition exists if the engine has not been rotated while the distributor was removed.

1. With a new O-ring on the distributor housing and the rotor aligned with the second mark on the housing, install the distributor, taking care to align the distributor body mark with the mark scribed on the engine. When fully installed, the rotor should turn and align with the first distributor housing mark and therefore point in the same direction as before removal. It may be necessary to lift the distributor and turn the rotor slightly to properly align the gears and the oil pump driveshaft.

2. With the respective marks aligned, install the hold-down clamp and bolt finger-tight.

3. If equipped, connect the vacuum hose to the distributor vacuum advance module.

4. Install and secure the distributor cap.

5. Engage the electrical connector(s) to the distributor or coil, as applicable.

6. If removed, connect the spark plug and coil wires as noted during removal.

7. Connect a timing light to the engine (following the manufacturer's instructions) and connect the negative battery cable. Start the engine, then check and adjust the timing, as necessary.

➡**If removed, be sure to install the air cleaner and hoses.**

8. Turn the engine **OFF** and tighten the distributor clamp bolt.

9. Start the engine and recheck the timing to verify it did not change while tightening the hold-down bolt, then stop the engine and remove the timing light.

4.3L MFI-TURBO

1. With a new O-ring on the distributor housing and the rotor aligned with the second housing mark, install the distributor, taking care to align the distributor body mark with the mark scribed on the engine. When fully installed, the rotor should turn and align with the first distributor mark and therefore point in the same direction as before removal. It may be necessary to lift the distributor and turn the rotor slightly to properly align the gears and the oil pump driveshaft.

2. With the marks aligned, install the hold-down clamp, washer and bolt. Tighten the bolt to 20 ft. lbs. (27 Nm).

3. Install and secure the distributor cap.

4. Connect the spark plug coil wires as noted during removal.

5. Install the upper intake manifold and tighten the bolts to 17 ft. lbs. (23 Nm).

6. Install the throttle body, cable bracket and bolts and tighten to 17 ft. lbs. (23 Nm).

7. Attach the upper intake manifold connectors and hoses.

8. Install the charge air cooler, then connect the cooler hoses and clamps.

9. Connect the negative battery cable.

10. Properly refill the charge air cooling system.

11. Connect a timing light to the engine (following the manufacturer's instructions). Start the engine, then check and adjust the timing as necessary. Turn the engine **OFF** and remove the timing light.

Disturbed Engine

This condition exists when the engine has been rotated with the distributor removed.

1. Install a new O-ring on the distributor housing.

2. Rotate the crankshaft to position the No. 1 cylinder on the TDC of it's compression stroke. This may be determined by inserting a rag into the No. 1 spark plug hole and slowly turn the engine crankshaft. When the timing mark on the crankshaft pulley aligns with the 0° mark on the timing scale and the rag is blown out by the compression, the No. 1 piston is at top-dead-center (TDC).

➡**If you are unsure when TDC is reached, remove the valve cover and watch the rocker arms for the No. 1 cylinder. If the valves move as the crankshaft timing marker approaches the scale, the No. 1 cylinder is on its exhaust stroke. If the valves remain closed as the timing mark approaches the scale, then the No. 1 cylinder is approaching TDC of the compression stroke.**

3. Turn the rotor so that it will point to the No. 1 terminal of the distributor cap.

4. Install the distributor into the engine block. It may be necessary to turn the rotor, a little in either direction, in order to engage the gears.

5. Tap the starter a few times to ensure that the oil pump shaft is mated to the distributor shaft.

6. Bring the engine to No. 1 TDC again and check to see that the rotor is indeed pointing toward the No. 1 terminal of the cap.

7. With the respective marks aligned, install the hold-down clamp and bolt finger-tight.

8. Install and secure the distributor cap.

9. Engage the electrical connector(s) to the distributor and, if equipped, the vacuum advance hose.

10. If removed, connect the spark plug and coil wires as noted during removal.

11. Connect a timing light to the engine (following the manufacturer's instructions) and connect the negative battery cable. Start the engine, then check and adjust the timing, as necessary.

➡**If removed, be sure to install the air cleaner and hoses.**

12. Turn the engine **OFF** and tighten the distributor clamp bolt.

13. Start the engine and recheck the timing to verify it did not change while tightening the hold-down bolt, then stop the engine and remove the timing light.

Alternator

The alternator used in the charging system of 1982–86 S/T trucks is the SI integral regulator alternator. The alternator will be one of the following types: 10-SI, 12-SI or 15-SI. Differences between the types are output current ratings, and drive end and slip ring end bearing stack up.

Starting in 1986, the CS-130 alternator was used in production. The CS-130 features a high ampere output per pound of weight. It has an integral regulator but DOES NOT use a diode trio. The stator, rectifier bridge, and rotor with slip rings and brushes are electrically similar to the SI model alternators.

The regulator voltage varies with temperature and limits system voltage by controlling rotor field current. It switches rotor field current on and off at a fixed frequency of about 400 cycles per second. By varying the on-off time, correct average field current for proper system voltage control is obtained. At high speeds, the on-time may be 10 percent and the off-time may be 90 percent. At low speeds, with high electrical loads, the on-off time may be 90 percent and 10 percent respectively.

➡**The CS-130 alternator is not serviceable. If the alternator is found to be defective, replacement is the only alternative. Even though the SI alternators may be serviced, purchasing a new or rebuilt component is often easier and more effective.**

ALTERNATOR PRECAUTIONS

To prevent damage to the on-board computer, alternator and regulator, the following precautionary measures must be taken when working with the electrical system.

• If the battery is removed for any reason, make sure it is reconnected with the correct polarity. Reversing the battery connections may result in damage to the one-way rectifiers. Always check the battery polarity visually. This is to be done before any connections are made to be sure that all of the connections correspond to the battery ground polarity.

• When utilizing a booster battery as a starting aid, always connect the positive to positive terminals and the negative terminal from the booster battery to a good engine ground on the vehicle being started.

• Never use a fast charger as a booster to start vehicles.

• Disconnect the battery cables when charging the battery with a fast charger; the charger has a tendency to force current through the diodes in the opposite direction for which they were designed. This burns out the diodes.

• Make sure the ignition switch is OFF when connecting or disconnecting any electrical component, especially on trucks equipped with an on-board computer control system.

• Never attempt to polarize the alternator.

• Do not use test lights of more than 12 volts when checking diode continuity.

• Do not short across or ground any of the alternator terminals.

• The polarity of the battery, alternator and regulator must be matched and considered before making any electrical connections within the system.

• Never separate the alternator on an open circuit. Make sure all connections within the circuit are clean and tight.

• Disconnect the battery ground terminal when performing any service on electrical components.

• Disconnect the battery if arc welding is to be done on the vehicle.

DIAGNOSIS

SI Alternator

A charge indicator lamp is used in most trucks to signal when there is a fault in the charging system. This lamp is located in the gauge package and is used in diagnosis. A voltmeter may be used instead of the charge indicator lamp in diagnosis.

CS-130 Alternator

1. Check drive belt(s) for wear and tension. Check wiring for obvious damage.
2. Go to Step 7 for vehicles without a charge indicator lamp.
3. With the ignition switch **ON** and the engine stopped, the lamp should be ON. If not, detach the wiring harness at the generator and ground the "L" terminal lead.
4. If the lamp illuminates, replace the alternator. If the lamp does not illuminate, locate the open circuit between the grounding lead and the ignition switch. Check the lamp, it may be open.
5. With the ignition switch **ON** and the engine running at moderate speed, the lamp should be OFF. If not, stop the engine, then turn the switch **ON** and detach the wiring harness at the alternator.
6. If the lamp goes out, replace the alternator. If the lamp stays ON, check for a grounded "L" terminal wire in the harness.
7. Determine if the battery is undercharged or overcharged.
• An undercharged battery is evidenced by slow cranking or a dark hydrometer.
• An overcharged battery is evidenced by excessive spewing of electrolyte from the vents.
8. Detach the wiring harness connector from the alternator.
9. With the ignition switch **ON**, and the engine not running, connect a voltmeter from ground to the "L" terminal in the wiring harness, and to the "I" terminal, if used.

10. A zero reading indicates an open circuit between the terminal and the battery. Repair the circuit as necessary.
11. Connect the harness connector to the alternator and run the engine at moderate speed with accessories OFF.
12. Measure the voltage across the battery. If above 16 volts, replace the alternator.
13. Connect an ammeter at the alternator output terminal, run the engine at moderate speed, turn ON all the accessories and load the battery with a carbon pile to obtain maximum amperage. Maintain voltage at 13 volts or above.
14. If the output is within 15 amps of the rated output of the alternator (stamped on the alternator case), the alternator is good. If the output is not within 15 amps, replace the alternator.

REMOVAL & INSTALLATION

V-Belt Equipped Engines

♦ See Figures 6 thru 13

1. Disconnect the negative battery cable to prevent diode damage and prevent the chance of shorting the battery cables.
2. Remove other components as necessary to gain access to the alternator.
3. Tag and disconnect the alternator wiring. Use a small screwdriver to release the locktab on the alternator connector, then use a wrench to loosen the stud nut and disconnect the terminal wiring.
4. Loosen the alternator lower though-bolt, then remove the alternator brace/adjuster bolt.
5. Pivot the alternator inward and remove the drive belt(s) from the pulley.

➡On some early model vehicles the heater hose(s) may interfere with alternator travel. If you are unable to pivot the alternator sufficiently to free the drive belt(s), partially drain the cooling system, disconnect and reposition the heater hose(s) for the necessary clearance.

6. If equipped, remove the rear mounting bolt from the engine alternator bracket.

Fig. 6 Depress the locktab and disengage the wiring connector from the alternator

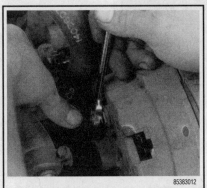

Fig. 7 Pull back the rubber boot, then loosen and remove the ring terminal retaining nut

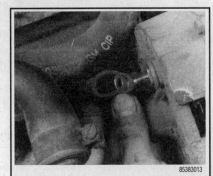

Fig. 8 With the nut removed, the ring terminal may be disconnected from the alternator

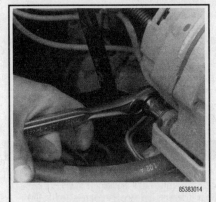

Fig. 9 Loosen the mounting/pivot bolt(s)

Fig. 10 Remove the alternator adjusting bolt

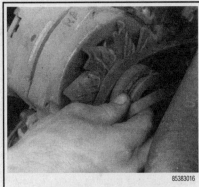

Fig. 11 Pivot the alternator inward and remove the drive belt(s) from the pulley

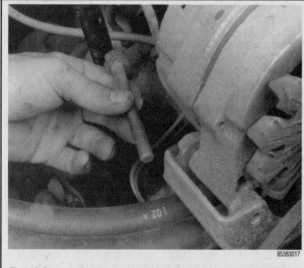

Fig. 12 Support the alternator and remove the mounting/pivot bolt(s)

Fig. 13 Remove the alternator from the vehicle

7. Support the alternator and remove the lower mount bolt(s), then remove the unit from the vehicle.

8. Installation is the reverse of removal. Refer to the belt adjustment procedures in Section 1.

Serpentine Belt Engines

▶ **See Figures 14 and 15**

Unlike the pivoting alternator used on many of the earlier vehicles covered by this manual, later model vehicles equipped with a serpentine drive belt utilize an alternator that is bolted into a fixed position.

1. Disconnect the negative battery cable.

2. For the 4.3L (VIN W) engine, remove the air inlet duct assembly, then remove the nut retaining the radiator hose brace to the back on the alternator.

3. If equipped, remove the retainers, then remove the brace from the engine and/or the alternator.

4. Disconnect the battery terminal boot wiring from the back of the alternator, then disengage the regulator wiring connector.

5. Carefully relieve the serpentine drive belt tension, then remove the belt from the alternator pulley. Do not allow the tensioner to snap back into position once the belt is off the pulley.

6. Support the alternator and remove the mounting bolts (usually 2) from either side of the alternator, then remove the alternator from the vehicle.

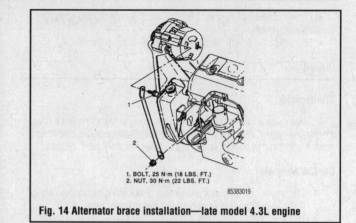

1. BOLT, 25 N·m (18 LBS. FT.)
2. NUT, 30 N·m (22 LBS. FT.)

85383019

Fig. 14 Alternator brace installation—late model 4.3L engine

1. BOLT, 50 N·m (36 LBS. FT.)
2. BOLT, 25 N·m (18 LBS. FT.)

85383020

Fig. 15 Common alternator mounting—4.3L engine

To install:

7. Position the alternator in the vehicle and loosely install using the mounting bolts.

8. If equipped, loosely install the brace to the engine and/or alternator.

9. Tighten the retaining bolts:

• For the 2.5L engine, tighten the nut on the lower mounting bolt to 37 ft. lbs. (50 Nm), the upper mounting bolt to 25 ft. lbs. (34 Nm) and the rear bolt to 20 ft. lbs. (27 Nm).

• For the 2.8L engine, tighten the lower mounting bolt to 26 ft. lbs. (35 Nm) for engines through 1990 or to 37 ft. lbs. (50 Nm) for 1991 and later engines. Tighten the upper mounting bolt to 18 ft. lbs. (25 Nm), then as applicable, tighten the AIR pump bracket bolt, rear brace bolt and/or stud nut to 18 ft. lbs. (25 Nm) and the rear brace-to-bracket nut to 37 ft. lbs. (50 Nm).

• For the 4.3L engine, tighten the left or front alternator bolt to 36 ft. lbs. (50 Nm), the right or rear alternator bolt to 18 ft. lbs. (25 Nm), the brace bolt to 18 ft. lbs. (25 Nm) and/or the brace nut (VIN W engine only) to 22 ft. lbs. (30 Nm), as applicable.

10. Connect and secure the alternator wiring.

11. Carefully relieve the serpentine drive belt tension and position the belt over the alternator pulley, then slowly release the tensioner into position.

12. If equipped with the 4.3L (VIN W) engine, install the air inlet duct assembly.

13. Connect the negative battery cable.

BELT ADJUSTMENT

For information on V-belt and serpentine drive belt installation, removal and adjustments, please refer to Section 1 of this manual.

Regulator

All vehicles covered in this manual were equipped with alternators which have built-in solid state voltage regulators. The regulator is in the end frame (inside) of the alternator. No adjustments are necessary or required on GM internal regulators.

ALTERNATOR SPECIFICATIONS

Year	Engine	Alternator	Part No.	Model	Field Current	Output (amps)
1982	1.9L	—	1100140	10SI	4.0–5.0	37
	1.9L	—	1100146	15SI	4.0–5.0	63
	2.8L	—	1100201	10SI	4.0–5.0	37
	2.8L	—	1100202	15SI	4.0–5.0	66
1983–85	1.9L	K85	1105185	10SI	4.0–5.0	37
	1.9L	K81	1100207	12SI	4.0–5.0	63
	1.9L	K64	1100209	12SI	4.0–5.0	78
	2.0L	K85	1100204	10SI	4.0–5.0	37
	2.0L	K81	1100275	12SI	4.0–5.0	66
	2.0L	K64	1100276	12SI	4.0–5.0	78
	2.8L	K85	1100227	10SI	4.0–5.0	37
	2.8L	K81	1100249	12SI	4.0–5.0	66
	2.8L	K64	1100273	12SI	4.0–5.0	78
1986–87	2.5L	—	1105627	12SI	4.0–5.0	78
	2.8L	100	1105663	CS130	5.4–6.4	85
1988–91	2.5L	100	1101346	CS130	6.0–7.5	96
	2.8L	100	1101259	CS130	4.8–5.7	85
	4.3L	100	1101317	CS130	5.7–7.1	85
	4.3L	100	1101293	CS130	6.0–7.5	100
1992	2.5L	100	1101618	CS130	5.7–7.5	96
	2.8L	100	1101259	CS130	4.8–5.7	85
	4.3L	100	10479801	CS130	4.8–5.7	85
1993	2.5L	100	1101618	CS130	5.7–7.5	96
	2.8L	100	10479974	CS130	6.0–7.5	100
	4.3L	100	10479802	CS130	6.0–7.5	100

85383023

Battery

The battery is normally mounted in front, side of the engine compartment. Most of these trucks were originally equipped with a no maintenance type that has side mounted terminals, although adapters are available so your truck could also be equipped with a top post mount battery. For more information regarding battery maintenance, testing or replacement, please refer to Section 1 of this manual.

Starter

The starter is usually located on the lower right-side (gasoline engines) or on the lower left-side (diesel engine). The diesel engine starter is a gear reduction type.

DIAGNOSIS

Before removing the starter for repair or replacement, check the condition of all circuit wiring for damage. Inspect all connection to the starter motor, solenoid, ignition switch, and battery, including all ground connections. Clean and tighten all connections as required.

Check all switches to determine their condition. Vehicles equipped with manual transmission have a clutch safety switch attached to the clutch pedal bracket which closes when the clutch is depressed. Vehicles equipped with automatic transmissions have a manual interlock in the steering column which does not allow the ignition switch to turn to the start position unless the transmission is in the Park or Neutral position.

Check the battery to ensure that it is fully charged. For more information on battery service, please refer to Section 1 of this manual.

Check the battery cables for excessive resistance as follows:

✻✻ CAUTION

To prevent possible injury from a moving vehicle or operating engine, engage the parking brakes, block the drive wheels, place the manual transmission in Neutral or the automatic transmission in Park, and disconnect the battery feed at the distributor before performing these tests.

• Check the voltage drop between the negative battery terminal and the vehicle frame by placing one lead of a voltmeter on the grounded battery post (not the cable clamp) and the other lead on the frame. Turn the ignition key to the START position and note the voltage drop.

• Check the voltage drop between the positive battery terminal (not the cable clamp) and the starter terminal stud. Turn the ignition key to the START position and note the voltage drop.

• Check the voltage drop between the starter housing and the frame. Turn the ignition key to the START position and note the voltage drop.

• If the voltage drop in any of the above is more than 1.0 volts, there is excessive resistance in the circuit. Clean and retest all cables not within specification. Replace as necessary.

No Load Test

▶ See Figure 16

Make the test connections as shown in the illustration. Close the switch and compare the rpm, current and voltage readings with the specification found on the chart located later in this section.

• Current draw and no load speed within specifications indicates normal condition of the starter motor.

• Low free speed and high current draw indicates worn bearings, a bent armature shaft, a shorted armature or grounded armature fields

• Failure to operate with high current draw indicates a direct ground in the terminal or fields, or frozen bearings.

• Failure to operate with no current draw indicates an open field circuit, open armature coils, broken brush springs, worn brushes or other causes which would prevent good contact between the commutator and the brushes.

• A low no load speed and low current draw indicates high internal resistance due to poor connections, defective leads or a dirty commutator.

• High free speed and high current draw usually indicate shorted fields or a shorted armature.

REMOVAL & INSTALLATION

▶ **See Figures 17 and 18**

Rear Wheel Drive Trucks

1. Disconnect the negative battery cable.

➡**When necessary for access from underneath the truck, raise and support the vehicle safely using jackstands.**

2. On 2.5L engines, remove the brush end mounting bracket from the starter motor.
3. Tag and disconnect the solenoid wiring.

➡**If the wiring is difficult to access with the starter installed, remove the bolts and partially lower the starter for access to the wiring. If this is done, be careful not to stretch or damage the wiring.**

4. Remove 1 of the starter mounting bolts, then support the starter and remove the other bolt.
5. Lower and remove the starter from the vehicle. Be careful, as the starter is heavier than it appears.
6. Note the position of any shims, if used, for installation purposes.

To install:

7. Position the starter in the vehicle (along with any shims which were removed) and support while threading the starter mounting bolts.
8. Tighten the starter mounting bolts to 30–33 ft. lbs. (40–45 Nm).
9. Engage the starter solenoid wiring as noted during removal.
10. On 2.5L engines, install the brush end mounting bracket.
11. Connect the negative battery cable.

Four Wheel Drive Trucks

▶ **See Figures 19 thru 25**

➡**When necessary for access from underneath the truck, raise and support the vehicle safely using jackstands.**

1. Disconnect the negative battery cable.

➡**On some vehicles access to the wiring may be easier from above. Before raising and supporting the vehicle, check to see if the solenoid wiring is accessible. If so, tag and disconnect it at this time.**

2. On 2.5L engines, remove the brush end mounting bracket from the starter motor.
3. Tag and disconnect the solenoid wiring.

➡**If the wiring is difficult to access with the starter installed, remove the bolts and partially lower the starter for access to the wiring. If this is done, be careful not to stretch or damage the wiring.**

4. If not done already, raise and support the front of the truck safely using jackstands.
5. If equipped, loosen the retaining bolts and remove the skid plate.
6. Remove the retainers and the brackets holding the brake line to the crossmember located just behind the oil pan. Reposition the brake line slightly in order to clear the crossmember.
7. Remove the crossmember retaining bolts, there are usually 3 on each side, then carefully lower the crossmember and remove it from the vehicle for access.

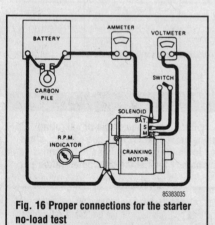

Fig. 16 Proper connections for the starter no-load test

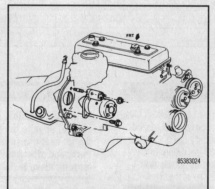

Fig. 17 Common starter mounting for early gasoline 4-cylinder engines

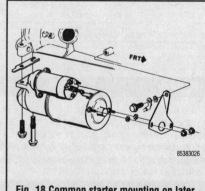

Fig. 18 Common starter mounting on later model 4-cylinder and 6-cylinder engines

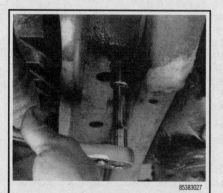

Fig. 19 Loosen the brake line bracket-to-crossmember retaining bolts

Fig. 20 Reposition the brake line away from the crossmember taking care not to damage the line

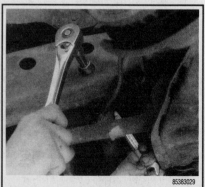

Fig. 21 Loosen and remove the crossmember bolts

Fig. 22 Begin lowering the crossmember from the vehicle, being careful not to snag the brake line

Fig. 23 Once the crossmember is clear of the brake line, remove it from the vehicle

Fig. 24 Loosen and remove starter retaining bolts

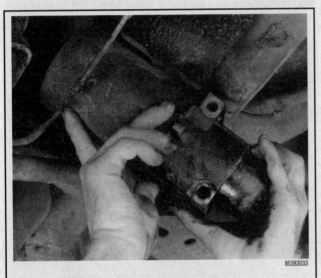

Fig. 25 Carefully lower the starter from the vehicle

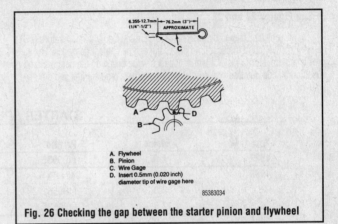

A. Flywheel
B. Pinion
C. Wire Gage
D. Insert 0.5mm (0.020 inch) diameter tip of wire gage here

Fig. 26 Checking the gap between the starter pinion and flywheel

8. As applicable and necessary, remove the bracket holding the transmission fluid cooler lines to the flywheel housing, brace rod to the flywheel housing and/or the lower flywheel housing.

9. Remove the starter-to-engine block bolts. When removing the last bolt, be sure to support the starter to keep it from falling and possibly injuring you.

➡On some vehicles, even with the crossmember removed clearance for starter removal is tight. As the starter is lowered, it may be necessary to rotate it upside down in order for the end to clear the motor mount, then lower the nose behind the bell housing and rotate it back so the solenoid is on top and the starter may be removed.

10. Carefully lower the starter and shims (if equipped) from the vehicle.

To install:

11. Position the starter in the vehicle (along with any shims which were removed) and support while threading the starter mounting bolts. Tighten the starter mounting bolts to 30–33 ft. lbs. (40–45 Nm).

12. Install the remaining components in the reverse of removal. For the 2.5L engine, install the brush end mounting bracket.

SHIMMING THE STARTER

◆ See Figure 26

Starter noise during cranking and after the engine fires is often a result of too much or tool little distance between the starter pinion gear and the flywheel. A high pitched whine during cranking (before the engine fires) can be caused by the pinion and flywheel being too far apart. Likewise, a whine after the engine starts (as the key is released) is often a result of the pinion-flywheel relationship being too close. In both cases flywheel damage can occur. Shims are available

in various sizes to properly adjust the starter on its mount. In order to check and adjust the shims, you will also need a flywheel turning tool, available at most auto parts stores or from any auto tool store or salesperson.

If your car's starter emits the above noises, follow the shimming procedure below:

1. Disconnect the negative battery cable.

2. Raise and support the vehicle safely using jackstands.

3. Remove the torque converter/flywheel cover from the bottom of the bell housing.

4. Using the flywheel turning tool, turn the flywheel and examine the flywheel teeth. If damage is evident, the flywheel should be replaced.

➡Most starters are equipped with an access hole in which a small screwdriver or prybar may be inserted to push the starter pinion outward into contact with the flywheel.

5. Move the starter pinion and clutch assembly so the pinion and flywheel teeth mesh. If necessary, rotate the flywheel so that a pinion tooth is directly in the center of the two flywheel teeth and on the centerline of the two gears, as shown in the accompanying illustration.

➡Normal pinion-to-flywheel clearance is about 0.01–0.06 in. (0.5–1.5mm).

6. Check the pinion-to-flywheel clearance by using a 0.020 in. (0.5mm) wire gauge (a spark plug wire gauge may work here, or you can make your own). Make sure you center the pinion tooth between the flywheel teeth and the gauge—NOT in the corners, as you may get a false reading. If the clearance is under this minimum, shim the starter away from the flywheel by adding 0.04 in. (1mm) shims one at a time to the starter mount. Check clearance after adding each shim, but do not use more than 2 shims.

7. If the clearance is over 0.060 in. (1.5mm), shim the starter towards the flywheel. Broken or severely mangled flywheel teeth are also a good indicator that the clearance here is too great. Shimming the starter towards the flywheel is done by adding shims to the outboard starter mounting pad only. Check the clearance after each shim is added. Add 0.013 in. (0.33mm) shims at this location, one at a time, but do NOT add a total of more than 4 shims.

SOLENOID REPLACEMENT

Most vehicles covered by this manual are equipped with replaceable solenoids. In all cases, the starter must first be removed from the vehicle for access.
1. Remove the starter and place it on a workbench.
2. Remove the screw and the washer from the motor connector strap terminal.
3. Remove the two solenoid retaining screws.
4. Twist the solenoid housing clockwise to remove the flange key from the keyway in the housing and remove.
5. Installation is the reverse of removal.

Sending Units and Sensors

REMOVAL & INSTALLATION

Engine Coolant Temperature

▶ See Figures 27 and 28

On all vehicles covered by this manual an Engine Coolant Temperature (ECT) sensor can be found threaded into one of the engine coolant passages. The sensor is a thermistor (a resistor which changes value based on temperature) and is used on all computer controlled fuel systems to help regulate fuel and emissions systems controlled by the computer module. The sensor may be found in various places on the engine. Most engines will likely have this sensor threaded into the intake manifold, often near the thermostat housing.

➡ **Care must be taken when handling engine control related sensors as damage to the sensor may adversely affect engine driveability and emissions.**

1. Disconnect the negative battery cable.
2. Drain the engine cooling system to a level below the sensor.
3. Release the locktab and disengage the sensor connector.
4. Using a special sensor tool or a deep 12-point socket, loosen the sensor, then carefully unthread and remove it from the engine.
   To install:
5. Thread the sensor into the engine by hand, then tighten using the socket or tool. If a replacement sensor came with instructions use a torque wrench to assure proper tightening.

➡ **On some engines, such as the Syclone's MFI 4.3L engine, the manufacturer suggests coating the coolant sensor threads with a sealant such as 1052080, or equivalent.**

6. Engage the sensor wiring harness.
7. Connect the negative battery cable.
8. Properly refill the engine cooling system, then run the engine and check for leaks.

STARTER SPECIFICATIONS

Year	Engine	Part No.	Series	No Load Test @ 10V	
				Amps	rpm
1982	2.8L	1109535	5MTPH3	45–70	7000–11900
1983	1.9L	94241705	—	—	—
	2.0L	1109561	5MTPH3	50–75	6000–11900
	2.8L	1109535	5MTPH3	45–70	7000–11900
1984–85	2.0L	1998431	5MTPH3	50–75	6000–11900
	2.8L	1998427	5MTPH3	50–75	6000–11900
1986–87	2.5L	1998532	5MT	50–75	6000–11900
	2.8L	1998524	5MT	50–75	6000–11900
1988–91	2.5L	1045018	5MT	50–70	6000–11900
	2.8L	10455016	SD200	50–75	6000–11900
	4.3L	9000735	PGMR ②	50–90	2330–2660 ①
1991	4.3L	10455013	SD260	50–62	8500–10700
1992	2.5L	10455018	SD-200	50–75	6000–11,900
	2.8L	10455016	SD-200	50–75	6000–11,900
	4.3L	10455013	SD-260	50–62	8500–10,700
1993	2.5L	10455018	SD-200	50–75	6000–11,900
	2.8L	10455016	SD-200	50–75	6000–11,900
	4.3L	10455013	SD-260	50–62	8500–10,700

① Drive speed
② SD200

85383036

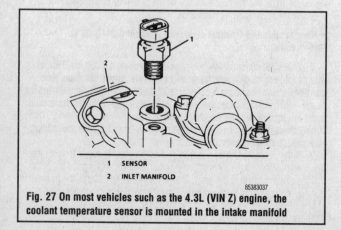

1 SENSOR
2 INLET MANIFOLD

85383037

Fig. 27 On most vehicles such as the 4.3L (VIN Z) engine, the coolant temperature sensor is mounted in the intake manifold

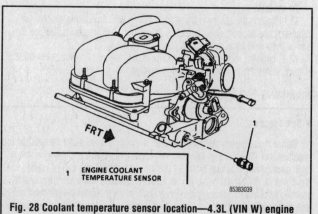

1 ENGINE COOLANT
TEMPERATURE SENSOR

85383039

Fig. 28 Coolant temperature sensor location—4.3L (VIN W) engine

Manifold Absolute Pressure (MAP) Sensor

▶ See Figures 29 and 30

The MAP sensor measures changes in the intake manifold pressure, resulting from changes in engine load and speed changes, then converts this to a voltage output. Other than checking for loose vacuum hoses or electrical connectors, the only service possible for this sensor is replacement, if testing shows the sensor is faulty.

1. Disconnect the negative battery cable.
2. Release the locktab, then disengage the sensor electrical connector.
3. Either tag and disconnect the hoses from the MAP sensor or disengage the entire vacuum harness assembly from the sensor, as applicable.
4. Either remove the retainers or release the lock tabs, then remove the sensor from the engine.

To install:

5. Install the sensor and secure in position using the retainers or lock tabs, as applicable.
6. Connect the vacuum harness or hoses to the sensor as noted during removal.
7. Engage the sensor electrical connector.
8. Connect the negative battery cable.

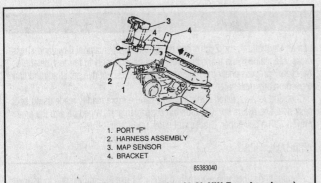

1. PORT "F"
2. HARNESS ASSEMBLY
3. MAP SENSOR
4. BRACKET

85383040

Fig. 29 Common MAP sensor mounting (4.3L VIN Z engine shown)

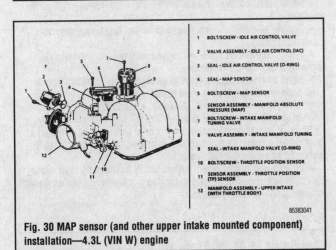

1. BOLT/SCREW - IDLE AIR CONTROL VALVE
2. VALVE ASSEMBLY - IDLE AIR CONTROL (IAC)
3. SEAL - IDLE AIR CONTROL VALVE (O-RING)
4. SEAL - MAP SENSOR
5. BOLT/SCREW - MAP SENSOR
6. SENSOR ASSEMBLY - MANIFOLD ABSOLUTE PRESSURE (MAP)
7. BOLT/SCREW - INTAKE MANIFOLD TUNING VALVE
8. VALVE ASSEMBLY - INTAKE MANIFOLD TUNING
9. SEAL - INTAKE MANIFOLD VALVE (O-RING)
10. BOLT/SCREW - THROTTLE POSITION SENSOR
11. SENSOR ASSEMBLY - THROTTLE POSITION (TP) SENSOR
12. MANIFOLD ASSEMBLY - UPPER INTAKE (WITH THROTTLE BODY)

85383041

Fig. 30 MAP sensor (and other upper intake mounted component) installation—4.3L (VIN W) engine

Oxygen Sensor

Almost all vehicles covered by this manual were equipped with an oxygen sensor for feedback carburetor control . Fuel injected engines, introduced to the S/T series in 1985 and used on all of these trucks built in 1986 and later also require an oxygen sensor for computer air/fuel mixture management. On vehicles so equipped, the oxygen sensor is usually mounted in an exhaust manifold. On some engines, the sensor is mounted at the end of the crossover pipe.

1. Disconnect the negative battery cable.
2. Locate the oxygen sensor. The sensor is usually mounted in the exhaust manifold or in the crossover pipe. If necessary, raise and support the front of the truck safely using jackstands.

3. Trace the wires leading from the oxygen sensor back to the first connector and then disengage the sensor harness connector.

➡The sensor may be extremely difficult to remove when engine temperature is below 120°F (48°C). Be careful as excessive force could damage threads in the exhaust manifold or pipe.

4. Using a special sensor tool or a socket, loosen the sensor, then carefully unthread and remove it from the engine. If sensor removal is difficult, spray a small amount of commercial heat riser solvent onto the sensor threads and allow it to soak in for at least five minutes, then attempt to loosen and remove the sensor again.

✳✳ CAUTION

Avoid using cleaning solvents of any type on the oxygen sensor. Keep the louvered end free of grease, dirt or other contaminants. Do not drop or roughly handle the sensor. If any of these cautions are ignored, the sensor could be damaged resulting in poor engine performance and excessive exhaust emissions.

To install:

5. New oxygen sensors will be packaged with a special anti-seize lubricant already applied to the threads. If a sensor is removed from the exhaust and is to be reinstalled for any reason, the sensor threads must be coated with a fresh anti-seize compound. Use a G.M. anti-seize compound no. 5613695, no. 3613695 or an equivalent compound made of liquid graphite and glass beads. This is not a conventional anti-seize paste, the graphite will tend to burn away but the glass beads will remain. The use of a regular compound may electrically insulate the sensor, rendering it inoperative. You must coat the threads with an electrically conductive anti-seize compound.

6. Carefully thread the sensor into the exhaust bore, then tighten to 30 ft. lbs. (41 Nm) using a torque wrench.
7. Engage the sensor harness.
8. If raised, remove the jackstands and carefully lower the truck.
9. Connect the negative battery cable, then start and run the engine to check for proper operation.

Intake Air Temperature/Manifold Air Temperature Sensor

▶ See Figures 31, 32 and 33

Most of the fuel injected vehicles covered by this manual are equipped with either an Intake Air Temperature (IAT) or an Manifold Air Temperature (MAT) sensor. The IAT sensor is normally installed into the air ducting somewhere near or before the throttle body. If equipped with a MAT sensor, it is typically threaded into the intake manifold.

1. Disconnect the negative battery cable.
2. Depress the locktab and disengage the sensor wiring.
3. Remove the sensor from the air duct or unthread it from the intake manifold, as applicable.

To install:

➡Before installing a manifold air temperature sensor, be sure to coat the THREADS of the sensor using 1052080 or an equivalent sealant.

4. Install and secure the sensor to the engine.
5. Engage the sensor wiring.
6. Connect the negative battery cable.

Knock Sensor

The Electronic Spark Control (ESC) knock sensor is normally mounted to the engine block or cylinder head. On these applications, the sensor can often be found on the side or end of the cylinder head. Also, on many of the se engines, the sensor is mounted in a hole which is exposes to engine coolant.

1. Disconnect the negative battery cable.
2. If the sensor is located in a coolant passage, drain the engine cooling system to a level below the sensor.

➡If you are not sure whether or not the sensor is threaded into a coolant passage, wait until the sensor is being loosened to determine if any coolant need to be drained. Loosen the sensor in small ¼ turn increments and see if coolant begins to seep from the threads. If coolant begins to seep, retighten the sensor and drain the cooling system.

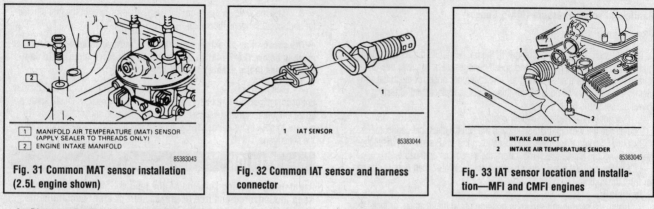

Fig. 31 Common MAT sensor installation (2.5L engine shown)

Fig. 32 Common IAT sensor and harness connector

Fig. 33 IAT sensor location and installation—MFI and CMFI engines

3. Disengage the wiring harness connector from the knock sensor
4. Loosen and remove the sensor from the engine.

To install:

5. Make sure the sensor threads are clean and free of debris. If the sensor is being threaded into a coolant passage, apply a water base caulk sealant to the sensor threads. DO NOT use a silicon tape as this may insulate the sensor from the engine block.

6. Install the sensor to the engine and tighten to 14 ft. lbs. (19 Nm).
7. Engage the sensor wiring harness.
8. Connect the negative battery cable and check for proper engine operation.

ENGINE MECHANICAL

Engine Overhaul Tips

Most engine overhaul procedures are fairly standard. In addition to specific parts replacement procedures and specifications for your individual engine, this section is also a guide to acceptable rebuilding procedures. Examples of standard rebuilding practice are given and should be used along with specific details concerning your particular engine.

Competent and accurate machine shop services will ensure maximum performance, reliability and engine life. In most instances it is more profitable for the do-it-yourself mechanic to remove, clean and inspect the component, buy the necessary parts and deliver these to a shop for actual machine work.

On the other hand, much of the rebuilding work (crankshaft, block, bearings, piston rods, and other components) is well within the scope of the do-it-yourself mechanic's tools and abilities. You will have to decide for yourself the depth of involvement you desire in an engine repair or rebuild.

TOOLS

The tools required for an engine overhaul or parts replacement will depend on the depth of your involvement. With a few exceptions, they will be the tools found in a mechanic's tool kit (see Section 1 of this manual). More in-depth work will require some or all of the following:

- A dial indicator (reading in thousandths) mounted on a universal base
- Micrometers and telescope gauges
- Jaw and screw-type pullers
- Scraper
- Valve spring compressor
- Ring groove cleaner
- Piston ring expander and compressor
- Ridge reamer
- Cylinder hone or glaze breaker
- Plastigage®
- Engine stand

The use of most of these tools is illustrated in this chapter. Many can be rented for a one-time use from a local parts jobber or tool supply house specializing in automotive work.

Occasionally, the use of special tools is called for. See the information on Special Tools and the Safety Notice in the front of this book before substituting another tool.

INSPECTION TECHNIQUES

Procedures and specifications are given in this chapter for inspecting, cleaning and assessing the wear limits of most major components. Other procedures such as Magnaflux® and Zyglo® can be used to locate material flaws and stress cracks. Magnaflux® is a magnetic process applicable only to ferrous materials. The Zyglo® process coats the material with a fluorescent dye penetrant and can be used on any material.

Checking for suspected surface cracks can be more readily made using spot check dye. The dye is sprayed onto the suspected area, wiped off and the area sprayed with a developer. Cracks will show up brightly.

OVERHAUL TIPS

Aluminum has become extremely popular for use in engines, due to its low weight. Observe the following precautions when handling aluminum parts:

- Never hot tank aluminum parts (the caustic hot tank solution will eat the aluminum.
- Remove all aluminum parts (identification tag, etc.) from engine parts prior to the tanking.
- Always coat threads lightly with engine oil or anti-seize compounds before installation, to prevent seizure.
- Never overtorque bolts or spark plugs especially in aluminum threads.

Stripped threads in any component can be repaired using any of several commercial repair kits (Heli-Coil®, Microdot®, Keenserts®, etc.).

When assembling the engine, any parts that will be exposed to frictional contact must be prelubed to provide lubrication at initial start-up. Any product specifically formulated for this purpose can be used, but engine oil is not recommended as a prelube in most cases.

When semi-permanent (locked, but removable) installation of bolts or nuts is desired, threads should be cleaned and coated with Loctite® or another similar, commercial non-hardening sealant.

REPAIRING DAMAGED THREADS

♦ **See Figures 34, 35, 36, 37 and 38**

Several methods of repairing damaged threads are available. Heli-Coil® (shown here), Keenserts® and Microdot® are among the most widely used. All involve basically the same principle—drilling out stripped threads, tapping the hole and installing a prewound insert—making welding, plugging and oversize fasteners unnecessary.

Two types of thread repair inserts are usually supplied: a standard type for most inch coarse, inch fine, metric course and metric fine thread sizes and a spark lug type to fit most spark plug port sizes. Consult the individual tool manufacturer's catalog to determine exact applications. Typical thread repair kits will contain a selection of prewound threaded inserts, a tap (corresponding to the outside diameter threads of the insert) and an installation tool. Spark plug inserts usually differ because they require a tap equipped with pilot threads and a combined reamer/tap section. Most manufacturers also supply blister-packed

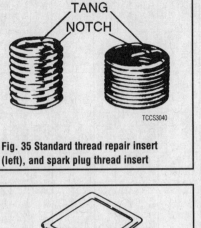

Fig. 34 Damaged bolt hole threads can be replaced with thread repair inserts

Fig. 35 Standard thread repair insert (left), and spark plug thread insert

Fig. 36 Drill out the damaged threads with the specified size bit. Be sure to drill completely through the hole or to the bottom of a blind hole

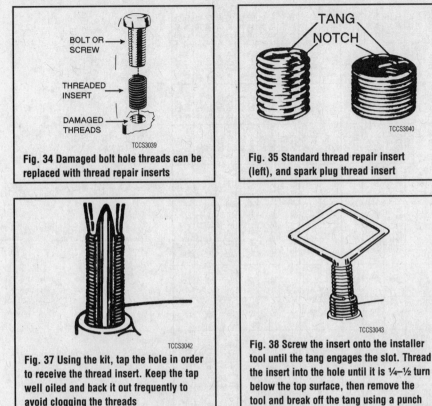

Fig. 37 Using the kit, tap the hole in order to receive the thread insert. Keep the tap well oiled and back it out frequently to avoid clogging the threads

Fig. 38 Screw the insert onto the installer tool until the tang engages the slot. Thread the insert into the hole until it is ¼–½ turn below the top surface, then remove the tool and break off the tang using a punch

Fig. 39 Remove the spark plugs from the engine

thread repair inserts separately in addition to a master kit containing a variety of taps and inserts plus installation tools.

Before attempting to repair a threaded hole, remove any snapped, broken or damaged bolts or studs. Penetrating oil can be used to free frozen threads. The offending item can usually be removed with locking pliers or using a screw/stud extractor. After the hole is clear, the thread can be repaired, as shown in the series of accompanying illustrations and in the kit manufacturer's instructions.

Checking Engine Compression

▶ See Figures 39 and 40

A noticeable lack of engine power, excessive oil consumption and/or poor fuel mileage measured over an extended period are all indicators of internal engine wear. Worn piston rings, scored or worn cylinder bores, blown head gaskets, sticking or burnt valves and worn valve seats are all possible culprits here. A check of each cylinder's compression will help you locate the problems.

As mentioned under Tools and Equipment in Section 1 of this manual, a screw-in type compression gauge is more accurate than the type you simply hold against the spark plug hole. Although it takes slightly longer to use, it's worth it to obtain a more accurate reading. Follow the procedures below.

1. Warm up the engine to normal operating temperature.
2. Remove all the spark plugs.
3. Disconnect the high tension lead from the ignition coil.
4. Screw the compression gauge into the No. 1 spark plug hole until the fitting is snug.

✳✳ WARNING

Be careful not to crossthread the plug hole. On aluminum cylinder heads use extra care, as the threads in these heads are easily ruined.

5. Ask an assistant to depress the accelerator pedal fully on both carbureted and fuel injected vehicles. Then, while you read the compression gauge, ask the assistant to crank the engine through 4–5 compression strokes (complete revolutions) until the highest compression is shown on the gauge.

6. Read the compression gauge at the end of each series of cranks, and record the highest of these readings. Repeat this procedure for each of the engine's cylinders. Compare the highest reading of each cylinder to the readings on the other cylinders. Readings should be similar for throughout the engine.

➡A cylinder's compression pressure is usually acceptable if it is not less than 80% of the highest reading. For example, if the highest reading is 150 psi, the lowest should be no lower than 120 psi. No cylinder should be less than 100 psi.

7. If a cylinder is unusually low, pour a tablespoon of clean engine oil into the cylinder through the spark plug hole and repeat the compression test. If the compression comes up after adding the oil, it appears that the cylinder's piston rings or bore are damaged or worn. If the pressure remains low, the valves may not be seating properly (a valve job is needed), or the head gasket may be blown near that cylinder. If compression in any two adjacent cylinders is low, and if the addition of oil doesn't help the compression, there is leakage past the head gasket. Oil and coolant water in the combustion chamber can result from this problem. There may be evidence of water droplets on the engine dipstick when a head gasket has blown.

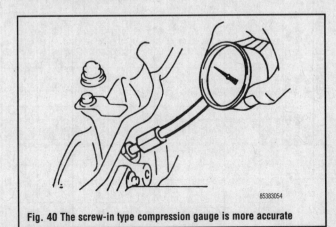

Fig. 40 The screw-in type compression gauge is more accurate

GENERAL ENGINE SPECIFICATIONS

Year	Engine ID/VIN	Engine Displacement Liters (cc)	Fuel System Type	Net Horsepower @ rpm	Net Torque @ rpm (ft. lbs.)	Bore × Stroke (in.)	Compression Ratio	Oil Pressure @ rpm
1982	A	1.9 (1949)	2 bbl	84 @ 4600	101 @ 3000	3.43 × 3.23	8.4:1	57 @ 2000
	B	2.8 (2835)	2 bbl	110 @ 4600	148 @ 2000	3.50 × 2.99	8.5:1	45 @ 2000
1983	A	1.9 (1949)	2 bbl	84 @ 4600	101 @ 3000	3.43 × 3.23	8.4:1	57 @ 2000
	Y	2.0 (1990)	2 bbl	83 @ 4600	108 @ 4200	3.50 × 3.15	9.3:1	45 @ 2000
	B	2.8 (2835)	2 bbl	110 @ 4800	148 @ 2000	3.50 × 2.99	8.5:1	45 @ 2000
1984	A	1.9 (1949)	2 bbl	84 @ 4600	101 @ 3000	3.43 × 3.23	8.4:1	57 @ 2000
	Y	2.0 (1990)	2 bbl	83 @ 4600	108 @ 4200	3.50 × 3.15	9.3:1	45 @ 2000
	B	2.8 (2835)	2 bbl	110 @ 4800	148 @ 2000	3.50 × 2.99	8.5:1	45 @ 2000
1985	A	1.9 (1949)	2 bbl	82 @ 4600	101 @ 3000	3.43 × 3.23	8.4:1	57 @ 2000
	E	2.5 (2474)	TBI	92 @ 4400	132 @ 2800	4.00 × 3.00	9.0:1	40-60 @ 2000
	B	2.8 (2835)	2 bbl	110 @ 4800	145 @ 2100	3.50 × 2.99	8.5:1	45 @ 2000
1986	E	2.5 (2474)	TBI	92 @ 4400	134 @ 2800	4.00 × 3.00	9.0:1	40-60 @ 2000
	R	2.8 (2835)	TBI	125 @ 4800	150 @ 2200	3.50 × 2.99	8.5:1	50 @ 2000
1987	E	2.5 (2474)	TBI	92 @ 4400	134 @ 2800	4.00 × 3.00	9.0:1	40-60 @ 2000
	R	2.8 (2835)	TBI	125 @ 4800	150 @ 2200	3.50 × 2.99	8.5:1	50 @ 2000
1988	E	2.5 (2474)	TBI	92 @ 4400	130 @ 3200	4.00 × 3.00	8.3:1	41 @ 2000
	R	2.8 (2835)	TBI	125 @ 4800	150 @ 2400	3.50 × 2.99	8.9:1	50 @ 2000
	Z	4.3 (4293)	TBI	150 @ 4000	230 @ 2400	4.00 × 3.48	9.3:1	30 @ 2000
1989	E	2.5 (2474)	TBI	92 @ 4400	130 @ 3200	4.00 × 3.00	9.0:1	36-41 @ 2000
	R	2.8 (2835)	TBI	125 @ 4800	150 @ 2400	3.50 × 2.99	8.9:1	50-55 @ 5000
	Z	4.3 (4293)	TBI	160 @ 4000	230 @ 2800	4.00 × 3.48	9.3:1	30-55 @ 5000
1990	A	2.5 (2474)	TBI	105 @ 4800	135 @ 3200	4.00 × 3.00	8.3:1	18 @ 2000
	R	2.8 (2835)	TBI	125 @ 4800	150 @ 2400	3.50 × 2.99	8.9:1	36-41 @ 2000
	W	4.3 (4293)	CMFI	195 @ 4500	260 @ 3600	4.00 × 3.48	9.05:1	25-50 @ 1200
	Z	4.3 (4293)	TBI	160 @ 4000	230 @ 2800	4.00 × 3.48	9.3:1	18 @ 2000
	Z	4.3 (4293)	Turbo	280 @ 4200	350 @ 3600	4.00 × 3.48	8.35:1	18 @ 2000
1991	A	2.5 (2474)	TBI	105 @ 4800	135 @ 3200	4.00 × 3.00	8.3:1	36-41 @ 2000
	R	2.8 (2835)	TBI	125 @ 4800	150 @ 2400	3.50 × 2.99	8.9:1	30-55 @ 5000
	W	4.3 (4293)	CMFI	195 @ 4500	260 @ 3600	4.00 × 3.48	9.05:1	25-50 @ 1200
	Z	4.3 (4293)	TBI	160 @ 4000	230 @ 2800	4.00 × 3.48	9.3:1	18 @ 2000
	Z	4.3 (4293)	Turbo	280 @ 4200	350 @ 3600	4.00 × 3.48	8.35:1	18 @ 2000
1992	A	2.5 (2474)	TBI	105 @ 4800	135 @ 3200	4.00 × 3.00	8.3:1	36-41 @ 2000
	R	2.8 (2835)	TBI	125 @ 4800	150 @ 2400	3.50 × 2.99	8.9:1	30-55 @ 5000
	W	4.3 (4293)	CMFI	195 @ 4500	260 @ 3600	4.00 × 3.48	9.05:1	25-50 @ 1200
	Z	4.3 (4293)	TBI	165 @ 4000	235 @ 2600	4.00 × 3.48	9.3:1	25-50 @ 1200
1993	A	2.5 (2474)	TBI	105 @ 4800	135 @ 3200	4.00 × 3.00	8.3:1	36-41 @ 2000
	R	2.8 (2835)	TBI	125 @ 4800	150 @ 2400	3.50 × 2.99	8.9:1	30-55 @ 5000
	W	4.3 (4293)	CMFI	195 @ 4500	260 @ 3600	4.00 × 3.48	9.05:1	25-50 @ 1200
	Z	4.3 (4293)	TBI	165 @ 4000	235 @ 2600	4.00 × 3.48	9.3:1	25-50 @ 1200

NOTE: Horsepower and torque are SAE net figures. They are measured at the rear of the transmission with all accessories installed and operating. Since the figures vary when a given engine is installed in different models, some are representative rather than exact.
2 bbl—Two barrel carburetor
DSL—Diesel
TBI—Throttle Body Injection
MFI—Multi-Port Fuel Injection
CMFI—Central Multi-Port Fuel Injection

8844R056

VALVE SPECIFICATIONS

Year	Engine ID/VIN	Engine Displacement Liters (cc)	Seat Angle (deg.)	Face Angle (deg.)	Spring Test Pressure (lbs. @ in.)	Spring Installed Height (in.)	Stem-to-Guide Clearance (in.) Intake	Stem-to-Guide Clearance (in.) Exhaust	Stem Diameter (in.) Intake	Stem Diameter (in.) Exhaust
1982	A	1.9 (1949)	45	45	②	②	0.0009-0.0079	0.0015-0.0097	0.3102 MIN	0.3091 MIN
	B	2.8 (2835)	46	45	88 @ 1.575	1.575	0.0010-0.0027	0.0010-0.0027	0.3410-0.3417	0.3410-0.3417
1983	A	1.9 (1949)	45	45	②	②	0.0009-0.0079	0.0015-0.0097	0.3102 MIN	0.3091 MIN
	Y	2.0 (1990)	46	45	77 @ 1.598	1.598	0.0011-0.0026	0.0014-0.0031	0.3410-0.3416	0.3410-0.3416
	B	2.8 (2835)	46	45	88 @ 1.575	1.575	0.0010-0.0027	0.0010-0.0027	0.3410-0.3417	0.3410-0.3417
1984	A	1.9 (1949)	45	45	②	②	0.0009-0.0079	0.0015-0.0097	0.3102 MIN	0.3091 MIN
	Y	2.0 (1990)	46	45	77 @ 1.598	1.598	0.0011-0.0026	0.0014-0.0031	0.3410-0.3416	0.3410-0.3416
	B	2.8 (2835)	46	45	88 @ 1.575	1.575	0.0010-0.0027	0.0010-0.0027	0.3410-0.3417	0.3410-0.3417
1985	A	1.9 (1949)	45	45	②	②	0.0009-0.0079	0.0015-0.0097	0.3102 MIN	0.3091 MIN
	E	2.5 (2474)	46	45	78-86 @ 1.66	1.690	0.0010-0.0027	②	0.3418-0.3425	0.3418-0.3425
	B	2.8 (2835)	46	45	88 @ 1.575	1.575	0.0010-0.0027	0.0010-0.0027	0.3410-0.3417	0.3410-0.3417
1986	E	2.5 (2474)	46	45	78-86 @ 1.66	1.690	0.0010-0.0027	0.0010-0.0027	0.3418-0.3425	0.3418-0.3425
	R	2.8 (2835)	46	45	88 @ 1.575	1.575	0.0010-0.0027	0.0010-0.0027	0.3410-0.3417	0.3410-0.3417
1987	E	2.5 (2474)	46	45	78-86 @ 1.66	1.690	0.0010-0.0027	0.0010-0.0027	0.3418-0.3425	0.3418-0.3425
	R	2.8 (2835)	46	45	88 @ 1.575	1.575	0.0010-0.0027	0.0010-0.0027	0.3410-0.3417	0.3410-0.3417
1988	E	2.5 (2474)	46	45	78-86 @ 1.66	1.690	0.0010-0.0027	0.0010-0.0027	0.3418-0.3425	0.3418-0.3425
	R	2.8 (2835)	46	45	88 @ 1.575	1.575	0.0010-0.0027	0.0010-0.0027	0.3410-0.3417	0.3410-0.3417
	Z	4.3 (4293)	46	45	76-84 @ 1.70	1.690-1.710	0.0010-0.0027	0.0010-0.0027	0.3410-0.3417	0.3410-0.3417
1989	E	2.5 (2474)	46	45	71-78 @ 1.44	1.44	0.0025-0.0027	0.0013-0.0030	0.3133-0.3138	0.3128-0.3135
	R	2.8 (2835)	46	45	88 @ 1.575	1.575	0.0010-0.0027	0.0010-0.0027	0.3410-0.3417	0.3410-0.3417
	Z	4.3 (4293)	46	45	76-84 @ 1.70	1.690-1.710	0.0010-0.0027	0.0010-0.0027	0.3410-0.3417	0.3410-0.3417

8844R057

CAMSHAFT SPECIFICATIONS

All measurements given in inches.

Year	Engine ID/VIN	Engine Displacement Liters (cc)	Journal Diameter 1	2	3	4	5	Elevation In.	Ex.	Bearing Clearance	Camshaft End Play
1982	A	1.9 (1949)	1.3362–1.3368	1.3362–1.3368	1.3362–1.3368	1.3362–1.3368	1.3362–1.3368	NA	NA	0.0016–0.0035	0.0020–0.0059
	B	2.8 (2835)	1.8677–1.8697	1.8677–1.8697	1.8677–1.8697	1.8677–1.8697	—	0.2310	0.2630	0.0010–0.0040	NA
1983	A	1.9 (1949)	1.3362–1.3370	1.3362–1.3370	1.3362–1.3370	1.3362–1.3370	1.3362–1.3370	NA	0.2630	1.3394–1.3406	0.0020–0.0059
	Y	2.0 (1990)	1.8677–1.8697	1.8677–1.8697	1.8677–1.8697	1.8677–1.8697	1.8677–1.8697	0.2630	0.2630	0.0010–0.0040	NA
	B	2.8 (2835)	1.8677–1.8697	1.8677–1.8697	1.8677–1.8697	1.8677–1.8697	—	0.2310	0.2630	0.0010–0.0040	NA
1984	A	1.9 (1949)	1.3362–1.3368	1.3362–1.3368	1.3362–1.3368	1.3362–1.3368	1.3362–1.3368	NA	NA	0.0016–0.0035	0.0020–0.0059
	Y	2.0 (1990)	1.8677–1.8697	1.8677–1.8697	1.8677–1.8697	1.8677–1.8697	—	0.2630	0.2630	0.0010–0.0040	NA
	B	2.8 (2835)	1.8677–1.8697	1.8677–1.8697	1.8677–1.8697	1.8677–1.8697	1.8677–1.8697	0.2310	0.2630	0.0010–0.0040	NA
1985	A	1.9 (1949)	1.3362–1.3368	1.3362–1.3368	1.3362–1.3368	1.3362–1.3368	1.3362–1.3368	NA	NA	0.0016–0.0035	0.0020–0.0059
	E	2.5 (2474)	1.8690	1.8690	1.8690	—	—	0.3980	0.3980	0.0007–0.0027	0.0015–0.0050
	B	2.8 (2835)	1.8677–1.8697	1.8677–1.8697	1.8677–1.8697	1.8677–1.8697	—	0.2310	0.2630	0.0010–0.0040	NA
1986	E	2.5 (2474)	1.8690	1.8690	1.8690	—	—	0.3980	0.3980	0.0007–0.0027	0.0015–0.0050
	R	2.8 (2835)	1.8677–1.8697	1.8677–1.8697	1.8677–1.8697	1.8677–1.8697	—	0.2310	0.2630	0.0010–0.0040	NA
1987	E	2.5 (2474)	1.8690	1.8690	1.8690	—	—	0.3980	0.3980	0.0007–0.0027	0.0015–0.0050
	R	2.8 (2835)	1.8677–1.8697	1.8677–1.8697	1.8677–1.8697	1.8677–1.8697	—	0.2310	0.2630	0.0010–0.0040	NA
1988	E	2.5 (2474)	1.8690	1.8690	1.8690	—	—	0.3980	0.3980	0.0007–0.0027	0.0015–0.0050
	R	2.8 (2835)	1.8677–1.8697	1.8677–1.8697	1.8677–1.8697	1.8677–1.8697	—	0.2310	0.2630	0.0010–0.0040	NA
	Z	4.3 (4293)	1.8682–1.8692	1.8682–1.8692	1.8682–1.8692	1.8682–1.8692	—	0.3570	0.3900	0.0010–0.0040	0.0040–0.0120
1989	E	2.5 (2474)	1.8690	1.8690	1.8690	—	—	0.3980	0.3980	0.0007–0.0027	0.0015–0.0050
	R	2.8 (2835)	1.8677–1.8697	1.8677–1.8697	1.8677–1.8697	1.8677–1.8697	—	0.2620	0.2730	0.0010–0.0040	NA
	Z	4.3 (4293)	1.8682–1.8692	1.8682–1.8692	1.8682–1.8692	1.8682–1.8692	—	0.3570	0.3900	0.0010–0.0030	0.0040–0.0120

8844R058

VALVE SPECIFICATIONS

Year	Engine ID/VIN	Engine Displacement Liters (cc)	Seat Angle (deg.)	Face Angle (deg.)	Spring Test Pressure (lbs. @ in.)	Spring Installed Height (in.)	Stem-to-Guide Clearance (in.) Intake	Exhaust	Stem Diameter (in.) Intake	Exhaust
1990	E	2.5 (2474)	46	45	71–78 @ 1.44	1.44	0.0010–0.0025	0.0010–0.0030	0.3133–0.3138	0.3128–0.3135
	R	2.8 (2835)	46	45	88 @ 1.575	1.575	0.0010–0.0027	0.0010–0.0027	0.3410–0.3417	0.3410–0.3417
	Z	4.3 (4293)	46	45	76–84 @ 1.70	1.690–1.710	0.0010–0.0027	0.0010–0.0027	0.3410–0.3417	0.3410–0.3417
1991	A	2.5 (2474)	46	45	71–78 @ 1.44	1.44	0.0010–0.0025	0.0013–0.0030	0.3133–0.3138	0.3128–0.3135
	E	2.5 (2474)	46	45	71–78 @ 1.44	1.44	0.0010–0.0025	0.0013–0.0030	0.3133–0.3138	0.3128–0.3135
	R	2.8 (2835)	46	45	88 @ 1.575	1.575	0.0010–0.0027	0.0010–0.0027	0.3410–0.3417	0.3410–0.3417
	Z	4.3 (4293)	46	45	76–84 @ 1.70	1.690–1.710	0.0010–0.0027	0.0010–0.0027	0.3410–0.3417	0.3410–0.3417
1992	A	2.5 (2474)	46	45	71–78 @ 1.68	1.679	0.0010–0.0025	⑦	0.3131–0.3138	⑦
	R	2.8 (2835)	46	45	88 @ 1.575	1.575	NA	0.0010–0.0027	NA	NA
	W	4.3 (4293)	46	45	76–84 @ 1.70	1.690–1.710	0.0011–0.0027	0.0011–0.0027	NA	NA
	Z	4.3 (4293)	46	45	76–84 @ 1.70	1.690–1.710	0.0010–0.0027	0.0010–0.0027	NA	NA
1993	A	2.5 (2474)	46	45	71–78 @ 1.68	1.679	0.0010–0.0025	⑦	0.3131–0.3138	⑦
	R	2.8 (2835)	46	45	88 @ 1.575	1.575	NA	0.0010–0.0027	NA	NA
	W	4.3 (4293)	46	45	76–84 @ 1.70	1.690–1.710	0.0011–0.0027	0.0011–0.0027	NA	NA
	Z	4.3 (4293)	46	45	76–84 @ 1.70	1.690–1.710	0.0010–0.0027	0.0010–0.0027	NA	NA

① Inner: 16–21 @ 1.516, Outer: 30–37 @ 1.614
② Free length, Inner: 1.784, Outer: 1.847
③ Inner: 11–14 @ 1.456, Outer: 40–49 @ 1.535
④ Free length, Inner: 1.805, Outer: 1.832- Minimums
⑤ Top: 0.0010–0.0027, Bottom: 0.0020–0.0037
⑥ Upper: 0.0013–0.0030, Lower: 0.0024–0.0041
⑦ Upper: 0.3129–0.3137, Lower: 0.3118–0.3126

8844R57A

CRANKSHAFT AND CONNECTING ROD SPECIFICATIONS

All measurements are given in inches.

Year	Engine ID/VIN	Engine Displacement Liters (cc)	Main Brg. Journal Dia.	Crankshaft Main Brg. Oil Clearance	Crankshaft Shaft End-play	Thrust on No.	Connecting Rod Journal Diameter	Connecting Rod Oil Clearance	Connecting Rod Side Clearance
1982	A	1.9 (1949)	2.1555-2.2050	0.0008-0.0025	0.0024-②	3	1.8799-1.9290	0.0007-0.0030	0.0137 MAX
	B	2.8 (2835)	2.1555-2.2050	0.0016-0.0032	0.0024-0.0083	3	1.9983-1.9994	0.0014-0.0037	0.0063-0.0173
1983	A	1.9 (1949)	2.1555-2.2050	0.0008-0.0025	0.0024-②	3	1.8799-1.9290	0.0007-0.0030	0.0137 MAX
	Y	2.0 (1990)	②	②	0.0020-0.0083	4	1.9983-1.9994	0.0010-0.0031	0.0039-0.0150
	B	2.8 (2835)	②	0.0016-0.0032	0.0024-0.0083	3	1.9983-1.9994	0.0014-0.0037	0.0063-0.0173
1984	A	1.9 (1949)	2.1555-2.2050	0.0008-0.0025	0.0024-②	3	1.8799-1.9290	0.0007-0.0030	0.0137 MAX
	Y	2.0 (1990)	②	②	0.0080	4	1.9983-1.9994	0.0010-0.0031	0.0040-0.0150
	B	2.8 (2835)	②	0.0016-0.0032	0.0024-0.0083	3	1.9983-1.9994	0.0014-0.0037	0.0063-0.0173
1985	A	1.9 (1949)	2.1555-2.2050	0.0008-0.0025	0.0024-②	3	1.8799-1.9290	0.0007-0.0030	0.0137 MAX
	E	2.5 (2474)	2.3000	0.0005-0.0022	0.0035-0.0085	5	2.000	0.0005-0.0026	0.0060-0.0220
	B	2.8 (2835)	②	0.0016-0.0032	0.0024-0.0083	3	1.9983-1.9994	0.0014-0.0037	0.0063-0.0173
1986	E	2.5 (2474)	2.3000	0.0005-0.0022	0.0035-0.0085	5	2.000	0.0005-0.0026	0.0060-0.0220
	R	2.8 (2835)	②	0.0016-0.0032	0.0024-0.0083	3	1.9983-1.9994	0.0014-0.0037	0.0063-0.0173
1987	E	2.5 (2474)	2.3000	0.0005-0.0022	0.0035-0.0085	5	2.000	0.0005-0.0026	0.0060-0.0220
	R	2.8 (2835)	②	0.0016-0.0032	0.0024-0.0083	3	1.9983-1.9994	0.0014-0.0037	0.0063-0.0252
1988	E	2.5 (2474)	2.3000	0.0005-0.0022	0.0035-0.0085	5	2.000	0.0005-0.0026	0.0060-0.0220
	R	2.8 (2835)	②	0.0016-0.0032	0.0024-0.0083	3	②	0.0014-0.0037	0.0063-0.0252
1989	E	2.5 (2474)	2.3000	0.0005-0.0022	0.0035-0.0085	5	2.000	0.0005-0.0026	0.0060-0.0220
	R	2.8 (2835)	②	0.0016-0.0032	0.0024-0.0083	3	②	0.0014-0.0037	0.0063-0.0252
	Z	4.3 (4293)	②	②	0.0020-0.0060	4	2.2487-2.2497	0.0013-0.0035	0.0060-0.0140

8844R059

CAMSHAFT SPECIFICATIONS

All measurements given in inches.

Year	Engine ID/VIN	Engine Displacement Liters (cc)	Journal Diameter 1	Journal Diameter 2	Journal Diameter 3	Journal Diameter 4	Journal Diameter 5	Elevation In.	Elevation Ex.	Bearing Clearance	Camshaft End Play
1990	E	2.5 (2474)	1.8690	1.8690	1.8690	—	—	0.2320	0.2320	0.0007-0.0027	0.0015-0.0050
	R	2.8 (2835)	1.8677-1.8697	1.8677-1.8697	1.8677-1.8697	1.8677-1.8697	—	0.2620	0.2730	0.0010-0.0040	NA
	Z	4.3 (4293)	1.8682-1.8692	1.8682-1.8692	1.8682-1.8692	1.8682-1.8692	—	0.3570	0.3900	0.0010-0.0030	0.0040-0.0120
1991	A	2.5 (2474)	1.8690	1.8690	1.8690	—	—	0.2510	0.2510	0.0007-0.0027	0.0015-0.0050
	E	2.5 (2474)	1.8690	1.8690	1.8690	—	—	0.3980	0.3980	0.0007-0.0027	0.0015-0.0050
	R	2.8 (2835)	1.8677-1.8697	1.8677-1.8697	1.8677-1.8697	1.8677-1.8697	—	0.2620	0.2730	0.0010-0.0040	NA
	Z	4.3 (4293)	1.8682-1.8692	1.8682-1.8692	1.8682-1.8692	1.8682-1.8692	—	0.3570	0.3900	0.0010-0.0030	0.0040-0.0120
1992	A	2.5 (2474)	1.8690	1.8690	1.8690	—	—	0.2510	0.2510	0.0007-0.0027	0.0015-0.0050
	R	2.8 (2835)	1.8677-1.8697	1.8677-1.8697	1.8677-1.8697	1.8677-1.8697	—	0.2620	0.2730	0.0010-0.0040	NA
	W	4.3 (4293)	1.8682-1.8692	1.8682-1.8692	1.8682-1.8692	1.8682-1.8692	—	0.2880	0.2940	NA	0.0010-0.0090
	Z	4.3 (4293)	1.8682-1.8692	1.8682-1.8692	1.8682-1.8692	1.8682-1.8692	—	0.3570	0.3900	NA	0.0040-0.0120
1993	A	2.5 (2474)	1.8690	1.8690	1.8690	—	—	0.2510	0.2510	0.0007-0.0027	0.0015-0.0050
	R	2.8 (2835)	1.8677-1.8697	1.8677-1.8697	1.8677-1.8697	1.8677-1.8697	—	0.2620	0.2730	0.0010-0.0040	NA
	W	4.3 (4293)	1.8682-1.8692	1.8682-1.8692	1.8682-1.8692	1.8682-1.8692	—	0.2880	0.2940	NA	0.0010-0.0090
	Z	4.3 (4293)	1.8682-1.8692	1.8682-1.8692	1.8682-1.8692	1.8682-1.8692	—	0.2340	0.2570	NA	0.0040-0.0120

8844R58A

PISTON AND RING SPECIFICATIONS

All measurements are given in inches.

Year	Engine ID/VIN	Engine Displacement Liters (cc)	Piston Clearance	Ring Gap Top Compression	Ring Gap Bottom Compression	Ring Gap Oil Control	Ring Side Clearance Top Compression	Ring Side Clearance Bottom Compression	Ring Side Clearance Oil Control
1982	E	1.9 (1949)	0.0018–0.0026	0.014–0.020	0.014–0.020	0.008–0.035	0.0059 MAX	0.0059 MAX	0.0059 MAX
	B	2.8 (2835)	0.0007–0.0017	0.0098–0.0197	0.0098–0.0197	0.020–0.055	0.0012–0.0028	0.0016–0.0037	0.0078 MAX
1983	A	1.9 (1949)	0.0018–0.0026	0.014–0.020	0.014–0.020	0.008–0.035	0.0059 MAX	0.0059 MAX	0.0059 MAX
	Y	2.0 (1990)	0.0007–0.0017	0.0098–0.0197	0.0098–0.0197	0.019–0.059	0.0012–0.0027	0.0012–0.0034	0.0078 MAX
	B	2.8 (2835)	0.0007–0.0017	0.0098–0.0197	0.0098–0.0197	0.020–0.055	0.0012–0.0028	0.0016–0.0037	0.0078 MAX
1984	A	1.9 (1949)	0.0018–0.0026	0.014–0.020	0.014–0.020	0.008–0.035	0.0059 MAX	0.0059 MAX	0.0059 MAX
	Y	2.0 (1990)	0.0007–0.0017	0.0098–0.0197	0.0098–0.0197	0.019–0.059	0.0012–0.0027	0.0012–0.0034	0.0078 MAX
	B	2.8 (2835)	0.0007–0.0017	0.0098–0.0197	0.0098–0.0197	0.020–0.055	0.0012–0.0028	0.0016–0.0037	0.0078 MAX
1985	A	1.9 (1949)	0.0018–0.0026	0.014–0.020	0.014–0.020	0.008–0.035	0.0059 MAX	0.0059 MAX	0.0059 MAX
	E	2.5 (2474)	0.0014–0.0022	0.010–0.022	0.010–0.027	0.015–0.055	0.0015–0.0030	0.0015–0.0030	NA
	B	2.8 (2835)	0.0007–0.0017	0.0098–0.0197	0.0098–0.0197	0.020–0.055	0.0012–0.0028	0.0016–0.0037	0.0078 MAX
1986	E	2.5 (2474)	0.0014–0.0022	0.010–0.020	0.010–0.020	0.020–0.060	0.0020–0.0030	0.0016–0.0030	0.015–0.055
	B	2.8 (2835)	0.0007–0.0017	0.0098–0.0197	0.0098–0.0197	0.020–0.055	0.0012–0.0028	0.0016–0.0037	0.0078 MAX
1987	E	2.5 (2474)	0.0014–0.0022	0.010–0.020	0.010–0.020	0.020–0.060	0.0020–0.0030	0.0010–0.0030	0.015–0.055
	R	2.8 (2835)	0.0007–0.0017	0.0098–0.0197	0.0098–0.0197	0.020–0.055	0.0012–0.0028	0.0016–0.0037	0.0078 MAX
1988	E	2.5 (2474)	0.0014–0.0022	0.010–0.020	0.010–0.020	0.020–0.060	0.0020–0.0030	0.0010–0.0030	0.015–0.055
	R	2.8 (2835)	0.0007–0.0017	0.0098–0.0197	0.0098–0.0197	0.020–0.055	0.0012–0.0028	0.0016–0.0037	0.0078 MAX
	Z	4.3 (4293)	0.0007–0.0017	0.010–0.020	0.010–0.025	0.015–0.055	0.0012–0.0032	0.0012–0.0032	0.002–0.007
1989	E	2.5 (2474)	0.00098–0.0022	0.010–0.020	0.010–0.020	0.020–0.060	0.0020–0.0030	0.0010–0.0030	0.015–0.055
	R	2.8 (2835)	0.0007–0.0017	0.0098–0.0197	0.0098–0.0197	0.020–0.055	0.0012–0.0028	0.0016–0.0037	0.0078 MAX
	Z	4.3 (4293)	0.0007–0.0017	0.010–0.020	0.010–0.025	0.015–0.055	0.0012–0.0032	0.0012–0.0032	0.002–0.007

8844R060

CRANKSHAFT AND CONNECTING ROD SPECIFICATIONS

All measurements are given in inches.

Year	Engine ID/VIN	Engine Displacement Liters (cc)	Crankshaft Main Brg. Journal Dia.	Crankshaft Main Brg. Oil Clearance	Crankshaft Shaft End-play	Crankshaft Thrust on No.	Connecting Rod Journal Diameter	Connecting Rod Oil Clearance	Connecting Rod Side Clearance
1990	E	2.5 (2474)	2.3000	0.0005–0.0022	0.0035–0.0085	5	2.000	0.0005–0.0026	0.0060–0.0220
	R	2.8 (2835)	②	0.0016–0.0032	0.0024–0.0083	3	④	0.0014–0.0037	0.0063–0.0252
	Z	4.3 (4293)	⑥	⑧	0.0020–0.0060	4	2.2487–2.2497	0.0013–0.0035	0.0060–0.0140
1991	A	2.5 (2474)	2.2992–2.2984	0.0005–0.0022	0.0050–0.0100	5	2.0001–1.9963	0.0005–0.0030	0.0060–0.0020
	E	2.5 (2474)	2.2300	0.0005–0.0022	0.0035–0.0085	5	2.000	0.0005–0.0026	0.0060–0.0020
	R	2.8 (2835)	②	0.0016–0.0032	0.0024–0.0083	3	④	0.0005–0.0026	0.0060–0.0020
	Z	4.3 (4293)	⑥	0.0013–0.0027	0.0020–0.0060	4	2.2487–2.2497	0.0013–0.0035	0.0063–0.0252
1992	A	2.5 (2474)	2.2992–2.2984	0.0005–0.0022	0.0050–0.0100	5	2.0001–1.9963	0.0005–0.0030	0.0060–0.0140
	R	2.8 (2835)	②	0.0016–0.0032	0.0024–0.0083	3	2.2487–2.2497	0.0011–0.0033	0.0060–0.0140
	W	4.3 (4293)	⑥	⑧	0.0020–0.0070	4	2.2487–2.2497	0.0013–0.0035	0.0142–0.0236
	Z	4.3 (4293)	⑥	0.0013–0.0027	0.0020–0.0060	4	2.2487–2.2497	0.0013–0.0035	0.0060–0.0140
1993	A	2.5 (2474)	2.2992–2.2984	0.0005–0.0022	0.0050–0.0100	5	2.0001–1.9963	0.0005–0.0030	0.0060–0.0140
	R	2.8 (2835)	②	0.0013–0.0027	0.0024–0.0083	3	2.2487–2.2497	0.0011–0.0033	0.0142–0.0236
	W	4.3 (4293)	⑥	⑧	0.0020–0.0070	4	2.2487–2.2497	0.0013–0.0035	0.0060–0.0140
	Z	4.3 (4293)	⑥	⑧	0.0020–0.0060	4	2.2487–2.2497	0.0013–0.0035	0.0060–0.0140

① Nos. 1–2, 4: 2.494–2.495
Nos. 3: 2.493–2.494
② Three dots: 2.64728–2.64759
Two dots: 2.64759–2.64790
One dot: 2.64790–2.64822
③ Two dots: 1.9983–1.9989
One dot: 1.9989–1.9994
④ No. 1: 2.4488–2.4495
Nos. 2–3: 2.4485–2.4494
No. 4: 2.4480–2.4489
⑤ Max. 0.0117
⑥ Nos. 1–4: 2.4945–2.4954
No. 5: 2.4937–2.4946
⑦ Nos. 1–4: 0.0010–0.0023
No. 5: 0.0018–0.0030
⑧ Nos. 1–4: 0.00006–0.0019
No. 5: 0.0014–0.0027
⑨ No. 1: 0.0008–0.0020
Nos. 2–3: 0.0011–0.0023
⑩ No. 4: 0.0017–0.0032

8844R59A

TORQUE SPECIFICATIONS

All readings in ft. lbs.

Year	Engine ID/VIN	Engine Displacement Liters (cc)	Cylinder Head Bolts	Main Bearing Bolts	Rod Bearing Bolts	Crankshaft Bolts	Flywheel Bolts	Manifold Intake	Manifold Exhaust
1982	A	1.9 (1949)	72①	72	43	87	76	17	16
	B	2.8 (2835)	40①	70	39	48-55	45-59	23	25
1983	A	1.9 (1949)	72	72	43	87	76	17	16
	Y	2.0 (1990)	65-75	70	36	66-88	45-59	25	26
	S	2.2 (2238)	②	116-130	62	124-151	70	10-17	10-17
	B	2.8 (2835)	40①	70	39	48-55	45-59	23	25
1984	A	1.9 (1949)	72	72	43	87	76	17	16
	Y	2.0 (1990)	65-75	72	36	66-88	45-59	25	26
	S	2.2 (2238)	②	116-130	62	124-151	70	10-17	10-17
	B	2.8 (2835)	40①	70	39	48-55	45-59	23	25
1985	A	1.9 (1949)	72	72	43	87	76	17	16
	S	2.2 (2238)	②	116-130	62	124-151	70	10-17	10-17
	E	2.5 (2474)	90	70	32	160	44	25①	32①
	B	2.8 (2835)	40①	70	39	48-55	45-59	23	25
1986	E	2.5 (2474)	90	70	32	160	55	25①	32①
	R	2.8 (2835)	40①	70	39	70	52	23	25
1987	E	2.5 (2474)	90	70	32	160	④	25①	32①
	R	2.8 (2835)	40①	70	39	70	52	23	25
1988	E	2.5 (2474)	90	70	32	160	④	25①	32①
	R	2.8 (2835)	40①	70	39	70	52	23	25
1989	Z	4.3 (4293)	65	80	45	70	75	35	20①
	E	2.5 (2474)	40①	70	32	160	④	25①	32①
	R	2.8 (2835)	40①	70	39	70	52	23	25
1990	Z	4.3 (4293)	65	80	45	70	75	35	20①
	E	2.5 (2474)	40①	70	32	160	52	25①	32①
	R	2.8 (2835)	40①	70	39	70	75	23	25
1991	Z	4.3 (4293)	65	80	45	70	75	35	20①
	A	2.5 (2474)	④	70	32	160	④	25①	32①
	E	2.5 (2474)	40①	70	32	160	④	25①	32①
	R	2.8 (2835)	40①	70	39	70	52	23	25
1992	Z	4.3 (4293)	65	80	45	70	75	35	20①
	A	2.5 (2474)	40①	70	32	160	52	25①	32①
	R	2.8 (2835)	40①	70	39	70	70	23	25
	W	4.3 (4293)	65	80	20⑤	70	75	35③	20⑥
	Z	4.3 (4293)	65	80	20⑤	70	75	35	20⑥

88446R061

PISTON AND RING SPECIFICATIONS

All measurements are given in inches.

Year	Engine ID/VIN	Engine Displacement Liters (cc)	Piston Clearance	Ring Gap Top Compression	Ring Gap Bottom Compression	Ring Gap Oil Control	Ring Side Clearance Top Compression	Ring Side Clearance Bottom Compression	Ring Side Clearance Oil Control
1990	E	2.5 (2474)	0.00098-0.0022	0.010-0.020	0.010-0.020	0.020-0.060	0.0020-0.0030	0.0010-0.0030	0.015-0.055
	R	2.8 (2835)	0.0007-0.0017	0.0098-0.0197	0.0098-0.0197	0.020-0.055	0.0012-0.0028	0.0016-0.0037	0.0078 MAX
	Z	4.3 (4293)	0.0007-0.0017	0.010-0.020	0.010-0.025	0.015-0.055	0.0012-0.0032	0.0012-0.0032	0.002-0.007
1991	A	2.5 (2474)	0.0015-0.0035	0.010-0.015	0.010-0.020	0.015-0.055	0.0015-0.0030	0.0015-0.0032	0.0005-0.007
	E	2.5 (2474)	0.0014-0.0022	0.010-0.020	0.010-0.020	0.020-0.060	0.0020-0.0030	0.0010-0.0030	0.015-0.055
	R	2.8 (2835)	0.0007-0.0017	0.0098-0.0197	0.0098-0.0197	0.020-0.055	0.0012-0.0028	0.0016-0.0037	0.0078 MAX
	Z	4.3 (4293)	0.0007-0.0017①	0.010-0.020	0.010-0.025	0.015-0.055	0.0012-0.0032	0.0012-0.0032	0.002-0.007
1992	A	2.5 (2474)	0.0015-0.0035	0.010-0.015	0.010-0.020	0.015-0.055	0.0015-0.0030	0.0015-0.0032	0.0005-0.007
	R	2.8 (2835)	0.0007-0.0017	0.0098-0.0197	0.0098-0.0197	0.011-0.050	0.0012-0.0028	0.0016-0.0037	0.0078 MAX
	W	4.3 (4293)	0.0007-0.0017	0.018-0.026	0.018-0.026	0.015-0.055	0.0014-0.0032	0.0014-0.0032	0.0014-0.0032
	Z	4.3 (4293)	0.0007-0.0017①	0.010-0.020	0.010-0.025	0.015-0.055	0.0012-0.0032	0.0012-0.0032	0.002-0.007
1993	A	2.5 (2474)	0.0015-0.0035	0.010-0.015	0.010-0.020	0.015-0.055	0.0015-0.0030	0.0015-0.0032	0.0005-0.007
	R	2.8 (2835)	0.0007-0.0017	0.0098-0.0197	0.0098-0.0197	0.011-0.050	0.0012-0.0028	0.0016-0.0037	0.0078 MAX
	W	4.3 (4293)	0.0007-0.0017	0.018-0.026	0.018-0.026	0.015-0.055	0.0014-0.0032	0.0014-0.0032	0.0014-0.0032
	Z	4.3 (4293)	0.0007-0.0017	0.010-0.020	0.010-0.025	0.015-0.055	0.0012-0.0032	0.0012-0.0032	0.002-0.007

① MFI-Turbo 0.0015-0.0030

88446OA

TORQUE SPECIFICATIONS
All readings in ft. lbs.

Year	Engine ID/VIN	Engine Displacement Liters (cc)	Cylinder Head Bolts	Main Bearing Bolts	Rod Bearing Bolts	Crankshaft Bolts	Flywheel Bolts	Manifold	
								Intake	Exhaust
1993	A	2.5 (2474)	⑦	70	32	160	⑤	25③	32④
	R	2.8 (2835)	40①	70	39	70	52	23	25
	W	4.3 (4293)	65	80	20⑧	70	75	35⑫	20⑥
	Z	4.3 (4293)	65	80	20⑧	70	75	35	20⑥

① Then tighten all bolts ¼ additional turn
② Torque bolts in two steps:
Step 1: 40–47 ft. lbs.
Step 2: New bolts: 54–61 ft. lbs.
Step 2: Used bolts: 61–69 ft. lbs.
③ If manifold is retained with bolts and studs tighten all fasteners to 25–37 ft. lbs.
④ Center retainers: 36 ft. lbs.
⑤ Automatic trans.: 55 ft. lbs.
Manual trans.: 65 ft. lbs.
⑥ Center exhaust tube: 26 ft. lbs.
All bolts on MFI-Turbo: 33 ft. lbs.

⑦ Step 1: Tighten all head bolts to 18 ft. lbs.
Step 2: Tighten all bolts to 26 ft. lbs. except No. 9
Retorque No. 9 to 18 ft. lbs.
Step 3: Tighten all an additional 90 degrees
⑧ Plus 70 degree turn
⑨ Upper intake on MFI-Turbo 18 ft. lbs.
⑩ Short bolts: 43 ft. lbs. plus 90 degrees
Long bolts: 46 ft. lbs. plus 90 degrees
⑪ Upper intake manifold: 22 ft. lbs.
⑫ Upper intake manifold: 124 inch lbs.

8844R61A

Engine

❊❊ CAUTION

Please refer to Section 1 before discharging the compressor or disconnecting air conditioning lines. Damage to the air conditioning system or personal injury could result. Consult your local laws concerning refrigerant discharge and recycling. In many areas it may be illegal for anyone but a certified technician to service the A/C system. Always use an approved recovery station when discharging the air conditioning.

The following procedures require the use of an engine hoist with sufficient capacity to safely lift and support 500–1000 lbs.

REMOVAL & INSTALLATION

Except 4.3L Engines

1. Properly relieve the fuel system pressure and disconnect the negative battery cable.

➡**Refer to Section 5 for special procedures to release fuel system pressure.**

2. Matchmark the hood hinges for installation reference and remove the hood.
3. Drain the cooling system and remove the upper and lower radiator hoses. Disconnect the coolant overflow hose. Disconnect the heater hoses at the engine.
4. Remove the upper and lower fan shrouds. On automatic transmission equipped vehicles, disconnect and plug the transmission cooler lines.
5. Remove the air cleaner assembly and cover the carburetor/throttle body with a rag.
6. Label and disconnect all necessary hoses, vacuum lines and wires from the engine, transmission and transfer case (if equipped).
7. Disconnect the throttle cable, transmission TV cable and cruise control cable (if equipped).
8. Raise and support the vehicle safely. Disconnect the exhaust pipes at the manifold.
9. Remove the front driveshaft and skid plates on 4WD vehicles.
10. If applicable, disconnect the strut rods at the bell housing.
11. For automatic transmission vehicles the body will have to be raised away from the engine in order for the top transmission-to-engine bolt(s) to clear the cowl. Remove the body mounting bolts, then use a floor jack to raise the front of the body away from the frame. Support the body using blocks of wood. Remove the top transmission-to-engine mounting bolts, then remove the wood and lower the body back into position.

➡**4WD vehicles equipped with automatic transmissions usually do not require transmission/transfer case removal when removing the engine. If equipped with a 2.8L engine, 4WD and a manual transmission, the transfer case and transmission must usually be removed prior to removing the engine. Please refer to the appropriate procedures located in Section 7 of this manual.**

12. Remove the rear driveshaft.
13. Support the transmission with a floor jack and remove the transmission crossmember.
14. For vehicles equipped with automatic transmissions:
• Remove the torque converter cover
• Remove the torque converter-to-flexplate attaching bolts
• If transmission removal is desired, remove the transmission shift linkage and, if equipped, the transfer case shift linkage. Remove the remaining transmission-to-engine mounting bolts, and remove the transmission and transfer case (if equipped) as an assembly
15. For vehicles equipped with manual transmissions:
• Remove the clutch slave cylinder and set aside
• If transmission removal is desired or necessary, remove the transmission shift linkage and shifter, and if equipped, remove the 4WD transfer case shift linkage and shifter.
• Remove the transmission-to-bellhousing bolts, if the transmission is being removed, carefully lower the transmission and transfer case (if equipped) as an assembly.

➡**If the manual transmission is removed, leave the bellhousing in place to protect the clutch during engine removal. Leaving the bell housing in place will also prevent the necessity of jacking the body off the frame to access the top bell housing-to-engine bolts which would otherwise be blocked by the cowl.**

16. Remove the accessory drive belts.
17. Remove the fan.
18. If equipped, remove the power steering pump, A/C compressor and air pump with their brackets and place aside in the engine compartment with the lines intact.

➡**DO NOT disconnect the fluid or refrigerant lines.**

19. Verify that nothing else is attached to the engine and, if necessary, disconnect the remaining component(s).
20. Attach a suitable lifting device to the engine and remove. Pause several times while lifting the engine to make sure no hoses or wiring have been snagged by the powerplant.
To install:
21. Using the lifting device, carefully lower the engine into position. Loosely install the engine mount bolts at this time to hold the engine in position.
22. If equipped, reposition and secure the power steering pump and/or A/C compressor to the engine.

23. Install the engine cooling fan and the accessory drive belts.

24. If removed, install the transmission and, if equipped, transfer case.

25. Install the transmission crossmember and remove the support. Install all accessible transmission-to-engine/bell housing bolts (as applicable) at this time.

26. Tighten the engine and transmission fasteners:
- Engine mount-to-engine: 35 ft. lbs. (47 Nm).
- Engine mount-to-frame mount: 52 ft. lbs. (70 Nm).
- Transmission mount-to-transmission: 45 ft. lbs. (61 Nm).
- Transmission mount-to-crossmember: 24 ft. lbs. (33 Nm).

27. For automatic transmission vehicles, install the torque converter-to-flex-plate bolts and install the torque converter cover.

28. If the transmission/transfer case was removed, reconnect the shift linkage.

29. For manual transmission vehicles, position and install the slave cylinder assembly.

30. Install the rear driveshaft.

31. Using a floor jack, carefully jack the front of the body away from the frame, then install the remaining transmission-to-engine bolts. Carefully lower the body back into position and secure the body mounts.

32. If applicable, connect the strut rods at the bell housing.

33. For 4WD vehicles, install the front driveshaft and, if equipped, the skid plates.

34. Connect the throttle cable, transmission TV cable and cruise control cable (if equipped).

35. Reconnect all necessary hoses, vacuum lines and wires from the engine, transmission and transfer case (if equipped), as noted during removal.

36. Remove the cover from the throttle body/carburetor, then install the air cleaner assembly.

37. For automatic transmission equipped vehicles, remove the plugs, then reconnect the transmission cooler lines.

38. Install the upper and lower fan shrouds.

39. Connect the upper and lower radiator hoses, the coolant overflow hose and the heater hoses at the engine.

40. Align and install the hood using the matchmarks made during removal.

41. Connect the negative battery cable, then proper refill the engine cooling system.

42. Check all powertrain fluid levels and add, as necessary.

4.3L Engines

2WD

1. Disconnect the negative battery cable and properly relieve the fuel system pressure.

2. Scribe matchmarks for installation purposes, then remove the hood.

3. Properly drain the engine cooling system, then disconnect the upper radiator hose from the radiator.

4. Disconnect the overflow hose, then remove the upper fan shroud.

5. If equipped, disconnect the automatic transmission cooler lines from the radiator assembly. Plug the openings to prevent system contamination or excessive fluid loss.

6. Remove the radiator assembly from the truck.

7. Remove the engine cooling fan, then disconnect and plug the heater hoses.

8. Remove the air cleaner assembly, then tag and disconnect all necessary vacuum hoses.

9. Tag and disconnect all necessary wires at the bulkhead, ground wires and main feed wires.

10. Disconnect the throttle and cruise control cables, as equipped.

11. Remove the distributor cap.

12. Raise and support the front of the vehicle safely using jackstands.

13. Remove the catalytic converter-to-exhaust pipe bolts, then disconnect the exhaust pipes at the manifold.

14. Disconnect the strut rods at the bell housing.

15. If equipped, remove the flywheel cover, then remove the torque converter bolts.

16. Remove the shield at the rear of the catalytic converter.

17. Disconnect the converter hanger at the exhaust pipe.

18. Remove the lower fan shroud.

19. Disconnect the fuel lines and loosen all fuel line clamps from the TBI unit and engine. Move the lines to the rear of the engine compartment and tie them in place, but take care not to stress or damage the lines.

20. Remove the 2 outer air dam bolts.

21. Remove the left body mount bolts, then carefully raise the body from the frame and support using an additional set of jackstands.

22. Remove the bell housing retaining bolts, then remove the jackstands and carefully lower the body back to the frame.

23. Remove the motor mount through bolts, then remove the jackstands and lower the truck.

24. Remove the A/C compressor and/or power steering pump from the engine, then position them aside with the lines intact. There is no need to disconnect the lines from either of these components.

25. Support the transmission using a floor jack, then install a suitable lifting device and carefully lift the engine from the vehicle. Pause several times while lifting the engine to make sure no wires or hoses have become snagged.

To install:

26. Carefully lower the engine into the vehicle and engage it with the transmission. Remove the floor jack from the transmission and the lifting device from the engine.

27. Raise and support the truck safely using jackstands.

28. Install the motor mount through bolts.

29. Use the floor jack to raise the body from the frame for access, then install and tighten the bell housing bolts. Lower the body back into position and install the body mount bolts.

30. If equipped, reposition and secure the power steering pump and/or A/C compressor.

31. Install and tighten the 2 outer air dam bolts.

32. Reposition the fuel lines and connect them to the TBI unit. Be sure to properly secure the lines using the clamps.

33. Install the lower fan shroud, then install the converter hanger to the exhaust pipe.

34. Install the shield at the rear of the converter

35. If applicable, install the torque converter bolts, then install the flywheel cover.

36. Connect the strut rods at the bell housing.

37. Connect the exhaust pipes to the manifolds, then install the converter-to-exhaust pipe bolts.

38. Remove the jackstands and carefully lower the truck.

39. Install the distributor cap.

40. Connect the throttle and, if equipped, cruise control cables.

41. Engage all wires at the bulkhead, ground wires and main feed wires as tagged during removal.

42. Install the vacuum hoses as noted during removal, then install the air cleaner assembly.

43. Connect the heater hoses, then install the fan.

44. Install the radiator and the upper fan shroud.

45. Connect the overflow hose, the radiator hoses and, if equipped, the transmission cooler lines.

46. Align and install the hood, then check all powertrain fluid levels.

47. Connect the negative battery cable, then properly fill the engine cooling system.

48. Start and run the engine, then check for leaks.

4WD; EXCEPT 1991–92 MFI-TURBO

1. Disconnect the negative battery cable and properly relieve the fuel system pressure.

2. If equipped, disconnect the underhood light.

3. Scribe matchmarks for installation purposes, then remove the hood.

4. Properly drain the engine cooling system, then raise and support the front of the truck safely using jackstands.

5. Loosen the front and remove the 2 body mounts located near or under the cab.

6. Remove the outer bolts from the front air dam.

7. Raise the body away from the frame to gain the necessary clearance for transmission bolt removal. Remove the top transmission-to-engine bolts, then carefully lower the body back into position.

8. Support the transmission using a floor jack, then remove the remaining transmission-to-engine bolts.

9. Remove the 2nd crossmember (located 2nd back from the front of the truck) from the vehicle.

10. Disconnect the exhaust pipes at the manifolds, then remove the catalytic converter hanger.

11. Remove the torque converter cover bolts and disconnect the front driveshaft from the front differential, then remove the torque converter cover.

12. Release the transmission oil cooler lines at the engine clips.

13. Remove the motor mount bolts.

14. Remove the flexplate-to-torque converter bolts.

15. Remove the front splash shield, then remove the lower fan shroud retaining bolts.

16. Remove the jackstands and carefully lower the truck.

17. Remove the upper fan shroud, then disconnect the hoses from the radiator.

18. Disconnect the oil filter pipe at the remote oil filter.

19. Remove the radiator assembly, then remove the engine cooling fan.

20. Remove the air cleaner assembly.

21. Remove the A/C compressor and/or power steering pump from the engine, then position them aside with the lines intact. There is no need to disconnect the lines from either of these components.

22. Disconnect the fuel lines and loosen all fuel line clamps from the TBI unit and engine. Move the lines to the rear of the engine compartment and tie them in place, but take care not to stress or damage the lines.

23. Tag and disconnect all necessary wires, vacuum lines and emission hoses.

24. Disconnect the accelerator cable and, if equipped, the cruise control cable.

25. Disconnect the engine wiring harness at the bulkhead connector.

26. Disconnect the heater hoses at the engine.

27. Make sure the transmission is supported using a floor jack, then install a suitable lifting device and carefully lift the engine from the vehicle. Pause several times while lifting the engine to make sure no wires or hoses have become snagged.

To install:

28. Carefully lower the engine into the vehicle and engage it with the transmission. Remove the floor jack from the transmission and the lifting device from the engine.

29. Raise and support the truck safely using jackstands.

30. Install the motor mount through bolts.

31. Use the floor jack to raise the body from the frame for access, then install and tighten the bell housing bolts. Lower the body back into position and install the body mount bolts.

32. Install the flexplate-to-torque converter bolts, then install the torque converter cover.

33. Install the front driveshaft assembly, then install the catalytic converter hanger.

34. Connect the exhaust pipe to the manifolds.

35. Install the crossmember.

36. Install the lower fan shroud retaining bolts, then install the front splash shield.

37. Secure the transmission oil cooler lines at the engine clips.

38. Install the front air dam bolts, then remove the jackstands and carefully lower the vehicle.

39. Engage the engine wiring harness at the bulkhead connector.

40. Connect the accelerator cable, and if equipped, the cruise control cable.

41. Connect the heater hoses, then connect the wires, vacuum lines and emission hoses as noted during removal.

42. Reposition and connect the fuel lines making sure they are properly routed in their clamps.

43. If equipped, reposition and secure the power steering pump and/or A/C compressor.

44. Install the engine cooling fan, then install the radiator assembly.

45. Connect the oil filter pipe at the remote oil filter using new O-rings.

46. Connect the radiator hoses and install the drive belt(s).

47. Install the upper fan shroud.

48. Install the hood and check all powertrain fluid levels.

49. Connect the negative battery cable and properly refill the engine cooling system.

50. Start and run the engine, then check for leaks.

1991–92 MFI-TURBO

1. Disconnect the negative battery cable, followed by the positive cable, then properly relieve the fuel system pressure.

2. Properly relieve the engine cooling system and the turbocharger air cooler system. Refer to Section 1 of this manual for details.

3. Scribe matchmarks for installation purposes, then remove the hood from the vehicle.

4. Remove the air cleaner and duct assembly.

5. Remove the turbocharger air inlet elbow.

6. Remove the upper fan shroud, then remove the fan and pulley nuts.

7. Remove the serpentine drive belt, then remove the fan and pulley.

8. Remove the battery tray and vacuum tank.

9. Raise and support the front of the truck safely using jackstands.

10. Remove the front tire and wheel assemblies, then remove the wheelhouse panels

11. Disconnect the mufflers and tailpipe from the catalytic converter, then remove the catalytic converter support bolts.

12. Remove the turbocharger outlet pipe bracket and outlet pipe nuts. Move the outlet pipe and catalytic converter away from the turbocharger.

13. Disengage the electrical wiring connector from the charge air cooler radiator temperature sensor, then disconnect the radiator hoses.

14. Remove the charge air cooler radiator.

15. Disconnect the exhaust crossover pipe. Underhood access is necessary, either install the front wheels and lower the vehicle, or adjust the jackstands for access.

16. Disconnect the transmission oil cooler lines from the radiator. Plug the openings to prevent system contamination or excessive fluid loss.

17. Remove the upper and lower radiator hoses.

18. Disconnect the engine oil cooler lines from the radiator. Plug the openings to prevent system contamination or excessive fluid loss.

19. Disconnect the heater hoses and the overflow hoses from the radiator.

20. Remove the radiator.

21. Disconnect the oil pipes at the filter adapter.

22. Remove the power steering pump hoses from the steering gear. Plug the openings to prevent system contamination or excessive fluid loss.

23. Remove the engine coolant reservoir.

24. Disconnect the A/C compress from the bracket and position aside with the lines intact.

25. Loosen the charge air cooler clamps, then disconnect the ducts and hoses.

26. Remove the charge air cooler from the supports.

27. Remove the throttle body, gasket and cable bracket from the upper intake manifold and position aside.

28. If not done already, disconnect the heater hose from the lower intake manifold.

29. Tag and disengage the electrical connectors from the upper intake manifold assembly.

30. Disconnect the fuel pipes from the fuel rail assembly.

31. Tag and disengage the remaining electrical connectors and vacuum hoses form the engine assembly.

32. If additional access is needed, further raise and support the front of the truck using the jackstands.

33. Remove the rear driveshaft.

34. Position a support under the transmission, then remove the transmission crossmember and mount.

35. Remove the front driveshaft.

36. Remove the torque converter cover, then disconnect the shift linkage from the transmission.

37. Remove the torque converter bolts.

38. Disconnect the fuel pipes from the hoses near the transfer case, then remove the fuel line bracket from the transfer case.

39. Disengage the fuel line clip and the electrical clips and connectors from the transmission and transfer case.

40. Remove the transfer case and gasket.

41. Disconnect the TV cable from the transmission.

42. Disconnect the transmission cooler lines from the transmission. Be sure to plug all openings.

43. Remove the torque converter housing bolts, then carefully lower the transmission from the vehicle.

44. Remove the transmission oil cooler lines from the oil pan.

45. Remove the fuel line clip, oil line and electrical harness clips from the cylinder heads.

46. Tag and disengage the starter motor electrical connections, then remove the starter from the engine.

47. Remove the engine mount through-bolts and nuts. Underhood access is necessary, either install the front wheels and lower the vehicle, or adjust the jackstands for access.

48. Disengage the electrical connections form the oil pressure and knock sensors, then remove the ground strap.

49. Install a suitable lifting device and carefully lift the engine from the vehicle. Pause several times while lifting the engine to make sure no wires or hoses have become snagged.

To install:

50. Carefully lower the engine into the vehicle.

51. Engage the electrical connections to the oil pressure and knock sensors, then install the ground strap.

52. Make sure the engine is properly positioned on the engine mounts, then route the wiring harnesses into position.

53. If further access is needed, further raise and support the front of the truck using the jackstands.

54. Install the engine mount through-bolts and nuts, then tighten the bolts to 61 ft. lbs. (83 Nm) or the nuts to 52 ft. lbs. (70 Nm).

55. Install the fuel line clip, oil line and electrical harness clips to the cylinder heads.

56. Install the starter motor and engage the wiring as noted during removal.

57. Carefully raise the transmission into position in the vehicle, then install the torque converter housing bolts and tighten to 35 ft. lbs. (41 Nm).

58. Connect the transmission oil cooler lines to the transmission housing and tighten to 21 ft. lbs. (28 Nm).

59. Connect the TV cable to the transmission.

60. Install the transfer case and gasket, then tighten the retaining bolts to 39 ft. lbs. (53 Nm).

61. Install the transmission cooler lines to the oil pan clip.

62. Install the fuel line pipes to the hoses, then connect the fuel line bracket to the transfer case. Tighten the fuel line hose fittings to 19 ft. lbs. (26 Nm) and the bracket bolt to 26 ft. lbs. (35 Nm).

63. Engage the fuel line clip and the electrical wiring clips and connectors to the transmission and transfer case.

64. Install the torque converter bolts and tighten to 46 ft. lbs. (63 Nm), then connect the shift linkage to the transmission.

65. Install the torque converter cover and tighten the retaining bolts to 35 ft. lbs. (47 Nm).

66. Install the front driveshaft and tighten the retaining bolts to 52 ft. lbs. (70 Nm).

67. Install the transmission crossmember and mount, then tighten the crossmember bolts to 35 ft. lbs. (47 Nm).

68. Install the rear driveshaft and tighten the retainers to 15 ft. lbs. (20 Nm).

69. Install the turbocharger outlet pipe and nuts, then install the turbocharger outlet pipe bracket. Tighten the pipe nuts to 41 ft. lbs (55 Nm) and the pipe support bolt to 22 ft. lbs. (30 Nm).

70. Install the catalytic converter support bolts, then install the mufflers and tailpipe to the converter. Tighten the support bolts to 25 ft. lbs. (34 Nm) and the tailpipe bolts to 24 ft. lbs. (32 Nm).

71. Connect the crossover pipe and tighten the nuts to 12 ft. lbs. (16 Nm).

72. Install the charge air cooler radiator, connect the cooler radiator hoses and engage the electrical connection.

73. Underhood access is necessary, either install the front wheels and lower the vehicle, or adjust the jackstands for access.

74. Engage the electrical connectors and vacuum lines to the engine.

75. Connect the fuel pipes to the fuel rail assembly, then install the upper intake manifold assembly and gasket. Tighten the upper intake manifold bolts (starting at the 2 middle bolts, moving outward to each side) to 18 ft. lbs. (24 Nm).

76. Engage the electrical connectors to the upper intake manifold assembly, then connect the heater hose to the lower intake manifold.

77. Install the throttle body, gasket and cable bracket to the upper intake manifold assembly. Tighten the throttle body bolts to 18 ft. lbs. (24 Nm).

78. Install the charge air cooler to the supports, then install the charge air cooler ducts and hoses (secure using the clamps).

79. Reposition the A/C compressor to the bracket and secure.

80. Install the engine coolant reservoir.

81. Install the power steering pump hoses to the steering gear and tighten the fittings to 21 ft. lbs. (28 Nm).

82. Install the oil pipes to the filter adapter and tighten the retaining bolt to 26 ft. lbs. (35 Nm).

83. Install the radiator assembly.

84. Connect the heater hoses and the overflow hose to the radiator.

85. Install the engine oil and transmission fluid cooler lines to the radiator. Tighten the engine oil line fittings to 26 ft. lbs. (35 Nm) and the transmission fluid lines to 20 ft. lbs. (27 Nm).

86. Connect the upper and lower radiator hoses.

87. Install the battery tray and vacuum tank.

88. Install the fan, pulley and nuts.

89. Install the serpentine drive belt, then tighten the pulley nuts to 18 ft. lbs. (24 Nm).

90. Install the upper radiator shroud.

91. Install the turbocharger air inlet elbow.

92. Install the air cleaner and duct.

93. Align and install the hood using the matchmarks made during removal.

94. Install the front wheelhouse panels.

95. Install the front tire and wheel assemblies, then remove the jackstands and carefully lower the vehicle.

96. Check all powertrain fluid levels and add, as necessary.

97. Connect the positive battery cable, followed by the negative battery cable.

98. Properly refill the charge air cooling system and bleed the air.

99. Properly refill the engine cooling system.

100. Start and run the engine, then check for leaks.

Rocker Arm (Valve) Cover

REMOVAL & INSTALLATION

▶ **See Figures 41 thru 52**

1.9L Engine

1. Disconnect the negative battery cable.
2. Remove the air cleaner assembly.
3. Tag and disconnect the spark plug wires, then remove the evaporator pipe.
4. Remove the rocker arm cover-to-engine nuts/washers.
5. Remove the rocker arm cover.

➡**DO NOT pry on the cover to remove it. If it sticks, use your palm or a rubber mallet to bump it rearwards, from the front.**

6. Using a putty knife, carefully clean the gasket mounting surfaces. Keep debris out of the engine.

7. To install, use a new gasket and reverse the removal procedures. Be careful not to overtighten the fasteners and either distort the valve cover (causing and leak) or break the fastener (causing more work).

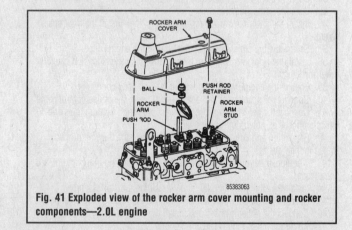

Fig. 41 Exploded view of the rocker arm cover mounting and rocker components—2.0L engine

2.0L Engine

1. Disconnect the negative battery cable.
2. Remove the air cleaner assembly and the distributor cap. If necessary, tag and disconnect the spark plug wires from the cap.
3. Remove the fuel vapor canister harness tubes from the rocker arm cover.
4. Disconnect the accelerator cable and remove the PCV valve.
5. Remove the rocker arm cover-to-cylinder head bolts, then remove the cover from the engine.

➡**DO NOT pry on the cover to remove it. If it sticks, use your palm or a rubber mallet to bump it rearwards, from the front.**

6. Using a putty knife, carefully clean the gasket mounting surfaces. Keep debris out of the engine.

7. To install, place a ⅛ in. bead of RTV sealant around the sealing rail of the cover and reverse the removal procedures. Torque the rocker arm cover-to-cylinder head bolts to 8 ft. lbs. (11 Nm). Be careful not to overtighten the fasteners and either distort the valve cover (causing and leak) or break the fastener (causing more work).

2.5L Engine

➡ **A rocker arm cover removal tool (J 34144-A or equivalent) is needed to properly perform this procedure and to prevent damage to the sealing rail of the rocker arm cover.**

1. Disconnect the negative battery cable.
2. Remove the air cleaner.
3. Disconnect the Positive Crankcase Ventilation (PCV) valve hose, the ignition wires from the rocker arm cover.
4. Remove the Exhaust Gas Recirculation (EGR) valve.
5. Label and disconnect the vacuum hoses. Disconnect and reposition the wiring harness, as necessary.
6. Remove the rocker arm cover-to-cylinder head bolts. Remove the cover using tool J 34144-A or equivalent to break the seal and drive the cover away from the cylinder head.

➡ **DO NOT pry on the cover to remove it. If it sticks, use your palm or a rubber mallet to bump it rearwards, from the front.**

7. Using a putty knife, carefully clean the gasket mounting surfaces. Keep debris out of the engine.

To install:

➡ **Be sure to use solvent to remove any oil or grease that may remain on the sealing surfaces.**

8. Place a ⅛ in. bead of RTV sealant around the sealing rail of the cover (or use a new gasket as applicable), then install the rocker arm cover to the cylinder head and tighten the retainers 75 inch lbs. (8 Nm). Be careful not to overtighten the fasteners and either distort the valve cover (causing and leak) or break the fastener (causing more work).
9. Connect the vacuum hoses as noted during removal. Reposition the wiring harness and re-engage any connectors.
10. Install the EGR valve.
11. Connect the PCV valve hose and the ignition wires to the rocker cover.
12. Install the air cleaner.
13. Connect the negative battery cable.

2.8L Engine

LEFT-SIDE

1. Disconnect the negative battery cable.
2. If equipped, disconnect the crankcase ventilation pipe.
3. Disconnect the air management hose, the vacuum hose(s), the electrical wires and the pipe bracket. Remove the spark plug wires and clips from the retaining studs.

4. If necessary, relieve the fuel system pressure and disconnect the fuel line(s) for clearance.
5. Remove the rocker arm cover-to-cylinder head bolts/nuts, reinforcements and the cover from the engine.

➡ **DO NOT pry on the cover to remove it. If it sticks, use your palm or a rubber mallet to bump it rearwards, from the front.**

6. Using a putty knife, carefully clean the gasket mounting surfaces. Keep debris out of the engine.

To install:

➡ **Be sure to use solvent to remove any oil or grease that may remain on the sealing surfaces.**

7. Place a ⅛ in. dab of RTV sealant at the points where the sealing area of the head meets the sealing area of the intake manifold. Install the cover and reinforcements using a new gasket, tighten the retainers 72 inch lbs. (8 Nm). Be careful not to overtighten the fasteners and either distort the valve cover (causing and leak) or break the fastener (causing more work).
8. If removed, connect the fuel lines.
9. Position the spark plug wires and clips back on the retaining studs.
10. Connect the hoses, wires and pipe bracket.
11. If equipped, connect the crankcase ventilation pipe.
12. Connect the negative battery cable.

RIGHT-SIDE (1982–87)

1. Disconnect the negative battery cable.
2. Disconnect the air management hoses, then remove the air management valve and coil bracket(s).
3. Disconnect the vacuum hose(s), the electrical wires and the pipe bracket, as applicable.
4. If equipped, remove the spark plug wires and clips from the retaining studs.
5. Disconnect the carburetor or throttle body linkage and controls and the brackets.
6. Remove the rocker arm cover-to-cylinder head bolts/nuts and the cover from the engine.

➡ **DO NOT pry on the cover to remove it. If it sticks, use your palm or a rubber mallet to bump it rearwards, from the front.**

7. Using a putty knife, carefully clean the gasket mounting surfaces. Keep debris out of the engine.

To install:

➡ **Be sure to use solvent to remove any oil or grease that may remain on the sealing surfaces.**

8. Place a ⅛ in. dab of RTV sealant at the points where the sealing area of the head meets the sealing area of the intake manifold. Install the cover and reinforcements using a new gasket, tighten the retainers 72 inch lbs. (8 Nm). Be careful not to overtighten the fasteners and either distort the valve cover (causing and leak) or break the fastener (causing more work).
9. Connect the throttle linkage and controls at the brackets.
10. If equipped, secure the spark plug wires and clips to the retaining studs.
11. Connect the vacuum hose(s), electrical wires and the pipe bracket, as applicable.

Fig. 42 If any component brackets interfere with cover removal, loosen the bracket retainers

Fig. 43 In this case the coil and air management valve bracket must be removed

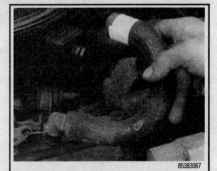

Fig. 44 Disconnect any vapor or breather hoses from the valve cover and/or air cleaner

Fig. 45 Release any wiring harnesses from cover mounted clips

Fig. 46 For the 2.8L engine, throttle return springs must be removed from the cover bracket

Fig. 47 If necessary, remove the throttle cable C-clip so the cable linkage may be disconnected

Fig. 48 With the C-clip removed, the linkage may be freed from the carburetor or throttle body

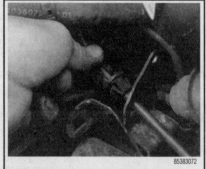

Fig. 49 Once the throttle linkage is disconnected, the cable may be removed from any cover mounted brackets

Fig. 50 Loosen and remove the valve cover retainers

Fig. 51 Lift the valve cover from the cylinder head

Fig. 52 Be careful not to get dirt or debris into the exposed cylinder head and oil passages

12. Install the air management valve and coil bracket(s), then connect the air management hoses.

13. Connect the negative battery cable.

RIGHT-SIDE (1988–93)

1. Disconnect the negative battery cable and remove the air cleaner assembly.

2. Remove the ignition coil and bracket.

3. Remove spark plug wires from the bracket on the rocker arm cover stud, then remove the PCV valve and vacuum pipe.

4. Remove the throttle, cruise control and TV cables (as applicable) along with the bracket at the throttle body.

5. Remove the alternator and lay it aside.

6. Remove the rocker arm cover-to-cylinder head bolts/nuts, reinforcements and the cover from the engine.

➡DO NOT pry on the cover to remove it. If it sticks, use your palm or a rubber mallet to bump it rearwards, from the front.

7. Using a putty knife, carefully clean the gasket mounting surfaces. Keep debris out of the engine.

To install:

➡Be sure to use solvent to remove any oil or grease that may remain on the sealing surfaces.

8. Place a ⅛ in. dab of RTV sealant at the points where the sealing area of the head meets the sealing area of the intake manifold. Install the cover and reinforcements using a new gasket, tighten the retainers 72 inch lbs. (8 Nm). Be careful not to overtighten the fasteners and either distort the valve cover (causing and leak) or break the fastener (causing more work).

9. Install the alternator.

10. Install the throttle, cruise control and TV cables (as applicable) along with the bracket.

11. Install the vacuum pipe and the PCV valve.

12. Position the spark plug wires in the bracket at the rocker arm cover stud.

13. Install the ignition coil and bracket.

14. Install the air cleaner assembly, then connect the negative battery cable.

4.3L Engine, Except MFI-Turbo

▶ **See Figure 53**

RIGHT SIDE

1. Disconnect the negative battery cable, then remove the air cleaner.

2. Remove PCV valve, then disconnect the heater pipe at the manifold.

3. Remove the emissions relays with their bracket and lay them aside.

4. Remove the wiring harness from the retaining clips and lay it aside.

5. Remove the spark plug wires from the clips.

6. Move the dipstick tube aside; on most vehicles you will have to first remove the dipstick tube bracket from the cylinder head.

7. Remove the rocker arm cover bolts, then remove the cover from the cylinder head.

➡**DO NOT pry on the cover to remove it. If it sticks, use your palm or a rubber mallet to bump it rearwards, from the front.**

8. Using a putty knife, carefully clean the gasket mounting surfaces. Keep debris out of the engine.

To install:

9. Install the rocker arm cover to the engine using a new gasket, then tighten the retainers to 90 inch lbs. (10 Nm). Be careful not to overtighten the fasteners and either distort the valve cover (causing and leak) or break the fastener (causing more work).

10. Reposition the dipstick guide tube and secure using the bracket.

11. Install the spark plug wires and the electrical wiring harness in the retaining clips.

12. Reposition and secure the emissions relays and bracket.

13. Connect the heater pipe to the manifold and install the PCV valve.

14. Install the air cleaner, then connect the negative battery cable.

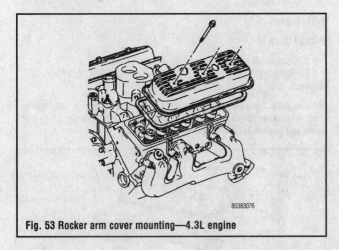

85383076

Fig. 53 Rocker arm cover mounting—4.3L engine

LEFT SIDE

1. Disconnect the negative battery cable and properly relieve the fuel system pressure.

2. Remove the air cleaner and heater (heat stove) pipe.

3. Remove the crankcase ventilation pipe.

4. Disconnect the fuel pipes at the throttle body, release the retaining clips and move the pipes aside.

5. Remove the alternator rear bracket.

6. Release the spark plug wires from the retaining clips, then disconnect the power brake vacuum line at the intake manifold.

7. Remove the rocker arm cover bolts, then remove the cover.

➡**DO NOT pry on the cover to remove it. If it sticks, use your palm or a rubber mallet to bump it rearwards, from the front.**

8. Using a putty knife, carefully clean the gasket mounting surfaces. Keep debris out of the engine.

To install:

9. Install the rocker arm cover to the engine using a new gasket, then tighten the retainers to 90 inch lbs. (10 Nm). Be careful not to overtighten the fasteners and either distort the valve cover (causing and leak) or break the fastener (causing more work).

10. Connect the power brake booster vacuum line to the intake manifold, then secure the spark plug wires to the retaining clips.

11. Install the alternator rear bracket.

12. Reconnect the fuel pipes to the throttle body, then secure the pipes using the retaining clips.

13. Install the crankcase ventilation pipe.

14. Install the air cleaner and heat stove.

15. Connect the negative battery cable.

4.3L MFI-Turbo

RIGHT SIDE

1. Disconnect the negative batter cable, then properly drain the engine cooling system and charge air cooling system.

2. Disconnect the charge air cooler clamps, hoses and ducts, then remove the charge air cooler.

3. Remove the PCV hoses and valves, then disconnect the turbocharger oil feed hose from the turbocharger.

4. Remove the air cleaner and duct, then disengage the oxygen sensor connector.

5. Disconnect the heater inlet hose from the lower intake manifold, then remove the charge air cooler lateral (center) support.

6. Remove the rocker arm cover retaining bolts, then remove the cover from the cylinder head.

➡**DO NOT pry on the cover to remove it. If it sticks, use your palm or a rubber mallet to bump it rearwards, from the front.**

7. Using a putty knife, carefully clean the gasket mounting surfaces. Keep debris out of the engine.

To install:

8. Install the rocker arm cover to the engine using a new gasket, then tighten the retainers to 89 inch lbs. (10 Nm). Be careful not to overtighten the fasteners and either distort the valve cover (causing and leak) or break the fastener (causing more work).

9. Connect the heater inlet hose, then connect the turbocharger oil feed hose and tighten the fitting to 16 ft. lbs. (22 Nm).

10. Install the PCV hoses and valves, then engage the oxygen sensor connector.

11. Install the charge air cooler lateral support to the lower intake manifold, then finger-tighten the nut.

12. Install the charge air cooler, then tighten the lateral support nut.

13. Install the charge air cooler clamps and hoses, then install the air cleaner and duct.

14. Connect the negative battery cable, then properly refill the engine cooling system and the charge air cooling system.

LEFT SIDE

1. Disconnect the negative battery cable, then drain the charge air cooling system.

2. Remove the serpentine drive belt, then unbolt the alternator and position it aside.

3. Disconnect the power brake hose.

4. Tag and disengage both the vacuum hoses and electrical connectors from the EVRV solenoid, ignition coil and the MAP sensor. All are located on the multi-use bracket.

5. Disconnect the charge air cooler inlet pipe, then remove the multi-use bracket.

6. Remove the rocker arm cover retaining bolts, then remove the cover from the cylinder head.

➡**DO NOT pry on the cover to remove it. If it sticks, use your palm or a rubber mallet to bump it rearwards, from the front.**

7. Using a putty knife, carefully clean the gasket mounting surfaces. Keep debris out of the engine.

To install:

8. Install the rocker arm cover to the engine using a new gasket, then tighten the retainers to 89 inch lbs. (10 Nm). Be careful not to overtighten the fasteners and either distort the valve cover (causing and leak) or break the fastener (causing more work).

9. Install the multi-use bracket, then connect the charge air cooler inlet pipe.

10. Engage the vacuum hoses and electrical wiring connectors to the components located on the multi-use bracket.

11. Connect the power brake hose.

12. Reposition and secure the alternator, then install the serpentine drive belt.

13. Connect the negative battery cable, then properly refill the charge air cooling system.

Rocker Arms and Pushrods

REMOVAL & INSTALLATION

1.9L Engine

▶ **See Figure 54**

1. Remove the rocker arm cover from the cylinder head.

2. Starting with the outer rocker arm shaft bracket, loosen the bracket nuts a little at a time (in sequence), then remove the nuts.

3. To disassemble the rocker arm shaft assembly, remove the spring from the rocker arm shaft, then the rocker arm brackets and arms.

➡**Valve train components which are to be reused MUST be installed in their original positions. If removed, be sure to tag or arrange all rocker arms and pushrods to assure proper installation.**

To install:

4. Inspect the rocker arm shafts for runout. Run-out should not exceed 0.0079 in. (0.20mm)

5. Measure the rocker arm to shaft clearance. Clearance should not exceed 0.0078 in. (0.20mm)

6. Check the face of the rocker arms for wear and/or damage, replace the rocker arms and/or shafts if not within specification.

7. Using clean engine oil or a suitable engine pre-lube, lubricate all of the moving parts. Pre-lube is better if the engine will sit for some time before it is started, while engine oil should be sufficient if the engine is to used immediately after repairs are completed.

8. Assemble the rocker arm shaft brackets and rocker arms to the shaft so that the cylinder number (on the upper face of the bracket) is pointed to the front of the engine.

9. Align the mark on the No. 1 rocker arm shaft bracket with the mark on the intake and exhaust valve side rocker arm shaft.

10. Check the amount of projection of the rocker arm shaft. The intake side should be longer when the holes in the shaft are aligned with the holes in the bracket.

11. Place the springs in position between the shaft bracket and rocker arm.

12. Check that the punch mark is turned upward, and install the shaft bracket assembly onto the head studs. Align the mark on the camshaft with the mark on the No. 1 rocker arm shaft bracket.

13. Tighten the bracket studs to 16 ft. lbs. (22 Nm) and adjust the valves.

➡**The valves are adjusted with the engine Cold.**

14. Using a wrench on the damper pulley bolt or using a remote starter button, turn the crankshaft until the No. 1 piston is at TDC of the compression stroke. You will know when the No. 1 piston is on it's compression stroke because both the intake and exhaust valves will remain closed as the crankshaft damper mark approaches the timing scale. If the rocker arms move, the engine is in the No. 4 firing position. Turn the engine over one revolution. Remove the distributor cap and ensure that the rotor is pointing to the No. 1 position on the cap.

➡**Another method to tell when the piston is coming up on the compression stroke is by removing the spark plug and placing your thumb over the hole, you will feel the air being forced out of the spark plug hole. Stop turning the crankshaft when the TDC timing mark on the crankshaft pulley is directly aligned with the timing mark pointer or the zero mark on the scale.**

15. With the No. 1 piston at TDC of the compression stroke, use a 0.006 in. (0.152mm) feeler gauge, to set intake valves of cylinders No. 1 & 2. Using a 0.010 in. (0.254mm) feeler gauge, set the exhaust valves of cylinders No. 1 & 3.

➡**When adjusting the valve clearance, loosen the locknut with an open-end wrench, then turn the adjuster screw with a screwdriver and retighten the locknut. The proper thickness feeler gauge should pass between the camshaft and the rocker with a slight drag when the clearance is correct.**

16. Rotate the engine one complete revolution, so that cylinder No. 4 is on the TDC of its compression stroke and the timing marks are aligned. This time the No. 4 cylinder valves remain closed as the timing mark approaches the scale.

17. With cylinder No. 4 on the TDC of the compression stroke, use a 0.006 in. (0.152mm) feeler gauge, to set intake valves of cylinders No. 3 & 4. Using a 0.010 in. (0.254mm) feeler gauge, set the exhaust valves of cylinders No. 2 & 4.

18. When the valves are properly adjusted, install the rocker arm cover.

19. Start and run the engine, then check ignition and carburetor adjustments.

2.0L Engine

▶ **See Figure 55**

1. Remove the rocker arm cover from the cylinder head.

2. Remove the rocker arm nuts, the ball washers and the rocker arms off the studs, then lift out the pushrods.

➡**Valve train components which are to be reused MUST be installed in their original positions. If removed, be sure to tag or arrange all rocker arms and pushrods to assure proper installation.**

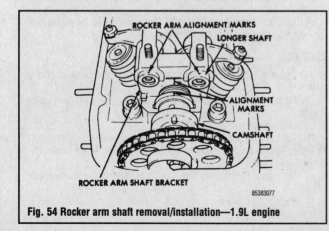

Fig. 54 Rocker arm shaft removal/installation—1.9L engine

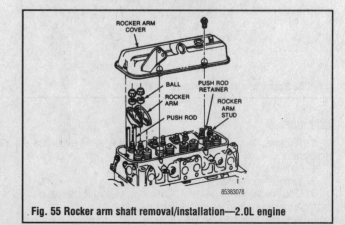

Fig. 55 Rocker arm shaft removal/installation—2.0L engine

To install:

3. Coat the bearing surfaces of the rocker arms and the rocker arm ball washers with Molykote® or equivalent pre-lube.

4. Install the pushrods making sure that they seat properly in the lifter.

5. Install the rocker arms, ball washers and the nuts, then tighten the rocker arm nuts until there is little or no valve lash.

➡**Each valve must be adjusted when the lifter is sitting on the base circle of the camshaft, not the raised section of the lobe.**

6. Rotate the crankshaft until the mark on the crankshaft pulley aligns with the **0** mark on the timing plate. Make sure that the No. 1 cylinder is positioned on the compression stroke. You will know when the No. 1 piston is on it's compression stroke because both the intake and exhaust valves will remain closed as the crankshaft damper mark approaches the timing scale. If the No. 1 valves move as the timing mark approaches TDC, the engine is in the No. 4 firing position; rotate the engine one complete revolution and it will be in the No. 1 position.

➡**Another method to tell when the piston is coming up on the compression stroke is by removing the spark plug and placing your thumb over the hole, you will feel the air being forced out of the spark plug hole. Stop turning the crankshaft when the TDC timing mark on the crankshaft pulley is directly aligned with the timing mark pointer or the zero mark on the scale.**

7. When the engine is on the No. 1 firing position, adjust the following valves:
• Exhaust—1, 3
• Intake—1, 2

8. To adjust the valves, back-out the adjusting nut until lash can be felt at the pushrod, then turn the nut until all of the lash is removed.

➡**To determine is all of the lash is removed, turn the pushrod with your fingers until the movement is removed.**

9. When all of the lash has been removed, turn the adjusting an additional 1½ turns; this will center the lifter plunger.

10. Crank the engine one complete revolution until the timing tab (0° mark) and the crankshaft pulley mark are again in alignment. Now the engine is in the No. 4 firing position. Adjust the following valves:
• Exhaust—2, 4
• Intake—3, 4

11. Install the rocker arm cover.

12. Start and run the engine, then check and adjust the timing and the idle speed, as necessary.

2.5L Engine

▶ See Figure 56

1. Remove the rocker arm cover from the cylinder head.

2. Using a socket wrench, remove the rocker arm bolts, the ball washer and the rocker arm.

➡**If only the pushrod is to be removed, back off the rocker arm bolt, swing the rocker arm aside and remove the pushrod. When removing more than one assembly, at the same time, be sure to keep them in order for reassembly purposes.**

3. If necessary, remove the pushrods and guides.

4. Inspect the rocker arms and ball washers for scoring and/or other damage, replace them (if necessary).

➡**If replacing worn components with new ones, be sure to coat the new parts with Molykote® or an equivalent pre-lube before installation.**

To install:

5. If removed, install the pushrods and guides.

6. Install the rocker arms, ball washers and retaining bolts. Tighten the rocker arm-to-cylinder head bolt for each valve to 22 ft. lbs. (30 Nm), but only tighten the bolt with the hydraulic lifter for that valve on the base circle of the camshaft. DO NOT tighten the bolts while the lifter is resting on the raised portion of the lobe and DO NOT overtighten the bolts.

➡**Valve lash is NOT adjustable on the 2.5L engine.**

7. Install the rocker arm cover to the cylinder head.

2.8L Engine

▶ See Figures 57, 58, 59, 60 and 61

1. Remove the rocker arm cover(s) from the cylinder head.

2. Remove the rocker arm nut, the rocker arm and the ball washer.

➡**If only the pushrod is to be removed, loosen the rocker arm nut, swing the rocker arm to the side and remove the pushrod.**

3. Withdraw the pushrod from the cylinder head.

To install:

4. Inspect and replace components if worn or damaged.

5. Coat the bearing surfaces of the rocker arms and the rocker arm ball washers with Molykote® or equivalent pre-lube.

6. Install the pushrods making sure that they seat properly in the lifter.

7. Install the rocker arms, ball washers and the nuts, then tighten the rocker arm nuts until there is little or no valve lash.

➡**Each valve must be adjusted when the lifter is sitting on the base circle of the camshaft, not the raised section of the lobe.**

8. Rotate the crankshaft until the mark on the crankshaft pulley aligns with the **0** mark on the timing plate. Make sure that the No. 1 cylinder is positioned on the compression stroke. You will know when the No. 1 piston is on it's compression stroke because both the intake and exhaust valves will remain closed as the crankshaft damper mark approaches the timing scale. If the No. 1 valves move as the timing mark approaches TDC, the engine is in the No. 4 firing position; rotate the engine one complete revolution and it will be in the No. 1 position.

➡**Another method to tell when the piston is coming up on the compression stroke is by removing the spark plug and placing your thumb over the hole, you will feel the air being forced out of the spark plug hole. Stop turning the crankshaft when the TDC timing mark on the crankshaft pulley is directly aligned with the timing mark pointer or the zero mark on the scale.**

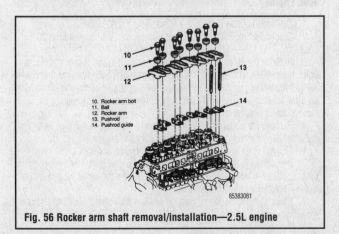

10. Rocker arm bolt
11. Ball
12. Rocker arm
13. Pushrod
14. Pushrod guide

85383081

Fig. 56 Rocker arm shaft removal/installation—2.5L engine

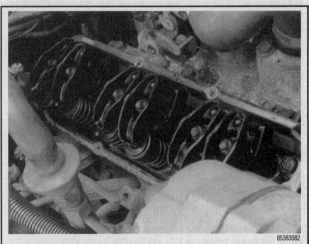

85383082

Fig. 57 For access to the rocker arms, remove the valve cover from the cylinder head

Fig. 58 Loosen the rocker arm retaining nut

Fig. 59 Remove the retaining nut and ball washer from the top of the rocker arm

Fig. 60 With the nut and washer removed, the rocker arm is free to be pulled from the stud

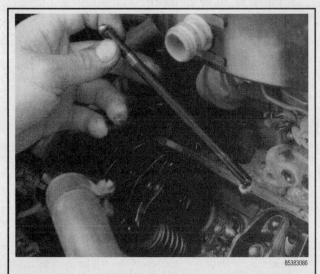

Fig. 61 The pushrod may now be pulled from the cylinder head

9. When the engine is on the No. 1 firing position, adjust the following valves:
- Intake—1, 5 & 6
- Exhaust—1, 2 & 3

10. To adjust the valves, back-out the adjusting nut until lash can be felt at the pushrod, then turn the nut until all of the lash is removed.

➡**To determine is all of the lash is removed, turn the pushrod with your fingers until the movement is removed.**

11. When all of the lash has been removed, turn the adjusting an additional 1½ turns; this will center the lifter plunger.

12. Crank the engine one complete revolution until the timing tab (0° mark) and the crankshaft pulley mark are again in alignment. Now the engine is in the No. 4 firing position. Adjust the following valves:
- Intake—2, 3 & 4
- Exhaust—4, 5 & 6

13. Install the rocker arm cover(s).

14. Start and run the engine, then check and adjust the timing and the idle speed, as applicable.

4.3L Engine

1. Remove the rocker arm cover(s) from the cylinder head.
2. Remove the rocker arm nut, the rocker arm and the ball washer.

➡**If only the pushrod is to be removed, loosen the rocker arm nut, swing the rocker arm to the side and remove the pushrod.**

3. Withdraw the pushrod from the cylinder head.

To install:

4. Inspect and replace components if worn or damaged.

5. Coat the bearing surfaces of the rocker arms and the rocker arm ball washers with Molykote® or equivalent pre-lube.

6. Install the pushrods making sure that they seat properly in the lifter.

7. Install the rocker arms, ball washers and the nuts.

8. For the 4.3L (VIN W) engine and any 1993 4.3L (VIN Z) engines which are equipped with screw-in type rocker arm studs with positive stop shoulders, Tighten the rocker arm adjusting nuts against the stop shoulders to 20 ft. lbs. (27 Nm). No further adjustment is necessary, or possible.

9. For all 1988–92 and most later 4.3L (VIN Z) engines (which are not equipped with screw-in type rocker arm studs and positive stop shoulders), properly adjust the valve lash. For details on valve lash adjustment, please refer to Section 1 of this manual.

10. Install the rocker arm cover(s) to the cylinder head.

11. Start and run the engine, then check for leaks and for proper ignition timing adjustment.

Thermostat

DIAGNOSIS

Make an operational check of the thermostat by hanging the it on a hook in a pot of warm water. Insert a thermometer into the water (neither the thermostat or thermometer should touch the metal sides or bottom of the pot) and heat the water to the thermostat opening temperature (stamped on the top of the thermostat). With the temperature within 10° of the opening temperature, the thermostat should open. If not, replace the thermostat.

REMOVAL & INSTALLATION

◆ **See Figures 62 thru 69**

1.9L Engine

1. Drain the cooling system to a level below the thermostat.

2. Disconnect the PCV hose, the ECS hose, the AIR hose and the TCA hose.

3. Remove the air cleaner-to-carburetor retainer(s) and loosen the clamp bolts, then lift the air cleaner and disconnect the TCA hose from the thermosensor (on the intake manifold). Remove the hoses from the air cleaner-to-carburetor slow actuator and the air cleaner-to-vacuum control (California), then remove the air cleaner assembly.

4. Remove the outlet pipe-to-inlet manifold bolts, the outlet pipe (with the radiator hose attached) and the thermostat from the engine.

5. Using a putty knife, clean the gasket mounting surfaces.

6. Installation is the reverse of removal. Use a new gasket and apply a thin coat of sealant to both surfaces of the gasket. Torque the outlet pipe-to-intake manifold bolts to 21 ft. lbs. (28 Nm).

7. Properly refill the engine cooling system, then start the engine and check for leaks.

Fig. 62 When draining coolant, remember to use a funnel in order to prevent a mess

Fig. 63 Loosen and remove the water outlet retainers

Fig. 64 Lift the outlet away from the thermostat and housing with the hose still attached

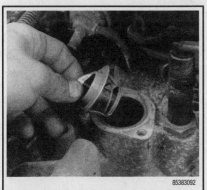

Fig. 65 Remove the old thermostat from the housing

Fig. 66 Be sure to clean the housing and outlet of all traces of old gasket/sealant

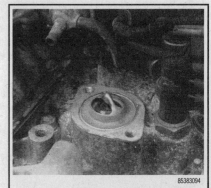

Fig. 67 Install the new thermostat to the housing

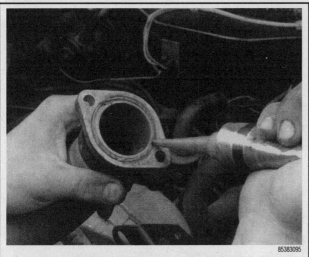

Fig. 68 For most vehicles covered by this manual, apply a thin coat of sealant to the outlet groove

Fig. 69 Install and tighten the bolts; using a torque wrench if a specification is given

2.0L Engine

▶ See Figure 70

The thermostat is connected to the water outlet and the thermostat housing, located at the top front-side of the engine.

1. Disconnect the negative battery cable.
2. Drain the cooling system to a level below the thermostat.
3. Remove the steel vacuum tubes.
4. Remove the water outlet-to-thermostat housing bolts, then lift the outlet from the thermostat housing and remove the thermostat.

To install:

5. Using a putty knife, clean the gasket mounting surfaces.
6. Place an 1/8 in. bead of RTV sealant on the water outlet. Place the thermostat, with the power element down, in the housing and install water outlet while the RTV is still wet.
7. Torque the water outlet-to-thermostat housing bolts to 15–22 ft. lbs. (20–30 Nm).
8. Install the steel vacuum tubes, then connect the negative battery cable.
9. Properly refill the engine cooling system, then check for leaks.

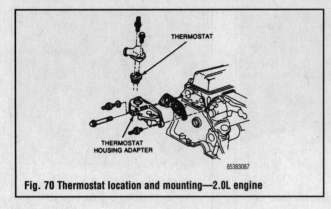

Fig. 70 Thermostat location and mounting—2.0L engine

2.5L Engine

The thermostat is located inside a housing attached to the front of the cylinder head.

1. Disconnect the negative battery cable.
2. Drain the cooling system to a level below the thermostat.
3. Remove the thermostat outlet-to-engine retainers, then remove outlet and the thermostat.

To install:

4. Using a putty knife, clean the gasket mounting surfaces.
5. Using RTV sealant or equivalent, place an ⅛ in. bead of sealant in the groove of the water outlet.
6. Installation is the reverse of removal, install the housing while the sealant is still wet.
7. Torque the thermostat housing-to-engine bolts to 18–20 ft. lbs. (24–27 Nm).
8. Refill the cooling system and check for leaks.

2.8L and 4.3L Engine

▶ See Figure 71

The thermostat is located between the water outlet and a housing built into the intake manifold.

1. Disconnect the negative battery cable.
2. Drain the cooling system to a level below the thermostat.
3. Remove the thermostat outlet-to-engine retainers (usually either 2 bolts or 1 bolt and 1 stud), then remove outlet from the intake manifold.
4. Remove the thermostat from the housing, noting the orientation for installation purposes.

To install:

5. Carefully clean the all traces of the old gasket or sealer from the housing and outlet.
6. Install the thermostat to the housing, oriented as noted during removal, then position a new gasket (if used).
7. Place a ⅛ in. bead of RTV sealant in the groove on the water outlet sealing surface, then install the outlet while the sealer is still wet.
8. Install the outlet retainers and tighten to 21 ft. lbs. (28 Nm) for the 2.8L and 4.3L (VIN Z) engine or to 14 ft. lbs. (19 Nm) for the 4.3L (VIN W) engine.
9. Properly fill the engine cooling system and check for leaks.

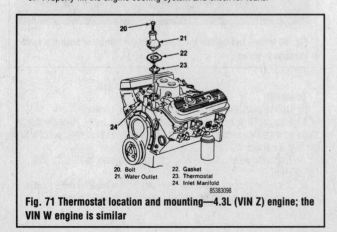

20. Bolt
21. Water Outlet
22. Gasket
23. Thermostat
24. Inlet Manifold

Fig. 71 Thermostat location and mounting—4.3L (VIN Z) engine; the VIN W engine is similar

Intake Manifold

REMOVAL & INSTALLATION

1.9L Engine

1. Disconnect the negative battery cable, then remove the air cleaner assembly.
2. Drain the engine cooling system to a level below the intake manifold.
3. Disconnect the upper radiator hose, the vacuum hose and the heater hose (from the rear of the intake manifold).
4. Disconnect the accelerator control cable. Disconnect the automatic choke and the solenoid electrical connectors.
5. From the distributor, disconnect the vacuum advance hose and the thermo-unit wiring electrical connector.
6. Disconnect the PCV valve from the rocker arm cover, then remove the oil level gauge guide tube-to-intake manifold bolt.
7. Disconnect the EGR pipe from the EGR valve adapter, the EGR valve and the adapter. Remove the nut from under the EGR valve.
8. Disconnect the AIR vacuum hose from the 3-way connector.
9. Remove the intake manifold-to-cylinder head nuts and the intake manifold from the engine.

To install:

10. Using a putty knife, clean the gasket mounting surfaces.
11. Inspect the manifold for cracks or damage. Using a straight edge and a feeler gauge, check manifold distortion on the sealing surfaces. Have the manifold surface ground if distortion exceeds 0.0157 in. (0.3988mm)
12. Install the intake manifold to the engine using a new gasket and sealant, then tighten the bolts to 17 ft. lbs. (23 Nm).
13. Connect the AIR vacuum hose to the 3-way connector.
14. Connect the EGR pipe to the EGR valve adapter, the EGR valve and the adapter.
15. Install the oil level gauge guide tube-to-intake manifold bolt, then connect the PCV valve to the rocker arm cover.
16. Engage the vacuum advance hose and the thermo-unit wiring electrical connector to the distributor.
17. Connect the accelerator control cable, then engage the automatic choke and the solenoid electrical connectors.
18. Connect the upper radiator hose, the vacuum hose and the heater hose (to the rear of the intake manifold).
19. Install the air cleaner assembly, then connect the negative battery cable.
20. Properly refill the engine cooling system, then check for leaks.

2.0L Engine

▶ See Figure 72

1. Disconnect the negative battery cable.
2. Remove the air cleaner, distributor cap, distributor hold-down nut and clamp.
3. Raise and support the front of the vehicle safely using jackstands. Remove the middle right hand bellhousing to block bolt and remove the wiring harness.

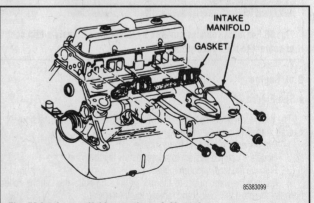

Fig. 72 Intake manifold mounting—2.0L engine

4. Drain the engine cooling system.

5. Tag and disconnect the vacuum hose and the primary wires from the coil.

6. Remove the fuel pump-to-engine bolts and allow the pump to hang. Be careful not to kink or damage the fuel lines.

7. If necessary for better underhood access, remove the jackstands and lower the vehicle.

8. Disconnect the accelerator cable, the fuel inlet line, then tag and disconnect the necessary vacuum hoses and wires. Remove the carburetor-to-intake manifold nuts, the carburetor and lift off the Early Fuel Evaporation (EFE) heater grid.

9. Disconnect the fuel vapor harness pipes from the cylinder head.

10. Disconnect the heater hose, bypass hose and any hoses and wires as necessary. Remove the intake manifold-to-cylinder head nuts/bolts, the intake manifold and the gasket.

To install:

11. Using a putty knife, clean the gasket mounting surfaces. Inspect the manifold for cracks, damage or distortion; if necessary, replace the intake manifold.

12. Install the intake manifold to the engine using a new gasket and sealant (as applicable), then tighten the intake manifold-to-cylinder head retainers to 25 ft. lbs. (34 Nm).

13. Connect the heater hose, bypass hose and any hoses and wires, which were removed from the intake.

14. Connect the fuel vapor harness pipes from the cylinder head.

15. Position the EFE grid and install the carburetor.

16. Connect the accelerator cable, the fuel inlet line, and the necessary vacuum hoses and wires.

17. Position the Early Fuel Evaporation (EFE) heater grid, then install the carburetor and secure with the carburetor-to-intake manifold nuts.

18. If lowered for underhood underhood access, raise and support the front of the truck safely using jackstands.

19. Reposition and secure the fuel pump.

20. Engage the vacuum hose and the primary wires to the coil.

21. Install the middle right hand bellhousing to block bolt and the wiring harness.

22. Remove the jackstands and carefully lower the truck.

23. Install the distributor distributor hold-down nut and clamp, then install the distributor cap.

24. Connect the negative battery cable and properly refill the engine cooling system.

25. Adjust the drive belts. Check and/or adjust the engine timing and idle speed, as necessary.

2.5L Engine

▶ See Figure 73

The intake manifold is located on the right-side of the cylinder head.

1. Properly relieve the fuel system pressure, then disconnect the negative battery cable.

2. Drain the engine cooling system and remove the air cleaner assembly.

3. Label and disconnect the wiring harnesses and connectors at the intake manifold.

4. Disconnect the accelerator, TVS, and cruise control cables (as equipped) with brackets.

5. Disconnect the EGR vacuum line.

6. Remove the emission sensor bracket at the manifold.

7. Tag and disconnect the fuel lines, vacuum lines and wiring from the TBI unit.

8. Disconnect the water pump bypass hose from the intake manifold.

9. Remove the alternator rear bracket.

10. Tag and disconnect the vacuum hoses and pipes from the intake manifold and the vacuum hold down at the thermostat and manifold.

11. If applicable, disconnect the heater hose at the intake.

12. Disconnect the coil wires.

13. Remove the intake manifold bolts, then remove the manifold from the engine.

To install:

14. Using a putty knife, clean the gasket mounting surfaces.

15. Installation the intake manifold to the engine using a new gasket and carefully thread the retainers.

16. Earlier model 2.5L engines use a manifold retained by bolts and studs, for these engines (used through the mid-1980's) tighten the retainers 25–37 ft. lbs. (34–50 Nm) using the sequence and torque values for each fastener as shown in the illustration. For later model engines which are retained only by bolts, slowly and evenly tighten all of the retainers to 25 ft. lbs. (34 Nm).

17. Engage the coil wires.

18. If applicable, connect the heater hose at the intake.

19. Connect the vacuum hoses and pipes to the manifold and the vacuum hold down at the thermostat as noted during removal.

20. Install the alternator rear bracket, then connect the coolant bypass hose.

21. Connect the fuel lines, vacuum lines and the wiring to the TBI unit.

22. Install the emissions sensor bracket, then connect the EGR valve hose.

23. Connect the accelerator, TVS and cruise control cables (as equipped) with brackets.

24. Engage and secure the wiring harness connectors at the intake, as noted during removal.

25. Install the air cleaner assembly, then connect the negative battery cable.

26. Properly refill the engine cooling system, then check for leaks.

2.8L Engine

▶ See Figures 74 thru 86

1. Properly relieve the fuel system pressure, then disconnect the negative battery cable.

2. Drain the engine cooling system and remove the air cleaner.

3. Tag and disengage the electrical connectors, vacuum hoses, fuel lines and accelerator cable(s) from the carburetor or TBI unit, as applicable.

4. If equipped with an AIR management system, remove the hose and the mounting bracket.

5. Label and disconnect the spark plug wires from the spark plugs and the electrical connectors from the ignition coil. Disconnect the coolant switch electrical connectors on the intake manifold.

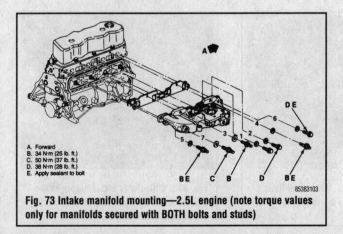

A. Forward
B. 34 N·m (25 lb. ft.)
C. 50 N·m (37 lb. ft.)
D. 38 N·m (28 lb. ft.)
E. Apply sealant to bolt

85383103

Fig. 73 Intake manifold mounting—2.5L engine (note torque values only for manifolds secured with BOTH bolts and studs)

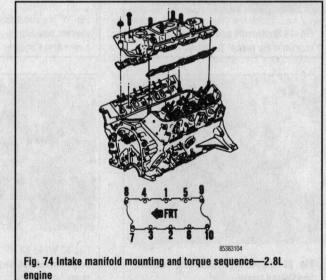

85383104

Fig. 74 Intake manifold mounting and torque sequence—2.8L engine

6. Remove the distributor cap (with the wires connected). Matchmark and remove the distributor from the intake manifold and engine. For details, please refer to the procedures located earlier in this Section.

➡**DO NOT crank the engine with the distributor removed or distributor installation will be more difficult.**

7. Disconnect the EGR vacuum line and the evaporative emission hoses. Remove the pipe brackets from the rocker arm covers.

8. Remove the heater and upper radiator hoses from the intake manifold.

9. If equipped, remove the power brake vacuum hoses from the intake manifold.

10. Remove the rocker arm covers.

11. Remove the intake manifold-to-engine nuts and bolts, then the intake manifold from the engine.

To install:

12. Using a putty knife, clean the mating surfaces of remaining gasket and sealer. Take extra care to keep gasket debris out of the lifter valley and the rest of the engine. Since the manifold is made from aluminum, be sure to inspect it for warpage and/or cracks; if necessary, replace it.

13. Position new intake manifold gaskets to the engine and apply a ³⁄₁₆ in. (5mm) bead of RTV sealant to the front and rear of the engine block.

➡**The gaskets are marked "Right-Side" and "Left-Side"; DO NOT interchange them. The gaskets may have to be cut slightly to fit past the center pushrods; DO NOT cut any more material than necessary. Hold the gaskets in place by extending the ridge bead of sealer ¼ in. onto the gasket ends.**

14. Position the intake manifold taking care not to disturb the gaskets. Make sure the areas between the case ridges and the intake manifold are completely sealed, then carefully thread the retainers. For 1993 engines, before threading the 2 center retainers (No.s 1 and 2 in the torque sequence) apply a coating of 9985427 or an equivalent sealer to the threads.

15. Tighten the intake manifold-to-cylinder head fasteners to 23 ft. lbs. (31 Nm) using the proper torque sequence.

Fig. 75 If it is easier, tag and disconnect the spark plug wires before removing the distributor cap

Fig. 76 Disengage the wiring from the ignition coil

Fig. 77 On 2.8L engines, there are usually 2 coil connectors (a small one which engages the top of the larger one)

Fig. 78 Matchmark and remove the distributor from the rear of the intake manifold

Fig. 79 Tag and disconnect all necessary vacuum connections, in this case the power brake booster

Fig. 80 Remove the coolant hose from the thermostat housing water outlet

Fig. 81 Remove the coolant hose from the front of the intake

Fig. 82 When all wires, hoses and lines are disconnected from the manifold, it is ready for removal

Fig. 83 If difficulty is encountered, make sure all bolts are removed, then use a prybar to help break the seal

Fig. 84 Carefully lift the manifold assembly from the engine

Fig. 85 Remove the old intake manifold gaskets from the block and cylinder heads

Fig. 86 Remove all gasket material, BE careful not to damage the surface (and keep debris out of the engine)

16. Install the rocker arm covers.

17. If equipped, connect the power brake vacuum hoses at the intake manifold.

18. Connect the heater and upper radiator hoses from the intake manifold.

19. Install the pipe brackets to the rocker arm covers, then Disconnect the EGR vacuum line and the evaporative emission hoses.

20. Align the marks made during removal and install the distributor assembly, then install the distributor cap and spark plug wires.

21. Engage the electrical connectors to the ignition coil and to the coolant switch on the intake manifold.

22. If equipped with an AIR management system, install the hose and the mounting bracket.

23. Engage the electrical connectors, vacuum hoses, fuel lines and the accelerator cable(s) to the carburetor or TBI unit, as applicable.

24. Install the air cleaner assembly, then connect the negative battery cable.

25. Properly refill the engine cooling system, then check for leaks.

26. Adjust the ignition timing, the idle speed (if possible) and check the coolant level after the engine has warmed up.

4.3L Engine

VIN Z ENGINE, EXCEPT MFI-TURBO

▶ See Figure 87

1. Disconnect the negative battery cable and properly relieve the fuel system pressure.

2. Drain the cooling system.

3. Remove the air cleaner and heat stove tube.

4. Remove the two braces at the rear of the serpentine drive belt tensioner.

5. Disconnect the upper radiator hose.

6. Remove the emissions relays along with the bracket, then disconnect the wiring harness from the retaining clips and position aside. Disconnect the ground cable from the intake manifold stud.

7. Remove the power brake vacuum pipe, then disconnect the heater hose pipe at the manifold and fuel lines at the TBI unit.

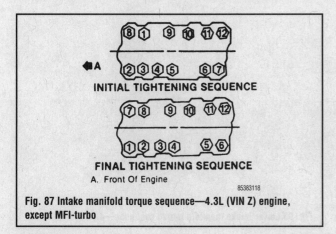

INITIAL TIGHTENING SEQUENCE

FINAL TIGHTENING SEQUENCE

A. Front Of Engine

Fig. 87 Intake manifold torque sequence—4.3L (VIN Z) engine, except MFI-turbo

8. Remove the ignition coil, then disengage the electrical connectors at the sensors on the manifold.

9. Matchmark and remove the distributor from the engine. For details, please refer to the procedure earlier in this section.

➡ **For ease of installation, DO NOT crank the engine with the distributor removed.**

10. Tag and disengage the wires and hoses from the TBI unit.

11. Disconnect the the EGR hose, then disconnect the throttle, TVS and cruise control cables (as equipped).

12. Remove the intake manifold retaining studs and/or bolts, then remove the manifold and gaskets.

To install:

13. Using a putty knife, carefully clean the gasket mounting surfaces. Be sure to inspect the manifold for warpage and/or cracks; if necessary, replace it.

14. Position the gaskets to the cylinder head with the port blocking plates to the rear, then apply a ³⁄₁₆ in. (5mm) bead of RTV sealant to the front and rear of the engine block at the block-to-manifold mating surface. Extend the bead ½ in. (13mm) up each cylinder head to seal and retain the gaskets.

15. Install the intake manifold taking care not to disturb the gaskets, then tighten the manifold retainers to 35 ft. lbs. (48 Nm) using the proper torque sequence.

16. Engage the TVS, cruise control and/or throttle cables, as equipped.

17. Connect the EGR hose then engage the wires and hoses at the TBI unit as noted during removal

18. Align and install the distributor assembly.

19. Install the ignition coil, then connect the fuel pipes.

20. Connect the heater hose pipe and the power brake vacuum pipe.

21. Connect the ground cable to the intake manifold stud, then position and secure the wiring harness using the clips.

22. Install the emissions relays along with their bracket, then connect the upper radiator hose.

23. Install the brace at the rear of the drive belt tensioner, then install the air cleaner and heat stove tube.

24. Connect the negative battery cable, then properly refill the engine cooling system.

25. Run the engine and check for leaks.

VIN Z MFI-TURBO ENGINE

▶ See Figures 88 and 89

1. Properly relive the fuel system pressure and disconnect the negative battery cable.

2. Drain the engine cooling system and the charge air cooling system.

3. Loosen the wing nut at the air cleaner, then position the air cleaner and duct aside.

4. Loosen the charge air cooler clamps, then remove the ducts and hoses.

5. Remove the charge air cooler from the supports, then remove the air cooler lateral (center) support.

6. Disengage the electrical connectors and hoses from the EVRV solenoid, the ignition coil and the MAP sensor located on the multi-use bracket.

7. Remove the multi-use bracket from the lower intake manifold assembly.

8. Tag and disengage the hoses and electrical connectors from the upper intake manifold assembly.

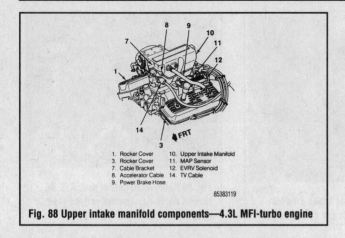

Fig. 88 Upper intake manifold components—4.3L MFI-turbo engine

1. Rocker Cover
3. Rocker Cover
7. Cable Bracket
8. Accelerator Cable
9. Power Brake Hose
10. Upper Intake Manifold
11. MAP Sensor
12. EVRV Solenoid
14. TV Cable

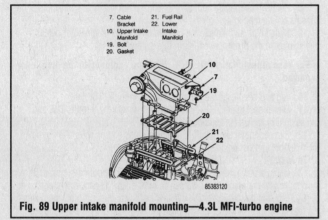

Fig. 89 Upper intake manifold mounting—4.3L MFI-turbo engine

7. Cable Bracket
10. Upper Intake Manifold
19. Bolt
20. Gasket
21. Fuel Rail
22. Lower Intake Manifold

9. Loosen the throttle body retaining bolts, then remove the throttle body, gasket and cable bracket from the upper intake manifold.

10. Remove the upper intake manifold retaining bolts, then remove the manifold and gasket.

11. Disconnect the heater hose from the lower intake manifold.

12. Remove the charge air cooler coolant inlet pipe from the lower intake manifold, then disconnect it from the radiator by loosening the clamp and disengaging the hose.

13. Tag and disengage the wiring connectors from the fuel injectors, then disconnect the fuel pipes from the fuel rail assembly.

14. Loosen and remove the retaining bolts, then remove the fuel rail assembly (rail and injectors) from the lower manifold.

15. If equipped, remove the rear A/C brace,.

16. Disconnect the turbocharger coolant return line, then remove the upper radiator hose from the lower intake manifold.

17. Remove the ground strap from the lower intake manifold, then disengage the coolant sensor connector.

18. Tag and disconnect the spark plug wires from the distributor, remove the distributor cap and remove the distributor from the engine. Be sure to matchmark the distributor and rotor with the engine before removal.

19. Remove the lower intake manifold bolts and studs, then remove the manifold from the engine.

To install:

20. Using a putty knife, carefully clean the gasket mounting surfaces. Be sure to inspect the manifold for warpage and/or cracks; if necessary, replace it.

21. Position the gaskets to the cylinder head with the port blocking plates to the rear, then apply a ³⁄₁₆ in. (5mm) bead of RTV sealant to the front and rear of the engine block at the block-to-manifold mating surface. Extend the bead ½ in. (13mm) up each cylinder head to seal and retain the gaskets.

22. Install the lower intake manifold taking care not to disturb the gaskets, then tighten the manifold retainers to 35 ft. lbs. (48 Nm).

23. Align the marks made during removal and install the distributor to the engine. Install the distributor cap and engage the spark plug wires.

24. Engage the coolant sensor electrical connector, then connect the ground strap.

25. Connect the upper radiator hose and the turbocharger coolant return line, then install the A/C compressor rear brace (if equipped).

26. Install the fuel rail and injectors, then connect the fuel pipes to the rail and engage the wiring connectors to the injectors. Tighten the fuel rail bolts to 58 inch lbs. (6.5 Nm) and the pipe fittings to 16 ft. lbs. (22 Nm).

27. Place the charge air cooler coolant inlet pipe into position on the lower intake manifold, then connect the hose and clamp from the radiator to the charge air cooler inlet pipe.

28. Connect the heater hose to the lower intake manifold.

29. Install the upper intake manifold using a new gasket, then tighten the retaining bolts (starting from the 2 middle bolts working outward to each side) to 18 ft. lbs. (24 Nm).

30. Install the throttle body and cable bracket using a new throttle body gasket, then tighten the retaining bolts to 18 ft. lbs. (24 Nm).

31. Engage the upper intake manifold connectors and hoses, then install the multi-use bracket. Engage the hoses and wiring to the MAP sensor, ignition coil and EVRV solenoid.

32. Install the charge air cooler lateral support and finger-tighten the retaining nut.

33. Install and secure the charge air cooler supports, then tighten the lateral support nut.

34. Install the charge air cooler hoses and ducts, then secure using the clamps.

35. Connect the negative battery cable.

36. Properly refill the charge air cooling system and the engine cooling system.

VIN W ENGINE

♦ See Figures 90 and 91

➡**If only the upper intake manifold is being removed, the fuel system pressure does not need to be released. ALWAYS release the pressure before disconnecting any fuel lines.**

1. Remove the plastic cover, then properly relieve the fuel system pressure and disconnect the negative battery cable.

2. Drain the engine cooling system, then remove the air cleaner and air inlet duct.

3. Disengage the wiring harness from the necessary upper intake components including:

- Throttle Position (TP) sensor
- Idle Air Control (IAC) motor
- Manifold Absolute Pressure (MAP) sensor
- Intake Manifold Tuning Valve (IMTV)

4. Disengage the throttle linkage from the upper intake manifold, then remove the ignition coil.

5. Disconnect the PCV hose at the rear of the upper intake manifold, then tag and disengage the vacuum hoses from both the front and rear of the upper intake.

6. Remove the upper intake manifold bolts and studs, making sure to note or mark the location of all studs to assure proper installation. Remove the upper intake manifold from the engine.

7. Disengage the distributor wiring and matchmark the distributor, then remove the assembly from the engine.

8. Disconnect the upper radiator hose at the thermostat housing and the heater hose at the lower intake manifold.

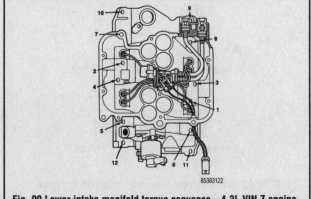

Fig. 90 Lower intake manifold torque sequence—4.3L VIN Z engine

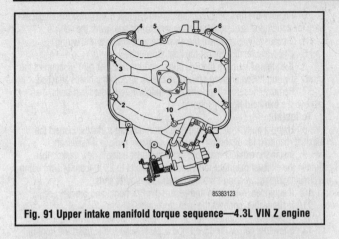

Fig. 91 Upper intake manifold torque sequence—4.3L VIN Z engine

9. Disconnect the fuel supply and return lines at the rear of the lower intake manifold.

10. Remove the pencil brace (A/C compressor bracket-to-lower intake manifold).

11. Disengage the wiring harness connectors from the necessary lower intake components including:
- Fuel injector
- Exhaust Gas Recirculation (EGR) valve
- Engine Coolant Temperature (ECT) sensor

12. Remove the lower intake manifold retaining bolts, then remove the manifold from the engine.

13. Using a putty knife, carefully clean the gasket mounting surfaces. Be sure to inspect the manifold for warpage and/or cracks; if necessary, replace it.

14. Position the gaskets to the cylinder head with the port blocking plates to the rear and the "this side up" stamps facing upward, then apply a ³⁄₁₆ in. (5mm) bead of RTV sealant to the front and rear of the engine block at the block-to-manifold mating surface. Extend the bead ½ in. (13mm) up each cylinder head to seal and retain the gaskets.

15. Install the lower intake manifold taking care not to disturb the gaskets, then tighten the manifold retainers to 35 ft. lbs. (48 Nm) using the proper torque sequence.

16. Engage the wiring harness to the lower manifold components, including the injector, EGR valve and ECT sensor.

17. Install the pencil brace to the A/C compressor bracket and the lower intake manifold.

18. Connect the fuel supply and return lines to the rear of the lower intake. Temporarily reconnect the negative battery cable, then pressurize the fuel system (by cycling the ignition without starting the engine) and check for leaks. Disconnect the negative battery cable and continue installation.

19. Connect the heater hose to the lower intake and the upper radiator hose to the thermostat housing.

20. Align the matchmarks and install the distributor assembly, then engage the wiring.

21. Position a new upper intake manifold gasket on the engine, making sure the green sealing lines are facing upward.

22. Install the upper intake manifold being careful not to pinch the fuel injector wires between the manifolds.

23. Install the manifold retainers, making sure the studs are properly positioned, then tighten them using the proper sequence to 124 inch lbs. (14 Nm).

24. Connect the PCV hose to the rear of the upper intake manifold and the vacuum hoses to both the front and rear of the manifold assembly.

25. Connect the throttle linkage to the upper intake, then install the ignition coil.

26. Engage the necessary wiring to the upper intake components including the TP sensor, IAC motor, MAP sensor and the IMTV.

27. Install the plastic cover, the air cleaner and air inlet duct.

28. Connect the negative battery cable, then properly refill the engine cooling system.

Exhaust Manifold

❊❊❊ CAUTION

ALWAYS use extreme caution when working around the exhaust system. Make sure the engine has had time to thoroughly cool or personal injury from exhaust system burns may occur. Also, be sure to wear safety goggles when working on exhaust parts and they are likely to rust and loose particle will be falling from them during the procedure.

REMOVAL & INSTALLATION

▸ **See Figures 92, 93 and 94**

1.9L Engine

1. Disconnect the negative battery cable, then remove the air cleaner assembly and hot air hose.

2. Raise and support the front of the vehicle safely using jackstands.

3. Disconnect the exhaust pipe and the EGR pipe from the exhaust manifold, then lower the vehicle.

4. If equipped with an A/C compressor or a P/S pump, remove the drive belt(s), the compressor/pump (move them aside) and the mounting brackets.

5. Remove the exhaust manifold shield and the heat stove (if equipped).

6. Remove the exhaust manifold-to-cylinder head nuts, then remove the manifold from the engine.

To install:

7. Using a putty knife, clean the gasket mounting surfaces. Inspect the exhaust manifold for distortion, cracks or damage; replace it, if necessary.

8. Install the exhaust manifold to the engine using a new gasket, then tighten the exhaust manifold-to-cylinder head nuts to 16 ft. lbs. (22 Nm). Tighten the nuts gradually using a sequence, starting with the center and working outwards.

9. Install the remaining components in the reverse order of removal, then remove the jackstands and carefully lower the truck.

10. Install the air cleaner and hot air hoses, then connect the negative battery cable.

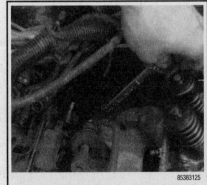

Fig. 92 Unbolt the exhaust pipe from the rear of the manifold

Fig. 93 Loosen and remove the manifold-to-cylinder head retainers (2.8L shown)

Fig. 94 Remove the exhaust manifold from the side of the cylinder head

2.0L Engine

▶ See Figure 95

1. Disconnect the negative battery cable and remove the air cleaner assembly.
2. Raise and support the front of the vehicle safely using jackstands.
3. Disconnect the exhaust pipe from the exhaust manifold.
4. If equipped with an air injection reaction (AIR) system, remove the AIR hose, the AIR pipe bracket bolt and the dipstick tube bracket.
5. Remove the fuel vapor canister harness (steel) pipes.
6. Remove the exhaust manifold-to-cylinder head bolts and the manifold from the engine.

To install:

7. Using a putty knife, clean the gasket mounting surfaces. Inspect the exhaust manifold for distortion, cracks or damage; replace it, if necessary.
8. Install the exhaust manifold to the engine using a new gasket, then tighten the exhaust manifold-to-cylinder head bolts to 26 ft. lbs. (35 Nm). Tighten the fasteners gradually in a sequence, starting at the center and working outwards.

2.5L Engine

▶ See Figure 96

The exhaust manifold is located on the left-side of the engine.

1. Disconnect the negative battery cable.
2. Remove the air cleaner and heat stove pipe.
3. Remove the A/C compressor (if equipped), drive belt, and the rear adjusting bracket (if used). Lay the compressor aside in the engine compartment.
4. Remove the dipstick tube and bracket.
5. Disconnect the exhaust pipe from the exhaust manifold.
6. Disengage the electrical connector from the oxygen sensor.
7. Remove the exhaust manifold-to-engine bolts/washers and the manifold from the engine.

To install:

8. Using a putty knife, clean the gasket mounting surfaces.
9. Install the manifold to the engine using a new gasket, then tighten the center retainers 36 ft. lbs. (49 Nm) and the outer retainers to 32 ft. lbs. (43 Nm).
10. Engage the oxygen sensor electrical connector, then connect and secure the exhaust pipe to the manifold.
11. Install the dipstick tube and bracket, then reposition and install the A/C compressor (if equipped), rear adjusting bracket (if used) and the drive belt.
12. Install the air cleaner and the heat stove pipe.
13. Connect the negative battery cable.

2.8L Engine

▶ See Figure 97

LEFT-SIDE

1. Disconnect the negative battery cable, then raise and support the front of the vehicle safely using jackstands.
2. Disconnect the exhaust pipe from the exhaust manifold.

3. Remove the rear exhaust manifold-to-cylinder head bolts, then if necessary for underhood access, remove the jackstands and lower the vehicle.
4. If necessary, disconnect the air management hoses and wiring.
5. If applicable, disconnect the heat stove tube.
6. If equipped, remove the P/S pump and bracket; DO NOT disconnect the power steering hoses, instead reposition the pump with the hoses attached.
7. Remove the remaining exhaust manifold-to-cylinder head bolts, then remove the manifold from the engine.

To install:

8. Using a putty knife, clean the gasket mounting surfaces. Inspect the exhaust manifold for distortion, cracks or damage; replace if necessary.
9. Install the exhaust manifold to the cylinder using a new gasket, then tighten the exhaust manifold-to-cylinder head bolts to 25 ft. lbs. (34 Nm) using a circular pattern, working from the center to the outer ends.
10. If equipped, reposition and secure the P/S pump and bracket
11. If applicable, connect the heat stove tube.
12. If necessary, reconnect the air management hoses and wiring.
13. If lowered earlier for underhood access, raise and support the front of the truck safely using jackstands.
14. Connect the exhaust pipe to the manifold.
15. Remove the jackstands and carefully lower the vehicle, then connect the negative battery cable.

RIGHT-SIDE

1. Disconnect the negative battery cable, then raise and support the front of the vehicle safely using jackstands.
2. Disconnect the exhaust pipe from the exhaust manifold.
3. Remove the rear exhaust manifold-to-cylinder head bolts, then if necessary for underhood access, remove the jackstands and lower the vehicle.
4. Remove the AIR system diverter valve and heat shield, then remove the AIR system pump and alternator brackets.
5. If necessary, disconnect the air management hoses and wiring.
6. Remove the remaining exhaust manifold-to-cylinder head bolts, then remove the manifold from the engine.

To install:

7. Using a putty knife, clean the gasket mounting surfaces. Inspect the exhaust manifold for distortion, cracks or damage; replace if necessary.
8. Install the exhaust manifold to the cylinder using a new gasket, then tighten the exhaust manifold-to-cylinder head bolts to 25 ft. lbs. (34 Nm) using a circular pattern, working from the center to the outer ends.
9. If necessary, reconnect the air management hoses and wiring.
10. Install the AIR system pump and alternator brackets, then install the AIR system diverter valve and heat shield.
11. If lowered earlier for underhood access, raise and support the front of the truck safely using jackstands.
12. Connect the exhaust pipe to the manifold.
13. Remove the jackstands and carefully lower the vehicle, then connect the negative battery cable.

4.3L Engine, Except MFI-Turbo

1. Disconnect the negative battery cable, then raise and support the front of the vehicle safely using jackstands.

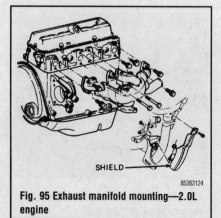

Fig. 95 Exhaust manifold mounting—2.0L engine

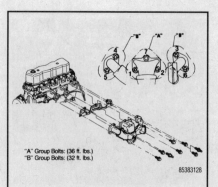

"A" Group Bolts: (36 ft. lbs.)
"B" Group Bolts: (32 ft. lbs.)

Fig. 96 Exhaust manifold installation—2.5L engine

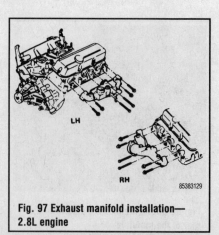

Fig. 97 Exhaust manifold installation—2.8L engine

➡It will be easier if the vehicle is only supported to a height where underhood access is still possible, the vehicle may be left in position for the entire procedure. If the vehicle is raised too high for underhood access, it will have to lowered, raised and lowered again during the procedure.

2. Disconnect the exhaust pipe from the exhaust manifold.

3. If necessary for underhood access, remove the jackstands and lower the vehicle.

4. Tag and disconnect the spark plug wires from the plugs and from the retaining clips.

5. If removing the left side manifold:

  a. Remove the air cleaner with heat stove pipe and cold air intake pipe.

  b. Remove the power steering/alternator rear bracket.

  c. Check for sufficient clearance between the manifold and the intermediate steering shaft. On some models it will be necessary to disconnect the intermediate shaft from the steering gear in order to reposition the shaft for clearance.

6. If necessary when removing the right side manifold, unbolt the A/C compressor and bracket, then position the assembly aside. DO NOT disconnect the lines or allow them to become kinked or otherwise damaged.

7. If necessary for the right side manifold, remove the spark plugs, dipstick tube and wiring.

8. Unbend the locktangs then remove the exhaust manifold retaining bolts, washers and tab washers. Remove the exhaust manifold, then remove and discard the old gaskets.

To install:

9. Using a putty knife, clean the gasket mounting surfaces. Inspect the exhaust manifold for distortion, cracks or damage; replace if necessary.

10. Install the exhaust manifold to the cylinder using a new gasket, then tighten the exhaust manifold-to-cylinder head bolts to 26 ft. lbs. (36 Nm) on the center exhaust tube and to 20 ft. lbs. (28 Nm) on the front and rear exhaust tubes. Once the bolts are tightened, bend the tabs on the washers back over the heads of all bolts in order to lock them in position.

11. If removed on the right side, install the spark plugs, dipstick tube and wiring.

12. If unbolted, reposition and secure the A/C compressor and bracket assembly.

13. If the left manifold was removed:

  a. If unbolted, reconnect the intermediate shaft to the steering gear.

  b. Install the power steering/alternator rear bracket.

  c. Install the air cleaner along with the heat stove pipe and cold air intake pipe.

14. Connect the spark plug wires to the retainer clips and to the plugs as noted during removal.

15. If lowered for underhood access, raise and support the front of the vehicle again using the jackstands.

16. Connect the exhaust pipe to the manifold.

17. Remove the jackstands and carefully lower the vehicle, then connect the negative battery cable.

4.3L MFI-Turbo Engine

LEFT SIDE

1. Disconnect the negative battery cable, then remove the air cleaner and duct.

2. Remove the turbocharger air inlet elbow, then remove the upper fan shroud.

3. Loosen the fan nuts, then remove the serpentine drive belt. Remove the fan and pulley assembly.

4. Using a suitable pulley remover (such as J-25034-B or equivalent) pull the power steering pump pulley from the pump.

5. Remove the rear brace from the alternator.

6. Raise and support the front of the truck safely using jackstands.

7. Remove the left tire and wheel, then remove the left wheelhouse panel.

8. Disconnect the power steering inlet and outlet hoses from the pump. Immediately plug all openings in order to prevent system contamination or excessive fluid loss.

9. Disconnect the oil filter line bracket from the power steering pump.

10. Disconnect the intermediate shaft.

11. Unbolt the exhaust crossover pipe from the manifold.

12. Remove the power steering pump and rear brace as an assembly from the front bracket.

13. Tag and disconnect the wires from the spark plugs, then remove the plugs from the left cylinder head.

14. Bend back the locktabs, then remove the exhaust manifold bolts, studs, locktabs, washers and heat shields. Remove the exhaust manifold.

To install:

15. Using a putty knife, clean the gasket mounting surfaces. Inspect the exhaust manifold for distortion, cracks or damage; replace if necessary.

16. Install the exhaust manifold to the cylinder using a new gasket, then tighten retainers to 33 ft. lbs. (45 Nm). Once the retainers are tightened, bend the tabs on the washers back over the hex-heads of all bolts/studs in order to lock them in position.

17. Install and tighten the spark plugs, then connect the spark plug wires.

18. Install the power steering pump and rear brace to the front bracket. Tighten the bracket bolts to 37 ft. lbs. (50 Nm) and the rear brace nut to 33 ft. lbs. (45 Nm).

19. Connect the crossover pipe and tighten the retaining nuts to 12 ft. lbs. (16 Nm).

20. Connect the intermediate shaft, then secure the oil filter line bracket to the power steering pump.

21. Remove the plugs, then connect the power steering outlet and inlet hoses to the pump. Tighten the hose fittings to 20 ft. lbs. (27 Nm).

22. Install the left wheelhousing panel, then install the left front tire and wheel assembly.

23. Remove the jackstands and carefully lower the vehicle.

24. Install the rear brace to the alternator and tighten the retaining bolt to 18 ft. lbs. (25 Nm).

25. Install the power steering pump pulley using a suitable installer tool.

26. Install the fan and pulley to the water pump, then install the serpentine drive belt. With the belt installed, tighten the fan and pulley nuts to 18 ft. lbs. (24 Nm).

27. Install the upper fan shroud, then install the turbocharger air inlet elbow.

28. Install the air cleaner and duct.

29. Connect the negative battery cable.

30. Refill the power steering pump and bleed air from the system.

RIGHT SIDE

1. Disconnect the negative battery cable, followed by the positive cable from the battery. Loosen the battery hold-down clamp and remove the battery from the vehicle.

2. Drain the engine cooling system, then remove the battery tray and vacuum tank.

3. Disconnect the turbocharger oil feed hose and the coolant return pipe.

4. Disengage the oxygen sensor connector, then raise and support the vehicle safely using jackstands.

➡It will be easier if the vehicle is only supported to a height where underhood access is still possible, the vehicle may be left in position for the entire procedure. If the vehicle is raised too high for underhood access, it will have to lowered, raised and lowered again during the procedure.

5. Remove the right front tire and wheel, then remove the right wheelhousing panel.

6. Disconnect the mufflers and tailpipe from the catalytic converter.

7. Remove the catalytic converter support bolts, then if necessary for underhood access, install the wheel, remove the jackstands and carefully lower the vehicle.

8. Disengage the turbocharger solenoid electrical connector and loosen the turbocharger coolant feed line.

9. If the vehicle was lowered, raise and support it safely using jackstands, then remove the turbocharger outlet pipe nuts.

10. Remove the turbocharger outlet pipe support bolt. Move the outlet pipe and catalytic converter away from the turbocharger.

11. Remove the turbocharger oil return pipe from the turbocharger, then remove the turbocharger mounting nuts.

12. Disconnect the coolant feed line from the turbocharger, then remove the turbocharger assembly.

13. Disconnect the exhaust crossover pipe from the manifold.

14. Tag and disconnect the wires from the spark plugs, then remove the plugs from the left cylinder head.

15. Remove the charger air cooler lower supports.

16. Bend back the locktabs, then remove the exhaust manifold bolts, studs, locktabs, washers and heat shields. Remove the exhaust manifold.

To install:

17. Using a putty knife, clean the gasket mounting surfaces. Inspect the exhaust manifold for distortion, cracks or damage; replace if necessary.

18. Install the exhaust manifold to the cylinder using a new gasket, then tighten retainers to 33 ft. lbs. (45 Nm). Once the retainers are tightened, bend the tabs on the washers back over the hex-heads of all bolts/studs in order to lock them in position.

19. Install and tighten the spark plugs, then connect the spark plug wires.

20. Install the charge air cooler lower supports.

21. Connect the exhaust crossover pipe to the manifold, then tighten the retaining nuts to 12 ft. lbs. (16 Nm).

22. Position the turbocharger, then connect the coolant feed pipe and loosely install the bolt.

23. Loosely install the turbocharger mounting nuts followed by the return pipe and bolts. Tighten the coolant feed pipe bolt to 26 ft. lbs. (35 Nm), then mounting nuts to 33 ft. lbs. (45 Nm) and the oil return pipe bolts to 35 inch lbs. (4 Nm).

24. Install the turbocharger outlet pipe and nuts along with the outlet pipe support bolt. Tighten the pipe nuts to 41 ft. lbs. (55 Nm) followed by the support bolt to 22 ft. lbs. (30 Nm).

25. Engage the turbocharger solenoid electrical connector.

26. Loosely install the catalytic converter support bolts, then engage the mufflers and tailpipe to the catalytic converter. Tighten the support bolts to 25 ft. lbs. (34 Nm), then tighten the tailpipe bolts to 24 ft. lbs. (32 Nm).

27. If reinstalled to lower the vehicle earlier, remove the tire and wheel assembly, then install the wheelhousing panel.

28. Install the tire and wheel assembly, then remove the jackstands and carefully lower the vehicle.

29. Engage the oxygen sensor electrical connector.

30. Connect the turbocharger oil feed hose and the coolant return pipe. Tighten the oil hose fitting to 13 ft. lbs. (17 Nm) and the coolant pipe fittings to 16 ft. lbs. (22 Nm).

31. Install the battery tray and vacuum tank.

32. Install the battery and secure using the hold-down clamp.

33. Connect the positive cable, then the negative cable to the battery.

34. Properly refill the engine cooling system.

Turbocharger

The special edition 1991–92 Syclone was equipped with a high performance 4.3L MFI-Turbo engine. The Turbocharger and multi-port fuel injection are special to this vehicle and require some service procedures which are unique to the rest of the S/T truck series.

PRECAUTIONS

Proper maintenance practices MUST be followed in order to prolong the performance and life of the turbocharger. Failures in the turbocharger system are often caused by oil lag, restriction or lack of oil flow, dirty oil or foreign objects entering the turbocharger.

When working on or around the turbocharger system always follow these precautions:

• DO NOT allow dust, sand or other foreign material to enter the turbocharger. Dust or sand will erode the compressor wheel blades, while uneven blade wear can produce shaft motion causing bearing failure. Large or heavy objects will completely destroy the turbocharger and could cause severe damage to the engine.

• The air cleaner system must be properly maintained. A plugged or restricted air cleaner will reduce air pressure and volume at the compressor air inlet. The pressure drop will lower turbocharger performance and may cause oil pullover during idle. Oil pullover is a compressor end oil seal leak without seal part failure.

• The oil lube system must be properly maintained. If dirt or foreign material is introduced into the turbocharger bearing system by lube oil, the center housing bearing bore surfaces will wear. Contaminants act as an abrasive cutting tool and will eventually wear through bearing surfaces causing turbocharger noise and poor performance. Excessive noise and/or oil smoke may be noticed. Remember that oil will completely bypass the filter if the element becomes clogged. Adhere closely to oil and filter change intervals on turbocharged vehicles.

• DO NOT allow sludge to build up in the turbocharger. Sludge may occur if oil oxidation or breakdown occurs. Possible causes would include, engine overheating, excessive combustion products from piston blow-by, non-compatible oils, engine coolant leakage into the oil, incorrect grade/quality of oil or improper oil change intervals. If turbine end oil leakage is noted, check the tur-

bocharger oil drain tube and the crankcase breathers. Remove any restrictions and check again for leaks.

• The charge air cooler system must be properly maintained. Only use the proper type and quantity of coolant in the system. If coolant becomes dirty or contaminated, the system must be flushed and refilled with fresh coolant. For system draining and refilling procedures, please refer to Section 1 of this manual.

REMOVAL & INSTALLATION

◗ **See Figures 98 and 99**

1. Drain the engine cooling system, then remove the air intake duct and the turbocharger air intake duct.

2. Disconnect the negative battery cable, followed by the positive cable from the battery. Loosen the battery hold-down clamp and remove the battery from the vehicle.

3. Remove the battery tray and vacuum tank.

4. Remove the nut and disconnect the turbocharger oil feed line, then disengage the electrical connector from the solenoid.

5. Loosen the turbocharger coolant return line clamp nut, then disconnect the coolant return line assembly.

6. Raise and support the front of the truck safely using jackstands.

7. Remove the right tire and wheel, then remove the wheelhouse panel retaining screws and remove the panel for access.

8. If necessary, disengage the oxygen sensor electrical connector, then remove the nut from the turbocharger and the bolt from the outlet pipe support bracket. Remove the clamp from the catalytic converter and bolts from the converter support, then remove the turbocharger outlet pipe.

9. Remove the retaining bolts from the turbocharger oil return pipe, then remove the return pipe and gasket from the turbocharger assembly.

10. Remove the turbocharger mounting nuts.

11. Disconnect the coolant feed line from the turbocharger, then remove the turbocharger assembly.

To install:

12. Inspect and clean the turbocharger and manifold mounting surfaces.

13. Position the turbocharger, then connect the coolant feed pipe with gaskets and loosely install the bolt.

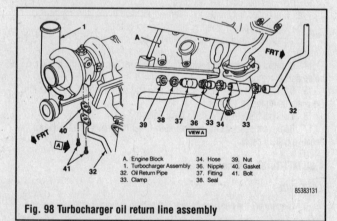

A. Engine Block	34. Hose	39. Nut
1. Turbocharger Assembly	36. Nipple	40. Gasket
32. Oil Return Pipe	37. Fitting	41. Bolt
33. Clamp	38. Seal	

85383131

Fig. 98 Turbocharger oil return line assembly

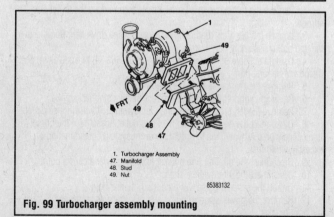

1. Turbocharger Assembly
47. Manifold
48. Stud
49. Nut

85383132

Fig. 99 Turbocharger assembly mounting

14. Loosely install the turbocharger mounting nuts followed by the oil feed pipe line fitting. Tighten the coolant feed pipe bolt to 26 ft. lbs. (35 Nm), then the turbocharger mounting nuts to 33 ft. lbs. (45 Nm) and the oil feed line fitting to 13 ft. lbs. (16 Nm).

15. Connect the turbocharger oil return pipe and gaskets, then tighten the line bolt to 35 inch lbs. (4 Nm).

16. Connect the turbocharger coolant return line assembly and tighten the line nut to 16 ft. lbs. (22 Nm). Secure the coolant return line clamp and tighten to 16 inch lbs. (1.8 Nm).

17. Install the turbocharger outlet pipe to the catalytic converter and turbocharger. Install the nuts to the turbocharger, then clamp to the converter, the bolts to the converter support and the the bolt to the outlet pipe bracket. Tighten the turbocharger nuts to 41 ft. lbs. (55 Nm), the converter clamp nuts to 42 ft. lbs. (57 Nm), the support bracket bolt to 22 ft. lbs. (30 Nm) and the converter support bolts to 25 ft. lbs. (34 Nm).

18. If disengaged, connect the oxygen sensor wiring to the harness.

19. Install the wheelhousing panel, then install the tire and wheel assembly. Remove the jackstands and carefully lower the vehicle.

20. Engage the turbocharger solenoid electrical connector.

21. Install the battery tray and vacuum tank.

22. Install the battery and secure using the hold-down clamp.

23. Install the air intake duct and the turbocharger air intake duct.

24. Connect the positive cable, then the negative cable to the battery.

25. Properly refill the engine cooling system.

Radiator

REMOVAL & INSTALLATION

▶ **See Figures 100 thru 109**

1. Disconnect the negative battery cable.
2. Drain the engine cooling system.
3. If equipped with the MFI-Turbo engine:

   a. Remove the air cleaner and duct, then remove the turbocharger inlet elbow.

   b. Disconnect the positive battery cable, then remove the battery and the battery tray.

   c. Disconnect the heater hose and clamp from the radiator.

4. Disconnect the overflow hose from the radiator, then disconnect the upper and lower radiator hoses.

5. If equipped with A/C, it may be necessary to remove the A/C hose retaining clip and reposition the hose for shroud and/or radiator removal. DO NOT disconnect any refrigerant fittings.

➡**If equipped with a 1 piece shroud, then shroud may be unbolted from the radiator support and pushed back over the cooling fan instead of removing it completely.**

6. All vehicles covered by this manual should be equipped with a 2 piece radiator/fan shroud. Remove the upper fan shroud-to-radiator support bolts and the upper fan shroud-to-lower fan shroud retainers. Remove the upper shroud from the vehicle.

7. If equipped with an A/T, disconnect and plug the fluid cooler lines at the radiator. Plug all openings to prevent system contamination or excessive fluid loss.

8. If equipped with a factory engine oil cooler which is integral to the radiator, disconnect and plug the oil cooler lines at the radiator. Plug all openings to prevent system contamination or excessive fluid loss. Plug all openings to prevent system contamination or excessive fluid loss.

9. Lift the radiator straight upward from the supports and from the vehicle. Be careful to lift the radiator straight upward and not to tilt it excessively as the radiator will still contain a significant amount of coolant and, if applicable, transmission fluid/engine oil.

To install:

10. Lower the radiator into position on the supports.

11. If equipped, remove the plugs, then connect the engine oil cooler lines and tighten the fittings.

12. If equipped with an A/T, remove the plugs, then connect the transmission fluid cooler lines and tighten the fittings.

13. Install the upper fan shroud and secure using the support and lower shroud retainers.

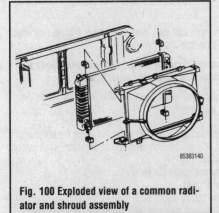

Fig. 100 Exploded view of a common radiator and shroud assembly

Fig. 101 Open the radiator petcock and drain the engine cooling system

Fig. 102 Slide the tension clamp back over the overflow hose

Fig. 103 Pull the overflow hose from the nipple on the filler neck

Fig. 104 Loosen the radiator hose retaining clamps

Fig. 105 Carefully pull the hoses from the radiator

Fig. 106 Loosen and remove the shroud-to-radiator support bolts

Fig. 107 Remove the upper shroud to lower shroud retainers

Fig. 108 Remove the upper shroud from the vehicle

Fig. 109 Lift the radiator assembly from the supports

14. If applicable, reposition the A/C refrigerant hose and secure using the retaining clip.
15. Connect the overflow hose, upper and lower radiator hoses.
16. If equipped with the MFI-Turbo engine:
   a. Connect the heater hose and clamp to the radiator.
   b. Install the battery tray, then install the battery and connect the positive battery cable
   c. Install the turbocharger inlet elbow, then install the air cleaner and duct.
17. Connect the negative battery cable.
18. Properly refill the engine cooling system.

Engine Cooling Fan/Clutch Fan

The vehicles covered by this manual are either equipped with a standard cooling fan (early models) or a clutch fan assembly (most later model vehicles). Standard cooling fans are simply bolted to the water pump hub, while on clutch fans, the fan blade assembly is bolted to a clutch assembly which is secured to water pump hub studs. Both fans are removed in a similar manner, but the clutch assembly requires a little more effort.

CLUTCH FAN DIAGNOSIS

Start the engine and listen for fan noise. Fan noise is usually evident during the first few minutes after start-up and when the clutch is engaged for maximum cooling (during idle). If fan noise is excessive, the fan cannot be rotated by hand while the engine is stopped or there is a rough grating feel as the fan is turned, replace the clutch.

Check a loose fan assembly for wear and replace as necessary. Under certain conditions, the fan may flex up to ¼ in. This is not cause for replacement.

The fan clutch is not affected by small fluid leaks which may occur in the area around the bearing assembly. If leakage appears excessive, replace the fan clutch. If the fan clutch free-wheels with no drag (revolves more than five times when spun by hand), replace the clutch.

REMOVAL & INSTALLATION

▶ See Figures 110, 111 and 112

➥DO NOT use or repair a damaged fan assembly. An unbalanced fan assembly could fly apart and cause personal injury or property damage. Replace damaged assemblies with new ones.

1. Disconnect the negative battery cable.
2. Remove the upper radiator shroud and, if desired for additional clearance, remove the radiator from the vehicle.

➥Although it is not necessary in most cases, the radiator may be removed from the vehicle for easier access to the fan retainers. If the radiator is left in place, use extra caution to prevent damage to the fragile radiator fins.

3. Remove the fan assembly attaching nuts (clutch type) or bolts (standard type), then remove the fan assembly from the engine.

➥Some vehicles use a space between the fan and the water pump pulley. If used, be sure to retain the spacer for installation.

4. If necessary, the clutch may be removed from the fan by removing the attaching nuts or bolts (as applicable).
To install:
5. If removed, install the fan to the clutch and secure using the fasteners.
6. Position the spacer (if used) and fan assembly to the water pump pulley and secure using the fasteners.
7. If removed for clearance, install the radiator.
8. Install the upper fan shroud.
9. Connect the negative battery cable.
10. If the radiator was removed, properly refill the engine cooling system.

Water Pump

DIAGNOSIS

Check the water pump operation by running the engine while squeezing the upper radiator hose. When the engine warms (thermostat opens) a pressure surge should be felt. Check for a plugged vent hole at the pump snout.

REMOVAL & INSTALLATION

▶ See Figures 113 thru 120

1.9L Engine

1. Disconnect the negative battery cable.
2. Raise and support the front of the vehicle safely using jackstands.

Fig. 110 Although usually not necessary, removing the radiator will often make fan removal easier

Fig. 111 For non-clutch type fans, loosen and remove the retaining bolts

Fig. 112 With the retainers removed, the fan assembly may be removed from the water pump pulley

Fig. 113 Loosen and remove the drive belts from the water pump pulley

Fig. 114 Some vehicles (like this early 2.8L engine) use a spacer between the fan and water pump pulley

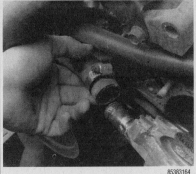

Fig. 115 Remove the pulley from the pump hub

Fig. 116 Loosen and remove all of the water pump retaining bolts

Fig. 117 For some engines it may be easier to remove the pump from the engine with a hose still attached

Fig. 118 This hose was easier to disconnect once the pump was removed

3. Remove the lower fan shroud/cover for access, then drain the engine cooling system.

4. If not equipped with A/C, remove the fan-to-water pump nuts and the fan from the vehicle. In most cases, it is easier to loosen the components and remove the drive belts before attempting to remove the pulley.

5. If equipped with A/C:

a. Loosen the air pump and alternator adjusting bolts, pivot them toward the engine and remove the drive belt(s).

b. Remove the fan-to-water pump nuts and the fan (with the fan and air pump drive pulley) from the vehicle.

c. Remove the fan set plate/pulley-to-water pump bolts, then remove the set plate and the pulley.

6. Disconnect the coolant hoses at the water pump.

7. Remove the water pump-to-engine bolts and the water pump from the engine.

To install:

8. Using a putty knife, clean the gasket mounting surfaces.

9. Install the water pump to the engine using a new gasket and sealant, then tighten the water pump bolts to 15–22 ft. lbs. (20–30 NM).

10. Connect the coolant hoses to the water pump.

11. If equipped with A/C, install the fan set plate/pulley to the water pump, then install the fan. Install the air pump and alternator drive belts, then adjust the belt tension.

12. If not equipped with A/C, install the fan assembly to the vehicle.

13. Make sure the radiator petcock is closed, then install the lower fan shroud/cover.

14. Remove the jackstands and carefully lower the vehicle.

15. Connect the negative battery cable and properly refill the engine cooling system.

16. Run the engine and check for leaks.

Fig. 119 Carefully clean all traces of gasket and sealant from the front of the engine

Fig. 120 If the old pump is to be reinstalled, clean the gasket mating surface of the pump as well

2.0L Engine

▶ See Figure 121

1. Disconnect the negative battery cable.
2. Drain the engine cooling system.
3. Remove the upper fan shroud and all of the necessary drive belts.
4. Disconnect the radiator and heater hoses from the water pump.
5. Remove the water pump-to-engine bolts, then remove the water pump from the vehicle.

To install:

6. Using a putty knife, clean the gasket mounting surfaces.
7. Install the water pump to the engine using a new gasket and sealant, then tighten the water pump bolts to 15–22 ft. lbs. (20–30 NM).
8. Connect the radiator and heater hoses to the water pump.
9. Install the necessary drive belts, then install the fan shroud.
10. Connect the negative battery cable and properly refill the engine cooling system.
11. Run the engine and check for leaks.

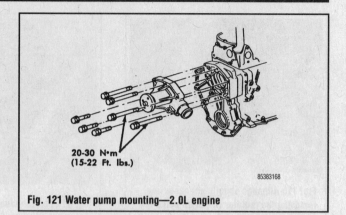

Fig. 121 Water pump mounting—2.0L engine

2.5L, 2.8L and 4.3L Gasoline Engines

▶ See Figures 122, 123 and 124

1. Disconnect the negative battery cable, then drain the engine cooling system.
2. Relieve the belt tension, then remove the accessory drive belts or the serpentine drive belt, as applicable.
3. Remove the upper fan shroud, then remove the fan or fan and clutch assembly, as applicable.
4. Remove the water pump pulley.
5. Loosen the clamp and disconnect the coolant hose(s) from the water pump.

➡On some engines, such as the heater hose on the early 2.8L, removal may be easier if the hose is left attached until the pump is free from the block. Once the pump is removed from the engine, the pump may be pulled (giving a better grip and greater leverage) from the tight hose connection.

6. Remove the retainers, then remove the water pump from the engine. Note the positions of all retainers as some engines will utilize different length fasteners in different locations and/or bolts and studs in different locations.

To install:

7. Using a putty knife, carefully clean the gasket mounting surfaces.

➡The water pumps on some of the earlier engines covered by this manual (early 2.8L's and 2.5L's for example) may have been installed using sealer only, no gasket, at the factory. If a gasket is supplied with the replacement part, it should be used. Otherwise, a 1/8 in. bead of RTV sealer should be used around the sealing surface of the pump.

8. Apply 1052080 or an equivalent sealant to the threads of the water pump retainers. Install the water pump to the engine using a new gasket, then thread the retainers in order to hold it in position.
9. Tighten the water pump retainers to specification:
   a. For the 2.5L engine, tighten the water pump-to-engine retainers to 17 ft. lbs. (23 Nm).
   b. For the 2.8L engine, tighten the retainers to 22 ft. lbs. (30 Nm) for all vehicles through 1992 or to 15 ft. lbs. (21 Nm) and 89 inch lbs. (10 Nm) depending on fastener location for 1993 vehicles. The central 3 lower bolts are tightened to the inch lbs. specification. Please refer to the illustration for clarification.
   c. For the 4.3L engine, tighten the bolts and studs to 30 ft. lbs. (41 Nm).
10. Connect the coolant hose(s) and secure using the retaining clamp(s).
11. Install the water pump pulley, then install the fan or fan and clutch assembly.
12. If equipped with a serpentine drive belt, position the belt over the pulleys, then carefully allow the tensioner back into contact with the belt.
13. If equipped with V-belts, install the accessory drive belts and adjust the tension.
14. Install the upper fan shroud, then connect the negative battery cable.
15. Properly refill the engine cooling system, then run the engine and check for leaks.

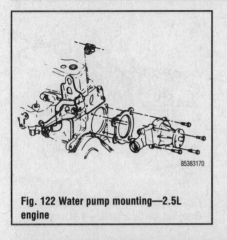

Fig. 122 Water pump mounting—2.5L engine

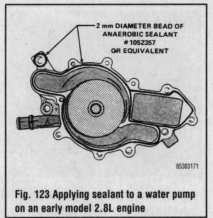

Fig. 123 Applying sealant to a water pump on an early model 2.8L engine

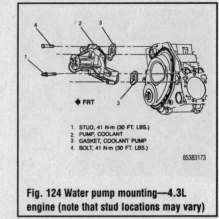

Fig. 124 Water pump mounting—4.3L engine (note that stud locations may vary)

Cylinder Head

REMOVAL & INSTALLATION

 **See Figures 125, 126, 127, 128 and 129**

➡The engine should be allowed to cool overnight before the cylinder head is removed in order to prevent warpage.

1.9L Engine

➤ **See Figures 130 and 131**

1. Disconnect the negative battery cable and drain the engine cooling system.
2. Remove the rocker arm cover from the cylinder head. For details, please refer to the procedure earlier in this section.
3. Remove EGR pipe clamp bolt at the rear of the cylinder head.
4. Raise and support the front of the truck safely using jackstands.
5. Disconnect the exhaust pipe from the manifold, then remove the jackstands and lower the vehicle.
6. Disconnect the heater hoses from the intake manifold and the front of the cylinder head.
7. If equipped with an A/C compressor and/or a P/S pump, disconnect them and lay them aside. DO NOT disconnect the refrigerant or P/S lines, but make sure they are not stretched, kinked or otherwise damaged when the component is repositioned.
8. Disconnect the accelerator linkage and the fuel line from the carburetor. Tag and disengage all necessary electrical connections, the spark plug wires and necessary vacuum lines.
9. Rotate the camshaft until the No. 4 cylinder is in the firing position. Remove the distributor cap and mark rotor-to-housing relationship, then remove the distributor.
10. Disconnect the fuel lines from the fuel pump, then remove the pump.
11. Using two pry bars, depress the timing chain adjuster lock lever to lock the automatic adjuster shoe in its fully retracted position.

12. Remove timing sprocket-to-camshaft bolt, the sprocket and the fuel pump drive cam from the camshaft. Keep the sprocket on the chain damper and tensioner—DO NOT remove the sprocket from the chain.
13. Disconnect the AIR hose and check valve from the air manifold.
14. Remove the cylinder head-to-timing cover bolts.
15. Using a suitable breaker bar, loosen and remove cylinder head-to-engine bolts. The bolts should be loosened gradually in a sequence, beginning with the outer bolts and working inward.
16. Remove the cylinder head, intake and exhaust manifold as an assembly.

To install:
17. Carefully clean and inspect the gasket mounting surfaces.

➡The gasket surfaces on both the head and block must be clean of any foreign matter and free of nicks or heavy scratches. The cylinder bolt threads in the block and thread on the bolts must be cleaned (dirt will affect the bolt torque).

18. Place a new gasket over the dowel pins with the side marked "TOP" facing upward, then carefully position the cylinder head over the gasket.

➡Be sure to lubricate the cylinder head bolts with engine oil before installing them.

19. Install the cylinder head bolts, then tighten them in several passes of the proper sequence (working from the inner towards the outer bolts) to a torque of 61 ft. lbs. (83 Nm). Then retighten the bolts in sequence to 72 ft. lbs. (98 Nm).
20. Install the cylinder head-to-timing cover bolts.
21. Connect the AIR hose and check valve to the air manifold.
22. Engage the timing sprocket and fuel pump drive cam to the camshaft, then install and tighten sprocket-to-camshaft bolt.
23. Unlock the timing chain adjuster lock lever to return it to its "free" position.
24. Install the fuel pump and Connect the fuel lines.
25. Align the marks made earlier, then install the distributor and check that it is still pointing to the No. 4 cylinder firing position.
26. Engage all necessary electrical connections, the spark plug wires and vacuum lines, as tagged during removal. Connect the accelerator linkage and the fuel line to the carburetor.

Fig. 125 Remove the rocker arm cover(s)

Fig. 126 On pushrod engines, loosen the rocker arms so the pushrods may be removed

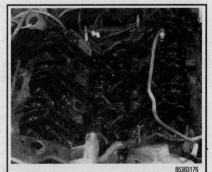

Fig. 127 On V-engines, remove the intake manifold from the block and cylinder heads

Fig. 128 During installation, use a torque wrench to tighten the cylinder head bolts

Fig. 129 An extension will be needed to reach the bolts on some cylinder heads

Fig. 130 Use 2 pry bars to lock the timing chain automatic adjuster—1.9L engine

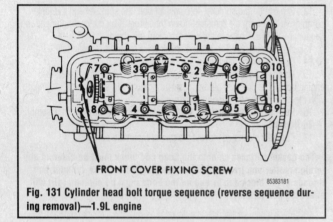

FRONT COVER FIXING SCREW

Fig. 131 Cylinder head bolt torque sequence (reverse sequence during removal)—1.9L engine

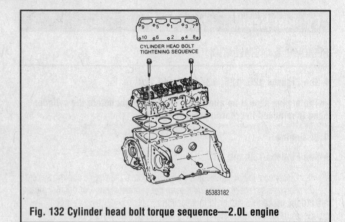

CYLINDER HEAD BOLT TIGHTENING SEQUENCE

Fig. 132 Cylinder head bolt torque sequence—2.0L engine

27. If equipped reposition and secure the A/C compressor and/or a P/S pump.

28. Connect the heater hoses to the intake manifold and the front of the cylinder head.

29. Raise and support the front of the truck safely using jackstands.

30. Connect the exhaust pipe to the manifold, then remove the jackstands and lower the vehicle.

31. Install EGR pipe clamp bolt to the rear of the cylinder head.

32. Install the rocker arm cover to the cylinder head.

33. Connect the negative battery cable, then properly refill the engine cooling system.

34. Run the engine, allow it to reach normal operating temperatures and check for leaks.

35. Check and/or adjust the engine timing and idle speed.

2.0L Engine

♦ See Figure 132

➡Let the vehicle sit overnight before attempting to remove the cylinder head. The engine must be cold.

1. Disconnect the negative battery cable.

2. Drain the engine cooling system, then remove the air cleaner assembly.

3. Raise and support the front of the truck safely using jackstands.

4. Remove the exhaust shield, then disconnect the exhaust pipe from the exhaust manifold.

5. Remove the jackstands and lower the vehicle.

6. Disconnect the accelerator linkage, then tag and disengage all necessary electrical wiring connectors and the vacuum lines.

7. Remove the fuel vapor canister harness (steel) pipes.

8. Remove the distributor cap, then matchmark the rotor-to-distributor housing and the distributor housing-to-engine. Remove the distributor from the engine.

9. Remove the rocker arm cover, then remove the rocker arms and the pushrods. For details, refer to the procedures earlier in this section.

10. Remove the upper radiator hose, the heater hose, the upper fan shroud and the fan.

11. Remove the AIR management valve, the air pump and the upper AIR bracket.

12. Disconnect the fuel line from the fuel pump and the wire from the rear of the cylinder head.

13. Remove the cylinder head-to-engine bolts, then carefully lift the cylinder head from the engine. If leverage must be used to break the gasket seal, be very careful not to damage the engine or score the gasket sealing surfaces.

To install:

14. Carefully clean and inspect the gasket mounting surfaces.

➡The gasket surfaces on both the head and block must be clean of any foreign matter and free of nicks or heavy scratches. The cylinder bolt threads in the block and thread on the bolts must be cleaned (dirt will affect the bolt torque).

15. Coat both sides of a new gasket with sealing compound No. 10520026, or equivalent, then position the gasket on the locating pins. Carefully lower the cylinder head into position on top of the gasket.

16. Install the cylinder head bolts, then tighten them in several passes of the proper sequence to 65–75 ft. lbs. (88–102 Nm).

17. Connect the fuel line to the fuel pump and the wire to the rear of the cylinder head.

18. Install the AIR management valve, the air pump and the upper AIR bracket.

19. Install the upper radiator hose, the heater hose, the upper fan shroud and the fan.

20. Install the rocker arms and pushrods, then install the rocker arm cover. For details, refer to the procedures earlier in this section.

21. Align the marks and install the distributor. Verify the marks are aligned, then install the distributor cap.

22. Install the fuel vapor canister harness (steel) pipes.

23. Engage all necessary electrical wiring connectors and the vacuum lines as tagged during removal, then connect the accelerator linkage,

24. Raise and support the front of the vehicle safely using jackstands.

25. Connect the exhaust pipe to the exhaust manifold, then install the exhaust shield.

26. Remove the jackstands and carefully lower the vehicle.
27. Install the air cleaner assembly.
28. Connect the negative battery cable, then properly refill the engine cooling system.
29. Run the engine, allow it to reach normal operating temperatures and check for leaks.
30. Check and/or adjust the engine timing and idle speed.

2.5L Engine

▶ See Figure 133

➡Let the vehicle sit overnight before attempting to remove the cylinder head. The engine must be cold.

☀☀ CAUTION

Relieve the pressure on the fuel system before disconnecting any fuel line connection. See Section 1 or 5 for the proper procedures.

VEHICLES THROUGH 1988

1. Properly relieve the fuel system pressure, then disconnect the negative battery cable.
2. Drain the engine cooling system, then remove the air cleaner assembly.
3. If equipped, remove and reposition the A/C compressor with the lines intact.
4. Disconnect the PCV hose and remove the EGR valve.
5. Tag and disengage the spark plug wires from the spark plugs, then remove them from the rocker arm cover.
6. Disconnect the vacuum line hold-down at the thermostat. Tag and disconnect the vacuum lines, fuel lines and wiring at the TBI unit. Remove the vacuum lines from the studs on the intake manifold.
7. Remove the rocker arm cover.
8. Disconnect the accelerator, the cruise control and the TVS cables, as equipped.
9. If equipped, remove the alternator rear brace.
10. Disconnect the water pump bypass and heater hoses from the intake manifold.
11. If equipped, remove the A/C compressor bracket.
12. Disconnect the exhaust pipe from the manifold.
13. If applicable, disengage the A/C line hold-down, but DO NOT disconnect the refrigerant lines.
14. Remove the alternator.
15. Disconnect the upper radiator hose.
16. Remove the fuel line bracket at the fuel filter, then disengage the fuel and vacuum lines near the filter.
17. Remove the dipstick tube, then disengage the wiring harness bracket at the rear of the cylinder head.
18. Remove the coil bracket from the cylinder head, then disengage the oxygen sensor wiring.
19. Loosen the rocker arms and remove the pushrods.
20. If equipped, remove the brace between the intake manifold and block.

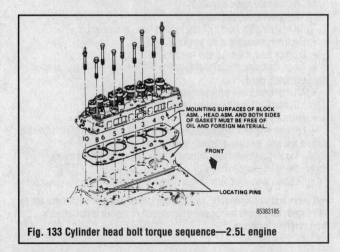

Fig. 133 Cylinder head bolt torque sequence—2.5L engine

MOUNTING SURFACES OF BLOCK ASM., HEAD ASM. AND BOTH SIDES OF GASKET MUST BE FREE OF OIL AND FOREIGN MATERIAL.

FRONT

LOCATING PINS

85383185

21. Remove the cylinder head-to-engine bolts, then remove the cylinder head from the engine (with the manifolds attached). If necessary, remove the intake and the exhaust manifolds from the cylinder head.

To install:

22. Carefully clean and inspect the gasket mounting surfaces.

➡The gasket surfaces on both the head and block must be clean of any foreign matter and free of nicks or heavy scratches. The cylinder bolt threads in the block and thread on the bolts must be cleaned (dirt will affect the bolt torque).

23. Place a new gasket over the dowel pins (DO NOT use any sealer on the gasket), then position the cylinder head on the block over the dowel pins and gasket.
24. Apply a coating of 1052080 or equivalent sealer to the heads and threads of all of the cylinder head bolts for 1985 vehicles, or to the threads of the bolts/studs at the front left and rear left positions (numbers 9 and 10 in the torque sequence, for 1986 and later vehicles. Thread the cylinder head bolts, then tighten them in the proper sequence to 90 ft. lbs. (125 Nm).
25. If equipped, install the brace between the intake manifold and block.
26. Install the pushrods and secure the rocker arms.
27. Install the coil bracket to the cylinder head.
28. Install the wiring harness bracket to the rear of the cylinder head, then install the dipstick tube.
29. Connect the fuel and vacuum lines near the fuel filter, then install the fuel line bracket at the filter.
30. Connect the upper radiator hose, then install the alternator.
31. If equipped, install the A/C refrigerant line hold-down.
32. Connect the exhaust pipe to the manifold.
33. If equipped, install the A/C compressor bracket.
34. Connect the water pump bypass and heater hoses, then install the alternator rear brace.
35. Connect the accelerator, TV and cruise control cables, as equipped.
36. Install the rocker arm cover.
37. Secure the vacuum lines at the intake manifold studs. Engage the vacuum lines, fuel lines and wiring connectors to the TBI unit as tagged during removal.
38. Install the vacuum line hold-down at the thermostat, then engage the spark plug wires.
39. Install the EGR valve, then connect the PCV hose.
40. If equipped, reposition and secure the A/C compressor.
41. Install the air cleaner assembly, then connect the negative battery cable.
42. Properly refill the engine cooling system, then check for leaks.

1989–93 VEHICLES

▶ See Figure 133

1. Properly relieve the fuel system pressure, then disconnect the negative battery cable.
2. Drain the engine cooling system, then remove the air cleaner assembly.
3. If equipped, remove and reposition the A/C compressor with the lines intact. Make sure the lines are not kinked or otherwise damaged.
4. Remove the rocker arm cover.
5. Loosen the rocker arms and remove the pushrods. For details, please refer to the procedure located earlier in this section.
6. Tag and disconnect the vacuum lines, fuel lines and wiring at the TBI unit. Remove the vacuum lines from the studs on the intake manifold.
7. Disconnect the accelerator, the cruise control and the TVS cables, as equipped.
8. Remove the alternator along with the brackets and position aside.
9. Remove the water pump bypass and heater hoses from the intake manifold.
10. Disconnect the exhaust pipe from the exhaust manifold.
11. Disconnect the upper radiator hose, then remove the vacuum tube from the coolant outlet stud.
12. Remove the fuel filter and fuel line bracket at the rear of the cylinder head.
13. Remove the dipstick tube, then disconnect the wiring harness and ground strap at the rear of the cylinder head.
14. Tag and disengage the wiring connectors from the sensors and the cylinder head and the thermostat housing.
15. Remove the ignition coil wires, then tag and disconnect the spark plug wires.

16. Disengage the oxygen sensor wiring connector.
17. Unfasten the cylinder head mounting bolts, then remove the head with the manifolds attached,
   To install:
18. Carefully clean and inspect the gasket mounting surfaces.

➡The gasket surfaces on both the head and block must be clean of any foreign matter and free of nicks or heavy scratches. The cylinder bolt threads in the block and thread on the bolts must be cleaned (dirt will affect the bolt torque).

19. Place a new gasket over the dowel pins, then position the cylinder head on the block over the dowel pins and gasket.
20. Apply a coating of 1052080 or equivalent sealer to the threads of the cylinder head bolts, then thread the bolts into position. Make sure the bolts are threaded within 15 minutes of the sealant application in order to allow the sealer to properly cure.
21. Tighten the cylinder head bolts to specification, using multiple passes of the proper sequence:
   • Torque all bolts gradually to 18 ft. lbs. (25 Nm).
   • Torque all bolts except the left front bolt (No. 9 in the sequence) to 26 ft. lbs. (35 Nm), then retorque number 9 to 18 ft. lbs. (25 Nm).
   • Torque all bolts an additional ¼ turn (90°).
22. Engage the oxygen sensor connector.
23. Connect the spark plug and ignition coil wiring.
24. Engage the wiring connectors to the sensors on the cylinder head and thermostat housing.
25. Connect the wiring harness bracket and ground strap to the rear of the cylinder head.
26. Install the dipstick tube, then install the fuel filter and fuel line bracket.
27. Secure the vacuum tube at the coolant outlet stud, then connect the upper radiator hose.
28. Connect the exhaust pipe to the manifold.
29. Connect the water pump bypass and heater hoses.
30. Reposition and secure the alternator with the brackets.
31. Connect the accelerator, cruise control and TVS cables, as equipped.
32. Secure the vacuum hoses to the intake manifold studs, then engage the vacuum hoses, fuel lines and electrical wires to the TBI unit as tagged during removal.
33. Install the pushrods and secure the rocker arms.
34. Install the rocker arm cover.
35. If equipped, reposition and secure the A/C compressor along with the brackets.
36. Install the air cleaner assembly, then connect the negative battery cable.
37. Properly refill the engine cooling system, then check for leaks.

2.8L Engine

♦ See Figure 134

❋❋ CAUTION

Relieve the pressure on the fuel system before disconnecting any fuel line connection. Please refer to Section 1 or 5 of this manual for the proper procedures.

1. Properly relieve the fuel system pressure, then connect the negative battery cable.
2. Drain the engine cooling system.
3. Remove the intake manifold assembly. For details, please refer to the procedure located earlier in this section..
4. If necessary, raise and support the front of the vehicle safely using jackstands. If you decide to disconnect the exhaust manifold and not the pipe in the next step, it may not be necessary to raise the vehicle.
5. Either disconnect the exhaust pipe from the exhaust manifold (so the manifold may be removed with the cylinder head) or, remove the exhaust manifold-to-cylinder block retainers and reposition the manifold out of the way.
6. If raised, remove the jackstands and carefully lower the vehicle.
7. If removing the left side cylinder head, remove the dipstick tube, then disconnect the ground strap and the sensor connector from the cylinder head.
8. If removing the right side cylinder head, remove the drive belt, alternator, and AIR pump with mounting bracket.

➡If valve train components, such as the pushrods, are to be reused, they must be tagged or arranged to insure installation in their original locations.

9. Loosen the rocker arm nuts, turn the rocker arms and remove the pushrods. Keep the pushrods in the same order as removed.
10. Loosen the cylinder head bolts using multiple passes in the reverse order of the tightening sequence.
11. Remove the cylinder head; DO NOT pry on the head to loosen it.
   To install:
12. Carefully clean and inspect the gasket mounting surfaces.

➡The gasket surfaces on both the head and block must be clean of any foreign matter and free of nicks or heavy scratches. The cylinder bolt threads in the block and thread on the bolts must be cleaned (dirt will affect the bolt torque).

13. Place a new gasket over the dowel pins with the words "This Side Up" facing upwards, then position the cylinder head on the block over the dowel pins and gasket.
14. Apply a coating of 1052080 or equivalent sealer to the threads of the cylinder head bolts, then thread the bolts into position and tighten them to specification using the proper torque sequence:
   • First, torque all bolts to 40 ft. lbs. (55 Nm).
   • Then, torque all bolts an additional ¼ turn (90°).
15. Install the pushrods, then reposition the rocker arms and adjust the valves.
16. For the right side, install the alternator and AIR pump along with mounting bracket, then install and tighten the drive belt.
17. For the left side, connect the ground strap and sensor connector, then install the dipstick tube.
18. If necessary, raise and support the front of the truck safely using jackstands.
19. Either connect the exhaust pipe to the manifold or the manifold to the cylinder head, as applicable. If raised, remove the jackstands and lower the truck.
20. Install the intake manifold assembly.
21. Connect the negative battery cable, then properly refill the engine cooling system.
22. Check and/or adjust the ignition timing and idle speed (if possible).

4.3L Engine

♦ See Figure 135

❋❋ CAUTION

Relieve the pressure on the fuel system before disconnecting any fuel line connection. Please refer to Section 1 or 5 of this manual for the proper procedures.

1. Properly relieve the fuel system pressure, then disconnect the negative battery cable.
2. Drain the engine cooling system.
3. Remove the rocker arm cover.
4. Remove the intake manifold.
5. Remove the exhaust manifold.
6. If removing the right cylinder head, remove or disconnect:
   • Electrical connector at the sensor.
   • Dipstick tube at the cylinder head bracket.
   • Air conditioning compressor (position it aside with the refrigerant lines attached), if equipped.
   • A/C compressor (if equipped)/belt tensioner bracket.
7. If removing the left cylinder head, remove or disconnect:
   • Alternator (position it aside).
   • Left side engine accessory bracket with power steering pump (position the pump aside with the lines attached) and brackets, if equipped.
8. Tag and disconnect the wiring from the spark plugs. If necessary, remove the spark plugs from the cylinder head.
9. Loosen the rocker arms and remove the pushrods.

➡If valve train components, such as the rocker arms or pushrods, are to be reused, they must be tagged or arranged to insure installation in their original locations.

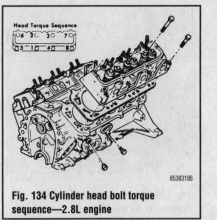

Fig. 134 Cylinder head bolt torque sequence—2.8L engine

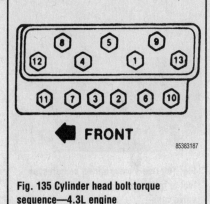

Fig. 135 Cylinder head bolt torque sequence—4.3L engine

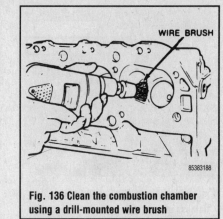

Fig. 136 Clean the combustion chamber using a drill-mounted wire brush

10. Remove the cylinder head bolts by loosening them in the reverse of the torque sequence, then carefully remove the cylinder head.

To install:

11. Carefully clean and inspect the gasket mounting surfaces.

➡**The gasket surfaces on both the head and block must be clean of any foreign matter and free of nicks or heavy scratches. The cylinder bolt threads in the block and thread on the bolts must be cleaned (dirt will affect the bolt torque).**

➡**DO NOT apply sealer to composition steel-asbestos gaskets.**

12. If using a steel only gasket, apply a thin and even coat of sealer to both sides of the gaskets.

13. Place a new gasket over the dowel pins with the bead or the words "This Side Up" facing upwards (as applicable), then carefully lower the cylinder head into position over the gasket and dowels.

14. Apply a coating of 1052080 or equivalent sealer to the threads of the cylinder head bolts, then thread the bolts into position until finger-tight. Using the proper torque sequence, tighten the bolts in 3 steps:

- First, tighten the bolts to 25 ft. lbs. (34 Nm).
- Next, tighten the bolts to 45 ft. lbs. (61 Nm).
- Finally, tighten the bolts to 65 ft. lbs. (90 Nm).

15. Install the pushrods, secure the rocker arms and adjust the valves.

16. If removed, install the spark plugs. Engage the spark plug wires.

17. If the left cylinder head was removed, reposition and secure the engine accessory bracket with the power steering pump and brackets, as equipped. Install the alternator.

18. If the right cylinder head was removed, install the A/C compressor (if equipped) and A/C compressor/belt tensioner bracket, then install the dipstick tube bracket and engage the sensor electrical connector.

19. Install the exhaust manifold.

20. Install the intake manifold.

21. Install the rocker arm cover.

22. Connect the negative battery cable, then properly refill the engine cooling system.

23. Run the engine to check for leaks, then check and/or adjust the ignition timing.

CLEANING & INSPECTION

◆ **See Figure 136**

1. With the valves installed to protect the valve seats, remove carbon deposits from the combustion chambers and valve heads with a drill-mounted wire brush. Be careful not to damage the cylinder head gasket surface. If the head is to be disassembled, proceed to Step 3. If the head is not to be disassembled, proceed to Step 2.

2. Remove all dirt, oil and old gasket material from the cylinder head with solvent. Clean the bolt holes and the oil passage. Be careful not to get solvent on the valve seals as the solvent may damage them. If available, dry the cylinder head with compressed air. Check the head for cracks or other damage, and check the gasket surface for burrs, nicks and flatness. If you are in doubt about the head's serviceability, consult a reputable automotive machine shop.

3. Remove the valves, springs and retainers, then clean the valve guide bores with a valve guide cleaning tool. Remove all dirt, oil and old gasket material from the cylinder head with solvent. Clean the bolt holes and the oil passage.

4. Remove all deposits from the valves with a wire brush or buffing wheel. Inspect the valves as described later in this section.

5. Check the head for cracks using a dye penetrant in the valve seat area and ports, head surface and top. Check the gasket surface for burrs, nicks and flatness. If you are in doubt about the head's serviceability, consult a reputable automotive machine shop.

➡**If the cylinder head was removed due to an overheating condition and a crack is suspected, do not assume that the head is not cracked because a crack is not visually found. A crack can be so small that it cannot be seen by eye, but can pass coolant when the engine is at operating temperature. Consult an automotive machine shop that has pressure testing equipment to make sure the head is not cracked.**

RESURFACING

◆ **See Figures 137 and 138**

Whenever the cylinder head is removed, check the flatness of the cylinder head gasket surface as follows:

1. Make sure all dirt and old gasket material has been cleaned from the cylinder head. Any foreign material left on the head gasket surface can cause a false measurement.

2. Place a straightedge straight across and diagonally across the gasket surface of the cylinder head (in the positions shown in the figures). Using feeler gauges, determine the clearance at the center of the straightedge.

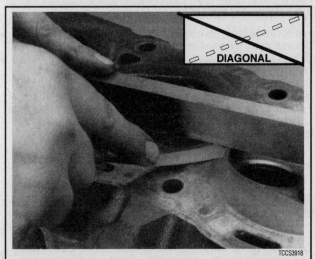

Fig. 137 Checking the cylinder head for flatness diagonally across the head surface

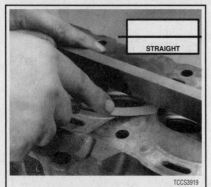

Fig. 138 Checking the cylinder head for flatness straight across the head surface

Fig. 139 Use a valve spring compressor tool to relieve spring tension from the valve caps

Fig. 140 A small magnet will help in removal of the valve keepers

Fig. 141 Be careful not to lose the valve keepers

Fig. 142 Once the spring has been removed, the O-ring (if used) may be removed from the valve stem

Fig. 143 After the seal and spring seat are removed, invert the cylinder head and withdraw the valve from the bore

3. If warpage exceeds the 0.004 in. (0.10mm) then the cylinder head should likely be resurfaced or replaced. Contact a reputable machine shop for machining service and recommendations.

➡When resurfacing the cylinder head(s), the intake manifold mounting position is altered and must be corrected by machining a proportionate amount from the intake manifold flange.

Valves

REMOVAL & INSTALLATION

▸ See Figures 139 thru 145

New valve seals must be installed when the valve train is put back together. Certain seals slip over the valve stem and guide boss, while others require that the boss be machined. In some applications Teflon guide seals are available. Check with a machinist and/or automotive parts store for a suggestion on the proper seals to use.

1. Remove the cylinder head(s), and place on a clean surface.
2. Using a suitable spring compressor (either a leverage or jawed type that is designed for pushrod overhead valve engines), compress the valve spring and remove the valve spring cap key. Carefully release the spring compressor and remove the valve spring and cap (and valve rotator on some engines).

➡Use care in removing the keys; they are easily lost.

3. Remove the valve seals and the spring seat (if applicable) from the valve guides. Throw these old seals away, as you'll be installing new seals during reassembly.
4. Slide the valves out of the head from the combustion chamber side.
5. Make a holder for the valves out of a piece of wood with drilled holes or cardboard. Make sure you number each hole in the holder to keep the valves in proper order; they MUST be installed in their original locations. Another method of sorting the valve components is to use numbered containers, and make sure the components from each valve is stored in a separate container.

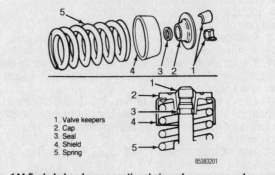

1. Valve keepers
2. Cap
3. Seal
4. Shield
5. Spring

Fig. 144 Exploded and cross-sectional view of a common valve component assembly

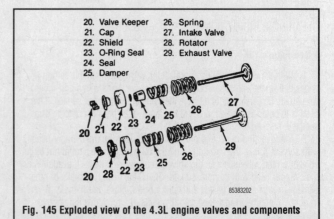

20. Valve Keeper
21. Cap
22. Shield
23. O-Ring Seal
24. Seal
25. Damper
26. Spring
27. Intake Valve
28. Rotator
29. Exhaust Valve

Fig. 145 Exploded view of the 4.3L engine valves and components

6. Use an electric drill and rotary wire brush to clean the intake and exhaust valve ports, combustion chamber and valve seats. In some cases, the carbon build-up will have to be chipped away. Use a blunt pointed drift for carbon chipping, being careful around valve seat areas.

7. Use a valve guide cleaning brush and suitable solvent to clean the valve guides.

8. Clean the valves with a revolving wire brush. Heavy carbon deposits may be removed with a blunt drift.

➡**When using a wire brush to remove carbon from the cylinder head or valves, make sure the deposits are actually removed and not just burnished.**

9. Wash and clean all valve springs, retainers etc., in safe solvent. Remember to keep parts from each valve separate.

10. Check the cylinder head for cracks. Cracks usually start around the exhaust valve seat because it is the hottest part of the combustion chamber. If a crack is suspected but cannot be detected visually, have the area checked by pressure testing, with a dye penetrant or other method by an automotive machine shop.

11. Inspect the valves, guides, springs and seats and machine or replace parts, as necessary.

To install:

12. Lubricate the valve stems with clean engine oil.

13. Install the valves in the cylinder head, one at a time, as numbered.

14. Lubricate and position the spring seats (if applicable), new seals and valve springs, again one valve at a time.

15. Install the spring caps, and compress the springs.

16. With the valve key groove exposed above the compressed valve spring, wipe some wheel bearing grease around the groove. This will retain the keys as you release the spring compressor.

17. Using needle nose pliers (or your fingers), carefully place the keys in the key grooves. The grease should hold the keys in place. Slowly release the spring compressor; the valve cap or rotator will raise up as the compressor is released, retaining the key.

18. Install the cylinder head(s).

INSPECTION

▶ See Figures 146 thru 151

➡**Excessive valve stem-to-bore clearance will cause excessive oil consumption and may cause valve breakage. Insufficient clearance will result in noisy and sticky functioning of the valve and disturb engine smoothness.**

Inspect the valve faces and seats (in the head) for pits, burned spots and other evidence of poor seating. Valves that are pitted must be refaced to the proper angle (45°). Valves that are warped excessively must be replaced. When a valve head that is warped excessively is refaced, a knife edge will be ground on part or all of the valve head due to the amount of material that must be removed to completely reface the valve. Knife edges lead to breakage, burning or preignition due to heat localizing on the knife edge. If the edge of the valve head is less than 1/32 in. after machining, replace the valve. We recommend that all machine work be performed by a reputable machine shop.

Make sure the valve stem is not bent. The valve may be rolled on a flat surface such as a mirror or glass. An even better indication of valve stem bending can be determined by carefully chocking the stem into an electric drill. Use the drill the spin the stem while you watch the valve head. A bent stem will be obvious by the wobbling of the head. Be very careful if this method is used. If the valve stem is not properly chocked in position it could come flying out of the drill and cause injury.

Some of the engines covered in this guide are equipped with valve rotators, which double as valve spring caps. In normal operation the rotators put a certain degree of wear on the tip of the valve stem; this wear appears as concentric rings on the stem tip. However, if the rotator is not working properly, the wear may appear as straight notches or **X** patterns across the valve stem tip. Whenever the valves are removed from the cylinder head, the tips should be inspected for improper pattern, which could indicate valve rotator problems. Valve stem tips will have to be ground flat if rotator patterns are severe.

Check the valve stem for scoring and burned spots. If not noticeably scored or damaged, clean the valve stem with solvent to remove all gum and varnish.

TCCS3142

Fig. 146 A dial indicator may be used to check valve stem-to-guide clearance

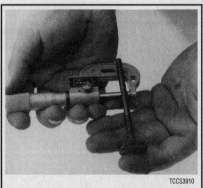

TCCS3910

Fig. 147 Use a micrometer to measure the valve stem diameter

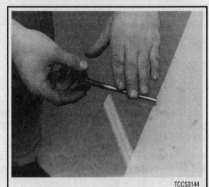

TCCS3144

Fig. 148 Valve stems may be rolled on a flat surface to check for bends

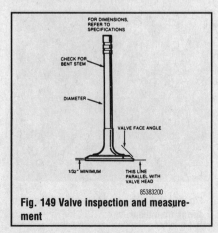

85383200

Fig. 149 Valve inspection and measurement

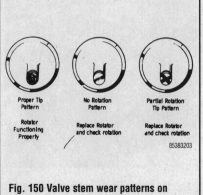

85383203

Fig. 150 Valve stem wear patterns on engines equipped with rotator cups

85383204

Fig. 151 A run-out (dial) gauge is used to check valve seat concentricity

Clean the valve guides using solvent and an expanding wire type valve guide cleaner. Check the valve stem-to-guide clearance in one or more of the following manners, but do not rely on the visual inspection alone:

1. A visual inspection can give you a fairly good idea if the guide, valve stem or both are worn. Insert the valve into the guide until the valve head is slightly away from the valve seat. Wiggle the valve sideways. A small amount of wobble is normal, excessive wobble means a worn guide and/or valve stem.

➡**If a dial indicator and micrometer are not available to you, take your cylinder head and valves to a reputable machine shop of inspection.**

2. If a dial indicator is on hand, mount the indicator so that gauge stem is 90° to the valve stem as close to the top of the valve guide as possible. Move the valve from the seat, and measure the valve guide-to-stem clearance by rocking the stem back and forth to actuate the dial indicator. Measure the valve stem using a micrometer and compare to specifications to determine whether stem or guide is causing excessive clearance.

3. If both a ball gauge and a micrometer are available, first, measure the inside diameter of the valve guide bushing at three locations using the ball gauge. Second, use the micrometer to measure the stem diameter. Finally, subtract the valve stem diameter from the corresponding valve guide inside diameter to arrive at the valve clearance. If clearance is greater than specification, the valve and guide bushing must be replaced.

The valve guide, if worn, must be repaired before the valve seats can be resurfaced. A new valve guide should be installed or, in some cases, knurled. Consult the automotive machine shop.

If the valve guide is okay, measure the valve seat concentricity using a runout gauge. Follow the manufacturers instructions. If runout is excessive, reface or replace the valve and machine or replace the valve seat.

➡**Valves and seats must always be machined together. Never use a refaced valve on a valve seat that has not been machined; never use a valve that has not been refaced on a machined valve seat.**

Valve Stem Seals

REPLACEMENT

Cylinder Head Installed

▸ **See Figures 152, 153, 154, 155 and 156**

The valve stem seals on most engines covered by this manual may be replaced with the cylinder head either on or off the engine. The removal procedure with the cylinder head installed utilizes compressed air in the cylinder to hold the valve in place and keep it from dropping into the cylinder once the valve key, cap and spring are removed.

➡**If air pressure is lost while the valve keepers are removed, the valve will drop into the cylinder. If this happens, the cylinder head must be removed in order to recover the valve.**

1. Disconnect the negative battery cable.
2. Remove the rocker arm cover.

➡**The cylinder must be on at TDC of it's compression stroke in order to follow this procedure. On the compression stroke, the cylinder's valves will be closed allowing the air pressure to hold the valve in position. The engine must therefore be turned slightly for each cylinder's valve seals.**

3. Remove the rocker arm and pushrod assemblies from the cylinders on which the valves are being serviced.

4. Remove the spark plug from the cylinder which is on it's compression stroke and install a spark plug air fitting adapter with an in-line gauge set between the adapter and air compressor. Apply compressed air to hold the valve in place.

5. Compress the valve spring using a suitable compressor tool and remove the valve key. Carefully release the spring tension, then remove the valve cap and spring.

➡**If the air pressure has forced the piston to the bottom of the cylinder, any removal of air pressure will allow the valves to fall into the cylinder. A rubber band, tape or string wrapped around the end of the valve stem will prevent this.**

6. Remove the old seal using a suitable removal tool.

To install:

7. Install the new seal using the valve stem seal tool.

8. Install the valve spring and cap, then compress the spring and install the valve key.

9. When the valve springs are properly installed, release the air pressure from the cylinder using the gauge set, then remove the spark plug adapter.

10. Install the spark plug and turn the engine sufficiently to work on the next cylinder. Repeat the above steps until all seals are replaced.

11. Install the rocker arm and pushrod assemblies, then install the rocker cover and connect the negative battery cable.

Cylinder Heads Removed

The valve stem oil seals are replaced as a part of normal valve service any time the valve stems are removed from the cylinder head. Refer to the valve procedure in this section for seal removal and installation when the cylinder head has been removed from the vehicle.

Valve Springs

REMOVAL & INSTALLATION

▸ **See Figures 157, 158, 159 and 160**

Removal or installation of the valve springs requires use of the following tools:
- Valve Spring Compressor tool (leverage type) No. J-5892-C or equivalent (2.0L, 2.5L, 2.8L and 4.3L engines)
- Valve Spring Compressor tool (jawed type) No. J-26513 or equivalent (1.9L engine)
- Valve Spring Compressor tool (leverage type) No. J-29760 or equivalent (2.2L diesel engine)

85383206

Fig. 152 Thread an adapter fitting into the spark plug bore so air pressure from a compressor may be used to hold the cylinder's valves in position

85383207

Fig. 153 Compress the valve spring and remove the valve keys

85383208

Fig. 154 With the keys removed, lift the spring from the valve

Fig. 155 Remove the old valve stem seal

Fig. 156 Install the replacement seal

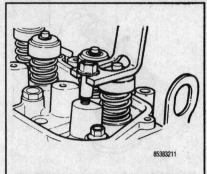

Fig. 157 Leverage type valve spring compressor tool—2.0L, 2.5L, 2.8L and 4.3L engines

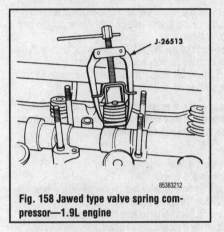

Fig. 158 Jawed type valve spring compressor—1.9L engine

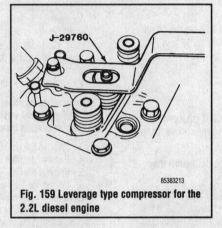

Fig. 159 Leverage type compressor for the 2.2L diesel engine

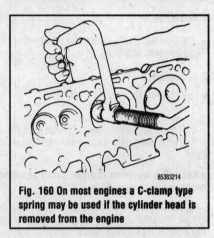

Fig. 160 On most engines a C-clamp type spring may be used if the cylinder head is removed from the engine

• GM Air Adapter tool No. J-23590 or equivalent to retain the valves if the cylinder head is to remain installed

The valve springs are removed and installed as part of the valve procedure found earlier in this section. If only a spring replacement is required, refer to the valve stem seal procedure with the cylinder head installed. The same air pressure method may be used to retain the valve while only a spring is replaced.

INSPECTION

▶ See Figures 161, 162, 163 and 164

1. Place the valve spring on a flat, clean surface next to a square.
2. Measure the height of the spring, and rotate it against the edge of the square to measure distortion (out-of-roundness). If spring height varies between springs by more than 1/16 in. or if the distortion exceeds 1/16 in., replace the spring.

A valve spring tester is needed to test spring test pressure, so the valve springs must usually be taken to a professional machine shop for this test. Spring pressure at the installed and/or compressed heights is checked, depending on the specification.

Valve Lifter

REMOVAL & INSTALLATION

▶ See Figures 165 and 166

When installing new lifters, a pre-lube should always be applied to the lifter body. It is also a good idea to prime hydraulic lifters by submerging them in clean engine oil a depressing the plunger using an old pushrod. This allows the internal components of the hydraulic lifter to coat with oil before initial operation in the engine. All lifters should be replaced when a new camshaft is installed.

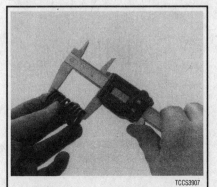

Fig. 161 A caliper gauge may be used to check the valve spring free-length

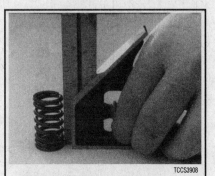

Fig. 162 Check the valve spring for squareness on a flat surface, a carpenters square can be used

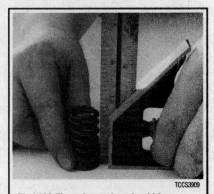

Fig. 163 The valve spring should be straight up and down when placed like this

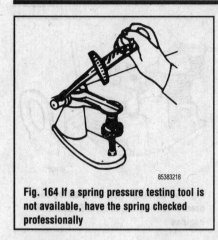

Fig. 164 If a spring pressure testing tool is not available, have the spring checked professionally

Fig. 165 Removing a lifter from the bore in the lifter valley on V-type engines

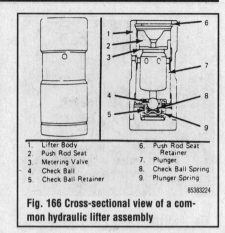

1. Lifter Body
2. Push Rod Seat
3. Metering Valve
4. Check Ball
5. Check Ball Retainer
6. Push Rod Seat Retainer
7. Plunger
8. Check Ball Spring
9. Plunger Spring

Fig. 166 Cross-sectional view of a common hydraulic lifter assembly

1.9L Engine

The camshaft directly actuates the rocker arms on the 1.9L engine, so no lifter assemblies are utilized.

2.0L Engine

▶ See Figure 167

1. Remove the rocker arm covers.
2. Loosen the rocker arms and remove the pushrods and guide plates.
3. Using Valve Lifter Removal tool J-29834, or equivalent, remove the valve lifters.

➡**Keep all components in order. If reusing components, install them into their original positions.**

4. For proper rotation during engine operation, the lifter bottom must be convex. Check the lifter bottom for proper shape using a straight edge. If the lifter bottom is not convex, replace the lifter. Chances are if lifters are in need of replacement, so is the camshaft.
5. Using the valve lifter tool, install the lifters into the block.
6. Installation is the reverse of removal. Adjust the valve lash.

2.5L Engine

▶ See Figure 168

1. Remove the rocker arm covers.
2. Remove the pushrod cover:
   a. Remove the alternator and bracket.
   b. Disengage the ignition coil wires, then remove the spark plug wires and bracket from the intake manifold.
   c. Remove the fuel pipes and clips from the pushrod cover.
   d. Remove the oil pressure gage sender, then remove the wiring harness brackets from the pushrod cover.
   e. Unscrew the nuts from the cover attaching studs, reverse 2 of the nuts so the washers face outward and screw them back onto the 2 inner studs.

f. Assemble the 2 remaining nuts to the same 2 inner studs with the washers facing inward, then using a small wrench on the inner nut (on each stud) jam the nuts slightly together.
g. Again using the wrench on the inner stud, unscrew the studs until the cover breaks loose, then remove the nuts from the studs and remove the cover from the engine. Remove the studs from the cover and reinstall them to the engine. Tighten the studs to 88 inch lbs. (10 Nm).

➡**Keep all components in order. If reusing components, install them into their original positions. If a new hydraulic lifter is being installed, all sealer coating inside the lifter must be removed.**

3. Remove the pushrods.
4. Remove the lifter studs and retainers.
5. Remove the lifter guides and lifters.
6. Inspect the lifter and lifter bore for wear and scuffing. Examine the roller for freedom of movement and/or flat spots on the roller surface.
7. Installation is the reverse of removal, be sure to lubricate the lifter and lifter body using clean engine oil. If installing new lifters, all sealer coating inside the lifter must first be removed.
8. When installing the pushrod cover, use a thin coating of RTV sealant around the entire cover flange. Install the cover retaining nuts and tighten to 106 inch lbs. (12 Nm) starting at the front of the engine and working toward the nuts in the rear.

2.8L Engine

▶ See Figure 169

Some engines have both standard size and 0.25mm (0.010 in.) oversize valve lifters. The cylinder block will be marked with a white paint mark and 0.25mm O.S. stamp where the oversize lifters are used.

If lifter replacement is necessary, use new lifters with a narrow flat along the lower ¾ of the body length. This provides additional oil to the cam lobe and lifter surfaces.

➡**Use of a Hydraulic Lifter Remover tool J-9290-1 (slide hammer type) or J-3049-A (plier type) will greatly ease the removal of stuck lifters.**

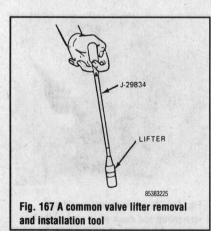

Fig. 167 A common valve lifter removal and installation tool

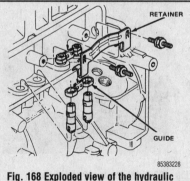

Fig. 168 Exploded view of the hydraulic lifter and related component installation— 2.5L engine

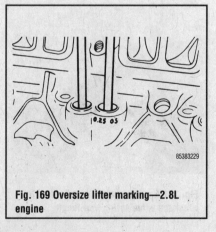

Fig. 169 Oversize lifter marking—2.8L engine

1. Remove the rocker arm covers.
2. Remove the intake manifold.
3. Remove the rocker arm nuts and balls.
4. Remove the rocker arms and pushrods.

➡**If any valve train components (lifters, pushrods, rocker arms) are to be reused, they must be tagged or arranged during removal to assure installation in their original locations.**

5. Remove the lifters from the bores.

To install:

6. For proper rotation during engine operation, the lifter bottom must be convex. Check the lifter bottom for proper shape using a straight edge. If the lifter bottom is not convex, replace the lifter. Chances are if lifters are in need of replacement, so is the camshaft.

7. Lubricate and install the lifters. If installing new lifters, coat the lifter body and foot using Molykote® or an equivalent prelube, then add 1051396 or an equivalent engine oil supplement to the crankcase.

8. Install the pushrods, rocker arms, rocker arm nuts and balls, then properly adjust the valve lash.

9. Install the intake manifold.
10. Install the rocker arm covers.

4.3L Engine

1. Remove the rocker arm cover.
2. Remove the intake manifold assembly.

➡**If any valve train components (lifters, pushrods, rocker arms) are to be reused, they must be tagged or arranged during removal to assure installation in their original locations.**

3. Remove the rocker arm and pushrod assemblies.
4. Remove the hydraulic lifter retainer bolts, them remove the retainers or retainers and restrictors, as equipped.
5. Remove the lifters from the engine.

To install:

6. Inspect the lifter and lifter bore for wear and scuffing. Examine the roller for freedom of movement and/or flat spots on the roller surface.

7. If new lifters are being installed, lubricate the lifters using a suitable pre-lube and add GM engine oil supplement or an equivalent additive to the crankcase.

8. Install the hydraulic lifters along with the restrictors and/or retainers. Secure the retainers using the bolts and tighten to 12 ft. lbs. (16 Nm).

9. Install the pushrods and rocker arm assemblies, then adjust the valve lash.

10. Install the intake manifold assembly.
11. Install the rocker arm covers.

Oil Pan

Pan removal is possible with the engine in the vehicle on some of the power-train combinations covered by this manual. If it is possible, it will often require the removal or repositioning of components including, the steering linkage assembly, the forward drive axle and crossmember (4WD) and/or the engine

mounts. It is a difficult and tedious task to remove the oil pan with the engine in the vehicle. The chances of contaminating the bearing surfaces or damaging other internal engine components is great. Also, working under the vehicle with the engine jacked up in the frame puts you at great risk for great personal injury. Therefore, it is desirable in most cases to remove the engine in order to gain access to the oil pan.

REMOVAL & INSTALLATION

1.9L Engine

▶ **See Figures 170 and 171**

1. Remove the engine from the vehicle.
2. Remove the bolts and nuts attaching the oil pan to the cylinder block, then remove the oil pan.
3. Remove the oil level gage guide tube from the intake manifold and the oil pan.

To install:

4. Using a putty knife, clean the gasket mounting surfaces. Make sure that the sealing surfaces on the pan, cylinder block and front cover are clean and free of oil.

5. Apply a thin coat of Permatex® number 2 or equivalent sealer to the front and rear pan-to-block sealing areas (shown in the illustration).

6. Install the new oil pan gasket, aligning the holes, and then install the oil pan.

7. Install and tighten the bolts and nuts evenly to 4 ft. lbs. (5 Nm).

8. Check the edge of the gasket to make certain the gasket is set in position correctly. If the projection of the gasket edge is beyond the oil pan flange is uneven, remove and reinstall.

9. Install the engine into the vehicle. Refill the crankcase with fresh oil. Start the engine, establish normal operating temperatures and check for leaks.

2.0L Engine

▶ **See Figure 172**

2-WHEEL DRIVE

1. Remove the engine from the vehicle.
2. Loosen the retainers, then remove the oil pan from the block.

To install:

3. Using a putty knife, clean the gasket mounting surfaces. Make sure that all sealing surfaces are clean and free of oil.

4. Apply a thin coat of RTV sealant to both ends of a new rear oil pan seal. Sealant must not extend beyond the tabs of the seal. Then install the seal firmly into the rear main bearing cap.

5. Apply a continuous ⅛ in. bead of RTV sealant on the oil pan side rails. This bead must be in line with the bolt holes and circled inboard at each hole location.

➡**DO NOT apply sealant to the rear oil pan seal mating surface.**

6. Apply RTV sealant to the oil pan surface which fits to the engine front cover. Ensure the sealant meets both side rail beads.

7. Using care to avoid disturbing the RTV beads, install the oil pan onto the cylinder block. The sealant must be wet during oil pan bolt torquing.

Fig. 170 Oil pan sealer location—1.9L engine

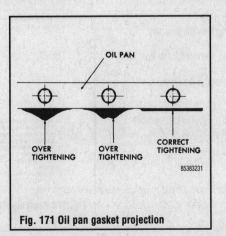

Fig. 171 Oil pan gasket projection

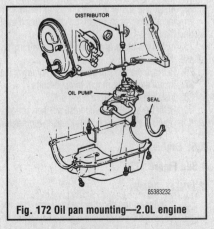

Fig. 172 Oil pan mounting—2.0L engine

8. Install and finger-tighten the oil pan retainers, then torque the attaching bolts to specification:
- Oil pan-to-cover: 6–9 ft. lbs. (8–12 Nm)
- Oil pan-to-side rail: 4–9 ft. lbs. (5–12 Nm)
- Oil pan-to-rear holes: 11–17 ft. lbs. (15–23 Nm)

9. Install the engine into the vehicle. Refill the crankcase with fresh oil. Start the engine, establish normal operating temperatures and check for leaks.

4-WHEEL DRIVE

1. Disconnect the negative battery cable.
2. Remove the starter front brace bolt.
3. Remove the motor mount through-bolts.
4. Raise and support the front of the vehicle safely using jackstands.
5. Remove the front splash shield, and the brake and fuel line clip retaining bolts.
6. Remove the crossmember bolts and crossmember. Rotate the cross-member around the lines.
7. Drain the engine oil.
8. Remove the starter bolts and support the starter aside using mechanic's wire.
9. Disconnect the steering damper at the frame.
10. Scribe the idler arm location and disconnect the idler arm and steering gear at the frame. Disconnect the front axle at the frame.
11. Disconnect the front driveshaft at the front differential, then slide the differential forward.
12. Remove the oil pan bolts.
13. Raise the engine slightly, as necessary, then remove the pan.

→Raising the engine too far could damage the EGR system. Watch for contact between the cowl and engine mounted components.

To install:

14. Using a putty knife, clean the gasket mounting surfaces. Make sure that all sealing surfaces are clean and free of oil.
15. Apply a thin coat of RTV sealant to both ends of a new rear oil pan seal. Sealant must not extend beyond the tabs of the seal. Then install the seal firmly into the rear main bearing cap.
16. Apply a continuous ⅛ in. bead of RTV sealant on the oil pan side rails. This bead must be in line with the bolt holes and circled inboard at each hole location.

→DO NOT apply sealant to the rear oil pan seal mating surface.

17. Apply RTV sealant to the oil pan surface which fits to the engine front cover. Ensure the sealant meets both side rail beads.
18. Using care to avoid disturbing the RTV beads, install the oil pan onto the cylinder block. The sealant must be wet during oil pan bolt torquing.
19. Install and finger-tighten the oil pan retainers, then torque the attaching bolts to specification:
- Oil pan-to-cover: 6–9 ft. lbs. (8–12 Nm)
- Oil pan-to-side rail: 4–9 ft. lbs. (5–12 Nm)
- Oil pan-to-rear holes: 11–17 ft. lbs. (15–23 Nm)

20. Reposition the differential, then connect the front driveshaft and connect the front drive axle at the frame.
21. Align the matchmarks made earlier, then connect the idler arm and steering gear at the frame.
22. Connect the steering damper to the frame.
23. Install the starter and secure using the retaining bolts.
24. Install the crossmember. Be careful when rotating the crossmember around the lines.
25. Install the brake and fuel line clip retaining bolts, then install the front splash shield.
26. Remove the jackstands and carefully lower the front of the truck.
27. Install the motor mount through-bolts.
28. Install the starter front brace bolt.
29. Refill the crankcase with fresh oil, then connect the negative battery cable. Start the engine, establish normal operating temperatures and check for leaks.

2.5L Engine

▶ See Figure 173

2-WHEEL DRIVE

1. Disconnect the negative battery cable.
2. Remove the power steering reservoir at the fan shroud.

3. Remove the radiator fan shroud.
4. Raise and support the front of the vehicle safely using jackstands.
5. Drain the engine oil.
6. Remove the strut rods.
7. Disconnect the exhaust pipes at the manifolds.
8. Remove the catalytic converter and exhaust pipe.
9. Remove the flywheel cover.
10. Remove the starter and brace.
11. Remove the brake line at the crossmember. Remove the engine mount through-bolts.
12. Carefully raise the engine, as necessary for clearance, then remove the oil pan bolts and pan.

To install:

13. Using a putty knife, clean the gasket mounting surfaces. Make sure that all sealing surfaces are clean and free of oil.
14. Apply RTV sealant to the oil pan flange and block as shown in the illustration.
15. Using care to avoid disturbing the RTV beads, install the oil pan onto the cylinder block. The sealant must be wet during oil pan bolt torquing.
16. Tighten oil pan bolts to 90 inch lbs. (10 Nm).
17. Carefully lower the engine into position, then install and tighten mount through-bolts.
18. Install the brake line to the crossmember.
19. Install the starter and brace.
20. Install the flywheel cover.
21. Install the converter and exhaust pipe, then connect the exhaust pipe to the manifolds.
22. Install the strut rods, then remove the jackstands and lower the vehicle.
23. Install the radiator/fan shroud, then install the power steering reservoir.
24. Refill the engine crankcase, then connect the negative battery cable.
25. Start the engine, establish normal operating temperatures and check for leaks.

4-WHEEL DRIVE

1. Disconnect the negative battery cable.
2. Remove the power steering reservoir at the fan shroud.
3. Remove the radiator fan shroud.
4. Remove the engine oil dipstick.
5. Raise and support the front of the vehicle safely using jackstands.
6. Drain the engine oil.
7. Remove the brake line at the crossmember, then remove the crossmember.
8. If equipped, remove the transmission cooler lines.
9. Disconnect the exhaust pipes at the manifolds.
10. Remove the catalytic converter hanger.
11. Remove the flywheel cover.
12. Remove the driveshaft splash shield.
13. Matchmark and remove the idler arm assembly.
14. Remove the steering gear bolts. Pull the steering gear and linkage forward.
15. Remove the differential housing mounting bolts at the bracket on the right side and at the frame on the left side.
16. Remove the starter and brace.
17. Remove the engine mount through-bolts.
18. Remove the oil pan bolts and pan.

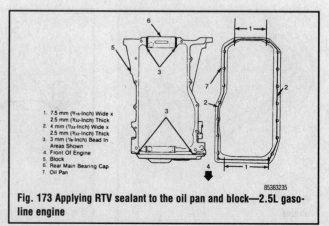

1. 7.5 mm (⁹⁄₁₆-Inch) Wide x 2.5 mm (³⁄₃₂-Inch) Thick
2. 4 mm (⁷⁄₃₂-Inch) Wide x 2.5 mm (³⁄₃₂-Inch) Thick
3. 3 mm (⅛-Inch) Bead In Areas Shown
4. Front Of Engine
5. Block
6. Rear Main Bearing Cap
7. Oil Pan

85383235

Fig. 173 Applying RTV sealant to the oil pan and block—2.5L gasoline engine

To install:

19. Apply RTV sealant to the oil pan flange and block as shown in the illustration.

20. Using care to avoid disturbing the RTV beads, install the oil pan onto the cylinder block. The sealant must be wet during oil pan bolt torquing.

21. Tighten oil pan bolts to 90 inch lbs. (10 Nm).

22. Install the engine mount through-bolts.

23. Install the starter and brace.

24. Install the differential housing mounting bolts at the bracket on the right side and at the frame on the left side.

25. Reposition the steering gear and linkage, then install the steering gear bolts.

26. Align and secure the idler arm assembly.

27. Install the driveshaft splash shield.

28. Install the flywheel cover.

29. Install the catalytic converter hanger.

30. Connect the exhaust pipes at the manifolds.

31. If equipped, connect the transmission cooler lines.

32. Install the crossmember, then secure the brake line at the crossmember.

33. Remove the jackstands and carefully lower the vehicle.

34. Install the engine oil dipstick.

35. Install the radiator fan shroud.

36. Install the power steering reservoir at the fan shroud.

37. Refill the engine crankcase, then connect the negative battery cable.

38. Start the engine, establish normal operating temperatures and check for leaks.

2.8L and 4.3L Engine

2-WHEEL DRIVE

1. Remove the engine from the vehicle.

2. Remove the oil pan retainers (nuts, studs and/or bolts) and rail reinforcements, if equipped. Remove the oil pan from the block.

To install:

3. Using a putty knife, clean the gasket mounting surfaces. Make sure that all sealing surfaces are clean and free of oil.

4. Apply 1052080 (4.3L), 1052914 (2.8L) or an equivalent sealant to the oil pan rail where it contacts the timing cover-to-block joint (front) and the crankshaft rear seal retainer-to-block joint (rear). Continue the bead of sealant about 1 in. (25mm) in both directions from each of the four corners.

➡**For the 2.8L engine, be sure all RTV is removed from the blind attaching holes to ensure proper fastener tightening can take place.**

5. Using a new gasket, install the oil pan, reinforcements (if equipped) and retainers. Tighten the retainers to specification:
   a. For 2.8L engines:
   • Two rear bolts (through 1992) and all bolts (1993): 18 ft. lbs. (25 Nm).
   • All other bolts (through 1992), studs and nuts: 7 ft. lbs. (10 Nm).
   b. For 4.3L engine:
   • Bolts: 100 inch lbs. (11 Nm).
   • Nuts at corners: 17 ft. lbs. (23 Nm)

6. Install the engine into the vehicle. Refill the crankcase with fresh oil. Start the engine, establish normal operating temperatures and check for leaks.

4-WHEEL DRIVE VEHICLES THROUGH 1991

▶ See Figures 174 thru 190

1. Disconnect the negative battery cable.

2. Remove the dipstick.

3. Raise and support the front of the vehicle safely using jackstands.

4. Remove the drive belt splash pan, the front axle shield and the transfer case shield, as equipped.

5. If necessary on early carbureted vehicles, disconnect the fuel lines and plug the openings.

6. Remove the brake line clips from the crossmember and the 2nd crossmember from the vehicle.

7. If equipped with an A/T, remove the converter hanger bolt, then disconnect the exhaust pipes at manifold and clamp from the catalytic converter. Slide the exhaust rearward.

8. Remove the front driveshaft-to-drive pinion nuts/bolts.

9. If equipped, disconnect the engine braces at the flywheel cover and loosen the braces at the block.

10. Remove the flywheel cover.

11. Remove starter-to-engine bolts, then remove the starter or support the starter aside using mechanic's wire.

12. Remove the steering shock absorber from the frame bracket. Using a scribing tool, mark the position of the idler arm-to-chassis, then remove the steering gear-to-chassis bolts along with the idler arm-to-chassis bolts. Slide the steering gear and linkage forward for clearance.

➡**A deeply offset wrench may be necessary to hold the differential housing nut. If the wrench cannot be fit fully over the nut, use a prybar to hold the wrench in position while the bolt is broken loose.**

13. Remove the front differential-to-bracket bolts from the sides of the chassis, then pull the front differential housing forward for clearance.

14. Remove the motor mount through-bolts.

15. Drain the engine oil.

➡**Use extreme caution when blocking the engine in position. Get out from underneath the truck and rock the engine slightly once the blocks are in place to be sure the engine is properly supported.**

16. Raise the engine slightly and block in position for safety.

17. Remove the oil pan-to-engine bolts, then remove the oil pan from the engine.

To install:

18. Using a putty knife, clean the gasket mounting surfaces. Make sure that all sealing surfaces are clean and free of oil.

➡**The oil pans on some early 2.8L engines may have been installed with no gasket, only RTV sealant. If a gasket is available during installation, it should be used. If not, use a ⅜ in. bead of RTV sealant around the entire oil pan sealing flange.**

19. If a gasket is available, apply 1052080 (4.3L), 1052914 (2.8L) or an equivalent sealant to the oil pan rail where it contacts the timing cover-to-block joint (front) and the crankshaft rear seal retainer-to-block joint (rear). Continue the bead of sealant about 1 in. (25mm) in both directions from each of the four corners.

Fig. 174 Loosen the brake line bracket-to-crossmember retaining bolts

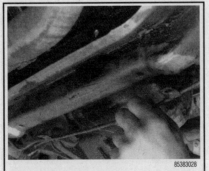

Fig. 175 Reposition the brake line away from the crossmember taking care not to damage the line

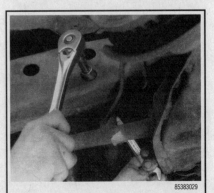

Fig. 176 Loosen and remove the crossmember bolts

Fig. 177 Begin lowering the crossmember from the vehicle, being careful not to snag the brake line

Fig. 178 Once the crossmember is clear of the brake line, remove it from the vehicle

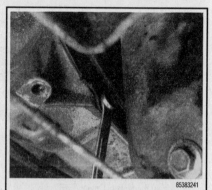

Fig. 179 Loosen and remove the flywheel cover retaining bolts

Fig. 180 With the bolts removed, carefully lower the flywheel cover from the vehicle

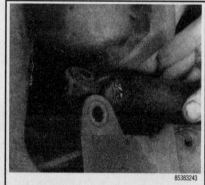

Fig. 181 Disengage the steering shock (steering damper) from the frame bracket

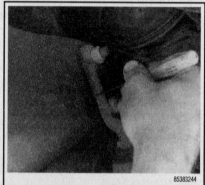

Fig. 182 Scribe the alignment of the idle arm bracket to the frame

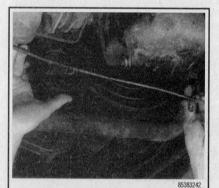

Fig. 183 Loosen the idler arm to to frame retainers (a backup wrench will be necessary for this)

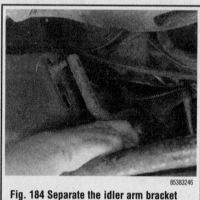

Fig. 184 Separate the idler arm bracket from the frame

Fig. 185 Loosen and remove the steering gear retainers

Fig. 186 Loosen and remove the front differential axle tube bracket retainers

Fig. 187 Remove the remaining front differential bracket retainers and the motor mount through bolts

Fig. 188 Loosen and remove the oil pan bolts

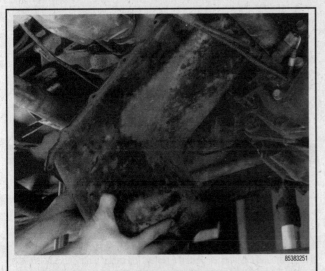

Fig. 189 Carefully lower the oil pan from the engine block

Fig. 190 BE CAREFUL, with the pan removed, the crank, oil pump and bearings are exposed to dirt or damage

➡For the 2.8L engine, be sure all RTV is removed from the blind attaching holes to ensure proper fastener tightening can take place.

20. Using a new gasket, install the oil pan, reinforcements (if equipped) and retainers. Tighten the retainers to specification:
    a. For 2.8L engines:
- Two rear bolts: 18 ft. lbs. (25 Nm).
- All other bolts, studs and nuts: 7 ft. lbs. (10 Nm)
    b. For 4.3L engine:
- Bolts: 100 inch lbs. (11 Nm).
- Nuts at corners: 17 ft. lbs. (23 Nm)
21. Remove the blocks and carefully lower the engine into position, then install the motor mount through-bolts.
22. Reposition the differential housing, then install the retaining bolts.
23. Reposition the steering linkage and align the marks made earlier, then install and tighten the retainers.
24. Install the steering shock absorber to the frame bracket.
25. Reposition and secure the starter motor, then install the flywheel cover.
26. If equipped, connect the engine braces at the flywheel cover and secure the braces at the block.
27. Connect the front driveshaft to the drive pinion.
28. If applicable, connect the exhaust pipes to the manifold, then install the converter hanger bolts and the exhaust pipe clamp.
29. Install the second crossmember to the vehicle, then secure the brake line clips at the crossmember.

30. If disengage, remove the plugs then reconnect the fuel lines.
31. As applicable, install the transfer case shield, front axle shield and/or drive belt splash shield.
32. Install the dipstick, then remove the jackstands and carefully lower the vehicle.
33. Refill the crankcase with fresh oil, then connect the negative battery cable.
34. Start the engine, establish normal operating temperatures and check for leaks.

4-WHEEL DRIVE VEHICLES 1992–1993

1. Disconnect the negative battery cable.
2. Remove the dipstick.
3. Raise and support the front of the vehicle safely using jackstands.
4. Remove the drive belt splash shield, the front axle shield, and the transfer case shield.
5. Remove the front skid plate and drain the engine crankcase oil, then remove the flywheel cover.
6. Remove the left and right motor mount through-bolts.
7. Raise the engine using a suitable lifting device and block in position. This may be accomplished using large wooden blocks between the motor mounts and brackets.

➡Use extreme caution when blocking the engine in position. Get out from underneath the truck and rock the engine slightly once the blocks are in place to be sure the engine is properly supported.

8. Disconnect the oil cooler line, then remove the oil filter adapter.
9. Remove the pitman arm bolt, then disconnect the pitman arm.
10. Remove the idler arm bolts, then disconnect the idler arm.
11. Remove the front differential through-bolts, then disconnect or remove the front driveshaft (as necessary).
12. Roll the differential assembly forward for clearance.
13. Remove the starter motor retaining bolts, then lower the starter and either remove it from the vehicle or suspend it out of the way using mechanic's wire.
14. Remove the oil pan bolts, nuts and reinforcements, then lower the oil pan and gasket from the vehicle.
To install:
15. Using a putty knife, clean the gasket mounting surfaces. Make sure that all sealing surfaces are clean and free of oil.
16. Apply 1052080, or an equivalent sealant to the oil pan rail where it contacts the timing cover-to-block joint (front) and the crankshaft rear seal retainer-to-block joint (rear). Continue the bead of sealant about 1 in. (25mm) in both directions from each of the four corners.
17. Using a new gasket, install the oil pan, reinforcements and retainers. Tighten the bolts to 100 inch lbs. (11 Nm) and the nuts at the corners to 17 ft. lbs. (23 Nm).
18. Install the starter motor and secure using the mounting bolts.
19. Roll the differential back into position, then install/connect the front driveshaft. Install the front differential through-bolts.
20. Connect the idler arm and secure using the retaining bolts, then connect the pitman arm and secure using the bolts.
21. Install the transfer case shield.
22. Install the flywheel cover, then install the front skid plate.
23. Install the front axle shield, then install the drive belt splash shield.
24. Remove the jackstands and carefully lower the truck.
25. Install the dipstick, then properly refill the engine crankcase.
26. Connect the negative battery cable.
27. Start the engine, establish normal operating temperatures and check for leaks.

Oil Pump

REMOVAL & INSTALLATION

Except 1.9L

▶ See Figures 191 and 192

1. Remove the oil pan.
2. Remove the oil pump attaching bolt and, if equipped, the pickup tube nut/bolt then remove the pump along with the pickup tube and shaft, as necessary.

To install:

3. Ensure that the pump pickup tube is tight in the pump body. If the tube should come loose, oil pressure will be lost and oil starvation will occur. If the pickup tube is loose it should be replaced.

4. Install the pump aligning the pump shaft with the distributor drive gear as necessary. Tighten oil pump/pickup tube retainer(s) to specification:
- 2.0L Engine: 25–38 ft. lbs. (34–51 Nm)
- 2.5L Engine: pump bolts 18 ft. lbs. (25 Nm) and pickup tube nut to 31 ft. lbs. (42 Nm)
- 2.8L Engine: 30 ft. lbs. (41 Nm)
- 4.3L Engine: 65 ft. lbs. (90 Nm)

5. Install the oil pan and refill the engine crankcase. Start the engine and make sure oil pressure builds immediately or engine damage could occur.

1.9L Engine

♦ See Figures 193, 194, 195 and 196

➡The oil pump in the 1.9L engine is bolted to the bottom of the engine front cover.

1. Remove the oil pan.
2. Either remove the oil pickup tube from the engine or from the oil pump.
3. If necessary, remove the distributor.
4. Remove the oil pump mounting bolt and remove the pump.

To install:

5. Rotate the crankshaft until the No. 1 and No. 4 cylinders are at TDC of the compression stroke. On most engines this can be identified when the mark on the camshaft is aligned with the mark on the No. 1 rocker arm shaft bracket and the notch in the crankshaft pulley is aligned with the "0" timing mark on the front cover.

6. Align the oil pump drive gear punch mark with the oil filter side of cover; then align the center of dowel pin with alignment mark on the oil pump case.

7. Install the pump by engaging the pinion gear with the oil pump drive gear on the crankshaft, then secure using the retainers.

8. Check that the punch mark on the oil pump drive gear is turned to the rear side (away from the water pump) as viewed through clearance between front cover and cylinder block.

9. Check that the slit at the end of the oil pump shaft is parallel with front face of cylinder block and that it is offset forward when viewed through the distributor fitting hole. If the distributor was not removed earlier, it should be removed for this step, then reinstalled.

10. Install the oil pickup tube.
11. Install the oil pan and refill the engine crankcase.
12. Check and/or adjust the engine timing. Inspect for leaks.

Crankshaft Damper/Pulley

REMOVAL & INSTALLATION

♦ See Figures 197, 198, 199, 200 and 201

Most of the engines covered in this manual are equipped with a crankshaft hub and pulley assembly. The pulley is usually mounted to the hub using 3 or so bolts around the inner circle of the pulley. The center mounting bolt is used to retain the hub to the crankshaft, but may also be used to retain the pulley. If the center mounting bolt also retains the pulley, a washer can normally be seen between the bolt head and the inner lip of the pulley.

1. Disconnect the negative battery cable.
2. Loosen and remove the accessory drive belts or serpentine drive belt from the crankshaft damper.
3. If necessary for access on certain models, remove the fan assembly.
4. Remove the pulley mounting bolts from the pulley and damper assembly. If the center mounting bolt is not used to retain the pulley, it may be separated from the hub at this time and removed from the engine.
5. Spray the damper bolt with penetrating oil and allow it to soak in for at least a few minutes. Loosen and remove the center crankshaft damper bolt. If the pulley was not removed earlier, it should be free now.

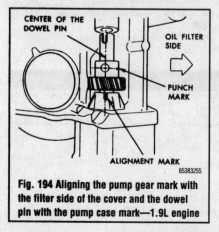

Fig. 191 The oil pan must be removed in order to access the oil pump

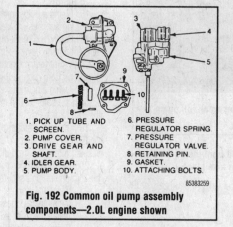

Fig. 192 Common oil pump assembly components—2.0L engine shown

1. PICK UP TUBE AND SCREEN.
2. PUMP COVER.
3. DRIVE GEAR AND SHAFT.
4. IDLER GEAR.
5. PUMP BODY.
6. PRESSURE REGULATOR SPRING
7. PRESSURE REGULATOR VALVE.
8. RETAINING PIN.
9. GASKET.
10. ATTACHING BOLTS.

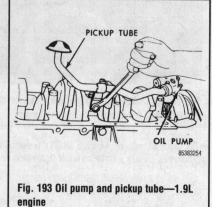

Fig. 193 Oil pump and pickup tube—1.9L engine

Fig. 194 Aligning the pump gear mark with the filter side of the cover and the dowel pin with the pump case mark—1.9L engine

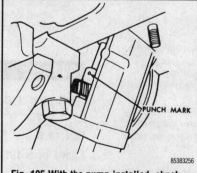

Fig. 195 With the pump installed, check that the punch mark faces to the rear (away from the water pump)—1.9L engine

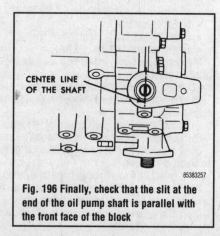

Fig. 196 Finally, check that the slit at the end of the oil pump shaft is parallel with the front face of the block

Fig. 197 Loosen the pulley and/or damper bolt(s)—in this case all must be removed before the pulley

Fig. 198 The damper retaining bolt is threaded into the center of the hub

Fig. 199 With the bolts removed, separate the pulley from the hub

Fig. 200 Use a threaded damper puller to draw the hub from the end of the crankshaft

Fig. 201 Once the hub is loosened carefully withdraw the hub from the end of the crankshaft

➡If damper bolt removal is difficult, various methods may be used to hold the crankshaft while loosening or tightening the bolt. One method involves installing a flywheel holding fixture to prevent the crankshaft from turning. A holding tool may be available for some dampers which threads into the pulley bolt holes. But most importantly of all, allow the penetrating oil to do the work when loosening an old damper bolt and reapply oil, as necessary. If you have the time, you might even want the oil to sit overnight.

6. Remove the damper from the end of the crankshaft using a suitable threaded damper puller, NOT a jawed-type puller which would most likely destroy dampers with bonded hubs.

✳✳ WARNING

The use of any other type of puller, such as a universal claw type which pulls on the outside of the hub, can destroy the balancer on some of these engines. Many of the vehicles covered in this manual use a balancer, the outside ring of which is bonded in rubber to the hub. Pulling on the outside will break the bond.

To install:

7. If removal of the damper was difficult, check the damper inner diameter and the crankshaft outer diameter for corrosion. A small amount of corrosion may be removed using steel wool, then the surface may be lubricated lightly using clean engine oil.

8. Coat the front cover seal contact edge of the damper lightly with clean engine oil, then apply a small amount of RTV sealant to the keyway in the damper hub. Install the damper on the end of the crankshaft (along with the pulley if the share the center retaining bolt), but DO NOT hammer it into position,

instead use a damper installation tool to slowly draw the hub into position. If the damper can be positioned far enough over the end of the crankshaft, the damper bolt may be used to draw it into position, but be careful that sufficient threads are in contact to prevent stripping the bolt or crankshaft.

9. Once the damper is fully seated, install and tighten the retaining bolt to specification.

10. If not done earlier, install the pulley and secure using the outer retaining bolts.

11. If removed for access, install the fan assembly.

12. Install the drive belt(s) to the crankshaft pulley.

13. Connect the negative battery cable.

Timing (Front) Cover

On most vehicles it is possible to replace the timing cover front seal without removing the timing cover. For details, please refer to the procedures found later in this section.

REMOVAL & INSTALLATION

1.9L Engine

1. Remove the cylinder head. Please refer to the procedures located earlier in this section for details.

2. Remove the oil pan. Please refer to the procedures located earlier in this section for details.

3. Remove the oil pickup tube from the oil pump.

4. Remove the crankshaft hub and pulley.

5. If not done already, remove the AIR pump drive belt.

6. If equipped with air conditioning, remove the compressor and mounting brackets and position aside with the lines intact. DO NOT disconnect the refrigerant lines.

7. Matchmark and remove the distributor assembly.

8. Remove the front cover attaching bolts, then remove the front cover.

9. If the crankshaft oil seal shows signs of wear or damage, carefully pry it from the cover using a suitable prytool.

To install:

10. If removed, install a new oil seal to the front cover using J-26587, or an equivalent seal driver tool. Be sure to support the rear of front cover in the seal area.

11. Check the front cover inner and outer faces for cracking or damage. Replace as necessary.

12. Install a new gasket onto the engine.

13. Align the oil pump drive gear punch mark with the oil filter side of cover; then align the center of dowel pin with alignment mark on the oil pump case.

14. Rotate the crankshaft until the No. 1 and No. 4 cylinders are at TDC of the compression stroke.

15. Install the front cover by engaging the pinion gear with the oil pump drive gear on the crankshaft. Loosely secure the cover using the retainers.

16. Check that the punch mark on the oil pump drive gear is turned to the rear side as viewed through clearance between front cover and cylinder block.

17. Check that the slit at the end of the oil pump shaft is parallel with front face of cylinder block and that it is offset forward.

18. Once the cover and oil pump components are verified as properly aligned, tighten the front cover retainers.

19. Align and install the distributor.

20. Install the crankshaft hub and pulley, then install the accessory drive belts.

21. Install the oil pickup tube to the pump.

22. Install the oil pan.

23. Install the cylinder head.

24. Refill the engine crankcase, then connect the negative battery cable.

25. Check and/or adjust the engine timing. Inspect for leaks.

2.0L Engine

▶ See Figure 202

1. Disconnect the negative battery cable, then drain the engine cooling system.

2. Remove the upper fan shroud.

3. Loosen the accessory drive belt adjusters and remove the drive belts from the crankshaft pulley.

4. Remove the cooling fan-to-water pump bolts and the pulley.

5. Disconnect the radiator hose and the heater hose from the water pump. Remove the water pump-to-engine bolts and the water pump from the engine.

6. Remove the pulley and hub from the end of the crankshaft.

7. Remove the front cover-to-engine bolts, then remove the cover from the engine.

8. If the crankshaft oil seal shows signs of wear or damage, carefully pry it from the cover using a suitable prytool.

To install:

9. If removed, install a new oil seal to the front cover using J-23042, or an equivalent seal driver tool. Be sure to support the rear of front cover in the seal area.

10. Using a putty knife, clean the gasket mounting surfaces. Using solvent, clean the oil and grease from the gasket mounting surfaces.

11. Apply a 2–3mm bead of RTV sealant to the front cover, oil pan and water pump sealing surfaces.

➡When applying RTV sealant to the front cover, be sure to keep it out of the bolt holes. The sealant must be wet to the touch when the bolts are torqued down.

12. Install the front cover and tighten the retaining bolts.

13. Install the pulley and hub to the end of the crankshaft.

14. Install the water pump, then connect the radiator hose and the heater hose to the water pump.

15. Install the cooling fan pulley and the fan-to-water pump bolts.

16. Install the accessory drive belts and adjust their tension.

17. Install the upper fan shroud.

18. Connect the negative battery cable, then properly refill the engine cooling system.

2.5L Engine

▶ See Figures 203 and 204

➡The following procedure requires the use of the GM Seal Installer/Centering tool No. J-34995 or equivalent.

1. Disconnect the negative battery cable.

2. Remove the power steering reservoir from the fan shroud, then remove the fan shroud.

3. Remove the accessory drive belts or the serpentine drive belt, as applicable.

4. Remove the alternator and brackets from the engine (lay them aside).

5. Remove the crankshaft pulley and hub.

➡The outer ring (weight) of the torsional damper is bonded to the hub with rubber. The damper must be removed with a puller which acts on the inner hub only. Pulling on the outer portion of the damper will break the rubber bond or destroy the tuning of the unit.

6. Drain the engine cooling system, then disconnect the lower radiator hose at the water pump.

7. Remove the timing cover bolts and cover. Check for bolts threaded from the front of the oil pan to the bottom of the cover. If present, these must be removed before attempting to loosen the cover.

8. If the front seal is to be replaced, it can be pried out of the cover with a small prytool.

To install:

9. If removed, use the GM seal installer/centering tool J-34995 or equivalent to install the replacement cover seal. Be sure to support the seal area of the cover when installing the new seal.

10. Clean all sealing surfaces and apply a ⅜ in. bead of RTV sealant to the oil pan and timing gear cover sealing surfaces.

11. Use the GM Seal Installer/Centering Tool J-34995 or equivalent align the front cover. Install the cover while the RTV sealant is still wet.

12. Install the cover (and pan) retaining bolts, then tighten the bolts to 90 inch lbs. (10 Nm). Remove the centering tool from the timing cover.

13. Connect the lower radiator hose to the water pump.

14. Install the crankshaft hub and pulley.

15. Reposition and secure the alternator and brackets.

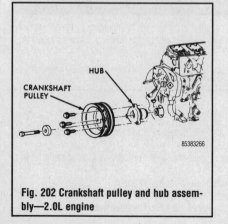

Fig. 202 Crankshaft pulley and hub assembly—2.0L engine

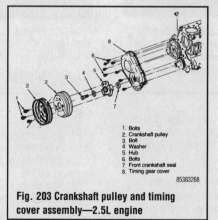

1. Bolts
2. Crankshaft pulley
3. Bolt
4. Washer
5. Hub
6. Bolts
7. Front crankshaft seal
8. Timing gear cover

Fig. 203 Crankshaft pulley and timing cover assembly—2.5L engine

Fig. 204 Applying sealer to the timing cover mating surface—2.5L engine

16. Install the serpentine drive belt or install and adjust the accessory drive belts, as applicable.

17. Install the upper fan shroud, then reposition and secure the power steering reservoir.

18. Connect the negative battery cable and properly refill the engine cooling system.

19. Run the engine until normal operating temperature is reached, then check for leaks.

2.8L Engine

▶ **See Figures 205 thru 214**

1. Disconnect the negative battery cable, then drain the engine cooling system.

2. Remove the accessory drive belts or the serpentine drive belt, as applicable.

3. Remove the water pump from the engine. For details, please refer to the procedure earlier in this section.

4. For early model engines equipped with A/C, remove the compressor from the mounting bracket and position it aside with the lines attached. Be careful not to kink or damage the refrigerant lines.

5. For late model engines, remove the power steering pump bracket.

6. Remove the crankshaft pulley bolt, crankshaft pulley and hub (torsional damper).

➡**The outer ring (weight) of the torsional damper is bonded to the hub with rubber. The damper must be removed with a puller which acts on the inner hub only. Pulling on the outer portion of the damper will break the rubber bond or destroy the tuning of the unit.**

7. Disconnect the lower radiator hose at the front cover.

8. Remove the timing cover bolts and cover. Check for bolts threaded from the front of the oil pan to the bottom of the cover. If present, these must be removed before attempting to loosen the cover.

9. If the front seal is to be replaced, it can be pried out of the cover with a small prytool.

Fig. 205 Remove the pulley from the crankshaft hub so a threaded puller may be installed

Fig. 206 Use a puller to free the damper hub from the crankshaft

Fig. 207 Disconnect the hose from the timing cover

Fig. 208 Loosen the timing cover retainers

Fig. 209 Remove the cover retainers, note the positions of studs and various length bolts

Fig. 210 Check for oil pan-to-front cover bolts and, if present, remove them

Fig. 211 Most bolts would be threaded upward from the oil pan to the front cover

Fig. 212 Once all of the bolts are removed, break the gasket seal and remove the front cover

Fig. 213 Remove all gasket material from the cover's mating surface . . .

Fig. 214 . . . then from the block and, if applicable, oil pan, but DO NOT allow debris to fall in the pan

To install:

10. Clean the gasket mating surfaces of the engine and cover of all remaining gasket or sealer material. Be careful not to score or damage the surfaces.

11. If removed, install a new seal to the cover using a suitable installation driver such as J-23042 (early model), J-35468 (late model) or equivalent. Be sure to support the back of the seal cover area during installation. Lightly coat the lips of the new seal with clean engine oil.

12. Lightly coat both sides of a new gasket using an anaerobic sealant, then position the gasket and cover to the engine. Install and tighten the retainers. On early model vehicles (or vehicles with a oil pan sealing lip on the cover), apply a bead of sealant to the front cover at the oil pan mating surface.

➡**If equipped, don't forget the oil pan-to-front-cover bolts.**

13. Install the water pump assembly to the engine.

14. Connect the lower radiator hose to the front cover.

15. Install the crankshaft hub and pulley.

16. Install the power steering pump bracket or the A/C compressor, as applicable.

17. Install the serpentine drive belt or install and adjust the accessory drive belts, as applicable.

18. Connect the negative battery cable, then properly refill the engine cooling system.

19. Run the engine until normal operating temperature has been reached, then check for leaks.

4.3L Engine

1. Disconnect the negative battery cable and drain the engine cooling system.

2. Remove the crankshaft pulley and damper. For details, please refer to the procedure earlier in this section.

➡**The outer ring (weight) of the torsional damper is bonded to the hub with rubber. The damper must be removed with a puller which acts on the inner hub only. Pulling on the outer portion of the damper will break the rubber bond or destroy the tuning of the unit.**

3. Remove the water pump assembly.

4. For 1988–91 vehicles:

   a. Remove the oil pan from the engine.

   b. Disconnect the upper radiator hose

   c. If equipped, remove the air conditioner compressor and position it aside with the lines attached. DO NOT disconnect any refrigerant lines but take caution not to kink or otherwise damage them.

   d. Remove the right side engine accessory bracket.

5. For 1992–93 vehicles, loosen the oil pan.

6. Remove the front cover bolts and, if equipped, the reinforcements, then remove the front cover from the engine.

7. If the front cover seal is to be replaced, it may be pried front the front cover using a suitable prytool.

To install:

8. Clean the gasket mating surfaces of the engine and cover of all remaining gasket or sealer material. Be careful not to score or damage the surfaces.

➡**Beginning in 1992, the manufacturer began suggesting you wait until the front cover is mounted to the engine before you install the replacement crankshaft oil seal. This may be to assure the cover is properly supported. On earlier vehicles, the manufacturer allowed for installation with the cover removed or installed, so waiting would be acceptable for all years of the 4.3L engine.**

9. If desired on early model engines, install a new seal to the cover using a suitable installation driver, such as J-35468 or equivalent. Be sure to support the back of the seal cover area during installation. Lightly coat the lips of the new seal with clean engine oil.

10. Position a new front cover gasket to the engine or cover using gasket cement to hold it in position. For 1992–93 vehicles, lubricate the front of the oil pan seal with engine oil to aid in reassembly.

11. Install the front cover to the engine. For 1992–93 vehicles, tale care while engaging the front of the oil pan seal with the bottom of the cover.

12. Install front cover retaining bolts and tighten to 124 inch lbs. (14 Nm).

13. If removed and not installed earlier, use the seal installation driver to install the new crankshaft seal at this time.

14. For 1992–93 vehicles, secure the oil pan.

15. For 1988–91 vehicles:

   a. Install the right side engine accessory bracket.

   b. If equipped, reposition and secure the A/C compressor.

   c. Install the oil pan.

16. Install the water pump.

17. Install the crankshaft damper and pulley.

18. Connect the negative battery cable, then properly refill the engine cooling system.

19. Run the engine until normal operating temperature has been reached, then check for leaks.

Timing (Front) Cover Oil Seal

On most gasoline engines covered by this manual it is possible to replace the timing cover front oil seal without removing the cover from the vehicle. For the 2.2L diesel engine the front seal is mounted to the timing pulley housing located under the timing belt assembly. The timing belt must be removed for seal replacement.

REMOVAL & INSTALLATION

♦ See Figures 215 and 216

If the timing front cover is to be removed from the engine for service, refer to the procedures earlier in this section regarding cover and seal replacement. If the timing cover does not need to be removed, replace the front seal as follows:

Fig. 215 Use a prybar to remove the old oil seal, but be careful not to distort the cover flange

Fig. 216 Install the seal to the cover using a suitable installation driver

1. Remove the crankshaft damper and pulley. For details, please refer to the procedure located earlier in this section.
2. Pry the seal out of the front cover using a small prytool. Be very careful not to distort the front cover or to score the end of the crankshaft.

To install:

3. Lightly coat the lips of the replacement crankshaft seal with clean engine oil, then position the seal with the open end facing inward the engine. Use a suitable seal installation driver to position the seal in the front cover.
4. Install the crankshaft damper and pulley.

Timing Chain and Gears

REMOVAL & INSTALLATION

1.9L Engine

♦ See Figures 217, 218 and 219

➡The following procedure requires the use of the puller tool No. J-25031 or equivalent, and timing sprocket installation tool No. J-26587 or equivalent.

1. Remove the timing (front) cover from the engine.
2. Lock the shoe on the automatic adjuster in fully retracted position by depressing the adjuster lock lever.

➡To remove the timing chain, it may be necessary to remove the camshaft sprocket. Before removing the timing chain, be sure to align the timing marks.

3. Remove timing chain from crankshaft sprocket.
4. Check the timing sprockets for wear or damage. If crankshaft sprocket must be replaced, remove the sprocket and the pinion gear from crankshaft using the puller tool No. J-25031 or equivalent.
5. Check timing chain for wear or damage; replace as necessary. Measure distance "L" (40 links) with the chain stretched with a pull of approximately 22 lbs. (98N). Standard "L" value is 15 in. (381mm); replace chain if "L" is greater than 15.16 in. (385mm).
6. Remove the automatic chain adjuster-to-engine bolt and the adjuster.
7. To check the operation of the automatic chain adjuster, push the shoe inwards, if it becomes locked, the adjuster is working properly. The adjuster assembly must be replaced if rack teeth are found to be worn excessively.
8. To remove the chain tensioner, remove the "E" clip and the tensioner. Check the tensioner for wear or damage; if necessary, replace it.
9. Inspect the tensioner pin for wear or damage. If replacement is necessary, remove the pin from the cylinder block using a pair of locking pliers. Lubricate the NEW pin tensioner with clean engine oil. Start the pin into block, then place the tensioner over the appropriate pin. Position the E-clip onto the pin, then (using a hammer) tap it into the block until clip just clears tensioner. Check the tensioner and adjuster for freedom of rotation on the pins.
10. Inspect the guide for wear or damage and plugged lower oil jet. If replacement or cleaning is necessary, remove the guide bolts, the guide and the oil jet. Install a new guide and upper attaching bolt. Install the lower oil jet and bolt, so that the oil port is pointed toward crankshaft.

To install:

11. Install the timing sprocket and the pinion gear (groove-side toward the front cover). Align the key groove with crankshaft key, then drive it into position using installation tool No. J-26587 or equivalent.
12. Turn the crankshaft so that key is turned toward the cylinder head-side (No. 1 and No. 4 pistons at TDC).
13. Install the timing chain, align the timing chain mark plate with the mark on the crankshaft timing sprocket. The side of the chain with the mark plate is on the front-side and the side of chain with the most links between mark plates is on the chain guide-side. Keep the timing chain engaged with the camshaft timing sprocket until the camshaft timing sprocket is installed on the camshaft.
14. Install the camshaft timing sprocket so that it's marked-side faces forward and it's triangular mark aligns with the chain mark plate.
15. Install the automatic chain adjuster.
16. Release the lock by depressing the shoe on adjuster by hand, and check to make certain the chain is properly tensioned when the lock is released.
17. Install the timing cover assembly.

2.0L Engine

♦ See Figure 220

➡The following procedure requires the use of the spring compressor tool No. J-33875 or equivalent, the gear puller tool No. J-22888-20 or equivalent.

1. Remove the timing cover from the engine.
2. Rotate the crankshaft to position the No. 4 piston on TDC of the compression stroke; the marks on the camshaft and crankshaft sprockets should be in alignment and positioned closest together in their travel.

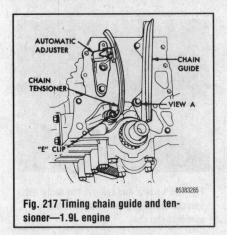

Fig. 217 Timing chain guide and tensioner—1.9L engine

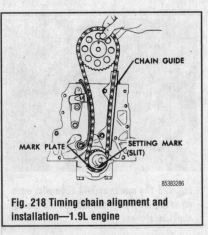

Fig. 218 Timing chain alignment and installation—1.9L engine

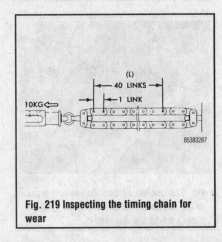

Fig. 219 Inspecting the timing chain for wear

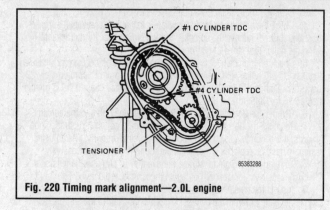

Fig. 220 Timing mark alignment—2.0L engine

3. Loosen the timing chain tensioner nut (as far as possible) without actually removing it.

4. Remove the camshaft sprocket-to-camshaft bolts and the sprocket; remove the timing chain with the sprocket. If the sprocket does not slide from the camshaft easily, a light blow with a soft mallet at the lower edge of the sprocket will dislodge it.

5. Using the gear puller tool No. J-22888-20 or equivalent, remove the crankshaft sprocket.

To install:

6. Using a putty knife, clean the gasket mounting surfaces. Inspect the timing chain and the sprocket teeth for wear and/or damage; replace the parts, if necessary.

7. Install the crankshaft sprocket onto the crankshaft, position the timing chain over the camshaft sprocket and then around the crankshaft sprocket. Make sure that the marks on the two sprockets are aligned. Lubricate the thrust surface with Molykote® or an equivalent pre-lube.

8. Align the dowel in the camshaft with the dowel hole in the sprocket and then install the sprocket onto the camshaft. Torque the camshaft sprocket-to-camshaft bolts to 66–88 ft. lbs. (90–120 Nm).

9. Lubricate the timing chain with clean engine oil. Using the spring compressor tool No. J-33875 or equivalent, position the tangs under the sliding block and pull the tool to compress the spring. Tighten the chain tensioner.

10. Install the timing cover to the engine.

2.8L and 4.3L Engine

◆ **See Figures 221 thru 226**

➡ **The following procedure requires the use of the Crankshaft Sprocket Removal tool No. J-5825-A or equivalent, and the Crankshaft Sprocket Installation tool No. J-5590 or equivalent.**

1. Remove the timing cover from the engine.

2. Rotate the crankshaft until the No. 4 cylinder is on the TDC of it's compression stroke and the camshaft sprocket mark aligns with the mark on the crankshaft sprocket (facing each other at a point closest together in their travel) and in line with the shaft centers.

3. Remove the camshaft sprocket-to-camshaft nut and/or bolts, then remove the camshaft sprocket (along with the timing chain). If the sprocket is difficult to remove, use a plastic mallet to bump the sprocket from the camshaft.

➡ **The camshaft sprocket (located by a dowel) is lightly pressed onto the camshaft and should come off easily. The chain comes off with the camshaft sprocket.**

4. If necessary use J-5825-A or an equivalent crankshaft sprocket removal tool to free the timing sprocket from the crankshaft.

To install:

5. Inspect the timing chain and the timing sprockets for wear or damage, replace the damaged parts as necessary.

6. Using a putty knife, clean the gasket mounting surfaces. Using solvent, clean the oil and grease from the gasket mounting surfaces.

7. If removed, use J-5590, or an equivalent crankshaft sprocket installation tool and a hammer to drive the crankshaft sprocket onto the crankshaft, without disturbing the position of the engine.

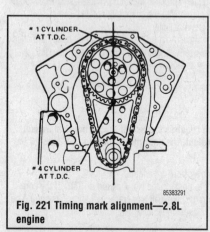

Fig. 221 Timing mark alignment—2.8L engine

Fig. 222 Timing mark alignment—4.3L engine

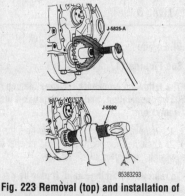

Fig. 223 Removal (top) and installation of the crankshaft timing gear

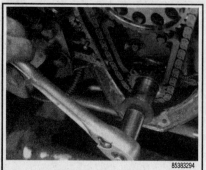

Fig. 224 Use the damper bolt to turn crank in the normal direction of rotation until the timing marks are aligned

Fig. 225 The marks should align with each other and the reference tabs on the timing chain tensioner

Fig. 226 Loosen and remove the camshaft sprocket bolts in order to remove the sprocket and chain

➥During installation, coat the thrust surfaces lightly with Molykote® or an equivalent pre-lube.

8. Position the timing chain over the camshaft sprocket. Arrange the camshaft sprocket in such a way that the timing marks will align between the shaft centers and the camshaft locating dowel will enter the dowel hole in the cam sprocket.

9. Position the chain under the crankshaft sprocket, then place the cam sprocket, with the chain still mounted over it, in position on the front of the camshaft. Install and tighten the camshaft sprocket-to-camshaft retainers to 17 ft. lbs. (23 Nm) for 2.8L engines or to 21 ft. lbs. (28 Nm) for 4.3L engines.

10. With the timing chain installed, turn the crankshaft two complete revolutions, then check to make certain that the timing marks are in correct alignment between the shaft centers.

11. Install the timing cover.

Timing Gear Assembly

Unlike the rest of the gasoline engines covered by this manual, the 2.5L engine does not use a timing chain assembly. Instead the camshaft timing gear is directly driven by the crankshaft timing gear. The timing gear (camshaft sprocket) is pressed onto the camshaft and requires the use of an arbor press to remove.

REMOVAL & INSTALLATION

◆ **See Figures 227 and 228**

➥The following procedure requires the use of an arbor press, a press plate, the GM gear removal tool No. J-971 or equivalent, and the GM gear installation tool No. J-21474-13, J-21795-1 or equivalent.

1. Remove the camshaft. For details, please refer to the procedure later in this section.

2. Using an arbor press, a press plate and the GM Gear Removal tool No. J-971 or equivalent, press the timing gear from the camshaft.

➥When pressing the timing gear from the camshaft, be certain that the position of the press plate does not contact the woodruff key.

3. To assemble, position the press plate to support the camshaft at the back of the front journal. Place the gear spacer ring and the thrust plate over the end of the camshaft, then install the woodruff key. Press the timing gear onto the camshaft, until it bottoms against the gear spacer ring.

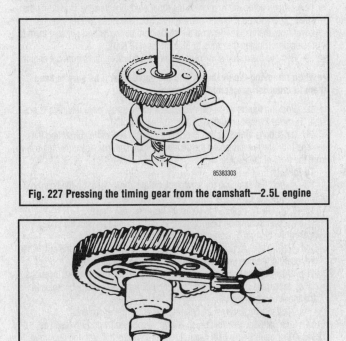

Fig. 227 Pressing the timing gear from the camshaft—2.5L engine

Fig. 228 Use a feeler gauge to check thrust plate clearance once the gear and thrust plate are assembled to the camshaft

➥The end clearance of the thrust plate should be 0.0015–0.005 in. (0.038–0.127mm). If less than 0.0015 in. (0.038mm), replace the spacer ring; if more than 0.005 in. (0.127mm), replace the thrust plate.

4. To complete the installation, align the marks on the timing gears and install the camshaft. For details, please refer to the procedure later in this section.

Camshaft and Bearings

REMOVAL & INSTALLATION

Most engines covered by this manual (except the 1.9L) utilize lifters between the camshaft and valve train. On all engines equipped with lifters, a complete new set of lifters must be installed whenever the camshaft is replaced in order to prolong the new camshaft's service life.

1.9L Engine

◆ **See Figures 229 and 230**

1. Remove the rocker (camshaft) cover from the engine. For details, please refer to the procedure earlier in this section.

2. Rotate camshaft until No. 4 cylinder is on the TDC of it's compression stroke.

3. Remove the distributor cap. Using a marking tool, mark the rotor-to-housing and the housing-to-engine positions, then remove the distributor from the engine.

4. Disconnect the fuel lines and remove the fuel pump from the engine.

5. Using two pry bars, depress the timing chain adjuster lock lever to lock the automatic adjuster shoe in its fully retracted position. After locking the automatic adjuster, check that the chain is in a free state.

6. Remove the timing sprocket-to-camshaft bolt, the sprocket and the fuel pump drive cam from the camshaft. Keep the timing sprocket on the chain damper and the tensioner without removing the chain from the sprocket.

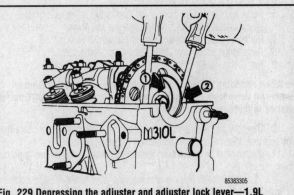

Fig. 229 Depressing the adjuster and adjuster lock lever—1.9L engine

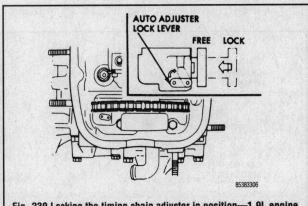

Fig. 230 Locking the timing chain adjuster in position—1.9L engine

7. Remove rocker arm, the shaft and the bracket assembly, the remove the camshaft assembly.

To install:

8. Using set of "V" blocks and a dial indicator, inspect the camshaft for damage and/or wear; replace it, if necessary.

9. Using a generous amount of clean engine oil or a suitable pre-lube, lubricate the camshaft and journals.

10. Install the camshaft, the rocker arm, the shaft and the bracket assembly.

11. Check that the mark on the No. 1 rocker arm shaft bracket is in alignment with the mark on the camshaft and that the crankshaft pulley groove is aligned with the TDC mark (0 degree) on the front cover.

12. Assemble the timing sprocket to the camshaft by aligning it with the pin on the camshaft; use care not to remove the chain from the sprocket.

13. Install the fuel pump drive cam, the sprocket retaining bolt and washer. Remove the half-moon seal in from end of head; then install torque wrench and torque bolt to 58 ft. lbs. (78 Nm); replace the half-moon seal in cylinder head.

14. Using the alignment marks, install the distributor.

15. Using a medium pry bar, depressing the adjuster shoe to release the lock, check the timing chain tension.

16. Check valve timing, the rotor and mark on distributor housing should be in alignment when the No. 4 cylinder on TDC. The timing mark on damper pulley should align with TDC mark (0 degree mark) on front cover.

17. To complete the installation, install the rocker arm cover and components. Adjust the drive belts. Refill the cooling system.

2.0L Engine

▶ **See Figure 231**

➡**If the camshaft bearings are to be replaced, the following procedure requires the use of the camshaft bearing removal/installation tool No. J-6098 or equivalent.**

1. Drain the engine cooling system.

2. Remove the timing chain and the rocker arm assemblies.

3. Remove the radiator hoses, the radiator-to-engine bolts and the radiator.

4. Remove the distributor cap, mark the rotor-to-housing and the housing-to-engine positions, then remove the distributor.

5. Raise and support the front of the truck safely using jackstands.

6. Disconnect the fuel lines and remove the fuel pump.

7. Remove the jackstands and carefully lower the vehicle.

8. Remove the rocker arm studs and the pushrod guides.

9. Remove the valve lifters.

➡**When removing the pushrods and the valve lifters, keep them in order. All valve train components which are to be reused MUST be reinstalled in their original locations.**

10. Carefully pull the camshaft from the front of the block, being sure that the camshaft lobes do not contact the bearings.

11. If removal of camshaft bearings is necessary, use the following procedure:

a. Using camshaft bearing removal/installation tool J-6098 or equivalent, install the tool with the shoulder toward the bearing. Ensure that enough threads are engaged.

b. Using two wrenches, hold the puller screw while turning the nut. When the bearing has been released from the bore, remove the tool.

c. Assemble the tool on the driver to remove the front and rear bearings.

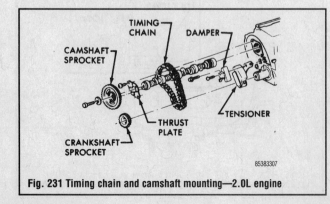

Fig. 231 Timing chain and camshaft mounting—2.0L engine

To install:

12. If the camshaft bearings were removed:

a. Install the rear and intermediate bearings with the oil hole between the 2 and 3 o'clock position. Install the front bearing with the holes at 11 o'clock and 2 o'clock.

b. Install a fresh camshaft bearing rear cover using sealant.

13. Lubricate the camshaft journals with clean engine oil or a suitable pre-lube, then install the camshaft into the block being extremely careful not to contact the bearings with the cam lobes.

➡**If installing a new camshaft, be sure to coat the lobes with GM Part No. 1051396 or equivalent.**

14. Install the camshaft sprocket and timing chain. Align the timing chain and sprockets and tighten the camshaft sprocket bolt.

15. Install the remaining components in the reverse order of removal.

16. Adjust the valve lash. Adjust the drive belts. Refill the cooling system.

2.5L Engine

▶ **See Figures 232, 233 and 234**

1. Disconnect the negative battery cable and drain the engine cooling system.

2. Remove the radiator from the vehicle.

3. If equipped with A/C, disconnect the condenser baffles and the condenser, then raise the condenser and set it aside without disconnecting the refrigerant lines.

4. Remove the grille and filler panel from the front of the vehicle.

5. Remove the timing cover from the engine.

6. Matchmark and remove the distributor.

7. Remove the oil pump drive shaft.

8. Remove the pushrod cover:

a. Remove the alternator and bracket.

b. Disengage the ignition coil wires, then remove the spark plug wires and bracket from the intake manifold.

c. Remove the fuel pipes and clips from the pushrod cover.

d. Remove the oil pressure gage sender, then remove the wiring harness brackets from the pushrod cover.

e. Unscrew the nuts from the cover attaching studs, reverse 2 of the nuts so the washers face outward and screw them back onto the 2 inner studs.

f. Assemble the 2 remaining nuts to the same 2 inner studs with the washers facing inward, then using a small wrench on the inner nut (on each stud) jam the nuts slightly together.

g. Again using the wrench on the inner stud, unscrew the studs until the cover breaks loose, then remove the nuts from the studs and remove the cover from the engine. Remove the studs from the cover and reinstall them to the engine. Tighten the studs to 88 inch lbs. (10 Nm).

9. Remove the rocker arm cover, pushrods and valve lifters from the engine.

➡**When removing the pushrods and the valve lifters, be sure to keep them in order for reassembly purposes.**

10. Position the camshaft gear so access to the thrust plate retainers is possible. Remove the camshaft thrust plate-to-engine bolts.

11. If not done already, align the timing marks, then while supporting the camshaft (to prevent damaging the bearing or lobe surfaces), carefully remove it from the front of the engine.

To install:

12. Inspect the camshaft for scratches, pitting and/or wear on the bearing and lobe surfaces. Check the timing gear teeth for damage.

13. If necessary, replace the camshaft bearings as follows:

a. Install a camshaft bearing removal/installation tool with the shoulder toward the bearing. Ensure that enough threads are engaged.

b. Using two wrenches, hold the puller screw while turning the nut. When the bearing has been released from the bore, remove the tool.

c. Assemble the tool on the driver to remove the front and rear bearings.

d. Install the bearings at the correct clocking to ensure the oil holes in the block and bearings align.

e. Install a fresh camshaft bearing rear cover using sealant.

14. Lubricate the camshaft using a high viscosity oil with zinc (such as 12345501 or equivalent), then carefully insert the camshaft into the engine while aligning the timing marks.

15. Turn the camshaft as necessary, then install the camshaft thrust plate-to-engine bolts to and tighten to 90 inch lbs. (10 Nm).

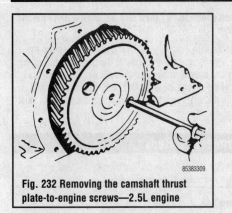

Fig. 232 Removing the camshaft thrust plate-to-engine screws—2.5L engine

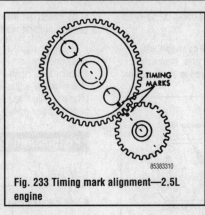

Fig. 233 Timing mark alignment—2.5L engine

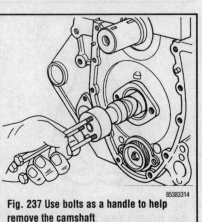

A. Apply A Continuous (5 mm ³/₁₆-Inch) Diameter Bead Of RTV As Shown

Fig. 234 Pushrod cover installation—2.5L engine

16. Install the valve lifters, then install the pushrods and rocker arms to the engine.

17. Using a thin bead of RTV sealant, install the pushrod cover to the engine, then tighten the stud nuts to 106 inch lbs. (12 Nm) starting at the front nut and working toward the rear of the engine. Reposition and secure the remaining components which were removed to access the pushrod cover.

18. Install the oil pump drive shaft.

19. Align and install the distributor.

20. Install the timing cover to the engine.

21. Install the the grille and filler panel to the front of the vehicle.

22. If equipped with A/C, reposition and secure the condenser and condenser baffles.

23. Install the radiator from the vehicle.

24. Connect the negative battery cable, then properly refill the engine cooling system.

2.8L and 4.3L Engines

♦ **See Figures 235, 236, 237 and 238**

1. Properly relieve the fuel system pressure, then disconnect the negative battery cable.

2. Drain the engine cooling system.

3. Remove the radiator from the vehicle.

4. Remove the rocker arm covers from the engine.

5. Remove the intake manifold assembly.

6. Remove the rocker arms, pushrods and lifters.

7. Remove the crankshaft pulley and hub.

8. Remove the engine front (timing) cover.

9. Align the timing marks on the crankshaft and camshaft sprockets.

10. Remove the camshaft sprocket and timing chain.

11. Remove the thrust plate screws, then remove the thrust plate.

12. Install the sprocket bolts or longer bolts of the same thread into the end of the camshaft as a handle, then remove the camshaft front the front of the engine while turning slightly from side to side, as necessary. Take care not to damage the camshaft bearings when removing the camshaft.

13. If removal of camshaft bearings is necessary, use the following procedure:

a. Install a camshaft bearing removal/installation tool with the shoulder toward the bearing. Ensure that enough threads are engaged.

b. Using two wrenches, hold the puller screw while turning the nut. When the bearing has been released from the bore, remove the tool.

c. Assemble the tool on the driver to remove the front and rear bearings.

d. Install the bearings so that the oil holes in the block and the bearing align.

e. Install a fresh camshaft bearing rear cover using sealant.

To install:

14. Lubricate the camshaft journals with clean engine oil or a suitable prelube, then install the camshaft into the block being extremely careful not to contact the bearings with the cam lobes.

15. Install the camshaft thrust plate and tighten the bolts to 105 inch lbs. (12 Nm).

16. Install the timing chain and camshaft sprocket.

17. Install the engine front (timing) cover.

18. Install the crankshaft pulley and hub.

19. Install the valve lifters, then install the pushrods and rocker arms. Properly adjust the valve clearance.

20. Install the intake manifold assembly.

21. Install the rocker arm covers to the engine.

22. Install the radiator to the vehicle.

23. Connect the negative battery cable and properly refill the engine cooling system.

INSPECTION

♦ **See Figure 239**

Using solvent, degrease the camshaft and clean out all of the oil holes. Visually inspect the cam lobes and bearing journals for excessive wear. If a lobe is questionable, check all of the lobes as indicated. If a journal or lobe is worn, the camshaft MUST BE reground or replaced.

➡**If a journal is worn, there is a good chance that the bearings are worn and need replacement.**

If the lobes and journals appear intact, place the front and rear journals in V-blocks and rest a dial indicator on the center journal. Rotate the camshaft to

Fig. 235 Aligning the timing marks—2.8L engine

A. Align Marks as Shown

Fig. 236 Aligning the timing marks—4.3L engine

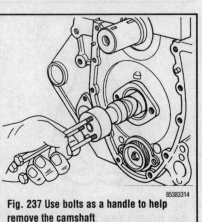

Fig. 237 Use bolts as a handle to help remove the camshaft

check the straightness. If deviation exceeds 0.001 in. (0.0254mm), the camshaft should likely be replaced.

➡On most engines lobe lift can be measured with the camshaft still installed. Simply remove the rocker cover and rocker arm, then use a dial gauge on the end of the pushrod. When the pushrod is at the bottom of its travel, set the dial gauge to "0" then turn the engine and note the gauge's highest reading.

Check the camshaft lobes with a micrometer, by measuring the across the lobe centerline from the nose to the base and again at the centerline across the diameter at 90° from the first measurement; (see illustration). The lobe lift is determined by subtracting the second measurement (diameter) from the first (diameter plug lobe lift). If the lobes vary from specification, the camshaft must be reground or replace.

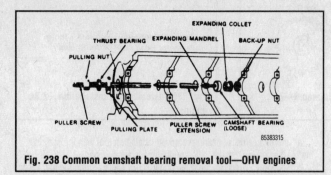

Fig. 238 Common camshaft bearing removal tool—OHV engines

Fig. 239 Checking the camshaft for straightness

Pistons and Connecting Rods

REMOVAL

◗ See Figures 240 thru 245

Although in some cases the pistons and connecting rods may be removed with the engine still in the vehicle, it is rarely worth the aggravation, especially when you are not working with a lift. On vehicles where this is possible (cylinder head and oil pan removal are both possible with the engine installed and there is sufficient working clearance) take EXTREME care to assure not dirt or contamination is allowed into the cylinders during assembly and installation.

Before removing the pistons, the top of the cylinder bore must be examined for a ridge. A ridge at the top of the bore is the result of normal cylinder wear, caused by the piston rings only traveling so far up the bore in the course of the piston stroke. The ridge can be felt by hand; it must be removed before the pistons are removed.

A ridge reamer is necessary for this operation. Place the piston at the bottom of its stroke, and cover it with a rag. Cut the ridge away with the ridge reamer, using extreme care to avoid cutting too deeply. Remove the rag, and remove the cuttings that remain on the piston with a magnet and a rag soaked in clean oil. Make sure the piston top and cylinder bore are absolutely clean before moving the piston. For more details, refer to the ridge removal and honing procedures later in this section.

1. Remove cylinder head or heads.
2. Remove the oil pan.
3. If necessary, remove the oil pump assembly.

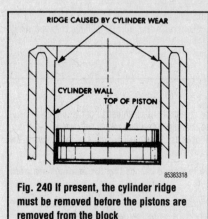

Fig. 240 If present, the cylinder ridge must be removed before the pistons are removed from the block

Fig. 241 Removing the ridge from the cylinder bore using a ridge cutter

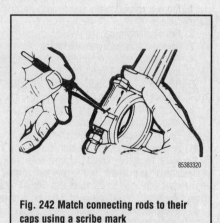

Fig. 242 Match connecting rods to their caps using a scribe mark

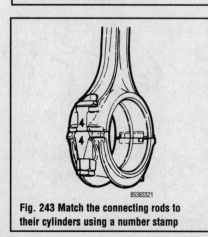

Fig. 243 Match the connecting rods to their cylinders using a number stamp

Fig. 244 Cut lengths of rubber hose for connecting rod bolt guides

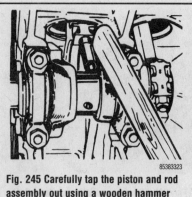

Fig. 245 Carefully tap the piston and rod assembly out using a wooden hammer handle

4. Matchmark the connecting rod cap to the connecting rod with a scribe; each cap must be reinstalled on its proper rod in the proper direction. Remove the connecting rod bearing cap and the rod bearing. Number the top of each piston with silver paint or a felt-tip pen for later assembly.

→The cylinders on a 4-cylinder engine are numbered 1-2-3-4 (front-to-rear); on the V6 (2.8L and 4.3L) engine, are numbered 1-3-5 (front-to-rear) on the right-side and 2-4-6 (front-to-rear) on the left-side.

5. Cut lengths of ⅜ in. diameter host to use as rod bolt guides. Install the hose over the threads of the rod bolts, to prevent the bolt threads from damaging the crankshaft journals and cylinder walls when the piston is removed.

6. Squirt some clean engine oil onto the cylinder wall from above, until the wall is coated. Carefully push the piston and rod assembly up and out of the cylinder by tapping on the bottom of the connecting rod with a wooden hammer handle.

7. Place the rod bearing and cap back on the connecting rod, and install the nut temporarily. Using a number stamp or punch, stamp the cylinder number on the side of the connecting rod and cap; this will help keep the proper piston and rod assembly on the proper cylinder.

8. Remove remaining pistons in similar manner.

9. Clean and inspect the engine block, the crankshaft, the pistons and the connecting rods.

CLEANING AND INSPECTION

▶ **See Figures 246 thru 251**

Pistons

A piston ring expander is necessary for removing piston rings without damaging them; any other method (screwdriver blades, pliers, etc.) usually results in the ring being bent, scratched or distorted, or the piston itself being damaged. When the rings are removed, clean the piston grooves using an appropriate ring groove cleaning tool, using care not to cut too deeply. Thoroughly clean all carbon and varnish from the piston with solvent.

Clean the varnish from the piston skirts and pins with a cleaning solvent. DO NOT WIRE BRUSH ANY PART OF THE PISTON. Clean the ring grooves with a groove cleaner and make sure that the oil ring holes and slots are clean.

Inspect the piston for cracked ring lands, scuffed or damaged skirts, eroded areas at the top of the piston. Replace the pistons that are damaged or show signs of excessive wear.

Inspect the grooves for nicks of burrs that might cause the rings to hang up.

Measure the piston in relation to cylinder diameter. Refer to the cylinder bore cleaning and inspection procedures later in this section.

Connecting Rods

Wash the connecting rods in cleaning solvent and dry with compressed air. Check for twisted or bent rods and inspect for nicks or cracks. Replace the connecting rods that are damaged.

Cylinder Bores

The piston should also be checked in relation to the cylinder diameter. Using a telescoping gauge and micrometer, or a dial gauge, measure the cylinder bore diameter perpendicular (90 degrees) to the piston pin, about 1–2½ in. below the cylinder block deck (surface where the block mates with the heads). Then, with the micrometer, measure the piston perpendicular to its wrist pin on the skirt. The difference between the two measurements is the piston clearance.

If the clearance is within specifications or slightly below (after the cylinders have been bored or honed), finish honing is all that is necessary, If the clearance is excessive, try to obtain a slightly larger piston to bring the clearance within specifications. If this is not possible obtain, the first oversize piston and

Fig. 246 Use a ring expander tool to remove the piston rings

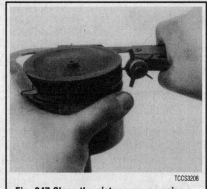
Fig. 247 Clean the piston grooves using a ring groove cleaner

Fig. 248 A telescoping gauge may be used to measure the cylinder bore diameter

Fig. 249 Measure the piston's outer diameter using a micrometer

Fig. 250 The cylinder bore may also be measured using a dial gauge

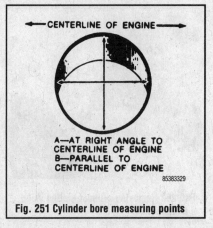
Fig. 251 Cylinder bore measuring points

hone the cylinder or (if necessary) bore the cylinder to size. Generally, if the cylinder bore is tapered more than 0.005 in. (0.127mm) or is out-of-round more than 0.003 in. (0.0762mm), it is advisable to rebore for the smallest possible oversize piston and rings. After measuring, mark the pistons with a felt-tip pen for reference and for assembly.

➡Boring of the cylinder block should be performed by a reputable machine shop with the proper equipment. In some cases, clean-up honing can be done with the cylinder block in the vehicle, but most excessive honing and all cylinder boring MUST BE done with the block stripped and removed from the vehicle.

RIDGE REMOVAL & HONING

◆ See Figures 252, 253 and 254

1. Before the piston is removed from the cylinder, check for a ridge at the top of the cylinder bore. This ridge occurs because the piston ring does not travel all the way to the top of the bore, thereby leaving an unworn portion of the bore.

2. Clean away any carbon buildup at the top of the cylinder with sand paper, in order to see the extent of the ridge more clearly. If the ridge is slight, it will be safe to remove the pistons without damaging the rings or piston ring lands. If the ridge is severe, and easily catches your fingernail, it will have to be removed using a ridge reamer.

➡A severe ridge is an indication of excessive bore wear. Before removing the piston, check the cylinder bore diameter with a bore gauge, as explained in the cleaning and inspection procedure. Compare your measurement with engine specification. If the bore is excessively worn, the cylinder will have to bored oversize and the piston and rings replaced.

3. Install the ridge removal tool in the top of the cylinder bore. Carefully follow the manufacturers instructions for operation. Only remove the amount of material necessary to remove the ridge. Place the piston at the bottom of its stroke, and cover it with a rag. Cut the ridge away with the ridge reamer, using extreme care to avoid cutting too deeply. Remove the rag, and remove the cuttings that remain on the piston with a magnet and a rag soaked in clean oil. Make sure the piston top and cylinder bore are absolutely clean before moving the piston.

❈❈ WARNING

Be very careful if you are unfamiliar with operating a ridge reamer. It is very easy to remove more cylinder bore material than you want, possibly requiring a cylinder overbore and piston replacement that may not have been necessary.

4. After the piston and connecting rod assembly have been removed, check the clearances as explained earlier in this section under the cleaning and inspection procedure, to determine whether boring and honing or just light honing are required. If boring is necessary, consult an automotive machine shop. If light honing is all that is necessary, proceed with the next step.

5. Honing is best done with the crankshaft removed, to prevent damage to the crankshaft and to make post-honing cleaning easier, as the honing process will scatter metal particles. However, if you do not want to remove the crankshaft, position the connecting rod journal for the cylinder being honed as far

away from the bottom of the cylinder bore as possible, and wrap a shop cloth around the journal.

6. Honing can be done either with a flexible glaze breaker type hone or with a rigid hone that has honing stones and guide shoes. The flexible hone removes the least amount of metal, and is especially recommended if your piston-to-cylinder bore clearance is on the loose side. The flexible hone is useful to provide a finish on which the new piston rings will seat. A rigid hone will remove more material than the flexible hone and requires more operator skill.

7. Regardless of which type of hone you use, carefully follow the manufacturers instructions for operation.

8. The hone should be moved up and down the bore at sufficient speed to obtain a uniform finish. A rigid hone will provide a definite cross-hatch finish; operate the rigid hone at a speed to obtain a 45–65 degree included angle in the cross-hatch. The finish marks should be clean but not sharp, free from embedded particles and torn or folded metal.

9. Periodically during the honing procedure, thoroughly clean the cylinder bore and check the piston-to-bore clearance with the piston for that cylinder.

10. After honing is completed, thoroughly wash the cylinder bores and the rest of the engine with hot water and detergent. Scrub the bores well with a stiff bristle brush and rinse thoroughly with hot water. Thorough cleaning is essential, for if any abrasive material is left in the cylinder bore, it will rapidly wear the new rings and the cylinder bore. If any abrasive material is left in the rest of the engine, it will be picked up by the oil and carried throughout the engine, damaging bearings and other parts.

11. After the bores are cleaned, wipe them down with a clean cloth coated with light engine oil, to keep them from rusting.

PISTON PIN REPLACEMENT

◆ See Figures 255 and 256

❈❈ WARNING

Do not use a wire brush or caustic solvent (Acids, etc.) on pistons. Inspect the pistons for scuffing, scoring, cracks, pitting, or excessive ring groove wear. If these are evident, the piston must be replaced.

Most engines covered by this manual utilize a piston and pin assembly which are pressed together. Disassembly will require an arbor press, a suitable support and the proper drivers.

➡The following procedure requires the use of the GM fixture/support assembly tool No. J-24086-20, GM piston pin removal tool No. J-24086-8, and the GM piston pin installation tool No. J-24086-9 or the equivalents.

Use care at all times when handling and servicing the connecting rods and pistons. To prevent possible damage to these units, DO NOT clamp the rod or piston in a vise since they may become distorted. DO NOT allow the pistons to strike one another, against hard objects or bench surfaces, since distortion of the piston contour or nicks in the soft aluminum material may result.

1. Using an arbor press, the GM fixture/support assembly tool No. J-24086-20 or equivalent, and the GM piston pin removal tool No. J-24086-8 or equivalent, place the piston assembly in the fixture/support tool and press the pin from the piston assembly.

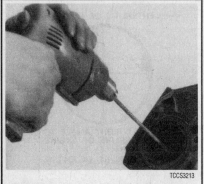

TCCS3213

Fig. 252 Removing cylinder glazing using a flexible hone

CROSS HATCH PATTERN

50°-60°

85383331

Fig. 253 Cylinder bore cross-hatch pattern

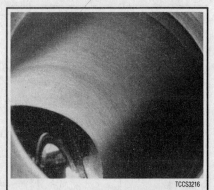

TCCS3216

Fig. 254 A properly cross-hatched cylinder bore

➡**The piston and the piston pin are a matched set which are not serviced separately.**

2. Using a suitable solvent, wash the varnish and oil from the parts, then inspect the parts for scuffing or wear.

3. Using a micrometer, measure the diameter of the piston pin. Using a inside micrometer or a dial bore gauge, measure the diameter of the piston bore.

➡**If the piston pin-to-piston clearance is in excess of 0.001 in. (0.0254mm), replace the piston and piston pin assembly.**

To install:

4. Lubricate the piston pin and the piston bore with engine oil.

5. Install the piston pin into the piston assembly, use an arbor press, the GM fixture/support assembly tool No. J-24086-20 or equivalent, and the GM piston pin installation tool No. J-24086-9 or equivalent, then press the piston pin into the piston/connecting rod assembly.

➡**When installing the piston pin into the piston/connecting rod assembly and the installation tool bottoms onto the support assembly, DO NOT exceed 5000 lbs. of pressure or structural damage may occur to the tool.**

6. After installing the piston pin, make sure that the piston has freedom of movement with the piston pin. The piston/connecting rod assembly is ready for installation into the engine block.

PISTON RING REPLACEMENT

Piston Ring End-Gap

Piston ring end-gap should be checked while the rings are removed from the pistons. Incorrect end-gap indicates the wrong size rings are being used; ring breakage could occur and engine damage could result.

Squirt clean engine oil into the cylinder, then carefully compress and insert the piston rings to be used in a cylinder, one at a time, into that cylinder. Position the rings approximately 1 in. (25mm) below the deck of the block at a point where bore diameter is smallest. The ring can be carefully positioned using the top of the piston, this will assure that the ring is properly squared to the cylinder walls. Measure the ring end-gap with a feeler gauge, and compare to the piston and ring chart earlier in this chapter. Carefully pull the ring out of the cylinder and, if a larger clearance is necessary, file the ends squarely with a fine file to obtain the proper clearance.

Piston Ring Side Clearance Check

◆ **See Figure 257**

Check the pistons to see that the ring grooves and oil return holes have been properly cleaned. Slide a piston ring into its groove, and check the side clearance with a feeler gauge. On used pistons, make sure you insert the gauge between the ring and its lower land (lower edge of the groove), because any wear that occurs forms a step at the inner portion of the lower land. If the piston grooves have worn to the extent that relatively high steps exist on the lower land, the piston should be replaced, because these will interfere with the operation of the new rings and ring clearance will be excessive. Piston rings are not furnished in oversize widths to compensate for ring groove wear.

Ring Installation

◆ **See Figures 258 thru 263**

Install the rings on the piston, lowest ring first, using a piston ring expander. There is a high risk of breaking or distorting the rings, or scratching the piston, if the rings are installed by hand or other means.

Position the rings on the piston as illustrated; spacing of the various piston ring gaps is crucial to proper oil retention and even cylinder wear. When installing new rings, refer to the installation diagram furnished with the new parts.

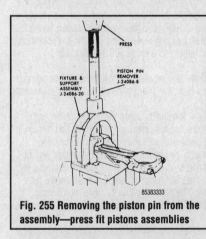

Fig. 255 Removing the piston pin from the assembly—press fit pistons assemblies

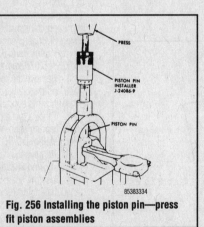

Fig. 256 Installing the piston pin—press fit piston assemblies

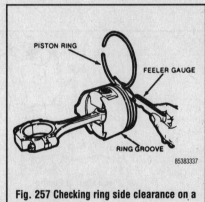

Fig. 257 Checking ring side clearance on a used piston

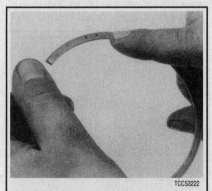

Fig. 258 Most rings are marked to show which side should face upward

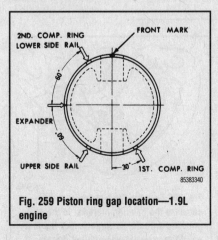

Fig. 259 Piston ring gap location—1.9L engine

Fig. 260 Piston ring gap location—2.0L and 2.5L engines

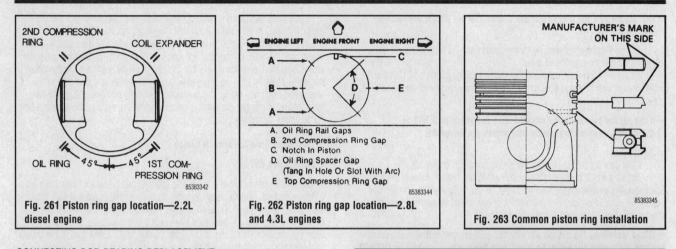

Fig. 261 Piston ring gap location—2.2L diesel engine

Fig. 262 Piston ring gap location—2.8L and 4.3L engines

Fig. 263 Common piston ring installation

CONNECTING ROD BEARING REPLACEMENT

▶ **See Figures 264, 265, 266 and 267**

Connecting rod bearings for the engines covered in this guide consist of two halves or shells which are usually interchangeable in the rod and cap. When the shells are placed in position, the ends extend slightly beyond the rod and cap surfaces so that when the rod bolts are torqued the shells will be clamped tightly in place to insure positive seating and to prevent turning. A tang holds the shells in place.

➡ **The ends of the bearing shells must never be filed flush with the mating surface of the rod and cap.**

If a rod bearing becomes noisy or is worn so that its clearance on the crank journal is sloppy, a new bearing of the correct undersize must be selected and installed since there is no provision for adjustment.

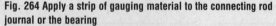

A. Place Gaging Plastic Parallel to Crankshaft

Fig. 264 Apply a strip of gauging material to the connecting rod journal or the bearing

Under no circumstances should the rod end or cap be filed to adjust the bearing clearance, nor should shims of any kind be used.

Inspect the rod bearings while the rod assemblies are out of the engine. If the shells are scored or show flaking, they should be replaced. If they are in good shape check for proper clearance on the crank journal (see below). Any scoring or ridges on the crank journal means the crankshaft must be replaced, or reground and fitted with undersized bearings.

Checking Bearing Clearance and Replacing Bearings

➡ **Make sure connecting rods and their caps are kept together, and that the caps are installed in the proper direction.**

Replacement bearings are available in standard size, and in undersizes for reground crankshaft. Connecting rod-to-crankshaft bearing clearance is checked using Plastigage® or an equivalent gauging material at either the top or bottom of each crank journal. The Plastigage® has a range of 0.001-0.003 in. (0.0254–0.0762mm).

1. Remove the rod cap with the bearing shell. completely clean the bearing shell and the crank journal, then blow any oil from the oil hole in the crankshaft; Plastigage® is soluble in oil.

2. Place a piece of Plastigage® lengthwise along the bottom center of the lower bearing shell, then install the cap with shell and torque the bolt or nuts to specification. DO NOT turn the crankshaft with Plastigage® in the bearing.

3. Remove the bearing cap with the shell. the flattened Plastigage® will be found sticking to either the bearing shell or crank journal. Do not remove it yet.

4. Use the scale printed on the Plastigage® envelope to measure the flattened material to its widest point. The number within the scale which most closely corresponds to the width of the Plastigage® indicates bearing clearance in thousandths of an inch.

5. Check the specifications chart earlier this section for the desired clearance. It is advisable to install a new bearing if clearance exceeds 0.003 in.;

Fig. 265 Install the bearing cap and tighten to specification

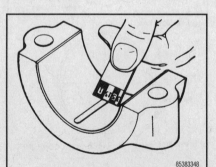

Fig. 266 Remove the bearing cap and compare the gauging material to the scale provided with the package (check the journal if the material was applied there)

Fig. 267 If necessary, remove the old bearing from the bearing cap for replacement

however, if the bearing is in good condition and is not being checked because of bearing noise, bearing replacement is not necessary.

6. If you are installing new bearings, try a standard size, then each under-size in order until one is found that is within the specified limits when checked for clearance with Plastigage®. Each undersize shell has its size stamped on it.

7. When the proper size shell is found, clean off the Plastigage® and oil the bearing thoroughly, then reinstall the cap with its shell and torque the rod fasteners to specification.

➡**With the proper bearing selected and the nuts torqued, it should be possible to move the connecting rod back and forth freely on the crank journal as allowed by the specified connecting rod end clearance. If the rod cannot be moved, either the rod bearing is too far undersize or the rod is misaligned.**

INSTALLATION

♦ **See Figures 268, 269 and 270**

➡**The following procedure requires the use of a ring compressor tool such as J-8037 or equivalent, and the ring expander (removal/installation) tool mentioned earlier.**

Assemble the piston, connecting rod and rings as detailed earlier in this section.

1. Make sure that the connecting rod big-end bearings (including the end cap) are of the correct size and are properly installed.

2. Fit rubber hoses over the connecting rod bolts to protect the crankshaft journals, as done during removal. Coat the rod bearings with clean oil.

➡**It is a good idea to lightly coat the walls of the cylinder bore with clean engine oil during assembly.**

3. Using the proper ring compressor, compress the rings around the piston head, then insert the piston assembly into the cylinder so that the notch (or other mark) in the top of the piston faces the front of the engine. This assumes that the dimple(s) or other markings on the connecting rods are in correct relation to the piston marking(s). The marks made during disassembly should serve as a guide here.

4. From beneath the engine, coat each crank journal with clean oil. Pull the connecting rod, with the bearing shell in place, into position against the crank journal.

5. Remove the rubber hoses from the studs. Install the bearing cap (with bearing shell) onto the connecting rod and the cap nuts. Torque the connecting rod cap nuts to the following:

- 1.9L engine: 43 ft. lbs. (59 Nm).
- 2.0L engine: 36 ft. lbs. (49 Nm)
- 2.2L diesel: 62 ft. lbs. (84 Nm)
- 2.5L engine: 32 ft. lbs. (43 Nm)
- 2.8L engine: 39 ft. lbs. (53 Nm)
- 4.3L engine: 45 ft. lbs. (61 Nm) for vehicles through 1990 or to 20 ft. lbs. (27 Nm), plus a 70 degree additional turn for 1991–93 vehicles.

➡**When more than one rod and piston assembly is being installed, the connecting rod cap attaching nuts should only be tightened enough to keep each rod in position until all have been installed. This will ease the installation of the remaining piston assemblies.**

6. Check the clearance between the sides of the connecting rods and crankshaft using a feeler gauge. Spread the rods slightly with a small prybar

and insert the gauge. If clearance is below the minimum tolerance, the rod may be machined to provide adequate clearance. If clearance is excessive, substitute an unworn rod, and recheck. If clearance is still outside specifications, the crankshaft must be welded and reground, or replaced.

7. If removed, install the oil pump
8. Install the oil pan.
9. Install the cylinder head(s), as applicable.
10. If removed, install the engine to the vehicle.

Freeze Plugs

On most cast iron blocks, round metal plugs are used to seal coolant jackets. These plugs allow for a certain amount of water and block expansion should water (without anti-freeze) ever be left in the coolant system. Although the cooling system should NEVER be filled with plain water only, an emergency and unavailability of coolant could force the situation to occur.

In the event that water only is placed in the cooling system and the engine is subject to sub-freezing temperatures, it is likely that the water will freeze and expand. It is also quite possible that the block will expand and crack. If you are lucky though, the expansion may only cause freeze plugs to become dislodged.

During engine block overhaul, it is often standard procedure to remove and replace all of the freeze plugs.

REMOVAL & INSTALLATION

♦ **See Figures 271 and 272**

1. Disconnect the negative battery cable, then properly drain the engine cooling system.

2. If equipped, remove the engine coolant drain plugs (located at the bottom of the block usually near the oil pan rail) and drain the coolant from the block. If the engine is not equipped with coolant drain plugs, drill a small hole in the leaking freeze plug and allow any remaining coolant to drain.

3. Remove any components that restrict access to the freeze plug or, if necessary, remove the engine from the vehicle for access to the freeze plug(s).

❊❊ CAUTION

Always wear proper eye protection when using a chisel, especially when attempting to dislodge a freeze plug.

4. Using a chisel, tap the bottom edge of the freeze plug to cock it in the bore. Remove the plug using pliers, but be careful not to score the block or the new freeze plug may not fit well. An alternate method is to drill an ⅛ in. hole in the plug and remove it using a dent puller.

To install:
5. Clean the bore of any debris and make sure it is free of any deep scratches which could cause a leak.

➡**Some auto part stores may offer easy to install freeze plugs consisting of a grommet with metal plates and an adjustment bolt. These plugs are positioned, then the bolt is tightened to expand the grommet sealing the block bore. Although these might be handy to get the vehicle home quickly, they should not be installed as a permanent fix.**

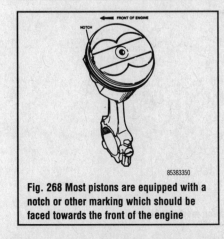

Fig. 268 Most pistons are equipped with a notch or other marking which should be faced towards the front of the engine

Fig. 269 Using a wooden hammer handle, carefully tap the piston down through the ring compressor and into the cylinder bore

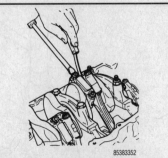

Fig. 270 Check the connecting rod side clearance using a feeler gauge. A small prybar should be used to carefully spread the connecting rods.

6. Freeze plugs are interference fitted to the block. Make sure you have the proper plug size and an equalled sized driver. The proper sized driver will ease the installation process by preventing the plug from cocking in the bore as it is driven into position.

7. Coat the plug with sealant, then position it to the bore and drive it into position.

8. Install the interfering components or the engine, as applicable.

9. Connect the negative battery cable and properly refill the engine cooling system, then check for leaks.

Rear Main Oil Seal

Replacing a rear main seal is a formidable task. Before replacing the seal, care should be taken in determining the exact source of the leak. Various manufacturers produce a fluorescent die oil additive which can be added to your crankcase. The engine is run, allowing the dyed oil to leak from the same source, then a black light is used to illuminate the leak so it can be traced.

REPLACEMENT

1.9L Engine

▶ **See Figures 273 and 274**

➡ **The following procedure requires the use of the seal Installer tool No. J-22928-A or equivalent**

1. Disconnect the negative battery cable.
2. Raise and support the front of the vehicle safely using jackstands.
3. Remove the starter motor and support it aside using mechanic's wire. DO NOT allow the starter to hang by the wires.
4. Remove driveshaft.
5. Support the rear of the engine and remove the transmission.
6. If equipped with a manual transmission, remove the clutch assembly.
7. Remove the flywheel-to-crankshaft bolts and the flywheel.
8. Remove the rear main seal retainer from the engine.

9. Using a medium pry bar, remove the rear main oil seal from the retainer and discard it. Be careful not to damage the retainer when removing the seal.

To install:

10. Lubricate the lips of the new seal and fill the space between the seal and the crankshaft with grease.

11. Using a seal Installer tool such as J-22928-A or equivalent, drive the new rear main oil seal into the housing.

12. Install the rear main seal retainer to the engine.

13. Position the flywheel, then secure using the flywheel-to-crankshaft bolts.

14. If equipped with a manual transmission, install the clutch assembly.

15. Install the transmission and remove the temporary support at the rear of the engine.

16. Install driveshaft.

17. Reposition and secure the starter motor.

18. Remove the jackstands and carefully lower the vehicle.

19. Connect the negative battery cable.

2.0L and 2.8L Engines

▶ **See Figure 275**

There are 2 sizes of seals used on these engines; 5mm and 11mm. The 5mm seal is available for 1 and 2 piece applications, while the 11mm seal is available only as a one piece design. Early models of the 2.0L and 2.8L engines may be equipped with any of these seals. Later models of the 2.0L engine will tend to be equipped with either of the 1 piece designs, while later models of the 2.8L engine are equipped with the 11mm one piece rear main seal.

To determine the type of oil seal on 2.0L engines, it will be necessary to look for an identification mark (oval) stamped on the right rear side of the engine where it connects to the transmission. If the oval appears, the engine uses an 11mm second design (one-piece) seal. If the oval does not appear the engine uses a 5mm first design seal. The first design seals may come in either a one or two piece configuration.

On 2.8L engines, the year of the engine (usually same as the vehicle) determines the seal used as follows:

- 1982–85 engines use a 5mm first design rear main seal.
- 1986–93 engines use an 11mm second design rear main seal.

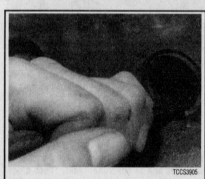

Fig. 271 Using a punch and hammer, the freeze plug can be cocked and loosened in the block

Fig. 272 Once the freeze plug has been cocked, it can be removed from the block

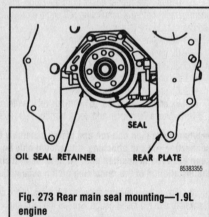

Fig. 273 Rear main seal mounting—1.9L engine

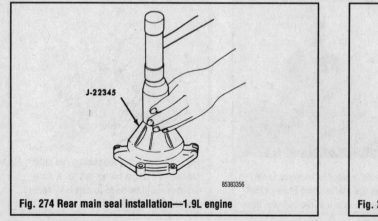

Fig. 274 Rear main seal installation—1.9L engine

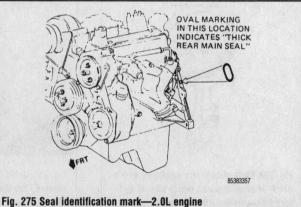

Fig. 275 Seal identification mark—2.0L engine

5MM TWO PIECE

▶ **See Figure 276**

1. Remove the oil pan.
2. Remove the oil pump.
3. Remove the rear main bearing cap.
4. Remove the upper and lower seal. Be careful when removing the upper seal not to score the crankshaft or sealing surface. Clean the seal channel of any oil.

To install:

➡ To install the replacement seal, you may need to loosen numbers 2, 3, and 4 rear main bearing caps.

5. Apply a very thin coat of gasket sealant to the outside diameter of the upper seal. Install the seal with the lip inward, turning the crankshaft to ease installation.
6. Install the lower seal in the rear main bearing cap after applying sealant to the outside diameter.
7. Check the bearing clearance of the rear main bearing with Plastigage®. Repair as necessary if out of specification.
8. Lightly oil the rear main bearing after removing the Plastigage®. Apply a 1mm bead of RTV to the rear main bearing cap between the rear main seal end and the oil pan rear seal groove. DO NOT allow sealant to come in contact with the rear main seal or the drain slot.
9. Lightly oil the rear main seal and install the rear main bearing cap. Torque the cap bolts to specification.
10. Install the oil pump.
11. Install the oil pan.

5MM ONE PIECE

▶ **See Figure 277**

1. Remove the engine from the vehicle.
2. Remove the oil pan, then remove the oil pump.
3. Remove the front (timing) cover and lock the chain tensioner with a pin.
4. Rotate the crankshaft until the timing marks on the cam and crank sprockets line up.
5. Remove the camshaft bolt, cam sprocket and timing chain.
6. Rotate the crankshaft to a horizontal position and remove the rod bearing nuts, caps and bearings.

➡ The rod bearings and caps must be replaced in order. DO NOT mix them up.

7. Remove the main bearing bolts, caps and bearings. Remove the crankshaft.
8. Remove the old rear main seal and clean the sealant from the crankshaft and block.

To install:

9. Apply a light coat of sealant to the outside diameter of the replacement seal.
10. Place a Seal Tool assembly on the rear area of the crankshaft. Position the seal tool so that the arrow points toward the engine. Place the crankshaft in the engine with the tool in this position. Remove and discard the tool.

11. Seal the rear main bearing split line (use sealant No. 1052756) and replace the rear main bearing and cap.
12. Replace the other bearings and caps, then tighten bolts to specification.
13. Replace the rod bearings and caps, then tighten the bolts to specification.
14. Install the oil pump.
15. Align the crank sprocket timing mark, then install the cam sprocket and timing chain.
16. Install the engine front cover.
17. Install the oil pan.
18. Install the engine.

11MM ONE PIECE

▶ **See Figures 278 and 279**

➡ The following procedure requires the use of a seal installation tool such as J-34686 or equivalent.

1. Remove the transmission assembly.
2. Remove the flywheel and verify the rear main seal is leaking.
3. Remove the seal by inserting a small prybar through the dust lip at an angle and prying the seal out. Be careful not to score the crankshaft sealing surface.

To install:

4. Check the crankshaft and seal bore for nicks or damage. Repair as necessary.
5. Lightly coat the inner diameter of the seal with clean engine oil.
6. Position the seal over the mandrel of the J-34686 or an equivalent installation tool. Make sure the dust lip (back of seal) is bottomed squarely against the collar of the tool.
7. Lightly coat the outer diameter of the seal using clean engine oil, then position the tool to the crankshaft while aligning the tool dowel pin with the crankshaft dowel pin hole. Tighten the screws to attach the tool and assure proper seal installation.
8. Turn the handle of the tool until the collar is tight against the case and the seal has been completely seated.
9. Turn the handle of the tool out until it stops, then remove the tool and verify that the is seated squarely in the bore.
10. Install the flywheel.
11. Install the transmission assembly.

2.5L and 4.3L Engine

➡ The following procedure requires the use of a seal installation tool (such as J-34924 for the 2.5L and J-35621 for the 4.3L) or equivalent.

1. Remove the transmission assembly.
2. If equipped, remove the clutch assembly.
3. Remove the flywheel and verify the rear main seal is leaking.
4. Remove the seal by inserting a small prybar through the dust lip at an angle and prying the seal out. Be careful not to score the crankshaft sealing surface.

To install:

5. Check the crankshaft and seal bore for nicks or damage. Repair as necessary.
6. Lightly coat the inner and outer diameters of the seal with clean engine oil, then position the seal on the installation tool.

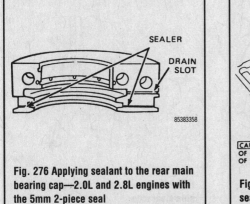

Fig. 276 Applying sealant to the rear main bearing cap—2.0L and 2.8L engines with the 5mm 2-piece seal

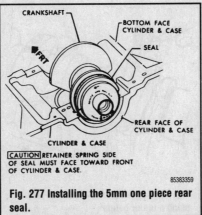

Fig. 277 Installing the 5mm one piece rear seal.

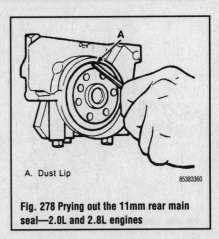

Fig. 278 Prying out the 11mm rear main seal—2.0L and 2.8L engines

7. Position the tool to the crankshaft and thread the tool's screws into the tapped holes. Tighten the screws securely using a screwdriver to attach the tool and assure proper seal installation.

8. Turn the handle of the tool until it bottoms and the seal has been completely seated.

9. Turn the handle of the tool out until it stops, then remove the tool and verify that the is seated squarely in the bore.

10. Install the flywheel to the engine.

11. If equipped, install the clutch assembly.

12. Install the transmission assembly.

Crankshaft and Main Bearings

REMOVAL & INSTALLATION

◆ **See Figures 280, 281, 282 and 283**

1. Drain the crankcase oil and remove the engine from the truck.

2. Remove the flywheel and mount the engine on a work stand in a suitable working area. Invert the engine, so the oil pan is facing up.

➡**If the cylinder heads are not being removed, the spark plugs should be removed in order to release engine compression and allow for easier rotation of the crankshaft when necessary.**

3. Remove the engine front (timing) cover.

4. Align the timing marks, then remove the timing chain and gears.

➡**After removing the timing gear or sprocket from the crankshaft, be sure to remove the woodruff key from the crankshaft.**

5. Remove the oil pan.

6. If necessary, remove the oil pump assembly.

7. Inspect the connecting rods and bearing caps for identification marks (numbers). If there are none, stamp the cylinder number on the machined surfaces of the bolt bosses of the connecting rods and caps for identification when reinstalling. If the pistons are to be removed eventually from the connecting rod, mark the cylinder number on the pistons with silver paint or felt-tip pen for proper cylinder identification and cap-to-rod location.

8. Remove the connecting rod nuts and caps, then store them in the order of removal. Place short pieces of rubber hose on the connecting rod studs to prevent damaging the crankshaft bearing surfaces.

9. Check the main bearing caps for identification marks (if not identified, mark them). Remove the main bearing caps and store them in order, for reassembly purposes; the caps must be reinstalled in their original position.

10. If equipped, remove the 1-piece rear main seal retainer from the engine.

11. Install rubber bands between a bolt on each connecting rod and oil pan bolts that have been reinstalled in the block (see illustration). This will keep the rods from banging on the block when the crank is removed.

12. Carefully lift the crankshaft out of the block. The rods will pivot to the center of the engine when the crank is removed.

To install:

13. Clean and inspect all parts for damage. Repair or replace, as necessary.

14. Install new bearing shell inserts and check the bearing clearances.

➡**If necessary, deliver the crankshaft to an automotive machine shop, have the crankshaft journals ground and new bearing shells matched.**

15. Lubricate all of the parts and oil seals with clean engine oil.

16. Using a feeler gauge and a medium pry bar, move the crankshaft forward-and-rearward. Check the crankshaft end-play by inserting a feeler gauge between the crankshaft and the thrust bearing shell. An alternate method is to use a dial indicator at the crankshaft snout. Install the indicator, move the crankshaft rearward, zero the indicator and then move the crankshaft forward. the dial indicator will read the end-play. Thrust bearing location varies with the engine:

- 1.9L engine: No. 3
- 2.0L engine: No. 4
- 2.5L engine: No. 5
- 2.8L engine: No. 3
- 4.3L engine: No. 4

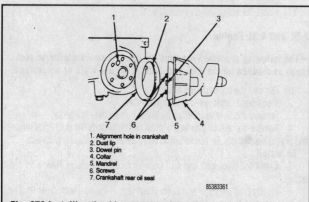

1. Alignment hole in crankshaft
2. Dust lip
3. Dowel pin
4. Collar
5. Mandrel
6. Screws
7. Crankshaft rear oil seal

85383361

Fig. 279 Installing the 11mm rear main seal

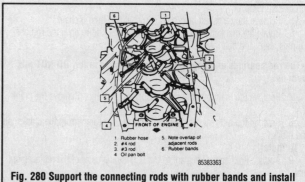

1. Rubber hose
2. #4 rod
3. #3 rod
4. Oil pan bolt
5. Note overlap of adjacent rods
6. Rubber bands

85383363

Fig. 280 Support the connecting rods with rubber bands and install rubber rod bolt caps to protect the crankshaft during removal and installation

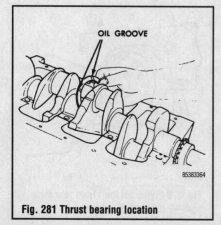

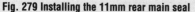

OIL GROOVE

85383364

Fig. 281 Thrust bearing location

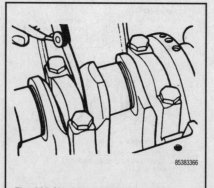

85383366

Fig. 282 Checking crankshaft end-play using a feeler gauge

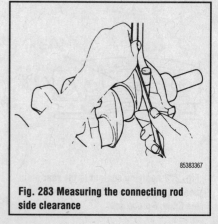

85383367

Fig. 283 Measuring the connecting rod side clearance

17. Tighten main bearing caps (in three steps) to specification:
- 1.9L engine: 72 ft. lbs. (98 Nm)
- 2.0L engine: 70 ft. lbs. (95 Nm)
- 2.5L engine: 70 ft. lbs. (95 Nm)
- 2.8L engine: 70 ft. lbs. (95 Nm)
- 4.3L engine: 80 ft. lbs. (108 Nm)

18. Remove the rubber hoses from the studs. Install the bearing cap (with bearing shell) onto the connecting rod and the cap nuts. Torque the connecting rod cap nuts to the following:
- 1.9L engine: 43 ft. lbs. (59 Nm).
- 2.0L engine: 36 ft. lbs. (49 Nm)
- 2.5L engine: 32 ft. lbs. (43 Nm)
- 2.8L engine: 39 ft. lbs. (53 Nm)
- 4.3L engine: 45 ft. lbs. (61 Nm) for vehicles through 1990;

to 20 ft. lbs. (27 Nm), plus a 60 degree additional turn for 1991–92 vehicles; to 20 ft. lbs. (27 Nm), plus a 70 degree additional turn for 1993 vehicles

➡**When more than one rod and piston assembly is being installed, the connecting rod cap attaching nuts should only be tightened enough to keep each rod in position until all have been installed. This will ease the installation of the remaining piston assemblies.**

19. Check connecting rod side clearance by inserting a feeler gauge between the side of the rod and the crankshaft. If not within specification, repair as necessary.

20. If necessary, install the pump assembly.

21. Install the oil pan.

22. Make sure the woodruff key is installed in the end of the crankshaft, then install the timing chain and gears.

23. Install the engine front (timing) cover.

24. Remove the engine from the work stand, then install the flywheel.

25. Refill the crankcase and install the engine to the truck.

CLEANING AND INSPECTION

▸ **See Figures 284, 285 and 286**

1. Clean the crankshaft with solvent and a brush. Clean the oil passages with a suitable brush, then blow them out with compressed air.

2. Inspect the crankshaft for obvious damage or wear. Check the main and connecting rod journals for cracks, scratches, grooves or scores. Inspect the crankshaft oil seal surface for nicks, sharp edges or burrs that could damage the oil seal or cause premature seal wear.

3. If the crankshaft passes a visual inspection, check journal runout using a dial indicator. Support the crankshaft in V-blocks as shown in the figure and check the runout as shown. Compare to specifications.

4. Measure the main and connecting rod journals for wear, out-of-roundness or taper, using a micrometer. Measure in at least 4 places around each journal and compare your findings with the journal diameter specifications.

5. If the crankshaft fails any inspection for wear or damage, it must be reground or replaced.

BEARING REPLACEMENT

▸ **See Figures 287 and 288**

➡**The following procedure requires the use of Plastigage® or a micrometer set consisting of inside and outside micrometers, and a dial indicator.**

1. Inspect the bearings for scoring, chipping or other wear.

2. Inspect the crankshaft journals as detailed in the Cleaning and Inspection procedure.

3. If the crankshaft journals appear usable, clean them and the bearing shells until they are completely free of oil. Blow any oil from the oil hole in the crankshaft.

4. To check the crankshaft/rod bearing clearances using a micrometer, perform the following procedures:

   a. Set the crankshaft on V-blocks. Using a dial indicator set on the center bearing journal, check the crankshaft runout. Repair or replace the crankshaft if out of specification.

   b. Using an outside micrometer, measure the crankshaft bearing journals for diameter and out-of-round conditions; if necessary, regrind the bearing journals.

   c. Install the bearings and caps and torque the nuts/bolts to specifications. Using an inside micrometer, check the bearing bores in the engine block. If out of specification, regrind the bearing bores to the next largest oversize.

   d. The difference between the two readings is the bearing clearance. If out of specification, inspect for the cause and repair as necessary.

5. To inspect the main bearing surfaces, using the Plastigage® method, perform the following procedures:

➡**NOTE: The journal surfaces and bearing shells must be completely free of oil to get an accurate reading with Plastigage®.**

   a. Place a strip of Plastigage® lengthwise along the bottom center of the lower bearing shell, then install the cap with the shell and torque the connecting rod nuts or main cap bolts to specification.

➡**When the Plastigage® material is installed on the bearing surfaces, DO NOT rotate the crankshaft.**

   b. Remove the bearing cap with the shell. The flattened Plastigage® will either be sticking to the bearing shell or the crankshaft journal.

   c. Using the printed scale on the Plastigage® package, measure the flattened Plastigage® at its widest point. The number on the scale that most closely corresponds to the width of the Plastigage® indicates the bearing clearance in thousandths of an inch or hundredths of a millimeter.

   d. Compare your findings with the bearing clearance specification. If the bearing clearance is excessive, the bearing must be replaced or the crankshaft must be ground and the bearing replaced.

➡**NOTE: Bearing shell sets over standard size are available to correct excessive bearing clearance.**

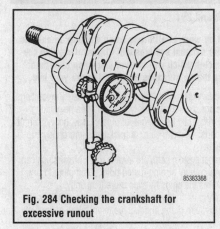

Fig. 284 Checking the crankshaft for excessive runout

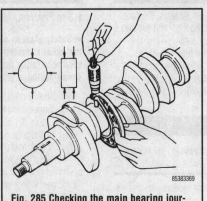

Fig. 285 Checking the main bearing journal using a micrometer

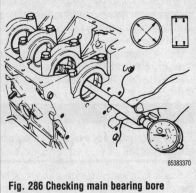

Fig. 286 Checking main bearing bore diameter with bearings installed

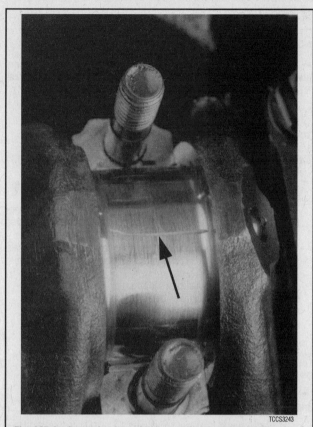

Fig. 287 Apply a strip of gauging material to the bearing, then install and torque the cap

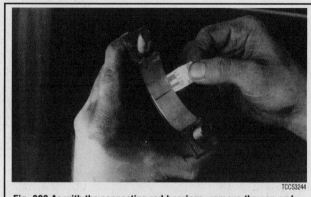

Fig. 288 As with the connecting rod bearings, remove the cap and compare the gauging material to the provided scale

e. After clearance measuring is completed, be sure to remove the Plasti-gage® from the crankshaft and/or bearing shell.

f. For final bearing shell installation, make sure the connecting rod and rod cap and/or cylinder block and main cap bearing saddles are clean and free of nicks or burrs. Install the bearing shells in the bearing saddles, making sure the bearing shell tangs are seated in the notches.

➡NOTE:Be careful when handling any plain bearings. Your hands and the working area should be clean. Dirt is easily embedded in the bearing surface and the bearings are easily scratched or damaged.

Flywheel/Flexplate

On most of the engines covered by this manual the flywheel and the ring gear are machined from one piece of metal and cannot be separated. On some of the engines (4.3L engine) the ring gear is a separate piece and can be driven from the flywheel once the gear is heated using a torch. If attempting this, first make certain that the ring gear is a separate piece, then uniformly heat it around the entire circumference. DO NOT heat the gear until it is red hot as this will change the metal structure.

REMOVAL & INSTALLATION

1. Remove the transmission assembly from the vehicle.
2. If equipped with a manual transmission, remove the clutch and pressure plate assembly.
3. Remove the flywheel-to-crankshaft bolts, then remove the flywheel from the engine.
   To install:
4. Inspect the flywheel for cracks, and inspect the ring gear for burrs or worn teeth. Replace the flywheel if any damage is apparent. Remove burrs with a mill file.
5. Install the flywheel. Most flywheels will only attach to the crankshaft in one position, as the bolt holes are unevenly spaced and/or the crankshaft is fitted with a dowel pin. Install the bolts and torque to specification using a criss-cross pattern.
6. If equipped, install the clutch and pressure plate assembly.
7. Install the transmission assembly.

EXHAUST SYSTEM

General Information

Two types of pipe connections are used on most exhaust systems, they are: the ball joint (to allow angular movement for alignment purposes) and the slip joint. Gaskets are used only with the ball joint type connections.

The system is supported by free hanging rubber mountings which permit some movement of the exhaust system but do not allow the transfer of noise and vibration into the passenger compartment. Any noise vibrations or rattles in the exhaust system are usually caused by misalignment of the parts.

❊ CAUTION

Before performing any operation on the exhaust system, be sure to allow it to cool.

As with many areas of service on your truck, the exhaust system presents it's own dangers. Always follow the safety precautions carefully during exhaust system service.

Safety Precautions

▶ **See Figures 289, 290 and 291**

➡**Safety glasses should be worn at all times when working on or near the exhaust system. Older exhaust systems will almost always be covered with loose rust particles which will shower you when disturbed. These particles are more than a nuisance and could injure your eye.**

Whenever working on the exhaust system always follow these safety precautions:

1. Support the truck extra securely. Not only will you often be working directly under it, but you'll frequently be using a lot of force, say, heavy hammer blows, to dislodge rusted parts. This can cause a truck that's improperly supported to shift and possibly fall.
2. Wear goggles. Exhaust system parts are always rusty. Metal chips can be dislodged, even when you're only turning rusted bolts. Attempting to pry pipes apart with a chisel makes the chips fly even more frequently.
3. If you're using a cutting torch, keep it a great distance from either the fuel tank or lines. Stop what you're doing and feel the temperature of the fuel

Fig. 289 A common exhaust flow—from the manifolds and crossover pipe to the catalytic converter, then gasses enters the intermediate pipe . . .

85383373

Fig. 290 . . . from the intermediate pipe, exhaust gases enter the muffler, then flow to the tailpipe . . .

85383374

Fig. 291 . . . most trucks direct the exhaust over the rear axle and out from underneath the bed

85383375

bearing pipes on the tank frequently. Even slight heat can expand and/or vaporize fuel, resulting in accumulated vapor, or even a liquid leak, near your torch.

4. Watch where your hammer blows fall and make sure you hit squarely. You could easily tap a brake or fuel line when you hit an exhaust system part with a glancing blow. Inspect all lines and hoses in the area where you've been working.

5. Check the complete exhaust system for open seams, holes loose connections, or other deterioration which could permit exhaust fumes to seep into the cab.

6. The exhaust system is supported by free-hanging rubber mountings which permits some movement of the exhaust system, but does not permit transfer of noise and vibration into the cab. Do not replace the rubber mounts with solid ones.

7. Before removing any component of the exhaust system, ALWAYS squirt a liquid rust dissolving agent onto the fasteners for ease of removal. A lot of knuckle skin will be saved by following this rule.

8. Annoying rattles and noise vibrations in the exhaust system are usually caused by misalignment of the parts. When aligning the system, leave all bolts and nuts loose until all parts are properly aligned, then tighten, working from front to rear.

9. When replacing a muffler and/or resonator, the tailpipe(s) should be checked. Often, the same wear or damage which caused a vehicle's muffler or resonator to fail will have taken the same toll on the tailpipe.

10. When installing exhaust system parts, make sure there is enough clearance between the hot exhaust parts and pipes and hoses that would be adversely affected by excessive heat. Also make sure there is adequate clearance from the floor pan to avoid possible overheating of the floor.

11. Exhaust pipe sealers should be used at all slip joint connections except at the catalytic convertor. Do not use any sealers at the convertor as the sealer will not withstand convertor temperatures.

✲✲ CAUTION

Be very careful when working on or near the catalytic converter. External temperatures can reach 1,500°F (816°C) and more, causing severe burns. Removal or installation should be performed only on a cold exhaust system.

Special Tools

A number of special exhaust system tools can be rented from auto supply houses or local rental stores that carry automotive equipment. A common one is a tailpipe expander, designed to enable you to join pipes of identical diameter. It may also be quite helpful to use solvents designed to loosen rusted bolts or flanges. Soaking rusted parts the night before you do the job can speed the work of freeing rusted parts considerably. Remember that these solvents are often flammable. Apply only to parts that have been allowed to cool!

Front Pipe/Crossover Pipe

REMOVAL & INSTALLATION

➡**Safety glasses should be worn at all times when working on or near the exhaust system. Older exhaust systems will almost always be cov-**

ered with loose rust particles which will shower you when disturbed. These particles are more than a nuisance and could injure your eye.

Except MFI-Turbo

1. Raise and support the front of the truck safely using jackstands.
2. Spray all fasteners which are to be disconnected using a penetrating oil.
3. Remove the front pipe(s)-to-manifold(s) nuts and separate (pry, if necessary) the front pipe (usually a ball joint fitting) from the exhaust manifold(s).
4. At the catalytic converter, loosen the front pipe-to-converter clamp nuts, then slide the clamp away from the converter and separate the front pipe from the converter.

➡**Use a twisting motion to separate the front pipe-to-converter slip joint connection. If the front pipe cannot be removed from the catalytic converter, use a hammer (to loosen the connection) or wedge tool to separate the connection.**

5. Inspect the pipe for holes, damage or deterioration; if necessary, replace the front pipe.
6. Installation is the reverse of removal.

➡**Be sure to use a sealing compound such as 1051249 or equivalent, at the slip joint connection.**

7. Lubricate the front pipe-to-manifold(s) studs/nuts and the front pipe-to-converter clamp threads. Torque the front pipe-to-exhaust manifold bolts to 15 ft. lbs. (20 Nm) and the front pipe-to-converter clamp nuts to 35 ft. lbs. (47 Nm).
8. Start the engine and check for exhaust leaks.

MFI-Turbo

1. Raise and support the front of the truck safely using jackstands.
2. Spray all fasteners which are to be disconnected using a penetrating oil.
3. Remove the nuts retaining the pipe to the left exhaust manifold.
4. Remove the nuts retaining the pipe to the right exhaust manifold.
5. Remove the manifold from the vehicle.

To install:

6. Install the pipe to the vehicle and loosely install the retaining nuts to the manifolds.
7. Tighten the manifold nuts evenly to 12 ft. lbs. (16 Nm).
8. Remove the jackstands and carefully lower the vehicle.
9. Start the engine and check for leaks.

Turbocharger Outlet Pipe

The 4.3L MFI-Turbo engine utilizes a turbocharger outlet pipe between the turbocharger and the catalytic converter.

REMOVAL & INSTALLATION

1. Raise and support the front of the truck safely using jackstands.
2. Remove the right front tire and wheel. Remove the wheelhouse panel screws, then remove the panel.

3. Spray all fasteners which are to be removed with a suitable penetrating lubricant.

4. Disengage the oxygen sensor electrical connector from the wiring harness.

5. Remove the nuts retaining the pipe to the turbocharger.

6. Remove the bolt from the outlet pipe support bracket.

7. Remove the clamp from the catalytic converter, then remove the bolts from the converter supports.

8. Remove the turbocharger outlet pipe.

To install:

9. Install the outlet pipe to the converter and turbocharger.

10. Loosely install the nuts to the turbocharger and the clamp to the converter.

11. Loosely install the bolts to the converter supports and the bolt to the outlet pipe support bracket.

12. Tighten the turbocharger nuts to 41 ft. lbs. (55 Nm), then tighten the clamp nuts to 42 ft. lbs. (57 Nm). Tighten the support bracket bolt to 22 ft. lbs. (30 Nm), followed by the converter support bolts to 25 ft. lbs. (34 Nm).

13. Engage the oxygen sensor connector to the electrical wiring harness.

14. Install the right wheelhouse panel, then install the tire and wheel assembly.

15. Remove the jackstands and carefully lower the vehicle.

16. Start and run the engine, then check for leaks.

Catalytic Converter

The catalytic converter is an emission control device added to the exhaust system to reduce the emission of hydrocarbon and carbon monoxide pollutants.

REMOVAL & INSTALLATION

➡**Safety glasses should be worn at all times when working on or near the exhaust system. Older exhaust systems will almost always be covered with loose rust particles which will shower you when disturbed. These particles are more than a nuisance and could injure your eye.**

1. Raise and support the front of the truck safely using jackstands.

2. Spray all fasteners which are to be disconnected using a penetrating oil.

3. Remove the catalytic converter-to-muffler bolts and separate the muffler from the converter.

➡**The connection between the converter and the muffler is usually a ball joint type, which can be easily separated.**

4. Remove the catalytic converter-to-front pipe clamp nuts and move the clamp forward.

5. Remove the converter-to-mounting bracket bolts, then twist the converter to separate it from the front pipe.

6. Inspect the condition of the catalytic converter for physical damage, replace it, if necessary.

➡**When installing the catalytic converter, be sure that it is installed with adequate clearance from the floor pan, to prevent overheating of the vehicle floor.**

7. Align the components and reverse the removal procedures.

➡**Be sure to use a sealing compound such as 1051249 or equivalent, at the slip joint connection.**

8. Tighten the fasteners taking care not to damage the pipe sealing surfaces when tightening the retaining clamps.

9. Remove the jackstands and carefully lower the truck.

10. Start the engine and check for exhaust leaks.

Muffler

REMOVAL & INSTALLATION

➡**Safety glasses should be worn at all times when working on or near the exhaust system. Older exhaust systems will almost always be covered with loose rust particles which will shower you when disturbed. These particles are more than a nuisance and could injure your eye.**

1. Raise and support the front of the truck safely using jackstands.

2. Spray all fasteners which are to be disconnected using a penetrating oil.

3. Remove the catalytic converter-to-muffler flange bolts and separate the items.

4. Remove the intermediate and rear tail pipe-to-bracket clamp nuts/bolts.

5. Remove the muffler bracket-to-chassis bolts and lower the muffler from the vehicle.

6. Coat the slip joints with GM Sealing Compound No. 1051249 or equivalent, and loosely install the components onto the vehicle.

7. After aligning the components, tighten the connecting bolts and clamps, taking care not to distort the sealing surfaces.

➡**When torquing the exhaust system connectors, be careful not to tighten the pipe clamps too tight.**

8. Remove the jackstands and carefully lower the vehicle.

9. Start the engine and check for exhaust leaks.

TORQUE SPECIFICATIONS

Component	U.S.	Metric
Intake manifold		
1.9L	17 ft. lbs.	23 Nm
2.0L	25 ft. lbs.	34 Nm
2.5L		
Early models (using bolts and studs)	25–37 ft. lbs.	34–50 Nm
Late model engines (using only bolts)	25 ft. lbs.	34 Nm
2.8L (using the proper sequence)	23 ft. lbs.	31 Nm
4.3L (using the proper sequence)		
Manifold/lower manifold (as applicable)	35 ft. lbs.	48 Nm
Upper intake manifold		
Turbo (from middle working outward)	18 ft. lbs.	24 Nm
CMFI (VIN W)	124 inch lbs.	14 Nm
Knock sensor	14 ft. lbs.	19 Nm
Main bearing caps (in three steps)		
1.9L	72 ft. lbs.	98 Nm
2.0L	70 ft. lbs.	95 Nm
2.5L	70 ft. lbs.	95 Nm
2.8L	70 ft. lbs.	95 Nm
4.3L	80 ft. lbs.	108 Nm
Oil pan		
1.9L (tighten evenly)	4 ft. lbs.	5 Nm
2.0L		
Oil pan-to-cover	6–9 ft. lbs.	8–12 Nm
Oil pan-to-side rail	4–9 ft. lbs.	5–12 Nm
Oil pan-to-rear holes	11–17 ft. lbs.	15–23 Nm
2.5L	90 inch lbs.	10 Nm
2.8L		
Through 1992		
Two rear bolts	18 ft. lbs.	25 Nm
All other bolts, studs and nuts	7 ft. lbs.	10 Nm
1993	18 ft. lbs.	25 Nm
4.3L engine		
Bolts	100 inch lbs.	11 Nm
Nuts at corners	17 ft. lbs.	23 Nm
Oil pump		
2.0L	25–38 ft. lbs.	34–51 Nm
2.5L		
Pump bolts	18 ft. lbs.	25 Nm
Pickup tube nut	31 ft. lbs.	42 Nm
2.8L	30 ft. lbs.	41 Nm
4.3L	65 ft. lbs.	90 Nm
Oxygen sensor	30 ft. lbs.	41 Nm
Connecting rod nuts		
1.9L	43 ft. lbs.	59 Nm
2.0L	36 ft. lbs.	44 Nm
2.5L	32 ft. lbs.	43 Nm
2.8L	39 ft. lbs.	53 Nm
4.3L		
Through 1990	45 ft. lbs.	61 Nm
1991 and 1992	20 ft. lbs. + 60° turn	27 Nm
1993	20 ft. lbs. + 70° turn	27 Nm

8844RT01

TORQUE SPECIFICATIONS

Component	U.S.	Metric
Pushrod cover (2.5L engine)		
Studs	88 inch lbs.	10 Nm
Cover retaining nuts	106 inch lbs.	12 Nm
Rocker arm cover		
2.0L	8 ft. lbs.	11 Nm
2.2L diesel	9–13 ft. lbs.	12–18 Nm
2.5L	75 inch lbs.	8 Nm
2.8L	72 inch lbs.	8 Nm
4.3L	89–90 inch lbs.	10 Nm
Rocker arm		
1.9L bracket studs	16 ft. lbs.	22 Nm
2.5L rocker arm bolt	22 ft. lbs.	30 Nm
4.3L (with positive stop shoulders only)	20 ft. lbs.	27 Nm
Starter		
Rear wheel drive trucks		
1982–93	30–33 ft. lbs.	40–45 Nm
Four-wheel drive trucks		
1983–93	30–33 ft. lbs.	40–45 Nm
Thermostat		
1.9L outlet pipe-to-intake manifold bolts	21 ft. lbs.	28 Nm
2.0L outlet-to-thermostat housing bolts	15–22 ft. lbs.	20–30 Nm
2.5L thermostat housing-to-engine bolts	18–20 ft. lbs.	24–27 Nm
2.8L and 4.3L (VIN Z) outlet retainers	21 ft. lbs.	28 Nm
4.3L (VIN W)	14 ft. lbs.	19 Nm
Valve lifter retainer/bracket		
Valve lifter retainer (4.3L)	12 ft. lbs.	16 Nm
Water pump		
1.9L and 2.0L engines	15–22 ft. lbs.	20–30 Nm
2.5L engine	17 ft. lbs.	23 Nm
2.8L engine		
Through 1992	22 ft. lbs.	30 Nm
1993 (refer to illustration in Section 3)		
All except central 3 lower bolts	15 ft. lbs.	21 Nm
Central 3 lower bolts	89 inch lbs.	10 Nm
4.3L	30 ft. lbs.	41 Nm

8844RT02

4

DRIVEABILITY AND EMISSION CONTROLS

EMISSION CONTROLS

▶ See Figure 1

There are three basic sources of automotive pollutants: crankcase fumes, exhaust gases and gasoline evaporation. he equipment that is used to limit these pollutants is commonly called emission control equipment.

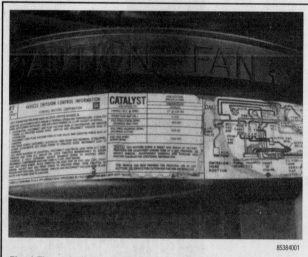

Fig. 1 The emission control label contains a vacuum diagram and engine control adjustment information

Positive Crankcase Ventilation

OPERATION

▶ See Figure 2

Before the years covered by this manual, Federal law mandated that oil fill caps on engines be sealed to prevent the escape of crankcase vapors into the atmosphere. The result was a closed crankcase ventilation system which is designed to control crankcase pressure, while preventing it from escaping into the atmosphere.

To supply this closed system with fresh air, a breather hose runs from the carburetor air cleaner to an inlet hole in the valve cover. The carburetor or throttle body end of the hose usually fits into a cup-shaped flame arrestor and breather filter in the air cleaner cover. In the event of a carburetor backfire, this arrestor prevents the spread of fire to the valve cover where it could create an explosion.

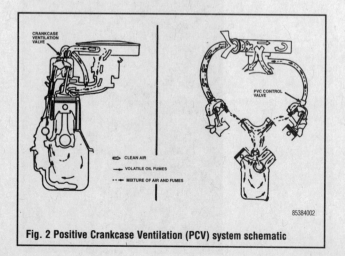

Fig. 2 Positive Crankcase Ventilation (PCV) system schematic

Included in the closed system is a Positive Crankcase Ventilation (PCV) valve that is usually mounted into an outlet hole in the top of the valve cover. A hose or hoses connects this valve to a vacuum outlet at the throttle body or intake manifold. Contained within the PCV housing is a unidirectional valve (pointed at one end, flat at the other) positioned within a coiled spring. The PCV valve meters the air flow rate, which varies under engine operation, depending on manifold vacuum. During idle or low speed operation, when manifold vacuum is highest, the valve spring tension is overcome by the high vacuum pull and, as a result, the valve is pulled up to very nearly seal off the manifold end of the valve housing. This restricts the flow of crankcase vapors to the intake manifold at a time when crankcase pressures are lowest and least disruptive to engine performance. The restricted flow also prevents the crankcase vapors from altering the idle mixture and thereby disrupting idle quality. At times of acceleration or constant speed, intake manifold vacuum is reduced to a point where it can no longer pull against the valve spring and so, spring force pulls the valve away from the housing outlet allowing crankcase vapors to escape through the hose to the intake manifold. Once inside the manifold, the gases enter the combustion chambers to be reburned. At times of engine backfire (at the carburetor), manifold vacuum ceases permitting the spring to pull the valve against the inlet (crankcase end) end of the valve housing. This seals off the inlet, thereby stopping the entrance of crankcase gases into the valve and preventing the possibility of a backfire spreading through the hose and valve to ignite these gases.

On the 1.9L engine, the blow by gases are forced back into the intake manifold through a closed system which consists of a baffle plate and an orifice mounted in the intake manifold.

A plugged PCV valve or hose may cause rough idle, stalling or slow idle speed, oil leaks, oil in the air cleaner or sludge in the engine. A leaking PCV valve or hose could cause rough idle, stalling or high idle speed.

Inspect the PCV system hose(s) and connections at each tune-up and replace any deteriorated hoses. Check the PCV valve at every tune-up and replace it at 30,000 mile intervals.

TESTING

▶ See Figure 3

1. Remove the PCV valve from the rocker arm cover, but leave the vacuum hose attached.
2. Operate the engine at idle speed.
3. Place your thumb over the end of the valve to check for vacuum. If no vacuum exists, check the valve, the hoses or the manifold port for a plugged condition.
4. Remove the valve from the hose(s), then shake it and listen for a rattling of the check needle (inside the valve); the rattle means the valve is working. If no rattle is heard the valve is stuck, and should be replaced.

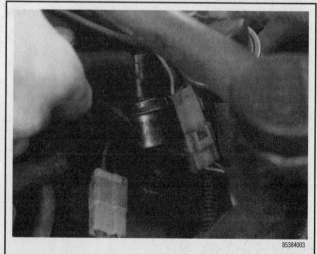

Fig. 3 To test for vacuum, remove the PCV valve from the grommet, with the hose attached

REMOVAL & INSTALLATION

PCV Valve

The large end of the valve is inserted into a rubber grommet in the valve cover. At the narrow end, it is inserted into a hose and usually clamped. To remove it, gently pull it out of the valve cover, then open the clamp with a pair of pliers. Hold the clamp open while sliding it an inch or two down the hose (away from the valve), and then remove the valve.

If the end of the hose is hard or cracked where it holds the valve, it may be feasible to cut the end off if there is plenty of extra hose. Otherwise, replace the hose. Replace the grommet in the valve cover if it is cracked or hard. Replace the clamp if it is broken or weak. In replacing the valve, make sure it is fully inserted in the hose, that the clamp is moved over the ridge on the valve so that the valve will not slip out of the hose, and that the valve is fully inserted into the grommet in the valve cover.

PCV Breather

Most breathers are located inside the air cleaner assembly, though they may be mounted directly to a valve cover. Although a breather may in some cases be removed and cleaned, it is an inexpensive part and it is wise to replace it if dirty. Breathers which are mounted directly to the valve cover may be simply grasped and pulled from the cover grommet. For breathers which are mounted inside the air cleaner follow the procedure listed below.

1. Loosen the wing nut or release the retainers, then remove the top of the air cleaner assembly.
2. Slide the rubber coupling that joins the tube coming from the valve cover to the breather off the breather nipple.
3. Slide the spring clamp off the breather nipple (if equipped) which is protruding from the air cleaner housing, then withdraw the breather from inside the air cleaner assembly.
4. Inspect the rubber grommet in the valve cover and the rubber coupling for brittleness or cracking. Replace parts as necessary.
5. Installation is the reverse of removal.

Evaporative Emission Control System (EECS)

OPERATION

The Evaporative Emission Control System (EECS) is designed to prevent fuel tank vapors from being emitted into the atmosphere. Gasoline vapors are absorbed and stored by a fuel vapor charcoal canister. The charcoal canister absorbs the gasoline vapors and stores them until certain engine conditions are met, then the vapors are purged and burned in the combustion process.

The charcoal canister purge cycle is normally controlled either by a thermostatic vacuum switch or by a timed vacuum source, though a few later model vehicles may use electronic regulation in the form of a purge control solenoid. The thermostatic vacuum switch is installed in a coolant passage and prevents canister purge when engine operating temperature is below approximately 115°F (46°C). A timed vacuum source uses a manifold vacuum-controlled diaphragm to control canister purge. When the engine is running, full manifold vacuum is applied to the top tube of the purge valve which lifts the valve diaphragm and opens the valve. If equipped with a purge solenoid, under proper engine operating conditions the ECM will signal the solenoid which will then open the vacuum line allowing manifold vacuum to control the purge diaphragm. Most solenoids used on these vehicles are normally closed and will open when the ECM provides a ground signal energizing the solenoid.

➡Remember that the fuel tank filler cap is an integral part of the system in that it is designed to seal in fuel vapors. If it is lost or damaged, make sure the replacement is of the correct size and fit so a proper seal can be obtained.

A vent, located in the fuel tank, allows fuel vapors to flow to the charcoal canister. A tank pressure control valve, used on high altitude applications, prevents canister purge when the engine is not running. The fuel tank cap does not normally vent to the atmosphere but is designed to provide both vacuum and pressure relief.

Poor engine idle, stalling and poor driveability can be caused by a damaged canister or split, damaged or improperly connected hoses.

Evidence of fuel loss or fuel vapor odor can be caused by a liquid fuel leak; a cracked or damaged vapor canister; disconnected, misrouted, kinked or damaged vapor pipe or canister hoses; a damaged air cleaner or improperly seated air cleaner gasket.

TESTING

⬥ See Figures 4 and 5

Charcoal Canister and Purge Valve

The fuel vapor canister is used to absorb and store fuel vapors from the fuel tank. Vacuum sources are generally ported, either through an internal or remote mounted purge control valve. Engines employing the timed vacuum source purge system usually use a canister purge valve which is integral to the vapor canister. The valve consists of a housing and tube molded into the canister cover, valve assembly, diaphragm and valve spring. The diaphragm cover has a built-in control vacuum signal tube.

1. Remove the vacuum hose from the lower tube of the purge valve and install a short length of tube, then try to blow through it (little or no air should pass, though a small amount may pass if the vehicles is equipped with a constant purge hole).

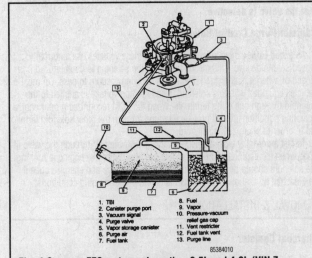

1. TBI
2. Canister purge port
3. Vacuum signal
4. Purge valve
5. Vapor storage canister
6. Purge air
7. Fuel tank
8. Fuel
9. Vapor
10. Pressure-vacuum relief gas cap
11. Vent restricter
12. Fuel tank vent
13. Purge line

85384010

Fig. 4 Common EEC system schematic—2.5L and 4.3L (VIN Z, except Turbo) engines shown

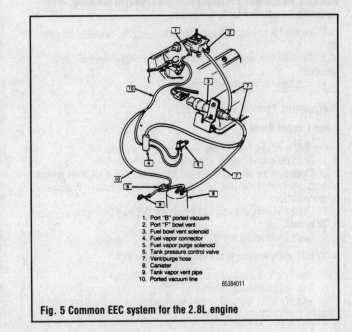

1. Port "B" ported vacuum
2. Port "F" bowl vent
3. Fuel bowl vent solenoid
4. Fuel vapor connector
5. Fuel vapor purge solenoid
6. Tank pressure control valve
7. Vent/purge hose
8. Canister
9. Tank vapor vent pipe
10. Ported vacuum line

85384011

Fig. 5 Common EEC system for the 2.8L engine

2. Using a vacuum source such as a hand vacuum pump, apply 15 in. Hg to the upper tube of the purge valve. The diaphragm should hold the vacuum for at least 20 seconds, if not replace the purge valve (remote mounted) or canister (internal mounted valve), as applicable.

3. While holding the vacuum on the upper tube, blow through the lower tube (an increased volume of air should now pass); if not, replace the valve or canister, as necessary.

➡**When testing valves by blowing air through them, be careful that you are blowing in the proper direction of flow. Many valves are designed to only allow air to flow in one direction and a proper working valve may seem defective if it is tested with air flow only in the wrong direction.**

Thermostatic Vacuum Switch (TVS)

➡**The number stamped on the base of the switch (valve) is the calibration temperature.**

1. With engine temperature below 100°F (38°C), apply vacuum to the manifold side of the switch. The switch should hold vacuum.

2. As the engine temperature increases above 122°F (50°C), vacuum should drop off.

3. Replace the switch if it fails either test.

➡**A leakage of up to 2 in. Hg/2 min. is allowable and does not mean that the valve is defective.**

Canister Purge Control Solenoid

As stated earlier, most solenoids found on these vehicles use a normally closed solenoid valve. This means that when the solenoid is de-energized it is closed or, when it is energized it will open allowing vacuum to pass. On most vehicles equipped with this solenoid, fused ignition voltage is applied to the solenoid through one of it's terminals. When the ECM recognizes proper engine operating conditions, it will provide a ground through the other solenoid terminal in order to energize the solenoid.

To test a normally closed solenoid valve, try blowing air through the valve fittings when the engine is **OFF**, air should not flow. When the engine is running the solenoid should de-energize during engine warm-up and energize once it has reached normal operating temperature and proper running conditions.

REMOVAL & INSTALLATION

Charcoal Canister

1. Tag and disconnect them from the canister assembly.

➡**If access to the vapor hoses is difficult with the canister installed, wait until the canister is released from the bracket or mounting, then reposition the canister for better access.**

2. Loosen the screw(s) fastening the canister retaining bracket to the vehicle.

3. Carefully remove the canister or canister and bracket assembly, as applicable.

4. Installation is the reverse of removal.

Thermostatic Vacuum Switch (TVS)

▶ **See Figures 6 and 7**

The TVS is located near the engine coolant outlet housing.
1. Drain the engine cooling system to a level below the TVS.
2. Disconnect the vacuum hose manifold from the TVS. If the hoses are not connected to a single manifold, be sure to tag them before removal to assure proper installation.
3. Using a wrench, unthread and remove the TVS from the engine.
To install:
4. Apply a soft setting sealant to the TVS threads.

➡**DO NOT apply sealant to the sensor end of the TVS.**

5. Install the TVS and tighten to 120 inch lbs. (13 Nm).
6. Reconnect the vacuum hoses.
7. Properly refill the engine cooling system, then run the engine and check for leaks.

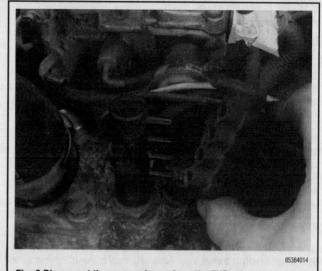

Fig. 6 Disconnect the vacuum hoses from the TVS

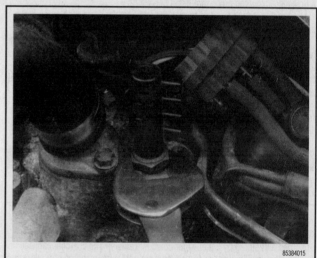

Fig. 7 Loosen and remove the thermostatic vacuum switch using a wrench

Exhaust Gas Recirculation (EGR) System

OPERATION

The EGR system is used to reduce oxides of nitrogen (NOx) emission levels caused by high combustion chamber temperatures. This is accomplished by the use of an EGR valve which opens, under specific engine operating conditions, to admit a small amount of exhaust gas into the intake manifold, below the throttle plate. The exhaust gas mixes with the incoming air charge and displaces a portion of the oxygen in the air/fuel mixture entering the combustion chamber. The exhaust gas does not support combustion of the air/fuel mixture but it takes up volume, the net effect of which is to lower the temperature of the combustion process.

The EGR valve is usually mounted on the intake manifold and has an opening into the exhaust manifold. Except for the fully electronic linear valve, the EGR valve is opened by manifold vacuum to permit exhaust gas to flow into the intake manifold. If too much exhaust gas enters, combustion will not occur. Because of this, very little exhaust gas is allowed to pass through the valve. The EGR system will be activated once the engine reaches normal operating temperature and the EGR valve will open when engine operating conditions are above idle speed and, in some applications, below Wide Open Throttle (WOT). The EGR system is deactivated on vehicles equipped with a Transmission Converter Clutch (TCC) when the TCC is engaged. There are 3 basic types of systems as described below.

Negative Backpressure EGR Valve

The negative backpressure EGR valve used on most or the earlier model vehicles covered by this manual and by later model vehicle engines such as the 2.5L engine. The negative backpressure valve is similar to the positive back-pressure EGR valve, except that the bleed valve spring is moved from above the diaphragm to below and the valve is normally closed. The negative backpressure valve varies the amount of exhaust gas flow into the intake manifold depending on manifold vacuum and variations in exhaust backpressure. The diaphragm on the valve has an internal air bleed hole which is held closed by a small spring when there is no exhaust backpressure. Engine vacuum opens the EGR valve against the pressure of a spring. When manifold vacuum combines with negative exhaust backpressure, the vacuum bleed hole opens and the EGR valve closes. This valve will open if vacuum is applied with the engine not running. Negative backpressure EGR valves will have an "N" stamped on the top side of the valve below the part number and after the date built.

Ported EGR Valve

The ported EGR valve is used on many of the later model engines covered by this manual including the versions of the 4.3L (VIN Z) engine, the 4.3L MFI-Turbo and some 2.8L TBI engines. This valve is controlled by a flexible diaphragm. It is spring-loaded in order to hold the valve closed. When ported vacuum is applied to the top side of the diaphragm, spring pressure is overcome and the valve in the exhaust gas port is opened. This allows the exhaust gas to be pulled into the intake manifold and enter the cylinders with the air/fuel mixture. Port EGR valves have no identification stamped below the part number. On most applications covered by this manual, the ported EGR valve will vacuum source will be controlled electronically through an Electronic Vacuum Regulator Valve (EVRV) or EGR vacuum solenoid.

Linear EGR Valve

Some late model versions of the 4.3L TBI (California emissions) and the all 4.3L CMFI (VIN W) engines utilize a linear EGR valve. This is a fully electronic EGR valve which is constantly monitored and controlled by the engine (power-train or vehicle) computer control module. The control module will monitor input from the TP, MAP, ECT and pintle positions sensors, then will send an output signal to the EGR valve indicating the proper amount of exhaust gas recirculation necessary to properly lower combustion temperatures. This electronic metering is about 10 times faster than vacuum-operated models and offers improved diagnostic capabilities.

ELECTRONIC EGR CONTROL

On certain vehicle applications (most late model and California emission vehicles), EGR flow is regulated by the ECM (linear valves) or by an ECM-controlled Electronic Vacuum Regulator Valve (EVRV)/EGR solenoid (ported or negative backpressure valves). On vacuum controlled valves, the vacuum supply is controlled by a solenoid using pulse width modulation. This means that the ECM turns the solenoid on and off many times a second and varies the amount of ON time (pulse width) which in turn varies the amount of vacuum and exhaust gas recirculation.

INCORRECT EGR OPERATION

Too much EGR flow at idle, cruise or during cold operation may result in the engine stalling after cold start, the engine stalling at idle after deceleration, vehicle surge during cruise and rough idle. If the EGR valve is always open, the vehicle may not idle. Too little or no EGR flow allows combustion temperatures to get too high which could result in spark knock (detonation), engine overheating and/or emission test failure.

TESTING (EXCEPT FUEL INJECTED ENGINES)

EGR Valve

1. Check hose routing (Refer to Vehicle Emission Control Information Label).
2. Check the EGR valve signal tube orifice for obstructions.
3. Connect a vacuum gauge between EGR valve and carburetor, then check the vacuum; the engine must be at operating temperature of 195°F (90°C). With the engine running at approximately 3000 rpm there should be at least 5 in. Hg.
4. Check the EGR solenoid for correct operation.
5. To check the valve, perform the following procedures:
    a. Depress the valve diaphragm.
    b. With the diaphragm still depressed hold finger over source tube and release the diaphragm.
    c. Check the diaphragm and seat for movement. The valve is good if it takes over 20 seconds for the diaphragm to move to the seated position (valve closed). Make sure the source tube is completely covered.
    d. Replace the EGR valve if it takes less than 20 seconds to move to the seated position.

EGR VALVE CLEANING

➡ **DO NOT wash valve assembly in solvents or degreaser—permanent damage to valve diaphragm may result. Also, sand blasting of the valve is not recommended since this can affect operation of the valve.**

1. Remove the EGR valve from the engine.
2. With a wire brush, remove the exhaust deposits from the mounting surface and around the valve.
3. On vacuum valves, depress the valve diaphragm and look at the valve seating area through the valve outlet for cleanliness. If the valve and/or seat are not completely clean, repeat Step 2.
4. Look for exhaust deposits in the valve outlet. Remove the deposit build-up with a small scraper.
5. Clean the mounting surfaces of the intake manifold and the valve assembly, then install the valve using a new gasket.

REMOVAL & INSTALLATION

◗ **See Figures 8 and 9**

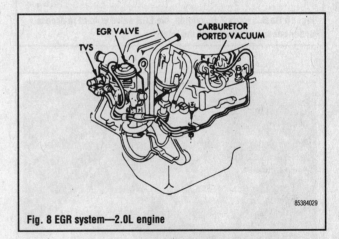

Fig. 8 EGR system—2.0L engine

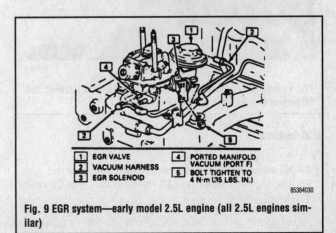

Fig. 9 EGR system—early model 2.5L engine (all 2.5L engines similar)

EGR Valve

▶ See Figures 10 and 11

1. If necessary for access, remove the air cleaner or duct, as applicable.
2. For vacuum actuated valves, detach the vacuum hose or line from the EGR valve.
3. For linear valves, disconnect the negative battery cable, then disengage the valve electrical connector.
4. If equipped on the 2.8L engine, disconnect the temperature switch from the EGR valve.
5. Remove the EGR valve flange retainers, then remove the valve from the manifold.
6. Installation is the reverse of removal.

Fig. 10 On this early 2.8L engine, the EGR valve is hard to access under hoses and wires over the intake

Fig. 11 Once the hoses are disconnected and the bolts removed, the EGR valve may be lifted from the engine

EGR Solenoid

1. Disconnect the negative battery cable.
2. If necessary for access, remove the air cleaner assembly or duct.
3. Disengage the electrical connector, then tag and disconnect the vacuum hoses from the solenoid.
4. Remove the retainer(s), then remove the solenoid from the engine.
5. If necessary (and applicable) remove the old filter from the solenoid. The filter should be grasped pulled out using rocking motion.

To install:

6. If removed, push a new filter into position in the solenoid, making sure the wire cut-out is properly aligned.
7. Install the solenoid to the engine and tighten the retainers to 17 ft. lbs. (24 Nm).
8. Engage the electrical connector and vacuum hoses to the solenoid.
9. If removed, install the air cleaner assembly or duct.
10. Connect the negative battery cable.

Back Pressure Transducer

1. Remove the back pressure transducer from the clamp bracket.
2. Remove the hoses from the transducer.
3. Inspect and/or replace the transducer.
4. Installation is the reverse of removal.

Thermostatic Air Cleaner (THERMAC)

OPERATION

▶ See Figure 12

Most of the carbureted and TBI engines covered by this manual use an air intake system which is designed to draw cool air from the exterior of the engine compartment during most engine operating conditions, but which draws heated air during engine warm-up. On these thermostatic controlled air cleaners, fresh air comes either from the snorkel, which supplies the engine with outside air, or a tube underneath the snorkel, which is connected to a heat stove surrounding the exhaust manifold. The purpose of the heat stove is to supply the engine with warm air during cold running to reduce choke-on time and bring the engine to normal operating temperature as quickly as possible.

An actuator motor in the snorkel operates the door which regulates the source of incoming air. The snorkel door is controlled either by a temperature sensor actuator or a vacuum diaphragm motor. The temperature sensor actuator is controlled by means of a self-contained, wax pellet assembly mounted in the air cleaner. When the engine is cold, the wax material sealed in the actuator is in a solid state, causing the damper to close off the cold air inlet. All air supplied to the engine is routed through the heat stove. As the incoming air warms the wax material, it changes to a liquid state and expands forcing out the piston to reposition the damper, allowing a hot/cold air mix or all cold air to enter the engine.

The vacuum diaphragm operated system uses a vacuum operated motor, mounted to the snorkel, to operate the damper door and a thermostatic bi-metal switch inside the air cleaner. When the engine is cold, the bi-metal switch is cold allowing vacuum to be supplied to the motor. As that the engine warms up, the bi-metal switch opens and bleeds off the vacuum. A spring inside the vacuum motor overcomes the vacuum and opens the damper door to the cold air inlet. Some applications use a delay valve on the hose connecting the vacuum

Fig. 12 Thermostatic air cleaner assemblies use a snorkel (such as this which runs to the grille)

motor to the temperature sensor. When vacuum in this hose drops for any reason, the check valve will bleed off the vacuum to the vacuum motor slowly. On most vehicles, the snorkel is connected to a tube, which is routed to the front of the vehicle in order to take in cooler air from outside the engine compartment.

Incorrect Thermostatic Air Cleaner (THERMAC) operation can result in warm up hesitation, lack of power or sluggishness on a hot engine. Inspect the system for any of the following:

1. Disconnected heat stove tube.
2. Vacuum diaphragm motor or temperature sensor actuator inoperative.
3. No damper door operation.
4. Absence of manifold vacuum source.
5. Air cleaner not seated properly.

REMOVAL & INSTALLATION

THERMAC Assembly

▶ See Figures 13, 14, 15 and 16

1. Remove the air cleaner cover and element from the housing assembly.
2. Disconnect the fresh air hose and heat stove pipe from the housing snorkel.
3. Tag and disconnect the hoses and vacuum lines, as necessary, from the air cleaner housing.
4. Remove the THERMAC housing assembly from the engine.
5. Installation is the reverse of removal.

Vacuum Motor

1. Remove the air cleaner housing assembly from the engine.
2. Disconnect the vacuum hose from the motor.
3. Drill out the spot welds with a ⅛ in. bit, then enlarge as necessary to remove the retaining strap.

4. Remove the retaining strap.
5. Lift up the motor and cock it to one side to unhook the motor linkage at the control damper assembly.

To install:

6. Drill a ⁷⁄₆₄ in. hole in the snorkel tube at the center of the vacuum motor retaining strap.
7. Insert and engage the vacuum motor linkage into the control damper assembly.
8. Use the motor retaining strap and a sheet metal screw to secure the retaining strap and motor to the snorkel tube.

➡**Make sure the screw does not interfere with the operation of the damper assembly. Shorten the screw if necessary.**

9. Connect the vacuum hose to the motor.
10. Install the air cleaner assembly to the vehicle making sure the hoses are properly seated. Pay close attention to the brittle heat stove to make sure it is not damaged and it is fully seated on both the exhaust manifold and the snorkel.

Temperature Sensor

1. Remove the air cleaner.
2. Disconnect the hoses from the sensor.
3. Pry up the tabs on the sensor retaining clip, then remove the clip and sensor from the air cleaner.
4. Installation is the reverse of removal.

Wax Pellet Actuator

1. Remove the THERMAC housing assembly from the engine.
2. If the application uses a plastic heat tube elbow, use a ⅛ in. drill bit to drill out the 2 rivets securing the heat tube and elbow.
3. Use a ⅛ in. drill bit to drill out the 2 rivets securing the wax pellet carrier assembly.

Fig. 13 Disconnect the fresh air hose from the snorkel and, if necessary, the vacuum hose from the motor

Fig. 14 Tag and disconnect the remaining hoses from the THERMAC air cleaner housing

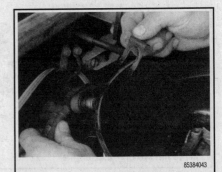

Fig. 15 On some engine, multiple lines connect to a common fitting, on these remove the fitting

Fig. 16 If equipped with a vacuum motor, don't forget the temp sensor line (often run underneath the housing)

4. Disconnect the blow down spring, then remove the wax pellet carrier assembly.
5. Installation is the reverse of removal.

Air Injection Reactor (AIR)

OPERATION

▶ See Figures 17, 18, 19 and 20

Many (though not all) of the vehicles covered by this manual are equipped with an Air Injector Reactor (AIR) or AIR management system. The AIR system uses an air pump, air check valve(s), a mixture control (deceleration) valve, an air switching (diverter) valve, and an air manifold (with air injector nozzles).

The air pump transmits filtered air received from the air cleaner assembly, through the air switching valve and the check valve, into an air manifold assembly which is mounted on the cylinder head. As the hot exhaust gas comes out from the combustion chamber, it meets with a blast of air from the air injection nozzle located in the exhaust port to burn some of the hydrocarbon and carbon monoxide emissions.

Upon receiving a high vacuum signal from the intake manifold, the mixture control valve introduces ambient air through the air filter into the intake mani-

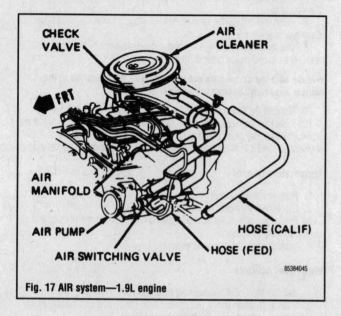

Fig. 17 AIR system—1.9L engine

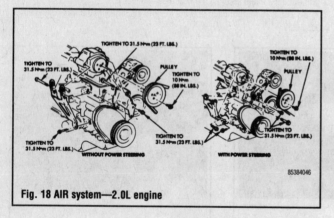

Fig. 18 AIR system—2.0L engine

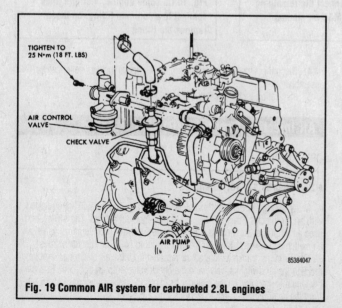

Fig. 19 Common AIR system for carbureted 2.8L engines

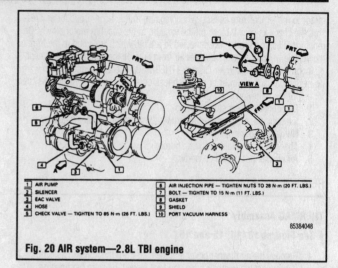

1	AIR PUMP	6	AIR INJECTION PIPE — TIGHTEN NUTS TO 28 N·m (20 FT. LBS.)
2	SILENCER	7	BOLT — TIGHTEN TO 15 N·m (11 FT. LBS.)
3	EAC VALVE	8	GASKET
4	HOSE	9	SHIELD
5	CHECK VALVE — TIGHTEN TO 85 N·m (26 FT. LBS.)	10	PORT VACUUM HARNESS

Fig. 20 AIR system—2.8L TBI engine

fold to dilute the momentarily rich fuel mixture that occurs on initial throttle closing. This eliminates backfire.

On most California and TBI models, the Electronic Control Module (ECM) operates an electric air control valve which directs the air flow to the engine exhaust manifold ports or the the air cleaner. When the engine is cold or in wide-open throttle, the ECM energizes the solenoid to direct the air flow into the exhaust manifold check valves. When the engine warms, operating at high speeds or deceleration, the ECM de-energizes the electric air control valve, changing the air flow from the exhaust manifold to the air cleaner. On some applications, at higher engine speeds air can be rediverted back to the air cleaner through a pressure relief valve, even though the solenoid is still energized. The diversion of the air flow to the air cleaner acts as a silencer.

A check valve(s) prevents back flow of the exhaust gases into the air pump, if there is an exhaust backfire or pump drive belt failure.

TESTING

Air Injection Pump

Accelerate the engine to approximately 1500 rpm and observe the air flow from hose(s). If the air flow increases as the engine is accelerated, the pump is operating satisfactorily. If the air flow does not increase or is not present, proceed as follows:

1. Check for proper drive belt tension. The Air Management System is not completely noiseless. Under normal conditions, noise rises in pitch as the engine speed increases. To determine if excessive noise is the present, operate the engine with the pump drive belt removed. If excessive noise does not exist with the belt removed, proceed as follows:
2. Check for a seized Air Injection Pump. DO NOT oil the air pump.
3. Check the hoses, the pipes and all connections for leaks and proper routing.
4. Check the air control valve.
5. Check air injection pump for proper mounting and bolt torque.
6. Repair irregularities in these components, as necessary.
7. If no irregularities exist and the air injection pump noise is still excessive, replace the pump.

Check Valves

1. The check valve should be inspected whenever the hose is disconnected from the check valve or whenever check valve failure is suspected (A pump that had become inoperative and had shown indications of having exhaust gases in the pump would indicate check valve failure).
2. With the check valve removed, blow through the check valve (toward the exhaust manifold side) then turn the valve around and attempt to blow back through it (toward the AIR pump). The flow should only be in one direction (toward the exhaust manifold). Replace the valve which does not function correctly.

Air Hoses and Injection Pipes

1. Inspect all hoses for deterioration or holes.
2. Inspect all air injection pipes for cracks of holes.

➡**When checking pipes and hoses, look at the routing, improper positioning and interference with other components may cause wear.**

3. Check all hose and pipe connections.
4. Check pipe and hose routing; interference may cause wear.
5. If a leak is suspected on the pressure side of the system or any hose has been disconnected on the pressure side, the connection should be checked for leaks with a soapy water solution. Look for bubbles which will form at any bad connections when the pump is operating.
6. If a hose, manifold and/or pipe assembly replacement is required, note the routing, then replace the item as required.
7. When installing the new item, be sure to connect the hoses correctly.

Air Switching (Diverter) Valve (ASV)

The diverter valve directs air to the exhaust ports unless there is a sudden rise in manifold vacuum due to deceleration. In such a case air is diverted to the intake manifold.

If the diverter valve is functioning properly, the secondary air will continue to blow out from the valve for a few seconds when the accelerator pedal is pressed to the floor and released quickly. If the secondary air continues to blow out for more than 5 seconds, replace the air switching valve.

Mixture Control (Deceleration) Valve

1. Install a tachometer to the engine and allow the engine to establish normal operating temperatures.
2. Remove the air cleaner and plug the air cleaner vacuum hose(s).
3. Operate the engine at idle speed, then remove the deceleration valve-to-intake manifold (diaphragm) hose.
4. Reconnect the hose and listen for a noticeable air flow (hiss) through the air cleaner-to-deceleration valve hose; there should also be a noticeable drop in idle speed.
5. If the air flow does not continue for at least one second or the engine speed does not drop, check the hoses (of the deceleration valve) for restrictions or leaks.
6. If no restrictions are found, replace the deceleration valve.

REMOVAL & INSTALLATION

Air Injection Pump

➡**The air pump is non-serviceable, it must be replaced as an assembly, if defective.**

1. Disconnect the negative battery cable.
2. Compress the drive belt to keep the pump pulley from turning, then loosen the pump pulley bolts.
3. Loosen the pump-to-mounting brackets, release the drive belt tension, then remove or reposition the belt.
4. Remove the hoses, the vacuum lines, the electrical connectors (if equipped) and the air control or diverter valve.
5. Unscrew the mounting bolts and then remove the pulley.
6. Unscrew the pump mounting bolts and then remove the pump.
7. If necessary, use a pair of needle nose pliers to pull the filter fan from the hub.
To install:
8. Install the AIR pump assembly and secure using the retaining bolts.
9. If removed, position a new filter fan on the pump hub. DO NOT drive the filter fan on with a hammer.
10. Install the spacer and pump pulley against the centrifugal filter fan.
11. Install the pulley bolts and tighten them evenly in order to compress the centrifugal filter fan onto the pump hole. DO NOT drive the filter fan on with a hammer. A slight amount of interference with the housing bore is normal. After a new filter fan is installed it may squeal upon initial operation or until the O.D. of the sealing lip has properly worn in. To break in the sealing lip the engine should be operated at various engine speeds once installation is complete.

12. Install the hoses, vacuum, lines, electrical connectors and air control or diverter valve, as applicable.
13. Install the drive belt and adjust the tension (unless equipped with a serpentine belt).
14. Connect the negative battery cable and check for proper pump operation.

Air Pump Pulley Replacement

1. Hold the pump pulley from turning by compressing the drive belt, then loosen the pump pulley bolts.
2. Loosen the pump-to-mounting brackets, release the drive belt tension, then remove or reposition the belt.
3. Unscrew the mounting bolts and then remove the pulley and pulley spacer.
To install:
4. Install the pump pulley and spacer with the retaining bolts hand-tight.
5. Install the drive belt and adjust (V-belts only) to proper tension.
6. Hold the pump pulley from turning by compressing the drive belt, then tighten the pump pulley bolts.
7. Recheck drive belt tension and adjust it, as necessary.

Air Pump Filter Fan Replacement

◗ **See Figure 21**

Before starting this operation, note the following:
- DO NOT allow any filter fragments to enter the air pump intake hole.
- DO NOT remove the filter fan by inserting a screwdriver between pump and filter fan. Damage to the pump air sealing lip will result.
- DO NOT remove the metal drive hub from the filter fan.
- It is seldom possible to remove the filter fan without destroying it. The fan should not be removed unless it is going to be replaced.
1. Remove the drive belt, the pump pulley and spacer.
2. Insert needle nose pliers and pull the filter fan from hub.
To install:
3. Position a new filter fan onto the pump hub.
4. Position the spacer and the pump pulley against the centrifugal filter fan.
5. Install the pump pulley bolts and tighten them evenly. This will compress the centrifugal filter fan into the pump hole. DO NOT drive the filter fan on with a hammer.

➡**A slight amount of interference with the housing bore is normal. After a new filter fan has been installed, it may squeal upon initial operation or until O.D. sealing lip has worn in. This may require a short period of pump operation at various engine speeds.**

6. Install the drive belt and check for proper tension.

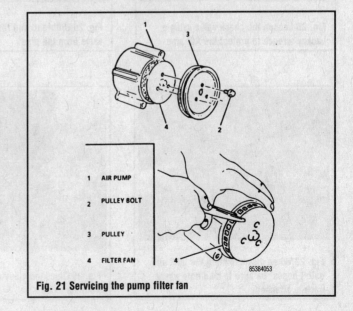

1	AIR PUMP
2	PULLEY BOLT
3	PULLEY
4	FILTER FAN

85384053

Fig. 21 Servicing the pump filter fan

Check Valve(s)

▶ See Figures 22, 23, 24, 25 and 26

1. Remove the clamp(s) and disconnect the hose from the valve(s).
2. Unscrew the valve(s) from the air injection pipe(s). Be sure to use a backup wrench to prevent damaging the injection pipe.

➡ **If difficulty is encountered loosening the valve, use a small amount of penetrating lubricant to help loosen the threads.**

3. To test the valve(s), air should pass in one direction only.
4. Installation is the reverse of removal.

Air Control/Diverter Valve

▶ See Figures 27, 28, 29 and 30

1. Disconnect the negative battery cable.
2. Loosen any retaining clamps, then disconnect the air inlet and outlet hoses from the valve.
3. Disconnect the electrical connector and/or the vacuum hose(s) at the valve.
4. Loosen the retaining bolts, then remove the electric air control or diverter valve, as equipped.

To install:

5. Position the valve and secure using the retaining bolts.

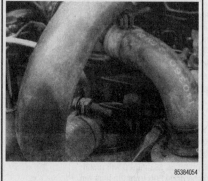
Fig. 22 Loosen the retaining clamp on the AIR hose

Fig. 23 Disconnect the hose from the check valve

Fig. 24 If removal is difficult, try a small amount of penetrating lubricant

Fig. 25 Loosen the check valve using a backup wrench to protect the AIR pipe

Fig. 26 Unthread and remove the check valve from the pipe

Fig. 27 Loosen the clamps and disconnect the hoses from the valve

Fig. 28 When disconnecting the inlet and outlet hoses, be sure to take note where each is attached

Fig. 29 Disconnect any vacuum hoses from the valve

Fig. 30 Remove the retaining bolts, then remove the valve from the engine

6. Engage the vacuum hose(s) and/or electrical connector, as applicable.

7. Make sure the hose clamps are on the hoses, then connect the inlet and outlet hoses to the valve. Secure the hoses using the clamps, but do not over-tighten them.

8. Connect the negative battery cable, then verify proper valve operation.

Mixture Control (Deceleration) Valve

1. Remove the vacuum hoses from the valve.
2. Remove the deceleration valve-to-engine bracket screws.
3. Remove the deceleration valve.
4. Installation is the reverse of removal.

Vacuum Switching Valve (VSV)

1. Disconnect the negative battery cable, then disengage the electrical wiring connector.
2. Disconnect the hoses from the valve.
3. Remove the vacuum switching valve.
4. Installation is the reverse of removal.

Electronic Spark Timing (EST) System

Most of the vehicles covered by this manual utilize an electronic control system for all spark timing changes. Many of the HEI distributor equipped engines use the EST system instead of mechanical or vacuum advance mechanisms. The HEI (EST) spark control system makes the ignition timing changes, necessary for emissions control, economy and performance. For more information on this system, please refer to Section 2 of this manual.

Electronic Spark Control (ESC) System

Because varying octane levels in gasoline can cause detonation (spark knock) in any engine, some of the fuel injected engines covered by this manual which are equipped with HEI (EST) are also equipped with an Electronic Spark Control (ESC) system. Spark knock is a condition caused by temperatures inside the cylinder rising so high as to ignite the air/fuel mixture prior to the spark plug firing. This early ignition causes a down force on the piston as it is rising in the cylinder toward TDC. In light cases, the only damage to the engine may be broken spark plug insulators. In extreme cases, pistons may become severely damaged (holes blown through the top of the piston) requiring the engine to be rebuilt.

The ESC is designed to detect detonation and retard spark timing up to 20° to reduce or eliminate detonation in the engine. This allows the engine to use maximum spark advance to improve driveability and fuel economy. For more information regarding the ESC system, please refer to Section 2 of this manual.

Transmission Converter Clutch (TCC) System

All vehicles equipped with an automatic transmission use the TCC system. The computer control module (ECM or PCM, as applicable) controls the converter by means of a solenoid mounted in the outdrive housing of the transmission. When the vehicle speed reaches a certain level, the computer module energizes the solenoid and allows the torque converter to mechanically couple the transmission to the engine. When the operating conditions (according to various sensors) indicate that the transmission should operate as a normal fluid coupled transmission, the module will de-energize the solenoid. Depressing the brake pedal will also return the transmission to normal automatic operation.

Early Fuel Evaporation (EFE) System

OPERATION

Carbureted engines covered by this manual should be equipped with an EFE system. The purpose of the system is to promote the vaporization of fuel droplets as they enter the intake manifold during cold engine operation. A heater grid is used to provide the heat necessary to promote vaporization of the air/fuel mixture which then ensures complete combustion providing the maximum power and minimum emissions output for the fuel used. In this way, the system provides quick fuel evaporation and more uniform fuel distribution during cold starts. The system also reduces the length of carburetor choking time, thus reducing exhaust emissions.

The system consists of a ceramic heater grid (located between the carburetor and the intake manifold) and a temperature switch (all non-ECM models) and/or a relay (ECM models and 1985 non-ECM models) which activates the heater during cold operation. The relay, usually located under the right fender, is operated by the ECM on most engines. Some 1985 non-ECM controlled models utilize the relay in the ignition circuit.

As the coolant temperature increases, the temperature switch (non-ECM models) or the relay (ECM models) turns Off the current to the ceramic heater, allowing the engine to operate normally.

➡**Operational checks should be made at normal maintenance intervals.**

REMOVAL & INSTALLATION

EFE Heater

▶ **See Figures 31, 32 and 33**

The EFE heater unit is located directly under the carburetor and is electrically operated.

1. Disconnect the negative battery terminal, then remove the air cleaner assembly.

2. From the carburetor, tag and disconnect the vacuum hoses, electrical wiring and fuel hoses. Disengage the EFE heater electrical connector from the wiring harness.

3. Remove the carburetor-to-intake manifold retainers, then carefully remove the carburetor from the manifold.

➡**Be careful once the carburetor is removed from the manifold not to allow anything (bolts, debris) to fall into the opening or the manifold may have to be removed.**

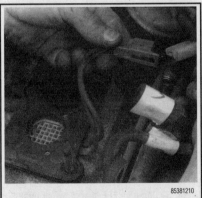

85381210

Fig. 31 Disengage the EFE wiring connector

85381211

Fig. 32 Carefully lift the EFE from the intake manifold

85381212

Fig. 33 When cleaning the gasket mounting surface, cover the opening to keep debris out of the engine

4. Lift the EFE heater unit from the intake manifold.

To install:

5. Using a putty knife, clean the gasket mounting surfaces carefully.

➡**During installation, replace all gaskets to assure proper seal and prevent vacuum leaks.**

6. Position the EFE heater unit to the intake manifold.

7. Install the carburetor to the intake, then tighten the carburetor-to-intake manifold retainers to 13 ft. lbs. (18 Nm).

8. Engage the EFE wiring connector to the harness.

9. Connect the fuel hoses, electrical wiring and vacuum hoses as noted during removal.

10. Install the air cleaner assembly and connect the negative battery terminal.

Temperature Switch (Non-ECM Models)

♦ **See Figures 34, 35, 36 and 37**

The temperature or heater switch is located near the thermostat housing (2.8L carbureted engine), on the bottom rear-side of the intake manifold (2.0L carbureted engine) or on the top right-side of the engine (1.9L carbureted engine).

1. Position a drain pan under the radiator, then open the drain cock and drain the coolant to a level below the heater switch.

2. Disengage the wiring harness connector from the EFE heater switch.

3. Remove the EFE heater switch (turn it counterclockwise) from the intake manifold.

To install:

➡**If replacing the temperature switch, refer to the calibration number stamped on the base.**

4. Coat the threads of the EFE heater switch with a soft setting sealant, then thread it into the intake and tighten to 10 ft. lbs. (14 Nm).

➡**When applying sealant to the EFE heater switch threads, be careful not to coat the sensor and/or the switch.**

5. Reconnect the wiring harness to the EFE heater switch.

6. Properly refill the cooling system. Coolant can be reused unless it is several years old or appears contaminated.

Relay (ECM Models and 1985 Non-ECM Models)

♦ **See Figures 38 and 39**

The heater switch relay is usually located on the left-fender.

1. Disconnect the negative battery cable.

2. Disengage the wiring harness connector(s) from the heater switch relay.

3. Remove the heater switch relay-to-bracket screw, then remove the relay from the truck.

4. To install, reverse the removal procedures.

Catalytic Converter

All gasoline engine vehicles covered by this manual are equipped with a catalytic converter in order to reduce tail pipe emissions. Most of the vehicles are also equipped with an electronically controlled closed loop fuel system which makes possible the use of a three-way reduction type catalytic converter instead of only an oxidizing catalyst converter. Though both converters act in a similar fashion, the three-way unit reduces additional emissions which a single oxidizing converter cannot. A three-way converter is used to reduce HC, CO and NOx in the engine's exhaust. The actual catalyst contains Platinum (Pt) and Rhodium (Rh). A few grams of catalyst is applied evenly onto a ceramic honeycomb, which is then installed into a stainless-steel enclosure. The unit is mounted in the exhaust system close to the engine for rapid warm-up to operating temperature.

The function of the catalytic converter is to reduce CO, HC, and NOx by causing these gasses to easily combine with oxygen forming mostly CO_2, N_2 and water. A very precise amount of exhaust gas oxygen is required for the

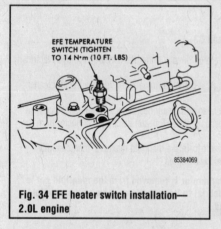

Fig. 34 EFE heater switch installation—2.0L engine

Fig. 35 Disengaging the EFE switch connector on a 2.8L engine

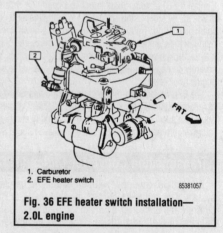

1. Carburetor
2. EFE heater switch

Fig. 36 EFE heater switch installation—2.0L engine

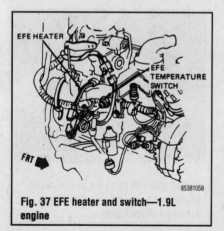

Fig. 37 EFE heater and switch—1.9L engine

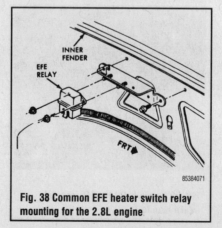

Fig. 38 Common EFE heater switch relay mounting for the 2.8L engine

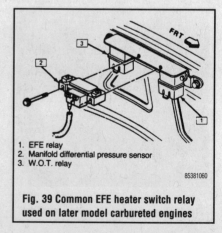

1. EFE relay
2. Manifold differential pressure sensor
3. W.O.T. relay

Fig. 39 Common EFE heater switch relay used on later model carbureted engines

three-way catalyst to function properly. On these vehicles a computer module (ECM, PCM or VCM) reads the oxygen sensor signal and then controls the carburetor mixture solenoid or fuel injector(s) so there is almost always the exact amount of oxygen required for proper catalyst operation.

A catalytic converter operates at temperatures up to 1500°F (815°C). It can be damaged by prolonged idling, a rich air/fuel ratio or by a constant misfire. Excess fuel will cause the unit to overheat and melt the ceramic substrate. Use of leaded fuel will quickly poison the catalyst and should be avoided. On vehicles sold in the US, catalytic converters are covered by factory warranty for 50,000 miles. However with proper care, on most vehicles a catalytic converter should still be effective for more than 100,000 miles.

1. Keep the engine in proper running condition at all times.
2. Use only unleaded fuel.
3. Avoid prolonged idling. Proper air flow past the catalytic converter is required to prevent overheating.
4. Do not disconnect any of the spark plug wires while the engine is running.
5. Make engine compression checks as quickly as possible to minimize the fuel pumped into the exhaust system.

If replacement of the catalytic converter or exhaust pipe components is necessary, refer to Section 3 of this manual for the relevant procedures.

ELECTRONIC ENGINE CONTROLS

Operation

The fuel injection or carburetor system, described in detail in Section No. 5 of this manual, is operated along with the ignition system to obtain optimum performance and fuel economy while producing a minimum of exhaust emissions. The various sensors described below are used by the computer control module (ECM, PCM or VCM depending upon application) for feedback to determine proper engine operating conditions.

➡**Although most diagnosis may be conducted using a Digital Volt/Ohm Meter (DVOM), certain steps or procedures may require use of the Tech 1® diagnostic scan tool (a specialized tester) or an equivalent scan/testing tool. If the proper tester is not available, the vehicle should be taken to a reputable service station which has the appropriate equipment.**

When dealing with the electronic engine control system, keep in mind that the system is sensitive to improperly connected electrical and vacuum circuits. The condition and connection of all hoses and wires should always be the first step when attempting to diagnose a driveability problem. Worn or deteriorated hoses and damaged or corroded wires may well make a good component appear faulty.

➡**When troubleshooting the system, always check the electrical and vacuum connectors which may cause the problem before testing or replacing a component.**

For more information on troubleshooting the electronic engine control system, please refer to the information on self-diagnostics later in this section.

Computer Control Module (ECM/PCM/VCM)

The heart of the electronic control system which is found on most vehicles covered by this manual is a computer control module. The module gathers information from various sensors, then controls fuel supply and engine emission systems. Most vehicles are equipped with an Engine Control Module (ECM) which, as its name implies, controls the engine and related emissions systems. Some ECMs may also control the Torque Converter Clutch (TCC) on automatic transmission vehicles or the manual upshift light on manual transmission vehicles. Later model vehicles may be equipped with a Powertrain Control Module (PCM) or a Vehicle Control Module (VCM). Both of these are similar to the original ECMs, but are designed to control additional systems as well. The PCM may control the manual transmission shift lamp or the shift functions of the electronically controlled automatic transmission. The VCM is used to control the manual shift lamp and electronic brake control functions.

Regardless of the name, all computer control modules are serviced in a similar manner. Care must be taken when handling these expensive components in order to protect them from damage. Carefully follow all instructions included with the replacement part. Avoid touching pins or connectors to prevent damage from static electricity.

All of these computer control modules contain a Programmable Read Only Memory chip or CALPAK that contains calibration information which is particular to the vehicle application. This chip is not supplied with a replacement module and must be transferred to the new module before installation. Late model vehicles equipped with a VCM utilize both a PROM chip and an Electronically Erasable Programmable Read Only Memory (EEPROM) which must be reprogrammed after installation.

✳ CAUTION

To prevent the possibility of permanent control module damage, the ignition switch MUST always be OFF when disconnecting power from or reconnecting power to the module. This includes unplugging the module connector, disconnecting the negative battery cable, removing the module fuse or even attempting to jump your dead battery using jumper cables.

REMOVAL & INSTALLATION

▶ **See Figure 40**

For most applications, the control module is located inside the passenger compartment, on the right side of the vehicle. For these vehicles it is usually found either under/behind the glove box or behind the kick panel. Some late model applications equipped with a VCM have the control module located in the engine compartment mounted on the right side, on/near the fender and wheel well. But not all VCMs are mounted in the engine compartment.

1. Make sure the ignition is turned **OFF**, then disconnect the negative battery cable.
2. Locate the computer control module. If not readily visible on the right side of the engine compartment, it is probably mounted under the dash.
3. If equipped with a passenger compartment mounted module, remove the dash panel located below the glove box and/or passenger side kick panel, as necessary.
4. Carefully disengage the connectors from the control module.

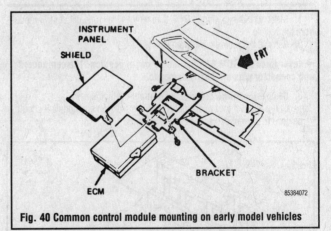

Fig. 40 Common control module mounting on early model vehicles

➡**On some modules, it may be easier to unfasten and rotate the module for easier access to the wiring. If necessary, do this before attempting to disengage the connectors.**

5. Loosen and remove the mounting hardware, then remove the module from the vehicle.

To install:

6. If the module is being replaced, remove the access covers and CAREFULLY replace the PROM chip or CALPAK. Refer to the procedure later in this section for details and cautions.

7. Make sure the access cover is properly installed.

❊❊ CAUTION

Remember, the ignition MUST be OFF when connecting the control module wiring.

8. Position the computer control module to the vehicle and secure using the hardware. If it was necessary to pivot the module for wire removal, then make sure the connectors are engaged before positioning the module.

9. Engage the wiring connectors to the module.

10. If removed for access, install the dash and/or kick panel.

11. Make sure the ignition is still **OFF**, then connect the negative battery cable.

12. If equipped with a VCM, the EEPROM must be reprogrammed using a suitable service system and the latest available software. In all likelihood, the vehicle must be towed to a dealer or repair shop containing the suitable equipment for this service.

13. Enter the self-diagnostic system and check for trouble codes to be sure the module and PROM/CALPACK are properly installed. For details, refer to the procedures for checking trouble codes, later in this section.

PROM/CALPAK REPLACEMENT

▶ See Figures 41, 42 and 43

As stated earlier, all computer control modules contain information regarding the correct parameters for engine and system operation based on vehicle applications. In most modules this information takes the form of a PROM chip or CALPAK, though some modules also store this information in an EEPROM. Since replacement modules are normally not equipped with this PROM/CALPAK, you must transfer the chip from the old component.

❊❊ CAUTION

The PROM/CALPAK chip and computer control module are EXTREMELY sensitive to electrical or mechanical damage. NEVER touch the connector pins or soldered components on the circuit board in order to prevent possible electrostatic discharge damage to the components.

1. Make sure the ignition is **OFF**, then remove the computer control module from the vehicle.

2. Remove the access cover from the module.

➡**Never force a PROM/CALPAK into or out of position. The component and connector pins are easily damaged.**

3. Remove the PROM chip or CALPAK from the module:

a. If a removal tool was supplied with the replacement module it should be used to prevent damage to the components.

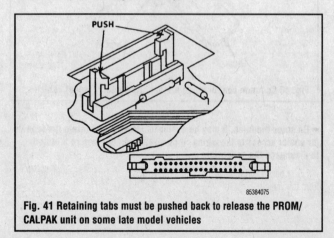

Fig. 41 Retaining tabs must be pushed back to release the PROM/CALPAK unit on some late model vehicles

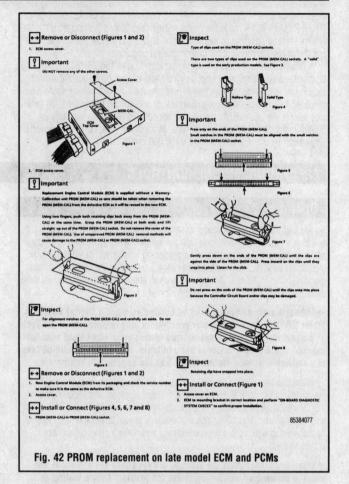

Fig. 42 PROM replacement on late model ECM and PCMs

b. Some early model units utilize a PROM and carrier assembly. On these components, the carrier and PROM should be removed together.

c. Some late model units are equipped with retaining tabs which must be pushed back to release the chip. Other models, such as the VCM, utilize a PROM unit with retaining tabs on either end, these must be gently squeezed as the unit is pulled upward.

To install:

➡**Use extra care to properly align the PROM during installation. In most cases, if the PROM is installed backwards and the ignition is turned ON, the PROM will be instantly destroyed.**

4. If equipped with a PROM carrier, position the chip at the top, flush with the top surface of the carrier.

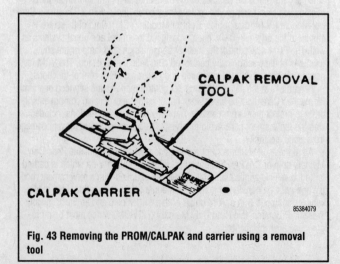

Fig. 43 Removing the PROM/CALPAK and carrier using a removal tool

➡If equipped with a PROM carrier, the carrier and chip (positioned at the top) should be carefully inserted into the module. Once the carrier is in place use a pencil eraser to gently push down on the top of the chip until the pins are properly in contact with the module.

5. Check the PROM/CALPAK chip or unit and carrier (if equipped) for alignment marks or tabs. Make sure the pins are properly aligned and carefully install the PROM/CALPAK to the module.

➡Except for VCMs equipped with a PROM unit with attached tabs, DO NOT press the PROM/CALPACK in until it clicks. The retaining tabs on ECM and PCM modules should be gently pushed over the edges of the unit after installation. Pressing on these PROM/CALPAKs until the tabs snap into place could cause circuit board or clip damage.

6. DO NOT force the PROM/CALPAK into position. Carefully press until the unit is seated. For VCMs equipped with a PROM unit, press until a light click is heard and the tabs are in place. For other late model units equipped with retaining tabs, the tabs must be gently positioned over the ends of the PROM/CAL-PAK.

7. Install the access cover to the module.

8. Make sure the ignition is **OFF**, then install the computer control module to the vehicle.

Engine Coolant Temperature (ECT) Sensor

The Engine Coolant Temperature (ECT) sensor, sometimes referred to as the Coolant Temperature Sensor (CTS), is a thermistor (resistor which changes value based on temperature) mounted in the engine coolant stream. Low coolant temperatures produce a high resistance—100,000ω at -40°F (-40°C), while high temperatures cause low resistance—70ω at 266°F (130°C).

The control module provides a 5 volt reference signal to the sensor through a resistor in the module and measures the voltage. The voltage will be high when the engine is cold and low when the engine is hot. By measuring the voltage, the control module knows the engine coolant temperature. The engine coolant temperature affects most other systems controlled by the module.

➡Removal and installation of the coolant temperature sensor is covered in Section 3 of this manual. Please refer there for further information.

Manifold Air Pressure (MAP) Sensor

♦ See Figure 44

The manifold absolute pressure sensor measures the changes in intake manifold pressure, which result from engine load and speed changes. The sensor converts this to voltage output. A closed throttle on an engine coastdown will produce a relatively low MAP output, while a wide open throttle will produce a relatively high output. This high output is produced because the pressure inside the manifold is the same as pressure outside the manifold, therefore 100 percent of the outside air pressure is measured.

The MAP sensor signal is opposite of what you would measure on a vacuum gauge. When manifold pressure is HIGH, vacuum is LOW. The MAP sensor is also used to measure barometric pressure under certain conditions, which allows the control module to automatically adjust for different altitudes.

The control module sends a 5 volt reference signal to the MAP sensor. As the manifold pressure changes, the electrical resistance of the sensor also changes. By monitoring the sensor output voltage, the control module can determine manifold pressure changes.

By using the MAP output signal, the control module can determine fuel ratio and ignition timing requirements. A high pressure reading would require more fuel, while a lower pressure reading would require less fuel.

➡Removal and installation of the manifold absolute pressure sensor is covered in Section 3 of this manual. Please refer there for further information.

Oxygen Sensor

♦ See Figure 45

The oxygen sensor is essentially a small variable battery; it has the ability to produce a low voltage signal that feeds information on engine exhaust oxygen content to the control module.

The sensor is constructed from a zirconia/platinum electrolytic element. Zirconia is an electrolyte that conducts electricity under certain chemical conditions. The element is made up of a ceramic material which acts as an insulator when cold. At operating temperatures of approximately 600°F (315°C), the element becomes a semiconductor. A platinum coating on the outer surface of the element stimulates further combustion of the exhaust gases right at the surface and this helps to keep the element up to the desired temperature.

The oxygen sensor has an inner cavity which is filled with reference (atmospheric) air. The atmosphere has approximately 21 percent oxygen in it. In the circuit, this inner cavity is the positive terminal, while the outer surface (exposed to the exhaust stream) is the negative or ground terminal.

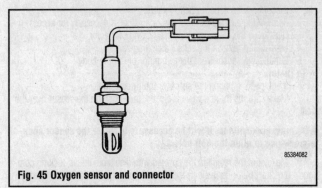

Fig. 45 Oxygen sensor and connector

Due to the element's electrolytic properties, oxygen concentration differences between the reference air and exhaust gases produce small voltages. A rich exhaust (excess fuel) has almost no oxygen. So when there is a large difference in the amount of oxygen touching the inside and outside surfaces, more conduction occurs and the sensor puts out a voltage signal above 0.6 V (600 mV). The signal may vary as high as 0.9 V (999 mV).

With a lean exhaust (excessive oxygen), there is about 2 percent oxygen in the gases. The smaller difference in oxygen content causes less conduction and the sensor produces a smaller voltage somewhere below 0.3 V (300 mV). The signal could drop as low as 0.1 V (100 mV). Commonly, values outside this range will cause a trouble code to set for most control systems.

Some late model vehicles are equipped with a heated oxygen sensor. This sensor has 3 wires in its pigtail instead of 1. The heated sensor works much in the same way as the standard oxygen sensor. The difference comes in the 2 other wires. On 1 wire, battery voltage is applied to a heating element located inside the sensor, while the other wire completes the heating elements circuit to ground. The heating element helps the sensor reach and maintain operating temperature faster, thereby allowing the fuel injection system to reach closed loop operation sooner.

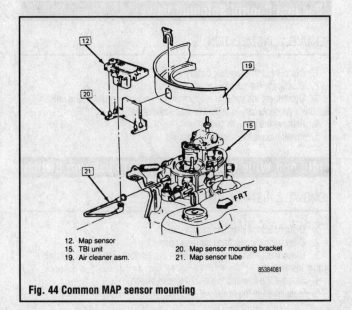

12. Map sensor
15. TBI unit
19. Air cleaner asm.
20. Map sensor mounting bracket
21. Map sensor tube

85384081

Fig. 44 Common MAP sensor mounting

➡Removal and installation of the oxygen sensor is covered in Section 3 of this manual. Please refer there for further information.

Intake Air Temperature (IAT)/Manifold Air Temperature (MAT) Sensors

The IAT or MAT sensor (as equipped), is a thermistor (resistor which changes value based on temperature) mounted either in the air intake snorkel or the manifold (depending on the application). Low intake air temperatures produce a high resistance—100,000ω at -40°F (-40°C), while high temperatures cause low resistance—70ω at 266°F (130°C).

The control module provides a 5 volt reference signal to the sensor through a resistor in the module and measures the voltage. The voltage will be high when the air is cold and low when the air is hot. By measuring the voltage, the control module knows the intake/manifold air temperature.

The air temperature signal is used by the control module to delay EGR until the temperature reaches approximately 40°F (5°C). The control module also uses the signal to retard ignition timing during high air temperatures.

➡Removal and installation of the air temperature sensor is covered in Section 3 of this manual. Please refer there for further information.

Throttle Position (TP) Sensor

▶ **See Figures 46 and 47**

The TP sensor is connected to the throttle shaft of the throttle body or carburetor. It is a potentiometer with one end connected to 5 volts from the control module and the other to ground. A third wire is connected to the control module in order to measure voltage from sensor. As the throttle angle is changed (the accelerator is pressed down), the output of the sensor changes.

At a closed throttle the output of the sensor is fairly low (0.5 V). As the throttle opens, the output voltage should rise towards 5 V. By monitoring the sensor output voltage the control module can determine fuel delivery based on throttle angle.

REMOVAL & INSTALLATION

1. Disconnect the negative battery cable.
2. Remove the air cleaner assembly or air duct, if necessary for access.
3. Disengage the TP sensor electrical wiring connector.
4. Loosen and remove the sensor attaching screws.
5. Remove the sensor from the carburetor or throttle body.

To install:
6. If equipped, position the seal over the throttle shaft.
7. Make sure the throttle valve is closed, then position the sensor over the shaft.

➡**On most applications, it will be necessary to rotate the sensor counterclockwise to align the bolt holes.**

8. Make sure the retainers are covered with a suitable thread-locking compound (Loctite®262 or equivalent) then install the bolts and tighten to 18 inch lbs (2 Nm).

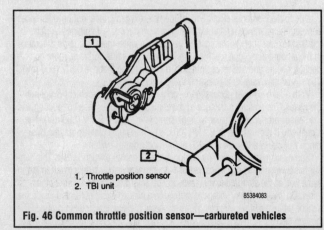

1. Throttle position sensor
2. TBI unit

85384083

Fig. 46 Common throttle position sensor—carbureted vehicles

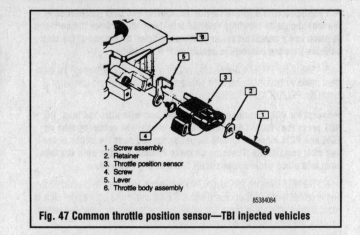

1. Screw assembly
2. Retainer
3. Throttle position sensor
4. Screw
5. Lever
6. Throttle body assembly

85384084

Fig. 47 Common throttle position sensor—TBI injected vehicles

➡**Some earlier model vehicles, such as some applications of the 2.8L engine, utilize an adjustable TP sensor. If so equipped, the sensor should be adjusted after the retainers are threaded, but BEFORE they are tightened. Please refer to Section 5 of this manual for TP sensor adjustment procedures.**

9. Engage the sensor electrical connector.
10. If removed, install the air cleaner assembly or duct, as applicable.
11. Connect the negative battery cable and check for proper operation. Please refer to

Power Steering Pressure Switch

Some 4-cylinder engines utilize a power steering pressure switch mounted on the steering gear or inlet pipe. The switch contacts will close when the steering is to the extreme left or right, this will signal the control module to increase idle speed and retard the spark timing in order to maintain a smooth idle.

REMOVAL & INSTALLATION

1. Disconnect the negative battery cable.
2. Locate the switch on the gear or inlet pipe. If necessary, raise the front of the truck and support safely using jackstands.
3. Disengage the switch connector.
4. Loosen and remove the switch from the vehicle. Have a rag handy to catch any fluid which might escape. If the new switch is not to be installed immediately, cap the opening to prevent system contamination or excessive fluid loss.
5. Installation is the reverse of removal.

Vacuum Control Solenoid Valve

REMOVAL & INSTALLATION

1. Disconnect the negative battery cable.
2. Disengage the solenoid valve electrical connector.
3. Disconnect the vacuum hoses from the vacuum regulator and solenoid. Tag them, as necessary to assure proper installation.
4. Remove the vacuum controller.
5. Installation is the reverse of removal.

Idle and Wide Open Throttle (WOT) Vacuum Switch

REMOVAL & INSTALLATION

1. Disconnect the negative battery cable.
2. Disengage the electrical harness connector.
3. Disconnect the vacuum hoses from the sensors. Tag them to assure proper installation.
4. Remove the idle and the WOT vacuum switch.
5. Installation is the reverse of removal.

SELF-DIAGNOSTICS

General Information

The computer control module (ECM, PCM or VCM) performs a continual self-diagnosis on many circuits of the engine control system. If a problem or irregularity is detected, the module will set a Diagnostic Trouble Code or DTC in the computer memory. A DTC indicates a suspected failure that currently exists or that has recently existed in a computer monitored system. A currently present code will usually illuminate the CHECK ENGINE or SERVICE ENGINE SOON light (as equipped), also known as the the Malfunction Indicator Lamp (MIL).

Diagnostic codes are stored in the computer module memory until they are manually erased by a scan tool or until power is disconnected from the module for a certain length of time. If a module detected problem is intermittent and disappears, the MIL will normally extinguish after 10 seconds, but the DTC will remain in diagnostic memory. Intermittent problems are often caused by corroded, dirty or loose electrical connections. A thorough inspection of the affected system should always be the first step in trouble shooting a DTC.

➡ **The CHECK ENGINE or SERVICE ENGINE SOON MIL will illuminate whenever the ignition is turned ON with the engine not running. This occurs for a bulb circuit check. As long as the light extinguishes after the engine is started, there are no currently detected trouble codes. Do not confuse the bulb check with a computer module detected DTC.**

Assembly Line Diagnostic Link (ALDL)/Diagnostic Link Connector (DLC)

▶ See Figure 48

There are many test procedures that require connecting a scan tool or connecting a jumper wire to terminals A and B of the 12-terminal ALDL/DLC (the main diagnostic tool connector). The connector is used during vehicle assembly to test the engine control systems before the vehicle leaves the assembly plant. The connector is also used throughout the vehicle's life to communicate with the computer control module.

➡ **When using a jumper wire at the connector to activate trouble code read out, the jumper must be connected during certain ignition switch conditions. On carbureted vehicles, the jumper should be connected with the ignition switch turned ON to begin code display. For fuel injected vehicles, the jumper should be connected with the ignition switch OFF, then with the jumpers in place, the switch should be turned ON to begin code read out. In both cases, the engine should not be running.**

The diagnostic connector is located in the passenger compartment. For most vehicles covered by this manual, the connector is located under the far left side of the dashboard. Terminal B is the diagnostic test terminal and is normally located on the top of the connector, second from right. Terminal A, located on the top right of the connector (to the right of terminal B), is the engine ground. When these terminals are jumpered together under the proper conditions, the MIL will flash Code 12. This indicates that the internal diagnostic system is operating. Terminal M, located on the bottom, far right of the connector, is usually the serial data terminal and is used by diagnostic scan tools to obtain and display information.

85384087

Fig. 48 ALDL/DLC terminal identification on most S/T series trucks

Entering Self-Diagnosis

To enter the diagnostics, either connect a scan tool to the ALDL/DLC connector (carefully following the tool manufacturer's instructions) or use a jumper wire to connect terminals A and B and begin flash diagnosis. On carbureted vehicles, the jumper should be connected with the ignition switch turned **ON** to begin code display. For fuel injected vehicles, the jumper should be connected with the ignition switch **OFF**, then with the jumpers in place, the switch should be turned **ON** to begin code read out. In both cases, the engine should NOT be;BS running. Once the jumper is properly connected, the control module will enter the diagnostic program and report trouble codes on the scan tool or by flashing the MIL.

All Codes are 2 digits between 12 and 82. Codes are displayed on the CHECK ENGINE or SERVICE ENGINE SOON light by flashing the MIL with short and long pauses to distinguish digits of 1 code from digits of another. The short pause is used between digits of the same code, long pauses are between codes. For Code 12, the sequence will be: flash, pause, flash-flash, long pause.

1. When the diagnostic mode is entered, Code 12 is displayed three times. This indicates that the internal diagnostic system is operating. If Code 12 is not displayed, the self-diagnostic program is not functioning properly. If no system malfunctions have been stored, Code 12 will continue to repeat.

➡ **On many applications, entering diagnostic mode will cause solenoids and relays to activate. Pulse-width modulated solenoids may be rapidly energized and de-energized, causing a clicking noise. Do not be startled by or concerned with this underhood noise during self-diagnosis code display.**

2. After code 12 flashes to indicate diagnostic display, any existing system fault codes are displayed in order from lowest to highest code number. Each code is displayed 3 times, followed by the next code, if any.
3. When all codes have been displayed, Code 12 will flash again.

Field Service Mode

For fuel injected engines, a special diagnostic mode is provided to help in oxygen sensor diagnosis. If the diagnostic terminal is grounded with the engine RUNNING, the system will enter field service mode. In this mode the MIL will display whether the engine control system is running in Open Loop or Closed Loop. When running in Closed Loop, the MIL will also display whether the engine is running lean or rich.

In Open Loop operation (during engine and oxygen sensor warm up) the MIL light will flash 2.5 times per second. Once the oxygen sensor is fully warmed and the control module decides that its feedback is reliable, the system will enter Closed Loop operation and the MIL will flash 1 time per second. During Closed Loop operation, if the MIL remains OFF most of the time, then the engine is running lean. If the MIL remains ON most of the time, the engine is running rich.

Clearing Codes

Codes should be cleared once repairs are completed to be assured that the fault is corrected and to make sure the code does not confuse a future attempt at troubleshooting. On most vehicles, the TECH 1®, or an equivalent scan tool may be used to clear codes from the control module memory. If a scan tool is unavailable or your tool does not have this capability, power must be removed from the module for a minimum of 30 seconds. The lower the ambient temperature, the longer period of time the power must be removed.

Remember, to prevent control module damage, the ignition must always be **OFF** when removing power. Power may be removed through various methods, depending on how the truck is equipped. The preferable method is to remove the control module fuse from the fuse box. The control module pigtail may also be unplugged. If necessary, the negative battery cable may be disconnected, but other on board data such as radio presets will be lost.

Control Module Learning Ability

Most of the later model control modules used in these vehicles contain a "learning" ability that allows the module to make corrections for minor variations in the fuel system and thereby improve driveability. Any time the module is replaced or power is removed from the module (to erase codes or during a repair), the "learning" process is reset and must begin again.

When the process is reset, a change may be noted in the vehicle's perfor-

mance. To "teach" the vehicle, start and run the engine until normal operating temperature is reached. Operate the vehicle using moderate acceleration and idle conditions until normal performance returns.

DIAGNOSTIC TROUBLE CODES

Below is a listing of the Diagnostic Trouble Codes (DTCs) for the various engine control systems covered in this manual. When using these charts along with the computer module's self-diagnostic system, remember that a code only points to the faulty circuit NOT necessarily to a faulty component. Loose, dam-

aged or corroded connections may contribute to a fault code on a circuit when the sensor or component is operating properly. Be sure that components are faulty before replacing them, especially the expensive ones.

Carbureted Vehicles

TROUBLE CODE IDENTIFICATION

The "CHECK ENGINE" light will only be "ON" if the malfunction exists under the conditions listed below. If the malfunction clears, the light will go out and a trouble code will be set in the ECM. Code 12 does not store in memory.

Any codes stored will be erased if no fault re-occurs within 50 engine starts.

The trouble codes indicate troubles as follows:

TROUBLE CODE 12	No ignition reference Pulses to the ECM. This code is not stored in memory and will only flash while the fault is present.	**TROUBLE CODE 25**	Air switching solenoid circuit open or grounded.
		TROUBLE CODE 31	No ignition reference pulses to the ECM for 10 seconds at part throttle, under road load. This code will store in memory.
TROUBLE CODE 13	Oxygen sensor circuit — The engine must run up 1 minute at part throttle, under road load, before this code will set. This code does not set when the coolant temperature is below 70°C and/or the time since engine start has not exceeded 2 minutes.	**TROUBLE CODE 44**	Lean oxygen sensor indication — The engine must run up to 2 minutes at part throttle, under road load, before this code will set. This code does not set when the coolant temperature is below 70°C and/or the air temperature in air cleaner is below 0°C.
TROUBLE CODE 14	Shorted coolant sensor circuit — The engine must run up to 2 minutes before this code will set.		
TROUBLE CODE 15	Open coolant sensor circuit — The engine must run up to 5 minutes before this code will set.	**TROUBLE CODE 45**	Rich System indication — The engine must run up to 2 minutes at part throttle, under road load, before this code will set. This code does not set when the engine exceeds 2500 rpm and/or the coolant temperature is below 70°C and/or the barometric pressure is below 23 in. Hg above 2500 m altitude. (8000 ft.)
TROUBLE CODE 21	Idle switch circuit open or WOT switch circuit shorted — The engine must run up to 10 seconds at following two conditions concurrently before this code will set. Idle switch output is in a low voltage state. WOT switch output is in a high voltage state.		
		TROUBLE CODE 51	Shorted fuel cut solenoid circuit and/or faulty ECM.
		TROUBLE CODE 52	Faulty ECM — Problem of RAM in ECM.
TROUBLE CODE 22	Fuel cut solenoid circuit open or grounded — The engine must run under the decelerating condition over 2000 engine rpm before this code will set.	**TROUBLE CODE 53**	Shorted air switching solenoid and/or faulty ECM.
		TROUBLE CODE 54	Shorted vacuum control solenoid and/or faulty ECM.
TROUBLE CODE 23	Vacuum control solenoid circuit open or grounded.	**TROUBLE CODE 55**	Faulty ECM — Fault of A/D converter in ECM.

85384088

Fig. 49 Diagnostic trouble codes—1.9L carbureted engine

TROUBLE CODE IDENTIFICATION

The "CHECK ENGINE" light will only be "ON" if the malfunction exists under the conditions listed below. It takes up to five seconds minimum for the light to come on when a problem occurs. If the malfunction clears, the light will go out and a trouble code will be set in the ECM. Code 12 does not store in memory.   Any codes stored will be erased if no problem reoccurs within 50 engine starts.

The trouble codes indicate problems as follows:

TROUBLE CODE 12 No distributor reference pulses to the ECM. This code is not stored in memory and will only flash while the fault is present. Normal code with ignition "on," engine not running.

TROUBLE CODE 13 Oxygen Sensor Circuit — The engine must run up to five minutes at part throttle, under road load, before this code will set.

TROUBLE CODE 14 Shorted coolant sensor circuit — The engine must run up to five minutes before this code will set.

TROUBLE CODE 15 Open coolant sensor circuit — The engine must run up to five minutes before this code will set.

TROUBLE CODE 21 Throttle position sensor circuit — The engine must run up to 25 seconds, at specified curb idle speed, before this code will set.

TROUBLE CODE 23 M/C solenoid circuit open or grounded.

TROUBLE CODE 24 Vehicle speed sensor (VSS) circuit — The vehicle must operate up to five minutes, at road speed, before this code will set.

TROUBLE CODE 32 Barometric pressure sensor (BARO) circuit low.

TROUBLE CODE 34 Vacuum sensor or Manifold Absolute Pressure (MAP) circuit — The engine must run up to five minutes, at specified curb idle, before this code will set.

TROUBLE CODE 35 Idle speed control (ISC) switch circuit shorted. (Over 50% throttle for over 2 seconds.)

TROUBLE CODE 41 No distributor reference pulses to the ECM at specified engine vacuum. This code will store in memory.

TROUBLE CODE 42 Electronic spark timing (EST) bypass circuit or EST circuit grounded or open.

TROUBLE CODE 43 Electronic Spark Control (ESC) retard signal for too long a time; causes retard in EST signal.

TROUBLE CODE 44 Lean exhaust indication — The engine must run up to five minutes, in closed loop and at part throttle, before this code will set.

TROUBLE CODE 45 Rich exhaust indication — The engine must run up to five minutes, in closed loop and at part throttle, before this code will set.

TROUBLE CODE 51 Faulty or improperly installed calibration unit (PROM). It takes up to 30 seconds before this code will set.

TROUBLE CODE 54 Shorted M/C solenoid circuit and/ or faulty ECM.

TROUBLE CODE 55 Grounded Vref (terminal "21"), high voltage on oxygen sensor circuit or ECM.

85384089

Fig. 50 Diagnostic trouble codes—2.0L and 2.8L carbureted engines

Fuel Injected Vehicles

"SCAN" DIAGNOSTIC CIRCUIT CHECK CODE DEFINITIONS (1 of 4)

THE 'DIAGNOSTIC CIRCUIT CHECK' SCAN DATA IS TYPICAL OF THAT DISPLAYED BY A PROPERLY DESIGNED AND CALIBRATED ALCL "SCAN" TOOL.

A "SCAN" TOOL THAT DISPLAYS FAULTY DATA SHOULD NOT BE USED AND THE PROBLEM REPORTED TO THE "SCAN" TOOL MANUFACTURER. THE USE OF A FAULTY "SCAN" TOOL CAN RESULT IN MISDIAGNOSIS AND UNNECESSARY PARTS REPLACEMENT.

CODE

DEFINITION

■ CODE 13
- "SCAN" IN "SPECIAL" MODE
- ENGINE AT 1200 RPM.
- "SCAN" OXYGEN SENSOR VOLTAGE.

HARD FAILURE -
OXYGEN SENSOR VOLTAGE FIXED BETWEEN .35 TO .55 V. OPEN CIRCUIT CONDITION.

INTERMITTENT CODE -
NORMAL "SCAN" VOLTAGE WILL VARY BETWEEN 100MV TO 999 MV (.1 AND 1.0 VOLT).

■ CODE 14
- IGNITION "ON".
- ENGINE STOPPED.
- "SCAN" COOLANT TEMPERATURE.

HARD FAILURE -
"SCAN" TOOL READS ABOVE 135°C. CIRCUIT SHORTED TO GROUND OR FAULTY SENSOR.

INTERMITTENT CODE -
"SCAN" TOOL READS ENGINE COOLANT TEMP. IN DEGREES CENTIGRADE. AFTER ENGINE IS STARTED, THE TEMPERATURE SHOULD RISE STEADILY TO ABOUT 85°C THEN STABILIZE WHEN THERMOSTAT OPENS.

■ CODE 15
- IGNITION "ON".
- ENGINE STOPPED.
- "SCAN" COOLANT TEMPERATURE.

HARD FAILURE -
"SCAN" TOOL READS BELOW -30°C. CIRCUIT OPEN OR FAULTY SENSOR.

INTERMITTENT CODE -
"SCAN" TOOL READS ENGINE COOLANT TEMPERATURE IN DEGREES CENTIGRADE.
AFTER ENGINE IS STARTED, THE TEMPERATURE SHOULD RISE STEADILY TO ABOUT 85°C, THEN STABILIZE WHEN THERMOSTAT OPENS.

85384090

Fig. 51 Diagnostic trouble codes—1985-87 2.5L engine

"SCAN" DIAGNOSTIC CIRCUIT CHECK CODE DEFINITIONS (2 of 4)

CODE

DEFINITION

■ CODE 21
- IGNITION "ON".
- ENGINE STOPPED.
- THROTTLE CLOSED
- "SCAN" TPS

OR

- ENGINE IDLING
- THROTTLE CLOSED
- "SCAN" TPS

HARD FAILURE -
"SCAN" TOOL READS OVER 4.5 VOLTS. GROUND WIRE OPEN, SIGNAL LINE SHORTED TO SENSOR REF. LINE, OR FAULTY SENSOR.

OR

HARD FAILURE -
"SCAN" TOOL READS OVER 2.5 VOLTS. GROUND WIRE OPEN OR FAULTY SENSOR.

INTERMITTENT CODE -
"SCAN" TOOL READS THROTTLE POSITION IN VOLTS. SHOULD READ BETWEEN 020-125 (200 MV AND 1.25 V). WITH THROTTLE CLOSED AND IGNITION ON OR AT IDLE. VOLTAGE SHOULD INCREASE AT A STEADY RATE AS THROTTLE IS MOVED TOWARD W.O.T.

■ CODE 22
- IGNITION "ON"
- ENGINE STOPPED.
- "SCAN" TPS

HARD FAILURE -
"SCAN" TOOL READS BELOW 020V (200 MV) OPEN OR SHORTED TO GROUND IN 5V REFERENCE OR SIGNAL CIRCUIT, OR FAULTY SENSOR.

INTERMITTENT CODE -
"SCAN" TOOL READS THROTTLE POSITION IN VOLTS. SHOULD READ BETWEEN 020-125 (200 MV AND 1.25 V). WITH THROTTLE CLOSED AND IGNITION ON OR AT IDLE. VOLTAGE SHOULD INCREASE AT A STEADY RATE AS THROTTLE IS MOVED TOWARD W.O.T.

■ CODE 24
- ENGINE RUNNING.
- DRIVE WHEELS TURNING.
- "SCAN" MPH.

HARD FAILURE -
"SCAN" TOOL READS 0 MPH. IF SPEEDOMETER IS WORKING OK, THEN THE VSS SIGNAL INPUT IS OPEN, SHORTED TO GROUND, OR THE BUFFER IS DEFECTIVE.

INTERMITTENT CODE -
"SCAN" TOOL READING SHOULD CLOSELY MATCH WITH SPEEDOMETER READING WITH DRIVE WHEELS TURNING.

85384091

Fig. 52 Diagnostic trouble codes—1985-87 2.5L engine continued

"SCAN" DIAGNOSTIC CIRCUIT CHECK
CODE DEFINITIONS (4 of 4)

CODE	DEFINITION
CODE 42 • CLEAR CODES, START AND • IDLE ENGINE FOR 1 MINUTE. • IF NO "SERVICE ENGINE SOON" LIGHT, REFER TO INTERMITTENTS IN SECTION "B".	**HARD FAILURE -** "SERVICE ENGINE SOON" ON, SCAN TOOL INDICATES CODE 42. **INTERMITTENT CODE -** THE "SCAN" DOES NOT HAVE THE ABILITY TO HELP DIAGNOSE A CODE 42 PROBLEM.
CODE 44 • "SCAN" TOOL IN "SPECIAL" MODE. • ENGINE IDLING AT 1000 RPM. • "SCAN" OXYGEN SENSOR VOLTAGE	**HARD FAILURE -** "SCAN" OXYGEN SENSOR VOLTAGE CONSISTENTLY BELOW .35V. CAUSED BY A LEAN EXHAUST OR SIGNAL CIRCUIT SHORTED TO GROUND. **INTERMITTENT CODE -** THE "SCAN" TOOL HAS SEVERAL POSITIONS THAT WILL INDICATE THE STATE OF THE EXHAUST GASES. CROSSCOUNTS, RICH-LEAN INDICATION, OXYGEN SENSOR VOLTAGE, INTEGRATOR, AND BLOCK LEARN.
CODE 45 • "SCAN" TOOL IN "SPECIAL" MODE • ENGINE IDLING AT 1000 RPM • "SCAN" OXYGEN SENSOR VOLTAGE	**HARD FAILURE -** "SCAN" OXYGEN SENSOR VOLTAGE CONSISTENTLY ABOVE .55V. RICH EXHAUST CAUSING A HIGH OXYGEN SENSOR VOLTAGE. **INTERMITTENT CODE -** THE "SCAN" TOOL HAS SEVERAL POSITIONS THAT WILL INDICATE THE STATE OF THE EXHAUST GASES. CROSSCOUNTS, RICH-LEAN INDICATION, OXYGEN SENSOR VOLTAGE, INTEGRATOR, AND BLOCK LEARN.
CODE 51 • CLEAR CODES • START ENGINE • CHECK FOR CODE	**HARD FAILURE -** CODE 51 RESETS WHICH INDICATES A FAULTY PROM.
CODE 55 • CLEAR CODES • START ENGINE • CHECK FOR CODE	**HARD FAILURE -** CODE 55 RESETS WHICH INDICATES THE ECM IS FAULTY. REPLACE ECM.

85384093

Fig. 54 Diagnostic trouble codes—1985–87 2.5L engine continued

"SCAN" DIAGNOSTIC CIRCUIT CHECK
CODE DEFINITIONS (3 of 4)

CODE	DEFINITION
CODE 33 • ENGINE IDLING. • "SCAN" MAP.	**HARD FAILURE -** "SCAN" TOOL READS ABOVE 2.5 VOLTS. SENSOR GROUND CIRCUIT OPEN, FAULTY SENSOR, LEAKING VACUUM HOSE OR, INSUFFICIENT MANIFOLD VACUUM. **INTERMITTENT CODE -** "SCAN" TOOL READS MANIFOLD PRESSURE IN VOLTS. LOW PRESSURE (HIGH VACUUM) READS A LOW VOLTAGE WHILE A HIGH PRESSURE (LOW VACUUM) READS A HIGH VOLTAGE. QUICK ACCELERATION SHOULD CAUSE A HIGH OUTPUT VOLTAGE WHILE A DECELERATION WILL SHOW A LOW VOLTAGE. IF ENGINE IDLE IS LOW.
CODE 34 • IGNITION "ON" • "SCAN" MAP.	**HARD FAILURE -** "SCAN" TOOL READS BELOW (200 MV) .2 VOLTS. SIGNAL WIRE OR 5V REFERENCE OPEN OR SHORTED TO GROUND OR FAULTY SENSOR. **INTERMITTENT CODE -** "SCAN" TOOL READS MANIFOLD PRESSURE IN VOLTS. LOW PRESSURE (HIGH VACUUM) READS A LOW VOLTAGE WHILE A HIGH PRESSURE (LOW VACUUM) READS A HIGH VOLTAGE. QUICK ACCELERATION SHOULD CAUSE A HIGH OUTPUT VOLTAGE WHILE A DECELERATION WILL SHOW A LOW VOLTAGE.
CODE 35 • A/C OFF. • ENGINE IDLING IN NEUTRAL. • COOLANT TEMP 70° TO 90°C • "SCAN" IN "SPECIAL" MODE. • INCREASE ENGINE RPM TO 2500 TO RESET IAC. CLOSE THROTTLE AND ALLOW IDLE AND IAC COUNTS STABILIZE.	**HARD FAILURE -** "SCAN" TOOL DISPLAYS IDLE SPEED 950 RPM OR ABOVE IAC COUNTS "0". THIS CONDITION IS USUALLY A SMALL VACUUM LEAK SUCH AS THERMAC OR CRUISE CONTROL HOSE DISCONNECTED. OR ENGINE SPEED 950 RPM OR BELOW OR IAC COUNTS ABOVE 80. **INTERMITTENT CODE -** FOLLOWING AN IAC RESET, RPM SHOULD STABILIZE AT 1000 ± 50 RPM IN SPECIAL MODE. DISCONNECTING "SCAN" TOOL WILL RESTORE NORMAL IDLE.

85384092

Fig. 53 Diagnostic trouble codes—1985–87 2.5L engine continued

"SCAN" DIAGNOSTIC
CIRCUIT CHECK
CODE DEFINITIONS
(2 of 4)

CODE	DEFINITION

■ CODE 21
- IGNITION "ON".
- ENGINE STOPPED.
- THROTTLE CLOSED
- "SCAN" TPS

OR

- ENGINE IDLING
- THROTTLE CLOSED
- "SCAN" TPS

HARD FAILURE -
"SCAN" TOOL READS OVER 4.5 VOLTS. GROUND WIRE OPEN, SIGNAL LINE SHORTED TO SENSOR REF. LINE, OR FAULTY SENSOR.

OR

HARD FAILURE -
"SCAN" TOOL READS OVER 2.5 VOLTS. GROUND WIRE OPEN OR FAULTY SENSOR.

INTERMITTENT CODE -
"SCAN" TOOL READS THROTTLE POSITION IN VOLTS. SHOULD READ BETWEEN 020-125 (200 MV AND 1.25 V). WITH THROTTLE CLOSED AND IGNITION ON OR AT IDLE. VOLTAGE SHOULD INCREASE AT A STEADY RATE AS THROTTLE IS MOVED TOWARD W.O.T.

■ CODE 22
- IGNITION "ON".
- ENGINE STOPPED.
- "SCAN" TPS

HARD FAILURE -
"SCAN" TOOL READS BELOW 020V (200 MV) OPEN OR SHORTED TO GROUND. IN 5V REFERENCE OR SIGNAL CIRCUIT, OR FAULTY SENSOR.

INTERMITTENT CODE -
"SCAN" TOOL READS THROTTLE POSITION IN VOLTS. SHOULD READ BETWEEN 020-125 (200 MV AND 1.25 V). WITH THROTTLE CLOSED AND IGNITION ON OR AT IDLE. VOLTAGE SHOULD INCREASE AT A STEADY RATE AS THROTTLE IS MOVED TOWARD W.O.T.

■ CODE 24
- ENGINE RUNNING.
- DRIVE WHEELS TURNING.
- "SCAN" MPH.

HARD FAILURE -
"SCAN" TOOL READS 0 MPH. IF SPEEDOMETER IS WORKING OK, THEN THE VSS SIGNAL INPUT IS OPEN, SHORTED TO GROUND, OR THE BUFFER IS DEFECTIVE.

INTERMITTENT CODE -
"SCAN" TOOL READING SHOULD CLOSELY MATCH WITH SPEEDOMETER READING WITH DRIVE WHEELS TURNING.

85384095

Fig. 56 Diagnostic trouble codes—1986–87 2.8L TBI engine continued

---

"SCAN" DIAGNOSTIC
CIRCUIT CHECK
CODE DEFINITIONS
(1 of 4)

THE 'DIAGNOSTIC CIRCUIT CHECK' SCAN DATA IS TYPICAL OF THAT DISPLAYED BY A PROPERLY DESIGNED AND CALIBRATED ALCL "SCAN" TOOL.

A "SCAN" TOOL THAT DISPLAYS FAULTY DATA SHOULD NOT BE USED AND THE PROBLEM REPORTED TO THE "SCAN" TOOL MANUFACTURER. THE USE OF A FAULTY "SCAN" TOOL CAN RESULT IN MISDIAGNOSIS AND UNNECESSARY PARTS REPLACEMENT.

CODE	DEFINITION

■ CODE 13
- "SCAN" IN "SPECIAL" MODE
- ENGINE IDLING AT 1000 RPM.
- "SCAN" OXYGEN SENSOR VOLTAGE.

HARD FAILURE -
OXYGEN SENSOR VOLTAGE FIXED BETWEEN .35 TO .55 V. OPEN CIRCUIT CONDITION.

INTERMITTENT CODE -
NORMAL "SCAN" VOLTAGE WILL VARY BETWEEN 100MV TO 999 MV (.1 AND 1.0 VOLT).

■ CODE 14
- IGNITION "ON".
- ENGINE STOPPED.
- "SCAN" COOLANT TEMPERATURE.

HARD FAILURE -
"SCAN" TOOL READS ABOVE 135°C. CIRCUIT SHORTED TO GROUND OR FAULTY SENSOR.

INTERMITTENT CODE -
"SCAN" TOOL READS ENGINE COOLANT TEMP. IN DEGREES CENTIGRADE. AFTER ENGINE IS STARTED, THE TEMPERATURE SHOULD RISE STEADILY TO ABOUT 85°C THEN STABILIZE WHEN THERMOSTAT OPENS.

■ CODE 15
- IGNITION "ON".
- ENGINE STOPPED.
- "SCAN" COOLANT TEMPERATURE.

HARD FAILURE -
"SCAN" TOOL READS BELOW -30°C. CIRCUIT OPEN OR FAULTY SENSOR.

INTERMITTENT CODE -
"SCAN" TOOL READS ENGINE COOLANT TEMPERATURE IN DEGREES CENTIGRADE. AFTER ENGINE IS STARTED, THE TEMPERATURE SHOULD RISE STEADILY TO ABOUT 85°C, THEN STABILIZE WHEN THERMOSTAT OPENS.

85384094

Fig. 55 Diagnostic trouble codes—1986–87 2.8L TBI engine

"SCAN" DIAGNOSTIC CIRCUIT CHECK
CODE DEFINITIONS (3 of 4)

CODE / **DEFINITION**

CODE 33
- ENGINE IDLING.
- "SCAN" MAP.

HARD FAILURE -
"SCAN" TOOL READS ABOVE 2.5 VOLTS. SENSOR GROUND CIRCUIT OPEN, FAULTY SENSOR, LEAKING VACUUM HOSE OR INSUFFICIENT MANIFOLD VACUUM.

INTERMITTENT CODE -
"SCAN" TOOL READS MANIFOLD PRESSURE IN VOLTS. LOW PRESSURE (HIGH VACUUM) READS A LOW VOLTAGE WHILE A HIGH PRESSURE (LOW VACUUM) READS A HIGH VOLTAGE. QUICK ACCELERATION SHOULD CAUSE A HIGH OUTPUT VOLTAGE WHILE A DECELERATION WILL SHOW A LOW VOLTAGE. IF ENGINE IDLE IS LOW.

CODE 34
- IGNITION "ON"
- "SCAN" MAP.

HARD FAILURE -
"SCAN" TOOL READS BELOW (200 MV) .2 VOLTS. SIGNAL WIRE OR 5V REFERENCE OPEN OR SHORTED TO GROUND OR FAULTY SENSOR.

INTERMITTENT CODE -
"SCAN" TOOL READS MANIFOLD PRESSURE IN VOLTS. LOW PRESSURE (HIGH VACUUM) READS A LOW VOLTAGE WHILE A HIGH PRESSURE (LOW VACUUM) READS A HIGH VOLTAGE. QUICK ACCELERATION SHOULD CAUSE A HIGH OUTPUT VOLTAGE WHILE A DECELERATION WILL SHOW A LOW VOLTAGE.

CODE 42
- CLEAR CODES. START AND
- IDLE ENGINE FOR 1 MINUTE.
- IF NO "SERVICE ENGINE SOON" LIGHT, REFER TO INTERMITTENTS IN SECTION "B".

HARD FAILURE -
"SERVICE ENGINE SOON" LIGHT ON, SCAN TOOL INDICATES CODE 42.

INTERMITTENT CODE -
THE SCAN DOES NOT HAVE THE ABILITY TO HELP DIAGNOSE A CODE 42 PROBLEM.

CODE 43
- "SCAN" TOOL IN SPECIAL MODE. ENGINE IDLING AT 1000 RPM. "SCAN" KNOCK RETARD OR OLD PA3.

HARD FAILURE -
KNOCK RETARD OR (OLD PA 3) WILL DISPLAY NUMBERS THAT ARE CONSTANTLY CHANGING (0 TO 255). FAULTY ESC CIRCUIT.

INTERMITTENT CODE -
NUMBERS SHOULD INCREASE WHEN KNOCK IS BEING DETECTED.

85384096

Fig. 57 Diagnostic trouble codes—1986-87 2.8L TBI engine continued

"SCAN" DIAGNOSTIC CIRCUIT CHECK
CODE DEFINITIONS (4 of 4)

CODE / **DEFINITION**

CODE 44
- "SCAN" TOOL IN "SPECIAL" MODE.
- ENGINE IDLING AT 1000 RPM.
- "SCAN" OXYGEN SENSOR VOLTAGE

HARD FAILURE -
"SCAN" OXYGEN SENSOR VOLTAGE CONSISTENTLY BELOW .35V. CAUSED BY A LEAN EXHAUST OR SIGNAL CIRCUIT SHORTED TO GROUND.

INTERMITTENT CODE -
THE "SCAN" TOOL HAS SEVERAL POSITIONS THAT WILL INDICATE THE STATE OF THE EXHAUST GASES. CROSSCOUNTS, RICH-LEAN INDICATION, OXYGEN SENSOR VOLTAGE, INTEGRATOR, AND BLOCK LEARN.

CODE 45
- "SCAN" TOOL IN "SPECIAL" MODE
- ENGINE IDLING AT 1000 RPM
- "SCAN" OXYGEN SENSOR VOLTAGE

HARD FAILURE -
"SCAN" OXYGEN SENSOR VOLTAGE CONSISTENTLY ABOVE .55V. RICH EXHAUST CAUSING A HIGH OXYGEN SENSOR VOLTAGE.

INTERMITTENT CODE -
THE "SCAN" TOOL HAS SEVERAL POSITIONS THAT WILL INDICATE THE STATE OF THE EXHAUST GASES. CROSSCOUNTS, RICH-LEAN INDICATION, OXYGEN SENSOR VOLTAGE, INTEGRATOR, AND BLOCK LEARN.

CODE 51
- CLEAR CODES
- START ENGINE
- CHECK FOR CODE

HARD FAILURE -
CODE 51 RESETS WHICH INDICATES A FAULTY PROM.

CODE 52
- CLEAR CODES
- START ENGINE
- CHECK FOR CODE

HARD FAILURE -
CODE 52 RESETS WHICH INDICATES CALPAK IS MISSING OR FAILED.

CODE 54
- CLEAR CODES
- START ENGINE
- CHECK FOR CODE

HARD FAILURE -
CODE 54 RESETS WHICH INDICATES LOW FUEL PUMP VOLTAGE.

CODE 55
- CLEAR CODES
- START ENGINE
- CHECK FOR CODE

HARD FAILURE -
CODE 55 RESETS WHICH INDICATES THE ECM IS FAULTY. REPLACE ECM.

85384097

Fig. 58 Diagnostic trouble codes—1986-87 2.8L TBI engine continued

DIAGNOSTIC TROUBLE CODE (DTC) IDENTIFICATION

The MIL (Service Engine Soon) will only be "ON" if the malfunction exists with the conditions listed below. If the malfunction clears, the lamp will go out and the DTC will be stored in the PCM. Any DTCs stored in the PCM will be erased if no problem reoccurs within 50 engine starts. Note: All DTCs with the sign * are transmission related DTCs.

Remember, always start with the lowest numerical DTC first, when diagnosing some engine DTCs trigger other transmission DTCs.

DTC AND CIRCUIT	PROBABLE CAUSE	DTC AND CIRCUIT	PROBABLE CAUSE
DTC 13 - Oxygen O2S Sensor Circuit (Open Circuit)	Indicates that the oxygen sensor circuit or sensor was open for one minute while off idle.	DTC 33 - Manifold Absolute Pressure (MAP) Sensor Circuit (Signal Voltage High - Low Vacuum)	MAP sensor output high for 5 seconds or an open signal circuit.
DTC 14 - Engine Coolant Temperature (ECT) Sensor Circuit (High Temperature Indicated)	Sets if the sensor or signal line becomes grounded or greater than 145°C (294°F) for 0.5 seconds.	DTC 34 - Manifold Absolute Pressure (MAP) Sensor Circuit (Signal Voltage Low - High Vacuum)	Low or no output from MAP sensor with engine operating.
DTC 15 - Engine Coolant Temperature (ECT) Sensor Circuit (Low Temperature Indicated)	Sets if the sensor, connections, or wires open or less than -33°C (-27°F) for 0.5 seconds.	DTC 35 - IAC	IAC error
DTC 16 - Transmission Output Speed Low	Open in CKT 1697/1716 or power loss to VSS buffer	*DTC 37 - Brake Switch Stuck On	With no voltage and vehicle speed is less than 5 mph for 6 seconds, then vehicle speed is 5 - 20 MPH for 6 seconds, then vehicle speed is greater than 20 MPH for 6 seconds, this must occur for 7 times.
DTC 21 - Throttle Position (TP) Sensor Circuit (Signal Voltage High)	TP voltage greater than 4.88 volts 4 seconds with less than 1200 RPM.	*DTC 38 - Brake Switch Stuck Off	With voltage and vehicle speed is greater than 20 MPH for 6 seconds, then vehicle speed is 5 - 20 MPH for 6 seconds. This must occur 7 times.
DTC 22 - Throttle Position (TP) Sensor Circuit (Signal Voltage Low)	A short to ground, open signal circuit, or TP voltage less than 0.16 volts for 4 seconds.	DTC 42 - Ignition Control (IC)	PCM detects an open or grounded IC or bypass circuit.
DTC 24 - Vehicle Speed Sensor (VSS) Signal Low	No vehicle speed sensor signal present during a road load decel.	DTC 43 - Knock Sensor (KS) Circuit	Signal to the PCM has remained low for too long, or the system has failed a functional system check.
DTC 28 - Fluid Pressure Switch Assembly	PCM detects 1 of 2 invalid combinations of the fluid pressure switch range signals	DTC 44 - Oxygen Sensor (O2S) Circuit (Lean Exhaust Indicated)	Vacuum switch shorted to ground on start up OR Switch not closed after the PCM has commanded EGR for a specified period of time.
DTC 32 - Exhaust Gas Recirculation (EGR) System	Vacuum switch shorted to ground on start up OR Switch not closed after the PCM has commanded EGR for a specified period of time. OR EGR solenoid circuit open for a specified period of time.	DTC 45 - Oxygen Sensor (O2S) Circuit (Rich Exhaust Indicated)	Sets if oxygen sensor voltage remains greater than 0.7 volt for about 1 minute.

Fig. 60 Diagnostic trouble codes—1993 PCM equipped vehicles

85384099

CODE IDENTIFICATION

The "Service Engine Soon" light will only be "ON" if the malfunction exists under the conditions listed below. If the malfunction clears, the light will go out and the code will be stored in the ECM. Any codes stored will be erased if no problem reoccurs within 50 engine starts.

CODE AND CIRCUIT	PROBABLE CAUSE	CODE AND CIRCUIT	PROBABLE CAUSE
Code 13 - O2 Sensor Open Oxygen Sensor Circuit	Indicates that the oxygen sensor circuit or sensor was open for one minute while off idle.	Code 33 - MAP Sensor Low Vacuum	MAP sensor output to high for 5 seconds or an open signal circuit.
Code 14 - Coolant Sensor High Temperature Indication	Sets if the sensor or signal line becomes grounded for 3 seconds.	Code 34 - MAP Sensor High Vacuum	Low or no output from sensor with engine running.
Code 15 - Coolant Sensor Low Temperature Indication	Sets if the sensor, connections, or wires open for 3 seconds.	Code 35 - IAC	IAC error
Code 21 - TPS Signal Voltage High	TPS voltage greater than 2.5 volts for 3 seconds with less than 1200 RPM.	Code 42 - EST	ECM has seen an open or grounded EST or Bypass circuit.
Code 22 - TPS Signal Voltage Low	A shorted to ground or open signal circuit will set code in 3 seconds.	Code 43 - ESC	Signal to the ECM has remained low for too long or the system has failed a functional check.
Code 23 - MAT Low Temperature Indication	Sets if the sensor, connections, or wires open for 3 seconds.	Code 44 Lean Exhaust Indication	Sets if oxygen sensor voltage remains below .2 volts for about 20 seconds.
Code 24 - VSS No Vehicle Speed Indication	No vehicle speed present during a road load decel.	Code 45 Rich Exhaust Indication	Sets if oxygen sensor voltage remains above .7 volts for about 1 minute.
Code 25 - MAT High Temperature Indication	Sets if the sensor or signal line becomes grounded for 3 seconds.	Code 51	Faulty MEM-CAL, PROM, or ECM.
Code 32 - EGR	Vacuum switch shorted to ground on start up OR Switch not closed after the ECM has commanded EGR for a specified period of time. OR EGR solenoid circuit open for a specified period of time.	Code 52	Fuel CALPAK missing or faulty.
		Code 53	System overvoltage. Indicates a basic generator problem.
		Code 54 - Fuel Pump Low voltage	Sets when the fuel pump voltage is less than 2 volts when reference pulses are being received.
		Code 55	Faulty ECM

Fig. 59 Diagnostic trouble codes—1988-92 engines (except MFI-urbo) and 1993 ECM equipped vehicles

85384098

DTC IDENTIFICATION

The MIL (Service Engine Soon) will only be "ON" if the malfunction exists under the conditions listed below. If the malfunction clears, the light will go out and the DTC will be stored in the VCM. Any DTC(s) stored will be erased if no problem reoccurs within 50 engine starts.

DTC AND CIRCUIT	PROBABLE CAUSE	DTC AND CIRCUIT	PROBABLE CAUSE
DTC 13 - Oxygen Sensor (O2S) Circuit (Open Circuit)	Indicates that the oxygen sensor circuit or sensor was open for one minute while off idle.	DTC 33 - Manifold Absolute Pressure (MAP) Sensor Circuit (Signal Voltage High-Low Vacuum)	MAP sensor output to high for 5 seconds or an open signal circuit.
DTC 14 - Engine Coolant Temperature (ECT) Sensor Circuit (High Temperature Indicated)	Sets if the sensor or signal line becomes grounded for 3 seconds.	DTC 34 - Manifold Absolute Pressure (MAP) Sensor Circuit (Signal Voltage Low-High Vacuum)	Low or no output from sensor with engine running.
DTC 15 - Engine Coolant Temperature (ECT) Sensor Circuit (Low Temperature Indicated)	Sets if the sensor, connections, or wires open for 3 seconds.	DTC 38 - Knock Sensor (KS) Line Open	Knock sensor line open for 3 seconds.
DTC 21 - Throttle Position (TP) Sensor Circuit (Signal Voltage High)	TP signal voltage greater than 2.5 volts for 3 seconds with less than 1200 RPM.	DTC 39 - Knock Sensor (KS) Line Shorted	Knock sensor line shorted for 3 seconds.
DTC 22 - Throttle Position (TP) Sensor Circuit (Signal Voltage Low)	A shorted to ground or open signal circuit will set code in 3 seconds.	DTC 42 - Ignition Control (IC)	VCM has seen an open or grounded IC or bypass circuit.
DTC 24 - Vehicle Speed Sensor (VSS)	No vehicle speed present during a road load decel.	DTC 43 - Knock Sensor (KS) Circuit	Signal to the VCM has remained low for too long or the system has failed a functional check.
DTC 26 - Quad-Driver (QDM) 1 Circuit	A shorted or open brake or MIL circuit for 3 seconds.	DTC 44 - Oxygen Sensor (O2S) Circuit (Lean Exhaust Indicated)	Sets if oxygen sensor voltage remains below .2 volt for about 20 seconds.
DTC 27 - Quad-Driver (QDM) 2 Circuit	A shorted or open electronic vacuum regulator valve, brake enable relay or shift lamp circuit for 3 seconds.	DTC 45 - Oxygen Sensor (O2S) Circuit (Rich Exhaust Indicated)	Sets if oxygen sensor voltage remains above .7 volt for about 1 minute.
DTC 32 - Exhaust Gas Recirculation (EGR) System	EGR valve closed and O2S fluctuating normally. The VCM will verify that short term fuel trim did increase.	DTC 53 - System Over Voltage	System over voltage. Indicates a basic generator problem.
		DTC 54 - Fuel Pump Circuit (Low Voltage)	Sets when the fuel pump voltage is less than 2 volts when reference pulses are being received.

85384101

Fig. 62 Diagnostic trouble codes—1993 VCM equipped vehicles

DIAGNOSTIC TROUBLE CODE (DTC) IDENTIFICATION

The MIL (Service Engine Soon) will only be "ON" if the malfunction exists with the conditions listed below. If the malfunction clears, the lamp will go out and the DTC will be stored in the PCM. Any DTCs stored will be erased if no problem reoccurs within 50 engine starts. Note: All DTCs with the sign * are transmission related DTCs. Remember, always start with the lowest numerical DTC first, when diagnosing some engine DTCs trigger other transmission DTCs.

DTC AND CIRCUIT	PROBABLE CAUSE	DTC AND CIRCUIT	PROBABLE CAUSE
DTC 51 - Faulty PROM (MEM-CAL) Problem	Faulty PROM (MEM-CAL) or PCM.	*DTC 69 - TCC Stuck "ON"	Slip > -20 and slip 20 TCC is not locked gear = 2, 3 or 4 TPS > 25%, not in P/R/N for 4 seconds.
DTC 53 - System Voltage High	System overvoltage of 19.5 volts for 2 seconds	*DTC 72 - Vehicle Speed Sensor Loss	Not in P/N • Output speed changes greater than 1000 RPM • P/N - Output speed changes greater than 2050 RPM for 2 seconds
DTC 54 - Fuel Pump Circuit (Low Voltage)	Sets when the fuel pump voltage is less than 2 volts when reference pulses are being received.	*DTC 73 - Pressure Control Solenoid	If return amperage varies more than 0.16 amps. from commanded amperage
DTC 55 - Faulty PCM	Faulty PCM.	*DTC 75 - System Voltage Low	System voltage < 7.3 at low temperature or < 11.7 at high temperature for 4 seconds.
*DTC 58 - Transmission Fluid Temperature High	Transmission fluid temperature greater than 154°C (309°F) for one second.	*DTC 79 - Transmission Fluid Over Temperature	Transmission fluid Temperature > 150°C and < 154°C for 15 minutes.
*DTC 59 - Transmission Fluid Temperature Low	Transmission fluid temperature greater than -33°C (-27°F) for one second.	*DTC 81 - 2-3 Shift Solenoid Circuit Fault	2-3 shift solenoid is command "ON", and circuit voltage is high for two seconds OR 2-3 shift solenoid is command "OFF", and circuit voltage is low for two seconds.
*DTC 66 - 3-2 Control Solenoid Circuit Fault	At High Duty Cycle the circuit voltage is high OR at Low Duty Cycle the Circuit Voltage is low for four seconds.	*DTC 82 - 1-2 Shift Solenoid Circuit Fault	1-2 shift solenoid is command "ON", and circuit voltage is high for two seconds OR 1-2 shift solenoid is command "OFF" and circuit voltage is low for two seconds.
*DTC 67 Torque Converter Clutch Circuit	TCC is commanded "ON" and circuit voltage remains high for two seconds OR TCC is commanded "OFF" and circuit voltage remains low for two seconds.		

85384100

Fig. 61 Diagnostic trouble codes—1993 PCM equipped vehicles, continued

MFI-TURBO ENGINE

- **Code 12**—Diagnostic system check
- **Code 13**—Oxygen sensor (open circuit)
- **Code 14**—Coolant temperature sensor (high temperature indicated)
- **Code 15**—Coolant temperature sensor (low temperature indicated)
- **Code 21**—Throttle position sensor (signal voltage high)
- **Code 22**—Throttle position sensor (signal voltage low)
- **Code 23**—Manifold air temperature sensor (low temperature indicated)
- **Code 24**—Vehicle speed sensor

- **Code 25**—Manifold air temperature sensor (high temperature indicated)
- **Code 31**—Turbocharger wastegate overboost
- **Code 32**—EGR circuit
- **Code 33**—MAP sensor (signal voltage high/vacuum low)
- **Code 34**—MAP sensor (signal voltage low/vacuum high)
- **Code 35**—Idle speed error
- **Code 42**—Electronic spark timing circuit
- **Code 43**—Electronic spark control circuit
- **Code 44**—Oxygen sensor circuit (lean exhaust indicated)
- **Code 45**—Oxygen sensor circuit (rich exhaust indicated)
- **Code 51**—PROM error (faulty or incorrect PROM)

VACUUM DIAGRAMS

Below is a listing of vacuum diagrams for most of the engine and emissions package combinations covered by this manual. Because vacuum circuits will vary based on various engine and vehicle options, always refer first to the vehicle emission control information label, if present. Should the label be missing, or should vehicle be equipped with a different engine from the car's original equipment, refer to the diagrams below for the same or similar configuration.

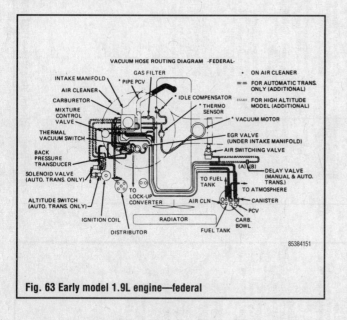

Fig. 63 Early model 1.9L engine—federal

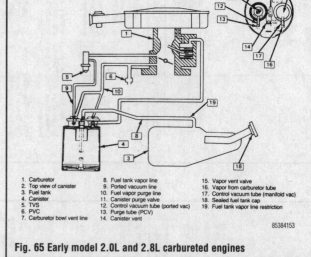

Fig. 65 Early model 2.0L and 2.8L carbureted engines

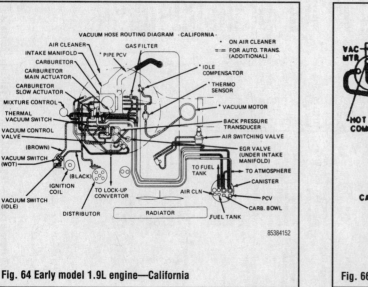

Fig. 64 Early model 1.9L engine—California

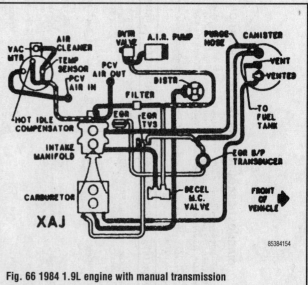

Fig. 66 1984 1.9L engine with manual transmission

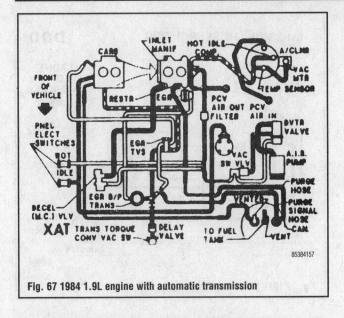

Fig. 67 1984 1.9L engine with automatic transmission

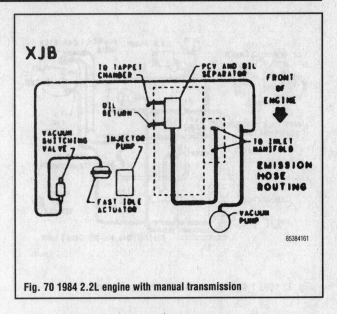

Fig. 70 1984 2.2L engine with manual transmission

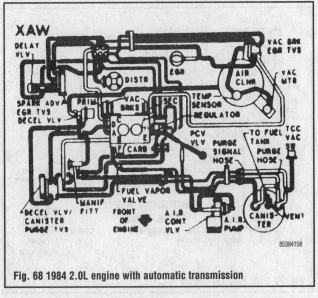

Fig. 68 1984 2.0L engine with automatic transmission

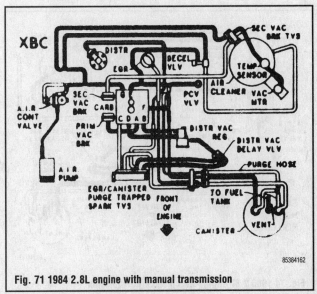

Fig. 71 1984 2.8L engine with manual transmission

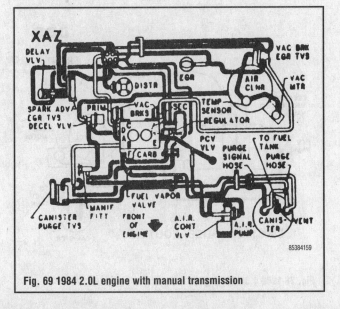

Fig. 69 1984 2.0L engine with manual transmission

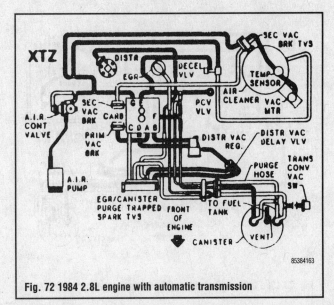

Fig. 72 1984 2.8L engine with automatic transmission

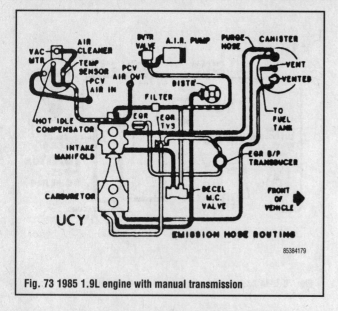

Fig. 73 1985 1.9L engine with manual transmission

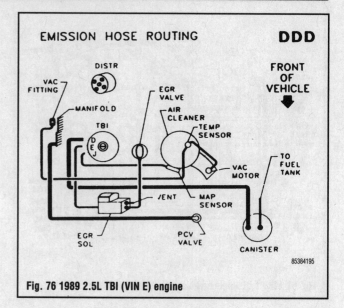

Fig. 76 1989 2.5L TBI (VIN E) engine

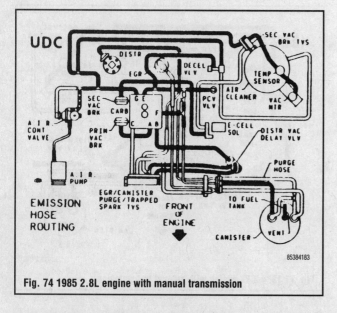

Fig. 74 1985 2.8L engine with manual transmission

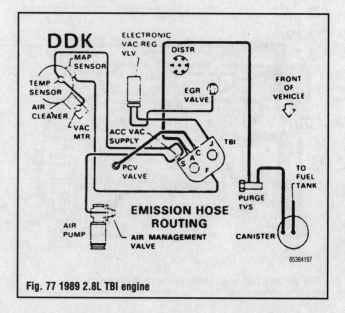

Fig. 77 1989 2.8L TBI engine

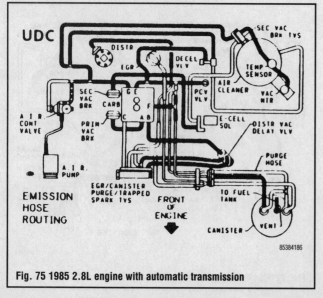

Fig. 75 1985 2.8L engine with automatic transmission

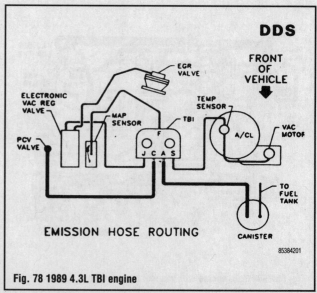

Fig. 78 1989 4.3L TBI engine

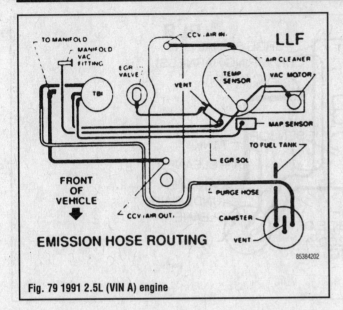

Fig. 79 1991 2.5L (VIN A) engine

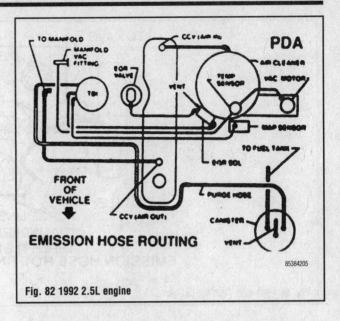

Fig. 82 1992 2.5L engine

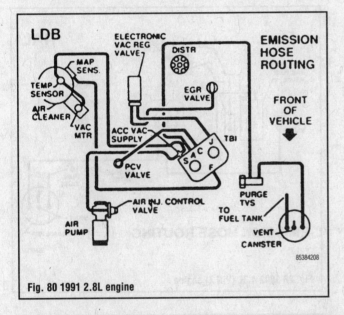

Fig. 80 1991 2.8L engine

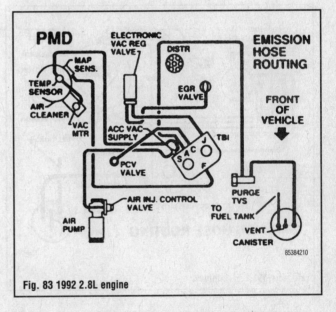

Fig. 83 1992 2.8L engine

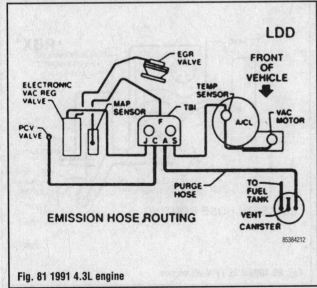

Fig. 81 1991 4.3L engine

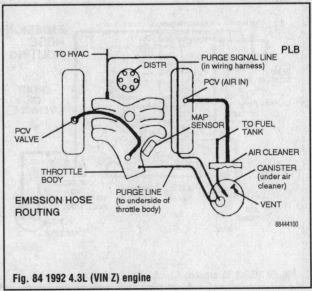

Fig. 84 1992 4.3L (VIN Z) engine

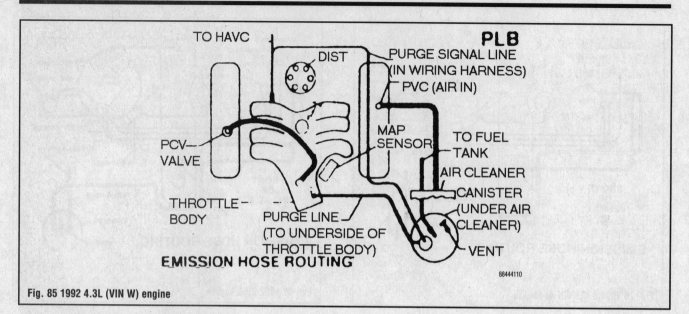

PLB

TO HAVC

DIST

PURGE SIGNAL LINE
(IN WIRING HARNESS)

PVC (AIR IN)

MAP
SENSOR

TO FUEL
TANK

AIR CLEANER

CANISTER
(UNDER AIR
CLEANER)

VENT

PCV
VALVE

THROTTLE
BODY

PURGE LINE
(TO UNDERSIDE OF
THROTTLE BODY)

EMISSION HOSE ROUTING

88444110

Fig. 85 1992 4.3L (VIN W) engine

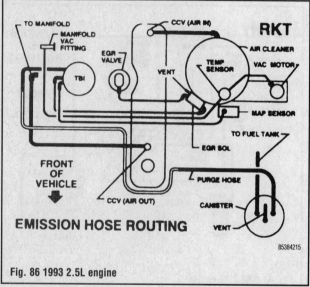

RKT

TO MANIFOLD

MANIFOLD
VAC
FITTING

CCV (AIR IN)

AIR CLEANER

EGR
VALVE

VENT

TEMP
SENSOR

VAC MOTOR

TBI

MAP SENSOR

TO FUEL TANK

FRONT
OF
VEHICLE

EGR SOL

PURGE HOSE

CANISTER

CCV (AIR OUT)

VENT

EMISSION HOSE ROUTING

85384215

Fig. 86 1993 2.5L engine

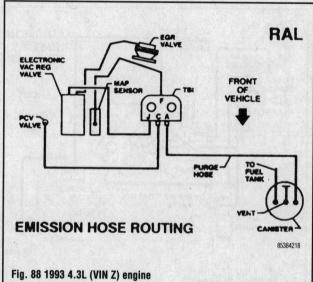

RAL

EGR
VALVE

ELECTRONIC
VAC REG
VALVE

MAP
SENSOR

TBI

F

C A

FRONT
OF
VEHICLE

PCV
VALVE

PURGE
HOSE

TO
FUEL
TANK

VENT

CANISTER

EMISSION HOSE ROUTING

85384218

Fig. 88 1993 4.3L (VIN Z) engine

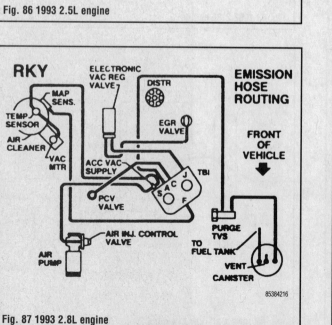

RKY

ELECTRONIC
VAC REG
VALVE

DISTR

**EMISSION
HOSE
ROUTING**

MAP
SENS.

TEMP
SENSOR

AIR
CLEANER

VAC
MTR

ACC VAC
SUPPLY

EGR
VALVE

TBI

J

S A C

F

FRONT
OF
VEHICLE

PCV
VALVE

AIR INJ. CONTROL
VALVE

PURGE
TVS

TO
FUEL TANK

AIR
PUMP

VENT

CANISTER

85384216

Fig. 87 1993 2.8L engine

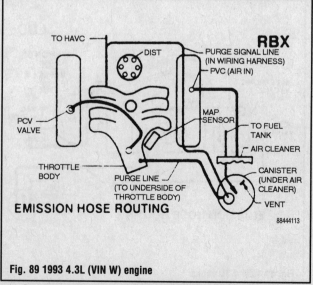

TO HAVC

DIST

RBX

PURGE SIGNAL LINE
(IN WIRING HARNESS)

PVC (AIR IN)

MAP
SENSOR

TO FUEL
TANK

AIR CLEANER

PCV
VALVE

THROTTLE
BODY

PURGE LINE
(TO UNDERSIDE OF
THROTTLE BODY)

CANISTER
(UNDER AIR
CLEANER)

VENT

EMISSION HOSE ROUTING

88444113

Fig. 89 1993 4.3L (VIN W) engine

5

FUEL SYSTEM

BASIC FUEL SYSTEM DIAGNOSIS

When there is a problem starting or driving a vehicle, two of the most important checks involve the ignition and the fuel systems. The 2 questions most mechanics attempt to answer first, "is there spark?" and "is there fuel?" will often lead to solving most basic problems. For ignition system diagnosis and testing, please refer to Section 2 of this manual. If the ignition system checks out (there is spark), then you must determine if fuel system is operating properly (is there fuel?).

CARBURETED FUEL SYSTEM

Fuel Pump

♦ **See Figures 1 and 2**

All carbureted engines use a mechanical fuel pump, driven off the camshaft and mounted on the engine block.

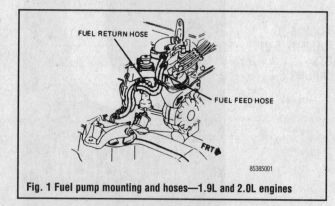

Fig. 1 Fuel pump mounting and hoses—1.9L and 2.0L engines

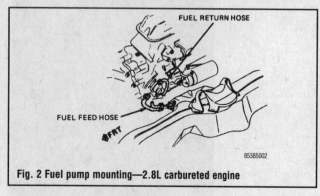

Fig. 2 Fuel pump mounting—2.8L carbureted engine

TESTING

To determine if the pump is in good condition, tests for both volume and pressure should be performed. The tests are made with the pump installed, and the engine at normal operating temperature and idle speed. Never replace a fuel pump without first performing these simple tests.

Be sure that the fuel filter has been changed at the specified interval. If in doubt, install a new filter first. The filter is an inexpensive maintenance item and should be replaced if old or suspect. Start the tests with a visual inspection. Check lines for damage, kinks or restrictions. Make sure all fittings are properly tightened and that there is no leakage from the system.

Pressure Test

1. Disconnect the fuel line from the carburetor and connect a fuel pump pressure gauge.
2. Start the engine and check the pressure with the engine at idle. If the pump has a vapor return hose, squeeze it off so that an accurate reading can be obtained. Pressure should not be below specification. Most of the carbureted engines covered by this manual are specified between 3–7 psi. Refer to the Tune-Up Specifications chart in Section 2 of this manual.
3. If the pressure is incorrect, replace the pump. It if is OK, perform the volume test.

Volume Test

1. Disconnect the fuel feed line from the carburetor.
2. Place the fuel line into a graduated container.
3. Run the engine at idle until one pint of gasoline has been pumped. One pint should be delivered in 30 seconds or less. There is normally enough fuel in the carburetor float bowl to perform this test, but refill it, if necessary.
4. If the delivery rate is below the minimum, check the lines for restrictions or leaks. If none are found, replace the pump.

REMOVAL & INSTALLATION

♦ **See Figures 3, 4, 5, 6 and 7**

➡**When you are disconnecting or connecting the fuel pump outlet fitting, always use 2 wrenches to avoid damaging the pump.**

1.9L and 2.0L Engines

The fuel pump is mounted to the front right side of the engine.
1. Disconnect the negative battery cable.
2. Matchmark and remove the distributor assembly.
3. Disconnect the fuel hoses from the fuel pump. If necessary, tag them to assure proper installation.
4. Remove the engine lifting hook.
5. Remove the fuel pump-to-engine bolts, then remove the fuel pump and discard the old gasket.
To install:

➡**Before installing the fuel pump, it may be helpful to rotate the crankshaft so that the cam lobe is on the down stroke. You may wish to temporarily reinstall the distributor in order to preserve ignition timing. New matchmarks should be made.**

6. Use a new gasket and RTV sealant, then install the pump to the engine.
7. Tighten the fuel pump-to-engine bolts to 15 ft. lbs. (20 Nm).
8. Install the engine lifting hook.
9. Connect the fuel hoses to the pump as noted during removal.
10. Align and install the distributor assembly.
11. Connect the negative battery cable, then check and/or adjust the timing.

Fig. 3 When fuel lines are disconnected, expect some fuel to leak out and keep a rag handy

Fig. 4 When removing the fuel pump, first disconnect all of the fuel lines

Fig. 5 Loosen and remove the pump retaining bolts

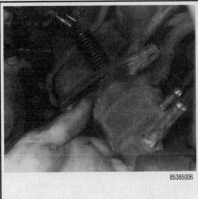

Fig. 6 Remove the pump from the engine

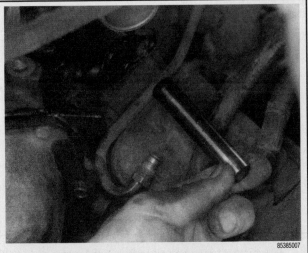

Fig. 7 If necessary, and applicable, remove the pushrod from the engine and check for damage

➡Some vehicles are equipped with a pushrod to actuate the fuel pump rocker arm. In some cases, this pushrod can be a nuisance during pump installation. If so equipped, a small screwdriver or thin plastic tool may be used to hold the pushrod up and out of the way while the fuel pump is installed. Make sure the pump rocker arm is properly located under or behind the pushrod, as applicable. Another method of retaining the pushrod it to pack it into position using grease, though this will only work on a cold engine

2.8L Engine

The fuel pump is located on the front left side of the engine.
1. Disconnect the negative battery cable.
2. Disconnect the fuel hoses the from pump. If necessary, tag the lines to assure proper installation.
3. Remove the fuel pump-to-engine bolts and remove the fuel pump from the engine, then remove and discard the old gasket.

➡Before installing the fuel pump, it may be helpful to rotate the crankshaft so that the cam lobe is on the down stroke.

4. Installation is the reverse of removal. Tighten the fuel pump-to-engine bolts to 15 ft. lbs. (20 Nm).

DCH340 Carburetor

The DCH340 carburetor should be found on the 1.9L engine which was installed in early model trucks covered by this manual.

ADJUSTMENTS

➡Please refer to Section 2 of this manual for Idle Speed and Mixture Adjustment procedures.

Float Level

♦ See Figure 8

The fuel level is normal if it is seen to be within the mark on the float bowl window. If not, remove the top of the carburetor and bend the float seat to regulate the level.

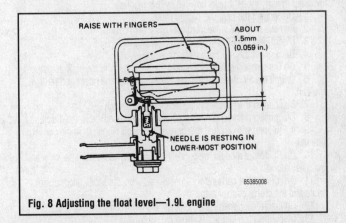

Fig. 8 Adjusting the float level—1.9L engine

Primary Throttle Valve

♦ See Figure 9

When the choke plate is completely closed, the primary throttle valve should be opened by the fast idle screw to an angle of 16° (M/T) or 18° (A/T). To check this adjustment:
1. Close the choke plate completely, then measure between the throttle plate and the air horn wall; the clearance should be 0.050–0.059 in. (1.3–1.5mm), M/T or 0.059–0.069 in. (1.50–1.75mm), A/T.

➡The measurement should be made at the center point of the choke plate.

2. If necessary, adjust the opening by turning the fast idle screw.

Throttle Linkage

♦ See Figure 10

1. Turn the primary throttle valve plate until the adjustment plate is in contact with the kickdown lever. This is a primary throttle plate opening of about 47°.
2. Measure the clearance between the center point of the primary throttle plate and the air horn wall; the clearance should be 0.24–0.30 in. (6.0–7.6mm). If not, bend the kickdown lever tab.

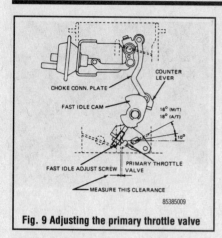

Fig. 9 Adjusting the primary throttle valve

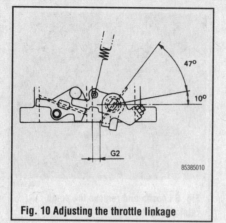

Fig. 10 Adjusting the throttle linkage

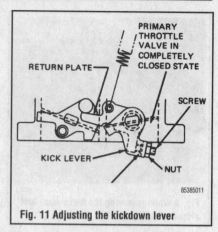

Fig. 11 Adjusting the kickdown lever

Kickdown Lever

▶ See Figure 11

1. Turn the primary throttle lever until the plate is completely closed. Back off the throttle adjustment screw, if necessary.
2. Loosen the locknut on the kickdown lever screw and turn the screw until it just contacts the return plate, then tighten the locknut.

REMOVAL & INSTALLATION

The DCH340 carburetor should be found on the 1.9L engine which was installed in early model trucks covered by this manual.
1. Disconnect the negative battery cable.
2. Remove the PCV valve from the rocker arm cover.
3. Disconnect the ECS hose from the air cleaner.
4. Disconnect the AIR hose from the pump.
5. On California models, disconnect the air hose from the slow actuator.
6. Unbolt the air cleaner, lift it slightly, disconnect the hoses and remove the unit.
7. Disconnect the rubber piping from the TVS switch.
8. Disconnect the vacuum advance hose (if equipped) from the distributor.
9. If equipped with an A/T, disconnect the vacuum hose from the converter housing.
10. On California models, disconnect the vacuum hoses from the slow and main actuators.
11. Disconnect the carburetor solenoid lead wire, the accelerator control cable and the cruise control cable.
12. On automatic transmission models, disconnect the control cable.
13. Disconnect the fuel line(s) from the carburetor.
14. Disconnect the ECS hose from the carburetor.
15. Remove the carburetor-to-intake manifold bolts and the carburetor; discard the mounting gasket.

➡ **Be sure to cover the opening in the intake manifold to prevent debris, foreign material or even a mishandled bolt from entering the engine.**

16. Installation is the reverse of removal. Make sure all of the linkage is properly adjusted and operates smoothly. Check that there are no leaks. Start and run the engine, then check and adjust the idle speed, as necessary.

2SE and E2SE Carburetor

The 2SE and E2SE carburetors are found on the 2.0L engine and early models of the 2.8L engines covered by this manual.

ADJUSTMENTS

Float Level

▶ See Figure 12

1. With the engine Cold, remove the top of the carburetor.
2. While holding a finger lightly (but firmly) on the float retainer, press down lightly on the float tab to seat the needle valve.

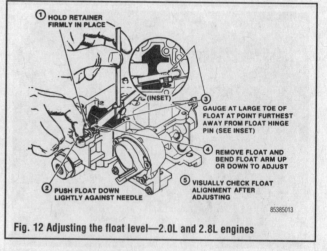

Fig. 12 Adjusting the float level—2.0L and 2.8L engines

3. Measure the distance between the float bowl gasket surface and the point on the float farthest from the needle valve.
4. If the measurement is not correct, remove the float and bend the tab.

Pump

1. With the throttle plate in the closed position and the fast idle screw off the steps of the fast idle cam, measure the distance from the air horn casting to the top of the pump stem.
2. To adjust, remove the retaining screw, the washer and the pump lever. Bend the end of the lever to correct the stem height. DO NOT twist the lever or bend it sideways.
3. Install the lever, washer and screw, then check the adjustment. When correct, open and close the throttle a few times to check the linkage movement and alignment.

Fast Idle

1. Set the ignition timing and curb idle speed, then disconnect and plug the hoses as directed on the emission control decal.
2. Position the fast idle screw on the highest step of the fast idle cam.
3. Start the engine and adjust the engine speed to specification with the fast idle screw.

Choke Coil Lever

▶ See Figure 13

➡ **The following procedure requires the use of the Choke Valve Angle Gauge tool No. J–26701, BT–7704 or equivalent.**

1. Remove the three retaining screws, the choke cover and coil. On models with a riveted choke cover, drill out the three rivets, then remove the cover and the choke coil.

➡ **A choke stat cover retainer kit is required for reassembly.**

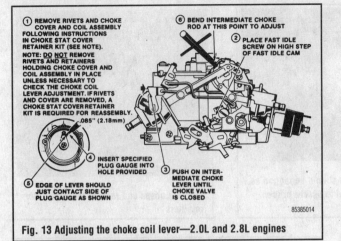

Fig. 13 Adjusting the choke coil lever—2.0L and 2.8L engines

2. Place the fast idle screw on the high step of the fast idle cam.
3. Close the choke plate by pushing in on the intermediate choke lever.
4. Insert a drill bit or plug gauge, of the specified size, into the hole in the choke housing. The choke lever in the housing should be up against the side of the gauge.
5. If the lever does not just touch the gauge, bend the intermediate choke rod to adjust.

Fast Idle Cam (Choke Rod)

▶ See Figures 14 and 15

➡The following procedure requires the use of the Choke Valve Angle Gauge tool No. J–26701, BT–7704 or equivalent.

1. First, adjust the choke coil lever and fast idle speed.
2. Rotate the degree scale until it is zeroed.
3. Close the choke and install the degree scale onto the choke plate. Center the leveling bubble.
4. Rotate the scale so that the specified degree is opposite the scale pointer.
5. Place the fast idle screw on the second step of the cam (against the high step). Close the choke by pushing in the intermediate lever.
6. Push on the vacuum break lever, to Open the choke, until the lever is against the rear tang on the choke lever.
7. Bend the fast idle cam rod at the U to adjust the angle to specifications.

Electric Choke

This procedure is only for those carburetors with choke covers retained by screws. Riveted choke covers are preset and nonadjustable.
1. Loosen the three retaining screws.

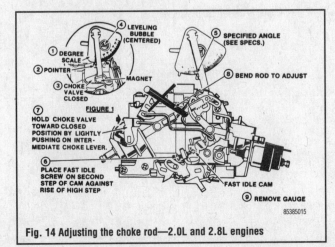

Fig. 14 Adjusting the choke rod—2.0L and 2.8L engines

Fig. 15 The fast idle screw must be properly set on the cam (which is not turned fully to the 2nd step here)

2. Place the fast idle screw on the high step of the cam.
3. Rotate the choke cover to align the cover mark with the specified housing mark.

Choke Unloader

▶ See Figure 16

1. Follow Steps 1–4 of the Fast Idle Cam Adjustment.
2. If removed, install the choke cover and the coil, then align the housing marks with the cover marks, as specified.
3. Hold the primary throttle valve Wide Open.
4. If the engine is Warm, push inward on the intermediate choke lever to close the choke valve.
5. Bend the unloader tang until the bubble is centered.

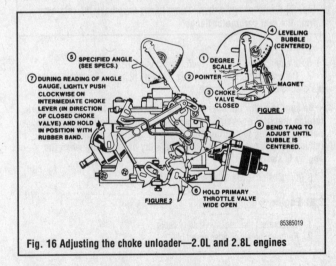

Fig. 16 Adjusting the choke unloader—2.0L and 2.8L engines

REMOVAL & INSTALLATION

▶ See Figures 17, 18, 19, 20 and 21

2.0L Engine

1. Disconnect the negative battery cable.
2. Remove the air cleaner and the gasket.
3. Disconnect the fuel pipe and all of the vacuum lines. Tag the vacuum lines to ensure proper installation.
4. Label and disengage all of the electrical connections.
5. Disconnect the downshift cable.

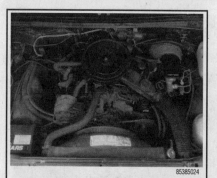

Fig. 17 The carb is located directly under the air cleaner (you remove few components for access)

Fig. 18 Vacuum lines should be tagged as they are disconnected to assure proper installation

Fig. 19 Loosen and remove the carburetor retainers

Fig. 20 A ratchet and extension are handy to remove the retainers from the rear carburetor flange

Fig. 21 With the retainers removed and all hoses/wiring disconnected, the carb can be lifted from the intake

6. If equipped with cruise control, disconnect the linkage.
7. Remove the carburetor-to-intake manifold bolts and the carburetor, then discard the old mounting gasket.

➡Be sure to cover the opening in the intake manifold to prevent debris, foreign material or even a mishandled bolt from entering the engine. Before installing the carburetor, fill the float bowl with gasoline to reduce the battery strain and the possibility of backfiring when the engine is started again.

8. Installation is the reverse of removal.

2.8L Engine

1. Disconnect the negative battery cable.
2. Remove the air cleaner assembly.

3. Disconnect the fuel and vacuum lines from the carburetor. Be sure to tag all vacuum lines for installation.
4. Disengage the electrical connectors from the carburetor.
5. Disconnect the linkage from the carburetor.
6. Remove the carburetor-to-intake manifold nuts and/or bolts, then remove the carburetor from the engine and discard the old gasket.

➡Be sure to cover the opening in the intake manifold to prevent debris, foreign material or even a mishandled bolt from entering the engine.

7. Installation is the reverse of removal.

CARBURETOR SPECIFICATIONS

Type DCH340 4-1.9L Engine

Primary Throttle Plate Gap (in.)	Primary Main Jet Number	Secondary Main Jet Number	Primary Slow Jet Number	Secondary Slow Jet Number	Power Jet Number	Primary Main Air Bleed Number	Secondary Main Air Bleed Number	Slow Air Bleed Number
.050-.059 (MT)	114 Fed.	170	50 Fed.	100	50	120 Fed.	70 Fed.	150 Fed.
.059-.069 (AT)	85 Cal.		54 Cal.			110 Cal.	90 Cal.	130 Cal.

Type E2SE 6-2.8L (Code B) (California)

Carb. Number	Float Level (in.)	Fast Idle Cam. (deg.)	Primary Vacuum Break (deg.)	Air Valve Rod (deg.)	Secondary Vacuum Break (deg.)	Choke Unloader (deg.)
17082356	13/32	22	25	1	30	30
17082357	13/32	22	25	1	32	30
17082358	13/32	22	25	1	30	30
17082359	13/32	22	25	1	32	30
17072683	9/32	28	25	1	35	45
17074812	9/32	28	25	1	35	45
17084356	9/32	22	25	1	30	30
17084357	9/32	22	25	1	30	30
17084358	9/32	22	25	1	30	30
17084359	9/32	22	25	1	30	30
17084368	1/8	22	25	1	30	30
17084370	1/8	22	26	1	30	30
17084430	11/32	15	26	1	38	42
17084431	11/32	15	26	1	38	42
17084434	11/32	15	26	1	38	42
17084435	11/32	28	25	1	35	45
17084452	5/32	28	25	1	35	45
17084453	5/32	28	25	1	35	45
17084455	5/32	28	25	1	35	45
17084456	5/32	28	25	1	35	45
17084458	5/32	28	25	1	35	45
17084532	5/32	28	25	1	35	45
17084534	5/32	28	25	1	35	45
17084535	5/32	28	25	1	35	45
17084537	5/32	28	25	1	35	45
17084538	5/32	28	25	1	35	45
17084540	5/32	28	25	1	35	45
17084542	1/8	28	25	1	35	45
17084632	9/32	28	25	1	35	45
17084633	9/32	28	25	1	35	45
17084635	9/32	28	25	1	35	45
17084636	9/32	28	25	1	35	45

85385029

Type 2SE 6-2.8L (Code B) (excluding California)

Carb. Number	Float Level (in.)	Fast Idle Cam. (deg.)	Primary Vacuum Break (deg.)	Air Valve Rod (deg.)	Secondary Vacuum Break (deg.)	Choke Unloader (deg.)
17082348	7/16	22	26	1	32	40
17082349	7/16	22	28	1	32	40
17082350	7/16	22	26	1	32	40
17082351	7/16	22	28	1	32	40
17082353	7/16	22	28	1	35	30
17082355	7/16	22	28	1	35	30
17083348	7/16	22	30	1	32	40
17083349	7/16	22	30	1	32	40
17083350	7/16	22	30	1	32	40
17083351	7/16	22	30	1	35	40
17083352	7/16	22	30	1	35	40
17083353	7/16	22	30	1	35	40
17083354	7/16	22	30	1	35	40
17083355	7/16	22	30	1	35	40
17083360	7/16	22	30	1	32	40
17083361	7/16	22	28	1	32	40
17083362	7/16	22	30	1	32	40
17083363	7/16	22	28	1	32	40
17083364	7/16	22	30	1	35	40
17083365	7/16	22	30	1	35	40
17083366	7/16	22	30	1	35	40
17083367	7/16	22	30	1	35	40
17083390	13/32	28	30	1	35	38
17083391	13/32	28	30	1	35	38
17083392	13/32	28	30	1	35	38
17083393	13/32	28	30	1	35	38
17083394	13/32	28	30	1	35	38
17083395	13/32	28	30	1	35	38
17083396	13/32	28	30	1	35	38
17083397	13/32	28	30	1	35	38
17084410	11/32	15	23	1	38	42
17084412	11/32	15	23	1	38	42
17084425	11/32	15	26	1	36	40
17084427	11/32	15	26	1	36	40
17084560	11/32	15	24	1	34	38
17084562	11/32	15	24	1	34	38
17084569	11/32	15	24	1	34	38

85385030

THROTTLE BODY FUEL INJECTION SYSTEM

General Information

♦ See Figures 22 and 23

Electronic fuel injection was introduced on these trucks for 1985 on the 2.5L engine. For the next model year (and all subsequent models covered by this manual) all S/T series trucks were equipped with fuel injection. Most of these late model fuel injected vehicles are equipped with a Throttle Body Injection (TBI) system. The system uses a TBI unit mounted centrally on the intake manifold where a carburetor would normally be found on older vehicles. The throttle body assembly is equipped with 1 (4-cylinder engines) or 2 (V6 engines) electronic fuel injectors in order to supply fuel to regulate the air/fuel mixture. All fuel injection and ignition functions are regulated by the computer control module, which is sometimes also referred to as the ECM, PCM or VCM, depending on the application. It accepts inputs from various sensors and switches, calculates the optimum air/fuel mixture and operates the various output devices to provide peak performance within specific emissions limits. The module will attempt to maintain the ideal air/fuel mixture of 14.7:1 in order to optimize catalytic converter operation. If a system failure occurs that is not serious enough to stop the engine, the module will illuminate the CHECK ENGINE or SERVICE ENGINE SOON light (as applicable) and will continue to operate the engine, although it may need to operate in a backup or fail-safe mode.

Fuel is supplied to the injector(s) through an electric fuel pump assembly which is mounted in the vehicle's fuel tank. The module provides a signal to operate the fuel pump though the fuel pump relay and oil pressure switch.

Other system components include a pressure regulator, an Idle Air Control (IAC) valve, a Throttle Position (TP) sensor, Manifold Air Temperature (MAT) or Intake Air Temperature (IAT) sensor, Engine Coolant Temperature (ECT) sensor, a Manifold Absolute Pressure (MAP) sensor and an oxygen sensor. The fuel injectors are solenoid valves that the control module pulse on and off many times per second to promote proper fuel atomization. The pulse width determines how long an injector is ON each cycle and this regulates the amount of fuel supplied to the engine.

The system pressure regulator is normally part of the TBI unit fuel meter cover. The regulator is designed to keep fuel pressure constant at the injector regardless of engine rpm. This is accomplished by controlling the flow in the return line (a calibrated bypass).

The idle air control valve is a stepper motor that controls the amount of air allowed to bypass the throttle plate. With this valve the computer control module can closely control idle speed even when the engine is cold or when there is a high engine load at idle.

The module used on TBI vehicles has a learning capability which is used to provide corrections for a particular engine's condition. If the battery is disconnected to clear diagnostic codes, or for safety during a repair, the learning process must start all over again. A change may be noted in vehicle performance. In order to "teach" the vehicle, make sure the vehicle is at normal operating temperature, then drive at part throttle, under moderate acceleration and idle conditions, until normal performance returns.

OPERATING MODES

Starting Mode

When the ignition switch is first turned **ON**, the fuel pump relay is energized by the module for 2 seconds in order to build system pressure. In the start mode, the computer module checks the ECT, TP sensor and crank signal in order to determine the best air/fuel ratio for starting. The modules on later model vehicles may also use the IAT or MAT (as equipped) and the MAP sensor. Ratios could range from 1.5:1 at approximately −33°F (−36°C), to 14.7:1 at 201°F (94°C).

Clear Flood Mode

If the engine becomes flooded, it can be cleared by opening the accelerator to the full throttle position. When the throttle is open all the way and engine rpm is less than 600, the computer module will pulse the fuel injector at an air/fuel ratio of 20:1 (early vehicles) or 16.5:1 (later model vehicles) while the engine is turning over in order to clear the engine of excess fuel. If throttle position is reduced below 80 percent (early vehicles) or 65 percent (later model vehicles), the module will return to the start mode.

Open Loop Mode

When the engine first starts and engine speed rises above 400 rpm, the computer module operates in the Open Loop mode until specific parameters are met. In Open Loop mode, the fuel requirements are calculated based on information from the MAP and ECT sensors. The oxygen sensor signal is ignored during initial engine operation because it needs time to warm up.

Closed Loop Mode

♦ See Figure 24

When the correct parameters are met, the computer module will use O_2 sensor output and adjust the air/fuel mixture accordingly in order to maintain a narrow band of exhaust gas oxygen concentration. When the module is correcting and adjusting fuel mixture based on the oxygen sensor signal along with the other sensors, this is known as feedback air/fuel ratio control. The computer module will shift into this Closed Loop mode when:

• Oxygen sensor output voltage is varied, indicating that the sensor has warmed up to operating temperature

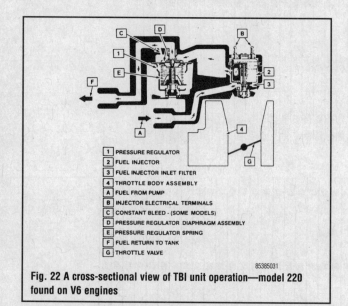

1	PRESSURE REGULATOR
2	FUEL INJECTOR
3	FUEL INJECTOR INLET FILTER
4	THROTTLE BODY ASSEMBLY
A	FUEL FROM PUMP
B	INJECTOR ELECTRICAL TERMINALS
C	CONSTANT BLEED - (SOME MODELS)
D	PRESSURE REGULATOR DIAPHRAGM ASSEMBLY
E	PRESSURE REGULATOR SPRING
F	FUEL RETURN TO TANK
G	THROTTLE VALVE

85385031

Fig. 22 A cross-sectional view of TBI unit operation—model 220 found on V6 engines

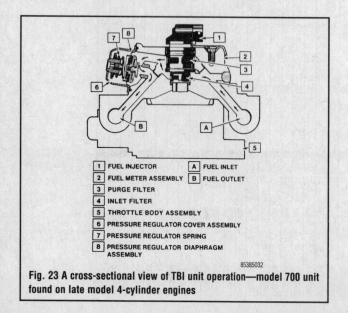

1	FUEL INJECTOR	A	FUEL INLET
2	FUEL METER ASSEMBLY	B	FUEL OUTLET
3	PURGE FILTER		
4	INLET FILTER		
5	THROTTLE BODY ASSEMBLY		
6	PRESSURE REGULATOR COVER ASSEMBLY		
7	PRESSURE REGULATOR SPRING		
8	PRESSURE REGULATOR DIAPHRAGM ASSEMBLY		

85385032

Fig. 23 A cross-sectional view of TBI unit operation—model 700 unit found on late model 4-cylinder engines

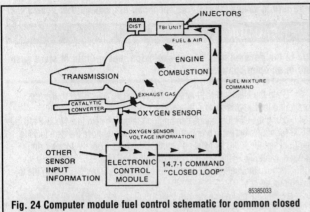

Fig. 24 Computer module fuel control schematic for common closed loop engine operation (same for PCMs and VCMs)

- The ECT shows an engine coolant temperature above a specified level.
- The engine has been operating for a programmed amount of time.

Acceleration Mode

If the throttle position and manifold pressure is quickly increased, the module will provide extra fuel for smooth acceleration.

Deceleration Mode

As the throttle closes and the manifold pressure decreases, fuel flow is reduced by the module. If both conditions remain for a specific number of engine revolutions indicating a very fast deceleration, the module may decide fuel flow is not needed and stop the flow by temporarily shutting off the injectors.

Highway Fuel Mode (Semi-Closed Loop)

On some late model vehicles, the computer control module is programmed to enter a special highway mode to improve fuel economy. If the module senses the correct ECT, ignition control, canister purge activity and a constant engine speed, it will enter highway mode. During this operation, there will be very little adjustment of the long and short term fuel trims, also, the oxygen sensor values will usually read below 100 millivolts.

Decel En-Leanment Mode

On some late model vehicles, the computer control module is programmed to further reduce emissions by leaning the fuel spray on deceleration. The module does this when a high MAP vacuum (low voltage or pressure) is sensed, BUT it should be noted that the module may do this when the vehicle is not moving. This mode of operation may be misdiagnosed as a lean condition. When diagnosing the control system using a scan tool with the transmission in Park, the oxygen sensor signal low (usually below 100 mV), and both fuel trim numbers around 128 counts, lower the engine speed to 1000 rpm. If the sensor and long term fuel trim numbers respond normally, it is possible that the system was fooled into decel en-leanment operation. If the oxygen sensor and long term numbers do not respond at the lower rpm, there are other problems with the vehicle.

Battery Low Mode

If the computer module detects a low battery, it will increase injector pulse width to compensate for the low voltage and provide proper fuel delivery. It will also increase idle speed to increase alternate output and, in some cases, ignition dwell time to allow for proper engine operation.

Field Service Mode

When the diagnostic terminal of the test connector is grounded with the engine running, the computer control module will enter the Field Service Mode. If the engine is running in Open Loop Mode, the CHECK ENGINE or SERVICE ENGINE SOON Malfunction Indicator Lamp (MIL) will flash quickly, about 2½ times per second. When the engine is in Closed Loop Mode, the MIL will flash only about once per second. If the light stays OFF most of the time in Close Loop, the engine is running lean. If the light is ON most of the time, the engine is running rich.

While the engine continues to operate in Field Service Mode certain conditions will apply:
- The distributor operates with a fixed spark advance (some early model vehicles).
- New trouble codes cannot be stored in computer memory.
- The closed loop timer is bypassed.

➡For more information concerning the computer control module, self-diagnosis systems and other electronic engine controls, please refer to Section 4 of this manual.

Fuel Pressure Relief

Prior to servicing any component of the fuel injection system, the fuel pressure must relieved. If fuel pressure is not relieved, serious injury could result.

TBI MODEL 300 OR 700 (2.5L ENGINE)

1. Place the transmission selector in PARK (automatic transmissions) or NEUTRAL (manual transmissions), then set the parking brake and block the drive wheels.
2. Loosen the fuel filler cap to relieve tank pressure.
3. Either remove the FUEL PUMP fuse from the fuse block in the passenger compartment (early model vehicles) or disengage the three terminal electrical connector at the fuel tank (late model vehicles). If you are unsure which method works for your truck, try removing the fuel pump fuse. If this does not disable the pump, the electrical connectors at the fuel tank must be disengaged.
4. Start the engine and allow to run until it stops due to lack of fuel.
5. Engage the starter (turn key to start) for three seconds to dissipate all pressure in the fuel lines.
6. Turn the ignition **OFF**, then re-engage the connector at the fuel tank or install the fuel pump fuse.
7. Disconnect the negative battery cable to prevent accidental fuel spillage should the ignition key accidentally be turned **ON** with a fuel fitting disconnected.
8. When fuel service is finished, tighten the fuel filler cap and connect the negative battery cable.

✳✳ CAUTION

To reduce the chance of personal injury when disconnecting a fuel line, always cover the fuel line with cloth to collect escaping fuel, then place the cloth in an approved container.

TBI MODEL 220 (2.8L AND 4.3L ENGINES)

1. Disconnect the negative battery cable.
2. Loosen fuel filler cap to relieve fuel tank pressure.
3. The internal constant bleed feature of the Model 220 TBI unit relieves fuel pump system pressure when the engine is turned **OFF**. Therefore, no further action is required.

➡Allow the engine to set for 5–10 minutes; this will allow the orifice (in the fuel system) to bleed off the pressure.

4. When fuel service is finished, tighten the fuel filler cap and connect the negative battery cable.

Electric Fuel Pump

The electric fuel pump is attached to the fuel sending unit, located in the fuel tank.

TESTING

▶ See Figure 25

1. Properly relieve the fuel system pressure.
2. If necessary for access, remove the air cleaner assembly and plug the vacuum port(s).

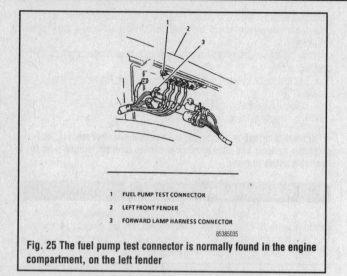

1 FUEL PUMP TEST CONNECTOR
2 LEFT FRONT FENDER
3 FORWARD LAMP HARNESS CONNECTOR

85385035

Fig. 25 The fuel pump test connector is normally found in the engine compartment, on the left fender

3. Disconnect the flexible fuel supply line, located in the engine compartment between the fuel filter and throttle body.

4. Install a fuel pressure gauge, such as J-29658 or equivalent, inline in-line between the fuel filter and throttle body unit (between the steel line and flexible hose). If necessary use an adapter or Tee fitting in order to connect the gauge and complete the fuel circuit.

➡A Tee fitting may be fabricated for this purpose. Depending on the fuel pressure gauge, short lengths of steel tubing, appropriately sized flare nuts and a flare nut adapter may be used.

5. If the engine will run, start the engine and allow it to run at normal idle speed. The fuel pressure should be 9–13 psi (62–90 kPa).

6. If the engine does not run, turn the ignition **ON**, but do not attempt to start the engine. Listen for the fuel pump to run. Within 2 seconds of turning the ignition **ON** pressure should be 9–13 psi (62–90 kPa). If necessary, cycle the ignition **OFF**, then **ON** again, in order to build up system pressure.

7. If the fuel pump did not run or system pressure did not reach specification, locate the fuel pump test connector. The test connector is usually found on the driver's side of the engine compartment (on or near the fender), with a single wire (usually red) leading from the relay to the connector. Using a jumper wire, apply battery voltage to the test connector in order to energize and run the fuel pump. The pump should run and produce fuel pressure of 9–13 psi (62–90 kPa). If the pump does not run, check the relay and fuel pump wiring.

8. If the pump pressure was lower than specification, first check for a restricted fuel line or filter and replace, as necessary. If no restrictions can be found, restrict the fuel supply line between the pressure gauge and the TBI unit (a flexible hose may be temporarily clamped to produce the restriction), then apply voltage to the test connector again. If pressure is now above 13 psi (90 kPa), replace the faulty pressure regulator. If pressure remains below 9 psi (62 kPa), then the problem is located in the fuel tank (the fuel pump, coupling hose or inlet filter).

9. If during Step 7, the pressure was higher than specification, disengage the injector connector, then disconnect the fuel return line flexible hose which connects the line from the throttle body to the tank line. Attach a ⁵⁄₁₆ ID flex hose to the fuel line from the throttle body and place the other end into an approved gasoline container. Cycle the ignition in order to energize the fuel pump and watch system pressure. If pressure is still higher, check for restrictions in the throttle body return line. Repair or replace the line if restrictions are found or replace the faulty pressure regulator if no other causes of high pressure are identified. If fuel pressure is normal only with the flexible hose-to-fuel tank line out of the circuit, check that line for restrictions and repair or replace, as necessary.

10. Once the test is completed, depressurize the fuel system and remove the gauge.

11. Secure the fuel lines and check for leaks.

12. If removed, install the air cleaner assembly.

REMOVAL & INSTALLATION

1. Properly relieve the fuel system pressure.
2. Connect the negative battery cable.

➡Be sure to keep a Class B (dry chemical) fire extinguisher nearby.

※※ **CAUTION**

Due to the possibility of fire or explosion, never drain or store gasoline in an open container.

3. Drain the fuel tank, then remove it from the vehicle. Refer to the procedure found later in this section for details.

4. Using the GM fuel gauge sending unit retaining cam tool No. J-24187, J-36608 (or equivalent) or a brass drift and a hammer, remove the cam locking ring (fuel sending unit) by twisting counterclockwise. With the locking ring released, carefully lift the sending unit from the fuel tank.

5. Remove the fuel pump from the fuel sending unit, by performing the following procedures:

a. Pull the fuel pump up into the mounting tube, while pulling outward (away) from the bottom support.

➡When removing the fuel pump from the sending unit, be careful not to damage the rubber insulator and the strainer.

b. When the pump assembly is clear of the bottom support, pull it out of the rubber connector.

6. Installation is the reverse of removal.

➡When installing the sending unit, be careful not to fold or twist the fuel strainer or it may restrict the fuel flow.

Fuel Pump Relay

The fuel pump relay is normally found on a relay bracket which is mounted to the left front fender in the engine compartment. Positioning within the bracket will vary according to model and application. Check for loose electrical connections; no other service is possible, except replacement.

REMOVAL & INSTALLATION

▶ See Figure 26

1. Disconnect the negative battery cable.
2. Disengage the relay/electrical connector assembly from the bracket.
3. Pull the fuel pump relay from the electrical connector.
4. If necessary, use a new relay, then reverse the removal procedures.

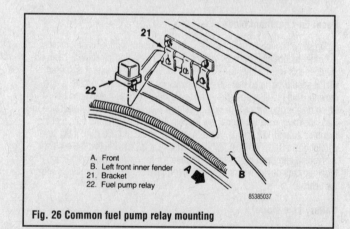

A. Front
B. Left front inner fender
21. Bracket
22. Fuel pump relay

85385037

Fig. 26 Common fuel pump relay mounting

Throttle Body

The Model 300 throttle body assembly is used on early 2.5L engines. It consists of three major casting assemblies:
• Fuel pressure cover with pressure regulator.
• Fuel metering body with fuel injectors.
• Throttle body with an Idle Speed Control (IAC) Valve and a Throttle Position (TP) sensor.

The Model 700 throttle body assembly is used on later 2.5L engines. It consists of two major casting assemblies:

- Fuel metering assembly with pressure regulator and fuel injector.
- Throttle body with an Idle Speed Control (IAC) Valve and a Throttle Position (TP) sensor.

The Model 220 throttle body assembly is used on the 2.8L and 4.3L engines. It consists of three major casting assemblies:
- Fuel pressure cover with pressure regulator.
- Fuel metering body with fuel injectors.
- Throttle body with an Idle Speed Control (IAC) Valve and a Throttle Position (TP) sensor.

The Throttle Position (TP) sensor is a variable resistor used to convert the degree of throttle plate opening to an electrical signal to the computer control module. The module uses this signal as a reference point of throttle valve position. In addition, an Idle Air Control (IAC) assembly, mounted in the throttle body is used to control idle speeds. A cone-shaped valve in the IAC assembly is located in an air passage in the throttle body that leads from the point beneath the air cleaner to below the throttle valve. The module monitors idle speeds and, depending on engine load, moves the IAC cone in the air passage to increase or decrease air bypassing the throttle valve to the intake manifold for control of idle speeds.

The operation of all throttle bodies is basically the same. Each is constantly monitored by the computer control module in order to produce a 14.7:1 air/fuel ratio, which is vital to the catalytic converter operation.

REMOVAL & INSTALLATION

◆ See Figures 27 and 28

1. Properly relieve the fuel system pressure, then disconnect the negative battery cable.
2. Remove the air cleaner assembly.
3. Disengage the electrical connectors from the idle air control valve, the throttle position sensor and the fuel injector(s). When disengaging the injector connectors, squeeze the plastic tabs and pull straight upward.
4. If applicable, remove the grommet with wires from the throttle body.
5. Disengage the throttle return spring(s) and linkage (including cruise control and/or throttle valve (as equipped).
6. Tag and disconnect the vacuum hoses from the throttle body.

➡**ALWAYS use a backup wrench on the TBI fuel line inlet nuts when disconnecting the fuel lines.**

7. Place a rag (to catch the excess fuel) under the fuel line-to-throttle body connection, then disconnect the fuel lines from the throttle body. Remove and discard the old O-rings from the lines.
8. Remove the TBI unit-to-manifold attaching hardware, then remove the throttle body and discard the old gasket.

➡**Be sure to place a cloth or plastic cover over the intake manifold opening to prevent dirt from entering the engine.**

9. To install, position the throttle body to the intake manifold using a new gasket, then thread the retainers and tighten to specification:
- For early 2.5L engines equipped with the model 300 TBI unit tighten bolts or nuts to 13 ft. lbs. (18 Nm) and studs to 45 inch lbs. (5 Nm).

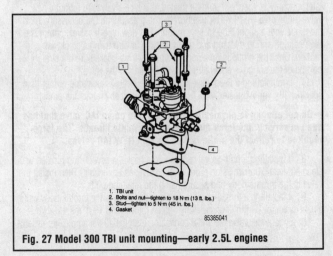

1. TBI unit
2. Bolts and nut—tighten to 18 N·m (13 ft. lbs.)
3. Stud—tighten to 5 N·m (45 in. lbs.)
4. Gasket

85385041

Fig. 27 Model 300 TBI unit mounting—early 2.5L engines

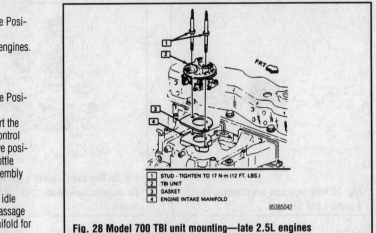

1	STUD - TIGHTEN TO 17 N·m (12 FT. LBS.)
2	TBI UNIT
3	GASKET
4	ENGINE INTAKE MANIFOLD

85385042

Fig. 28 Model 700 TBI unit mounting—late 2.5L engines

- For late 2.5L engines equipped with the model 700 TBI unit: 12 ft. lbs. (17 Nm).
- For 2.8L engines (model 220 TBI unit): 18 ft. lbs. (25 Nm).
- For 4.3L engines (model 220 TBI unit): 12 ft. lbs. (16 Nm).

➡**ALWAYS use a backup wrench on the TBI fuel line inlet nuts when connecting the fuel lines.**

10. Depress the accelerator pedal to the floor and release it, to see if the pedal returns freely. Turn the ignition switch **ON** and check for fuel leaks.

INJECTOR REPLACEMENT

◆ See Figures 29, 30 and 31

❊❊ CAUTION

When removing the injector(s), be careful not to damage the electrical connector pins (on top of the injector), the injector fuel filter and the nozzle. The fuel injector is serviced as a complete assembly ONLY, it is an electrical component and should not be immersed in any kind of cleaner.

1. Properly relieve the fuel system pressure, then disconnect the negative battery cable.
2. Remove the air cleaner assembly.
3. At the injector connector(s), squeeze the two tabs together and pull straight up to disengage connector from the injector.
4. Except for the model 700 TBI unit, loosen the fuel meter cover retaining screws, then remove the cover from the fuel meter body, but leave the cover gasket in place.
5. For the model 700 TBI unit, loosen the injector retainer screw, then remove the screw and retainer from the top of the throttle body.
6. Using a small prybar and a round fulcrum, carefully pry the injector until it is free, then remove the injector from the fuel meter body.
7. Remove the small O-ring from the nozzle end of the injector. If equipped and removal is necessary, carefully rotate the injector's fuel filter back and forth to remove it from the base of the injector.
8. Except for model 700 TBI unit, remove and discard the fuel meter cover gasket.
9. Remove the large O-ring and back-up washer (if equipped) from the top of the counterbore of the fuel meter body injector cavity.

To install:

10. If removed, with the larger end of the filter facing the injector (so that the filter covers the raised rib of the injector base) install the filter by twisting it into position on the injector.
11. Lubricate the new O-rings with clean automatic transmission fluid, then install the small O-ring on the nozzle end of the injector. Be sure the O-ring is pressed up against the injector or injector filter (as applicable).
12. Install the steel backup washer (if equipped) in the top counterbore of the fuel meter body's injector cavity, then install the new large O-ring directly over the backup washer. Make sure the O-ring is properly seated in the cavity and is flush with the top of the fuel meter body casting surface.

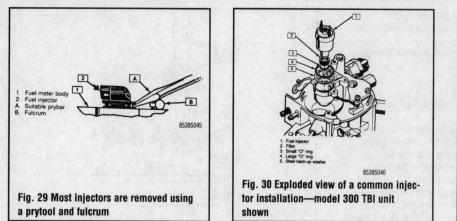

Fig. 29 Most injectors are removed using a prytool and fulcrum

Fig. 30 Exploded view of a common injector installation—model 300 TBI unit shown

Fig. 31 Removing the injectors from the model 220 TBI unit (2.8L and 4.3L engines)

→If the backup washer and large O-ring are not properly installed BEFORE the fuel injector, a fuel leak will likely result.

13. For the model 220 TBI unit, install the fuel injector into the cavity by aligning the raised lug on the injector base with the cast notch in the fuel meter body cavity. Once the injector is aligned, carefully push down on the injector by hand until it is fully seated in the cavity. When properly aligned and installed, the injector terminals will be approximately parallel to the throttle shaft.

14. For the model 300 or model 700 TBI units, carefully align and install the injector to the cavity. Push straight down until the injector is properly seated. For the model 700 unit, the injector connector should be installed parallel to the casting support rib and facing in the general direction of the cut-out in the fuel meter body provided for the wire grommet.

15. Except for the model 700 TBI unit, position a new fuel meter cover gasket, then install the cover to the body, making sure the gasket remains in position. Using a suitable threadlocking compound, install and tighten the cover retainers to 30 inch lbs. (4 Nm).

16. For the model 700 TBI unit, install the injector retainer and coat the retainer screw threads with a suitable threadlocking compound, then install and tighten the screw to secure the injector.

17. Engage the injector electrical connector(s).

18. Connect the negative battery cable, then turn the **ON** to pressurize the fuel system and check for leaks.

19. Install the air cleaner assembly, then start the engine and check for leaks.

IDLE AIR CONTROL (IAC) VALVE REPLACEMENT

▶ See Figures 32 and 33

1. Disconnect the negative battery cable.
2. Remove the air cleaner assembly from the engine.
3. Disengage the electrical connector from the idle air control valve.
4. If the valve is threaded into the throttle body, use a 1¼ (32mm) wrench or an IAC removal tool to loosen and remove the idle air control valve from the throttle body unit.

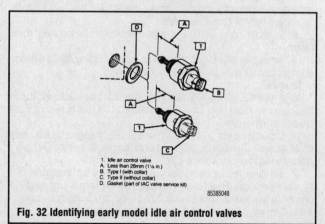

1. Idle air control valve
A. Less than 28mm (1⅛ in.)
B. Type I (with collar)
C. Type II (without collar)
D. Gasket (part of IAC valve service kit)

Fig. 32 Identifying early model idle air control valves

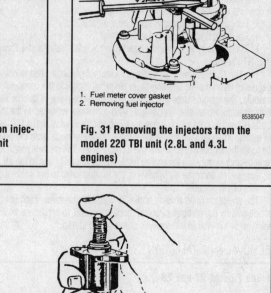

Fig. 33 Retracting the pintle on a NEW IAC valve (late model or early model type I)

5. If the valve is bolted to the throttle body, loosen and remove the retaining bolts, then remove the valve and gasket from the TBI unit.
To install:

✳✳ WARNING

Before installing a new idle air control valve, measure the distance that the valve extends (from the motor housing to the end of the cone); the distance should be no greater than 1⅛ in. (28mm). If it is extended too far, damage may occur to the valve when it is installed.

6. Measure the valve pintle extension. If a threaded valve pintle length is excessive, identify the valve as a type-I or type-II for all vehicles through the late 1980's. The type I valve has a collar at the electric terminal end while the type-II does not. If the valve is a bolt-on (not thread on) or the vehicle is a 1989 or later model type, then it should be treated as a type-I valve. To retract a new valve pintle on a type-I valve, use firm thumb pressure and, if necessary, rock the pintle with a slight side-to-side motion. For new type-II valves, compress the retaining spring by hand and turn the valve inward using a clockwise motion. Once the pintle is retracted for type-II valves, make sure the straight portion of the spring is again aligned with the flat on the valve.

7. If reinstalling a used valve on which the pintle is extended further than specification, an IAC tester MUST be used to electrically retract the pintle.

→Do not attempt to physically retract a pintle on an IAC valve that has been in service, the force may damage the pintle threads. The force required to retract the pintle is only safe on NEW IAC valves.

8. If installing a bolt-on valve, position a gasket a new O-ring (coated with clean automatic transmission fluid) on the valve, as applicable. Then install the valve to the throttle body and secure using the retaining bolts.

9. If installing a threaded valve, position the valve to the throttle body using a new gasket or O-ring, then carefully tighten the valve to 13 ft. lbs. (18 Nm).

10. Engage the valve electrical connector, then install the air cleaner assembly.

11. Connect the negative battery cable, then reset the IAC valve pintle:

   a. For vehicles through 1988, connect the negative battery cable, then start and run the engine until it reaches normal operating temperature. Shut the engine **OFF** and the computer module will reset the IAC valve pintle.

   b. For 1989 and later vehicles equipped with a model 700 TBI unit (2.5L engine), connect the negative battery cable. Depress the accelerator pedal slightly, then start and run the engine for 5 seconds. Turn the ignition **OFF** for 10 seconds, then restart the engine and check for proper idle operation.

   c. For 1989 and later vehicles equipped with a model 220 TBI unit (2.8 and 4.3L engines), connect the negative battery cable. Turn the ignition **ON** (engine NOT running) for 5 seconds, then turn the ignition **OFF** for 10 seconds. Start the engine and check for proper idle operation.

THROTTLE POSITION (TP) SENSOR SERVICE

▶ **See Figures 34 and 35**

The throttle position sensor used on most of the engines covered by this manual is non-adjustable. Some early 2.8L engines (certain models used pre-1989) may be equipped with an adjustable sensor. If so, the sensor can be rotated when the fasteners are loosened. If sensor problems are suspected, test sensor output using a scan tool or voltmeter. If readings are out of specification, the sensor must be adjusted (if possible) or replaced.

Adjustment & Testing

The TP sensor wiring should consist of a 3 wire harness connector. The gray wire is normally the 5 volt reference signal from the computer control module. The dark blue wire should be the TP signal and the black wire is ground.

1. If available, connect a scan tool to the ALDL/DLC. If a scan tool is not available, use a digital voltmeter to backprobe the TP sensor connector terminals for the ground (black wire on end of connector) and sensor signal (dark blue wire usually at center of connector). By backprobing the connector a voltage reading can be taken without disconnecting the circuit and without piercing the wires.

2. Turn the ignition **ON**, but do not start the engine. Check the voltmeter or scan tool for TP sensor output.

   a. On all engines with a non-adjustable sensor, voltage should be 1.25 volts or less with the throttle closed. Open the throttle and watch for a smooth change as the voltage increases. Voltage may go as high as 4.5 volts at wide open throttle. If voltage with the throttle closed is greater than 1.25 volts, or if the voltage does not increase smoothly as the throttle is opened, replace the sensor.

   b. For early model 2.8L engines with an adjustable sensor, rotate the sensor (with the throttle closed) until a reading of 0.420–0.450 volts is obtained. Tighten the retaining screws and retest to verify proper adjustment. Open the

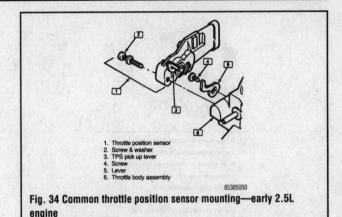

1. Throttle position sensor
2. Screw & washer
3. TPS pick up lever
4. Screw
5. Lever
6. Throttle body assembly

85385050

Fig. 34 Common throttle position sensor mounting—early 2.5L engine

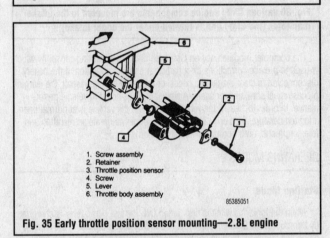

1. Screw assembly
2. Retainer
3. Throttle position sensor
4. Screw
5. Lever
6. Throttle body assembly

85385051

Fig. 35 Early throttle position sensor mounting—2.8L engine

throttle and look for a smooth increase. If proper adjustment cannot be obtained, the sensor must be replaced.

Replacement

➡ **The throttle position sensor is an electrical component. Do NOT soak it or clean it with solvent or the sensor could be damaged.**

For sensor removal and installation, please refer to electronic engine control information in Section 4 of this manual.

CENTRAL MULTI-PORT FUEL INJECTION SYSTEM

General Information

▶ **See Figure 36**

Available in the S/T series pick-up for the 1992–93 model years, the 4.3L (VIN W) engine is equipped with a Central Multi-port Fuel Injection (CMFI) system. The system functions similarly to the TBI system in that an injection assembly (CMFI unit) is centrally mounted on the engine intake manifold. The major differences come in the incorporation of a split (upper and lower) intake manifold assembly with a variable tuned plenum (using an intake manifold tuning valve) and the CMFI unit's single fuel injector which feeds 6 poppet valves (1 for each individual cylinder).

The non-repairable CMFI assembly or injection unit consists of a fuel meter body, gasket seal, fuel pressure regulator, fuel injector and six poppet nozzles with fuel tubes. The assembly is housed in the lower intake manifold. Should a failure occur in the CMFI assembly, the entire component must be replaced as a unit.

As with other fuel injection systems, all injection and ignition functions are controlled by the computer control module. The module accepts inputs from various sensors and switches, calculates the optimum air/fuel mixture and operates the various output devices to provide peak performance within specific emissions limits. The module will attempt to maintain the ideal air/fuel mixture of 14.7:1 in order to optimize catalytic converter operation. If a system failure

occurs that is not serious enough to stop the engine, the module will illuminate the SERVICE ENGINE SOON light and will continue to operate the engine, although it may need to operate in a backup or fail-safe mode.

Fuel is supplied to the injector through an electric fuel pump assembly which is mounted in the vehicle's fuel tank. The module provides a signal to operate the fuel pump though the fuel pump relay and oil pressure switch. The CMFI unit internal pressure regulator maintains a system pressure of approximately 55–61 psi (380–420 kPa). When the injector is energized by the control module, an armature lifts allowing pressurized fuel to travel down the 6 fuel tubes to the poppet valves. In the poppet valves, fuel pressure (working against the extension spring force) will cause the nozzle ball to open from its seat and fuel will flow from the nozzle. It takes approximately 51 psi (350 kPa) to force fuel from the poppet nozzle. Once the module de-energizes the injector, the armature will close, allowing fuel pressure in the tubes to drop and the spring force will close off fuel flow.

Other system components include a pressure regulator, an Idle Air Control (IAC) valve, a Throttle Position (TP) sensor, Intake Air Temperature (IAT) sensor, Engine Coolant Temperature (ECT) sensor, a Manifold Absolute Pressure (MAP) sensor and an oxygen sensor.

The idle air control valve is a stepper motor that controls the amount of air allowed to bypass the throttle plate. With this valve the computer control module can closely control idle speed even when the engine is cold or when there is a high engine load at idle.

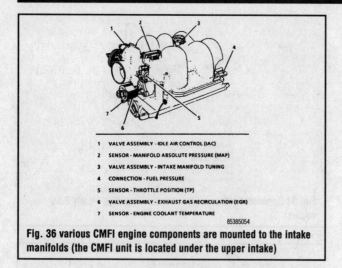

1	VALVE ASSEMBLY - IDLE AIR CONTROL (IAC)
2	SENSOR - MANIFOLD ABSOLUTE PRESSURE (MAP)
3	VALVE ASSEMBLY - INTAKE MANIFOLD TUNING
4	CONNECTION - FUEL PRESSURE
5	SENSOR - THROTTLE POSITION (TP)
6	VALVE ASSEMBLY - EXHAUST GAS RECIRCULATION (EGR)
7	SENSOR - ENGINE COOLANT TEMPERATURE

85385054

Fig. 36 various CMFI engine components are mounted to the intake manifolds (the CMFI unit is located under the upper intake)

The computer module used on CMFI vehicles has a learning capability which is used to provide corrections for a particular engine's condition. If the battery is disconnected to clear diagnostic codes, or for safety during a repair, the learning process must start all over again. A change may be noted in vehicle performance. In order to "teach" the vehicle, make sure the vehicle is at normal operating temperature, then drive at part throttle, under moderate acceleration and idle conditions, until normal performance returns.

OPERATING MODES

Starting Mode

When the ignition switch is first turned **ON**, the fuel pump relay is energized by the module for 2 seconds in order to build system pressure. In the start mode, the computer module checks the ECT, IAT, TP sensor, MAP and crank signal in order to determine the best air/fuel ratio for starting. Ratios could range from 1.5:1 at approximately –33°F (–36°C), to 14.7:1 at 201°F (94°C).

Clear Flood Mode

If the engine becomes flooded, it can be cleared by opening the accelerator to the full throttle position. When the throttle is open all the way and engine rpm is less than 600, the computer module will pulse the fuel injector at an air/fuel ratio of 16.5:1 while the engine is turning over in order to clear the engine of excess fuel. If throttle position is reduced below 65 percent, the module will return to the start mode.

Open Loop Mode

When the engine first starts and engine speed rises above 400 rpm, the computer module operates in the Open Loop mode until specific parameters are met. In Open Loop mode, the fuel requirements are calculated based on information from the MAP and ECT sensors. The oxygen sensor signal is ignored during initial engine operation because it needs time to warm up.

Closed Loop Mode

When the correct parameters are met, the computer module will use O₂ sensor output and adjust the air/fuel mixture accordingly, in order to maintain a narrow band of exhaust gas oxygen concentration. When the module is correcting and adjusting fuel mixture based on the oxygen sensor signal along with the other sensors, this is known as feedback air/fuel ratio control. The computer module will shift into this Closed Loop mode when:

- Oxygen sensor output voltage is varied, indicating that the sensor has warmed up to operating temperature
- The ECT shows an engine coolant temperature above a specified level.
- The engine has been operating for a programmed amount of time.

Acceleration Mode

If the throttle position and manifold pressure is quickly increased, the module will provide extra fuel for smooth acceleration.

Deceleration Mode

As the throttle closes and the manifold pressure decreases, fuel flow is reduced by the module. If both conditions remain for a specific number of engine revolutions indicating a very fast deceleration, the module may decide fuel flow is not needed and stop the flow by temporarily shutting off the injectors.

Highway Fuel Mode (Semi-Closed Loop)

The computer control module is programmed to enter a special highway mode to improve fuel economy. If the module senses the correct ECT, ignition control, canister purge activity and a constant engine speed, it will enter highway mode. During this operation, there will be very little adjustment of the long and short term fuel trims, also, the oxygen sensor values will usually read below 100 millivolts.

Decel En-Leanment Mode

The computer control module is programmed to further reduce emissions by leaning the fuel spray on deceleration. The module does this when a high MAP vacuum (low voltage or pressure) is sensed, BUT it should be noted that the module may do this when the vehicle is not moving. This mode of operation may be misdiagnosed as a lean condition. When diagnosing the control system using a scan tool with the transmission in Park, the oxygen sensor signal low (usually below 100 mV), and both fuel trim numbers around 128 counts, lower the engine speed to 1000 rpm. If the sensor and long term trim numbers respond normally, it is possible that the system was fooled into decel en-leanment operation. If the oxygen sensor and long term numbers do not respond at the lower rpm, there are other problems with the vehicle.

Battery Low Mode

If the computer module detects a low battery, it will increase injector pulse width to compensate for the low voltage and provide proper fuel delivery. It will also increase idle speed to increase alternate output and ignition dwell time to allow for proper engine operation.

Field Service Mode

When the diagnostic terminal of the test connector is grounded with the engine running, the computer module will enter the Field Service Mode. If the engine is running in Open Loop Mode, the SERVICE ENGINE SOON Malfunction Indicator Lamp (MIL) will flash quickly, about 2½ times per second. When the engine is in Closed Loop Mode, the MIL will flash only about once per second. If the light stays OFF most of the time in Close Loop, the engine is running lean. If the light is ON most of the time, the engine is running rich.

While the engine continues to operate in Field Service Mode certain conditions will apply:

- New trouble codes cannot be stored in computer memory.
- The closed loop timer is bypassed.

➡️**For more information concerning the computer control module, self-diagnosis systems and other electronic engine controls, please refer to Section 4 of this manual**

Fuel Pressure Relief

▶ **See Figure 37**

Prior to servicing any component of the fuel injection system, the fuel pressure must relieved. If fuel pressure is not relieved, serious injury could result.

A schrader valve is provided on this fuel system in order to conveniently test or release the fuel system pressure. A fuel pressure gauge and adapter will be necessary to connect the gauge to the fitting. The CMFI system covered here uses a valve located on the inlet pipe fitting, immediately before it enters the CMFI assembly (towards the rear of the engine).

1. Disconnect the negative battery cable to assure the prevention of fuel spillage if the ignition switch is accidentally turned **ON** while a fitting is still disconnected.
2. Loosen the fuel filler cap to release the fuel tank pressure.
3. Make sure the release valve on the fuel gauge is closed, then connect the fuel gauge to the pressure fitting located on the inlet fuel pipe fitting.

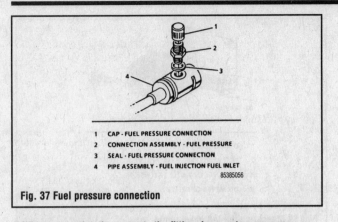

1 CAP - FUEL PRESSURE CONNECTION
2 CONNECTION ASSEMBLY - FUEL PRESSURE
3 SEAL - FUEL PRESSURE CONNECTION
4 PIPE ASSEMBLY - FUEL INJECTION FUEL INLET

85385056

Fig. 37 Fuel pressure connection

➡ **When connecting the gauge to the fitting, be sure to wrap a rag around the fitting to avoid spillage. After repairs, place the rag in an approved container.**

4. Install the bleed hose portion of the fuel gauge assembly into an approved container, then open the gauge release valve and bleed the fuel pressure from the system.

5. When the gauge is removed, be sure to open the bleed valve and drain all fuel from the gauge assembly.

Electric Fuel Pump

The electric pump is attached to the fuel sending unit, located in the fuel tank.

TESTING

1. Properly relieve the fuel system pressure.
2. Leave the gauge attached to the pressure fitting on the fuel inlet pipe.
3. If disconnected during the fuel pressure relief procedure, reconnect the negative battery terminal.
4. If the engine will run, start the engine and allow it to run at normal idle speed. The fuel pressure should be 55–61 psi (380–420 kPa). Once the engine is at normal operating temperature, open the throttle quickly while noting fuel pressure; it should quickly approach 61 psi (40 kPa) if all components are operating properly (there is no need to proceed further). If the pressure was in specification before, but does not approach 61 psi (420 kPa) on acceleration, the pressure regulator in the CMFI unit is faulty and the assembly should be replaced.
5. If the engine does not run, turn the ignition **ON**, but do not attempt to start the engine. Listen for the fuel pump to run. Within 2 seconds of turning the ignition **ON** pressure should be 55–61 psi (380–420 kPa) while the pump is running. Once the pump stops, pressure may vary by several pounds, then it should hold steady. If the pressure does not hold steady, wait 10 seconds and repeat this step, but pinch the fuel pressure line flexible hose and watch if the pressure holds. If it still does not hold, the CMFI unit should be replaced. If the pressure holds with the pressure line pinched, check for a partially disconnected fuel dampener (pulsator) or faulty in-tank fuel pump.
6. If the fuel pump did not run or system pressure did not reach specification, locate the fuel pump test connector. The test connector is usually found on the driver's side of the engine compartment (on or near the fender), with a single wire (usually red) leading from the relay to the connector. Using a 10 amp fused jumper wire, apply battery voltage to the test connector in order to energize and run the fuel pump. The pump should run and produce fuel pressure of 55–61 psi (380–420 kPa). If the pump does not run, check the relay and fuel pump wiring.
7. If the pump pressure was lower than specification, first check for a restricted fuel line, filter or a disconnected fuel pulse dampener (pulsator) and repair/replace, as necessary. If no restrictions can be found, restrict the flexible fuel return line (by gradually pinching it) until the pressure rises above 61 psi (420 kPa), but DO NOT allow pressure to exceed 75 psi (517 kPa). If the fuel pressure rises above specification with the return line restricted, then the pressure regulator is faulty and the CMFI assembly should be replaced. If pressure still does not reach specification, check for a faulty fuel pump, partially disconnected fuel pulse dampener (pulsator), partially restricted pump strainer or an incorrect pump.
8. If during the previous steps, the fuel pressure was higher than specification, relieve the system pressure, then disconnect the engine compartment fuel return line. Attach a ⁵⁄₁₆ ID flex hose to the fuel line from the throttle body and

place the other end into an approved gasoline container. Cycle the ignition in order to energize the fuel pump and watch system pressure. If pressure is still higher, check for restrictions in the line between the pressure regulator and the point where it was disconnected. Repair or replace the line if restrictions are found or replace the CMFI assembly with the faulty internal pressure regulator if no other causes of high pressure are identified. If fuel pressure is normal only with the rest of the return line out of the circuit, check that remaining line for restrictions and repair or replace, as necessary.

9. Once the test is completed, depressurize the fuel system and remove the gauge.

REMOVAL & INSTALLATION

Removal and installation of the fuel pump and sending unit assembly is the same on CMFI vehicles as it is for TBI vehicles. Please refer to the TBI procedures earlier in this section for electric fuel pump replacement.

Fuel Pump Relay

For CMFI vehicles, the fuel pump relay is normally found in the convenience center, located under the center of the dashboard.

If a problem is suspected, first check for loose electrical connections; no other service is possible, except replacement.

REMOVAL & INSTALLATION

▶ **See Figure 38**

1. Disconnect the negative battery cable.
2. Remove the retainer, if equipped.
3. Disengage the relay electrical connector.
4. Remove the relay by depressing the bracket clip at the rear of the relay, or removing the bolts from the retaining bracket, as applicable.
5. If necessary, use a new relay, then reverse the removal procedures.

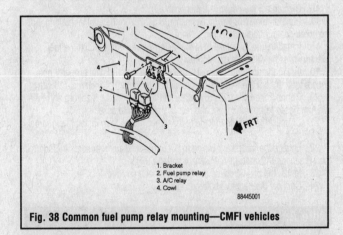

1. Bracket
2. Fuel pump relay
3. A/C relay
4. Cowl

88445001

Fig. 38 Common fuel pump relay mounting—CMFI vehicles

CMFI Assembly

REMOVAL & INSTALLATION

The CMFI assembly is mounted to the lower intake manifold. The upper intake manifold assembly must be removed for access. The CMFI assembly includes a fuel meter body, gasket seal, fuel pressure regulator, fuel injector and six poppet nozzles with fuel tubes. Should a failure occur in any components of the CMFI unit, the entire assembly must be replaced.

1. Remove the plastic cover and properly relieve the fuel system pressure.
2. Disconnect the negative battery cable, then remove the air cleaner and air inlet duct.
3. Disengage the wiring harness from the necessary upper intake components including:
   • Throttle Position (TP) sensor
   • Idle Air Control (IAC) motor

- Manifold Absolute Pressure (MAP) sensor
- Intake Manifold Tuning Valve (IMTV)

4. Disengage the throttle linkage from the upper intake manifold, then remove the ignition coil.

5. Disconnect the PCV hose at the rear of the upper intake manifold, then tag and disengage the vacuum hoses from both the front and rear of the upper intake.

6. Remove the upper intake manifold bolts and studs, making sure to note or mark the location of all studs to assure proper installation. Remove the upper intake manifold from the engine.

7. Disengage the injector wiring harness connector at the CMFI assembly.

8. Remove and discard the fuel fitting clip.

9. Disconnect the fuel inlet and return tube and fitting assembly. Discard the old O-rings.

10. Squeeze the poppet nozzle locktabs together while lifting each nozzle out of the casting socket. Once all six nozzles are released, carefully lift the CMFI assembly out of the casting.

To install:

11. Align the CMFI assembly grommet with the casting grommet slots and push downward until it is seated in the bottom guide hole.

❊❊ CAUTION

To reduce the risk of fire and personal injury, be ABSOLUTELY SURE that the poppet nozzles are firmly seated and locked into their casting sockets. An unlocked poppet nozzle could work loose from its socket resulting in a dangerous fuel leak.

12. Carefully insert the poppet nozzles into the casting sockets. Make sure they are FIRMLY SEATED and locked into the casting sockets.

13. Position new O-ring seals (lightly coated with clean engine oil), then connect the fuel inlet and return tube and fitting assembly.

14. Install a new fuel fitting clip.

15. Temporarily connect the negative battery cable, then pressurize the fuel system by cycling the ignition switch **ON** for 2 seconds, then **OFF** for 10 seconds and repeating, as necessary. Once the fuel system is pressurized, check for leaks.

16. Disconnect the negative battery cable.

17. Position a new upper intake manifold gasket on the engine, making sure the green sealing lines are facing upward.

18. Install the upper intake manifold being careful not to pinch the fuel injector wires between the manifolds.

19. Install the manifold retainers, making sure the studs are properly positioned, then tighten them using the proper sequence to 124 inch lbs. (14 Nm).

20. Connect the PCV hose to the rear of the upper intake manifold and the vacuum hoses to both the front and rear of the manifold assembly.

21. Connect the throttle linkage to the upper intake, then install the ignition coil.

22. Engage the necessary wiring to the upper intake components including the TP sensor, IAC motor, MAP sensor and the IMTV.

23. Install the plastic cover, the air cleaner and air inlet duct.

24. Connect the negative battery cable.

Idle Air Control (IAC) Valve

REMOVAL & INSTALLATION

▶ **See Figure 39**

1. Disconnect the negative battery cable.
2. Disengage the electrical connector from the idle air control valve.
3. Loosen and remove the IAC valve retaining bolts, then remove the valve from the engine.

To install:

❊❊ WARNING

Before installing a new idle air control valve, measure the distance that the valve extends (from the motor housing to the end of the cone); the distance should be no greater than 1⅛ in. (28mm). If it is extended too far, damage may occur to the valve when it is installed.

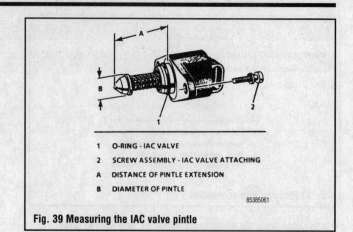

1	O-RING - IAC VALVE
2	SCREW ASSEMBLY - IAC VALVE ATTACHING
A	DISTANCE OF PINTLE EXTENSION
B	DIAMETER OF PINTLE

85385061

Fig. 39 Measuring the IAC valve pintle

4. Measure the valve pintle extension. To retract the pintle on a NEW valve, use firm thumb pressure and, if necessary, rock the pintle with a slight side-to-side motion. BUT, if reinstalling a used valve on which the pintle is extended further than specification, an IAC tester MUST be used to electrically retract the pintle.

➠**Do not attempt to physically retract a pintle on an IAC valve that has been in service, the force may damage the pintle threads. The force required to retract the pintle is only safe on NEW IAC valves.**

5. Lightly coat the IAC valve O-ring with clean engine oil.

6. Inspect the retaining screw threads for threadlocking material. If there is no longer sufficient material on the threads, clean the threads and apply Loctite®262 or equivalent. DO NOT use a stronger compound or future bolt removal may be difficult.

7. Install the IAC valve and tighten the retaining bolts to 27 inch lbs. (3.0 Nm).

8. Engage the valve electrical connector.

9. Connect the negative battery cable.

10. Reset the IAC valve pintle: turn the ignition **ON** (engine NOT running) for 5 seconds, then turn the ignition **OFF** for 10 seconds. Start the engine and check for proper idle operation.

Throttle Position (TP) Sensor

ADJUSTMENT & TESTING

The TP sensor wiring should consist of a 3 wire harness connector. The gray wire is normally the 5 volt reference signal from the computer control module. The dark blue wire should be the TP signal and the black wire is ground.

Because the TP sensor on these engines is bolted into a fixed position, no adjustment is necessary or possible. If the sensor does not give proper readings (and other problems with the circuit are not to blame), the faulty TP sensor must be replaced.

1. If available, connect a scan tool to the ALDL/DLC. If a scan tool is not available, use a digital voltmeter to backprobe the TP sensor connector terminals for the ground (black wire on end of connector) and sensor signal (dark blue wire usually at center of connector). By backprobing the connector a voltage reading can be taken without disconnecting the circuit and without piercing the wires.

2. Turn the ignition **ON**, but do not start the engine. Check the voltmeter or scan tool for TP sensor output. Voltage should be 1.25 volts or less with the throttle closed. Open the throttle and watch for a smooth change as the voltage increases. Voltage may go as high as 4.5 volts at wide open throttle. If voltage with the throttle closed is greater than 1.25 volts, or if the voltage does not increase smoothly as the throttle is opened, replace the sensor.

REPLACEMENT

➠**The throttle position sensor is an electrical component. Do NOT soak it or clean it with solvent or the sensor could be damaged.**

For sensor removal and installation, please refer to electronic engine control information in Section 4 of this manual.

MULTI-PORT FUEL INJECTION SYSTEM

General Information

▶ **See Figure 40**

Multi-port fuel injection first became available in the S/T series pick-up with the special edition Syclone for the 1991–92 model years. The Syclone was equipped with a 4.3L MFI-Turbo engine. MFI was likely chosen for it's combination of efficiency and power. The 4.3L MFI-Turbo offered performance which could not be expected in the S/T series previously.

The MFI system functions with electronic engine control like most fuel injection systems. A throttle body is used to meter intake air, but unlike TBI systems, the fuel is delivered further downstream of the air flow. The defining feature of a MFI system is that a separate fuel injector is used for each cylinder. A fuel rail and injector assembly is mounted to the intake manifold. Fuel is delivered (through the fuel rail assembly) to each of the injectors.

As with other fuel injection systems, all injection and ignition functions are controlled by the computer control module. The module accepts inputs from various sensors and switches, calculates the optimum air/fuel mixture and operates the various output devices to provide peak performance within specific emissions limits. The module will attempt to maintain the ideal air/fuel mixture of 14.7:1 in order to optimize catalytic converter operation. If a system failure occurs that is not serious enough to stop the engine, the module will illuminate the CHECK ENGINE OR SERVICE ENGINE SOON light (as equipped) and will continue to operate the engine, although it may need to operate in a backup or fail-safe mode.

Fuel is supplied to the injectors through an electric fuel pump assembly which is mounted in the vehicle's fuel tank. The module provides a signal to operate the fuel pump though the fuel pump relay and oil pressure switch. The fuel pressure regulator, mounted to the end of the fuel rail, maintains a constant system pressure by metering flow to the fuel return line. A spring diaphragm is capable of restricting flow until sufficient pressure is achieved, then preventing over-pressurization by allowing increased flow in the return line, as necessary. When the fuel injectors are energized by the control module, the ball valve will open to allow pressurized fuel through the nozzle. Fuel is sprayed in a conical pattern towards the intake valve.

Other system components include a pressure regulator, an Idle Air Control (IAC) valve, a Throttle Position (TP) sensor, Intake Air Temperature (IAT) sensor, Engine Coolant Temperature (ECT) sensor, a Manifold Absolute Pressure (MAP) sensor and an oxygen sensor.

The idle air control valve is a stepper motor that controls the amount of air allowed to bypass the throttle plate. With this valve the computer control module can closely control idle speed even when the engine is cold or when there is a high engine load at idle.

The computer module used on all MFI vehicles has a learning capability which is used to provide corrections for a particular engine's condition. If the battery is disconnected to clear diagnostic codes, or for safety during a repair, the learning process must start all over again. A change may be noted in vehicle performance. In order to "teach" the vehicle, make sure the vehicle is at normal operating temperature, then drive at part throttle, under moderate acceleration and idle conditions, until normal performance returns.

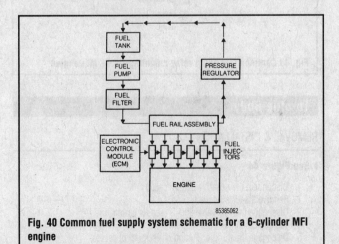

Fig. 40 Common fuel supply system schematic for a 6-cylinder MFI engine

OPERATING MODES

Starting Mode

When the ignition switch is first turned **ON**, the fuel pump relay is energized by the module for 2 seconds in order to build system pressure. In the start mode, the computer module checks the ECT and TP sensor in order to determine the best air/fuel ratio for starting. Ratios could range from 1.5:1 at approximately −33°F (−36°C), to 14.7:1 at 201°F (94°C).

Clear Flood Mode

If the engine becomes flooded, it can be cleared by opening the accelerator to the full throttle position. When the throttle is open all the way and engine rpm is less than 600, the computer module will pulse the fuel injector at an air/fuel ratio of 20:1 (4.3L) while the engine is turning over in order to clear the engine of excess fuel. If throttle position is reduced below 80 percent, the module will return to the start mode.

Open Loop Mode

When the engine first starts and engine speed rises above 400 rpm, the computer module operates in the Open Loop mode until specific parameters are met. In Open Loop mode, the fuel requirements are calculated based on information from the MAP and ECT sensors. The oxygen sensor signal is ignored during initial engine operation because it needs time to warm up.

Closed Loop Mode

▶ **See Figure 41**

When the correct parameters are met, the computer module will use O₂ sensor output and adjust the air/fuel mixture accordingly in order to maintain a narrow band of exhaust gas oxygen concentration. When the module is correcting and adjusting fuel mixture based on the oxygen sensor signal along with the other sensors, this is known as feedback air/fuel ratio control. The computer module will shift into this Closed Loop mode when:

• Oxygen sensor output voltage is varied, indicating that the sensor has warmed up to operating temperature
• The ECT shows an engine coolant temperature above a specified level.
• The engine has been operating for a programmed amount of time.

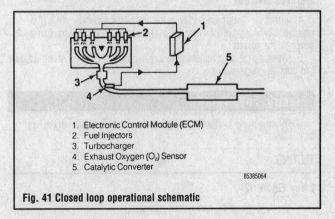

1. Electronic Control Module (ECM)
2. Fuel Injectors
3. Turbocharger
4. Exhaust Oxygen (O₂) Sensor
5. Catalytic Converter

Fig. 41 Closed loop operational schematic

Acceleration Mode

If the throttle position and manifold pressure is quickly increased, the module will provide extra fuel for smooth acceleration.

Deceleration Mode

As the throttle closes and the manifold pressure decreases, fuel flow is reduced by the module. If both conditions remain for a specific number of engine revolutions indicating a very fast deceleration, the module may decide fuel flow is not needed and stop the flow by temporarily shutting off the injectors.

Battery Low Mode

If the computer module detects a low battery, it will increase injector pulse width to compensate for the low voltage and provide proper fuel delivery. It will also increase idle speed to increase alternate output and ignition dwell time to allow for proper engine operation.

Field Service Mode

When the diagnostic terminal of the test connector is grounded with the engine running, the computer module will enter the Field Service Mode. If the engine is running in Open Loop Mode, the CHECK ENGINE or SERVICE ENGINE SOON (as applicable) Malfunction Indicator Lamp (MIL) will flash quickly, about 2½ times per second. When the engine is in Closed Loop Mode, the MIL will flash only about once per second. If the light stays OFF most of the time in Close Loop, the engine is running lean. If the light is ON most of the time, the engine is running rich.

While the engine continues to operate in Field Service Mode certain conditions will apply:
- New trouble codes cannot be stored in computer memory.
- The closed loop timer is bypassed.

➡**For more information concerning the computer control module, self-diagnosis systems and other electronic engine controls, please refer to Section 4 of this manual.**

Fuel Pressure Relief

Prior to servicing any component of the fuel injection system, the fuel pressure must be relieved. If fuel pressure is not relieved, serious injury could result.

A valve is provided on these fuel systems in order to conveniently test or release the fuel system pressure. A fuel pressure gauge and adapter will be necessary to connect to the fitting. The 4.3L MFI system uses a valve located on the fuel rail assembly, immediately before the pressure regulator in the fuel circuit.

1. Disconnect the negative battery cable to assure the prevention of fuel spillage if the ignition switch is accidentally turned **ON** while a fitting is still disconnected.
2. Loosen the fuel filter cap to release the fuel tank pressure.
3. Make sure the release valve on the fuel gauge is closed, then connect the fuel gauge to the pressure fitting located on the fuel rail.

➡**When connecting the gauge to the fitting, be sure to wrap a rag around the fitting to avoid spillage. After repairs, place the rag in an approved container.**

4. Install the bleed hose portion of the fuel gauge assembly into an approved container, then open the gauge release valve and bleed the fuel pressure from the system.
5. When the gauge is removed, be sure to open the bleed valve and drain all fuel from the gauge assembly.

Electric Fuel Pump

The electric pump is attached to the fuel sending unit, located in the fuel tank.

TESTING

▶ **See Figure 42**

1. Properly relieve the fuel system pressure.
2. Leave the gauge attached to the pressure fitting on the fuel inlet pipe.
3. If disconnected during the fuel pressure relief procedure, reconnect the negative battery terminal.
4. Disconnect the vacuum hose from the regulator.
5. Turn the ignition **ON** and listen for the pump to run (is should run for 2 seconds). If necessary, cycle the ignition **OFF** for 10 seconds and then **ON** again in order to build maximum system pressure. Check that pressure is at specification:
   a. Note the pressure after the pump stops, it should be 35–38 psi (245–256 kPa) and should hold steady. If not, refer to the accompanying fuel system diagnostic charts.

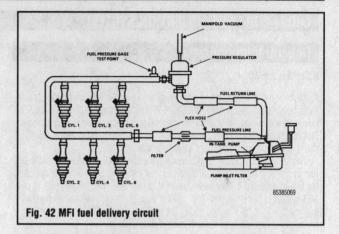

Fig. 42 MFI fuel delivery circuit

REMOVAL & INSTALLATION

Removal and installation of the fuel pump and sending unit assembly is the same on MFI vehicles as it is for TBI vehicles. Please refer to the TBI procedures earlier in this section for electric fuel pump replacement.

Fuel Pump Relay

The fuel pump relay can be found on a bracket mounted to the cowl. If a problem is suspected, first check for loose electrical connections; no other service is possible, except replacement.

REMOVAL & INSTALLATION

▶ **See Figure 43**

1. Disconnect the negative battery cable.
2. Remove the retainer, if equipped.
3. Disengage the relay electrical connector.
4. Remove the relay from the bracket and from the vehicle.
5. If necessary, use a new relay, then reverse the removal procedures.

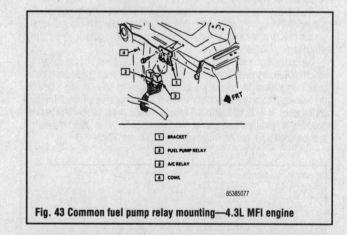

Fig. 43 Common fuel pump relay mounting—4.3L MFI engine

Throttle Body

REMOVAL & INSTALLATION

▶ **See Figure 44**

1. Disconnect the negative battery cable.
2. Remove the air inlet duct.
3. Disengage the IAC valve and TP sensor connectors.
4. Tag and disconnect the vacuum lines.
5. Disengage the throttle, TV and cruise control cables.

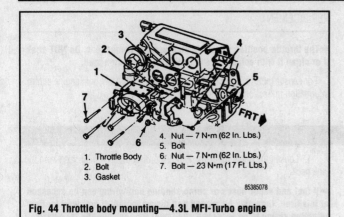

Fig. 44 Throttle body mounting—4.3L MFI-Turbo engine

4. Nut — 7 N·m (62 In. Lbs.)
5. Bolt
1. Throttle Body   6. Nut — 7 N·m (62 In. Lbs.)
2. Bolt   7. Bolt — 23 N·m (17 Ft. Lbs.)
3. Gasket

85385078

6. Remove the throttle body retaining bolts, then remove the throttle body and discard the old gasket.

To install:

7. Position the throttle body to the intake using a new gasket.
8. Install the throttle body retaining bolts and tighten to 17 ft. lbs. (23 Nm).
9. Engage the throttle, TV and cruise control cables.
10. Engage the vacuum lines as tagged during removal.
11. Engage the IAC and TP sensor connectors.
12. Install the air inlet duct.
13. Connect the negative battery cable.

Fuel Injectors

REMOVAL & INSTALLATION

➡Take care when servicing the fuel rail assembly to prevent dirt or contaminants from entering the fuel system. ALL openings in the fuel lines and passages should be capped or plugged while disconnected.

1. Before disassembly, clean the fuel rail assembly with a spray type cleaner such as AC Delco® X-30A, or equivalent. After removal, DO NOT immerse the fuel rail in liquid solvent.
2. Properly relieve the fuel system pressure and disconnect the negative battery cable.
3. Remove the air intake duct, as necessary for access.
4. Tag and disengage the fuel injector electrical connectors.
5. Disengage the fuel pressure regulator vacuum line, then tag and disengage all other necessary vacuum hoses.
6. Loosen and remove the fuel rail retaining bolts.
7. If necessary to remove the fuel rail assembly completely from the engine compartment, or to prevent stressing and damaging the fuel lines, disconnect the fuel lines from the rail assembly.
8. Carefully lift the fuel rail assembly and fuel injectors from the intake.
9. Carefully release and separate the fuel injectors from the rail assembly.
10. Remove and discard ALL old O-rings from the fuel injectors and, if disconnected, the fuel lines.

To install:

11. Lightly coat the new O-rings with clean engine oil, then position them to the injectors and, if applicable, fuel fittings.
12. Install the injectors to the fuel rail assembly.
13. Carefully install the fuel rail and injectors to the intake manifold. Make sure the injectors are properly seated in their bores, but DO NOT force them into position.
14. Install and tighten the rail retaining bolts to 62 inch lbs. (7 Nm).
15. If removed, connect the fuel lines to the rail assembly and secure the fittings.
16. Engage the fuel pressure regulator and any other vacuum lines, as noted during removal.
17. Engage the injector electrical connectors.
18. Connect the negative battery cable and cycle the ignition switch (without attempting to start the engine) in order to pressurize the fuel system, then check for leaks.
19. Install the air intake duct.

Fuel Pressure Regulator

REMOVAL & INSTALLATION

1. Properly relieve the fuel system pressure and disconnect the negative battery cable.
2. Disengage the vacuum line from the pressure regulator.
3. If applicable, disengage the fuel line(s) from the regulator.
4. Remove the retaining bolts, then separate the regulator from the fuel rail assembly.
5. Installation is the reverse of removal. Connect the negative battery cable, then pressurize the fuel system by cycling the ignition (without attempting to start the engine) and check for leaks.

Idle Air Control Valve

REMOVAL & INSTALLATION

1. Disconnect the negative battery cable.
2. Disengage the electrical connector from the idle air control valve.
3. Loosen and remove the threaded IAC control valve and gasket using either a 1¼ in. (32mm) wrench, J-33031, or equivalent.

To install:

❈❈ WARNING

Before installing a new idle air control valve, measure the distance that the valve extends (from the motor housing to the end of the cone); the distance should be no greater than 1⅛ in. (28mm). If it is extended too far, damage may occur to the valve when it is installed.

4. Measure the valve pintle extension. To retract the pintle on a NEW valve, use firm thumb pressure and, if necessary, rock the pintle with a slight side-to-side motion. BUT, if reinstalling a used valve on which the pintle is extended further than specification, an IAC tester MUST be used to electrically retract the pintle.

➡Do not attempt to physically retract a pintle on an IAC valve that has been in service, the force may damage the pintle threads. The force required to retract the pintle is only safe on NEW IAC valves.

5. Install the IAC valve and gasket to the throttle body and tighten to 13 ft. lbs (18 Nm).
6. Engage the valve electrical connector.
7. Connect the negative battery cable.
8. Reset the IAC valve pintle:
   a. There are 2 possible methods to resetting the IAC valve. First, depress the accelerator pedal slightly, then start and run the engine for 5 seconds. Shut the engine **OFF** for 10 seconds, then restart it and check for proper idle operation. If this does not work, start and run the engine until it reaches normal operating temperature. Drive the vehicle and the IAC valve will reset once vehicle speed is above 35 mph.

Throttle Position (TP) Sensor

ADJUSTMENT & TESTING

The TP sensor wiring should consist of a 3 wire harness connector. The gray wire is normally the 5 volt reference signal from the computer control module. The dark blue wire should be the TP signal and the black wire is ground.

Because the TP sensor on these engines is bolted into a fixed position, no adjustment is necessary or possible. If the sensor does not give proper readings (and other problems with the circuit are not to blame), the faulty TP sensor must be replaced.

1. If available, connect a scan tool to the ALDL/DLC. If a scan tool is not available, use a digital voltmeter to backprobe the TP sensor connector terminals for the ground (black wire on end of connector) and sensor signal (dark blue wire usually at center of connector). By backprobing the connector a volt-

age reading can be taken without disconnecting the circuit and without piercing the wires.

2. Turn the ignition **ON**, but do not start the engine. Check the voltmeter or scan tool for TP sensor output. Voltage should be 1.25 volts or less with the throttle closed. Open the throttle and watch for a smooth change as the voltage increases. Voltage may go as high as 4.5 volts at wide open throttle. If voltage with the throttle closed is greater than 1.25 volts, or if the voltage does not increase smoothly as the throttle is opened, replace the sensor.

FUEL TANK

Service

DRAINING

1. Remove the tank filler cap in order to release vapor pressure in the tank.

➡**If the pump device is equipped with a static ground wire, be sure to connect it to a metal part of the gas tank before you begin draining the fuel.**

2. Use a hand operated pump device to remove fuel through the filler neck. If difficulty is encountered, disconnect the filler hose from the tank neck and insert the pump hose directly into the tank.

3. The hand pump may not be able to completely drain the tank, but do your best to remove as much as possible.

4. On vehicles equipped with an electric fuel pump, disconnect the feed line (somewhere between the tank and engine, wherever access is convenient), then connect a length of rubber hose to the feed line. Place the other end of the rubber hose in an approved container, then operate the fuel pump to further drain the tank. On most of these vehicles, the easiest method of energizing the fuel pump is to use a 10 amp fused jumper wire to apply battery voltage to the fuel pump test connector. The connector is usually located in the engine compartment, often on the left fender.

REMOVAL & INSTALLATION

♦ **See Figures 45, 46, 47, 48 and 49**

Except Late Model Vehicles Equipped With Shield Package

1. Properly drain the fuel tank, then disconnect the negative battery cable.
2. If not done already, raise and support the rear of the truck safely using jackstands.
3. If equipped on late-model vehicles, loosen and remove the tank plastic shield.

REPLACEMENT

➡**The throttle position sensor is an electrical component. Do NOT soak it or clean it with solvent or the sensor could be damaged.**

For sensor removal and installation, please refer to electronic engine control information in Section 4 of this manual.

4. Loosen the retaining clamp and disconnect the tank filler hose from the tank neck.

➡**If fuel and vapor hoses or pump/sending unit wiring can be accessed at this time, they may be tagged and disconnected. If not, wait for the retaining straps to be loosened and lower the tank slightly for access.**

5. Tag and disconnect and accessible wiring or hoses from the top of the fuel tank.

6. Have an assistant support the fuel tank, then remove the fuel tank-to-vehicle straps and, if equipped, the isolation strips. If no assistant is available, position a floor jack to support the tank while the straps are removed.

7. Lower the tank slightly, then remove the sending unit or sending unit/pump wires, hoses and ground strap. Be sure to label all connections to ease installation.

8. Carefully lower the fuel tank from the vehicle and store in a safe place.

To install:

9. Raise the tank partially into position in the vehicle. If you are working without an assistant, you may wish to loosely install one of the retaining straps and use a floor jack to support the tank at an angle so there is access to the sending unit or sending unit/pump assembly (as applicable).

10. Connect the fuel/vapor hoses and wiring to the top of the fuel tank, as tagged during removal.

11. Carefully raise the fuel tank so it is fully into position and loosely secure the retaining straps. Make sure the wires and hoses are not pinched or damaged when raising the tank. Also, be sure that the isolation strips (if used) are positioned between the retaining straps and the fuel tank.

12. It may be easier to connect the fuel filler hose to the tank neck at this time. If desired, connect the hose and secure the clamp.

13. Tighten the fuel tank retaining strap fasteners.

14. If not done earlier, connect the tank filler hose to the tank neck and secure using the clamp.

15. If equipped, install and secure the tank plastic shield.

16. Remove the jackstands and carefully lower the rear of the truck.

17. Refill the fuel tank and install the filler cap, then check for leaks.

18. Connect the negative battery cable.

85385100

Fig. 45 Failure to tag the fuel lines could lead to confusion during installation

85385101

Fig. 46 One of the retaining straps may be used to help retain the tank while connecting hoses and wires

vFig. 47 If equipped, make sure the isolators are positioned between the straps and tank

Fig. 48 Secure the retaining straps using the fasteners

Fig. 49 Most tanks on these vehicles are retained using 2 straps

Late Model Vehicles Equipped With Shield Package

1. Properly drain the fuel tank, then disconnect the negative battery cable.
2. Raise and support the rear of the truck safely using jackstands.
3. Remove the shield forward support and bracket.
4. While supporting the shield and tank assembly with the help of both an assistant and a floor jack, remove the remaining bolts holding the assembly to the frame, then lower it sufficiently for access to the hoses and wires.
5. Tag and disengage the hoses and wires from the sending unit assembly.
6. Carefully lower the fuel tank and shield from the vehicle, then if necessary for service or replacement, separate the tank from the shield.

To install:

7. If separated, install the tank to the shield.
8. Carefully raise the tank and shield assembly partially into position with the help of an assistant and a floor jack.
9. Connect the wiring and hoses to the sending unit assembly, as tagged during removal.
10. Raise the tank and shield assembly fully into position, then secure to the frame using the lower retaining bolts.
11. Install the shield forward support bracket.
12. Remove the jackstands and carefully lower the rear of the truck.
13. Refill the fuel tank and install the filler cap, then check for leaks.
14. Connect the negative battery cable.

SENDING UNIT REPLACEMENT

▶ **See Figures 50, 51, 52, 53 and 54**

➡ **The following procedure covers sending unit replacement only. For all fuel injected vehicles, which are equipped with a sending unit/pump assembly, please refer to the electric fuel pump procedure located under TBI fuel injection, earlier in this section.**

1. Properly drain the fuel tank, then disconnect the negative battery cable.
2. Remove the fuel tank assembly from the truck.
3. Release the sending unit lockring cam using J-24187, or an equivalent locking tool to turn it counterclockwise. If no tool is available, a hammer and a brass drift may be used to CAREFULLY turn the lockring and release it from the tabs. DO NOT force the ring or tank/sending unit damage may occur.
4. Remove the sending unit from the top of the fuel tank. Be careful not to damage the float or pick-up while removing the unit.
5. Remove and discard the old sending unit-to-tank O-ring.

To install:

6. Position a new O-ring on the top of the tank opening.

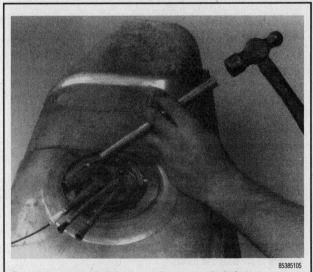

Fig. 50 Loosen the lockring by turning counterclockwise

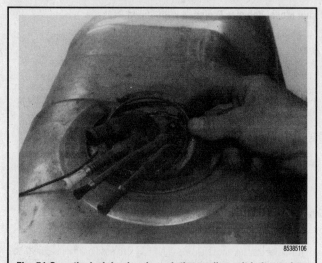

Fig. 51 Once the lockring is released, the sending unit is free to be removed from the tank

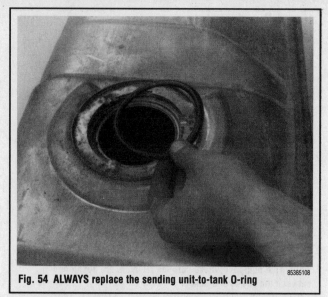

Fig. 54 ALWAYS replace the sending unit-to-tank O-ring

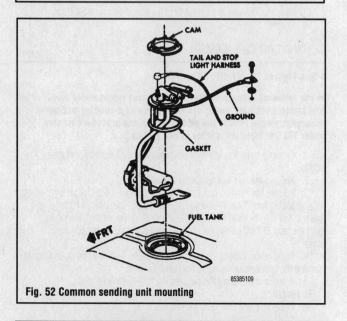

Fig. 52 Common sending unit mounting

7. Carefully insert the sending unit to the tank, making sure that the unit is properly aligned so the bottom or sides of the tank do not interfere with the float or pickup. If necessary, carefully tilt the unit to insert the bottom, then straighten it out as it is inserted into the tank.

8. Make sure the sending unit and O-ring are properly installed, then position the lockring. Use the removal/installation tool to turn the lockring clockwise and secure the sending unit.

9. Install the fuel tank to the vehicle, then refill it and check for leaks.

10. Connect the negative battery cable and check for proper sending unit operation.

Fig. 53 Tilt the sending unit during removal in order to prevent damage to the float and pickup

6

CHASSIS ELECTRICAL

UNDERSTANDING AND TROUBLESHOOTING ELECTRICAL SYSTEMS

Basic Electrical Theory

▶ **See Figure 1**

For any 12 volt, negative ground, electrical system to operate, the electricity must travel in a complete circuit. This simply means that current (power) from the positive (+) terminal of the battery must eventually return to the negative (-) terminal of the battery. Along the way, this current will travel through wires, fuses, switches and components. If, for any reason, the flow of current through the circuit is interrupted, the component fed by that circuit will cease to function properly.

Perhaps the easiest way to visualize a circuit is to think of connecting a light bulb (with two wires attached to it) to the battery—one wire attached to the negative (-) terminal of the battery and the other wire to the positive (+) terminal. With the two wires touching the battery terminals, the circuit would be complete and the light bulb would illuminate. Electricity would follow a path from the battery to the bulb and back to the battery. It's easy to see that with longer wires on our light bulb, it could be mounted anywhere. Further, one wire could be fitted with a switch so that the light could be turned on and off.

The normal automotive circuit differs from this simple example in two ways. First, instead of having a return wire from the bulb to the battery, the current travels through the frame of the vehicle. Since the negative (-) battery cable is attached to the frame (made of electrically conductive metal), the frame of the vehicle can serve as a ground wire to complete the circuit. Secondly, most automotive circuits contain multiple components which receive power from a single circuit. This lessens the amount of wire needed to power components on the vehicle.

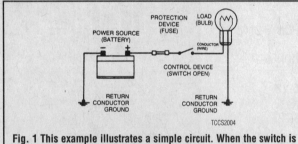

Fig. 1 This example illustrates a simple circuit. When the switch is closed, power from the positive (+) battery terminal flows through the fuse and the switch, and then to the light bulb. The light illuminates and the circuit is completed through the ground wire back to the negative (-) battery terminal. In reality, the two ground points shown in the illustration are attached to the metal frame of the vehicle, which completes the circuit back to the battery

HOW DOES ELECTRICITY WORK: THE WATER ANALOGY

Electricity is the flow of electrons—the subatomic particles that constitute the outer shell of an atom. Electrons spin in an orbit around the center core of an atom. The center core is comprised of protons (positive charge) and neutrons (neutral charge). Electrons have a negative charge and balance out the positive charge of the protons. When an outside force causes the number of electrons to unbalance the charge of the protons, the electrons will split off the atom and look for another atom to balance out. If this imbalance is kept up, electrons will continue to move and an electrical flow will exist.

Many people have been taught electrical theory using an analogy with water. In a comparison with water flowing through a pipe, the electrons would be the water and the wire is the pipe.

The flow of electricity can be measured much like the flow of water through a pipe. The unit of measurement used is amperes, frequently abbreviated as amps (a). You can compare amperage to the volume of water flowing through a pipe. When connected to a circuit, an ammeter will measure the actual amount of current flowing through the circuit. When relatively few electrons flow through a circuit, the amperage is low. When many electrons flow, the amperage is high.

Water pressure is measured in units such as pounds per square inch (psi);

The electrical pressure is measured in units called volts (v). When a voltmeter is connected to a circuit, it is measuring the electrical pressure.

The actual flow of electricity depends not only on voltage and amperage, but also on the resistance of the circuit. The higher the resistance, the higher the force necessary to push the current through the circuit. The standard unit for measuring resistance is an ohm. Resistance in a circuit varies depending on the amount and type of components used in the circuit. The main factors which determine resistance are:

• Material—some materials have more resistance than others. Those with high resistance are said to be insulators. Rubber materials (or rubber-like plastics) are some of the most common insulators used in vehicles as they have a very high resistance to electricity. Very low resistance materials are said to be conductors. Copper wire is among the best conductors. Silver is actually a superior conductor to copper and is used in some relay contacts, but its high cost prohibits its use as common wiring. Most automotive wiring is made of copper.

• Size—the larger the wire size being used, the less resistance the wire will have. This is why components which use large amounts of electricity usually have large wires supplying current to them.

• Length—for a given thickness of wire, the longer the wire, the greater the resistance. The shorter the wire, the less the resistance. When determining the proper wire for a circuit, both size and length must be considered to design a circuit that can handle the current needs of the component.

• Temperature—with many materials, the higher the temperature, the greater the resistance (positive temperature coefficient). Some materials exhibit the opposite trait of lower resistance with higher temperatures (negative temperature coefficient). These principles are used in many of the sensors on the engine.

OHM'S LAW

There is a direct relationship between current, voltage and resistance. The relationship between current, voltage and resistance can be summed up by a statement known as Ohm's law.

Voltage (E) is equal to amperage (I) times resistance (R): $E = I \times R$
Other forms of the formula are $R = E/I$ and $I = E/R$

In each of these formulas, E is the voltage in volts, I is the current in amps and R is the resistance in ohms. The basic point to remember is that as the resistance of a circuit goes up, the amount of current that flows in the circuit will go down, if voltage remains the same.

The amount of work that the electricity can perform is expressed as power. The unit of power is the watt (w). The relationship between power, voltage and current is expressed as:

Power (w) is equal to amperage (I) times voltage (E): $W = I \times E$

This is only true for direct current (DC) circuits; The alternating current formula is a tad different, but since the electrical circuits in most vehicles are DC type, we need not get into AC circuit theory.

Electrical Components

POWER SOURCE

Power is supplied to the vehicle by two devices: The battery and the alternator. The battery supplies electrical power during starting or during periods when the current demand of the vehicle's electrical system exceeds the output capacity of the alternator. The alternator supplies electrical current when the engine is running. Just not does the alternator supply the current needs of the vehicle, but it recharges the battery.

The Battery

In most modern vehicles, the battery is a lead/acid electrochemical device consisting of six 2 volt subsections (cells) connected in series, so that the unit is capable of producing approximately 12 volts of electrical pressure. Each subsection consists of a series of positive and negative plates held a short distance apart in a solution of sulfuric acid and water.

The two types of plates are of dissimilar metals. This sets up a chemical reaction, and it is this reaction which produces current flow from the battery when its positive and negative terminals are connected to an electrical load. The power removed from the battery is replaced by the alternator, restoring the battery to its original chemical state.

The Alternator

On some vehicles there isn't an alternator, but a generator. The difference is that an alternator supplies alternating current which is then changed to direct current for use on the vehicle, while a generator produces direct current. Alternators tend to be more efficient and that is why they are used.

Alternators and generators are devices that consist of coils of wires wound together making big electromagnets. One group of coils spins within another set and the interaction of the magnetic fields causes a current to flow. This current is then drawn off the coils and fed into the vehicles electrical system.

GROUND

Two types of grounds are used in automotive electric circuits. Direct ground components are grounded to the frame through their mounting points. All other components use some sort of ground wire which is attached to the frame or chassis of the vehicle. The electrical current runs through the chassis of the vehicle and returns to the battery through the ground (-) cable; if you look, you'll see that the battery ground cable connects between the battery and the frame or chassis of the vehicle.

➡️It should be noted that a good percentage of electrical problems can be traced to bad grounds.

PROTECTIVE DEVICES

▶ See Figure 2

It is possible for large surges of current to pass through the electrical system of your vehicle. If this surge of current were to reach the load in the circuit, the surge could burn it out or severely damage it. It can also overload the wiring, causing the harness to get hot and melt the insulation. To prevent this, fuses,

circuit breakers and/or fusible links are connected into the supply wires of the electrical system. These items are nothing more than a built-in weak spot in the system. When an abnormal amount of current flows through the system, these protective devices work as follows to protect the circuit:

• Fuse—when an excessive electrical current passes through a fuse, the fuse "blows" (the conductor melts) and opens the circuit, preventing the passage of current.

• Circuit Breaker—a circuit breaker is basically a self-repairing fuse. It will open the circuit in the same fashion as a fuse, but when the surge subsides, the circuit breaker can be reset and does not need replacement.

• Fusible Link—a fusible link (fuse link or main link) is a short length of special, high temperature insulated wire that acts as a fuse. When an excessive electrical current passes through a fusible link, the thin gauge wire inside the link melts, creating an intentional open to protect the circuit. To repair the circuit, the link must be replaced. Some newer type fusible links are housed in plug-in modules, which are simply replaced like a fuse, while older type fusible links must be cut and spliced if they melt. Since this link is very early in the electrical path, it's the first place to look if nothing on the vehicle works, yet the battery seems to be charged and is properly connected.

✳️ CAUTION

Always replace fuses, circuit breakers and fusible links with identically rated components. Under no circumstances should a component of higher or lower amperage rating be substituted.

SWITCHES & RELAYS

▶ See Figures 3 and 4

Switches are used in electrical circuits to control the passage of current. The most common use is to open and close circuits between the battery and the various electric devices in the system. Switches are rated according to the amount of amperage they can handle. If a sufficient amperage rated switch is not used in a circuit, the switch could overload and cause damage.

Some electrical components which require a large amount of current to operate use a special switch called a relay. Since these circuits carry a large amount of current, the thickness of the wire in the circuit is also greater. If this large wire were connected from the load to the control switch, the switch would have to carry the high amperage load and the fairing or dash would be twice as large to accommodate the increased size of the wiring harness. To prevent these problems, a relay is used.

Relays are composed of a coil and a set of contacts. When the coil has a current passed though it, a magnetic field is formed and this field causes the contacts to move together, completing the circuit. Most relays are normally open, preventing current from passing through the circuit, but they can take any electrical form depending on the job they are intended to do. Relays can be considered "remote control switches." They allow a smaller current to operate devices that require higher amperages. When a small current operates the coil, a larger

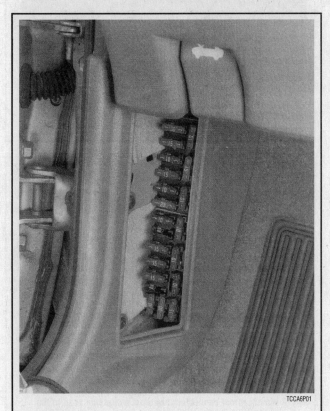

Fig. 2 Most vehicles use one or more fuse panels. This one is located on the driver's side kick panel

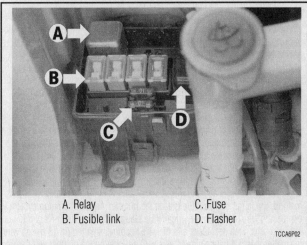

A. Relay   C. Fuse
B. Fusible link   D. Flasher

Fig. 3 The underhood fuse and relay panel usually contains fuses, relays, flashers and fusible links

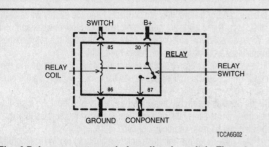

Fig. 4 Relays are composed of a coil and a switch. These two components are linked together so that when one operates, the other operates at the same time. The large wires in the circuit are connected from the battery to one side of the relay switch (B+) and from the opposite side of the relay switch to the load (component). Smaller wires are connected from the relay coil to the control switch for the circuit and from the opposite side of the relay coil to ground

current is allowed to pass by the contacts. Some common circuits which may use relays are the horn, headlights, starter, electric fuel pump and other high draw ciruits.

LOAD

Every electrical circuit must include a "load" (something to use the electricity coming from the source). Without this load, the battery would attempt to deliver its entire power supply from one pole to another. This is called a "short circuit." All this electricity would take a short cut to ground and cause a great amount of damage to other components in the circuit by developing a tremendous amount of heat. This condition could develop sufficient heat to melt the insulation on all the surrounding wires and reduce a multiple wire cable to a lump of plastic and copper.

WIRING & HARNESSES

The average vehicle contains meters and meters of wiring, with hundreds of individual connections. To protect the many wires from damage and to keep them from becoming a confusing tangle, they are organized into bundles, enclosed in plastic or taped together and called wiring harnesses. Different harnesses serve different parts of the vehicle. Individual wires are color coded to help trace them through a harness where sections are hidden from view.

Automotive wiring or circuit conductors can be either single strand wire, multi-strand wire or printed circuitry. Single strand wire has a solid metal core and is usually used inside such components as alternators, motors, relays and other devices. Multi-strand wire has a core made of many small strands of wire twisted together into a single conductor. Most of the wiring in an automotive electrical system is made up of multi-strand wire, either as a single conductor or grouped together in a harness. All wiring is color coded on the insulator, either as a solid color or as a colored wire with an identification stripe. A printed circuit is a thin film of copper or other conductor that is printed on an insulator backing. Occasionally, a printed circuit is sandwiched between two sheets of plastic for more protection and flexibility. A complete printed circuit, consisting of conductors, insulating material and connectors for lamps or other components is called a printed circuit board. Printed circuitry is used in place of individual wires or harnesses in places where space is limited, such as behind instrument panels.

Since automotive electrical systems are very sensitive to changes in resistance, the selection of properly sized wires is critical when systems are repaired. A loose or corroded connection or a replacement wire that is too small for the circuit will add extra resistance and an additional voltage drop to the circuit.

The wire gauge number is an expression of the cross-section area of the conductor. Vehicles from countries that use the metric system will typically describe the wire size as its cross-sectional area in square millimeters. In this method, the larger the wire, the greater the number. Another common system for expressing wire size is the American Wire Gauge (AWG) system. As gauge number increases, area decreases and the wire becomes smaller. An 18 gauge wire is smaller than a 4 gauge wire. A wire with a higher gauge number will carry less current than a wire with a lower gauge number. Gauge wire size refers to the size of the strands of the conductor, not the size of the complete wire with

insulator. It is possible, therefore, to have two wires of the same gauge with different diameters because one may have thicker insulation than the other.

It is essential to understand how a circuit works before trying to figure out why it doesn't. An electrical schematic shows the electrical current paths when a circuit is operating properly. Schematics break the entire electrical system down into individual circuits. In a schematic, usually no attempt is made to represent wiring and components as they physically appear on the vehicle; switches and other components are shown as simply as possible. Face views of harness connectors show the cavity or terminal locations in all multi-pin connectors to help locate test points.

CONNECTORS

▶ **See Figures 5 and 6**

Three types of connectors are commonly used in automotive applications—weatherproof, molded and hard shell.

• Weatherproof—these connectors are most commonly used where the connector is exposed to the elements. Terminals are protected against moisture and dirt by sealing rings which provide a weathertight seal. All repairs require the use of a special terminal and the tool required to service it. Unlike standard blade type terminals, these weatherproof terminals cannot be straightened once they are bent. Make certain that the connectors are properly seated and all of the sealing rings are in place when connecting leads.

• Molded—these connectors require complete replacement of the connector if found to be defective. This means splicing a new connector assembly into the harness. All splices should be soldered to insure proper contact. Use care when probing the connections or replacing terminals in them, as it is possible to create a short circuit between opposite terminals. If this happens to the wrong

Fig. 5 Hard shell (left) and weatherproof (right) connectors have replaceable terminals

Fig. 6 Weatherproof connectors are most commonly used in the engine compartment or where the connector is exposed to the elements

terminal pair, it is possible to damage certain components. Always use jumper wires between connectors for circuit checking and NEVER probe through weatherproof seals.

• Hard Shell—unlike molded connectors, the terminal contacts in hardshell connectors can be replaced. Replacement usually involves the use of a special terminal removal tool that depresses the locking tangs (barbs) on the connector terminal and allows the connector to be removed from the rear of the shell. The connector shell should be replaced if it shows any evidence of burning, melting, cracks, or breaks. Replace individual terminals that are burnt, corroded, distorted or loose.

Test Equipment

Pinpointing the exact cause of trouble in an electrical circuit is most times accomplished by the use of special test equipment. The following describes different types of commonly used test equipment and briefly explains how to use them in diagnosis. In addition to the information covered below, the tool manufacturer's instructions booklet (provided with the tester) should be read and clearly understood before attempting any test procedures.

JUMPER WIRES

✳✳ CAUTION

Never use jumper wires made from a thinner gauge wire than the circuit being tested. If the jumper wire is of too small a gauge, it may overheat and possibly melt. Never use jumpers to bypass high resistance loads in a circuit. Bypassing resistances, in effect, creates a short circuit. This may, in turn, cause damage and fire. Jumper wires should only be used to bypass lengths of wire or to simulate switches.

Jumper wires are simple, yet extremely valuable, pieces of test equipment. They are basically test wires which are used to bypass sections of a circuit. Although jumper wires can be purchased, they are usually fabricated from lengths of standard automotive wire and whatever type of connector (alligator clip, spade connector or pin connector) that is required for the particular application being tested. In cramped, hard-to-reach areas, it is advisable to have insulated boots over the jumper wire terminals in order to prevent accidental grounding. It is also advisable to include a standard automotive fuse in any jumper wire. This is commonly referred to as a "fused jumper". By inserting an in-line fuse holder between a set of test leads, a fused jumper wire can be used for bypassing open circuits. Use a 5 amp fuse to provide protection against voltage spikes.

Jumper wires are used primarily to locate open electrical circuits, on either the ground (-) side of the circuit or on the power (+) side. If an electrical component fails to operate, connect the jumper wire between the component and a good ground. If the component operates only with the jumper installed, the ground circuit is open. If the ground circuit is good, but the component does not operate, the circuit between the power feed and component may be open. By moving the jumper wire successively back from the component toward the power source, you can isolate the area of the circuit where the open is located. When the component stops functioning, or the power is cut off, the open is in the segment of wire between the jumper and the point previously tested.

You can sometimes connect the jumper wire directly from the battery to the "hot" terminal of the component, but first make sure the component uses 12 volts in operation. Some electrical components, such as fuel injectors or sensors, are designed to operate on about 4 to 5 volts, and running 12 volts directly to these components will cause damage.

TEST LIGHTS

◆ See Figure 7

The test light is used to check circuits and components while electrical current is flowing through them. It is used for voltage and ground tests. To use a 12 volt test light, connect the ground clip to a good ground and probe wherever necessary with the pick. The test light will illuminate when voltage is detected. This does not necessarily mean that 12 volts (or any particular amount of voltage) is present; it only means that some voltage is present. It is advisable before using the test light to touch its ground clip and probe across the battery posts or terminals to make sure the light is operating properly.

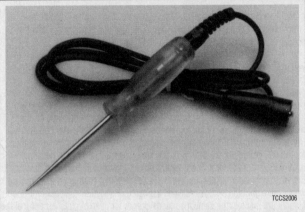

TCCS2006

Fig. 7 A 12 volt test light is used to detect the presence of voltage in a circuit

✳✳ WARNING

Do not use a test light to probe electronic ignition, spark plug or coil wires. Never use a pick-type test light to probe wiring on computer controlled systems unless specifically instructed to do so. Any wire insulation that is pierced by the test light probe should be taped and sealed with silicone after testing.

Like the jumper wire, the 12 volt test light is used to isolate opens in circuits. But, whereas the jumper wire is used to bypass the open to operate the load, the 12 volt test light is used to locate the presence of voltage in a circuit. If the test light illuminates, there is power up to that point in the circuit; if the test light does not illuminate, there is an open circuit (no power). Move the test light in successive steps back toward the power source until the light in the handle illuminates. The open is between the probe and a point which was previously probed.

The self-powered test light is similar in design to the 12 volt test light, but contains a 1.5 volt penlight battery in the handle. It is most often used in place of a multimeter to check for open or short circuits when power is isolated from the circuit (continuity test).

The battery in a self-powered test light does not provide much current. A weak battery may not provide enough power to illuminate the test light even when a complete circuit is made (especially if there is high resistance in the circuit). Always make sure that the test battery is strong. To check the battery, briefly touch the ground clip to the probe; if the light glows brightly, the battery is strong enough for testing.

➡**A self-powered test light should not be used on any computer controlled system or component. The small amount of electricity transmitted by the test light is enough to damage many electronic automotive components.**

MULTIMETERS

Multimeters are an extremely useful tool for troubleshooting electrical problems. They can be purchased in either analog or digital form and have a price range to suit any budget. A multimeter is a voltmeter, ammeter and ohmmeter (along with other features) combined into one instrument. It is often used when testing solid state circuits because of its high input impedance (usually 10 megaohms or more). A brief description of the multimeter main test functions follows:

• Voltmeter—the voltmeter is used to measure voltage at any point in a circuit, or to measure the voltage drop across any part of a circuit. Voltmeters usually have various scales and a selector switch to allow the reading of different voltage ranges. The voltmeter has a positive and a negative lead. To avoid damage to the meter, always connect the negative lead to the negative (-) side of the circuit (to ground or nearest the ground side of the circuit) and connect the positive lead to the positive (+) side of the circuit (to the power source or the nearest power source). Note that the negative voltmeter lead will always be black and that the positive voltmeter will always be some color other than black (usually red).

• Ohmmeter—the ohmmeter is designed to read resistance (measured in ohms) in a circuit or component. Most ohmmeters will have a selector switch which permits the measurement of different ranges of resistance (usually the selector switch allows the multiplication of the meter reading by 10, 100, 1,000 and 10,000). Some ohmmeters are "auto-ranging" which means the meter itself will determine which scale to use. Since the meters are powered by an internal battery, the ohmmeter can be used like a self-powered test light. When the ohmmeter is connected, current from the ohmmeter flows through the circuit or component being tested. Since the ohmmeter's internal resistance and voltage are known values, the amount of current flow through the meter depends on the resistance of the circuit or component being tested. The ohmmeter can also be used to perform a continuity test for suspected open circuits. In using the meter for making continuity checks, do not be concerned with the actual resistance readings. Zero resistance, or any ohm reading, indicates continuity in the circuit. Infinite resistance indicates an opening in the circuit. A high resistance reading where there should be none indicates a problem in the circuit. Checks for short circuits are made in the same manner as checks for open circuits, except that the circuit must be isolated from both power and normal ground. Infinite resistance indicates no continuity, while zero resistance indicates a dead short.

✳✳ WARNING

Never use an ohmmeter to check the resistance of a component or wire while there is voltage applied to the circuit.

• Ammeter—an ammeter measures the amount of current flowing through a circuit in units called amperes or amps. At normal operating voltage, most circuits have a characteristic amount of amperes, called "current draw" which can be measured using an ammeter. By referring to a specified current draw rating, then measuring the amperes and comparing the two values, one can determine what is happening within the circuit to aid in diagnosis. An open circuit, for example, will not allow any current to flow, so the ammeter reading will be zero. A damaged component or circuit will have an increased current draw, so the reading will be high. The ammeter is always connected in series with the circuit being tested. All of the current that normally flows through the circuit must also flow through the ammeter; if there is any other path for the current to follow, the ammeter reading will not be accurate. The ammeter itself has very little resistance to current flow and, therefore, will not affect the circuit, but it will measure current draw only when the circuit is closed and electricity is flowing. Excessive current draw can blow fuses and drain the battery, while a reduced current draw can cause motors to run slowly, lights to dim and other components to not operate properly.

Troubleshooting Electrical Systems

When diagnosing a specific problem, organized troubleshooting is a must. The complexity of a modern automotive vehicle demands that you approach any problem in a logical, organized manner. There are certain troubleshooting techniques, however, which are standard:

• Establish when the problem occurs. Does the problem appear only under certain conditions? Were there any noises, odors or other unusual symptoms? Isolate the problem area. To do this, make some simple tests and observations, then eliminate the systems that are working properly. Check for obvious problems, such as broken wires and loose or dirty connections. Always check the obvious before assuming something complicated is the cause.

• Test for problems systematically to determine the cause once the problem area is isolated. Are all the components functioning properly? Is there power going to electrical switches and motors. Performing careful, systematic checks will often turn up most causes on the first inspection, without wasting time checking components that have little or no relationship to the problem.

• Test all repairs after the work is done to make sure that the problem is fixed. Some causes can be traced to more than one component, so a careful verification of repair work is important in order to pick up additional malfunctions that may cause a problem to reappear or a different problem to arise. A blown fuse, for example, is a simple problem that may require more than another fuse to repair. If you don't look for a problem that caused a fuse to blow, a shorted wire (for example) may go undetected.

Experience has shown that most problems tend to be the result of a fairly simple and obvious cause, such as loose or corroded connectors, bad grounds or damaged wire insulation which causes a short. This makes careful visual inspection of components during testing essential to quick and accurate troubleshooting.

Testing

OPEN CIRCUITS

▸ **See Figure 8**

This test already assumes the existence of an open in the circuit and it is used to help locate the open portion.

1. Isolate the circuit from power and ground.
2. Connect the self-powered test light or ohmmeter ground clip to the ground side of the circuit and probe sections of the circuit sequentially.
3. If the light is out or there is infinite resistance, the open is between the probe and the circuit ground.
4. If the light is on or the meter shows continuity, the open is between the probe and the end of the circuit toward the power source.

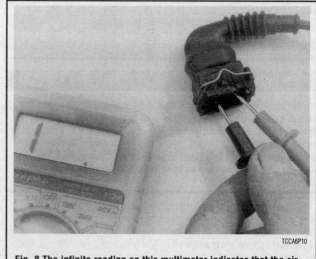

TCCA6P10

Fig. 8 The infinite reading on this multimeter indicates that the circuit is open

SHORT CIRCUITS

➡**Never use a self-powered test light to perform checks for opens or shorts when power is applied to the circuit under test. The test light can be damaged by outside power.**

1. Isolate the circuit from power and ground.
2. Connect the self-powered test light or ohmmeter ground clip to a good ground and probe any easy-to-reach point in the circuit.
3. If the light comes on or there is continuity, there is a short somewhere in the circuit.
4. To isolate the short, probe a test point at either end of the isolated circuit (the light should be on or the meter should indicate continuity).
5. Leave the test light probe engaged and sequentially open connectors or switches, remove parts, etc. until the light goes out or continuity is broken.
6. When the light goes out, the short is between the last two circuit components which were opened.

VOLTAGE

This test determines voltage available from the battery and should be the first step in any electrical troubleshooting procedure after visual inspection. Many electrical problems, especially on computer controlled systems, can be caused by a low state of charge in the battery. Excessive corrosion at the battery cable terminals can cause poor contact that will prevent proper charging and full battery current flow.

1. Set the voltmeter selector switch to the 20V position.
2. Connect the multimeter negative lead to the battery's negative (-) post or terminal and the positive lead to the battery's positive (+) post or terminal.
3. Turn the ignition switch **ON** to provide a load.

4. A well charged battery should register over 12 volts. If the meter reads below 11.5 volts, the battery power may be insufficient to operate the electrical system properly.

VOLTAGE DROP

▶ See Figure 9

When current flows through a load, the voltage beyond the load drops. This voltage drop is due to the resistance created by the load and also by small resistances created by corrosion at the connectors and damaged insulation on the wires. The maximum allowable voltage drop under load is critical, especially if there is more than one load in the circuit, since all voltage drops are cumulative.

1. Set the voltmeter selector switch to the 20 volt position.
2. Connect the multimeter negative lead to a good ground.
3. Operate the circuit and check the voltage prior to the first component (load).
4. There should be little or no voltage drop in the circuit prior to the first component. If a voltage drop exists, the wire or connectors in the circuit are suspect.
5. While operating the first component in the circuit, probe the ground side of the component with the positive meter lead and observe the voltage readings. A small voltage drop should be noticed. This voltage drop is caused by the resistance of the component.
6. Repeat the test for each component (load) down the circuit.
7. If a large voltage drop is noticed, the preceding component, wire or connector is suspect.

Fig. 10 Checking the resistance of a coolant temperature sensor with an ohmmeter. Reading is 1.04 kilohms

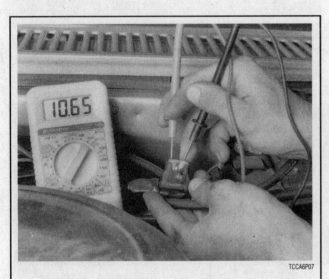

Fig. 9 This voltage drop test revealed high resistance (low voltage) in the circuit

RESISTANCE

▶ See Figures 10 and 11

※ WARNING

Never use an ohmmeter with power applied to the circuit. The ohmmeter is designed to operate on its own power supply. The normal 12 volt electrical system voltage could damage the meter!

1. Isolate the circuit from the vehicle's power source.
2. Ensure that the ignition key is **OFF** when disconnecting any components or the battery.
3. Where necessary, also isolate at least one side of the circuit to be checked, in order to avoid reading parallel resistances. Parallel circuit resistances will always give a lower reading than the actual resistance of either of the branches.
4. Connect the meter leads to both sides of the circuit (wire or component) and read the actual measured ohms on the meter scale. Make sure the selector switch is set to the proper ohm scale for the circuit being tested, to avoid misreading the ohmmeter test value.

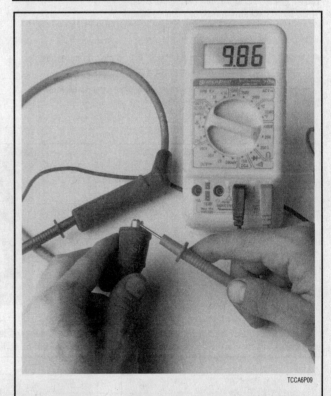

Fig. 11 Spark plug wires can be checked for excessive resistance using an ohmmeter

Wire and Connector Repair

Almost anyone can replace damaged wires, as long as the proper tools and parts are available. Wire and terminals are available to fit almost any need. Even the specialized weatherproof, molded and hard shell connectors are now available from aftermarket suppliers.

Be sure the ends of all the wires are fitted with the proper terminal hardware and connectors. Wrapping a wire around a stud is never a permanent solution and will only cause trouble later. Replace wires one at a time to avoid confusion. Always route wires exactly the same as the factory.

➡️ **If connector repair is necessary, only attempt it if you have the proper tools. Weatherproof and hard shell connectors require special tools to release the pins inside the connector. Attempting to repair these connectors with conventional hand tools will damage them.**

HEATING AND AIR CONDITIONING

❄ CAUTION

Please refer to Section 1 of this manual before discharging/recovering the A/C system or disconnecting air conditioning lines. Damage to the air conditioning system or personal injury could result. Consult your local laws concerning refrigerant discharge and recycling. In many areas it may be illegal for anyone but a certified technician to service the A/C system. Always use an approved recovery station when discharging the air conditioning.

Blower Motor

REMOVAL & INSTALLATION

▶ **See Figures 12, 13, 14 and 15**

1. Disconnect the negative battery cable.
2. If necessary on MFI-Turbo vehicles, remove the charge air cooler. For details, please refer to Section 3 of this manual.
3. Disconnect the blower motor cooling tube.
4. Disengage the electrical connector(s) from the blower motor, as necessary.

➡**On some earlier models equipped with A/C, it may be necessary to remove the A/C vacuum tank and move it aside.**

5. Remove the blower motor-to-case screws, then carefully withdraw the blower motor from the case.
6. Installation is the reverse of removal.

Heater Core

The heater core is removable from under the right side of the instrument panel.

REMOVAL & INSTALLATION

▶ **See Figures 16 thru 23**

1. Disconnect the negative battery cable.
2. Position a drain pan under the radiator, open the drain cock and drain the cooling system to a level below the heater core.

➡**Plug the heater core tubes to avoid spilling coolant in the passenger compartment during removal.**

3. Disconnect the heater-to-engine coolant hoses from the core tubes on the fire wall, in the engine compartment.

➡**On some early model vehicles, the cabin light mounted under the dash may interfere with cover removal. If necessary, loosen the retaining bolt and reposition the light housing with the wiring attached.**

4. From the passenger compartment (under the dash) remove the heater core rear case cover-to-cowl screws, then remove the cover from the vehicle.

➡**On a few of the early model vehicles covered by this manual, some of the heater core cover screws may be partially/fully covered by the dashboard. Be sure that all are removed before attempting to remove the cover. If necessary, unbolt and reposition all/part of the dashboard for better access.**

85386002

Fig. 12 Disconnect the blower motor cooling tube

85386003

Fig. 13 Disengage the necessary electrical connector(s) from the blower motor

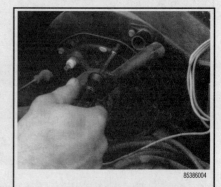
85386004

Fig. 14 Loosen and remove the blower motor retaining screws

85386005

Fig. 15 Withdraw the blower motor from the case

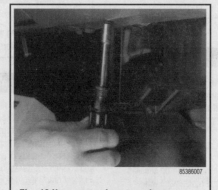
85386007

Fig. 16 If necessary loosen and remove the under dash cabin light retaining bolt

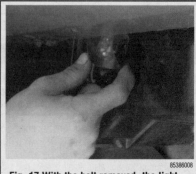
85386008

Fig. 17 With the bolt removed, the light and housing may be repositioned out of the way

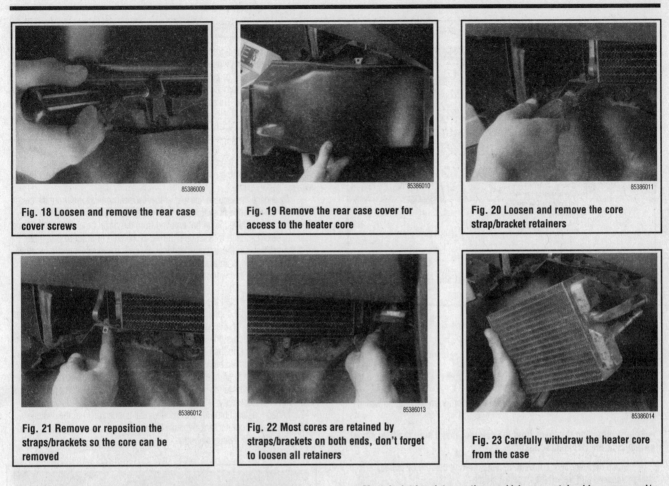

Fig. 18 Loosen and remove the rear case cover screws

Fig. 19 Remove the rear case cover for access to the heater core

Fig. 20 Loosen and remove the core strap/bracket retainers

Fig. 21 Remove or reposition the straps/brackets so the core can be removed

Fig. 22 Most cores are retained by straps/brackets on both ends, don't forget to loosen all retainers

Fig. 23 Carefully withdraw the heater core from the case

5. Remove the straps or brackets from each end of the heater core.

6. Carefully remove the heater core from the cowl and case.

7. Installation is the reveres of removal. Run the engine at normal operating temperatures and check for leaks.

Control Head

REMOVAL & INSTALLATION

1. Disconnect the negative battery cable.

2. Remove the instrument panel trim plate or accessory trim plate, as applicable.

➡Most dash trim plates on these vehicles are retained by screws and/or snap fasteners. Make sure all screws are removed before attempting to remove the trim plate. If retained by snap fasteners, it may be necessary to pry the plate loose, BUT take care not to force and break the usually fragile plastic pieces.

3. Remove the control head-to-instrument panel screws, then pull the control head from the instrument panel.

4. Disconnect the vacuum hoses, electrical connectors and/or the control cables from the control head, as applicable. Make sure each connection may be only made 1 way, or tag hoses/wires and cables before removal.

5. Remove the control head assembly from the vehicle.

6. If necessary, remove the blower switch knob and spring clip, then remove the switch form the control head.

7. To install, reverse the removal procedures.

CRUISE CONTROL

Cruise Control Actuator Switch

REMOVAL & INSTALLATION

The cruise control actuator switch on most S/T vehicles with factory or dealer installed systems is part of the multi-function lever located on the steering column.

Vehicles Through 1992

▶ See Figure 24

1. Disconnect the negative battery cable.

2. Disengage the lever electrical connector (down towards the base of the column).

3. Remove or reposition the harness protector cover for access, then attach a length of piano or mechanic's wire to the connector.

➡On some vehicles removal and installation of the wiring and lever assembly may be easier if the shift lever is positioned in Low, the turn signal switch is in the RIGHT TURN position and tilt columns are placed in the FULL UP position.

4. Carefully pull the multi-function lever from the turn signal switch. Once the lever is free from the steering column, carefully pull the harness connector and length of wire through the column. Leave the wire in the column to pull the wiring into position during installation.

To install:

5. Attach the lever connector and wiring to the length of wire in the steering column, then carefully pull the harness through the column and into position.

6. Insert the multi-function lever to the turn signal.

7. Remove the length of wire from the harness connector, then reposition and secure the protector cover.

8. Engage the lever wiring harness connector.

9. Connect the negative battery cable and check for proper lever operation.

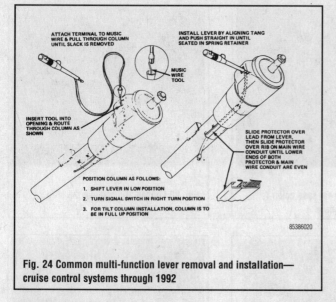

Fig. 24 Common multi-function lever removal and installation— cruise control systems through 1992

1993 Vehicles

▶ **See Figure 25**

1. Disconnect the negative battery cable.
2. Unsnap and remove the housing cover cap from the steering column for access to the wiring.
3. Disengage the cruise control wiring connectors from the column wiring harness.

➡ **Before removing the lever from the column, make sure the turn signal switch is in the OFF/center position.**

4. Grasp the lever and remove it from the steering column by pulling straight outward and from the turn signal switch.

To install:

5. With the switch in the center/OFF position, carefully push the lever into the turn signal switch on the column.
6. Engage the cruise control wiring connectors to the column wiring.
7. Snap the housing cover cap into position on the column.
8. Connect the negative battery cable and check for proper operation.

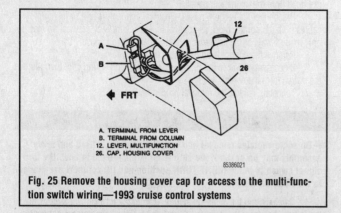

A. TERMINAL FROM LEVER
B. TERMINAL FROM COLUMN
12. LEVER, MULTIFUNCTION
26. CAP, HOUSING COVER

Fig. 25 Remove the housing cover cap for access to the multi-function switch wiring—1993 cruise control systems

Brake/Clutch Release Switches

All factory or dealer installed cruise control systems for these vehicles are equipped with either a brake or clutch release switch. The purpose of the switch is to deactivate the system when the driver begins to depress the pedal. Most of the switches found on earlier models are vacuum break switches (vacuum release valves) which will therefore have a vacuum line attached to the rear or side of the switch. A vacuum break switch is used to quickly vent vacuum to the atmosphere so a vacuum controlled servo may return the throttle to the idle position. Later models may use a vacuum switch, an electric switch or a com-

bined vacuum and electric switch, depending upon the model and application. Some vehicles may combine the cruise control release and stoplamp (brake light) switches into a single component with multiple connections. Electric switches are commonly used to disengage the cruise control by either completing/breaking a circuit or by signalling a control module.

All switches are normally mounted using an interference clip which holds ribs on the switches neck. These switches are self-adjusting when installed properly.

REMOVAL & INSTALLATION

▶ **See Figure 26**

1. If equipped with an electric or vacuum/electric switch, disconnect the negative battery cable.
2. Disengage the vacuum line and/or the electrical connector(s) from the switch.
3. For interference fit switches, grasp the switch and withdraw it from the clip. If necessary the clip can be removed from the pedal bracket as well. Some clips are designed with lock tangs and may be pivoted in order to pull them from the bracket. On these, you may twist the switch and retainer clip together and withdraw them as an assembly. Other clips are also an interference fit and must be squeezed and withdrawn.

To install:

4. If removed, install the retainer to the pedal bracket.
5. With the pedal depressed so it will not interfere, insert and fully seat the switch into the clip on the pedal bracket.
6. In order to adjust the switch, grasp the pedal and pull it fully back against the stop. While pulling the pedal backwards, a clicking sound should be heard as the switch is pushed backwards in the clip until it is in the proper position. Make sure the switch plunger is seated when the pedal is released and that the plunger fully extends as the pedal is depressed. Check the switch operation and adjust again, if necessary.
7. Engage the vacuum line and/or electrical connector(s) to the switch.
8. If removed, connect the negative battery cable.
9. Verify proper switch operation.

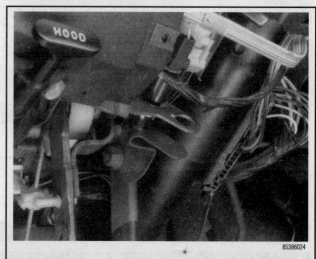

Fig. 26 View of an early model, combined cruise control/brake light switch

ADJUSTMENT

Clip mounted switches should be found on all factory and dealer installed systems through 1993. Clip mounted switches are automatically adjusted during installation. The clip holds the switch in position by the raised ribs located on the switch's neck.

Vacuum Servo

Most factory or dealer installed cruise control systems for these vehicles utilize a vacuum servo to rotate the throttle plate and hold engine speed. The servo is connected to the throttle plate by linkage, either a chain, rod or cable.

REMOVAL & INSTALLATION

▶ **See Figure 27**

1. Disconnect the negative battery cable.
2. Disengage the electrical connector(s) from the servo, as applicable.
3. Disconnect the vacuum line from the servo assembly.
4. Disconnect the servo linkage.
5. Remove the servo and bracket assembly retaining bolts, then remove the servo from the vehicle.

To install:

6. Install the servo and bracket assembly, then secure using the retaining bolts.
7. Connect and adjust the servo linkage.
8. Install the vacuum line to the servo assembly.
9. Engage the necessary electrical connector(s).
10. Connect the negative battery cable.

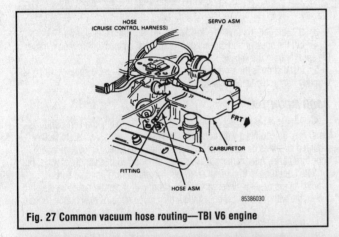

Fig. 27 Common vacuum hose routing—TBI V6 engine

ADJUSTMENT

The vacuum servo linkage is usually adjusted either by jamnuts or by a servo blade which contains various adjustment holes. In either case, once the engine is fully warmed, position the cable or rod so it is tight, with little slack, but NOT holding the throttle open. For vehicles equipped with the servo blade, if the desired hole seems to open the throttle, take the next hole on the blade in order to leave the required slack. It would be better for the adjustment to be on the loose side rather than on the tight side of proper adjustment.

Cruise Control Module

REMOVAL & INSTALLATION

The cruise control module is used to control operation of the system. The module monitors speed and servo position and operates the vacuum and vent valves located in the servo in order to maintain the desired speed. The module is usually located on or near the pedal bracket, under the instrument panel.

1. Disconnect the negative battery cable.
2. Disengage the electrical wiring from the module.

➡**On most applications, the module is retained by a clip. Pry back on the clip in and slide the module from the bracket.**

3. Remove the module from the retaining bracket.
4. If necessary, remove the bracket from the vehicle.

To install:

5. If removed, install the retaining bracket.
6. Install the module to the bracket.
7. Engage the electrical wiring to the module.
8. Connect the negative battery cable.

ENTERTAINMENT SYSTEMS

Radio

REMOVAL & INSTALLATION

▶ **See Figures 28 thru 34**

1. Disconnect the negative battery cable.
2. Remove the ash tray.
3. Remove the accessory trim plate.

➡**Most dash trim plates on these vehicles are retained by screws and/or snap fasteners. Make sure all screws are removed before attempting to remove the trim plate. If retained by snap fasteners, it may be necessary to pry the plate loose, BUT take care not to force and break the usually fragile plastic pieces.**

❊❊ WARNING

On early model vehicles, DO NOT let the antenna cable touch the clock connector. It is very important when changing speakers or performing any radio work to avoid pinching the wires. A short circuit-to-ground from any wire will cause damage to the output circuit in the radio.

4. Remove the radio bracket-to-instrument panel bracket screws or nuts, then carefully pull the radio forward.
5. Disengage the antenna lead and electrical connectors, as necessary.
6. Remove the radio from the vehicle.
7. Installation is the reverse of removal.

Fig. 28 Remove the accessory trim plate retainers

Fig. 29 With the retainers removed or snap fasteners released, pull the trim plate from the dash

Fig. 30 On most vehicles, access to the control head and radio is possible with the trim plate removed

Fig. 31 Loosen and remove the radio fasteners

Fig. 32 Pull the radio forward to access the electrical connections

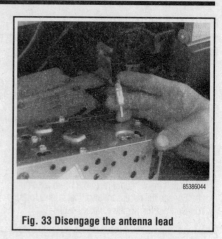

Fig. 33 Disengage the antenna lead

Fig. 34 Disengage the electrical connector(s) and remove the radio from the vehicle

Speakers

REMOVAL & INSTALLATION

Front

INSTRUMENT PANEL MOUNTED

Most early model trucks were equipped with instrument panel (dash) mounted speakers.
1. Disconnect the negative battery cable
2. Remove the front speaker grille screws, then lift and remove the grille.

➡On most earlier models, the grille screws retained the speaker as well. But, always check to make sure no additional fasteners were hidden under the grilles.

3. If equipped, remove the speaker-to-instrument panel screws,
4. Lift the speaker and disengage the electrical connection(s), then remove the speaker from the vehicle.
5. Installation is the reverse of the removal. Make sure the speaker wiring is properly connected before attempting to test the radio.

DOOR MOUNTED

Some later model trucks (or early model trucks with aftermarket sound systems) may be equipped with door mounted radio speakers. Access to factory mounted speakers on late model vehicles usually requires removal of inner door trim panel. Aftermarket speakers may be mounted in a variety of ways, but will often not require trim panel removal. In order to save time, be sure removal of the panel is necessary before starting. If the grille fasteners are accessible with the trim panel installed, then panel removal may not be necessary.
1. Disconnect the negative battery cable
2. For late-model vehicles, remove the door trim panel. On early model vehicles, check for any accessible fasteners on the speaker grille. If the grille can be removed, do that first to see if the speaker may be removed without removing the trim panel. For details on door trim panel removal, please refer to the procedures in Section 10 of this manual.
3. Drill out the heads of the old speaker retaining rivets. Again, aftermarket systems may not contain rivets. If equipped with screws, unthread and remove them.
4. Pull the speaker from the door and disengage the electrical connectors, then remove the speaker from the vehicle.
5. Installation is the reverse of removal. If the speaker was retained with rivets, use new ones to fasten it to the door.

Rear

1. Disconnect the negative battery cable
2. Remove the necessary trim panel for access to the speaker. Lower trim (most regulator cab) or the upper trim panel (extended cab).
3. Disengage the necessary wiring.
4. Remove the speaker retaining nuts.
5. Remove the speaker from the vehicle.
6. Installation is the reverse of removal.

WINDSHIELD WIPERS

Blade and Arm

REMOVAL & INSTALLATION

♦ **See Figures 35, 36 and 37**

1. Matchmark the base of the wiper arm to the linkage. This will assure the arm is installed in the proper position. If the arm is being replaced, transfer the matchmark from the old component to the new one before installation. This can be done by placing the new arm on top of the old one and copying the mark.
2. Most wiper arms are retained by a spring clip. Some are equipped with a release tab at the center which should be depressed to release the arm. If no tab is provided, use a small prybar or a wiper arm removal tool such as J-8966 to depress the spring and release the arm. Remove the arm from the vehicle.
3. Some late model vehicles (all 1993 and some earlier models) are equipped with a wiper arm that utilizes a small release hole at the base of the wiper arm. If equipped, insert a $\frac{1}{8}$ in. drift pin into the tool access hole to

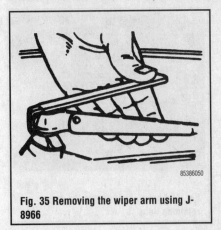

Fig. 35 Removing the wiper arm using J-8966

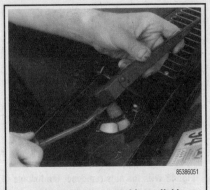

Fig. 36 If no wiper arm tool is available, use a small prytool to depress the spring

Fig. 37 With the spring released, pull the wiper arm from the linkage

release the locking device and allow the arm to be easily pulled from the transmission. If necessary, use a gentle rocking motion to remove the arm.

4. Installation is the reverse of removal. Operate the wipers and verify proper alignment.

Wiper Motor

REMOVAL & INSTALLATION

▶ **See Figures 38 thru 47**

1. Disconnect the negative battery cable.
2. Remove the wiper arms from the linkage so the cowl may be removed.

3. Remove the cowl vent grille and screen. On early model vehicles, the windshield washer hose may be connected to a hard plastic fitting located under the cowl grille. If the hose connection is very tight it may make removing the cowl grille difficult. Take your time if difficulty is encountered. If possible, reach underneath the grille to disconnect the hose from the fitting.

4. Loosen but DO NOT remove the nuts which hold the drive link to the motor crank arm. Detach the drive link from the crank arm.

5. Disengage the wiring from the wiper motor.

6. Remove the wiper motor-to-cowl screws. Carefully rotate the motor and guide the drive link from the hole in the cowl, then remove the motor from the vehicle.

7. Installation is the reverse of removal. Connect the negative battery cable and verify proper operation.

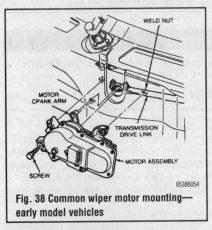

Fig. 38 Common wiper motor mounting—early model vehicles

Fig. 39 Loosen and remove the cowl grille retainers

Fig. 40 The grille may also be bolted along its lower lip

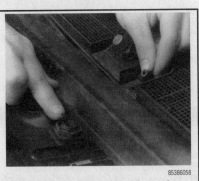

Fig. 41 To remove this grille, the washer hose had to be disconnected from the grille mounted fitting

Fig. 42 Remove the cowl screen

Fig. 43 Disengage the wiper motor electrical wiring

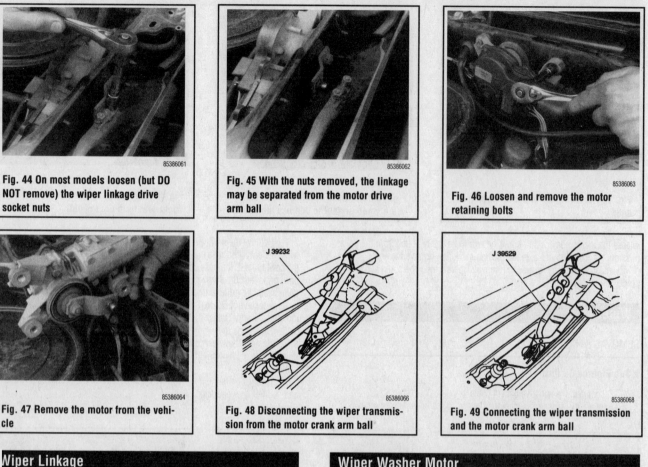

Fig. 44 On most models loosen (but DO NOT remove) the wiper linkage drive socket nuts

Fig. 45 With the nuts removed, the linkage may be separated from the motor drive arm ball

Fig. 46 Loosen and remove the motor retaining bolts

Fig. 47 Remove the motor from the vehicle

Fig. 48 Disconnecting the wiper transmission from the motor crank arm ball

Fig. 49 Connecting the wiper transmission and the motor crank arm ball

Wiper Linkage

REMOVAL & INSTALLATION

▶ **See Figures 48 and 49**

1. Disconnect the negative battery cable.
2. Remove the wiper arms from the linkage so the cowl may be removed.
3. Remove the cowl vent grille and screen. On early model vehicles, the a windshield washer hose may be connected to a hard plastic fitting located under the cowl grille. If the hose connection is very tight it may make removing the cowl grille difficult. Take your time if difficulty is encountered, if possible, reach underneath the grille to disconnect the hose from the fitting.
4. Loosen but DO NOT remove the nuts which hold the drive link to the motor crank arm. Detach the drive link from the crank arm.
5. Remove the transmission linkage-to-cowl retaining screws, then carefully remove the linkage through the top of the cowl.
6. Installation is the reverse of removal. Connect the negative battery cable and verify proper wiper operation.

Wiper Washer Motor

The vehicles covered by this manual utilize a small electric washer pump which is mounted to the bottom of the washer reservoir.

REMOVAL & INSTALLATION

1. Disconnect the negative battery cable.
2. Use a siphon or hand pump to drain the washer fluid from the reservoir. If you are using a siphon, be careful not to inhale or swallow the fluid. The stuff tastes nasty, and like with most fluids in your truck, can be harmful if swallowed.
3. Disengage the electrical connector and washer hose from the pump.
4. Remove the washer fluid reservoir mounting screws, then remove the reservoir from the vehicle.
5. Remove the washer pump from the reservoir.

To install:

6. Install the washer pump to the reservoir. Make sure the pump is fully inserted into the washer reservoir seal.
7. Install the reservoir to the vehicle and secure using the retaining screws.
8. Engage the washer hose and electrical connector to the pump.
9. Refill the reservoir with fluid. Add just a little at first, and check for leaks. Refill the reservoir when you are certain the pump seal is secure.
10. Connect the negative battery cable and check for proper pump operation.

INSTRUMENTS AND SWITCHES

Instrument Cluster

REMOVAL & INSTALLATION

▶ **See Figures 50 and 51**

1. Disconnect the negative battery cable.
2. If equipped (such as on the MFI-Turbo) remove the fog lamp switch retaining screws.

3. Remove the lamp switch trim plate-to-instrument panel screws and the trim plate, then disengage the electrical connector from the lamp switch.
4. Remove the air conditioning/heater control assembly-to-instrument panel screws and the assembly, the disengage the electrical connector from the lamp switch.
5. Remove the filler panel (under the steering column) to instrument panel screws and the filler panel.
6. If equipped, disconnect the shift indicator cable from the lower shift bowl.

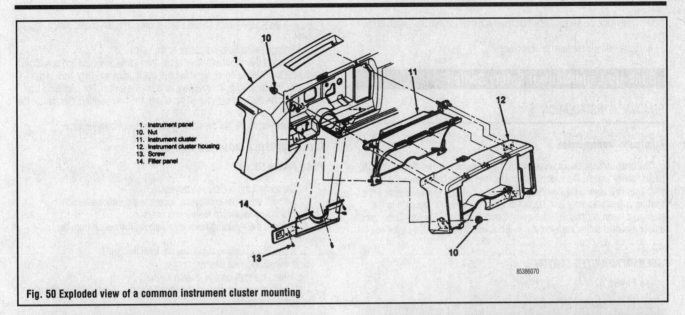

1. Instrument panel
10. Nut
11. Instrument cluster
12. Instrument cluster housing
13. Screw
14. Filler panel

85386070

Fig. 50 Exploded view of a common instrument cluster mounting

85386071

Fig. 51 Most instrument clusters are easily accessed once the trim plate is removed

➡️**Some late model vehicles may use a single multi-pin connector to which the instrument cluster is mounted. On these vehicles, pulling the cluster outward should disengage the necessary connections. Be careful not to damage the connector during removal and installation. Do not force the cluster, but make sure it is firmly seated when installed.**

7. Remove the instrument cluster housing nuts, then carefully pull the instrument cluster forward for access to the connectors.

8. Disengage the speedometer cable and/or electrical connectors from the rear of the cluster, as applicable.

9. Remove the instrument housing and/or cluster from the vehicle.

To install:

10. Position the instrument housing and/or cluster assembly in front of the instrument panel.

11. Engage the speedometer cable and/or electrical connectors to the rear of the cluster, as applicable.

12. Position the cluster and secure the housing retaining nuts.

13. If equipped, connect the shift indicator cable to the lower shift bowl.

14. Install the filler panel (under the steering column).

15. Install the air conditioning/heater control assembly.

16. Install the lamp switch trim plate.

17. If equipped, install the fog lamp switch retaining screws.

18. Connect the negative battery cable.

Windshield Wiper Switch

The windshield wiper switch is located deep inside the steering column assembly and is actuated by the multi-function lever on the left of the steering column. For details concerning removal and installation, please refer to the steering column procedures located in Section 8 of this manual.

Headlight Switch

The headlight switch is located on the left side of the instrument panel. A rheostat dial, usually located just above the headlight/parking light switch, is used to control the illumination of the instrument panel lighting.

A dimmer switch is mounted on the lower back of the steering column (near the ignition switch) and is actuated by the multi-function lever. For dimmer switch removal and installation, please refer to the steering column procedures located in Section 8 of this manual.

REMOVAL & INSTALLATION

1. Disconnect the negative battery cable.

2. From under the headlight switch assembly, remove the trim plate/switch assembly retaining screws.

➡️**For some vehicles equipped with a fog lamps, the lamp switch may have to be removed in order to access the headlight trim plate/switch screw.**

3. Pull the switch trim plate from the instrument panel. On late model vehicles, pivot the trim plate outward at the bottom, then pull the plate downward to release it.

4. Disengage the electrical wiring connectors from the rear of the switch/trim plate assembly.

5. Remove the headlight switch from the trim plate assembly; if necessary, replace the switch.

6. To install, reverse the removal procedures.

Fog Lamp Switch

REMOVAL & INSTALLATION

When equipped with factory or dealer installed fog lamps, the switch is usually located on the left side of the instrument panel, underneath the headlight switch assembly.

1. Disconnect the negative battery cable.

2. Remove the switch attaching screws (from underneath the switch assembly).

3. Disengage the switch electrical connector, then remove the switch from the vehicle.

4. Installation is the reverse of removal.

Back-Up Light/Neutral Safety Switch

REMOVAL & INSTALLATION

Automatic Transmission

The back-up light switch on automatic transmission vehicles also acts as the neutral safety switch. The switch will activate the reverse lights when the gear shift lever is placed in the Reverse position, and it will prevent the engine from starting unless the shifter is in Neutral or Park. The switch is mounted to the steering column on most vehicles covered by this manual. The MFI-Turbo uses a floor mounted shifter, therefore the switch is relocated under the center console on these vehicles.

COLUMN MOUNTED SWITCH

▶ **See Figure 52**

Two type of switches are generally found on these vehicles. Some early models will be equipped with adjustable switches which are bolted into position. Most vehicles covered by this manual should be equipped with ratcheting self-adjusting switches.

1. Disconnect the negative battery cable.
2. If necessary for access, remove the steering column insulator/filler panel for access to the switch.
3. Disengage the electrical harness connector from the switch.
4. Certain early model vehicles utilize a switch which is bolted in position. If equipped, remove the retaining bolts.
5. Remove the switch by grasping and pulling it straight out of the steering column jacket.

To install:

6. If equipped with an early model switch which is bolted into position, the switch should be equipped with a gauge hole for adjustment. If equipped, loosely install the switch to the column and adjust following the procedures in the illustration.
7. Most vehicles covered by this manual utilize a self-adjusting (ratcheting) switch. To install:
   a. Align the actuator on the switch with the holes in the shift tube.
   b. Set the parking brake and place the gear selector in Neutral.
   c. Press down on the front of the switch until the tangs snap into the rectangular holes in the steering column jacket.
   d. Adjust the switch by moving the gear selector to Park. The main hous-

ing and the housing back should ratchet, providing the proper switch adjustment.

8. Engage the harness connector to the switch.
9. Connect the negative battery cable, then verify proper switch operation. Make sure the Reverse lights work and that the ignition will only work in the Neutral or Park positions. If necessary, readjust the switch. For ratcheting type switches, move the gear selector all the way to the Low position, then repeat the adjustment.

10. If applicable, install the steering column insulator/filler panel.

FLOOR CONSOLE MOUNTED SWITCH

▶ **See Figure 53**

1. Disconnect the negative battery cable.
2. Remove the center console for access to the switch assembly.
3. Disengage the switch electrical connector.
4. Remove the retaining nuts, then remove the switch from the vehicle.
5. If necessary, remove the gauge pin from the switch.
6. If installing a new switch:
   a. Place the shift control lever in Neutral.
   b. Align the carrier tang on the back-up lamp/neutral safety switch with the slot on the shifter.

➡**Replacement switches are pinned in the Neutral position to ease installation. If the switch has been rotated or the switch is broken, install the switch using the "old switch" installation and adjustment procedure.**

   c. Tighten the switch retaining nuts to 30 inch lbs. (3.4 Nm), then engage the switch connector.
   d. Move the shift control lever out of Neutral in order to shear the plastic pin, then remove the accessible piece(s) of the gauge pin.
7. If installing an old switch, install and adjust the switch to assure proper operation:
   a. Place the shift control lever in Neutral.
   b. Align the carrier tang on the switch with the slot on the shifter.
   c. Loosely install the retaining switch nuts and engage the wiring connector.
   d. Rotate the switch to align the service adjustment hole with the carrier tang hold, then use a 0.09 in. (2.34mm) gauge pin to complete adjustment. Insert the pin in the service adjustment hole and rotate the switch until it drops to a depth of 0.59 in. (15mm). Hold the switch in this position and tighten the retaining nuts to 30 inch lbs. (3.4 Nm).
8. Install the center console.
9. Connect the negative battery cable.
10. Verify proper switch operation.

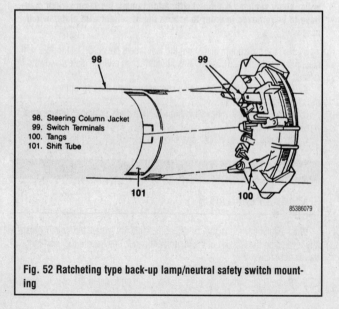

98. Steering Column Jacket
99. Switch Terminals
100. Tangs
101. Shift Tube

85386079

Fig. 52 Ratcheting type back-up lamp/neutral safety switch mounting

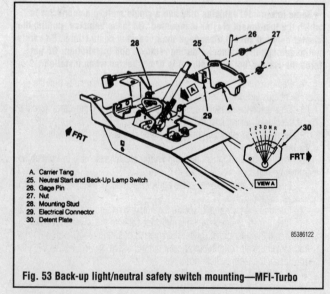

A. Carrier Tang
25. Neutral Start and Back-Up Lamp Switch
26. Gage Pin
27. Nut
28. Mounting Stud
29. Electrical Connector
30. Detent Plate

85386122

Fig. 53 Back-up light/neutral safety switch mounting—MFI-Turbo

Manual Transmission

On manual transmissions, the back-up light switch is normally mounted to the transmission. The safety switch is replaced by a clutch switch which is mounted to the clutch pedal. For replacement procedures, please refer to Section 7 of this manual.

Speedometer Cable

REMOVAL & INSTALLATION

Some early model vehicles are equipped with a speedometer cable. Later vehicles utilize a vehicle speed sensor to electronically deliver speed information to the computer control unit and the speedometer.

1. Disconnect the negative battery cable.
2. Remove the instrument cluster for access to the cable. For details, please refer to the procedure located earlier in this section.

3. From the rear of the instrument cluster, remove the speedometer cable-to-head fitting.
4. If replacing ONLY the speedometer cable core, perform the following procedures:
   a. Disconnect the speedometer casing from the speedometer head.
   b. Pull the speedometer cable core from the speedometer casing.
   c. Using a graphite-based lubricant, lubricate a new speedometer cable and install the cable into the casing.
5. If replacing the speedometer cable assembly, perform the following procedures:
   a. Disconnect the speedometer casing from the speedometer head.
   b. Disconnect the speedometer casing from the transmission.
   c. Remove the various speedometer cable/casing retaining clips.
   d. Remove the speedometer cable/casing assembly from the vehicle.
6. To install the speedometer cable, reverse the removal procedures.

LIGHTING

Headlights

REMOVAL & INSTALLATION

Sealed Beam

▶ See Figures 54 thru 59

Most vehicles covered by this manual are equipped with 1-piece sealed beam headlamps. The lamps are held in position against an adjuster housing

using a retaining ring. On older vehicles a headlight bezel must be removed to access the ring. On newer vehicles (starting around 1990), the grille and bezels became a single piece. On newer vehicles, the retaining ring fasteners should be accessible with the grille in position. If difficulty is encountered however, the grille should be removed to ease access and prevent damage to components.

➡ **If some or all of the headlight bulbs being replaced still operate, refer to the headlight aiming procedure later in this section to ease checking or adjustment of the headlights after installation.**

1. Disconnect the negative battery cable.
2. If equipped with separate headlight bezels, loosen and remove the retaining screws, then remove the headlight bezel from the front of the vehicle.
3. If equipped with a 1-piece bezel and grille assembly (most 1990 and later vehicles), determine if grille removal is necessary for access to the retaining ring. If necessary, remove the grille from the vehicle.
4. The headlight bulb retaining ring is only held on to the adjuster housing by retaining screws. Remove the bulb retaining ring screws. These are the screws which hold the thin metal ring which holds the bulb against the adjusting plate. Do not touch the two headlight aiming screws, at the center of the top and side of the retaining ring (these screws will have different heads), or the headlight aim will have to be re-adjusted.

➡ **One way to identify the retaining ring screws is that they will be threaded through a lip on the outer edge of the retaining ring before threading through the adjusting plate housing. One the other hand, the adjustment screws are first threaded through the adjustment plate and then an adjuster located underneath the housing.**

5. Pull the bulb and ring forward and then separate them. Unplug the electrical connector from the rear of the bulb and remove the bulb from the vehicle.
6. Installation is the reverse of removal.

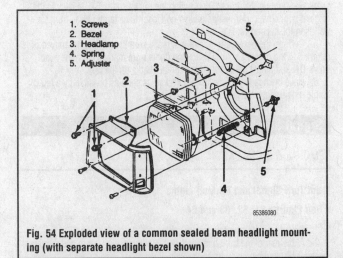

1. Screws
2. Bezel
3. Headlamp
4. Spring
5. Adjuster

85386080

Fig. 54 Exploded view of a common sealed beam headlight mounting (with separate headlight bezel shown)

85386081

Fig. 55 Loosen and remove the headlight bezel retaining screws/bolts

85386082

Fig. 56 Some of screws may require Torx® head drivers

85386083

Fig. 57 Loosen and remove the retaining ring screws

Fig. 58 Don't forget the ring screws located under the light

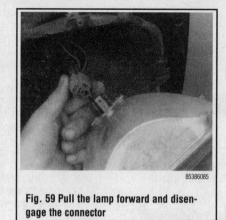

Fig. 59 Pull the lamp forward and disengage the connector

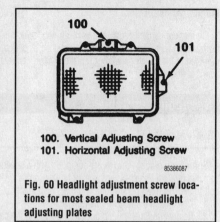

100. Vertical Adjusting Screw
101. Horizontal Adjusting Screw

Fig. 60 Headlight adjustment screw locations for most sealed beam headlight adjusting plates

HEADLIGHT AIMING

♦ **See Figure 60**

The headlights must be properly aimed to provide the best, safest road illumination. The lights should be checked for proper aim and adjusted as necessary. Certain state and local authorities have requirements for headlight aiming; these should be checked before adjustment is made.

Headlight adjustment may be temporarily made using a wall, as described below, or on the rear of another vehicle. When adjusted, the lights should not glare in oncoming car or truck windshields, nor should they illuminate the passenger compartment of vehicles driving in front of you. These adjustments are rough and should always be fine-tuned by a repair shop which is equipped with headlight aiming tools. Improper adjustments may be both dangerous and illegal.

For most S/T vehicles, horizontal and vertical aiming of each sealed beam unit is provided by two adjusting screws which move the retaining ring and adjusting plate against the tension of a coil spring. There is no adjustment for focus; this is done during headlight manufacturing.

➡**Because the composite headlight assembly is bolted into position, no adjustment should be necessary or possible. Some applications however may be bolted to an adjuster plate or may be retained used adjusting screws. If so, follow this procedure when adjusting the lights, BUT always have the adjustment checked by a reputable shop.**

Before removing the headlight bulb or disturbing the headlamp in any way, note the current settings in order to make adjusting the headlights upon reassembly easier. If the high or low beam setting of the old lamp still works, this can be done using the wall of a garage or a building:

1. Park the truck on a level surface, with the fuel tank no more than ½ full and with the vehicle empty of all extra cargo (unless normally carried). The vehicle should be facing a wall which is no less then 6 feet high and 12 feet wide. The front of the vehicle should be about 25 feet from the wall.

➡**The truck's fuel tank should be about half full when adjusting the headlights. Tires should be properly inflated, and if a heavy load is normally carried in the bed, it should remain there.**

2. If this is be performed outdoors, it is advisable to wait until dusk in order to properly see the headlight beams on the wall. If done in a garage, darken the area around the wall as much as possible by closing shades or hanging cloth over the windows.

3. Turn the headlights **ON** and mark the wall at the center of each light's low beam, then switch on the brights and mark the center of each light's high beam. A short length of masking tape which is visible from the front of the truck may be used. Although marking all 4 positions is advisable, marking 1 position from each light should be sufficient.

4. If neither beam on 1 side of the vehicle is working, park another like-sized truck in the exact spot where the truck was and mark the beams using the same side light on that truck. Then switch the trucks so the S/T is back in the original spot. The truck must be parked no closer to or farther away from the wall than the second vehicle.

5. Perform the necessary repairs, but make sure the truck is not moved or is returned to the exact spot from which the lights were marked. Turn the headlights **ON** and adjust the beams to match the marks on the wall.

6. Have the headlight adjustment checked as soon as possible by a reputable repair shop.

Signal and Marker Lights

REMOVAL & INSTALLATION

Front Turn Signal and Parking Lights

♦ **See Figures 61, 62, 63 and 64**

1. Disconnect the negative battery cable.
2. At the rear of the front bumper, turn the bulb socket ¼ turn and remove the socket from the parking brake housing.

Fig. 61 Common front turn signal/parking light mounting

Fig. 62 Twist and remove the bulb socket from the back of the turn signal/parking light lens

Fig. 63 If lens removal is necessary, loosen and remove the retaining bolts

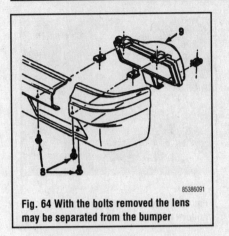

Fig. 64 With the bolts removed the lens may be separated from the bumper

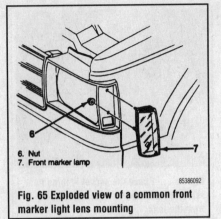

6. Nut
7. Front marker lamp

Fig. 65 Exploded view of a common front marker light lens mounting

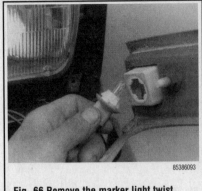

Fig. 66 Remove the marker light twist socket from the back of the lens

3. Remove the bulb from the socket; if necessary, replace the bulb.

4. If lens replacement is necessary, remove the retaining bolts and remove the lens from the bumper.

5. To install, reverse the removal procedures. Check the turn signal/parking light operations.

Front Marker Lights

▶ See Figures 65, 66 and 67

On most vehicles covered by this manual, the front marker lights are mounted in a lens attached to the headlight bezel (pre-1990) or the one piece headlight bezel/grille assembly (1990 and later vehicles). Replacement usually requires removal of the bezel or bezel/grille assembly for access to the bulb twist socket.

1. Disconnect the negative battery cable.

2. If equipped with a separate headlight bezel, remove the headlight bezel-to-fender screws and the bezel; allow the bezel to hang by the turn signal/marker light wires.

3. If equipped with a 1-piece bezel/grille assembly, remove the grille assembly and support it on the bumper as you work.

4. At the rear of the bezel mounted lens, turn the marker bulb socket ¼ turn and remove it from the headlight bezel.

5. Remove the bulb from the turn signal/marker bulb socket; if necessary, replace the bulb.

6. To install, use a new bulb (if necessary) and reverse the removal procedures. Check the turn signal/marker light operations.

Rear Turn Signal, Brake, Parking and Reverse Lights

▶ See Figures 68 thru 77

Most vehicles covered by this manual use 2 tail light assemblies (1 on either side) to house the rear turn signal, brake, parking and reverse lights. A few late model vehicles may also be equipped with a center high-mounted

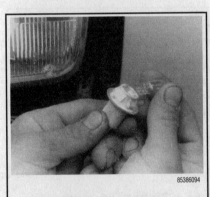

Fig. 67 If replacement is necessary, remove the bulb from the socket

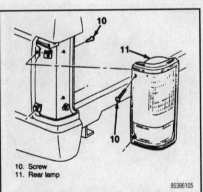

10. Screw
11. Rear lamp

Fig. 68 Exploded view of a common tail light assembly mounting

Fig. 69 Loosen and remove the tail light lens assembly retaining screws

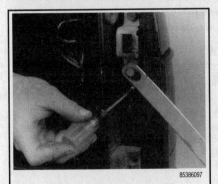

Fig. 70 Don't forget most vehicles will have screws hidden behind the tail gate.

Fig. 71 With all screws loosened, the lens is free for removal . . .

Fig. 72 . . . carefully pull the lens assembly away from the body for access to the wires.

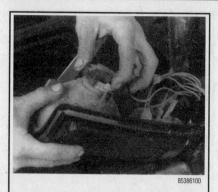

Fig. 73 To remove the twist sockets, grasp and give them a ¼ turn . . .

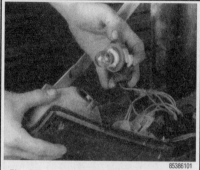

Fig. 74 . . . once the socket is turned and released, withdraw the socket and bulb from the lens

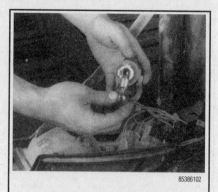

Fig. 75 If replacement is necessary, remove the bulb from the socket

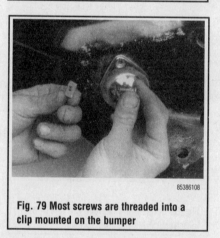

Fig. 76 The other bulb (marker/reverse as applicable) twist sockets may be removed in the same manner

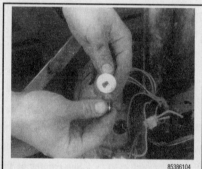

Fig. 77 Again, bulb replacement is possible once the socket is removed from the lens

Fig. 78 If the bulb housing must be removed for access, loosen and remove the retaining screws

Fig. 79 Most screws are threaded into a clip mounted on the bumper

Fig. 80 Remove the housing cover, lens and gasket, as applicable

Fig. 81 Remove the license plate bulb from the socket

brake light (covered later in this section) on the top of the cab. To replace any of the bulbs housed in the rear tail light assemblies, then lens must be removed for access.

1. Disconnect the negative battery cable.
2. Remove the rear lamp assembly-to-vehicle screws, then carefully pull the lamp housing away from the vehicle for access to the bulb twist sockets. On most vehicles, lamp screws can be found on the outer edge of the lamp and behind the tailgate. Make sure all screws are removed and DO NOT force the lens.
3. Turn the bulb twist socket ¼ turn and remove the socket from the lamp housing.
4. Remove the bulb from the bulb socket; if necessary, replace the bulb.
5. To install, reverse the removal procedures. Check the turn signal/brake/parking light operations.

License Plate Light

REMOVAL & INSTALLATION

▶ See Figures 78, 79, 80 and 81

Vehicles covered by this manual utilize a license plate bulb which is covered by a housing which is mounted adjacent to the license plate using 1 or more retaining screws. On most vehicles covered by this manual, replacement is possible by reaching under the bumper, twisting and withdrawing the socket and bulb from the rear of the housing. If access is not possible or the housing is not equipped with a twist socket, the housing retaining screws should be removed and the housing should be lifted off to access the bulb. Remove the bulb from the socket and replace using a new part.

Cargo Light

REMOVAL & INSTALLATION

▶ **See Figure 82**

Some vehicles may be equipped with a cargo light mounted to the top rear of the cab. On most applications, the bulb is easily accessible once the lens is removed.

1. Disconnect the negative battery cable.
2. Remove the lens-to-housing screws and the lens.
3. Remove the bulb from the cargo light housing; if necessary, replace the bulb.
4. To install, reverse the removal procedures.

Fog Lamps

REMOVAL & INSTALLATION

➡ **If removing or replacing the fog lamps (not just the bulb) and 1 or both of the fog lamps still operate, refer to the aiming procedure later in this section to ease checking or adjustment of the fog lamps after installation.**

Most fog lamp bulbs are easily replaced by removing the lens cover (standard bulbs) or lens trim panels (halogen bulbs) for access. Most later model vehicles are equipped with Halogen bulbs which require extra care. Handling a Halogen bulb improperly could cause it to shatter into flying glass fragments. To help avoid personal injury follow the precautions closely.

Whenever handling Halogen bulb ALWAYS follow these precautions:
- Turn the lamp switch OFF and allow the bulb to cool before changing it. Leave the switch OFF until the change is complete.
- ALWAYS wear eye protection when changing a Halogen bulb.
- DO NOT drop or scratch the bulb. Keep moisture away.
- Place the use bulb in the new bulb's carton and dispose of it properly.

1. Disconnect the negative battery cable.
2. If replacing a standard bulb, remove the screws and lens for access to the bulb. Free the bulb from the socket and replace.
3. If replacing a Halogen bulb (all 1992 and later equipped vehicles and some earlier models):
   a. Remove the lens trim panel screws from the front of the lamp, then pull the lamp and lens assembly forward from the case and turn it over.
   b. Disengage the white wire connector inside the braided insulator (leave the ground wire connected). Note the position of the wire clip at the lamp and lens assembly, then squeeze the edges of the clip together and remove it.
   c. Lift out the wire and the halogen bulb assembly.
4. If the lamp assembly is being replaced:

➡ **When replacing lamp assemblies, if possible mark the beams of one or both lamps on a wall as a reference. Please see the aiming procedure later in this section for details.**

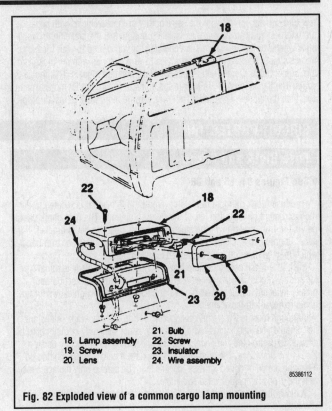

18. Lamp assembly
19. Screw
20. Lens
21. Bulb
22. Screw
23. Insulator
24. Wire assembly

85386112

Fig. 82 Exploded view of a common cargo lamp mounting

a. Disengage the electrical wiring from the fog lamp.
b. Remove the lamp assembly retaining screws. On early applications the lamp was usually fastened to the bumper and air deflector. Make sure all retaining screws are unthreaded, then remove the lamp assembly from the vehicle.

To install:
5. If the lamp assembly was removed:
   a. Position the lamp assembly to the vehicle and secure using the retaining screws.
   b. Engage the electrical wiring.
   c. Check fog lamp aiming and adjust, as necessary.
6. If only the Halogen bulb is being replaced:
   a. Install the white wire connector to the wiring in the brained insulator.
   b. Install the bulb into the back of the lamp and lens assembly.
   c. Install the wire clip to hold the bulb in place. Make sure the clip is firmly in position and the bulb is not loose.
   d. Install the lens and lamp assembly into the case, then secure the trim panels using the retaining screws.
7. If only a standard bulb was replaced, install the bulb, then secure lens cover to the housing.
8. Connect the negative battery cable and check for proper operation.

TRAILER WIRING

➡ **For more information on towing a trailer please refer to Section 1 of this manual.**

Wiring the truck for towing is fairly easy. There are a number of good wiring kits available and these should be used, rather than trying to design your own. All trailers will need brake lights and turn signals as well as tail lights and side marker lights. Most states require extra marker lights for overly wide trailers. Also, most states have recently required back-up lights for trailers, and most trailer manufacturers have been building trailers with back-up lights for several years. Additionally, some Class I, most Class II and just about all Class III trailers will have electric brakes. Add to this number an accessories wire, to operate trailer internal equipment or to charge the trailer's battery, and you can have as many as seven wires in the harness.

Determine the equipment on your trailer and buy the wiring kit necessary. The kit will contain all the wires needed, plus a plug adapter set which included the female plug, mounted on the bumper or hitch, and the male plug, wired into, or plugged into the trailer harness. When installing the kit, follow the manufacturer's instructions. The color coding of the wires tends to be standard throughout the industry.

One point to note: some domestic vehicles, and most imported vehicles, have separate turn signals. On most domestic vehicles, the brake lights and rear turn signals operate with the same bulb. For those vehicles with separate turn signals, you can purchase an isolation unit so that the brake lights won't blink whenever the turn signals are operated, or you can go to your local electronics supply house and buy four diodes to wire in series with the brake and turn signal bulbs. Diodes will isolate the brake and turn signals. The choice is yours. The isolation units are simple and quick to install, but far more expensive than the diodes. The diodes, however, require more work to install prop-

erly, since they require the cutting of each bulb's wire and soldering in place of the diode.

One final point, the best kits are those with a spring loaded cover on the vehicle mounted socket. This cover prevent dirt and moisture from corroding the terminals. Never let the vehicle socket hang loosely; always mount it securely to the bumper or hitch.

CIRCUIT PROTECTION

Fuse Block and Fuses

♦ **See Figures 84, 85 and 86**

The fuse block on most models covered by this manual is located under the instrument panel to the left of the steering column. The fuse block should be visible from underneath the steering column, near the pedal bracket. If the panel is not visible, check for a removable compartment door or trim panel which may be used on later models to hide the block.

Each fuse block uses miniature fuses (normally plug-in blade terminal type for these vehicles) which are designed for increased circuit protection and greater reliability. The compact plug-in or blade terminal design allows for fingertip removal and replacement.

Although most fuses are interchangeable in size, the amperage values are not. Should you install a fuse with too high a value, damaging current could be allowed to destroy the component you were attempting to protect by using a fuse in the first place. The plug-in type fuses have a bold number molded on them and are color coded for easy identification. Be sure to only replace a fuse with the proper amperage rated substitute.

A blown fuse can easily be checked by visual inspection or by continuity checking.

FUSE REPLACEMENT

♦ **See Figure 87**

1. Pull the fuse from the fuse block.
2. Inspect the fuse element (through the clear plastic body) to the blade terminal for defects.

➡**When replacing the fuse, DO NOT use one of a higher amperage.**

3. Once repairs are completed, install a replacement fuse of the same amperage.

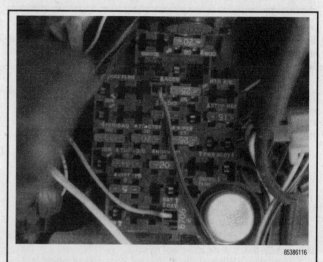

Fig. 85 View of an early model fuse block—notice that most terminals are labelled

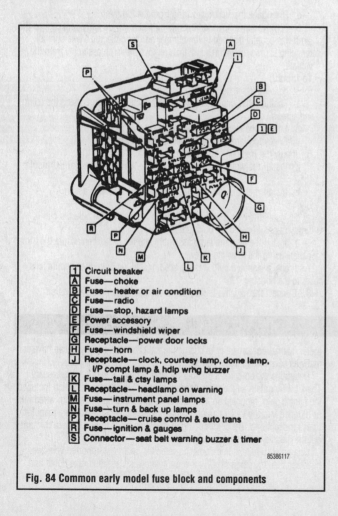

1	Circuit breaker
A	Fuse—choke
B	Fuse—heater or air condition
C	Fuse—radio
D	Fuse—stop, hazard lamps
E	Power accessory
F	Fuse—windshield wiper
G	Receptacle—power door locks
H	Fuse—horn
J	Receptacle—clock, courtesy lamp, dome lamp, I/P compt lamp & hdlp wrhg buzzer
K	Fuse—tail & ctsy lamps
L	Receptacle—headlamp on warning
M	Fuse—instrument panel lamps
N	Fuse—turn & back up lamps
P	Receptacle—cruise control & auto trans
R	Fuse—ignition & gauges
S	Connector—seat belt warning buzzer & timer

Fig. 84 Common early model fuse block and components

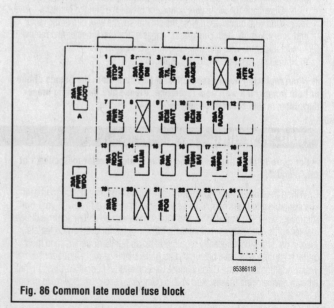

Fig. 86 Common late model fuse block

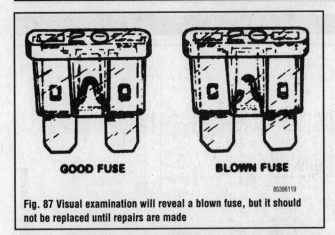

Fig. 87 Visual examination will reveal a blown fuse, but it should not be replaced until repairs are made

Fusible Links

A fusible link is a protective device used in an electrical circuit and acts very much like a standard fuse. The major difference lies in that fusible links are larger and capable of conducting a higher amperage than most fuses. When the current increases beyond the rated amperage for a given link, the fusible metal of the wire link will melt, thus breaking the electrical circuit and preventing further damage to any other components or wiring. Whenever a fusible link is melted because of a short circuit, correct the cause before installing a new one. There are 4 different gauge sizes commonly used and they are usually color coded so that they may be easily installed in their original positions.

REPLACING FUSIBLE LINKS

▶ **See Figure 88**

1. Disconnect the negative battery cable, followed by the positive cable.
2. Locate the burned out link.
3. If both ends of the link are ring terminal connectors which are easily accessed:
   a. Measure the installed length necessary for the new link.
   b. Unbolt and remove the link and connector pieces.

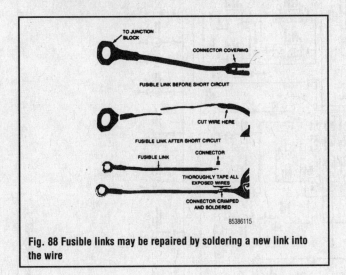

Fig. 88 Fusible links may be repaired by soldering a new link into the wire

c. Obtain a suitable length of link, then strip the insulation off the harness wire back ½ in (12.7mm) to allow soldering of the new connectors.
   d. Position the new connector around the new link and crimp it securely. Then, solder the connection, using rosin core solder and sufficient heat to guarantee a good connection. Repeat for the remaining connection.

➡**Whenever splicing a new wire, always bond the splice with rosin core solder, then cover with electrical tape. Using acid core solder may cause corrosion.**

4. If the ends of the connector are not easily accessed, repair the length in the vehicle.
   a. Strip away the melted insulation and cut the burned link ends from the wire.
   b. Strip the wire back ½ in. (12.7mm) to allow soldering of the new link.
   c. Using a new fusible link of appropriate gauge and length, solder it into the circuit.
5. Tape all exposed wiring with electrical tape and seal with silicone or use a heat shrink tube, if available to weatherproof the repair.
6. If removed from the vehicle, install the link and secure the connectors.
7. Reconnect the positive, followed by the negative battery cables.

Circuit Breakers

One device used to protect electrical components from burning out due to excessive current is a circuit breaker. Circuit breakers open and close the flow path for the electricity rapidly in order to protect the circuit if current is excessive. A circuit breaker is used on components which are more likely to draw excessive current such as a breaker often found in the light switch that protects the headlight circuit. Circuit breakers may be found in various locations on the vehicle including on/in the protected component, on a firewall bracket, the convenience center and/or the fuse block.

Convenience Center

▶ **See Figure 89**

The convenience center is used to centrally locate various buzzers, relays, flashers and/or circuit breakers. On some earlier vehicles, it is box-like, swing-down unit located on the underside of the instrument panel. Later vehicles use a bracket like strip, mounted under the instrument panel to the right of the steering column. All components located in the convenience center are serviced by plug-in replacements.

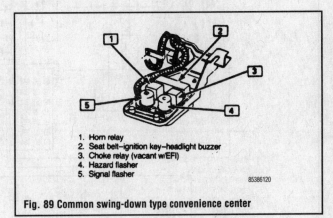

1. Horn relay
2. Seat belt–ignition key–headlight buzzer
3. Choke relay (vacant w/EFI)
4. Hazard flasher
5. Signal flasher

Fig. 89 Common swing-down type convenience center

WIRING DIAGRAMS

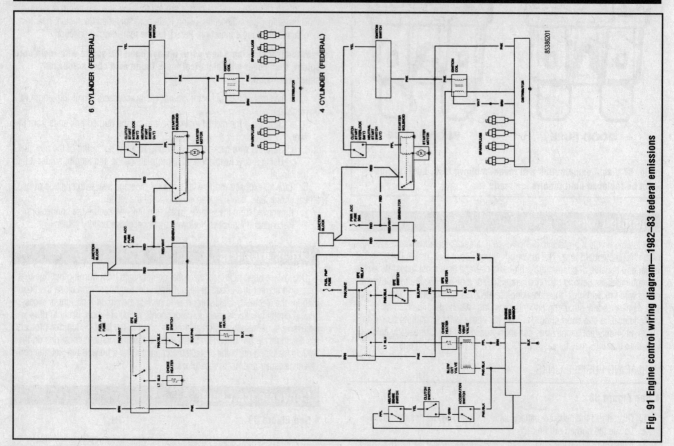

Fig. 91 Engine control wiring diagram—1982–83 federal emissions

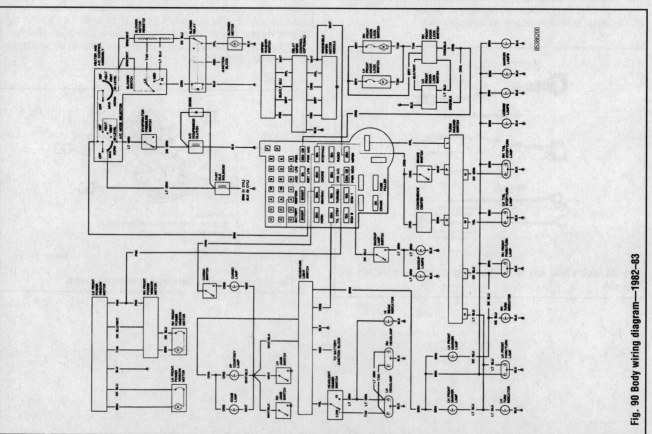

Fig. 90 Body wiring diagram—1982–83

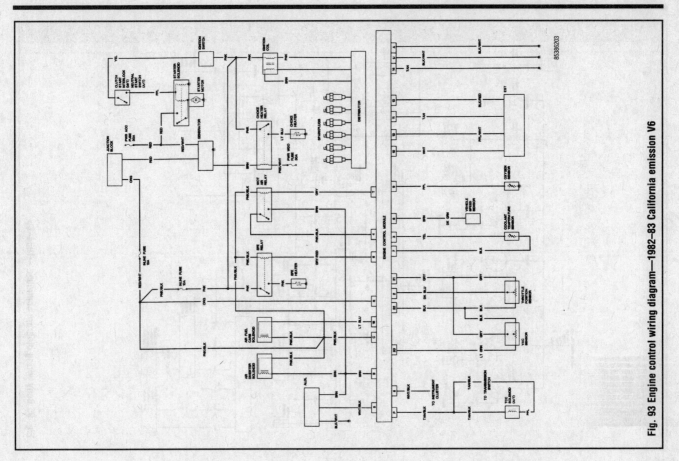

Fig. 93 Engine control wiring diagram—1982–83 California emission V6

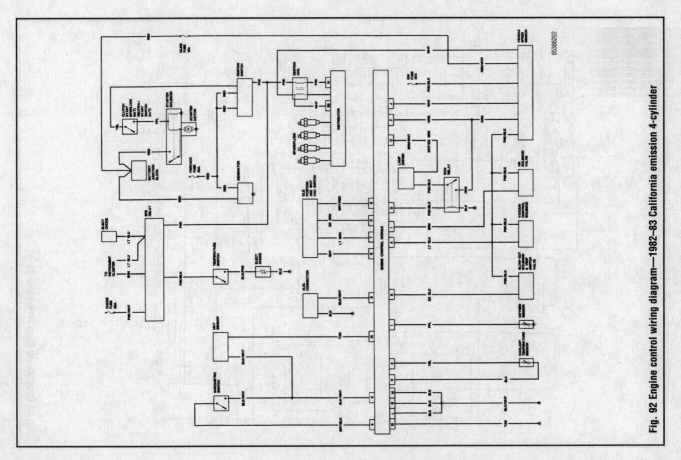

Fig. 92 Engine control wiring diagram—1982–83 California emission 4-cylinder

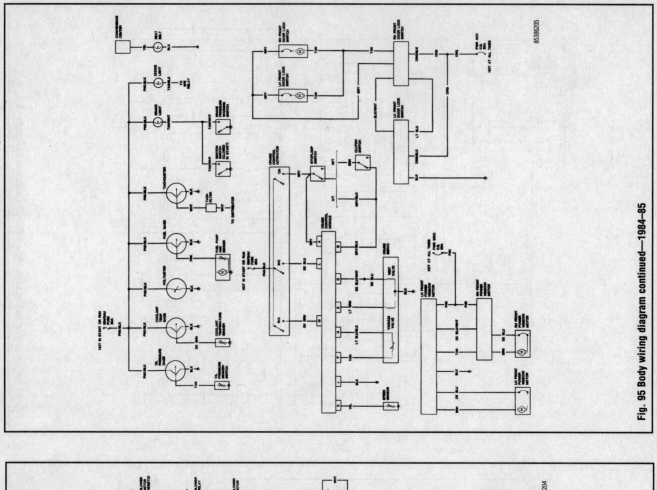

Fig. 95 Body wiring diagram continued—1984–85

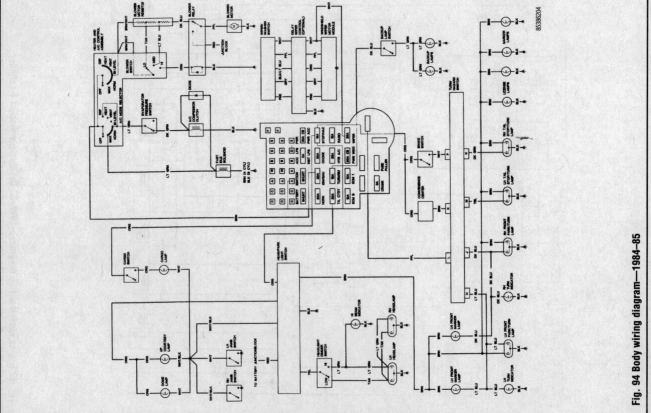

Fig. 94 Body wiring diagram—1984–85

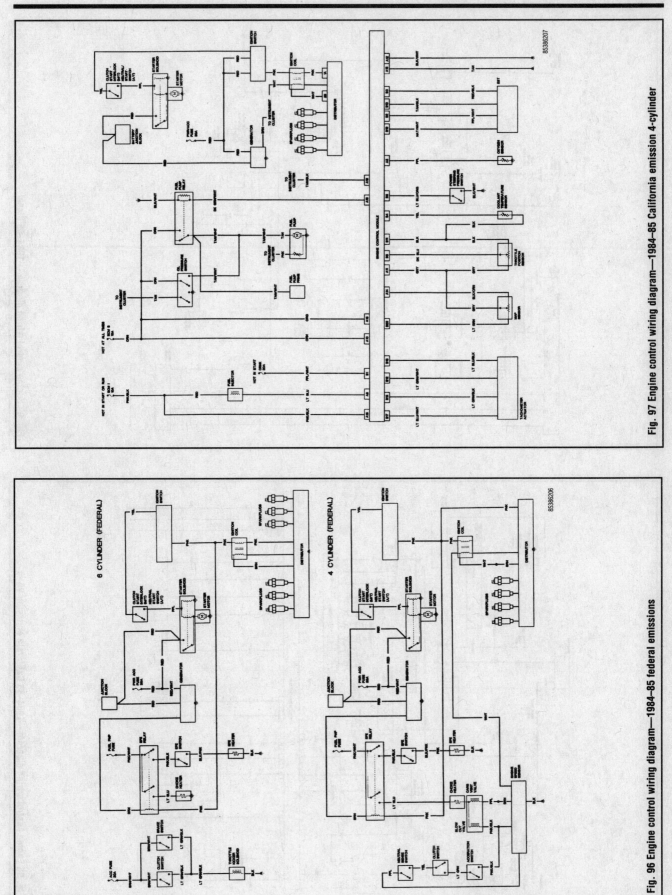

Fig. 97 Engine control wiring diagram—1984-85 California emission 4-cylinder

Fig. 96 Engine control wiring diagram—1984-85 federal emissions

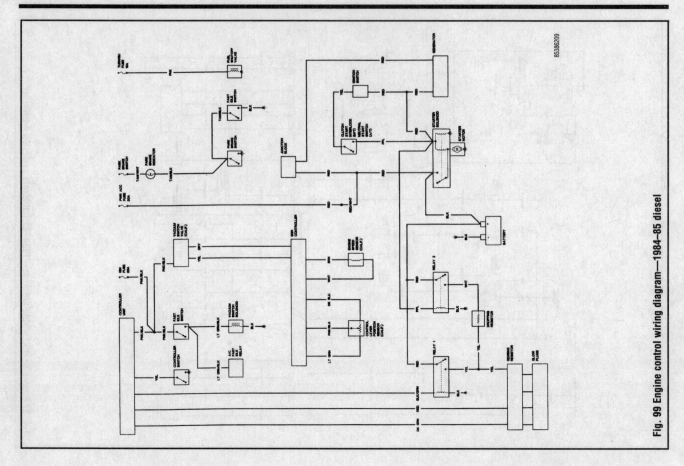

Fig. 99 Engine control wiring diagram—1984–85 diesel

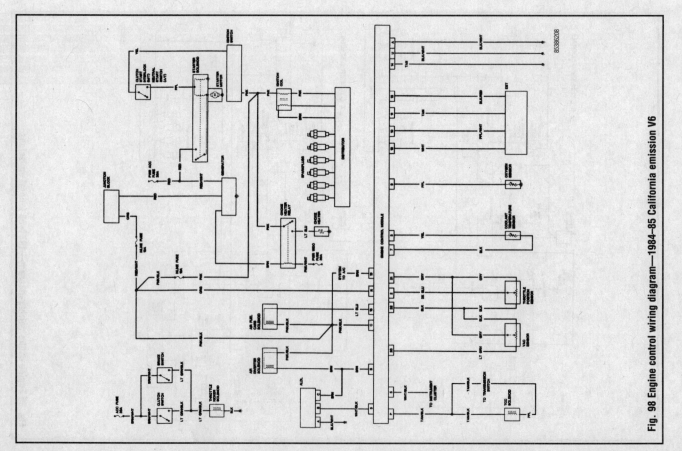

Fig. 98 Engine control wiring diagram—1984–85 California emission V6

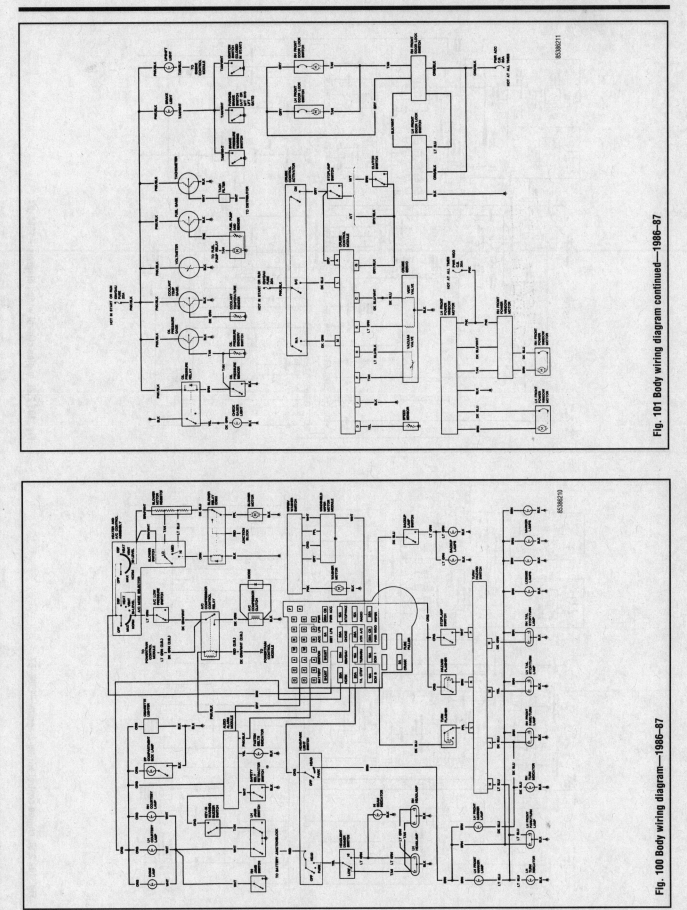

Fig. 101 Body wiring diagram continued—1986-87

Fig. 100 Body wiring diagram—1986-87

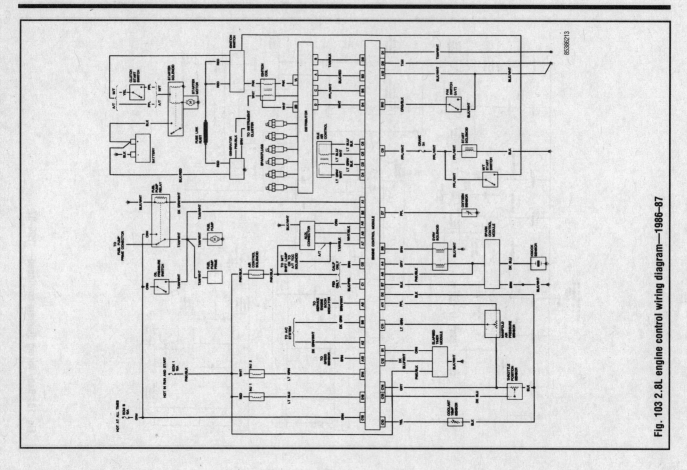

Fig. 103 2.8L engine control wiring diagram—1986-87

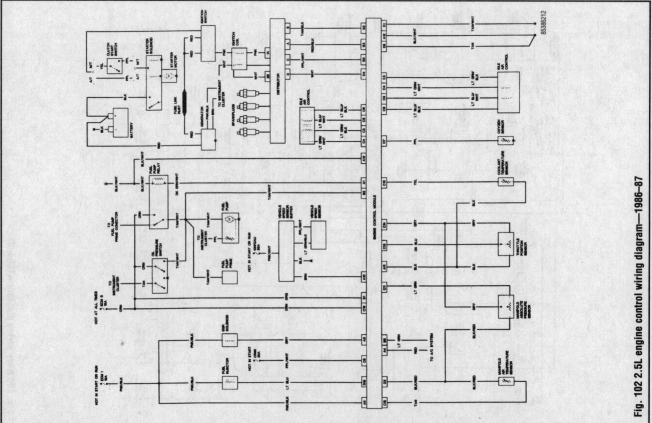

Fig. 102 2.5L engine control wiring diagram—1986-87

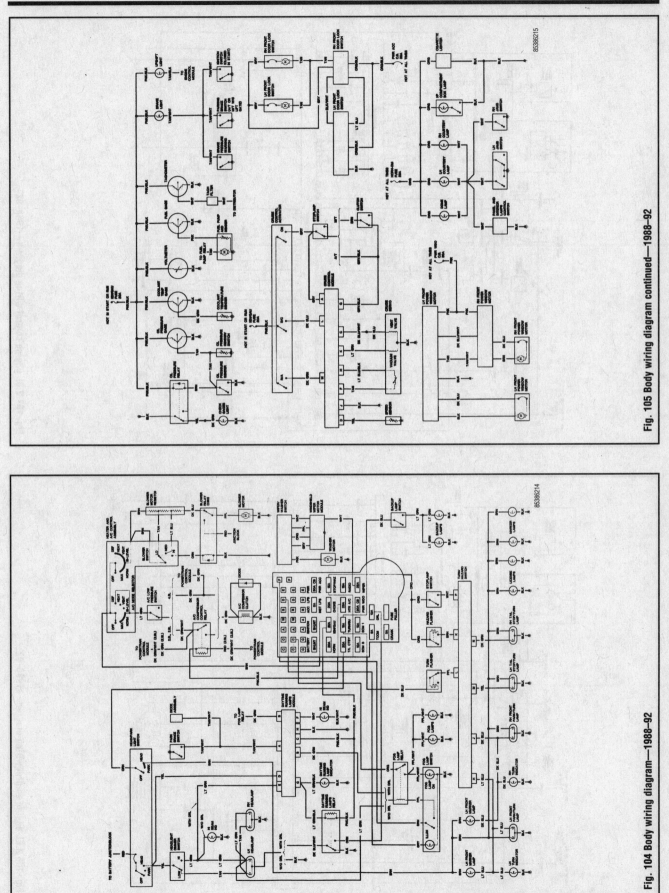

Fig. 105 Body wiring diagram continued—1988–92

Fig. 104 Body wiring diagram—1988–92

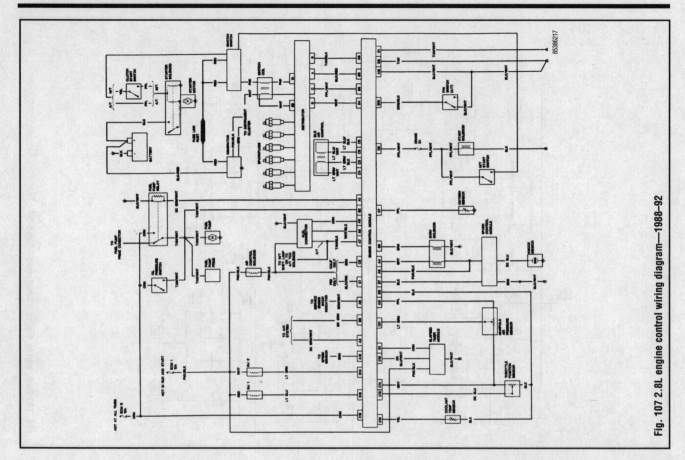

Fig. 107 2.8L engine control wiring diagram—1988–92

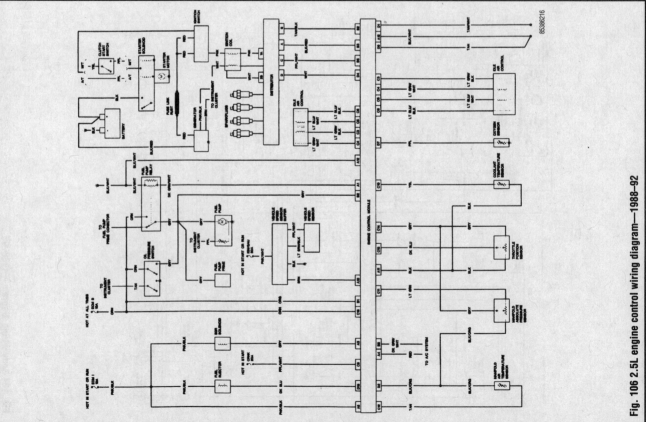

Fig. 106 2.5L engine control wiring diagram—1988–92

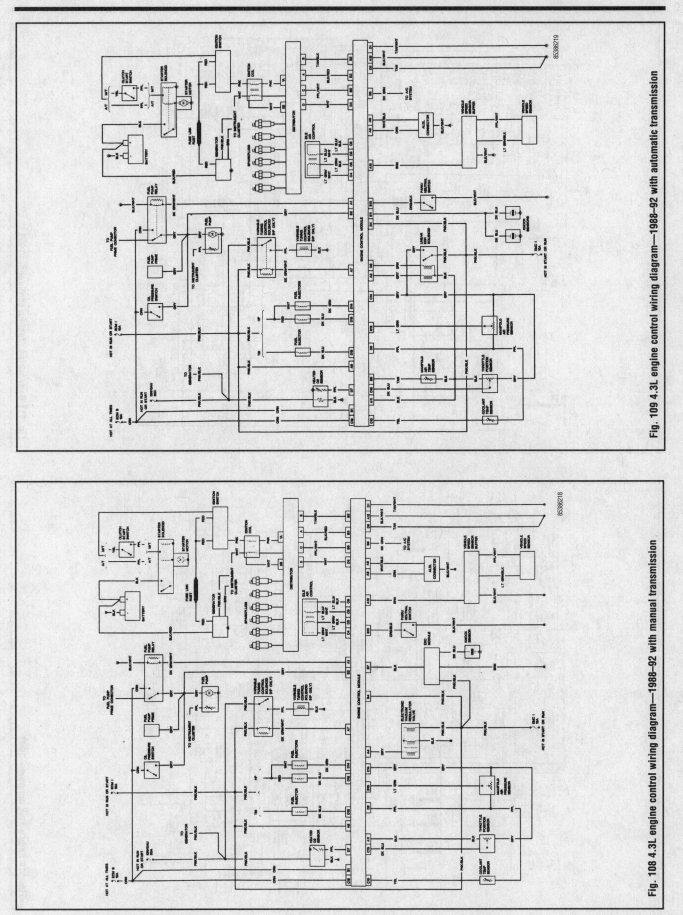

Fig. 109 4.3L engine control wiring diagram—1988–92 with automatic transmission

Fig. 108 4.3L engine control wiring diagram—1988–92 with manual transmission

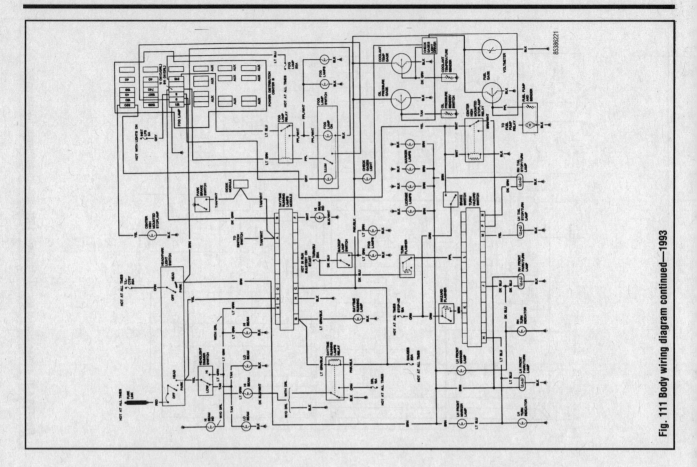

Fig. 111 Body wiring diagram continued—1993

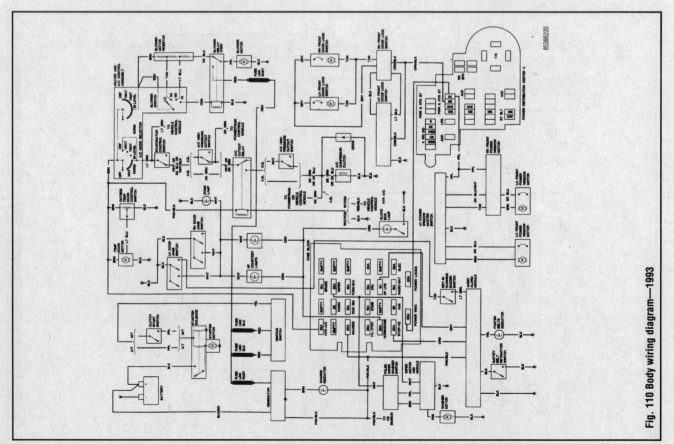

Fig. 110 Body wiring diagram—1993

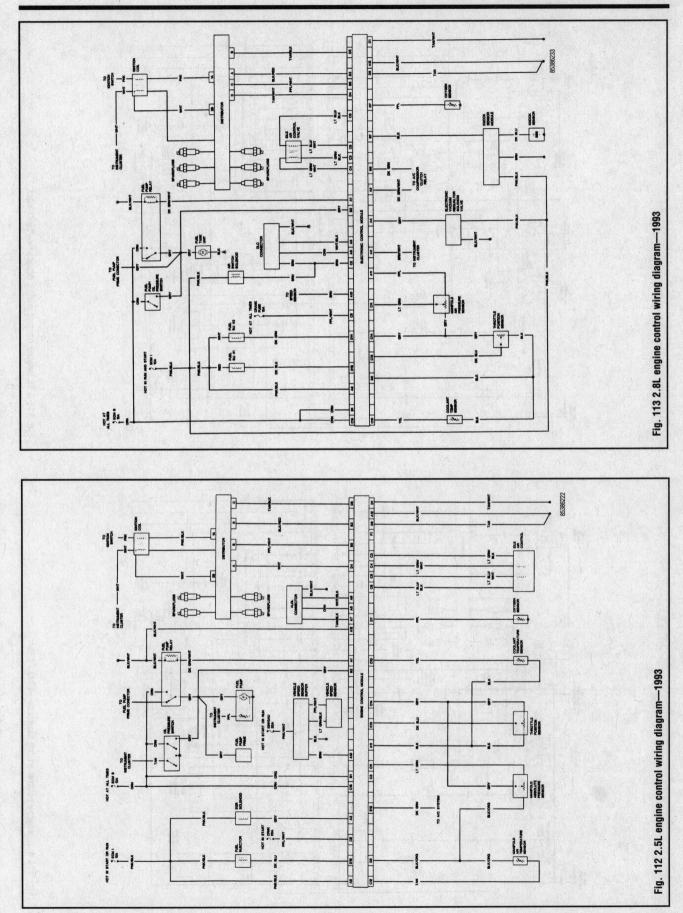

Fig. 113 2.8L engine control wiring diagram—1993

Fig. 112 2.5L engine control wiring diagram—1993

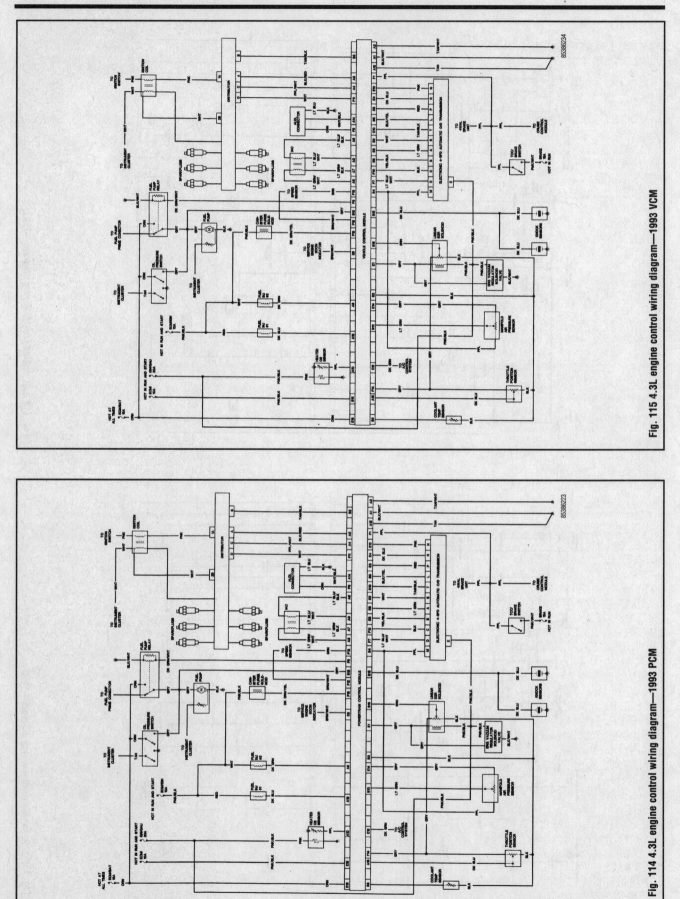

Fig. 115 4.3L engine control wiring diagram—1993 VCM

Fig. 114 4.3L engine control wiring diagram—1993 PCM

7

DRIVE TRAIN

MANUAL TRANSMISSION

Adjustments

SHIFTER

Because the shifter on most manual transmissions covered by this manual is bolted directly to the top of the transmission housing, no shifter/linkage adjustments should be necessary or possible. If shift trouble is encountered, check for a worn clutch or a damaged shifter assembly.

STARTER CLUTCH SWITCH

◆ **See Figures 1 and 2**

A clutch switch is located under the instrument panel and attached to the top of the clutch pedal. Its function is to prevent starter operation unless the clutch pedal is depressed. Some vehicles may be equipped with a separate cruise control release clutch switch or the switch may be combined with the starter safety switch, depending on the model and application. For information regarding the cruise control switch, please refer to Section 6 of this manual.

For most vehicles covered by this manual, the clutch (starter safety) switch is bolted in position. For most later model vehicles no adjustment is necessary or possible. However, on some early model vehicles (most carbureted and diesel along with early fuel injected engines), the switch must be adjusted for reliable starter operation.

1. Remove the lower steering column-to-instrument panel cover for access.
2. Disengage the electrical connector from the clutch switch.

➥**Be sure to leave any carpets and floor mats in place when making the adjustment.**

3. At the clutch switch, move the slider (A) rearward (towards the clutch switch) on the clutch switch shaft (B).
4. Push the clutch pedal to the floor. A clicking noise will be heard as the switch adjusts itself.
5. Release the clutch pedal; the adjustment is complete.
6. Reconnect the switch and test for proper operation.

Shift Lever

REMOVAL & INSTALLATION

◆ **See Figure 3**

Most vehicles covered by this manual utilize a 2-piece shift lever assembly. The upper portion of the shift lever is threaded to the lower portion and locked in position using a jamnut. If equipped, the upper portion may removed without unbolting the rest of the shifter lever/housing from the top of the transmission

housing. In fact, on most later model vehicles, the shift lever housing cannot or should not be removed with transmission installed. On some transmissions, such as the New Venture Gear 3500 the shift lever is retained to a shift lever socket inside the transmission using a roll pin. On vehicles equipped with a 1-piece lever, the entire assembly (shift lever/lever housing) must be removed from the transmission as a unit.

1. Position the transmission in Neutral, this will prevent stressing the internal shift forks when working on the shift lever components.
2. Unthread the shift knob and nut (if equipped) from the top of the shift lever. The nut is usually used as a jamnut to hold the shift knob in position, so knob removal may be easier if you turn the nut slightly to ease tension from the knob before attempting to unthread it. This will most likely mean turning the nut clockwise to thread it further down on the top of the shift lever.
3. If equipped with a shifter boot retainer, loosen and remove the retaining screws.
4. Remove the shifter boot along with the retainer (if equipped).

➥**On most models covered by this manual there is a locknut (jamnut) at the base of the shift lever (where the lower portion of the shift lever enters the transmission housing. This locknut is used on 2 piece shift levers, if removal of only the upper portion is desired, it may be unthreaded from the lower portion at this time.**

5. On models equipped with a 2-piece shift lever, hold the lower locknut from turning and use the wrench slots in the base of the upper shift lever to unthread and remove it from the vehicle. If removal is difficult, it is advised that you back the nut off of the upper lever by turning it clockwise, then unthread the lever by turning it (the lever) counterclockwise.
6. If equipped with a 1-piece lever, loosen and remove the retaining bolts. Carefully remove the shift lever/housing from the transmission housing assembly.

To install:

7. If equipped with a 1-piece lever, clean the gasket mating surface taking care not to allow debris inside the transmission. Lightly lubricate the shifter with moly grease, then install the assembly to the top of the transmission using a new gasket or silicone sealer (as applicable). Install the retaining bolts and tighten to 10 ft. lbs. (13 Nm).
8. If equipped with a 2-piece lever, thread the locknut all the way on to the base of the lower shift lever (do not tighten it), then thread the upper shift lever to the lower portion. Secure the upper lever by holding the lever using the wrench slots and tightening the locknut up against the base of the upper lever Tighten the locknut to 35 ft. lbs. (48 Nm).
9. Install the shifter boot along with the retainer (if equipped). On vehicles equipped with a boot retainer, install and tighten the bolts.
10. If equipped with an upper locknut, thread the nut all of the way onto the top of the upper shift lever, but do not tighten it. Thread the shift knob onto the lever, then turn the knob as necessary to align the shift pattern. Hold the knob aligned as desired and tighten the knob jamnut against the knob to retain the position.

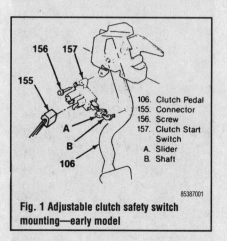

106. Clutch Pedal
155. Connector
156. Screw
157. Clutch Start Switch
A. Slider
B. Shaft

Fig. 1 Adjustable clutch safety switch mounting—early model

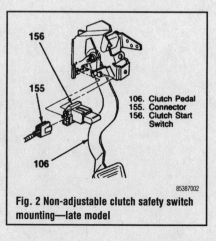

106. Clutch Pedal
155. Connector
156. Clutch Start Switch

Fig. 2 Non-adjustable clutch safety switch mounting—late model

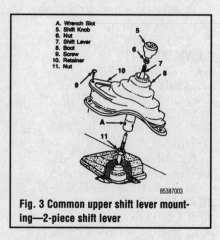

A. Wrench Slot
5. Shift Knob
6. Nut
7. Shift Lever
8. Boot
9. Screw
10. Retainer
11. Nut

Fig. 3 Common upper shift lever mounting—2-piece shift lever

Back-Up Light Switch

REMOVAL & INSTALLATION

1. Disconnect the negative battery cable.
2. Locate the switch on the left or right rear of the transmission housing (depending on the application), the back-up light switch is threaded into the transmission case. The speed sensor is held in with a separate bracket. Disengage the electrical connector from the back-up light switch.
3. Remove the back-up light switch from the transmission.
4. To install, reverse the removal procedures.
5. With the engine NOT running (for safety), place the gear shift lever in the reverse position and check that the back-up lights work.

Extension Housing Seal

The extension housing seal (located in the tail section of the transmission assembly) controls oil leakage around the driveshaft. Continued failure of this seal usually indicates a worn output shaft bushing. If so, there will be signs of the same wear on the driveshaft, at the point where it contacts the seal and bushing. The seal is a fairly simple component to install, but it requires the proper driver tool to assure proper installation and prevent the danger of component damage.

1. Raise and support the rear of the truck safely using jackstands. If the rear of the vehicle is supported sufficiently, transmission oil loss will be minimized during the procedure. Keep a drain pan handy though, just to be sure.
2. Matchmark and remove the driveshaft from the truck. Refer to the procedure later in this section for details.
3. Pry the seal out of the transmission extension housing. Be careful not to score and damage the housing sealing surface when removing the seal.

To install:
4. Coat the outside of the replacement seal using a suitable locking compound.
5. Fill between the seal lips with chassis grease and drive the seal into position using J-21426, or an equivalent seal installation tool.
6. Align and install the driveshaft.
7. Lower the rear of the truck or raise and support the front as well so the vehicle is level, then check the transmission fluid and add, as necessary. Remove the jackstands and carefully lower the vehicle.

Transmission

REMOVAL & INSTALLATION

♦ See Figures 4 and 5

Manual transmission removal on most vehicles covered by this manual can be done through the following, fairly straightforward procedures. In most cases, the transmission can be removed leaving the bellhousing and the clutch assembly in position. The bellhousing on the 77.5mm 4-speed and MW2 (New Venture Gear) 5-speed is integral with the transmission casing and therefore must be unbolted in order to remove the transmission assembly. Of course, if the transmission is being removed for clutch replacement, the bellhousing must be removed anyway.

On many of the vehicles covered by this manual, the upper bellhousing-to-engine bolts (especially the upper left) may be difficult to access and withdraw due to the close proximity of the cowl sheet metal. Even if a wrench fits over the bolt, there may be insufficient room to fully unthread it. The factory recommended procedure to access these bolts is to remove the left body mount bolt(s) from under the cab and loosen the radiator support mounting, then carefully jack the body up off the frame until sufficient clearance exists. Place wooden blocks between the body and frame to support the body (this is to prevent damage and for SAFETY) during service. In some cases, this may be unnecessary if the engine will pivot downward sufficiently on the motor mount to allow bolt access or if the motor mounts are removed and the engine is supported using a lifting device. BUT DO NOT try this if it appears that the mounts will be damaged by the stress. Also, be sure the engine is properly supported at ALL times and that no components will be damaged. Watch that the distributor does not contact the cowl and that the cooling fan remains clear of the radiator and shroud assembly. When in doubt, unbolt and raise the body for access.

Vehicles Through 1988

2-WHEEL DRIVE

1. Disconnect the negative battery terminal from the battery.
2. If the bellhousing is being removed with the transmission (77.5mm 4-speed) remove the starter. The 77mm 4-speed and 5-speed can be removed without removing the bellhousing.
3. Shift the transmission into Neutral. Remove the shift lever boot-to-console screws and slide the boot up the shift lever.
4. Remove the shift lever.
5. Raise and safely support the truck on jackstands. Remove the drain plug and drain the oil. Dispose of old oil properly at a reclamation center, such as a gas station or parts retailer.
6. Disconnect the speedometer cable and/or the electrical wiring connectors from the transmission.
7. Remove the driveshaft. Refer to the Driveline section if necessary.
8. Disconnect the exhaust pipe-to-exhaust manifold nuts and separate the exhaust pipe from the manifold.
9. On the 1982–83 models, disconnect the clutch cable from the clutch lever. On the 1984–91 models, remove the clutch slave cylinder from the clutch release lever. It can be secured out of the way without disconnecting the hydraulic line.
10. Position a floor jack under the transmission and support the transmission. Secure the jack to the transmission so it won't slip
11. Remove the transmission-to-crossmember mount bolts.
12. Remove the catalytic converter-to-chassis hanger bolts.
13. Remove the crossmember-to-chassis bolts and the crossmember from the vehicle.
14. If the bellhousing is being removed, remove the clutch cover from the front of the housing.

➡On some vehicles, access to and removal of the upper bellhousing bolts may be difficult. Refer to the text at the beginning of the transmission removal procedures for suggestions.

15. Unbolt the bellhousing from the engine, or the transmission from the bellhousing and carefully roll the floor jack straight back away from the engine. Carefully lower it from the vehicle.
16. Installation is the reverse of removal. Lightly coat the input shaft spline with high temperature or molybdenum grease. Don't use too much or the clutch disc will be ruined. On 4-cylinder engines with the 77.5mm transmission, torque the bellhousing-to-engine bolts to 25 ft. lbs. (34 Nm). On all others, torque the bolts to 55 ft. lbs. (75 Nm). Install the cross member and torque the bolts to 25 ft. lbs. (34 Nm).

85387006

Fig. 4 View of the transmission crossmember (upper or forward of the 2 visible members)

4-WHEEL DRIVE

1. Shift the transfer case into **4H**.
2. Disconnect the negative battery cable.
3. Raise and support the vehicle safely using jackstands. Remove the skid plate.
4. Drain the lubricant from the transfer case.
5. Mark the transfer case front output shaft yoke and driveshaft for assembly reference. Disconnect the front driveshaft from the transfer case.
6. Mark the rear axle yoke and driveshaft for assembly reference. Remove the rear driveshaft.
7. Disconnect the speedometer cable and vacuum harness at the transfer case. Remove the shift lever from the transfer case.
8. Remove the catalytic converter hanger bolts at the converter.
9. Raise the transmission and transfer case and remove the transmission mount attaching bolts. Remove the mount and catalytic converter hanger and lower the transmission and transfer case.
10. If the bellhousing is being removed, remove the clutch cover from the front of the housing.

➡ **On some vehicles, access to and removal of the upper bellhousing bolts may be difficult. Refer to the text at the beginning of the transmission removal procedures for suggestions.**

11. Unbolt the bellhousing from the engine, or the transmission from the bellhousing and carefully roll the floor jack straight back away from the engine. Carefully lower it from the vehicle.
12. Installation is the reverse of removal. Lightly coat the input shaft spline with high temperature or molybdenum grease. Don't use too much or the clutch disc will be ruined. On 4-cylinder engines with the 77.5mm transmission, torque the bellhousing-to-engine bolts to 25 ft. lbs. (34 Nm). On all others, torque all the bolts to 55 ft. lbs. (75 Nm). Install the crossmember and torque the bolts to 25 ft. lbs. (34 Nm).

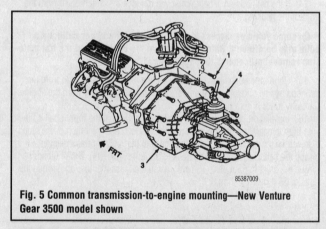

85387009

Fig. 5 Common transmission-to-engine mounting—New Venture Gear 3500 model shown

1989–93 Vehicles

1. Disconnect the negative battery cable.
2. Remove the shift lever. For details, please refer to the procedure earlier in this section.
3. Raise and support the vehicle safely using jackstands.
4. Disconnect the parking brake cable for clearance. Before disconnecting the cable, you may want to measure the adjustment or scribe marks to ease adjustment after installation.
5. Matchmark and remove the driveshaft. For details, please refer to the procedure later in this section.
6. If equipped, remove the skid plate.
7. On 4wd vehicles, remove the transfer case and shift lever. For details, please refer to the procedure later in this section.
8. Tag and disengage the necessary wiring connectors, including the reverse (backup) light switch and Vehicle Speed Sensor (VSS) connectors.
9. For 1992–93 4.3L engines, properly relieve the fuel system pressure, then disconnect the fuel lines at the engine.
10. Disconnect the exhaust pipes.

➡ **On some vehicles, access to and removal of the upper bellhousing bolts may be difficult. Refer to the text at the beginning of the transmission removal procedures for suggestions.**

11. Remove the slave cylinder from the transmission. If the cylinder can be repositioned with the hydraulics intact, simply support it out of the way, but make sure the line is not stretched, kinked or otherwise damaged. If necessary, disconnect the line and remove the cylinder completely.
12. Support the transmission carefully using a floor jack. If possible, secure the transmission to the jack to keep it from shifting suddenly and falling.
13. Remove the transmission mount retainers.
14. If necessary, remove the catalytic converter support hanger.
15. Disconnect or remove the necessary support braces.
16. If necessary, unbolt and remove the transmission crossmember.
17. Make sure the transmission is properly supported, then remove the transmission-to-bellhousing or transmission-to-engine bolts, as necessary.
18. Carefully pull the transmission assembly, straight back to disengage the input shaft splines, DO NOT allow the transmission to hang on the clutch. For 4.3L engines it may be necessary to rotate the transmission counterclockwise, then pull back and disengage it from the engine. Once the transmission is disengaged, slowly lower the jack and transmission to remove it from the vehicle.
19. Installation is the reverse of removal. Place a THIN coat of high-temperature grease on the main drive gear (input shaft) splines, then shift the transmission into height gear. Once the transmission is properly positioned, install the retaining bolts and tighten to 55 ft. lbs. (75 Nm).

➡ **For 4.3L engines, it may be necessary to rotate the transmission clockwise while inserting it to the clutch hub.**

CLUTCH

Adjustment

Since the hydraulic system provides automatic clutch adjustment, no adjustment of the clutch linkage or pedal height is required on vehicles equipped with the master and slave cylinder actuator system.

CLUTCH CABLE

Vehicles not equipped with a hydraulic clutch actuator system (1982–83) are equipped with a linkage or cable system. The clutch cable should be adjusted in order to provide proper pedal feel and clutch actuation/engagement.

The early model vehicles equipped with a clutch cable utilize a self-adjuster which is easily reset:

1. Lift up on the pedal to allow the self adjuster to adjust the cable length.
2. Depress the pedal several times to set the pawl into mesh with the detent teeth.
3. Make sure the clutch is working properly. If troubles are found, check the linkage for lost motion caused by loose or worn swivels, mounting brackets or a damaged cable.

Clutch Disc and Pressure Plate

REMOVAL & INSTALLATION

▸ **See Figures 6, 7, 8 and 9**

✳✳ CAUTION

The clutch plate contains asbestos, which has been determined to be a cancer causing agent. Never clean the clutch surfaces with compressed air! Avoid inhaling any dust from any clutch surface! When cleaning clutch surfaces, use a commercially available brake cleaning fluid. If a spray cleaning fluid is not available, use a water dampened (NOT SOAKED) cloth to wipe away dust from the assembly.

1. Remove the manual transmission assembly from the vehicle. For details, refer to the procedures located earlier in this section.

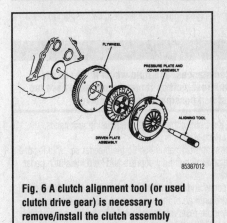

Fig. 6 A clutch alignment tool (or used clutch drive gear) is necessary to remove/install the clutch assembly

Fig. 7 Using a slide-hammer puller tool to remove the pilot bearing from the flywheel

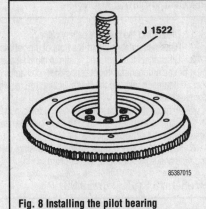

Fig. 8 Installing the pilot bearing

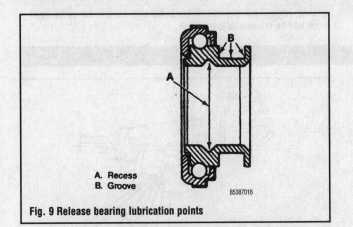

A. Recess
B. Groove

Fig. 9 Release bearing lubrication points

2. If equipped with a clutch cable (1982–83) and not performed for transmission removal, disconnect the cable from the clutch lever and move it aside.

3. If equipped with a hydraulic clutch system (1984–93) and not performed for transmission removal, disconnect the slave cylinder from the clutch release fork and move it aside.

4. If the bellhousing was not removed with the transmission, remove the inspection cover (if equipped), then loosen the retaining bolts and remove the bellhousing from the rear of the engine assembly.

5. Remove the clutch fork from the ball stud (by carefully prying it free) and the dust boot (if applicable). Except for vehicles equipped with a New Venture Gear transmission, carefully pry the retainer out of the clutch fork (if it is not damaged). On late model vehicles, or as necessary, remove the ball stud.

➡A used clutch drive gear may be used as an alignment tool. This may be available inexpensively from a junk yard or a transmission rebuilding shop.

6. Insert a clutch alignment tool such as No. J-33169 (V6 and late-model 4-cylinders), J-33034 (early model 4-cylinders), or equivalent, into the crankshaft pilot bearing to support the clutch assembly.

7. Check for an "X" or other painted mark on the pressure plate and flywheel. If no marks are readily visible, matchmark the flywheel, clutch cover and pressure plate lug for installation purposes.

8. Loosen the pressure plate-to-flywheel bolts, evenly and alternately, a little at a time, until the spring tension is released. Remove the pressure plate, driven clutch plate and alignment tool.

To install:

9. Check the flywheel for cracks, wear, scoring or other damage. Check the pilot bearing for wear. If necessary, replace the bearing by removing it with a slide-type bearing puller and driving in a new one with a wood or plastic hammer. Lubricate the new pilot bearing with a few drops of machine oil.

10. If available, check the driven plate for run-out using a dial gauge. Run-out should not exceed 0.02 in. (5.08mm).

11. Using the clutch alignment tool to support the clutch, align and install the clutch plate and cover assembly. If a new clutch is being installed align the manufacturer's marks as directed.

12. Install the washers and bolts, then tighten each bolt one turn at a time to avoid warping the clutch cover. If spring washers were used, new ones should be installed. Once the bolts are fully threaded, tighten each one to 15 ft. lbs. (20 Nm) for vehicles through 1991 or to 30 ft. lbs. (40 Nm) for 1992–93 vehicles. Remove the clutch alignment tool.

13. If removed, install the ball stud. Pack the seat and coat the rounded end of the ball stud with high temperature (wheel-bearing) grease.

➡The clutch release bearing used on most vehicles covered by this manual is permanently packed with lubricant and should NOT be soaked in cleaning solvent as this will dissolve the lubricant.

14. Install the release bearing and the clutch fork. Pack the inside recess (A) and coat the outside groove (B) of the release bearing with high-temperature wheel-bearing grease. Please refer to the illustration for lubrication points.

15. If separate, install the flywheel housing and install the retaining bolts.

16. If removed, install the inspection cover.

17. For vehicles equipped with a hydraulic clutch system (and the flywheel housing is already installed), reposition and secure the slave cylinder.

18. For vehicles equipped with a clutch cable (and the flywheel housing is already installed), install and adjust the clutch cable.

19. Install the manual transmission assembly. For details, please refer to the procedures located earlier in this section.

Master Cylinder and Reservoir

The clutch master cylinder is located in the engine compartment, on the left-side of the firewall, above or near the steering column.

REMOVAL & INSTALLATION

1. Disconnect the negative battery cable.
2. Remove hush panel or lower filler panel from under the dash.
3. If necessary, remove the lower left A/C duct.
4. Remove the push rod retainer, then disconnect push rod from clutch pedal.
5. Either disconnect the reservoir hose (if the reservoir is not being removed or if there is no clearance for reservoir removal with the hose installed) or remove the reservoir retainers.
6. Disconnect slave cylinder hydraulic line from the clutch master cylinder. Immediately plug all openings to prevent system contamination or excessive fluid loss.
7. Remove the master cylinder-to-cowl brace nuts. Remove master cylinder and overhaul (if necessary).
8. Installatuion is the reverse of removal. Tighten the retainers to 13 ft. lbs. (18 Nm). Properly refill the master cylinder reservoir, then bleed the system of air and check for fluid leaks.

Slave (Secondary) Cylinder

The slave cylinder is located on the left side of the bellhousing and controls the clutch release fork operation. For more information, please refer to understanding the clutch, earlier in this section.

REMOVAL & INSTALLATION

1. Disconnect the negative battery cable.
2. Raise and safely support the front of the vehicle safely using jackstands.
3. Disconnect the hydraulic line from clutch master cylinder. Immediately plug or cap all openings to prevent system contamination or excessive fluid loss. If equipped, remove the hydraulic line-to-chassis screw and the clip from the chassis.
4. Remove the slave cylinder-to-bellhousing nuts.
5. Remove the push rod and the slave cylinder assembly from the vehicle, then overhaul it (if necessary).
6. Install the slave cylinder to the bellhousing, then secure using the retaining nuts and tighten to 13 ft. lbs. (18 Nm).

HYDRAULIC SYSTEM BLEEDING

Bleeding air from the hydraulic clutch system is necessary whenever any part of the system has been disconnected or the fluid level (in the reservoir) has been allowed to fall so low, that air has been drawn into the master cylinder.

1. Fill master cylinder reservoir with new brake fluid conforming to Dot 3 specifications.

> **✳✳ CAUTION**
>
> **Never, under any circumstances, use fluid which has been bled from a system to fill the reservoir as it may be aerated, have too much moisture content and possibly be contaminated.**

2. Raise and support the front of the vehicle safely using jackstands.
3. Remove the slave cylinder retainers.
4. Hold slave cylinder at approximately 45° so the bleeder screw is located at the highest point. Have an assistant fully depress and hold the clutch pedal, then open the bleeder screw.
5. Close the bleeder screw and have your assistant release the clutch pedal.
6. Repeat the procedure until all of the air is evacuated from the system. Check and refill master cylinder reservoir as required to prevent air from being drawn through the master cylinder.

➡ **Never release a depressed clutch pedal with the bleeder screw open or air will be drawn into the system.**

AUTOMATIC TRANSMISSION

Adjustments

SHIFT LINKAGE

▶ **See Figures 10 and 11**

The shift linkage should be adjusted so that transmission is in the proper gear when the selector is in the shift gate. The shift indicator position should not be relied on, instead, make sure the shifter properly engages each gate position when the transmission is shifted to each gear. After adjustment, check the back-up light/neutral safety switch adjustment to be sure the engine will only start when the transmission is in the Park or Neutral positions.

1. Firmly apply the parking brake and chock the rear wheels.
2. Raise and safely support the front of the vehicle on jackstands.
3. At the left-side of the transmission, loosen the shift rod swivel-to-equalizer lever nut or retaining bolt, as equipped.
4. At the steering column, place the gear selector lever into the Neutral position.

➡ **When positioning the gear selector lever, DO NOT use the steering column indicator to find the Neutral position. Instead rely on the mechanical shift gate.**

5. Rotate the transmission shift lever counterclockwise (forward) to the 1st detent (Park) position, then turn it clockwise (rearward) to the 2nd detent (Neutral) position.
6. Tightly, hold the shifting rod (swivel) in position, then torque the

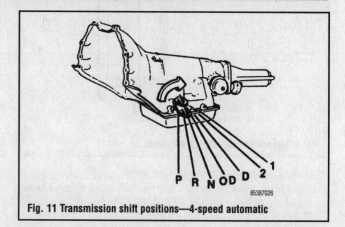

Fig. 11 Transmission shift positions—4-speed automatic

adjusting nut to 11 ft. lbs. (15 Nm) or the bolt to 18 ft. lbs. (25 Nm), as applicable.

7. Place the gear selector lever (on the steering column) in the Park position and check the adjustment. Move the gear selector lever into the various positions; the engine must start in the Park and the Neutral positions.

➡ **If the engine will not start in the Neutral and/or Park positions (or will start in gear), refer to back-up light switch adjustment procedures in Section 6 of this manual, then properly adjust the switch.**

> **✳✳ CAUTION**
>
> **With the gear selector lever in the Park position, the parking pawl should engage the rear internal gear lugs or output ring gear lugs to prevent the vehicle from rolling and possibly causing personal injury.**

8. Align the gear selector lever indicator, if necessary. Remove the jackstands and carefully lower the vehicle.

THROTTLE VALVE (TV) CABLE

▶ **See Figures 12 and 13**

The non-electronically controlled transmissions covered by this manual utilize a throttle valve and TV cable. If the TV cable is broken, sticking, misadjusted or if an incorrect part is installed for the model, the vehicle may exhibit various malfunctions, such as: delayed or full throttle shifts.

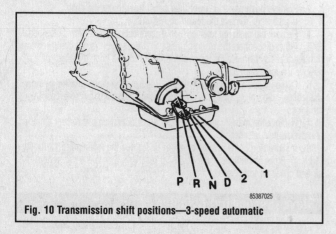

Fig. 10 Transmission shift positions—3-speed automatic

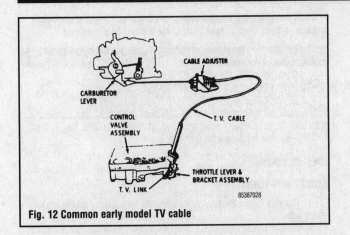

Fig. 12 Common early model TV cable

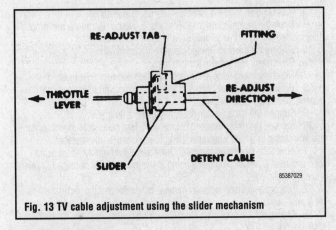

Fig. 13 TV cable adjustment using the slider mechanism

Preliminary Checks

1. Inspect and/or correct the transmission fluid level.
2. Make sure that the brakes are not dragging and that the engine is operating correctly.
3. Make sure that the cable is connected at both ends.
4. Make sure that the correct cable is installed.

Adjustment

1. If necessary for access, remove the air cleaner assembly.
2. If the cable has been removed and installed, pull on the upper end of the cable. It should travel a short distance with light resistance caused by the small return spring on the TV lever. When released, check to see that the cable slider returns to the zero or the fully adjusted position; if not, adjust the cable and slider:
   a. Depress and hold the readjust tab on the end of the TV cable.
   b. Move the slider back on the cable (away from the throttle lever) until it stops against the fitting.
   c. Release the readjust tab.
3. Rotate the throttle lever by hand (DO NOT use the accelerator pedal) to the full throttle stop (wide open throttle) position. The slider must move (ratchet) toward the lever in order to adjust the cable when the lever is rotated.
4. Release the throttle lever and check for proper operation.

➡**The throttle valve cable adjustment should be rechecked with the engine at normal operating temperature. A cable may appear to function properly while the engine is cold, but no work properly when warmed.**

Back-Up Lamp/Neutral Safety Switch

The back-up lamp/neutral safety switch assembly is mounted either on the steering column or on the floor shifter assembly, under the console, depending on the vehicle and application. Most models utilize a steering column mounted shifter for the automatic transmission, therefore the switch will be found on the steering column for most vehicles covered by this manual. For the removal,

installation and adjustment procedures, please refer to the back-up lamp/neutral safety switch procedures in Section 6, of this manual.

Extension Housing Seal

REMOVAL & INSTALLATION

▶ **See Figure 14**

1. Raise and support the vehicle safely using jackstands. If the rear of the vehicle is supported significantly higher than the front of the truck, the transmission fluid may not have to be drained for this service.
2. Remove the transmission fluid pan and drain the fluid from the vehicle. This step is recommended, but may not be necessary if the rear of the vehicle is held higher than the front. What is important is that the sealing surface in the extension housing may be cleaned of fluid and debris before installing the new seal. If fluid continues to run out of the housing once the old seal is removed, then the fluid should be drained to allow for proper seal installation.
3. Matchmark and remove the driveshaft. Most vehicles covered in this manual should be equipped with a slip yoke and the front of the driveshaft. In order to remove the shaft, disconnect it from the rear axle, then carefully withdraw the splined yoke from the rear of the transmission.
4. Carefully distort the seal using a punch, then pry the seal from the rear of the transmission housing. Be careful not to damage the sealing surface of the housing.
   To install:
5. Clean and DRY the sealing surface in the rear of the transmission housing.
6. Coat the outside of the new seal with a non-hardening sealing compound.
7. Carefully drive the new seal into position using a proper seal installation tool. Be careful not to damage the housing or the transmission output shaft upon installation.
8. Align and install the driveshaft assembly.
9. Remove the jackstands and carefully lower the vehicle.
10. Immediately check and, if necessary, add fresh transmission fluid.
Please refer to Section 1 of this manual for details concerning proper methods and type of automatic transmission fluid.

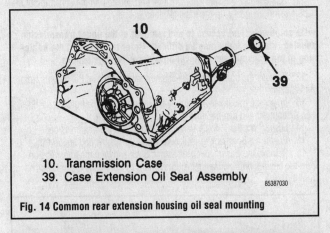

10. Transmission Case
39. Case Extension Oil Seal Assembly

Fig. 14 Common rear extension housing oil seal mounting

Transmission

REMOVAL & INSTALLATION

On many of the vehicles covered by this manual, the upper transmission-to-engine bolts (especially the upper left) may be difficult to access and withdraw due to the close proximity of the cowl sheet metal. Even if a wrench fits over the bolt, there may be insufficient room to fully unthread it. The factory recommended procedure to access these bolts is to remove the left body mount bolt(s) from under the cab and loosen the radiator support mounting, then carefully jack the body up off the frame until sufficient clearance exists. Place wooden blocks between the body and frame to support the body (this is to prevent damage and for SAFETY) during service. In some cases, this may be unnecessary if the engine will pivot downward sufficiently on the motor mount to allow bolt access or if the motor mounts are removed and the engine is supported using a lifting device. BUT DO NOT try this if it appears that the mounts will be damaged by the stress. Also, be sure the engine is properly supported at ALL times and that no components will be damaged. Watch that the distributor does not contact the cowl and that the cooling fan remains clear of the radiator and shroud assembly. When in doubt, unbolt and raise the body for access.

Vehicles Through 1991

EXCEPT MFI-TURBO

♦ See Figure 15

➡ The following procedure requires the use of the Torque Converter Holding Strap tool No. J-21366 or equivalent.

1. Disconnect the negative battery cable.
2. Remove the air cleaner assembly.
3. Disconnect the Throttle Valve (TV) cable from the throttle linkage.

➡ If equipped with a 4-cylinder engine, remove the upper starter bolt.

4. Raise and support the truck safely using jackstands.
5. Remove the driveshaft-to-differential bolts, then slide the driveshaft from the transmission (2wd) or transfer case (4wd).

➡ On 4wd vehicles, the transfer case will be removed along with the transmission as an assembly.

6. Disconnect the speedometer cable, the dipstick tube (and seal), the shift linkage (transmission and transfer case, on 4wd) and the electrical wiring connectors from the transmission.
7. Remove the transmission-to-catalytic converter support brackets and the engine-to-transmission support brackets, if equipped.
8. Remove the transmission-to-crossmember nuts/bolts, slide the crossmember rearward and remove it from the vehicle.
9. Remove the torque converter cover, then match-mark the torque converter-to-flywheel.
10. Remove the torque converter-to-flywheel bolts. Using the converter holding strap tool No. J-21366 or equivalent, secure the torque converter to the transmission.
11. Using a transmission jack, position and secure it to the underside of the transmission, then take up the transmissions weight.

➡ On some vehicles, access to and removal of the upper transmission housing retaining bolts may be difficult. Refer to the text at the beginning of the transmission removal procedures for suggestions.

12. Remove the transmission-to-engine mount bolts and the mounts from the vehicle.
13. Lower the transmission slightly to gain access to the fluid cooler lines, then disconnect and cap the fluid lines.
14. Disconnect the Throttle Valve (TV) cable from the transmission.
15. Position a floor jack or jackstand under the engine and support it.
16. Remove the transmission-to-engine bolts and then the transmission from the engine; pull the transmission rearward to disengage it and lower it from the truck.

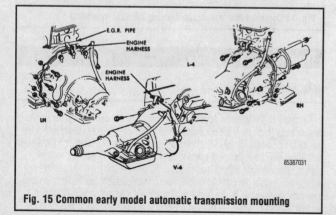

Fig. 15 Common early model automatic transmission mounting

➡ When removing the transmission, be careful not to allow the transmission to hang from the pilot shaft, for it could become bent.

17. Installation is the reverse of removal. Tighten the transmission-to-engine bolts to specification
- 1.9L engine: 25 ft. lbs. (35 Nm)
- 2.5L and 2.8L engines through 1988: 55 ft. lbs. (75 Nm)
- 2.5L and 2.8L engines 1989–91: 75 ft. lbs. (101 Nm)
18. Install all the converter–to–flywheel bolts finger tight, then tighten the bolts to 35 ft. lbs. (50 Nm) for vehicles through 1988 or to 62 ft. lbs. (84 Nm) for 1989–91 vehicles. Install the converter cover.

1992–93 Vehicles

EXCEPT MFI-TURBO

1. Properly relieve the fuel system pressure, then disconnect the negative battery cable.
2. Remove the air cleaner assembly. If equipped (4L60 model) disconnect the TV cable from the TBI unit.
3. Raise and support the vehicle safely using jackstands.
4. Drain the transmission fluid. For details, please refer to the pan procedure located earlier in this section or in Section 1 of this manual.
5. Disconnect the shift linkage from the transmission.
6. Disconnect and remove the fuel lines.
7. Matchmark and remove the front (if used) and rear driveshafts.
8. Remove the support bracket at the catalytic converter. Remove any components necessary for clearance.
9. Support the transmission assembly using a floor jack.
10. Remove the transmission crossmember. Take care not to stretch or damage any cables or wiring when attempting to remove the crossmember.
11. Lower the transmission slightly for access, then remove the dipstick tube and seal. Cover or plug the opening in the transmission housing to prevent system contamination.
12. Disengage the speedometer harness connector and the vacuum modulator line, if used.
13. Disengage the necessary electrical wiring connectors from the transmission assembly.
14. Disconnect the transmission fluid cooler lines. Plug or cap all openings to prevent system contamination or excessive fluid spillage.
15. On 4wd vehicles, disengage the transfer case shifter and position it aside.
16. Remove the transmission support braces. Be sure to tag or note the location of all support braces as they must be installed in their original positions.
17. Remove the torque converter housing cover.
18. Matchmark the flywheel-to-torque converter relationship, then remove the retaining bolts.
19. Support the engine using a jackstand and a block of wood.
20. Remove the transmission-to-engine retaining bolts. Note the positions of any brackets or clips and move them aside.
21. Using the floor jack, slide the transmission straight back off the locating pins. Be careful not to drop the torque converter, then as soon as access is possible, install a torque converter retaining strap.
22. Carefully lower the transmission from the vehicle.
23. Installation is the reverse of removal. Install and finger-tighten the converter bolts, then tighten them to 50 ft. lbs. (68 Nm). Tighten the transmission-to-engine retainers and the dipstick tube retainer, then tighten the bolts to 23 ft. lbs. (32 Nm).

MFI-Turbo

1. Disconnect the negative battery cable.
2. Raise and support the vehicle safely using jackstands.
3. Remove the transfer case from the vehicle. For details, please refer to the procedures located later in this section.
4. Loosen and remove the retainers, then remove the torque converter cover.
5. Disengage the shift control cable from the transmission.
6. Remove the bolt and retaining clip, then reposition the fuel lines and speed sensor harness.
7. Disconnect the TV cable.

8. Remove the retaining nuts, then disconnect the oil cooler lines from the transmission.

9. Disconnect the vent hose by removing the retaining strap, then pulling the hose through the clip.

10. Remove the dipstick from the filler tube. Remove the filler tube retaining bracket and bolt, then carefully pull the tube from the transmission. Keep track of the oil seal located on the base of the tube.

11. Loosen the nuts from the transmission-to-engine studs located on the right side of the housing, then remove the bracket.

TRANSFER CASE

Identification

An identification tag, which is usually attached to the rear half of the case (lower portion of case on Borg Warner model), gives the model number, low range reduction ratio and assembly number. Most vehicles covered by this manual use one of two units: the New Process 207 and the New Process 231. Early model vehicles equipped with a floor mounted transfer case shifter are equipped with the 207, while late model vehicles with the floor shift are equipped with the 231. Some later model vehicles covered by this manual (1991–93) may be equipped with an electronic shift transfer case, the New Process 233. The MFI-Turbo was equipped with a Borg Warner 4472 transfer case.

The Model 207 transfer case is an aluminum case, chain drive, 4 position unit providing 4wd High and Low ranges, a 2wd High range and a Neutral position. The 207 is a part-time 4wd unit. Range positions are selected by a floor mounted shift lever. Dexron® II automatic transmission fluid, or equivalent, is usually the recommended lubricant for this unit, though some models may use SAE 80W or SAE-80W-90 GL5. Be sure to check your owners manual to be certain if Dexron®II is correct for your model.

The Model 231 is a part-time transfer case with a built in low range gear reduction system. A front axle disconnect mechanism is used for 2-wheel drive operation. The 231 has three operating ranges — 2-wheel drive High and 4-wheel drive High and Low, plus Neutral. The 4-wheel drive operating ranges are undifferentiated. Dexron® II automatic transmission fluid, or equivalent, is used as a lubricant.

The Model 233 is an electronic shift transfer case that has 3 modes of operation: 2wd range, 4wd High, and 4wd Low. Gear reduction for low range is provided by a planetary gear set. The floor mounted shifter has been replaced by a dash mounted switch for these units.

The Borg Warner 4472 transfer case is a 2-piece aluminum case, chain driven, viscous clutch type transfer case. This produces a system in which all wheel drive is engaged all of the time. Torque is transmitted through a planetary gear set which distributes torque at a ratio of ⅓ front and ⅔ rear.

Adjustments

SHIFT LEVER/LINKAGE

Only the 207 and 231 model transfer cases are equipped with a shift lever. In order to adjust the lever/linkage assembly, then floor console must be removed for access. The original floor shift mechanism was used on vehicles covered by this manual.

▶ **See Figure 16**

1. Remove the center console for access to the shift lever retainers.
2. Raise the floor shift lever boot upward on the lever.
3. Loosen the detent switch bracket retaining bolt and the floor shift lever pivot bolt (also threaded through the detent switch bracket).
4. Manually place the transfer case lever in the 4 High position (refer to the illustration).
5. Install a suitable lock bolt to hold the transfer case lever in position. (refer to the illustration).
6. Insert a ⁵⁄₁₆ in. (8mm) drill bit (gauge pin) through the hole in the shift lever and into the upper corner of the switch bracket. This will assure that the switch is aligned with 4 High position.
7. Tighten the floor shift lever pivot bolt to 75 ft. lbs. (102 Nm) and the detent switch bracket retaining bolt to 30 ft. lbs. (40 Nm).
8. Remove the lock bolt and the gauge pin/drill bit.

12. Make sure the transmission is securely supported by a floor jack, then remove the engine-to-transmission bolts and studs.

13. Remove the transmission by carefully pulling the assembly back and, once it is disengaged from the converter, by lowering it from the vehicle.

14. Installation is the reverse of removal.. Tighten the transmission-to-engine retainers to 35 ft. lbs. (47 Nm). Position the bracket over the studs on the right side of the housing, then install the retaining nuts and tighten to 22 ft. lbs. (30 Nm).

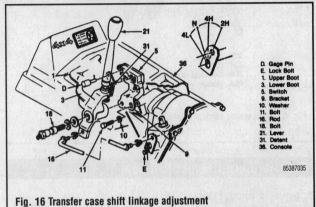

D.	Gage Pin
E.	Lock Bolt
1.	Upper Boot
3.	Lower Boot
5.	Switch
9.	Bracket
10.	Washer
11.	Bolt
16.	Rod
18.	Bolt
21.	Lever
31.	Detent
36.	Console

Fig. 16 Transfer case shift linkage adjustment

9. Verify proper shifting action.
10. Reposition the floor shift lever boot and install the center console.

Shift Motor

REMOVAL & INSTALLATION

The Model 233 transfer case, available on some late model vehicles covered by this manual, utilizes an electronic shifter. The motor is attached to the lower side of the transfer case.

1. Disconnect the negative battery cable.
2. Raise and support the vehicle safely using jackstands.
3. If equipped, remove the transfer case shield for access.
4. Disengage the motor electrical connector.
5. Matchmark and remove the front driveshaft and the output shaft yoke. For details, please refer to the procedure later in this section.
6. Remove the motor-to-transfer case retaining bolts, then remove the motor from the case.
7. Installation is the reverse of removal. Tighten the retaining bolts to 13 ft. lbs. (18 Nm).

Shift Motor Control Module

REMOVAL & INSTALLATION

▶ **See Figure 17**

The Model 233 transfer case, available on some late model vehicles covered by this manual, utilizes an electronic shifter. The motor control module is located behind the cowl panel, attached to the ECM bracket.

1. Disconnect the negative battery cable.
2. Remove the ECM from the vehicle for access to the module. Take extreme care when handling the computer control module. Refer to Section 4 for details and safety precautions.
3. Disengage the electrical wiring from the module.
4. Loosen the retainers, then remove the module from the vehicle.
5. Installation is the reverse of removal. MAKE SURE the ignition remains **OFF** when installing the ECM. On all vehicles, the ignition MUST be **OFF** whenever you connect or disconnect the negative battery cable.

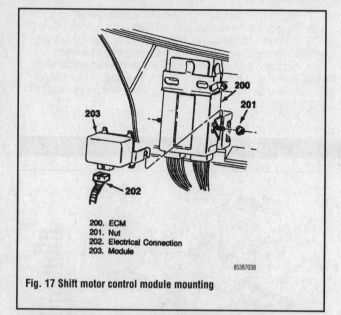

200. ECM
201. Nut
202. Electrical Connection
203. Module

85387038

Fig. 17 Shift motor control module mounting

Transfer Case Output Shaft Seal

REMOVAL & INSTALLATION

▶ **See Figure 18**

1. Raise and support the vehicle safely using jackstands.
2. Matchmark and remove the front or rear driveshaft, as applicable.
3. Remove the shaft yoke nut and washers, then remove the yoke and shield for access to the seal.
4. Pry out the old seal using a small suitable prytool. Be careful not to damage the seal bore.

To install:

5. Lubricate the lips of the new seal using automatic transmission fluid or petroleum jelly, whichever is at hand.
6. Position the seal and carefully drive it into position using a suitable seal installer tool.
7. Install the shield and shaft yoke, then install the washers and yoke nut. Tighten the nut to 110 ft. lbs. (149 Nm).
8. Align and install the driveshaft to the vehicle.
9. Remove the jackstands and carefully lower the vehicle.

Transfer Case

REMOVAL & INSTALLATION

▶ **See Figures 19, 20 and 21**

Vehicles Through 1991

1. Disconnect the negative battery cable.
2. Shift the transfer case into the 4wd High range.
3. Raise and support the vehicle safely using jackstands.
4. If equipped, remove the skid plate bolts and remove the skid plate from under the transmission/transfer case assembly.
5. On Model 231 transfer cases, remove the plug and drain the transfer case fluid.
6. Matchmark and remove the front and rear driveshafts from the transfer case.
7. Disconnect the speedometer cable(s), the vacuum harness and/or the electrical connectors, as necessary.
8. Disconnect the shift linkage from the case. If necessary for access from above, remove the center console from the vehicle.
9. Remove the catalytic converter front bracket bolts, then loosen the front converter clamp.

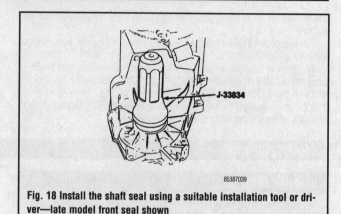

85387039

Fig. 18 Install the shaft seal using a suitable installation tool or driver—late model front seal shown

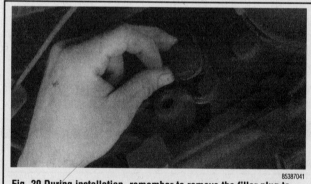

85387040

Fig. 19 It is recommended that the fluid be drained from most transfer cases before removal

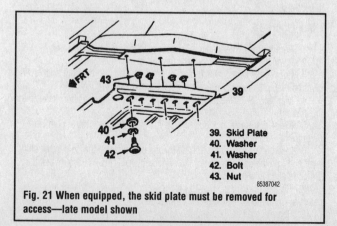

85387041

Fig. 20 During installation, remember to remove the filler plug to check the level and, if necessary, add fluid

39. Skid Plate
40. Washer
41. Washer
42. Bolt
43. Nut

85387042

Fig. 21 When equipped, the skid plate must be removed for access—late model shown

10. Support the transmission using a floor jack, then remove the transmission rear mounting bolts.

11. Carefully raise the transmission/transfer case assembly and remove the catalytic converter front bracket, then lower the assembly. Position a support (such as a jackstand) to keep the transmission in place.

12. Reposition the floor jack to support the transfer case, then remove transfer case retaining bolts. On vehicles equipped with automatic transmissions, remove the bolts from the shift lever bracket and position the bracket aside. This will permit access to the upper left transfer case attaching bolt.

13. Carefully lower the transfer case from the vehicle, then remove all traces of the old gasket from the mating surface.

To install:

14. Use a new transfer case-to-transmission gasket and mount the unit to the transmission. Torque the bolts to 23 ft. lbs. (31 Nm).

15. If removed, install the shift lever bracket bolts.

16. Remove the floor jack from the transfer case, then reposition the jack under the transmission. Remove the transmission support.

17. Raise the transmission/transfer case assembly in order to install the catalytic converter front hanger.

18. Once the converter front bracket is positioned, lower the assembly and remove the floor jack. Secure the transmission rear mounting bolts and the converter front bracket bolts. Don't forget to tighten the converter clamp.

19. Install the remaining components in the reverse of removal.

1992–93 Vehicles

1. Disconnect the negative battery cable.
2. Shift the transfer case into the 4wd High range.

3. Raise and support the vehicle safely using jackstands.

4. If equipped, remove the skid plate bolts, then remove the skid plate from under the transmission/transfer case assembly.

5. Remove the plug and drain the transfer case fluid.

6. Matchmark and remove the front and rear driveshafts from the transfer case.

7. Tag and disconnect the vacuum lines and/or the electrical connectors, as equipped.

8. If applicable, disconnect the transfer case shift rod from the case.

9. If applicable, remove the support brace-to-transfer case bolts.

10. Support the transfer case using a floor jack, then remove the transfer case-to-transmission retaining bolts

11. Slide the transfer case rearward and off the transmission output shaft, then careful lower it from the vehicle.

12. Remove all traces of old gasket material from the mating surfaces.

To install:

13. Using the floor jack, carefully raise the transfer case into position behind the transmission. Position a new gasket, using sealer to hold it in position, then slide the transfer case onto the transmission output shaft.

14. Install the transfer case-to-transmission retaining bolts, then tighten to 24 ft. lbs. (33 Nm).

15. If equipped, install the support brace bolts and tighten to 35 ft. lbs. (47 Nm).

16. Install the remaining components in the reverse of removal.

DRIVELINE

On all models covered by this manual, conventional, open type driveshafts are used. Located at either end of the driveshaft is a universal joint (U-joint), which allows the driveshaft to move up and down (within designed limits) in order to match the motion of the rear axle. The shaft is designed and built with yoke lugs (ears) in line with each other in order to produce the smoothest possible running shaft. Because some vehicles covered by this manual utilize 2-pieces shafts and splined yokes, it may be possible to reinstall the shaft incorrectly or "out of the phase" which would cause vibration. Many of these vehicles will utilize a keyed slip yoke to prevent this, but DO NOT risk improper installation. ALWAYS matchmark the shaft ends to the yokes before removal or installation.

Since the truck can be obtained in either 2wd or 4wd and in various cab/bed combinations (long and short beds, standard and extended cabs), four types of driveshafts may be employed. Some models will be equipped with a one-piece rear driveshaft, while others have a two-piece rear driveshaft which uses a center support bearing. Most 4wd vehicles are equipped with a front shaft which is a two piece telescopic type with internal splines. The MFI-Turbo is equipped with a similar front shaft, but the joint at each end is attached to a companion flange which is bolted to the front axle or transfer case, as applicable (much in the way a halfshaft is bolted to a companion flange on the front drive axle). The rear (transfer case end) joint on the MFI-Turbo front driveshaft is a Double Cardan joint instead of a typical spider U-joint.

On the front of the rear one or two-piece driveshafts, the U-joints connect the driveshaft to a slip-jointed yoke. This yoke is internally splined and allows the driveshaft to move in and out on the transmission splines (one-piece) or the shaft splines (two-piece). On the rear of the one or two-piece driveshaft, the U-joint is clamped to the rear axle pinion. It is usually attached to the rear axle pinion by use of bolted straps.

For the front driveshaft on 4wd vehicles, the U-joints are secured to the transfer case and the front differential by the use of bolted straps (except for the MFI-Turbo). Located in the center of the driveshaft is a slip-joint, which allows the driveshaft to move in and out on its own splines.

On production U-joints, nylon is injected through a small hole in the yoke during manufacture and flows along a circular groove between the U-joint and the yoke, creating a non-metallic snapring. Since plastic retaining rings must be sheared for removal and no snapring grooves are supplied, the production joints must be replaced as an assembly whenever they are removed from the shaft.

Bad U-joints, requiring replacement, will produce a clunking sound when the vehicle is put into gear and when the transmission shifts from gear-to-gear. This is due to worn needle bearings or scored trunnion ends. U-joints require no periodic maintenance and therefore have no lubrication fittings.

On many early model 4wd vehicles, a grease fitting is supplied near the front (axle end) of the front driveshaft. A similar fitting is found near the slip yoke at the middle of the two-piece rear driveshaft assemblies. This fitting is to provide lubrication for the center slip joint. Chassis grease should be used at this fitting. The rear (transfer case end) joint on the MFI-Turbo front driveshaft is a Double Cardan joint which is equipped with a grease fitting. Unlike the permanently lubricated U-joints found on the rest of these trucks, it should be lubricated periodically using a grease gun and chassis grease such as GM-6031-M, or equivalent.

Front Driveshaft and U-Joints

REMOVAL & INSTALLATION

Except MFI-Turbo

♦ **See Figures 22 and 23**

➡**DO NOT pound on the original driveshaft ears (unless the U-joints are being replaced) or the injected nylon U-joints may fracture.**

1. Raise and support the front of the truck safely using jackstands.

2. Matchmark the relationship of the driveshaft to the front axle and the transfer case flanges.

3. Remove the driveshaft-to-retainer bolts and the retainers, first from the transfer case, then from the front axle.

4. Collapse the driveshaft so it may be disengaged from the transfer case flange.

5. Move the driveshaft rearward (between the transfer case and the chassis) to disengage it from the front axle.

➡**Use care when handling the driveshaft to avoid dropping the U-joint cap assemblies and loosing portions of the bearing assemblies.**

6. Wrap a length of tape around the loose caps to hold them in place.

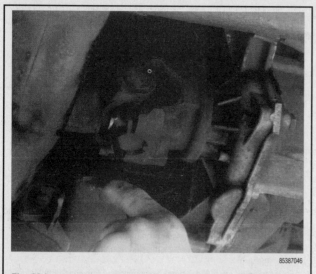

Fig. 22 Loosen and remove the U-joint retainers from the flanges

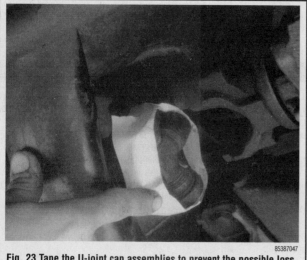

Fig. 23 Tape the U-joint cap assemblies to prevent the possible loss of components

To install:

7. Carefully insert the driveshaft into position in the vehicle.

8. Align the matchmarks made earlier, then remove the tape from the U-joints cap assemblies and position them to the flanges. Loosely install the retainers to hold the shaft in position.

9. Verify that the marks are properly aligned then tighten the retainers to 15 ft. lbs. (20 Nm) for vehicles through 1991 or to 92 ft. lbs. (125 Nm) for the transfer case flange bolts and to 53 ft. lbs. (72 Nm) for front axle flange bolts on 1992–93 vehicles.

10. Remove the jackstands and carefully lower the vehicle.

MFI-Turbo

1. Raise and support the front of the vehicle safely using jackstands.
2. Remove the retaining bolts from the flange at the transfer case.
3. Remove the retaining bolts from the flange at the front axle.
4. Pull the axle forward and downward, then remove it from the vehicle.

To install:

5. Inspect the shroud and boot for cracking or deterioration. Replace the entire assembly if evidence of damage is found. Also, check the front shaft for dents or bending.

6. Carefully install the shaft to the vehicle while aligning the matchmarks made during removal. Loosely install the retaining bolts to hold the shaft in position.

7. Tighten the transfer case flange bolts, followed by the axle flange bolts to 52 ft. lbs. (70 Nm).

8. Remove the jackstands and carefully lower the vehicle.

U-JOINT REPLACEMENT

With the exception of the size socket/pipe which must be used to support the trunnion yoke on some earlier model driveshafts, U-joint replacement is identical between the front and rear driveshaft assemblies. Please refer to the procedure found later for the rear driveshaft to service the U-joints. Make sure an appropriately sized socket is used as a support on early model front driveshafts, these will require a 1¼ in. socket as opposed to the 1⅛ in. socket used by later models and most rear driveshafts.

Rear Driveshaft and U-Joints

REMOVAL & INSTALLATION

◆ **See Figures 24, 25 and 26**

➡ **DO NOT** pound on the original propeller shaft yoke ears (unless the U-joints are being replaced) or the injected nylon joints may fracture.

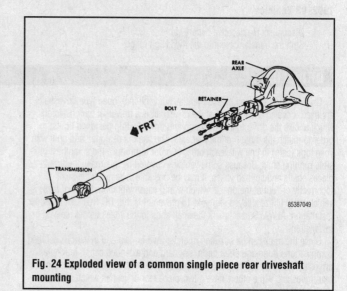

Fig. 24 Exploded view of a common single piece rear driveshaft mounting

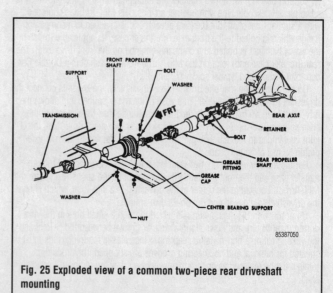

Fig. 25 Exploded view of a common two-piece rear driveshaft mounting

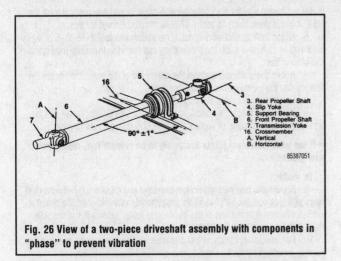

Fig. 26 View of a two-piece driveshaft assembly with components in "phase" to prevent vibration

3. Rear Propeller Shaft
4. Slip Yoke
5. Support Bearing
6. Front Propeller Shaft
7. Transmission Yoke
16. Crossmember
A. Vertical
B. Horizontal

85387051

1. Raise and support the rear of the truck safely using jackstands.
2. Matchmark relationship of the driveshaft-to-pinion flange and the slip yoke-to-front driveshaft or transmission/transfer case housing, as necessary. ALL shaft components which are being removed should be installed in their original positions, this includes slip yokes and U-joints ears. Disconnect the rear universal joint by removing retainers. If the bearing caps are loose, tape them together to prevent dropping and loss of bearing rollers.
3. If equipped with a one-piece driveshaft, perform the following procedures:
   a. Slide the driveshaft forward to disengage it from the rear axle flange.
   b. Move the driveshaft rearward to disengage it from the transmission slip-joint, passing it under the axle housing.
4. If equipped with a two-piece driveshaft, perform the following procedures:
   a. Slide the rear driveshaft half forward to disengage it from the rear axle flange.
   b. Slide the driveshaft rearward to disengage it from slip-joint of the front driveshaft half passing it under the axle housing.
   c. Remove the center bearing support nuts and bolts.
   d. Slide the front driveshaft half rearward to disengage it from the transfer case/transmission slip-joint.

➡**DO NOT allow the driveshaft to drop or allow the universal joints to bend to extreme angles, as this might fracture injected joint internally. Support propeller shaft during removal.**

To install:

5. Inspect the slip-joint splines for damage, burrs or wear, for this will damage the transmission seal. Apply engine oil to all splined propeller shaft yokes.
6. DO NOT use a hammer to force the driveshaft into place. Check for burrs on transmission output shaft spline, twisted slip yoke splines or possibly the wrong U-joint. Make sure the splines agree in number and fit. To prevent trunnion seal damage, DO NOT place any tool between yoke and splines.
7. If installing a one-piece driveshaft, perform the following procedures:
   a. Align the matchmarks made during removal, then slide driveshaft into the transmission/transfer case.
   b. Align the rear universal joint-to-rear axle pinion flange, make sure the bearings are properly seated in the pinion flange yoke.
   c. Install the rear driveshaft-to-pinion fasteners and verify all marks are aligned. Torque the fasteners to 15 ft. lbs. (20 Nm).
8. If installing a two-piece driveshaft, perform the following procedures:
   a. Install the front driveshaft half into the transmission/transfer case (aligning the marks made during removal) and bolt the center bearing support in position. Torque the center bearing to support nuts and bolts to 25 ft. lbs. (34 Nm).

➡In most cases, the yoke on the front driveshaft half must be bottomed out in the transmission (fully forward) before installation to the support.

   b. Rotate the shaft as necessary so the front U-joint trunnion is in the correct position to align the matchmarks for the rear driveshaft half.
➡Before installing the rear driveshaft, align the U-joint trunnions using the matchmarks made earlier (in some cases a "key" in the output spline of the front driveshaft half will align with a missing spline in the rear yoke).

   c. Attach the rear U-joint to the axle, then torque the retainers to 15 ft. lbs. (20 Nm).
9. Remove the jackstands and carefully lower the vehicle.
10. Road test the vehicle.

U-JOINT REPLACEMENT

▶ **See Figures 27 thru 33**

As mentioned earlier in this section, these vehicles utilize 2 different types of U-joint assemblies. At the factory, most vehicles are equipped with a Nylon injected assembly. Because these assemblies contain no snapring grooves, and the very action of removing them destroys their retainers, they cannot be reused. Once removed, Nylon injected U-joints should be discarded. If your vehicle has already received U-joint service, then it will be equipped with a snapring retained assembly. Once properly removed, these assemblies may be reused if they are in good condition.

Snapring Type

1. Matchmark and remove the driveshaft assembly from the vehicle. Refer to the procedure earlier in this section.

✳✳ WARNING

NEVER clamp the driveshaft tube in a vise, for this may dent the tube. Support the driveshaft horizontally and clamp on the yokes of the universal joints using a soft-jawed vise or blocks of wood to protect the yokes.

2. Remove the snaprings from the yoke by pinching the ends together with a pair of pliers. If the snapring is difficult to remove, tap the end of the bearing cap lightly to relieve pressure from snapring.
3. Support the propeller shaft horizontally in line with the base plate of a bench vise, but never clamp the driveshaft tube.
4. Place the universal joint so the lower ear of the yoke is supported on a 1¼ in. or 1⅛ inch socket (or ID pipe), depending on the application. Most rear driveshafts and late model driveshafts require the 1⅛ in support. Press the

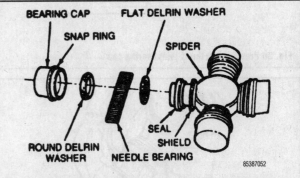

BEARING CAP
SNAP RING
FLAT DELRIN WASHER
SPIDER
ROUND DELRIN WASHER
NEEDLE BEARING
SEAL
SHIELD

85387052

Fig. 27 Exploded view of a replacement U-joint assembly—internal snapring type

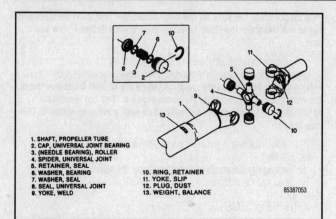

1. SHAFT, PROPELLER TUBE
2. CAP, UNIVERSAL JOINT BEARING
3. (NEEDLE BEARING), ROLLER
4. SPIDER, UNIVERSAL JOINT
5. RETAINER, SEAL
6. WASHER, BEARING
7. WASHER, SEAL
8. SEAL, UNIVERSAL JOINT
9. YOKE, WELD
10. RING, RETAINER
11. YOKE, SLIP
12. PLUG, DUST
13. WEIGHT, BALANCE

85387053

Fig. 28 Exploded view of a replacement U-joint assembly—external snapring type

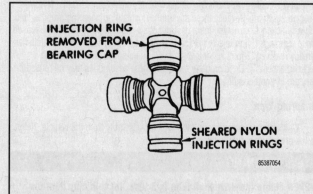

INJECTION RING REMOVED FROM BEARING CAP

SHEARED NYLON INJECTION RINGS

85387054

Fig. 29 Production Nylon type U-joint

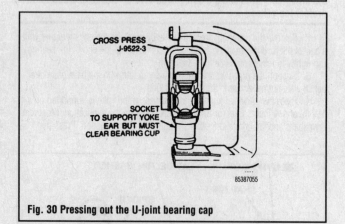

CROSS PRESS J-9522-3

SOCKET TO SUPPORT YOKE EAR BUT MUST CLEAR BEARING CUP

85387055

Fig. 30 Pressing out the U-joint bearing cap

TRUNNION

SPACER J-9522-5

BEARING CUP

85387056

Fig. 31 Positioning the spacer tool to assist in bearing cap removal

trunnion bearing against the socket/pipe in order to partially press it from the yoke. A cross press such as tool J-9522-3 should be used for this.

5. Grasp the cap and work it out, if necessary use tool J–9522–5 or equivalent spacer to further push the the bearing cap from the trunnion, then grasp and work it free.

6. Rotate the shaft and support the other side of the yoke, then press the bearing cap from the yoke as in previous steps.

7. Remove the trunnion from the driveshaft yoke.

8. Clean and check the condition of all parts. Use U-joint repair kits to replace all the worn parts or replace the assembly using a new U-joint.

➥**If the used universal joints are going to be reinstalled, repack with new grease.**

To install:

9. Repack the bearings with chassis grease and replace the trunnion dust seals after any operation that requires disassembly of the U-joint. Be sure the lubricant reservoir at the end of the trunnion is full of lubricant. Fill the reservoirs with lubricant from the bottom.

10. Partially insert the cross into the yoke so 1 trunnion seats freely in the bearing cap, then rotate the shaft so this trunnion is on the bottom.

11. Install the opposite bearing cap part way. Be sure both trunnions are started straight into the bearing caps.

12. Press against opposite bearing caps, working the cross constantly to be sure the trunnions are free in the bearings. If binding occurs, check the needle rollers to be sure 1 or more needles have not become lodged under an end of the trunnion.

13. As soon as 1 bearing retainer groove is exposed, stop pressing and install the bearing retainer snapring.

➥**It may be necessary to strike the yoke with a hammer to align the seating of the bearing retainers.**

14. Continue to press until the opposite bearing retainer can be installed. If difficulty installing the snaprings is encountered, tap the yoke with a hammer to spring the yoke ears slightly.

15. Once the driveshaft and U-joints are properly assembled, align the matchmarks and install the driveshaft to the vehicle.

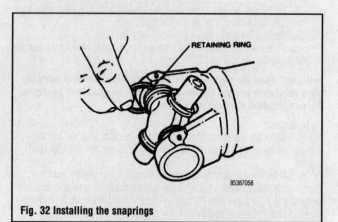

RETAINING RING

85387058

Fig. 32 Installing the snaprings

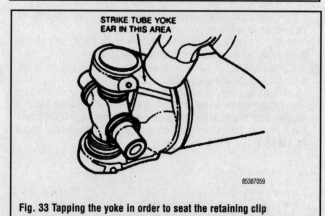

STRIKE TUBE YOKE EAR IN THIS AREA

85387059

Fig. 33 Tapping the yoke in order to seat the retaining clip

Nylon Injected Type

➡️Don't disassemble these joints unless replacing the complete U-joint. These factory installed joints cannot be reused and should instead be replaced by snapring type U-joints.

1. Matchmark and remove the driveshaft assembly from the vehicle. Refer to the procedure earlier in this section.

✷✷ WARNING

NEVER clamp the driveshaft tube in a vise, for this may dent the tube. Support the driveshaft horizontally and clamp on the yokes of the universal joints using a soft-jawed vise or blocks of wood to protect the yokes.

2. Support the propeller shaft horizontally in line with the base plate of a bench vise, but never clamp the driveshaft tube.

3. Place the universal joint so the lower ear of the yoke is supported on a 1¼ in. or 1⅛ inch socket (or ID pipe), depending on the application. Most rear driveshafts and late model driveshafts require the 1⅛ in support.

4. Press the lower bearing cap out of the yoke ear, this will shear the nylon injected ring retaining the lower bearing cap.

5. If the bearing cap is not completely removed, lift the cross (J–9522–3) and insert J–9522–5 or equivalent spacer, then press the cap completely out.

6. Rotate the driveshaft, shear the opposite plastic retainer, and press the other bearing cap out in the same manner.

7. Remove the cross from the yoke.

➡️**Production U-joints cannot be reassembled. There are no bearing retainer grooves in the caps. Discard all parts that were removed and substitute those in the overhaul kit.**

8. If the front U-joint is being removed, separate the bearing caps from the slip yoke in the same manner.

REAR AXLE

Identification

◆ **See Figure 34**

The rear axle identification code and manufacturer's code must be known before attempting to adjust or repair axle shafts or rear axle case assembly. Rear axle ratio, differential type, manufacturer, and build date information is normally stamped on the right axle tube on the forward side.

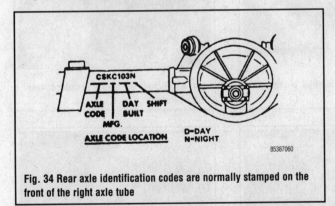

Fig. 34 Rear axle identification codes are normally stamped on the front of the right axle tube

Axle Shaft, Bearing and Seal

REMOVAL & INSTALLATION

◆ **See Figures 35 thru 46**

Although the axle shaft is easily removed using common hand tools, special tools are required if the bearings are also to be serviced.

9. Remove the sheared plastic bearing retainer from the yoke. If necessary, drive a small pin or punch through the injection holes to aid removal.

10. Install the new snapring U-joints. Refer to the snapring type installation procedure found earlier in this section.

Center Support Bearing

REMOVAL & INSTALLATION

On all early model vehicles and some late model vehicles covered by this manual that are equipped with a two-piece rear driveshaft assembly, the center support bearing may be removed for replacement. To be sure if your late model driveshaft may be serviced, check with your local parts supplier or dealer for parts availability information.

1. Matchmark and remove the rear driveshaft assembly. For details, please refer to the procedure earlier in this section.

2. Remove the strap retaining the rubber cushion from the bearing support.

3. Pull the support bracket from the rubber cushion and the cushion from the bearing.

4. Press the bearing assembly from half-shaft.

To install:

5. Assemble the center support bearing to the driveshaft:

a. If removed, install the inner deflector onto the front shaft half and prick punch the deflector at 2 opposite points to make sure it is tight on the shaft.

b. Fill the space between the inner dust shield and bearing with lithium soap grease.

c. Start the bearing and slinger assembly straight onto the shaft journal. Support the shaft and using a length of pipe over the splined end of the shaft, press the bearing and inner slinger against the shoulder of the front shaft half.

d. Install the bearing retainer (rubber cushion onto bearing, bracket onto cushion and retaining strap).

6. Align and install the driveshaft assembly to the vehicle.

1. Raise and support the rear of the vehicle safely using "jackstands.
2. Remove the rear wheel and brake drum.

✷✷ CAUTION

Brake shoes contain asbestos, which has been determined to be a cancer causing agent. Never clean the brake surfaces with compressed air! Avoid inhaling any dust from any brake surface! When cleaning brake surfaces, use a commercially available brake cleaning fluid.

3. Using a wire brush, clean the dirt/rust from around the rear axle cover. This should be done to help prevent foreign material from entering the rear axle and possibly damaging the differential.

4. Place a catch pan under the differential, then unscrew the retaining bolts and remove the rear cover. When removing the cover, a small prytool may be used at the base of the cover to gently pry it back from the axle housing, breaking the gasket seal and allowing the lubricant to drain out into the container. Be careful not to use excessive force and damage the cover or housing.

5. Remove the rear pinion shaft lock bolt and the pinion shaft from the differential.

6. Push the axle shaft inward, then remove the C-lock from the button end of the axle shaft.

7. Remove the axle shaft from the axle housing by pulling straight back on the shaft hub, be careful not to damage the oil seal with the shaft splines.

➡️**It is recommended, when the axle shaft is removed, to replace the oil seal.**

8. If the bearing and/or oil seal is being replaced, use a medium pry bar to carefully pry the old oil seal from the end of the rear axle housing. DO NOT score or damage the housing oil seal surface.

9. If the wheel bearing is being removed, use the GM slide hammer tool No. J-2619, along with adapter No. J-2619-4 and the axle bearing puller No. J-22813-01, or the equivalent tools to pull the bearing from the tube. Be sure to install the tool assembly so that the tangs engage the outer race of the bearing,

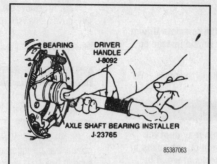

Fig. 35 Use a slide hammer, bearing puller and adapter to remove the old axle bearing

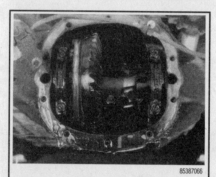

Fig. 36 Drive the axle bearing into position using a suitable installer and driver handle

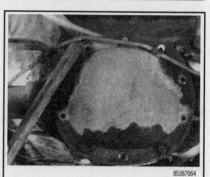

Fig. 37 Clean all dirt or corrosion from the differential housing and cover in order to prevent contamination

Fig. 38 Loosen and remove the cover retaining bolts, then carefully break the gasket seal allowing oil to drain

Fig. 39 Once the fluid has drained, remove the cover from the differential housing

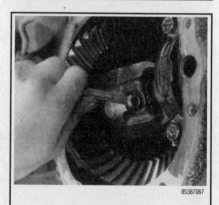

Fig. 40 Loosen pinion shaft lock screw

Fig. 41 Remove the lock screw in order to free the pinion shaft

Fig. 42 Once the shaft is freed, withdraw it from the differential

Fig. 43 Remove the C-lock in order to free the axle shaft

Fig. 44 Remove the shaft by pulling it straight back and from the housing tube

Fig. 45 If necessary, remove the old seal using a prybar, but be careful not to damage the sealing surface

Fig. 46 Install a new seal using a suitable installation tool or driver

then use the action of the slide hammer to withdraw the wheel bearing from the axle housing.

To install:

10. Clean and inspect the axle tube housing.

11. If the bearing was removed, thoroughly clean the wheel bearing using solvent, then blow dry with compressed air. DO NOT spin the bearing with the compressed air or damage may occur. Inspect the wheel bearing for excessive wear or damage. If it feels rough, replace it.

12. With a new or the reused bearing, place a blob of heavy grease in the palm of your hand, then work the bearing into the grease until it is thoroughly lubricated. Using an axle shaft bearing installer such as No. J-34974, J-23765 or equivalents, drive the bearing into the axle housing until it bottoms against the seat.

13. If the bearing and/or seal was removed, use an axle shaft seal installer tool such as No. J-33782, J-23771 or equivalents to drive the new seal into the housing until it is flush with the axle tube. If a seal installer is not available, a suitably sized driver or socket may be used, just make sure the surface in contact with the seal is smooth so that it won't damage the seal.

14. Using gear oil, lubricate the new seal lips.

15. Using a putty knife, clean the gasket mounting surfaces on the housing and cover. Take care to keep material out of the differential housing. If necessary, place a rag or paper towels over the differential while cleaning the housing flange.

➡**When installing the axle shaft(s), be careful not to cut the oil seal lips.**

16. Slide the axle shaft into the rear axle housing, taking care not to damage the seal, then engage the splines of the axle shaft with the splines of the rear axle side gear.

17. Install the C-lock retainer on the axle shaft button end. After the C-lock is installed, pull the axle shaft outward to seat the C-lock retainer in the counterbore of the side gears.

18. Install the pinion shaft through the case and the pinions, then install a new pinion shaft lock bolt. Torque the new lock bolt to 25 ft. lbs. (34 Nm).

➡**When adding oil to the rear axle, be aware that some locking differentials require the use of a special gear lubricant additive GM No. Seal Replacement**

19. Install the rear cover using a new gasket and sealant. Tighten the retaining bolts using a crosswise pattern to 20 ft. lbs. (27 Nm).

➡**Make sure the vehicle is level before attempting to add fluid to the rear axle or an incorrect fluid level will result.**

20. Refill the rear axle housing using the proper grade and quantity of lubricant as detailed in Section 1 of this manual. Install the filler plug, operate the vehicle and check for any leaks.

Pinion Oil Seal

REPLACEMENT

▸ **See Figures 47, 48 and 49**

➡**The following procedure requires the use of the Pinion Holding tool No. J-8614-10 or equivalent, the Pinion Flange Removal tool No. J-8614-1, J-8614-2, J-8614-3 or equivalent, and the Pinion Oil Seal Installation tool No. J-23911 or equivalent.**

1. Matchmark the driveshaft and pinion flange to assure they are reassembled in the same position.

2. Disconnect the driveshaft from rear axle pinion flange and support the shaft up in body tunnel by wiring the driveshaft to the exhaust pipe. If the U-joint bearings are not retained by a retainer strap, use a piece of tape to hold bearings on their journals.

3. Mark the position of the pinion stem, flange and nut for reference. On vehicles through 1991 this will reference mark will be used to set pre-load during assembly.

4. For 1992–93 vehicles, use an inch lbs. torque wrench to measure the amount of torque necessary to turn the pinion, then note this measurement as it is the combined pinion bearing, seal, carrier bearing, axle bearing and seal preload.

5. Using a pinion holding tool such as No. J-8614-10, and the appropriate

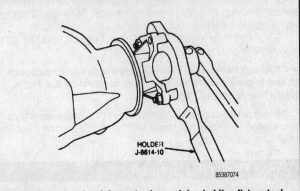

Fig. 47 Removing the pinion nut using a pinion holding fixture tool

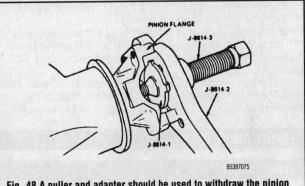

Fig. 48 A puller and adapter should be used to withdraw the pinion from the housing

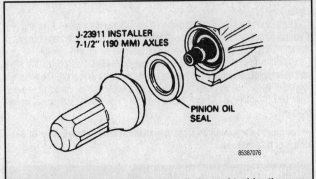

Fig. 49 Use the appropriately sized installation tool to drive the new seal into position.

pinion flange removal tool No. J-8614-1, J-8614-2, J-8614-3 (as applicable) or equivalents, remove the pinion flange nut and washer.

6. With suitable container in place to hold any fluid that may drain from rear axle, remove the pinion flange.

7. Remove the oil seal by driving it out of the differential with a blunt chisel; DO NOT damage the carrier.

8. Examine the seal surface of pinion flange for tool marks, nicks or damage, such as a groove worn by the seal. If damaged, replace flange as outlined later in this section.

9. Examine the carrier bore and remove any burrs that might cause leaks around the O.D. of the seal.

10. Apply GM seal lubricant No. 1050169 or equivalent to the outside diameter of the pinion flange and sealing lip of new seal. Drive the new seal into place using a correctly sized installation tool.

11. Install the pinion flange and tighten nut to the same position as marked in Step 3. Tighten the nut a little at a time and turn the pinion flange several times after each tightening in order to set the rollers.

12. For 1992–93 vehicles, measure the torque necessary to turn the pinion and compare this to the reading taken during removal. Tighten the nut additionally, as necessary to achieve the same preload as measured earlier.

13. For vehicles through 1991 hold the pinion flange and tighten the nut 1/16 in. (1.6mm) beyond the original alignment marks.

➡️**If fluid was lost from the differential housing during this procedure, be sure to check and add additional fluid, as necessary. For details, please refer to Section 1 of this manual.**

14. Remove the support then align and secure the driveshaft assembly to the pinion flange. The original matchmarks MUST be aligned to assure proper shaft balance and prevent vibration.

Pinion Flange Replacement

REMOVAL & INSTALLATION

1. Raise and safely support the rear of the truck safely using jackstands.
2. Remove both rear wheels and drums.
3. Matchmark the driveshaft and pinion flange, then disconnect the rear U-joint and support the driveshaft out of the way. If the U-joint bearings are not retained by a retainer strap, use a piece of tape to hold bearing caps on their journals.
4. The pinion rides against a tapered roller bearing. Check the pre-load by reading how much torque is required to turn the pinion. Use an inch pound torque wrench on the pinion flange nut and record the reading. This will give combined pinion bearing, carrier bearing, axle bearing and seal pre-load.
5. Remove pinion flange nut and washer. A suitable pinion holding tool should be used keep the flange from turning when loosening the nut.
6. With a suitable container in place to hold any fluid that may drain from the rear axle, remove the pinion flange.

To install:

7. Apply GM seal lubricant No. 1050169 or equivalent, to the outside diameter of the new pinion flange, then install the pinion flange.

➡️**DO NOT hammer on the pinion flange in order to install it to the stem.**

8. Install the washer and a new pinion flange nut finger tight.
9. While holding the pinion flange, tighten the nut a little at a time and turn the drive pinion several revolutions after each tightening to set the rollers. Check the pre-load of bearings each time with an inch pound torque wrench until the same pre-load is achieved as the reading that was obtained in Step 4. For vehicles through 1991, tighten the nut an additional 3–5 inch lbs. (0.3–0.6 Nm) past this point.
10. Remove the support then align and secure the driveshaft assembly to the pinion flange. The original matchmarks MUST be aligned to assure proper shaft balance and prevent vibration.

➡️**If fluid was lost from the differential housing during this procedure, be sure to check and add additional fluid, as necessary. For details, please refer to Section 1 of this manual.**

11. Install the rear drums and wheels.
12. Remove the jackstands and carefully lower the vehicle.

FRONT DRIVE AXLE

Identification

The front axle assembly used on most 4wd models covered by this manual utilizes a central disconnect type front axle/transfer case system which allows shifting in and out of 4wd when the vehicle is moving under most driving conditions. The axle has an aluminum carrier which includes a vacuum activated center lock feature.

The axle on the MFI-Turbo is designed for full-time four wheel drive and therefore is not equipped with a disengagement feature. With this one exception, the MFI-Turbo and standard 4wd front axle assemblies are very similar.

The drive axles employ completely flexible assemblies which consist of inner and outer constant velocity (CV) joints connected by an axle shaft. The inner CV joint is a "tri-pot" design, which is completely flexible and can move in and out. The outer CV joint is a "Rzeppa" design which is also flexible but cannot move in or out.

➡️**For more information on front axle identification, please refer to Section 1 of this manual.**

Halfshafts (Drive Axle)

REMOVAL & INSTALLATION

▶ **See Figures 50 thru 59**

Vehicles Through 1991

EXCEPT MFI-TURBO

1. Disconnect the negative battery cable.
2. Unlock the steering column so the linkage is free to move, then raise and support the front of the vehicle safely using jackstands.
3. Remove the tire and wheel assembly.
4. Remove brake caliper from the bracket and support out of the way using safety wire. Be careful not to stretch, kink or otherwise damage the brake line.
5. Disengage the tie rod at the steering knuckle. For details, please refer to Section 8 of this manual.
6. Remove the lower shock absorber retainers, then push the shock out of the way. If necessary, compress the shock and secure it using safety wire.
7. Matchmark the inner shaft flange, then loosen and remove the retaining bolts. If necessary, hold the axle from turning by installing 2 of the lug nuts and using a prybar across the nuts on the hub.
8. Remove the cotter pin and retainer from the hub end of the shaft. Hold the hub from turning and loosen the axle nut. Once the nut is loosened unthread it and remove the washer.
9. Move the inside of the drive axle forward and support it away from the frame.
10. Using a suitable axle remover such as J-28733 or equivalent, drive the axle shaft from the hub.
11. Remove the axle from the vehicle. If the boots are not being serviced, take care not to damage or rip the CV-boots during removal.

To install:

12. Install the axle to the vehicle taking care not to damage the CV-boots. Insert the shaft end into the hub.
13. Install the washer and retaining nut, then tighten the nut to 160–200 ft. lbs. (220–270 Nm).
14. Install the retainer and a new cotter pin over the axle nut. DO NOT back off or exceed specification in order to insert the cotter pin.
15. Align the hub flange, then install the retaining bolts and tighten to 60 ft. lbs. (80 Nm).
16. Reposition the shock absorber and secure using the retaining bolts.
17. Install the tie rod end to the steering knuckle and secure.
18. Remove the support, then install the brake caliper.
19. Install the tire and wheel assembly.
20. Remove the jackstands and carefully lower the vehicle.
21. Make sure the ignition is **OFF**, then connect the negative battery cable.

MFI-TURBO

1. Disconnect the negative battery cable.
2. Unlock the steering column so the linkage is free to move, then raise and support the front of the vehicle safely using jackstands.
3. Remove the tire and wheel assembly.
4. Remove the cotter pin and retainer from the hub end of the axle shaft.
5. Hold the hub from turning and loosen the axle nut. Once the nut is loosened unthread it and remove the washer. The hub may be held by installing 2 lug nuts and using a large prybar.

6. Place a jackstand or a floor jack under the lower control arm for support.

7. Remove the lower shock absorber retainers, then reposition the shock for access.

8. Matchmark the output shaft flange, then remove the output shaft flange-to-drive axle bolts. If necessary, hold the hub from turning using the prybar or insert a drift through the opening in the top of the brake caliper into the vanes of the rotor.

9. Using a axle driver/removal tools such as the Posilock Puller Model 110, or equivalent, drive the axle shaft from the hub.

10. Remove the drive axle from the vehicle. If the boots are not being serviced, take care not to damage or rip the CV-boots during removal.

To install:

11. Install the axle to the vehicle taking care not to damage the CV-boots. Insert the shaft end into the hub.

12. Install the washer and retaining nut, then tighten the nut to 180 ft. lbs. (245 Nm).

13. Install the retainer and a new cotter pin over the axle nut. If necessary, tighten the nut additionally in order to insert the cotter pin, but DO NOT back off specification.

14. Align the hub flange, then install the retaining bolts and tighten to 59 ft. lbs. (80 Nm).

15. Reposition the shock absorber and secure using the retaining bolts.

16. Install the tire and wheel assembly.

17. Remove the jackstands and carefully lower the vehicle.

18. Make sure the ignition is **OFF**, then connect the negative battery cable.

Fig. 50 A torn CV-boot requires removal of the driveshaft for overhaul

Fig. 51 On most vehicles. the caliper should be removed and supported out of

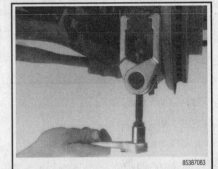
Fig. 52 Also on most vehicles, the tie rod end should be separated from the steering knuckle

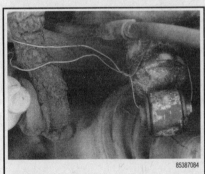
Fig. 53 Once the lower shock fasteners are removed it may be compressed and wired up out of the way

Fig. 54 Loosen and remove the flange bolts

Fig. 55 Remove the cotter pin and retainer so the axle nut may be loosened

Fig. 56 A prybar may be used across to of the lug nuts in order to keep the hub from turning while loosening the nut

Fig. 57 Use a suitable axle shaft removal tool to drive the shaft from the hub

Fig. 58 If a driver tool is not available, thread the nut just flush with the shaft end and tab gently with a rubber or brass mallet

Fig. 59 During assembly, hold the hub from turning and torque the axle nut to specification

1992–93 Vehicles

EXCEPT MFI-TURBO

▶ See Figure 60

1. Disconnect the negative battery cable.
2. Unlock the steering column so the linkage is free to move, then raise and support the front of the vehicle safely using jackstands.
3. If equipped, remove the front skid plate for access
4. Remove the tire and wheel assembly.
5. Insert a drift through the brake caliper into one of the brake rotor vanes to prevent the drive axle from turning.
6. Remove the cotter pin and retainer from the hub end of the shaft. Hold the hub from turning and loosen the axle nut. Once the nut is loosened unthread it and remove the washer.
7. Matchmark the inner shaft flange, then loosen (but DO NOT remove) the bolts retaining the inner joint flange to the output shaft companion flange.
8. Remove the brake line support bracket from the upper control arm in order to allow for additional knuckle travel. If necessary, remove the brake caliper and support aside.
9. Remove the cotter pin and nut from the outer tie rod end, then disengage the tie rod at the steering knuckle using J-24319-B, or an equivalent jawed tie rod puller. Push the linkage out toward the opposite side of the vehicle, then support the outer tie rod out of the way to provide the necessary clearance for shaft removal.
10. Remove the lower shock absorber retainers, then compress the shock and secure it out of the way using safety wire.

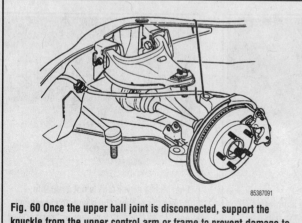

Fig. 60 Once the upper ball joint is disconnected, support the knuckle from the upper control arm or frame to prevent damage to the brake line and/or lower ball joint

11. Position a jackstand between the spring seat and lower control arm ball joint for maximum leverage, then use the vehicle's weight to relieve the spring tension on the upper control arm.
12. Remove the cotter pin and retainer, then loosen and remove the upper ball joint stud nut away from the knuckle. Tip the knuckle out and toward the rear of the vehicle. Suspend the knuckle from the upper control arm or frame in order to prevent straining and damaging the brake line.
13. Using a suitable axle remover such as J-28733-B or equivalent, drive the axle shaft from the hub.
14. Remove the inboard flange bolts which were removed earlier.
15. Remove the axle from the vehicle. If the boots are not being serviced, take care not to damage or rip the CV-boots during removal.

✳✳ CAUTION

DO NOT allow the vehicle's weight to load the front wheels or attempt to operate the vehicle when the drive axle(s) or hub nut(s) are removed. To do so may cause the front wheel bearing inner races to separate resulting in damage to the front brake and suspension components and/or personal injury.

To install:

16. Prior to shaft installation, cover the shock mounting bracket, lower control arm ball stud and ALL other sharp edges with a cloth or rag to help protect the boot.
17. Install the axle to the vehicle taking care not to damage the CV-boots. Insert the shaft end into the hub making sure to properly align the shaft splines.
18. Install the washer and retaining nut, if the nut can be fully threaded, it may be used to help draw the shaft into position in the hub.
19. Align the inboard flange to the output shaft companion flange, then loosely install the retainers.

➡ Neither the flange retainers or the axle end nut should be fully tightened at this time. Thread the retainers to hold the axle shaft in position and reassemble the other components.

20. Install the upper ball joint to the steering knuckle, then install the nut and tighten to 61 ft. lbs. (83 Nm). Install a new cotter pin, but DO NOT back of the specified torque. Lube the ball joint until grease appears at the seals, then remove the support from underneath the lower control arm.
21. Reposition and secure the lower shock absorber fasteners. Tighten the nut and bolt to 47 ft. lbs. (64 Nm).
22. Install the tie rod end to the steering knuckle, then tighten the nut to 35 ft. lbs. (47 Nm). Align the cotter pin hole by rotating the retainer, DO NOT back off the specified torque OR exceed specification in order to install the cotter pin. Install the new cotter pin once the retainer is aligned.
23. Install the brake line support bracket and tighten the retainer(s) to 13 ft. lbs. (17 Nm). Make sure the brake hose is not twisted, kinked or otherwise damaged before securing the bracket.
24. Insert a drift through the brake caliper to prevent the drive axle from turning, then tighten the inboard flange bolts to 60 ft. lbs. (80 Nm).
25. Tighten the hub nut on the end of the axle to 180 ft. lbs. (245 Nm), then install the retainer and a new cotter pin. Rotate the retainer, as necessary to install the cotter pin. DO NOT back off or exceed specification to install the cotter pin.
26. If removed, reposition and secure the caliper.
27. Install the tire and wheel assembly.
28. If applicable, install the skid plate.
29. Remove the jackstands and carefully lower the vehicle.
30. Make sure the ignition is **OFF**, then connect the negative battery cable.

CV-JOINT OVERHAUL

▶ See Figure 61

Outer CV-Joint

▶ See Figures 62, 63, 64 and 65

1. Remove the drive axle from the vehicle.
2. Place the axle in a vise using a protective covering on the vise jaws to prevent axle damage.

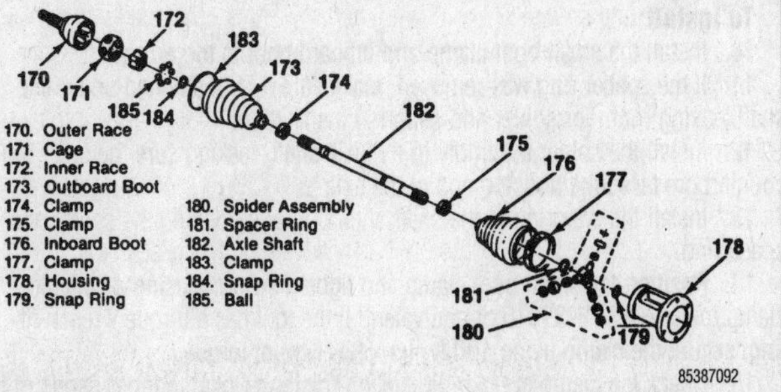
172
183
170
171
173
174
185
184
182
170. Outer Race
171. Cage
172. Inner Race
173. Outboard Boot
174. Clamp
175. Clamp
176. Inboard Boot
177. Clamp
178. Housing
179. Snap Ring
180. Spider Assembly
181. Spacer Ring
182. Axle Shaft
183. Clamp
184. Snap Ring
185. Ball
175
176
177
178
181
180
179
85387092

Fig. 61 Exploded view of the drive axle and CV-joints

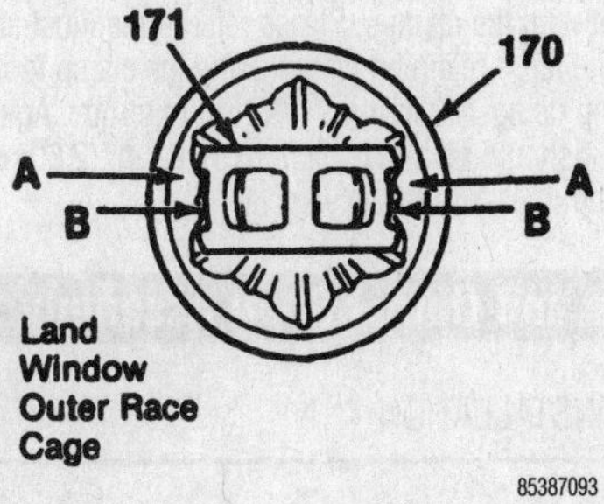
171
170
A
B
B
A
A. Land
B. Window
170. Outer Race
171. Cage
85387093

Fig. 62 Aligning the cage windows with the outer race lands so the cage (and inner race) may be removed

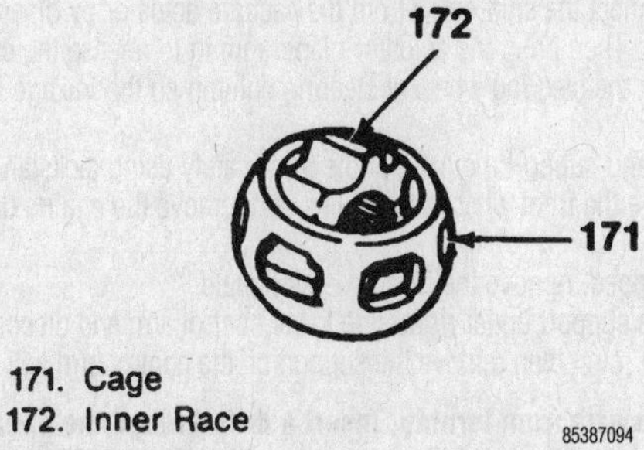
172
171
171. Cage
172. Inner Race
85387094

Fig. 63 Rotating the inner race up and out of the cage

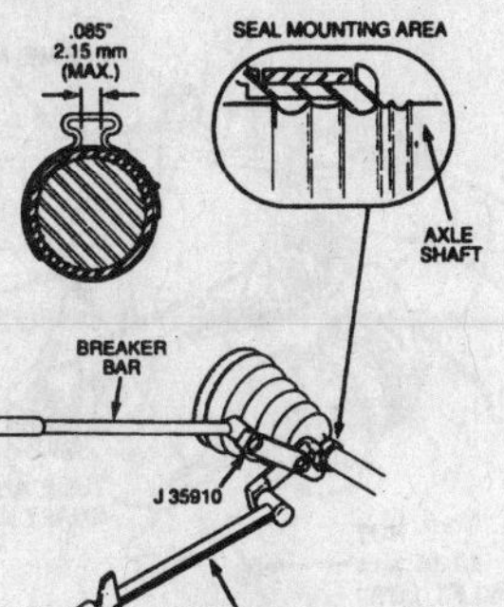
.085"
2.15 mm
(MAX.)
SEAL MOUNTING AREA
AXLE
SHAFT
BREAKER
BAR
J 35910
TORQUE WRENCH
85387095

Fig. 64 Small retaining clamp installation and ear dimension

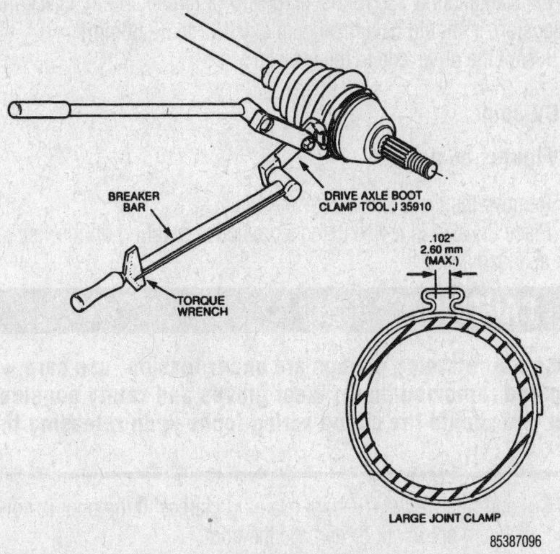
BREAKER
BAR
DRIVE AXLE BOOT
CLAMP TOOL J 35910
.102"
2.60 mm
(MAX.)
TORQUE
WRENCH
LARGE JOINT CLAMP
85387096

Fig. 65 Large retaining clamp installation and ear dimension—outer joint shown (inner joint uses same dimension)

CAUTION

Because the retaining clamps are under tension, use care when cutting and removing them. Wear gloves and safety goggles to protect you should the clamp spring loose upon releasing the tension.

3. Cut and remove the CV-boot retaining clamps. If the boot is not being replaced, use care not to cut or damage the boot.

➡Some late-model vehicles are equipped with a swage ring. In order to remove the ring, use a hand grinder to cut through the ring. Take care not to damage the outer race while cutting the swage ring free.

4. Once the clamps are removed, reposition the boot and wipe the grease away in order to locate the snapring.
5. Remove the snapring using a suitable pair of snapring pliers, such as J-8059 or equivalent.
6. Remove the joint assembly from the axle shaft.
7. Using a brass drift and hammer, tap the cage until it tilts sufficiently to remove the first ball, remove the remaining balls in the same manner.
8. Pivot the cage so the inner race is 90 degrees to the centerline of the outer race, then align the cage windows with the outer race lands and lift the cage (along with the inner race) from the outer race. Please refer to the illustration for clarification.
9. Rotate the inner race up and out of the cage.
10. Thoroughly clean all parts in an approved solvent, then check for wear or damage and replaces, as necessary.

To install:

11. Apply a suitable grease to the ball grooves of the inner and outer races.
12. Install the inner race to the cage by inserting and rotating.
13. Align the cage windows with the outer race lands, then install the cage (along with the inner race) to the outer race. Make sure the retaining ring side of the inner race faces outward.
14. Use the brass drift to tap the cage to a tilted position, then install the balls.
15. Pack the joint using a suitable grease.
16. Position the small boot clamp onto the outboard boot, then install the boot the axle shaft. Tighten the small clamp securely using a suitable clamp tool such as J-35910 or equivalent. If the tool has a torque wrench fitting, secure the clamp using 100 ft. lbs. (136 Nm) of torque.
17. Check the clamp ear gap dimension (distance that the inner bends of the crimp should be from each other), it should be a maximum of 0.085 in. (2.15mm). Please refer to the illustration for clarification.
18. Install the joint assembly to the shaft and secure using the snapring. Pack the boot and outer joint assembly with the premeasured amount of the grease supplied with the service kit, then snap the boot onto the outer joint assembly and manipulate it to remove excess air.
19. Install the large retaining clamp using the clamp tool and torque wrench.

Secure the clamp using 130 ft. lbs. (176 Nm) of torque. Again, check the clamp ear dimension, it should be a maximum of 0.102 in. (2.60mm)

20. Install the drive axle to the vehicle.

Inner CV-Joint

▶ See Figures 66 and 67

1. Remove the drive axle from the vehicle.
2. Place the axle in a vise using a protective covering on the vise jaws to prevent axle damage.

✳✳ CAUTION

Because the retaining clamps are under tension, use care when cutting and removing them. Wear gloves and safety goggles to protect you should the clamp spring loose upon releasing the tension.

3. Cut and remove the CV-boot retaining clamps. If the boot is not being replaced, use care not to cut or damage the boot.

➡**Some late-model vehicles are equipped with a swage ring. In order to remove the ring, use a hand grinder to cut through the ring. Take care not to damage the outer race while cutting the swage ring free.**

4. Remove the axle shaft with spider assembly from the housing.

➡**Handle the spider assembly with care. The tripot needle rollers may separate from the spider trunions.**

5. Grasp the space ring using J-8059, or an equivalent pair of snaring pliers, then slide the ring back on the axle shaft in order to provide clearance to move the spider assembly.
6. Move the spider assembly back on the shaft in order to expose the retaining snapring.
7. Remove the snapring using a suitable pair of snaping pliers, such as J-8059 or equivalent.
8. Remove the spider assembly.

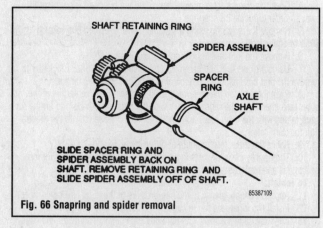

Fig. 66 Snapring and spider removal

9. Thoroughly clean all grease from the housing. Check for rust at the boot mounting grooves, if found remove with a wire brush.

To install:

10. Install the small boot clamp and inboard boot to the axle shaft.
11. If the spacer ring was removed, make sure it is positioned up on the shaft leaving room for spider and snapring installation.
12. Install the spider assembly to the axle shaft, making sure the snapring counterbore faces the housing end of the axle.
13. Install the snapring to the shaft, then properly position the spider and space ring.
14. Position the small boot clamp and tighten securely using a suitable clamp tool such as J-35910 or equivalent. If the tool has a torque wrench fitting, secure the clamp using 100 ft. lbs. (136 Nm) of torque.
15. Check the clamp ear gap dimension (distance that the inner bends of the crimp should be from each other), it should be a maximum of 0.085 in. (2.15mm). Please refer to the illustration for clarification.
16. Repack the housing using about half of the premeasured grease supplied with the service kit, then place the remainder of grease in the boot. Coat the inside of the boot sealing lips with grease.
17. Make sure the joint/boot are assembled to the proper dimension of 6 ¼ in. (160mm) between the clamps. Please refer to the illustration for clarification.
18. Install the large retaining clamp using the clamp tool and torque wrench. Secure the clamp using 130 ft. lbs. (176 Nm) of torque. Again, check the clamp ear dimension, it should be a maximum of 0.102 in. (2.60mm).
19. Install the drive axle to the vehicle.

Axle Tube and Output Shaft Assembly

REMOVAL & INSTALLATION

Except MFI-Turbo

▶ See Figures 68, 69 and 70

➡**The following procedure requires the use of the Shift Cable Housing Seal Installer tool No. J-33799 or equivalent.**

1. Disconnect the negative battery cable.
2. Disconnect the shift cable from the vacuum actuator by disengaging the locking spring. Then push the actuator diaphragm in to release the cable.
3. Unlock the steering wheel at steering column so the linkage is free to move.
4. Raise and support the front of the truck safely using jackstands.
5. Remove the front wheel assemblies and remove the engine drive belt shield.
6. If equipped, remove the front axle skid plate.
7. Place a support under right-side lower control arm and disconnect right-side upper ball joint, then remove the support so the control arm will hang free.

➡**To keep the axle from turning, insert a drift through the opening in the top of the brake caliper, into the corresponding vane of the brake rotor.**

8. Matchmark the right-side drive axle to the output shaft. Remove the right-side drive axle shaft-to-tube assembly bolts and separate the drive axle

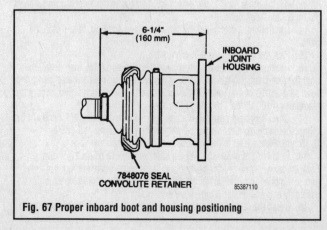

Fig. 67 Proper inboard boot and housing positioning

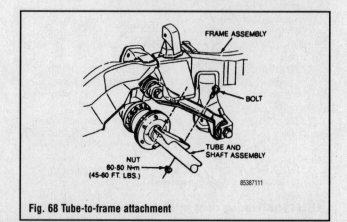

Fig. 68 Tube-to-frame attachment

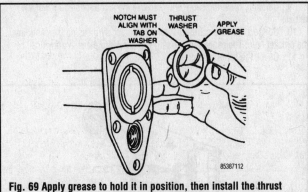

Fig. 69 Apply grease to hold it in position, then install the thrust washer to the output shaft tube

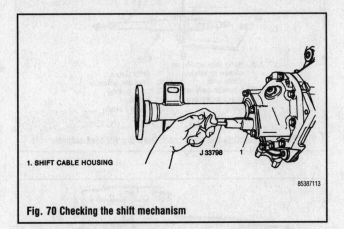

1. SHIFT CABLE HOUSING

Fig. 70 Checking the shift mechanism

from the tube assembly, then remove the drift from the brake caliper and rotor.

9. Disengage the 4wd indicator lamp electrical connector from the switch.

10. Remove the three bolts securing the cable and switch housing-to-carrier and pull the housing away to gain access to the cable locking spring. DO NOT unscrew the cable coupling nut unless the cable is being replaced.

11. Disconnect the cable from the shift fork shaft by lifting spring over slot in shift fork.

12. Remove the 2 bolts securing the tube bracket to the frame.

13. Remove the remaining 2 upper bolts securing the tube assembly to the carrier. The other 3 were removed with the shift cable housing.

14. Remove the tube assembly by working around the drive axle. Be careful not to allow the sleeve, thrust washers, connector and output shaft to fall out of carrier or be damaged when removing the tube.

To install:

15. Apply a bead of sealant on the tube-to-carrier mating surface.

16. Make sure the sleeve, thrust washers, connector and output shaft are in position in the carrier. Apply grease to the thrust washer to hold it in place during assembly, then position the washer to the tube.

17. Install the tube and shaft assembly-to-carrier, then thread and finger-tighten a bolt at one o'clock position but DO NOT torque. Pull the assembly down, then install the cable/switch housing and the remaining bolts. Torque the bolts to 36 ft. lbs. (48 Nm).

18. Install the tube-to-frame nuts/bolts and torque to 55 ft. lbs. (75 Nm).

19. Using the hub engagement tool No. J-33798 or equivalent, check the operation of the 4wd mechanism. Insert tool into the shift fork and check for the rotation of the axle shaft.

20. Remove the engagement tool, then install the shift cable switch housing by pushing the cable through into fork shaft hole. The cable will automatically snap into place. Please refer to shift cable replacement, later in this section for details.

21. Engage the 4wd indicator light wiring connector to the switch.

22. Install the support under the right-side lower control arm to raise arm and connect upper ball joint. For details, please refer to Section 8 of this manual.

23. Align and install right-side drive axle to the axle tube output shaft by installing one bolt first, then, rotate the axle to install and finger-tighten the remaining bolts. Torque the bolts to 60 ft. lbs. (80 Nm).

➡To hold the axle from turning, insert a drift through the opening in the top of the brake caliper into the corresponding vane of the brake rotor. If the caliper was removed, either temporarily install it or use a prybar across 2 installed lug nuts.

24. If equipped, install the front axle skid plate.

25. Install the drive belt shield, then install the front wheel assemblies.

26. Remove the jackstands and carefully lower the vehicle.

27. Connect the shift cable-to-vacuum actuator by pushing the cable end into the vacuum actuator shaft hole. The cable will snap into place, automatically. For details, please refer to shift cable replacement, late in this section.

28. Make sure the ignition is **OFF**, then connect the negative battery cable.

MFI-Turbo

1. Remove the right drive axle (halfshaft) from the vehicle. For details, please refer to the procedure located earlier in this section.

2. Remove the support bracket-to-frame nuts and washers.

3. Remove the tube-to-carrier retaining bolts.

➡Before removing the shaft and tube assembly, position a drain pan to catch any escaping fluid.

4. Attach a slide hammer to the output shaft and pull the shaft free, then remove the shaft and tube assembly from the vehicle.

To install:

5. Thoroughly clean the mating surfaces of the carrier and tube.

6. Apply a bead of sealer such as Loctite®514 or equivalent to the carrier sealing surface.

7. Install the shaft and tube assembly to the carrier.

8. Install the tube-to-carrier bolts, then tighten to 35 ft. lbs. (58 Nm).

9. Install the support bracket nuts and washers, then tighten to 55 ft. lbs. (75 Nm).

10. Install the right drive axle to the output shaft. For details, please refer to the procedure earlier in this section.

Output Shaft Pilot Bearing & Seal

REMOVAL & INSTALLATION

▶ **See Figure 71**

Except MFI-Turbo

➡The following procedures requires the use of the Pilot Bearing Remover tool No. J-34011 and the Pilot Bearing Installer tool No. J-33842, or equivalents.

1. Remove the axle tube and output shaft assembly from the vehicle. For details, please refer to the procedure located earlier in this section.

2. Remove the pilot bearing from the tube using J-34011 or an equivalent pilot bearing remover tool.

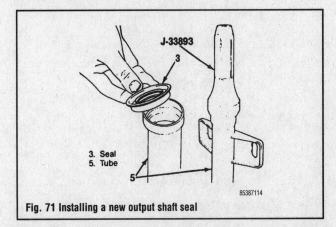

J-33893

3. Seal
5. Tube

Fig. 71 Installing a new output shaft seal

To install:

3. Lubricate the new seal lips and the new bearing using fresh axle lubricant.

4. Install the new bearing using a pilot bearing installer tool such as J-33842, or equivalent.

5. Install the new seal using J-33893, or an equivalent seal installer.

6. Install the axle tube and output shaft assembly.

MFI-Turbo

1. Remove the axle tube and output shaft assembly. For details, please refer to the procedure located earlier in this section.

2. Remove the shaft along with the deflector and retaining ring. Strike the inside of the shaft flange with a brass hammer to dislodge it.

3. Remove the shaft seal and bearing using a slide hammer and axle tube bearing remover such as J-29369-2.

To install:

4. Lubricate the seal lips, bearings and bearing surfaces using axle lubricant.

5. Install the bearing using J-33844 or an equivalent bearing installer.

6. Install the seal using J-33893, or an equivalent seal installer.

7. Install the shaft to the tube taking care not to cut the seal with the splines.

8. Install the axle tube and output shaft assembly to the vehicle.

Shift Cable

REMOVAL & INSTALLATION

▶ **See Figures 72 and 73**

1. Disengage the shift cable from the vacuum actuator by disengaging the locking spring (bend the tang on the spring as shown in the illustration), then, push the actuator diaphragm in to release the cable. Using a pair of pliers, squeeze the two cable locking fingers, then pull the cable out of the bracket hole.

2. Raise and safely support the front of the truck safely using jackstands.

3. Remove cable housing-to-carrier bolts and pull housing away to gain access to the cable locking spring.

➡ **DO NOT unscrew the coupling nut at this time.**

4. Disconnect the cable from the shift fork shaft by lifting the spring over shift fork slot.

5. Unscrew the cable from the housing by unscrewing the coupling nut.

6. Remove the cable from the truck.

To install:

7. Install the cable housing-to-carrier bolts. Torque the bolts to 36 ft. lbs. (48 Nm).

8. Guide the cable through the housing into the fork shaft hole and push the cable inward; the cable will automatically snap into place. Start turning the coupling nut by hand, to avoid cross threading, then torque the nut to 90 inch lbs. (10 Nm). DO NOT overtorque the nut as this will cause thread damage to the housing.

9. Carefully route the cable, then remove the jackstands and lower the vehicle.

10. Connect the shift cable-to-vacuum actuator by pressing the cable into the bracket hole. The cable and housing will snap into place, automatically.

11. Check the cable operation.

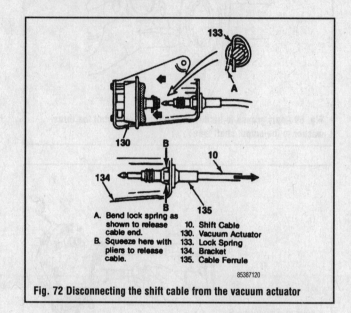

A. Bend lock spring as shown to release cable end.
B. Squeeze here with pliers to release cable.

10. Shift Cable
130. Vacuum Actuator
133. Lock Spring
134. Bracket
135. Cable Ferrule

85387120

Fig. 72 Disconnecting the shift cable from the vacuum actuator

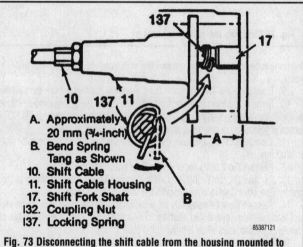

A. Approximately 20 mm (³⁄₄-inch)
B. Bend Spring Tang as Shown
10. Shift Cable
11. Shift Cable Housing
17. Shift Fork Shaft
132. Coupling Nut
137. Locking Spring

85387121

Fig. 73 Disconnecting the shift cable from the housing mounted to the carrier

8

SUSPENSION AND STEERING

WHEELS

2 and 4-Wheel Drive

REMOVAL & INSTALLATION

▶ **See Figures 1 and 2**

The vehicles covered by this manual use a variety of wheel styles, but from the factory they are all one piece rims with 5 bolt holes in a bolt circle of 4.75 in. (120.6mm) for vehicles through 1991 or 5 in. (127mm) for 1992–93 vehicles. Wheels are also available in a variety of standard sizes from 14 x 6 in. (355.6 x 152.4mm) to 15 x 7 in. (381 x 177.8mm). The MFI-Turbo was equipped with 16 x 8 in. (406.4 x 203.2mm). Most vehicles are equipped with a space saver spare, for EMERGENCY USE ONLY, which comes in a 16 x 4 in. (406.4mm x 101.6mm) and 15 x 4 in. (381 x 101.6mm) sizes.

1. When removing a wheel, loosen all the lug nuts with the wheel on the ground, then raise and safely support the vehicle. If you are working at home (not on a roadside emergency) support the truck safely using jackstand(s).

2. If the wheel is stuck or rusted on the hub, make all the lug nuts finger tight, then back each one off 2 turns. Put the truck back on the ground and rock it side to side. Get another person to help if necessary. This is far safer than hitting a stuck wheel with the vehicle on a jack or jackstands.

3. When installing a wheel, tighten the lug nuts in a rotation, skipping every other one.

4. Always use a torque wrench to avoid uneven tightening, which will distort the brake drum or disc. For vehicles through 1991 (except MFI-Turbo) tighten the lug nuts on steel wheels to 73 ft. lbs. (100 Nm) and the nuts on aluminum alloy wheels to 90 ft. lbs. (120 Nm). For 1992 stock wheels, tighten the nuts to 90 ft. lbs. (120 Nm). For 1991–92 MFI-Turbo wheels, tighten the lug nuts to 100 ft. lbs. (140 Nm). On 1993 vehicles equipped with the stock wheels, tighten the lug nuts to 95 ft. lbs. (130 Nm).

INSPECTION

▶ **See Figures 3 and 4**

Wheels can be distorted or bent and not effect dry road handling to a noticeable degree. Out of round wheels will show up as uneven tire wear, or will make it difficult to balance the tire. Wheel runout can be checked with the wheel on or off the truck and with the tire on or off the rim. If measurement is to be made with the wheel off the truck, you will need an accurate mounting surface such as a wheel balancer.

Both lateral and radial runout should be measured using a dial gauge. Lateral runout is a sideways vibration causing a twist or wobble and is measured on a side surface. On a tire and wheel assembly, measure the sidewall of the tire, as close as possible to the tread shoulder design edge. On a rim, measure the runout on the flange.

Radial runout is the egg-shaped difference from a perfect circle. On a tire and wheel assembly, measure radial runout from the center of the tire tread rib, although other tread ribs can be measured, if necessary. The rim may be measured on either flange if the tire is removed.

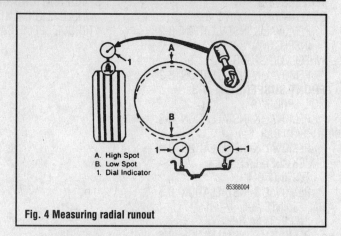

A. High Spot
B. Low Spot
1. Dial Indicator

85388004

Fig. 4 Measuring radial runout

1. Use a dial gauge to measure the runout of the wheel or tire and wheel assembly, as applicable.

2. For steel wheels, the lateral runout limit is 0.045 in. (1.143mm), the radial runout limit is 0.040 in. (1.015mm).

3. For aluminum alloy wheels, the limit for both runout directions is 0.030 in. (0.762mm).

Wheel Lug Studs

REMOVAL & INSTALLATION

Front Wheels on 2wd Vehicles

▶ **See Figure 5**

1. Raise and support the front of the vehicle safely using jackstands, then remove the wheel.

2. Remove the brake pads and caliper. Support the caliper aside using wire or a coat hanger. For details, please refer to Section 9 of this manual.

3. Remove the outer wheel bearing and lift the rotor off the axle. For details on removal, installation and adjustment, please refer to Section 1 of this manual.

4. Properly support the rotor using press bars, then drive the stud out using an arbor press.

To install:

5. Clean the stud hole with a wire brush and start the new stud with a hammer and drift pin. Do not use any lubricant or thread sealer.

6. Finish installing the stud with the press.

7. Install the rotor and adjust the wheel bearing.

8. Install the brake caliper and pads.

9. Install the tire, then remove the jackstands and carefully lower the vehicle.

85388001

Fig. 1 Most trucks are equipped with a spare tire mounted to a hanger bracket under the bed

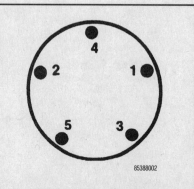

85388002

Fig. 2 Wheel lug tightening sequence for a 5-lug wheel

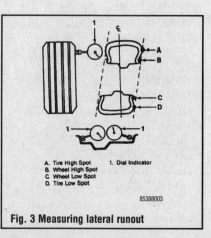

A. Tire High Spot
B. Wheel High Spot
C. Wheel Low Spot
D. Tire Low Spot
1. Dial Indicator

85388003

Fig. 3 Measuring lateral runout

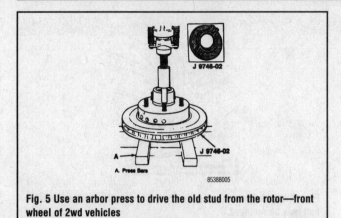

Fig. 5 Use an arbor press to drive the old stud from the rotor—front wheel of 2wd vehicles

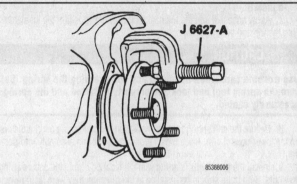

Fig. 6 On many vehicles a stud press tool may be used with the hub still installed on the vehicle

Rear Wheels and Front Wheels on 4wd Vehicles

▶ See Figure 6

1. Raise and support the vehicle safely using jackstands, then remove the wheel.

2. On front wheels, remove the brake, caliper and rotor. Support the caliper from the suspension using wire or a coat hanger. For details, please refer to Section 9 of this manual.

3. On rear wheels, remove the brake drum.

➡When replacing the front hub bolts on vehicles with 4 wheel anti-lock brakes, remove and replace only one wheel lug stud at a time to avoid misaligning the speed sensor exciter ring.

4. Do not hammer the wheel stud to remove it. This will ruin the wheel bearing. Use the stud press tool such as J-6627A or equivalent to press the stud out of the hub.

To install:

5. Clean the hole with a wire brush and start the new stud into the hole. Do not use any lubricant or thread sealer.

6. Stack 4 or 5 washers onto the stud and then put the nut on. Tighten the nut to draw the stud into place.It should be easy to feel when the stud is seated.

7. Reinstall the rotor and caliper or drum, as applicable.

8. Install the tire, then remove the jackstands and carefully lower the vehicle.

FRONT SUSPENSION

▶ See Figure 7

Coil Spring

The 2wd vehicles covered by this manual use a coil spring support for the front suspension.

REMOVAL & INSTALLATION

▶ See Figures 8 and 9

➡The following procedure requires the use of a coil spring removal and installation tool such as No. J-23028 or equivalent.

1. Raise and support the front of the vehicle safely using jackstands so that the front wheels hang free.

2. Remove the shock absorber-to-lower control arm bolts, then push the shock up through the control arm and into the spring.

3. Secure a coil spring tool (such as J-23028 or equivalent), to the end of a jack, then position it to cradle the inner control arm bushings.

4. Remove the stabilizer bar link from the lower control arm.

5. Properly remove the lower control arm pivot bolts in order to pivot the arm and remove spring:

a. Raise the jack to remove the tension from the lower control arm pivot bolts.

b. Install a chain around the spring and through the control arm as a safety measure.

➡During removal, note the direction in which the pivot bolts are mounted.

c. Remove the lower control arm-to-frame pivot nuts and bolts—remove the rear pivot bolt first.

d. Lower the control arm by slowly lowering the jack.

6. When all of the compression is removed from the spring, remove the safety chain and the spring.

➡DO NOT apply force to the lower control arm and/or ball joint to remove the spring. Proper maneuvering of the spring will allow for easy removal.

Fig. 7 View of the 4wd front suspension—visible are the lower control arms and sway bar

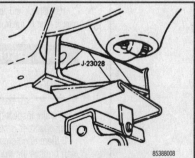

Fig. 8 With the spring tool secured to a jack, raise the control arm in order to relieve tension from the control arm pivot bolts

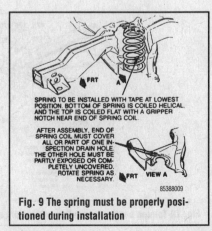

SPRING TO BE INSTALLED WITH TAPE AT LOWEST POSITION. BOTTOM OF SPRING IS COILED HELICAL AND THE TOP IS COILED FLAT WITH A GRIPPER NOTCH NEAR END OF SPRING COIL.

AFTER ASSEMBLY, END OF SPRING COIL MUST COVER ALL OR PART OF ONE IN-SPECTION DRAIN HOLE. THE OTHER HOLE MUST BE PARTLY EXPOSED OR COMPLETELY UNCOVERED. ROTATE SPRING AS NECESSARY.

Fig. 9 The spring must be properly positioned during installation

To install:

7. Apply adhesive into the insulators groove, then position the insulators onto the top and bottom of the spring.

✳✳ CAUTION

Use extreme care when installing and compressing the spring. Be sure the spring tool and jack and properly installed and the spring is securely seated.

8. Secure the coil spring tool, then position the coil spring and insulators on the lower control arm. Raise the control arm and spring assembly into position.

9. Install the pivot bolts, starting with the front bolt first, and secure using new nuts. Both bolts should be installed in the direction they were facing when removed, which usually means they are inserted from the front of the vehicle.

10. Install and secure the stabilizer bar link to the lower control arm.

11. Position and secure the shock absorber.

12. Remove the jackstands and carefully lower the vehicle.

Torsion Bar

Instead of the coil spring used on the front suspension of 2wd trucks, the 4wd vehicles covered by this manual are equipped with a torsion bar.

REMOVAL & INSTALLATION

▶ **See Figures 10 and 11**

➡ **The following procedure requires the use of the torsion bar unloader tool No. J-22517-C (early model vehicles), J-36202 (late model vehicles), or equivalent.**

1. Raise and support the front of the vehicle safely using jackstands.

2. Install a torsion bar unloader tool to relax the tension on the torsion bar adjusting arm screw; record the number of turns necessary to properly install the tool. Remove the adjusting screw.

3. For vehicles through 1991:

a. Remove the torsion support-to-insulator nut/bolt, the support insulator-to-frame nuts/bolts, the insulator retainer and the insulator from the support.

b. Slide the torsion bar(s) forward into the control arm(s) to clear the support.

c. Remove the adjusting arm, the adjusting arm screw and the nut from the support.

d. Remove the torsion bar from the control arm and the support.

4. For 1992–93 vehicles:

a. Remove the adjuster arms.

b. Remove the nut and square washer (raise the support out of the way) from the retainer, then remove the retainer bolts from underneath the frame.

c. Slide the insulator off the support and remove it from the vehicle.

d. Disconnect the muffler flange from the converter, loosen the rear exhaust hanger and lower the rear exhaust.

e. Remove the torsion support from the frame.

f. Remove the torsion bars from the lower control arms.

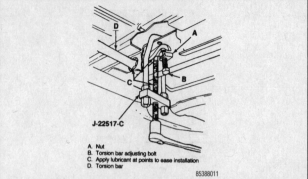

A. Nut
B. Torsion bar adjusting bolt
C. Apply lubricant at points to ease installation
D. Torsion bar

85388011

Fig. 11 Use the torsion bar unloader to ease tension so the adjuster bolt may be removed

To install:

5. For 1992–93 vehicles:

a. Position the torsion bars with the lower control arms. If installing a replacement component, be sure the tag is facing forward.

b. Install the support.

c. Install and secure the rear exhaust system to the proper height, then connect the muffler flange to the converter.

d. Install the insulator, making sure the mount studs are positioned through the support and the insulator locator tabs are indexed to the support (facing forward).

e. Install and finger-tighten the square washer and nut.

f. Install the insulator mounting retainers, then tighten the bolts to 26 ft. lbs. (35 Nm) and/or the nuts to 25 ft. lbs. (34 Nm).

g. Install the adjuster arms, then connect the torsion bars to the arms. With the torsion bars installed, check for an assembled clearance from the end of the bar to the support of 0.236 in. (6.0mm).

h. Lubricate the top of the adjusting arm and the adjusting bolt, then install the nuts and adjuster bolts.

6. For vehicles through 1991:

a. Lubricate the top of the adjusting arm, then install the arm to the support.

b. Install the adjusting bolt nut to the support, then lubricate the adjusting bolt and loosely install it to the retaining nut.

c. Install the insulator to the support end, then install the support to the frame.

d. Install the nut to the retainer and the retainer to the support, then secure the bolts to the retainer from underneath the frame.

e. Install the retainer nuts to the bolts from above the retainer, then install the top center retainer bolt. Tighten the retainer nuts (or bolts from below the frame) to 26 ft. lbs. (35 Nm) and the center retainer bolt to 25 ft. lbs. (35 Nm).

f. Slide the torsion bar into the lower control arm.

g. Raise and slide the torsion bar into the adjusting arm making sure the torsion bar clearance at the support is 0.236 in. (6mm).

7. Attach the torsion bar unloader tool using the same number of turns as recorded during removal, then thread the adjusting screw in until contact is just made with the adjusting arm.

8. Remove the torsion bar unloader tool.

9. Remove the jackstands and carefully lower the vehicle.

10. Check and adjust the trim height ("Z" adjustment), as necessary. For details, please refer to the front end alignment procedures found later in this section.

Shock Absorbers

TESTING

Visually inspect the shock absorber. If there is evidence of leakage and the shock absorber is covered with oil the shock is defective and should be replaced.

If there is no sign of excessive leakage (a small amount of weeping is normal) bounce the truck at one corner by pressing down on the bumper and releasing it. When you have the truck bouncing as much as you can, release the bumper. The truck should stop bouncing after the first rebound. If the bouncing continues past the center point of the bounce more than once, the shock absorbers are worn and should be replaced.

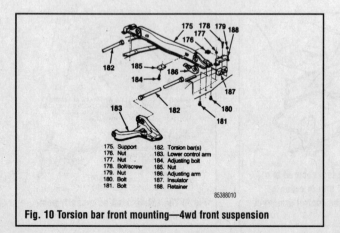

175. Support	182. Torsion bar(s)
176. Nut	183. Lower control arm
177. Nut	184. Adjusting bolt
178. Bolt/screw	185. Nut
179. Nut	186. Adjusting arm
180. Bolt	187. Insulator
181. Bolt	188. Retainer

85388010

Fig. 10 Torsion bar front mounting—4wd front suspension

REMOVAL & INSTALLATION

2wd Vehicles

▶ **See Figure 12**

1. Raise and support the front of the truck safely using jackstands.
2. Using an open end wrench, hold the shock absorber upper stem from turning, then remove the upper stem retaining nut, the retainer and rubber grommet.
3. Remove the shock absorber-to-lower control arm retaining bolts and lower the shock absorber assembly from the bottom of the control arm.
4. Inspect and test the shock absorber; replace it, if necessary.

To install:

5. Fully extend the shock absorber stem, then push it up through the lower control arm and spring so that the upper stem passes through the mounting hole in the upper control arm frame bracket.
6. Install the upper shock absorber nut and tighten to 100 inch lbs. (11 Nm). Be careful not to crush the rubber bushing.
7. Install the shock absorber-to-lower control arm retaining bolts and tighten to 20 ft. lbs. (27 Nm).
8. Remove the jackstands and carefully lower the vehicle.

4wd Vehicles

▶ **See Figures 13 and 14**

1. Raise and support the front of the truck safely using jackstands.
2. Remove the tire and wheel assembly to ease access.
3. Remove the shock absorber-to-lower control arm nut and bolt (using a backup wrench), then collapse the shock absorber.
4. Remove the upper shock absorber-to-frame nut and bolt (again, using a backup wrench).
5. Inspect and test the shock absorber; replace it, if necessary.

To install:

6. Position the shock absorber to the mounting brackets.

7. Install the upper and lower retaining bolts (inserted from the front of the vehicle).
8. Install the retaining nuts to the bolts, then torque the retainers to 54 ft. lbs. (73 Nm).
9. Install the tire and wheel assembly, then remove the jackstands and carefully lower the vehicle.

Ball Joints

INSPECTION

▶ **See Figures 15, 16, 17 and 18**

➡ **Before performing this inspection, make sure that the wheel bearings are adjusted correctly and that the control arm bushings are in good condition.**

1. Make sure the vehicle is parked on a level surface.
2. Raise and support the front of the vehicle safely by placing jackstands under each lower control arm as close as possible to each lower ball joint (as far outboard as possible). Make sure that the vehicle is stable and the control arm bumpers are not contacting the frame.
3. Wipe the ball joints clean and check the seals for cuts or tears. If a seal is cut or torn, then ball joint MUST be replaced.
4. If necessary on 2wd vehicles, adjust the wheel bearings before proceeding.
5. Check the ball joints for horizontal deflection (looseness):
   a. Position a dial indicator against the lowest outboard point on the rim.
   b. Grasp the tire (top and bottom), then pull outward on the top and push inward on the bottom; record the reading on the dial indicator.
   c. Grasp the tire (top and bottom), then pull outward on the bottom and push inward on the top; record the reading on the dial indicator.
   d. The difference in the dial indicator reading is the horizontal deflection of both joints. If the reading exceeds 0.125 in. (3.2mm), the lower ball joint should be checked for wear in order to determine what component(s) must be replaced.

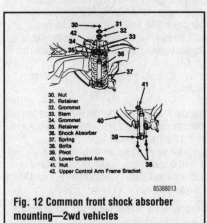

30. Nut
31. Retainer
32. Grommet
33. Stem
34. Grommet
35. Retainer
36. Shock Absorber
37. Spring
38. Bolts
39. Pivot
40. Lower Control Arm
41. Nut
42. Upper Control Arm Frame Bracket

85388013

Fig. 12 Common front shock absorber mounting—2wd vehicles

85388014

Fig. 13 Loosen and remove the shock absorber lower mounting bolt

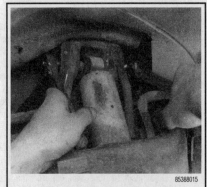

85388015

Fig. 14 Then loosen the upper mounting bolt and remove the shock from the vehicle

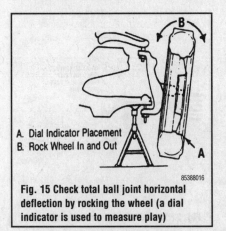

A. Dial Indicator Placement
B. Rock Wheel In and Out

85388016

Fig. 15 Check total ball joint horizontal deflection by rocking the wheel (a dial indicator is used to measure play)

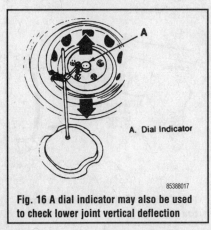

A. Dial Indicator

85388017

Fig. 16 A dial indicator may also be used to check lower joint vertical deflection

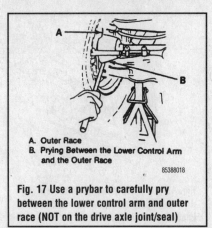

A. Outer Race
B. Prying Between the Lower Control Arm and the Outer Race

85388018

Fig. 17 Use a prybar to carefully pry between the lower control arm and outer race (NOT on the drive axle joint/seal)

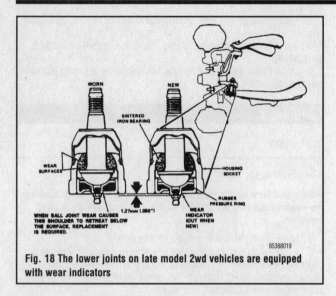

Fig. 18 The lower joints on late model 2wd vehicles are equipped with wear indicators

➡️ **The lower ball joints used on 2wd vehicles use wear indicators.**

6. On 4wd vehicles (no wear indicators), check the lower ball joint for wear:

a. With the vehicle still supported by jackstands, place a dial indicator against the spindle in order to measure vertical movement.

➡️ **DO NOT pry between the lower control arm and the drive axle seal or damage to the seal will result.**

b. Pry between the lower control arm and the outer bearing race while reading the dial indicator. This reading will show vertical deflection (looseness).

c. The lower ball joint is not a pre-loaded joint and may show some looseness, but it should be replaced if movement exceeds 0.125 in. (3.2mm).

7. For 2wd vehicles check for lower ball joint wear using the indicators:

a. Visually inspect the positioning of the grease fitting on the ball joint. The fitting is threaded into a small housing nub which projects approximately 0.050 in. (1.27mm) beyond the surface of the ball joint cover on new parts. As the joint wears, the nub will slowly retreat inward. If the housing nub is visible above the cover, then the joint is still good.

b. If necessary, scrape a screwdriver or fingernail across the ball joint cover and feel for the housing nub. If the housing is flush or inside the cover surface, the joint is worn and should be replaced.

8. Finally, if the joints failed the initial combined test, but the lower joint is found good, the upper ball joint should be checked for looseness as it is probably the culprit:

a. Disconnect the upper ball joint from the steering knuckle.

b. Check for any looseness or if the stud can be twisted by hand. If so, the joint should be replaced.

REMOVAL & INSTALLATION

2wd Vehicles

UPPER

▶ **See Figures 19, 20, 21, 22 and 23**

➡️ **The following procedure requires the use of a ball joint separator tool such as GM No. J-23742 or equivalent.**

1. Raise and support the front of the vehicle safely by placing jackstands securely under the lower control arms. Because the vehicle's weight is used to relieve spring tension on the upper control arm, the floor stands must be positioned between the spring seats and the lower control arm ball joints for maximum leverage.

> ※❀ **CAUTION**
>
> **With components unbolted, the jackstand is holding the lower control arm in place against the coil spring. Make sure the jackstand is firmly positioned and cannot move, or personal injury could result.**

2. Remove the tire and wheel assembly.

3. Remove the brake caliper and support it from the vehicle using a coat hanger or wire. Make sure the brake line is not stretched or damaged and that the caliper's weight is NOT supported by the line.

4. Remove the cotter pin and retaining nut from the upper ball joint.

5. Position J-23742 or an equivalent ball joint separator tool between upper joint stud and the lower joint/control arm. Use the tool to separate the upper ball joint from the steering knuckle. Pull the steering knuckle free of the ball joint after removal.

➡️ **After separating the steering knuckle from the upper ball joint, be sure to support the steering knuckle/hub assembly to prevent damaging the brake hose.**

6. Remove the riveted upper ball joint from the upper control arm:

a. Drill a ⅛ in. (3mm) hole, about ¼ in. (6mm) deep into each rivet.

b. Then use a ½ in. (13mm) drill bit, to drill off the rivet heads.

c. Using a pin punch and the hammer, drive out the rivets in order to free the upper ball joint from the upper control arm assembly, then remove the upper ball joint.

7. Clean and inspect the steering knuckle hole. Replace the steering knuckle if the hole is out of round.

To install:

8. Position the joint in the upper control arm, then install the joint retaining nuts and bolts. Position the bolts threaded upward from under the control arm. Tighten the ball joint retainers to 17 ft. lbs. (23 Nm).

9. Remove the support from the steering knuckle, then install the ball joint to the knuckle. Make sure the joint is seated, then install the stud nut and tighten to 65 ft. lbs. (90 Nm) for vehicles through 1986 or to 61 ft. lbs. (83 Nm) for 1987–93 vehicles. Install a new cotter pin.

➡️ **When installing the cotter pin, never loosen the castle nut to expose the cotter pin hole.**

Fig. 19 Use a ball joint separator tool to drive the upper ball joint from the steering knuckle

Fig. 20 Drill a small guide hole into each ball joint rivet

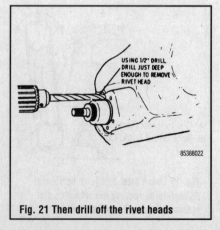

Fig. 21 Then drill off the rivet heads

10. If not installed already, thread the grease fitting into the ball joint. Use a grease gun to lubricate the upper ball joint.

11. Reposition and secure the brake caliper.

12. Install the tire and wheel assembly.

13. Remove the jackstands and carefully lower the vehicle.

14. Check and adjust the front end alignment, as necessary.

LOWER

▶ **See Figures 24, 25, 26, 27 and 28**

➡**The following procedure requires the use of a ball joint remover/installer set (the particular set may vary upon application but must include a clamping-type tool with the appropriately sized adapters) and a ball joint separator tool, such as J-23742 or equivalent.**

1. Raise and support the front of the vehicle safely using jackstands under the frame so the control arms hang free.

2. Remove the tire and wheel assembly.

3. Position a floor jack under the spring seat of the lower control arm, then raise the jack to support the arm.

➡**The floor jack MUST remain under the lower control arm, during the removal and installation procedures, to retain the arm and spring positions. Make sure the jack is securely positioned and will not slip or release during the procedure or personal injury may result.**

4. Remove the brake caliper and support it aside using a hanger or wire. Make sure the brake line is not stressed or damaged.

5. Remove and discard the lower ball joint cotter pin, then loosen and remove the stud nut.

6. Position J-23742 or an equivalent ball joint separator tool between lower joint stud and the upper joint/control arm. Use the tool to separate the lower ball joint from the steering knuckle.

7. Carefully guide the lower control arm out of the opening in the splash shield using a putty knife. Position a block of wood between the frame and upper control arm to keep the knuckle out of the way.

8. Remove the grease fitting from the control arm.

9. Use the ball joint remover set along with the appropriate adapters to drive the ball joint from the control arm.

To install:

10. Clean the tapered hole in the steering knuckle of any dirt or foreign matter, then check the hole to see if it is out of round, deformed or otherwise damaged. If a problem is found, then knuckle must be replaced.

11. Using a suitable installation set, press the new ball joint until it bottoms in the control arm. Make sure the grease seal is facing inboard.

12. Position the ball joint stud into the steering knuckle, then install the retaining nut and tighten to 90 ft. lbs. (120 Nm) for vehicles through 1988 or to 83 ft. lbs. (113 Nm) for 1989–93 vehicles. Install a new cotter pin.

➡**When installing the cotter pin, never loosen the castle nut to expose the cotter pin hole.**

13. If not installed already, thread the grease fitting into the ball joint, then use a grease gun to lubricate the joint.

14. Reposition and secure the brake caliper.

15. Install the tire and wheel assembly.

16. Remove the jackstands and carefully lower the vehicle.

17. Check and adjust the front end alignment, as necessary.

4wd Vehicles

▶ **See Figures 20, 21, 22, 23 and 29**

On 4wd vehicles both the upper and lower ball joints are removed in the same manner. Once the joint is separated from the steering knuckle the rivets are drilled and punched to free the joint from the control arm. Service joints are bolted into position with the retaining bolts threaded upward from beneath the control arm. In this manner, the joint is replaced in an almost identical fashion to the upper joints on 2wd vehicles.

1. Raise and support the front of the vehicle safely using jackstands.

2. Remove the tire and wheel assembly.

3. Remove the cotter pin from the ball joint, then loosen the retaining nut.

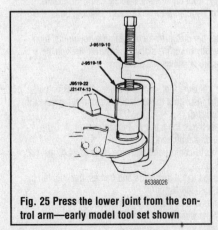

Fig. 22 Punch the rivets out and remove the ball joint

Fig. 23 Service ball joints are bolted to the control arm

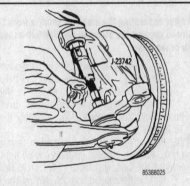

Fig. 24 Use a ball joint separator to drive the lower joint from the knuckle

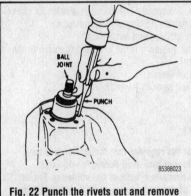

Fig. 25 Press the lower joint from the control arm—early model tool set shown

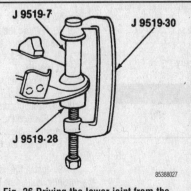

Fig. 26 Driving the lower joint from the control arm—Late model tool set

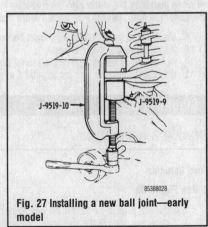

Fig. 27 Installing a new ball joint—early model

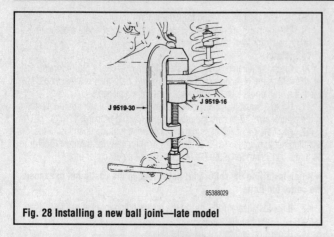

Fig. 28 Installing a new ball joint—late model

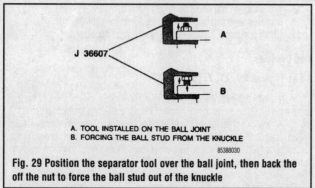

A. TOOL INSTALLED ON THE BALL JOINT
B. FORCING THE BALL STUD FROM THE KNUCKLE

Fig. 29 Position the separator tool over the ball joint, then back the off the nut to force the ball stud out of the knuckle

4. Position a suitable ball joint separator tool such as J-34026, or equivalent, then carefully loosen the joint in the steering knuckle. Remove the tool and the retaining nut, then remove the joint from the knuckle.

➡**After separating the steering knuckle from the upper ball joint, be sure to support the steering knuckle/hub assembly to prevent damaging the brake hose.**

5. Remove the riveted ball joint from the control arm:
    a. Drill a ⅛ in. (3mm) hole, about ¼ in. (6mm) deep into each rivet.
    b. Then use a ½ in. (13mm) drill bit, to drill off the rivet heads.
    c. Using a pin punch and the hammer, drive out the rivets in order to free the ball joint from the control arm assembly, then remove the ball joint.
    To install:
6. Position the joint in the control arm, then install the joint retaining nuts and bolts. Position the bolts threaded upward from under the control arm. Tighten the ball joint retainers to 17 ft. lbs. (23 Nm).
7. Remove the support from the steering knuckle, then install the ball joint to the knuckle. Make sure the joint is seated, then install the stud nut and tighten to 70 ft. lbs. (95 Nm). Install a new cotter pin.

➡**When installing the cotter pin, never loosen the castle nut to expose the cotter pin hole, but DO NOT tighten more than an additional ⅙ turn.**

8. Use a grease gun to lubricate the upper ball joint.
9. Install the tire and wheel assembly.
10. Remove the jackstands and carefully lower the vehicle.
11. Check and adjust the front end alignment, as necessary.

Stabilizer Bar

REMOVAL & INSTALLATION

2wd Vehicles

▶ **See Figure 30**

1. Raise and support the front of the vehicle safely using jackstands.
2. If necessary, remove the front wheels for additional access.

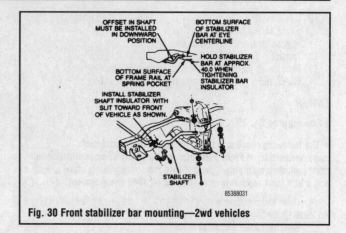

Fig. 30 Front stabilizer bar mounting—2wd vehicles

3. Loosen the nut from the top of one of the the link bolts, then remove the retainer and grommet so the stabilizer may be separated from the link bolt. If necessary, remove the link bolt, washers and grommets, but make sure all components remain in order on the link bolt once it is removed in order to ease installation.
4. Loosen the nut from the top of the other link bolt and separate it from the stabilizer in the same fashion. If the link bolt and components are completely removed, be sure to tag or arrange everything to assure installation on the same side.
5. Loosen and remove the bolts retaining the stabilizer brackets to the frame, then remove the stabilizer bar from the vehicle.
6. If necessary, remove the rubber bushings (insulators).
To install:
7. If removed, install the rubber bushings to the stabilizer bar, making sure they are positioned with the slits facing toward the front of the vehicle.
8. Position the stabilizer shaft, then install the brackets over the bushings to retain the shaft. Tighten the bracket bolts to 24 ft. lbs. (33 Nm).
9. Install the link bolts making sure the positioning of the grommets, retainers and washers is correct. If necessary, refer to the illustration for classification. But keep in mind the grommets are normally surrounded by washers/retainers or components (control arm or stabilizer).
10. Install the upper grommet, retainer and nut to the top of each link bolt, then tighten to 13 ft. lbs. (17 Nm).
11. If removed, install the front wheels.
12. Remove the jackstands and carefully lower the truck.

4wd Vehicles

▶ **See Figures 31, 32 and 33**

➡**Installation of the stabilizer bar requires that the torsion bar be unloaded using a special unloader tool used during tension bar removal. Do not attempt this procedure without the unloader. For details on the unloader and its use, please refer to the tension bar procedure found earlier in this section.**

1. Raise and support the front of the vehicle safely using jackstands.
2. Remove the stabilizer bar clamp-to-control arm retaining bolts, then remove the clamps.
3. Remove the stabilizer bar clamp-to-frame retaining bolts/nuts, then remove the clamps and carefully lower the stabilizer bar from the vehicle.
4. If necessary remove the bushings (insulators).
To install:
5. Using a tension bar unloader tool, properly unload the tension bar.
6. If removed, install the insulators to the stabilizer bar, making sure the slits in the insulators face forward.
7. Position the stabilizer bar to the frame and lower control arm, then loosely install the clamps and retaining bolts.
8. Tighten the bar clamp-to-control arm retaining bolts to 24 ft. lbs. (33 Nm).
9. Install the frame clamps to the insulators and frames, then tighten the retaining bolts/nuts to 35 ft. lbs. (48 Nm).
10. Remove the jackstands and carefully lower the vehicle.
11. Check and/or adjust the vehicle trim height, as necessary.

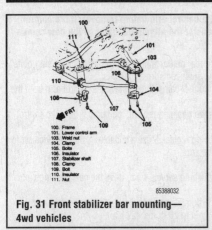

Fig. 31 Front stabilizer bar mounting—4wd vehicles

Fig. 32 When removing the 4wd stabilizer bar, first loosen the control arm clamp bolts

Fig. 33 Loosen and remove the frame clamp retainers

Upper Control Arm

REMOVAL & INSTALLATION

2wd Vehicles

▶ See Figures 34, 35 and 36

➡ The following procedure requires the use of a ball joint separator tool such as J-23742 or equivalent.

1. Raise and support the front of the vehicle safely by placing jackstands securely under the lower control arms. Because the vehicle's weight is used to relieve spring tension on the upper control arm, the floor stands must be positioned between the spring seats and the lower control arm ball joints for maximum leverage.

❊❊ CAUTION

With components unbolted, the jackstand is holding the lower control arm in place against the coil spring. Make sure the jackstand is firmly positioned and cannot move, or personal injury could result.

2. Remove the tire and wheel assembly.
3. Remove the brake caliper and support it from the vehicle using a coat hanger or wire. Make sure the brake line is not stretched or damaged and that the caliper's weight is NOT supported by the line.
4. Remove the cotter pin and retaining nut from the upper ball joint.
5. Position J-23742 or an equivalent ball joint separator tool between upper joint stud and the lower joint/control arm. Use the tool to separate the upper ball joint from the steering knuckle. Pull the steering knuckle free of the ball joint after removal.

➡ After separating the steering knuckle from the upper ball joint, be sure to support the steering knuckle/hub assembly to prevent damaging the brake hose.

6. Remove the upper control arm-to-frame nuts and bolts, then lift and remove the upper control arm from the vehicle.

➡ Tape the shims together and identify them to assure that they are re-installed in the same place

7. Clean and inspect the steering knuckle hole. Replace the steering knuckle if any out of roundness is noted.
8. If replacement is necessary, mount the control arm in a vise, then remove the pivot shaft nuts and washers. Use a control arm bushing fixture (C-clamp like tool) along with a slotted washer and a piece of pipe (slightly larger than the bushing) to remove the old bushings.

   To install:
9. If removed, position the pivot shaft to the control arm and install the bushing using the fixture tool, washer and a length of pipe with the same outer diameter as the bushing. Tighten the tool until the bushing is positioned on the shaft as shown in the illustration. Loosely install the bushing retaining nuts and washers. For 1987–93 vehicles, tighten bushing nuts to 85 ft. lbs. (115 Nm). For 1986 and earlier vehicles, wait until the control arm is installed with the vehicle's weight on the suspension.
10. Loosely install the control arm to the frame using the bolts and nuts. Position the shims as noted during removal, then tighten the retainers to 45 ft. lbs. (60 Nm) for vehicles through 1986 or to 65 ft. lbs. (88 Nm) for 1987–93 vehicles.

➡ On most vehicles, the left upper control arm shaft must have the depression facing inboard.

11. Remove the support from the steering knuckle, then install the ball joint to the knuckle. Make sure the joint is seated, then install the stud nut and tighten to 65 ft. lbs. (90 Nm) for vehicles through 1986 or to 61 ft. lbs. (83 Nm) for 1987–93 vehicles. Install a new cotter pin.

➡ When installing the cotter pin, never loosen the castle nut to expose the cotter pin hole.

12. Reposition and secure the brake caliper.
13. Install the tire and wheel assembly.

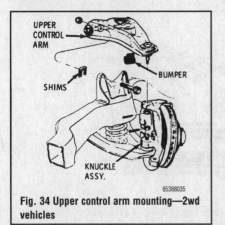

Fig. 34 Upper control arm mounting—2wd vehicles

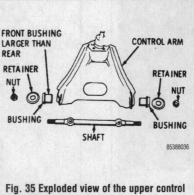

Fig. 35 Exploded view of the upper control arm and bushing components

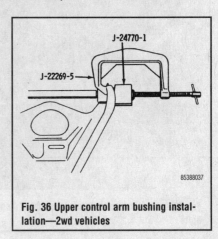

Fig. 36 Upper control arm bushing installation—2wd vehicles

14. Remove the jackstands and carefully lower the vehicle.
15. If the control arm bushings were replaced on 1986 and earlier vehicles, tighten the pivot shaft nuts to 65 ft. lbs. (88 Nm).
16. Check and adjust the front end alignment, as necessary.

4wd Vehicles

♦ **See Figures 37 and 38**

1. Raise and support the front of the vehicle safely using jackstands.
2. Remove the tire and wheel assembly.
3. Remove the cotter pin from the ball joint, then loosen the retaining nut.

➡**After separating the steering knuckle from the upper ball joint, be sure to support the steering knuckle/hub assembly to prevent damaging the brake hose.**

4. Position a suitable ball joint separator tool such as J-34026, or equivalent, then carefully loosen the joint in the steering knuckle. Remove the tool and the retaining nut, then remove the joint from the knuckle.

➡**The 4wd vehicles covered by this manual do not use shims to adjust the front wheel alignment. Instead, the upper control arm bolts are equipped with cams which are rotated to achieve caster and camber adjustments. In order to preserve adjustment and ease installation,** matchmark the cams to the control arm before removal. If the control arm is being replaced, transfer the alignment marks to the new component before installation.

5. Remove the front and rear nuts retaining the control arm retaining bolts to the frame, then remove the outer cams from the bolts.
6. Remove the bolts and inner cams, then remove the control arm from the vehicle.
7. If necessary, remove the retaining nut and the bumper from the control arm.
8. If the bushings are being replaced, use a suitable bushing service set to remove the bushings from the arm.

To install:

9. If removed, use the bushing service set to drive the new bushings into the control arm.
10. If removed, install the bumper and retaining nut to the control arm. Tighten the bumper retaining nut to 20 ft. lbs. (27 Nm).
11. Position the control arm to the vehicle, then install the retaining bolts (from the inside of the frame brackets facing outward) and the inner cams. The inner cams must be positioned on the bolts before they are inserted through the control arm and frame brackets.
12. Position the outer cams over the retaining bolts, then install the nuts to the ends of the bolts at the front and rear of the control arm. Align the cams to the reference marks made earlier, then tighten the end nuts to 70 ft. lbs. (95 Nm).
13. Remove the support from the steering knuckle, then install the ball joint to the knuckle. Make sure the joint is seated, then install the stud nut and tighten to 70 ft. lbs. (95 Nm). Install a new cotter pin.

➡**When installing the cotter pin, never loosen the castle nut to expose the cotter pin hole, but DO NOT tighten more than an additional ⅛ turn.**

14. Install the tire and wheel assembly.
15. Remove the jackstands and carefully lower the vehicle.
16. Check and adjust the front end alignment, as necessary.

Lower Control Arm

REMOVAL & INSTALLATION

2wd Vehicles

♦ **See Figure 39**

1. Remove the coil spring from the vehicle. For details, please refer to the procedure located earlier in this section.
2. If not done already, remove the tire and wheel assembly.
3. Remove the brake caliper and support it from the vehicle using a coat hanger or wire. Make sure the brake line is not stretched or damaged and that the caliper's weight is NOT supported by the line.
4. Remove the cotter pin and retaining nut from the upper ball joint.
5. Position J-23742 or an equivalent ball joint separator tool between upper joint stud and the upper joint/control arm. Use the tool to separate the ball joint from the steering knuckle. Pull the steering knuckle free of the ball joint after removal.

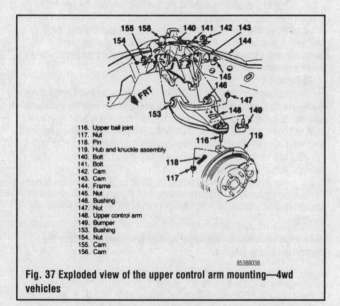

116. Upper ball joint
117. Nut
118. Pin
119. Hub and knuckle assembly
140. Bolt
141. Bolt
142. Cam
143. Cam
144. Frame
145. Nut
146. Bushing
147. Nut
148. Upper control arm
149. Bumper
153. Bushing
154. Nut
155. Cam
156. Cam

85388038

Fig. 37 Exploded view of the upper control arm mounting—4wd vehicles

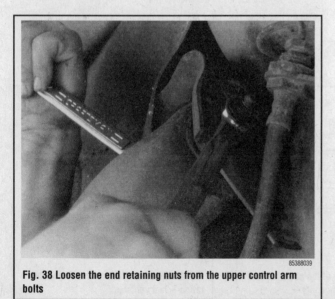

85388039

Fig. 38 Loosen the end retaining nuts from the upper control arm bolts

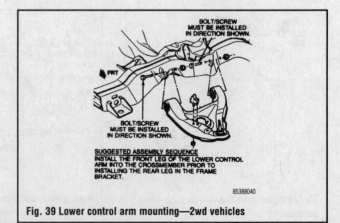

85388040

Fig. 39 Lower control arm mounting—2wd vehicles

➡**After separating the steering knuckle from the upper ball joint, be sure to support the steering knuckle/hub assembly to prevent damaging the brake hose. Also, support the lower control arm and guide it out of the opening in the splash shield.**

6. Remove the jam nuts from the back of each lower control arm pivot bolt.

7. Remove the pivot bolts (noting the direction in which they are facing), then remove the control arm from the vehicle.

8. If the bushings are beings replaced, use a suitable bushing service set to remove the bushings from the control arm. The front bushing is normally flared and the flare must be driven down flush with the rubber using a blunt chisel before attempting removal.

To install:

9. If the bushings were removed, use the bushing service set to install them to the control arms. If the front bushing is the flared type, use a flaring tool to produce an approximate flare of 45 degrees.

10. Position the control arm to the vehicle.

11. Install the pivot bolts as noted during removal. For most vehicles covered by this manual, that means they should be installed with the heads forward, facing the rear.

12. Install the jam nuts and tighten to 94 ft. lbs. (127 Nm) for the front nut on vehicles through 1992, and/or to 67 ft. lbs. for the rear nut on vehicles through 1992 or both nuts on 1993 vehicles.

13. Remove the support from the steering knuckle, then install the ball joint to the knuckle. Make sure the joint is seated, then install the stud nut and tighten to 65 ft. lbs. (90 Nm) for vehicles through 1986 or to 61 ft. lbs. (83 Nm) for 1987–93 vehicles. Install a new cotter pin.

➡**When installing the cotter pin, never loosen the castle nut to expose the cotter pin hole.**

14. Reposition and secure the brake caliper.

15. Install the tire and wheel assembly.

16. Remove the jackstands and carefully lower the vehicle.

17. Check and adjust the front end alignment, as necessary.

4wd Vehicles

▶ **See Figure 40**

1. Raise and support the front of the vehicle safely using jackstands.

2. Remove the tire and wheel assembly.

3. Remove the stabilizer bar. For details, please refer to the procedures earlier in this section. Installation of the stabilizer bar will require use of a torsion bar unloader tool.

4. Remove the shock absorber.

5. Remove the lower control arm-to-frame nuts, then withdraw the bolts, noting the direction they were facing for installation purposes. Remove the lower control arm from the truck.

6. If necessary, use a suitable bushing service set to remove the bushings from the lower control arm.

To install:

7. If removed, use the service set to install new bushings to the lower control arm.

8. Position the control arm in the vehicle, installing the front leg of the lower control arm into the crossmember before installing the rear leg into the frame bracket.

9. Insert the control arm retaining bolts in the direction noted during removal. For most vehicles, they should be inserted from the rear of the truck facing forward. On vehicles through 1992 the bolts may be threaded into a fitting on the frame/crossmember, if so they should be tightened to 148 ft. lbs. (200 Nm) while the suspension is at normal trim height.

➡**When tightening the lower control arm fasteners for these vehicles, the suspension must be held at normal trim height. This can be accomplished in various ways, including using a floor jack or jackstands to support the control arm at the proper height or loosely tightening the fasteners, installing the remaining components and placing the vehicle's weight on the wheels. If the second option is chosen, make sure the fasteners are tightened sufficiently to prevent components from pulling apart while the vehicle is supported by the wheels. Also, for safety should components come loose, position jackstands under the vehicle, in contact with the suspension but not taking any significant weight away from the wheels.**

10. Install the lower control arm retaining nuts and tighten them with the suspension at normal trim height to 92 ft. lbs. (125 Nm) for vehicles through 1992 or to 70 ft. lbs. (95 Nm) for 1993 vehicles.

11. Install the shock absorber.

12. Properly unload the torsion bar, then install the stabilizer bar. Adjust the torsion bar, as necessary. For details, please refer to the procedures located earlier in this section.

13. Install the tire and wheel assembly.

14. Remove the jackstands and carefully lower the vehicle.

Steering Knuckle and Spindle

REMOVAL & INSTALLATION

2wd Vehicles

▶ **See Figure 41**

1. Raise and support the front of the vehicle frame using jackstands.

➡**When supporting the vehicle on jackstands, DO NOT place the jackstands under the lower control arms as spring tension will be used to help separate the ball joint studs from the knuckle. Place the jackstands under the frame and use a suitable floor jack under the control arm for safety.**

2. Remove the tire and wheel assembly.

3. Remove the brake caliper from the steering knuckle and hang it from the vehicle using wire or a coat hanger. Make sure the brake line is not stretched or otherwise damaged.

4. Remove the grease cup, the cotter pin, the castle nut and the hub-and-rotor assembly. For details, please refer to the the brake rotor (disc) procedure located in Section 9 of this manual.

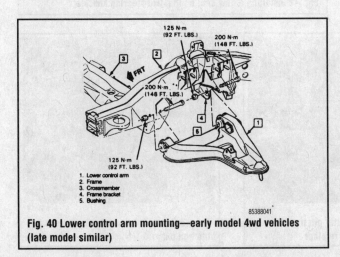

Fig. 40 Lower control arm mounting—early model 4wd vehicles (late model similar)

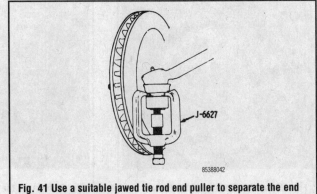

Fig. 41 Use a suitable jawed tie rod end puller to separate the end from the steering knuckle

5. Remove the splash shield-to-steering knuckle bolts and separate the shield from the knuckle.

6. At the tie rod end-to-steering knuckle stud, remove the cotter pin and the nut. Use a suitable jawed tie rod end puller tool such as J-6627, J-24319-01 or equivalent to separate the tie rod end from the steering knuckle.

7. Position a floor jack under the spring seat of the lower control arm in order to retain the spring seat. Raise the floor jack until it just contacts the arm.

8. Remove the cotter pins from the upper and lower ball joint studs, then loosen the retaining nuts.

9. Use a ball joint separator such as J-23742 or equivalent to separate the upper ball joint from the steering knuckle. Remove the nut and pivot the upper control arm free of the knuckle.

10. Use the ball joint tool to separate the lower ball joint from the steering knuckle, then remove the nuts and lift the steering knuckle from the lower control arm.

11. Clean and inspect the steering knuckle and spindle for signs of wear or damage; if necessary, replace the steering knuckle. If any out-of-roundness is found in the tapered knuckle hole it MUST be replaced.

To install:

12. Position the steering knuckle onto the lower ball joint stud, then lift the upper control arm to insert the upper ball joint stud into the steering knuckle. Loosely install both ball joint stud nuts to hold the components in position.

13. Properly tighten the upper and lower ball joint stud nuts, then install new cotter pins. For details, please refer to the procedures located earlier in this section.

➡**When installing a cotter pin, never loosen the castle nut to expose the cotter pin hole.**

14. If equipped, position a new steering knuckle gasket.

15. Install the splash shield to the knuckle and secure the retaining bolts.

16. Install the tie rod end to the steering knuckle, then tighten the stud nut to specification and install a new cotter pin.

17. Install the hub and rotor assembly and castle nut. Properly adjust the wheel bearings, then install a new cotter pin followed by the grease cup. For wheel bearing adjustment procedures, please refer to Section 1 of this manual.

18. Remove the support, then reposition and secure the brake caliper.

19. Install the tire and wheel assembly.

20. Remove the jackstands and carefully lower the vehicle.

21. Check and/or adjust the front end alignment, as necessary.

4wd Vehicles

◆ **See Figures 42 thru 49**

➡**The following procedure requires the use a universal steering linkage puller J-24319-01, an axle shaft boot seal protector J-28712, a ball joint separator tool J-34026 and a steering knuckle seal Installation tool J-28574 or their equivalents.**

1. Raise and support the front of the vehicle safely using jackstands.

2. Properly unload the torsion bar. For details, please refer to the torsion bar procedure located earlier in this section.

3. Remove the tire and wheel assembly.

4. Install an axle shaft boot seal protector to the tri-pot axle joint.

5. Remove the brake caliper and support aside using wire or a coat hanger. Make sure the brake line is not stretched or damaged.

6. Remove the brake disc from the wheel hub.

7. At the wheel hub, remove the cotter pin, the retainer, the castle nut, the thrust washer. If necessary, hold the hub from turning using a prybar across 2 installed lug nuts.

8. Remove the cotter pin and castle nut from the tie-rod end, then use the steering linkage puller to separate the tie rod end from the knuckle..

9. Remove the hub/bearing assembly-to-steering knuckle retaining bolts from the rear of the knuckle, then remove the hub/bearing assembly from the steering knuckle.

➡**When removing the steering knuckle and wheel hub, be careful not to damage the splined surface of the half shaft.**

10. Remove the splash shield.

11. Remove the cotter pins from the upper and lower ball joints, then back off the castle nut(s).

12. Use the ball joint separator tool J-34026 or equivalent to loosen the ball joints in the steering knuckle.

13. Remove the ball joint nuts, then separate the ball joints from the knuckle and remove the knuckle from the vehicle.

14. Remove the spacer and the seal from the steering knuckle.

15. Clean and inspect the parts for nicks, scores and/or damage, then replace them as necessary.

To install:

16. Install a new seal into the steering knuckle, using a knuckle seal installation tool such as J-28574 or equivalent.

17. Install the spacer, then position the knuckle and insert the upper and lower ball joints.

18. Install the upper and lower ball joint stud nuts and tighten to specification, then install new cotter pins. For details, please refer to the ball joint procedures located earlier in this section.

19. Position the splash shield to the steering knuckle, then install the wheel hub/bearing assembly while aligning the threaded holes. Tighten the hub/bearing assembly retaining bolts to 86 ft. lbs. (116 Nm).

20. Install the tie rod end to the steering knuckle, then secure using the retaining nut and cotter pin.

21. Install the thrust washer and the castle nut to the drive axle and tighten to 180 ft. lbs. (245 Nm). Install the retainer and a new cotter pin (DO NOT back off the torque specification).

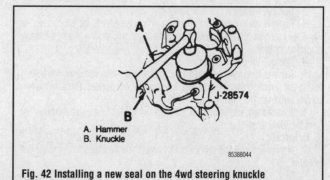

A. Hammer
B. Knuckle

Fig. 42 Installing a new seal on the 4wd steering knuckle

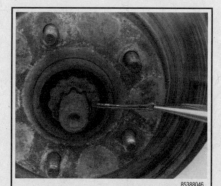

Fig. 43 Remove the wheel in order to access the steering knuckle components

Fig. 44 Remove the cotter pin from the drive axle end nut and retainer

Fig. 45 Remove the retainer for access to the end nut

Fig. 46 Loosen the drive axle nut—here the caliper is installed so a drift could be inserted to keep the disc from spinning

Fig. 47 The various ball studs must be removed from the steering knuckle as well

Fig. 48 Remove the cotter pin (in this case from the tie rod end)

Fig. 49 Loosen and remove the retaining nut so the tie rod may be separated

22. Install the brake disc.
23. Reposition and secure the brake caliper.
24. Remove the axle boot protector and the torsion bar unloader tool.
25. Install the tire and wheel assembly.
26. Remove the jackstands and carefully lower the truck.

Front Wheel Bearings

REMOVAL & INSTALLATION

2wd Vehicles

For wheel bearing removal, packing, installation and adjustment procedures on 2wd vehicles, please refer to

4wd Vehicles

➡The wheel bearing is installed in the wheel hub assembly and is serviced by replacement only.

Please refer to the appropriate portion of the steering knuckle procedure earlier in this section in order to replace the wheel hub assembly.

Wheel Alignment

If the tires are worn unevenly, if the vehicle is not stable on the highway or if the handling seems uneven in spirited driving, the wheel alignment should be checked. If an alignment problem is suspected, first check for improper tire inflation and other possible causes. These can be worn suspension or steering components, accident damage or even unmatched tires. If any worn or damaged components are found, they must be replaced before the wheels can be properly aligned. Wheel alignment requires very expensive equipment and involves minute adjustments which must be accurate; it should only be performed by a trained technician. Take your vehicle to a properly equipped shop.

Following is a description of the alignment angles which are adjustable on most vehicles and how they affect vehicle handling. Although these angles can apply to both the front and rear wheels, usually only the front suspension is adjustable.

CASTER

▶ **See Figure 50**

Looking at a vehicle from the side, caster angle describes the steering axis rather than a wheel angle. The steering knuckle is attached to a control arm or strut at the top and a control arm at the bottom. The wheel pivots around the line between these points to steer the vehicle. When the upper point is tilted back, this is described as positive caster. Having a positive caster tends to make the wheels self-centering, increasing directional stability. Excessive positive caster makes the wheels hard to steer, while an uneven caster will cause a pull to one side. Overloading the vehicle or sagging rear springs will affect caster, as will raising the rear of the vehicle. If the rear of the vehicle is lower than normal, the caster becomes more positive.

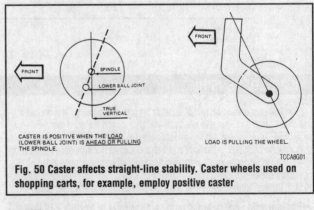

Fig. 50 Caster affects straight-line stability. Caster wheels used on shopping carts, for example, employ positive caster

CAMBER

▶ **See Figure 51**

Looking from the front of the vehicle, camber is the inward or outward tilt of the top of wheels. When the tops of the wheels are tilted in, this is negative camber; if they are tilted out, it is positive. In a turn, a slight amount of negative camber helps maximize contact of the tire with the road. However, too much negative camber compromises straight-line stability, increases bump steer and torque steer.

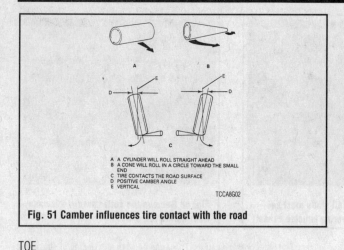

A A CYLINDER WILL ROLL STRAIGHT AHEAD
B A CONE WILL ROLL IN A CIRCLE TOWARD THE SMALL END
C TIRE CONTACTS THE ROAD SURFACE
D POSITIVE CAMBER ANGLE
E VERTICAL

TCCA8G02

Fig. 51 Camber influences tire contact with the road

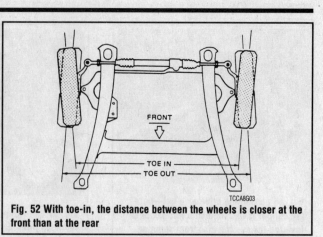

TCCA8G03

Fig. 52 With toe-in, the distance between the wheels is closer at the front than at the rear

TOE

▶ **See Figure 52**

Looking down at the wheels from above the vehicle, toe angle is the distance between the front of the wheels, relative to the distance between the back of the wheels. If the wheels are closer at the front, they are said to be toed-in or to have negative toe. A small amount of negative toe enhances directional stability and provides a smoother ride on the highway.

WHEEL ALIGNMENT

Year	Caster Range (deg.)	Caster Preferred Setting (deg.)	Camber Range (deg.)	Camber Preferred Setting (deg.)	Toe-in (in.)	Steering Axis Inclination (deg.)
1982	0–4P	2P	0.7N–2.3P	0.8P	1/16	NA
1983	0–4P	2P	0.7N–2.3P	0.8P	1/16	NA
1984	1P–3P	2P	0–1.6P	0.8P	1/16	NA
1985	1P–3P	2P	0–1.6P	0.8P	1/16	NA
1986	1P–3P	2P	0–1.6P	0.8P	1/16	NA
1987	1P–3P	2P	0–1.6P	0.8P	1/16	NA
1988	1P–3P	2P	0–1.6P	0.8P	1/16	NA
1989	1P–3P	2P	0–1.6P	0.8P	1/16	NA
1990	1P–3P	2P	0–1.6P	0.8P	1/16	NA
1991–92	1P–3P①	2P①	0–1.6P①	0.8P①	1/16①	NA①
	2.5P–4.5P②	3.5P②	0.8N–0.8P②	0②	1/16②	NA②
1993	1P–3P	2P	0–1.6P	0.8P	1/16	NA

① Except MFI-Turbo
② MFI-Turbo

85388058

REAR SUSPENSION

The rear suspension system consists of 3 major components: The double acting shock absorbers, variable rate multi-leaf springs and the solid rear axle assembly. The multi-leaf springs are connected to the frame by a hanger assembly with integral bushings in the front and a shackle assembly with integral bushings in the rear. In response to different road and payload conditions, the shackle assembly allows the leaf spring to "change its length". The rear axle is connected to both the leaf springs and the shock absorbers by various attaching parts.

➡**For rear axle service procedures, please refer to Section 7 of this manual.**

Leaf Springs

REMOVAL & INSTALLATION

▶ **See Figures 53 and 54**

➡**The following procedure requires the use of two sets of jackstands.**

1. Raise and support the rear frame of the vehicle safely using jackstands. Support the rear axle with the second set of jackstands.

➡**When supporting the rear of the vehicle, support the axle and the body separately in order to relieve the load on the rear spring.**

2. Remove the tire and wheel assembly.
3. Remove the shock absorber.
4. For vehicles through 1988:
   a. At the rear of the spring, loosen (but DO NOT remove) the shackle-to-frame bolt and the shackle-to-spring bolt.
   b. Remove the nut and bolt from the front hanger, then carefully disconnect the spring from the hanger.
   c. Support the spring, then remove the shackle.
   d. Remove the U-bolts and anchor plate.
5. For 1989–93 vehicles:
   a. Remove the U-bolt nuts, washers, anchor plate and bolts.
   b. On 1993 vehicles, remove the spare tire, if equipped.
   c. Remove the shackle-to-frame bolt, washers and nut.

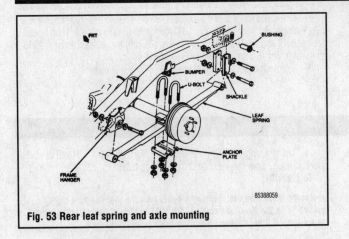

Fig. 53 Rear leaf spring and axle mounting

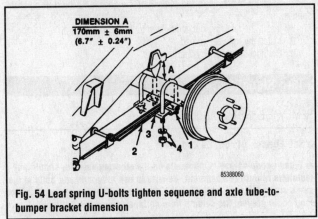

Fig. 54 Leaf spring U-bolts tighten sequence and axle tube-to-bumper bracket dimension

d. For 1993 vehicles, remove the fuel tank, if necessary. For details, please refer to Section 5 of this manual.

e. Remove the front bracket nut, washers and bolt.

6. Carefully remove the spring from the vehicle.

7. If necessary on 1989 and later vehicles, remove the shackle-to-spring nut, washers and bolts, then remove the shackle from the spring.

To install:

8. If removed on 1989 and later vehicles, install the shackle to the rearward spring eye using the bolt, washers and nut, but do not fully tighten at this time.

9. Position the spring assembly to the vehicle.

10. For 1989–93 vehicles:

a. Install the spring to the front bracket using the retaining bolt, washers and nut, but do not fully tighten at this time.

b. If removed, install the fuel tank.

c. Install the shackle-to-frame bolt, washers and nut, but do not fully tighten at this time. If used, remove the spring support.

d. Install the U-bolts, anchor plate, washers and U-bolt nuts. Tighten the U-bolt nuts using 2 passes of a diagonal sequence. First tighten the nuts to 18 ft. lbs. (25 Nm), then tighten them to 85 ft. lbs. (115 Nm).

11. For vehicles through 1988:

a. Install the anchor plate and U-bolts.

b. Tighten the U-bolts using 2 passes of a diagonal sequence. First tighten the nuts to 18 ft. lbs. (25 Nm), then tighten them to 85 ft. lbs. (115 Nm).

c. Loosely install the shackle-to-spring fasteners.

d. Loosely install the spring to the front hanger.

12. Position the axle to achieve an approximate gap of 6.46–6.94 in.. (164–176mm) between the axle housing tube and the metal surface of the rubber frame bumper bracket. Measure from the housing between the U-bolts to the metal part of the rubber bump stop on the frame.

13. While supporting the axle in this position, torque the front and rear spring mounting fasteners to 88 ft. lbs. (120 Nm) for vehicles through 1988 or to 92 ft. lbs. (125 Nm) for 1989–93 vehicles.

14. Install the shock absorber.

15. Remove the jackstands and carefully lower the vehicle.

Shock Absorbers

TESTING

There are 2 possible clues that the shock absorbers are worn and may need replacement. The first is how the vehicle rides and the second is how the shocks appear. The shocks should be checked if the ride of your vehicle has become increasingly bouncy or if oil is visible on the shock, indicating possible fluid leakage.

Visually inspect the shock absorber if trouble or wear is suspected. If the shock absorber is covered with oil and there is evidence of leakage, the shock is defective and should be replaced.

If there is no sign of excessive leakage (a small amount of weeping is normal) but the ride is still suspect, bounce the truck at one corner by pressing down on the rear bumper and releasing. When you have the truck bouncing as much as you can, release the fender or bumper. The truck should stop bouncing after the first rebound. If the bouncing continues past the center point of the bounce more than once, the shock absorbers are worn and should be replaced.

REMOVAL & INSTALLATION

◆ **See Figures 55 and 56**

1. Raise and support the rear of the truck safely using jackstands. Support the rear axle securely using a jackstands or a floor jack. The axle must be supported to prevent overextension and damage to the brake lines once the shock is removed.

2. Remove the shock absorber-to-frame retainers at the top of the shock.

Fig. 55 Loosen the retainers from the upper shock mount—a backup wrench is usually needed

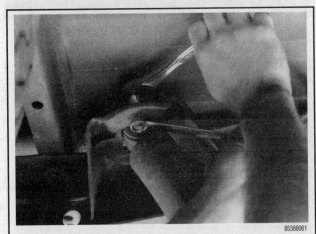

Fig. 56 Loosen and remove the lower shock mount

3. Remove the shock-to-axle retainers at the bottom of the shock.

4. Remove the shock absorber from the vehicle.

To install:

5. Position the shock in the vehicle and loosely install the upper mounting fasteners to retain it.

6. Align the lower-end of the shock absorber with the axle mounting, then loosely install the retainers.

7. Torque the upper shock absorber retainers to 15 ft. lbs. (20 Nm) for vehicles through 1988 or to 17 ft. lbs. (23 Nm) for 1989–93 vehicles. Then tighten lower shock absorber fastener to 50 ft. lbs. (70 Nm) for vehicles through 1988 or to 47 ft. lbs. (64 Nm) for 1989–93 vehicles.

8. Remove the jackstands and carefully lower the vehicle.

STEERING

The steering box (manual or power) utilizes a recirculating ball system, which transmits force from the worm gear to the sector gear. A relay type steering linkage is used with a pitman arm connected to one end of the relay rod. The relay rod is supported on the other end by an idler arm assembly; the idler arm pivots on a support which is attached to the frame. The relay rod is connected to the steering arms by two adjustable tie rods.

These trucks are equipped with a collapsible steering column which is designed to absorb an impact by collapsing, thereby reducing possible chest injuries during accidents. When making any repairs to the steering column or steering wheel, excessive pressure or force capable of collapsing the column must be avoided. The ignition switch, ignition lock and antitheft system are built into each column.

On the automatic transmission, the ignition key cannot be removed unless the shift lever is in the Park position and the ignition switch is in the Lock position. Placing the key in the Lock position activates a rod within the column which locks the steering wheel and shift lever.

Steering Wheel

REMOVAL & INSTALLATION

▶ **See Figures 57 thru 63**

1. Disconnect the negative battery cable.

2. Position the steering wheel so that it is in the horizontal position and the front wheel are straight.

3. If equipped with a horn cap (most late models), pry the cap from the center of the steering wheel. If equipped with a steering wheel shroud (most early models), remove the screw from the rear of the steering wheel and remove the shroud.

➡ **If the horn cap or shroud is equipped with an electrical connector it must be disengaged in order to remove the cap/shroud from the steering column.**

4. Remove the steering wheel-to-steering shaft retainer clip (snapring), then loosen and remove the nut.

➡ **Since the steering column is designed to collapse upon impact, NEVER hammer on it!**

5. Matchmark the relationship of the steering wheel to the steering shaft. Some late model vehicles may already be equipped with one or more alignment marks. If not, make your own using a permanent marker.

6. Using a suitable steering wheel puller, such as No. J-1859-03 or equivalent, carefully draw the wheel from the steering column.

To install:

➡ **Before installing the steering wheel, be sure that the turn signal switch is in the Neutral position. DO NOT misalign the steering wheel more than 0.8 in. (20mm) from the horizontal centerline.**

7. Align the matchmarks and carefully fit the wheel onto the steering shaft splines.

8. Install the retaining nut and tighten to 30 ft. lbs. (40 Nm).

9. Install the horn cap or pad.

10. Connect the negative battery cable.

Turn Signal Switch

REMOVAL & INSTALLATION

▶ **See Figures 64, 65, 66 and 67**

➡ **When servicing any components on the steering column, should any fasteners require replacement, be sure to use only nuts and bolts of the same size and grade as the original fasteners. Using screws that are too long could prevent the column from collapsing during a collision.**

➡ **The following procedures require the use of a lock plate compressor tool such as J-23653 or equivalent.**

Vehicles Through 1991

1. Disconnect the negative battery cable.

2. Matchmark and remove the steering wheel. Please refer to the procedure earlier in this section for details.

➡ **If necessary, the steering column may be removed for this service, but turn signal switch replacement should be possible with the column installed on most vehicles covered by this manual.**

3. Insert a small prytool into the slots between the steering shaft lock plate cover and the steering column housing, then pry upward to remove the cover from the lock plate.

4. Position a lock plate compressor tool such as J-23653-A or equivalent, by screwing the tool's center shaft onto the steering shaft (as far as it will go), then screw the center post nut clockwise until the lock plate is compressed.

Fig. 57 On vehicles equipped with a steering wheel shroud, loosen the retainer and remove the shroud

Fig. 58 Remove the snapring retainer clip from the steering shaft

Fig. 59 Once the clip is removed, loosen and remove the wheel retaining nut

Fig. 60 Use a suitable threaded puller to loosen the steering wheel from the shaft

Fig. 61 If the shroud is equipped with a wiring lead it must be disconnected in order to remove the shroud

Fig. 62 When the wheel is removed, be careful not to loosen the horn spring (if equipped)

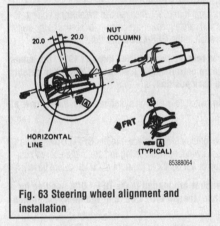

Fig. 63 Steering wheel alignment and installation

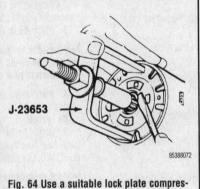

Fig. 64 Use a suitable lock plate compressor tool when removing the shaft lock

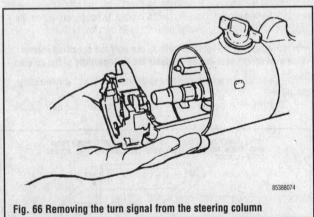

Fig. 66 Removing the turn signal from the steering column

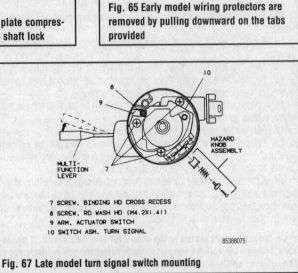

7 SCREW, BINDING HD CROSS RECESS
8 SCREW, RD WASH HD (M4.2X1.41)
9 ARM, ACTUATOR SWITCH
10 SWITCH ASM, TURN SIGNAL

Fig. 67 Late model turn signal switch mounting

Fig. 65 Early model wiring protectors are removed by pulling downward on the tabs provided

5. Pry the locking plate snapring from the steering shaft slot.

➥If the steering column is being disassembled on a bench, the steering shaft is free to slide out of the mast jacket when the snapring is removed.

6. Carefully release and remove the lock plate compressor tool, then remove the lock plate.

7. Loosen the retaining screw, then remove the turn signal lever.

8. Remove the hazard warning knob; press the knob inward and then unscrew it.

9. Remove the turn signal switch assembly-to-steering column retaining screws.

➥Whenever wiring and connectors must be pulled through the steering column, attach a length of mechanic's wire to the connector before beginning. Once the wiring and connector has been pulled through the column, leave the length of mechanic's wire in place (through the col-

umn) so it can be used to draw the connector back into position during installation.

10. Pull the switch connector out of the bracket on the jacket and feed the switch connector through the column support bracket. Pull the switch straight up, guiding the wiring harness through the column housing and protector.

11. If equipped with a tilt column, position the housing in the "low" position.

12. Remove the wiring protector by pulling downward and out of the column using a pair of pliers on the tab provided.

13. Remove the switch and wiring harness from the column.

To install:

➥If used, the length of mechanic's wire may be used to help route the wiring harness.

14. Install the turn signal assembly to the column by first routing the connector harness:

a. On non-tilt columns, be sure that the electrical connector is on the protector, then feed it and the cover down through the housing and under the mounting bracket.

b. On tilt columns, feed the electrical connector down through the housing and under the mounting bracket, then install the cover onto the housing.

15. Position the turn signal and clip the connector to the bracket on the jacket. Secure the turn signal using the retaining screws, then install the trim plate.

16. Install the hazard warning knob, then install the turn signal lever and retaining screws.

17. Position the turn signal in the Neutral or non-signalling position, then pull out the hazard warning knob to the hazard On position.

18. Install the washer, upper bearing preload spring and the cancelling cam onto the upper end of the shaft.

19. Position the lock plate and a NEW snapring over the shaft, then position the compressor tool. Use the tool to compress the lock plate as far as it will go, then slide the new snapring down the shaft and into the groove. Carefully release the compressor tool and make sure the lock plate is properly positioned.

20. Snap the lock plate cover into position.

21. Align and install the steering wheel.

22. Make sure the ignition is **OFF**, then connect the negative battery cable.

1992–93 Vehicles

1. Disconnect the negative battery cable.

2. Matchmark and remove the steering wheel. Please refer to the procedure earlier in this section for details.

3. Remove the shaft lock cover.

4. Push downward on the shaft lock assembly until the snapring is exposed using the shaft lock compressor tool.

5. Remove the shaft lock retaining snapring, then carefully release the tool and remove the shaft lock from the column.

6. Remove the turn signal cancelling cam assembly.

7. For standard columns, remove the upper bearing spring and thrust washer.

8. For tilt columns, remove the upper bearing spring, inner race seat and inner race.

9. Move the turn signal lever upward to the "Right Turn" position.

10. Remove the access cap and disengage the multi-function lever harness connector, then grasp the lever and pull it from the column.

11. Loosen and remove the hazard knob retaining screw, then remove the screw, button, spring and knob.

12. Remove the screw and the switch actuator arm.

13. Remove the turn signal switch retaining screws, then pull the switch forward and allow it to hang from the wires. If the switch is only being removed for access to other components, this may be sufficient.

14. If the switch is being completely removed, disengage the wiring at the base of the column. Attach a length of mechanic's wire to the switch harness connector, then pull the harness through the column, leaving the mechanic's wire in place for installation purposes.

➡ **On some vehicles access to the connector may be difficult. If necessary, remove the column support bracket assembly and properly support the column, and/or remove the wiring protectors.**

15. Remove the switch and wiring harness from the vehicle.

To install:

16. Install the switch and wiring harness to the vehicle. If the switch was completely removed, use the length of mechanic's wire to pull the switch harness through the column, then engage the connector.

➡ **If the column support bracket or wiring protectors were removed, install them before proceeding.**

17. Position the switch in the column and secure using the retaining screws. Tighten the screws to 30 inch lbs. (3.4 Nm).

18. Install the switch actuator arm and retaining screw, then tighten the screw to 20 inch lbs. (2.3 Nm).

19. Install the hazard knob assembly, then install the multi-function lever.

20. Install the thrust washer and upper bearing spring (standard columns) or the inner race, upper bearing race seat and upper bearing spring (tilt columns), as applicable.

21. Lubricate the turn signal cancelling cam using a suitable synthetic grease (usually included in the service kit), then install the cam assembly.

22. Position the shaft lock and a NEW snapring, then use the lock compressor to hold the lock down while you seat the new snapring. Make sure the ring is firmly seated in the groove, then carefully release the tool.

23. Install the shaft lock cover.

24. Align and install the steering wheel.

25. Make sure the ignition is **OFF**, then connect the negative battery cable.

Ignition Switch

For anti-theft reasons, the ignition switch is located on top of the steering column assembly and is completely inaccessible without first lowering the steering column. The switch is actuated by a rod and rack assembly. A gear on the end of the lock cylinder engages the toothed upper end of the actuator rod.

REMOVAL & INSTALLATION

▶ **See Figure 68**

1. Disconnect the negative battery cable.

2. Remove the lower column trim panel, then remove the steering column-to-instrument panel fasteners and carefully lower the column for access to the switch.

3. Place the ignition switch in the **OFF-LOCK** position.

➡ **If the lock cylinder was removed on vehicles through 1991, the actuating rod should be pulled up until it stops, then moved down one detent; the switch is now in the Lock position.**

4. Remove the ignition switch-to-steering column retainers, then remove the assembly.

To install:

5. Before installing the ignition switch, place it in the **OFF-LOCK** position, then make sure that the lock cylinder and actuating rod are in the Locked position (1st detent from the top or 1st detent to the right of far left detent travel).

➡ **Most replacement switches are pinned in the OFF-LOCK position for installation purposes. If so, the pin MUST be removed after installation or damage may occur.**

6. Install the activating rod into the ignition switch and assemble the switch onto the steering column. Once the switch is properly positioned, tighten the ignition switch-to-steering column retainers to 35 inch lbs. (4.0 Nm).

➡ **When installing the ignition switch, use only the specified screws since over length screws could impair the collapsibility of the column.**

7. Raise the column into position and secure, then install any necessary trim plates.

8. Make sure the ignition is **OFF**, then connect the negative battery cable.

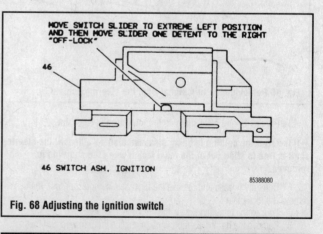

MOVE SWITCH SLIDER TO EXTREME LEFT POSITION AND THEN MOVE SLIDER ONE DETENT TO THE RIGHT "OFF-LOCK"

46

46 SWITCH ASM. IGNITION

85388080

Fig. 68 Adjusting the ignition switch

Headlight Dimmer Switch

The headlight dimmer switch is mounted on top of the steering column with the ignition switch. In some cases, these 2 switches may even share retainers, requiring the partial removal of the ignition switch in order to remove the dimmer switch.

The switch locations makes replacement unlikely without first lowering the steering column. The switch is actuated by the multi-function lever through a rod.

REMOVAL & INSTALLATION

▶ **See Figure 69**

1. Disconnect the negative battery cable.
2. Remove the lower column trim panel, then remove the steering column-to-instrument panel fasteners and carefully lower the column for access to the switch.

➡ **If the ignition switch shares fasteners with the dimmer switch it may be necessary to remove it first. For details, please refer to the procedure located earlier in this section.**

3. Remove the dimmer switch-to-steering column retainers, then remove the switch from the column.
   To install:
4. Position the switch to the column and loosely install the retainers.
5. Insert a ³⁄₃₂ in. drill bit into the adjustment hole provided in the switch to limit travel, then push the switch up against the actuator rod in order to remove lash.
6. Tighten the switch retainers, then remove the drill bit.
7. If removed for access, install the ignition switch.
8. Raise the column into position and secure, then install any necessary trim plates.
9. Make sure the ignition is **OFF**, then connect the negative battery cable.

Ignition Lock Cylinder

REMOVAL & INSTALLATION

▶ **See Figure 70**

1. Disconnect the negative battery cable.
2. Matchmark and remove the steering wheel.
3. Remove the turn signal switch from the column and allow it to hang from the wires (leaving them connected). For details, please refer to the procedure located earlier in this section.
4. For vehicles through 1991, place the lock cylinder in the **Run** position.
5. For 1992–93 vehicles, remove the buzzer switch assembly.
6. Carefully remove the lock cylinder screw and the lock cylinder. If possible, use a magnetic tipped screwdriver on the screw in order to help prevent the possibility of dropping it.

❊❊ CAUTION

If the screw is dropped upon removal, it could fall into the steering column, requiring complete disassembly in order to retrieve the screw and prevent damage.

To install:
7. Align and install the lock cylinder set. On vehicles through 1991 it will be necessary to rotate the switch clockwise to align the cylinder key with the keyway in the housing.
8. Push the lock cylinder all the way in, then carefully install the retaining screw. Tighten the screw to 22 inch lbs. (2.5 Nm) on tilt columns or to 40 inch lbs. (4.5 Nm) on standard non-tilt columns.
9. If necessary, install the buzzer switch assembly.
10. Reposition and secure the turn signal switch assembly
11. Align and install the steering wheel.
12. Make sure the ignition is **OFF**, then connect the negative battery cable.

Steering Linkage

▶ **See Figures 71 and 72**

The steering linkage consists of: a forward mounted linkage, crimp or prevailing torque nuts at the inner pivots, castellated nuts at the steering knuckle arm, an idler arm, a steering gear pitman arm, a relay rod and a steering damper (4wd vehicles). Grease fittings are equipped with each joint, for durability. Depending on the application, the relay rod may only be equipped with holes to accept ball studs, or the rod may itself contain ball studs for connection with the pitman/idler arms.

REMOVAL & INSTALLATION

Pitman Arm

▶ **See Figure 73**

1. Raise and support the front of the vehicle safely using jackstands.
2. For 1991–93 vehicles:

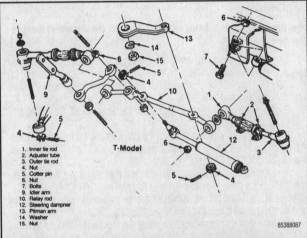

1. Inner tie rod
2. Adjuster tube
3. Outer tie rod
4. Nut
5. Cotter pin
6. Nut
7. Bolts
8. Idler arm
10. Relay rod
12. Steering dampner
13. Pitman arm
14. Washer
15. Nut

T-Model

85388087

Fig. 72 Common 4wd steering linkage components (with steering damper)

85388088

Fig. 73 Remove the pitman arm using a suitable pitman puller tool

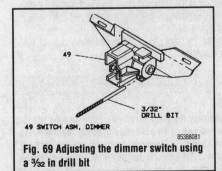

85388081

Fig. 69 Adjusting the dimmer switch using a ³⁄₃₂ in drill bit

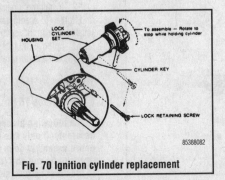

85388082

Fig. 70 Ignition cylinder replacement

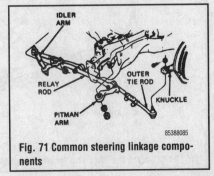

85388085

Fig. 71 Common steering linkage components

a. If necessary, remove the air snorkle for access to the intermediate shaft.

b. Matchmark the upper and lower intermediate shaft joints, then remove the retainers and remove the intermediate shaft.

c. Disconnect the oil cooler pipes at the crossmember.

d. If equipped, remove the splash shield.

3. Remove the nut from ball stud at the relay rod-to-pitman arm connection.

4. Using a suitable universal steering linkage puller, such as J-24319-01 or equivalent, separate the relay rod from the pitman arm. Pull down on the relay rod and separate the stud.

5. For 1991–93 vehicles where access to the pitman arm/nut is restricted, remove the 2 lower steering gear bolts (leaving on the top bolt which should be loosened), then pivot the steering gear for pitman arm clearance at the frame crossmember. Support the gear using a block of wood.

6. Remove the pitman arm-to-pitman shaft nut, then matchmark the relationship of the arm to the shaft to assure proper alignment during assembly.

7. Using a pitman arm remover such as J-6632 or equivalent, separate the pitman arm from the pitman shaft and remove it from the vehicle.

➡ **When separating the pitman arm from the shaft, DO NOT use a hammer or apply heat to the arm.**

To install:

➡ **If the pitman arm is being replaced, transfer the alignment mark to the new component.**

8. Install the pitman arm while aligning the arm-to-pitman shaft matchmark. Use a steering linkage installer such as J-29193 (12mm), J-29194 (14mm) or equivalent (as applicable) to properly seat the arm on the shaft, install the correct one onto the shaft and torque it to 40 ft. lbs. (54 Nm) to seat the taper.

9. Remove the installer tool, then install the pitman shaft nut and tighten to 185 ft. lbs. (250 Nm).

10. On 1991–93 vehicles on which the gear was pivoted for access, pivot the gear back into position and install the lower retaining bolts. Tighten all of the retaining bolts to 55 ft. lbs. (75 Nm).

11. Connect the pitman arm to the relay rod (make sure that the seal is on the stud). Use a steering linkage installer such as J-29193 (12mm), J-29194 (14mm) or equivalent (as applicable), install the correct one onto the ball stud and torque it to 40 ft. lbs. (54 Nm) to seat the taper.

12. After seating, remove the tool, install the lock washer and nut and torque to 60 ft. lbs. (82 Nm). If a prevailing torque nut was used a NEW nut MUST be installed.

13. On 1991–93 vehicles install the splash shield, oil cooler pipes, intermediate shaft and air duct, as applicable.

14. Remove the jackstands and carefully lower the vehicle.

15. Check and adjust toe, as necessary.

Idler Arm

▶ **See Figure 74**

1. Raise and support the front of the vehicle safely using jackstands under the frame so the wheels are free to turn.

➡ **Jerking the right wheel assembly back and forth is not an acceptable testing procedure; there is no control on the amount of force being applied to the idler arm. Before suspecting idler arm shimmying complaints, check the wheels for imbalance, runout, force variation and/or road surface irregularities.**

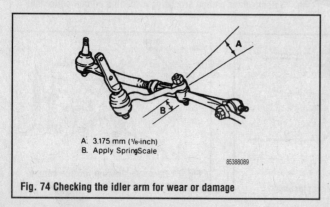

A. 3.175 mm (1/8-inch)
B. Apply Spring Scale

85388089

Fig. 74 Checking the idler arm for wear or damage

2. To inspect for a defective idler arm:

a. Position the wheels in the straight ahead position.

b. Position a spring scale near the relay rod end of the idler arm, then exert 25 ft. lbs. (110 Nm) of force upward and then downward. Measure the distance between the upward and downward directions that the idler arm moves. The allowable deflection is 1/8 in. (3.18mm) for each direction for a total difference of 1/4 in. (6.35mm); if the idler arm deflection is beyond the allowable limits, replace it.

3. Remove the idler arm-to-frame bolts/nuts.

4. Remove the nut from the idler arm-to-relay rod ball joint.

5. Use a suitable steering linkage puller such as J-24319-01 or equivalent to separate the relay rod from idler arm.

6. Remove the idler arm assembly from the vehicle.

To install:

7. Install the idler arm, then tighten the arm assembly-to-frame bolts to 60 ft. lbs. (82 Nm).

8. Connect the relay rod to the idler arm. Use a steering linkage installer such as J-29193 (12mm), J-29194 (14mm) or equivalent (as applicable) to seat the relay rod-to-idler arm ball joint stud. Tighten the tool to 40 ft. lbs. (54 Nm), then remove the tool.

9. Install the idler arm-to-relay rod stud nut and torque it to 35 ft. lbs. (47 Nm) for 2wd vehicles or 60 ft. lbs. (81 Nm) for 4wd vehicles.

10. Remove the jackstands and carefully lower the vehicle.

11. Check and/or adjust the toe-in, as necessary.

Relay Rod (Centerlink)

1. Raise and support the vehicle safely using jackstands.

2. Remove the inner tie rod stud nuts, then separate the tie rods from the relay rod using a suitable linkage puller. For details, please refer to the tie rod procedure located later in this section.

3. On vehicles equipped with a steering damper, remove the shock absorber ball stud nut, then separate the shock from the relay rod using a suitable linkage puller, such as J-24319-01 or equivalent.

4. Remove the ball stud nut from the pitman arm-to-relay rod connection, then use a suitable steering linkage puller, such as J-24319-01 or equivalent, to disconnect the pitman rod from the idler arm.

5. Remove the ball stud nut from the idler arm-to-relay rod connection, then use a suitable steering linkage puller, such as J-24319-01 or equivalent, to disconnect the relay rod from the idler arm.

6. Once the linkage components have been removed from the relay rod, it is free to be removed from the vehicle.

To install:

7. Clean and inspect the threads on the tie rod, the tie rod ends and the ball joints for damage, and replace them (if necessary). Inspect the ball joint seals for excessive wear, and replace them (if necessary).

8. Connect the relay rod to the idler arm. Use a steering linkage installer such as J-29193 (12mm), J-29194 (14mm) or equivalent (as applicable) to seat the relay rod-to-idler arm ball joint stud. Tighten the tool to 40 ft. lbs. (54 Nm), then remove the tool.

9. Install the idler arm-to-relay rod stud nut and torque it to 35 ft. lbs. (2wd) or 60 ft. lbs. (4wd).

10. Connect the pitman arm to the relay rod (make sure that the seal is on the stud). Use a steering linkage installer such as J-29193 (12mm), J-29194 (14mm) or equivalent (as applicable), install the correct one onto the ball stud and torque it to 40 ft. lbs. (54 Nm) to seat the taper.

11. After seating, remove the tool, install the lock washer and nut and torque to 60 ft. lbs. (82 Nm). If a prevailing torque nut was used, a NEW nut MUST be installed.

12. Install the inner tie rods to the relay rod, then install the mounting nuts and tighten to specification. For details, please refer to the tie rod procedure located later in this section.

13. Remove the jackstands and carefully lower the vehicle, then check the steering linkage for proper operation.

Tie Rod

▶ **See Figures 75 thru 81**

➡ **The following procedure may be used to remove the entire tie rod assembly. If only one tie rod end of an assembly is being replaced, the entire assembly does not have to be removed from the vehicle. The opposite tie rod end (the end not being replaced) may remain attached to the steering linkage/knuckle, as applicable.**

1. Raise and support the front frame of the vehicle safely using jackstands.
2. Remove the cotter pin from the tie rod-to-steering knuckle stud, then loosen and remove the retaining nut.
3. Remove the nut from the tie rod-to-relay rod connection.

➡DO NOT attempt to separate the tie rod-to-steering knuckle joint by driving a wedge type tool between the joint and knuckle or seal damage could result.

4. Using a suitable tie rod remover such as the wheel stud/tie rod tool No. J-6627-A or equivalent, separate the outer tie rod stud from the steering knuckle and the inner tie from the relay rod.
5. Remove the tie rod from the vehicle.
6. If one or both of the tie rod ends are being replaced:

➡Tie rod adjustment components tend to rust in service. If the torque required to remove the nut from the bolt exceeds 62 inch lbs. (9 Nm), the nuts should be replaced. Also, the components should be lubricated with a penetrating oil, then the clamps should be rotated until the move freely. Pay attention to the clamp positioning before loosening or removing them.

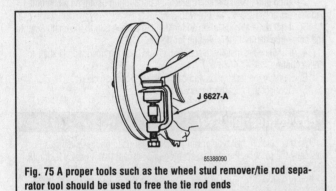

Fig. 75 A proper tools such as the wheel stud remover/tie rod separator tool should be used to free the tie rod ends

a. Measure the installed length of the tie rod end(s) for installation purposes.
b. Loosen the adjuster tube clamp bolt(s).
c. Unscrew the tie rod end from the adjuster tube; count the number of turns necessary to remove the tie rod end. This can be used to help preserve the toe adjustment during installation.

To install:

7. If one or both of the tie rod ends were removed:
a. Clean, inspect and lubricate the adjuster tube threads.
b. Thread the tie rod end into the adjuster tube using the same number of turns necessary to remove it. Once installed, measure the length of the tie rod end, as done during removal to help assure toe adjustment.
c. Position the clamp bolts between the adjuster tube dimples (located at each end) and in the proper location. Torque the adjuster tube clamp bolt 14 ft. lbs. (19 Nm).
8. Position the tie rod ends to the steering knuckle and/or the relay rod. Use a steering linkage installer such as J-29193 (12mm), J-29194 (14mm) or equivalent (as applicable), install the correct one onto the ball stud and torque it to 40 ft. lbs. (54 Nm) to seat the taper(s).
9. Once the ends are properly seated, remove the tool and install the retaining nut(s).
10. Tighten the inner and/or outer tie rod end retaining nuts to 35 ft. lbs. (47 Nm).
11. Install a new cotter pin to the castle nut(s), as applicable.
12. Check and adjust the toe, as necessary.
13. Remove the jackstands and carefully lower the vehicle, then check the steering linkage for proper operation.

Damper Assembly

▶ **See Figure 82**

The damper assembly is used to remove steering wheel vibration and vehicle wander; not all vehicles are equipped with it, though most 4wd vehicles should come with a damper assembly.
1. Raise and support the front frame of the vehicle safely using jackstands.
2. Remove the damper assembly-to-relay rod cotter pin and nut.

Fig. 76 When removing a tie rod end, first straighten the ends of the old cotter pin

Fig. 77 Then pull the cotter pin from the ball stud and retaining nut

Fig. 78 Loosen and remove the stud nut

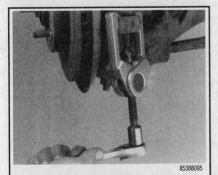

Fig. 79 Use a suitable puller to push the tie rod end free. DO NOT drive a wedge-type tool between the linkage

Fig. 80 Once the ball stud has be unseated, withdraw the tie rod end from the component (knuckle or relay rod, as applicable)

Fig. 81 If replacing a tie rod end (in this case still on the vehicle), loosen the adjuster clamp bolt/nut

3. Use a suitable universal steering linkage puller such as J-24319-01 or equivalent to separate the damper assembly from the relay rod.

4. Remove the cotter pin (if equipped) and the damper assembly-to-frame bracket nut/bolt, then remove the damper assembly from the vehicle.

To install:

5. Install the damper assembly to the frame bracket, then secure using the retainers. Tighten the bolt/nut to 26 ft. lbs. (35 Nm). If equipped, install a new cotter pin.

6. Position the damper assembly to the relay rod. Use a steering linkage installer such as J-29193 (12mm), J-29194 (14mm) or equivalent (as applicable), install the correct one onto the stud and torque it to 40 ft. lbs. (54 Nm) to seat the taper.

7. Remove the installation tool, then install retaining nut and tighten to 45 ft. lbs. (62 Nm). Install a new cotter pin.

8. Remove the jackstands and carefully lower the vehicle.

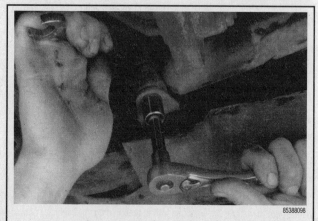

Fig. 82 Disconnecting the damper assembly from the frame bracket

Manual Steering Gear

REMOVAL & INSTALLATION

▶ **See Figure 83**

1. Disconnect the negative battery cable.

2. Raise and support the front of the vehicle safely using jackstands under the frame. Turn the wheels so they are facing in the straight ahead position.

3. On late model vehicles (or as equipped), remove the retainers and the shield from the base of the intermediate shaft.

4. Matchmark the intermediate shaft-to-steering gear connection in order to assure proper installation.

5. Remove the intermediate shaft-to-steering gear pinch bolt.

6. Matchmark and remove the pitman arm from the pitman shaft. For details, please refer to the procedure located earlier in this section. On some late model vehicles it may be easier to save this step for later as access to the pitman arm/shaft may be difficult unless the gear is loosened or removed.

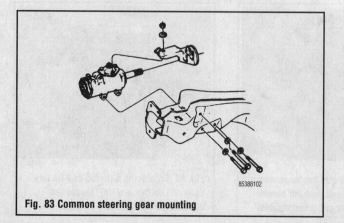

Fig. 83 Common steering gear mounting

➡ **When separating the pitman arm from the shaft, DO NOT use a hammer or apply heat to the arm.**

7. Remove the steering gear-to-frame mounting bolts and washers, then remove the gear from the vehicle.

8. If note done already on late model vehicles and, if necessary, remove the pitman shaft from the gear at this time.

To install:

9. If necessary on late model vehicles, align and install the pitman shaft to the gear.

10. Position the steering gear to the frame and secure by threading the retaining bolts. On some late model vehicles, if not done already, it will be necessary to align and install the pitman arm to the shaft at this time.

11. Install the gear retaining bolts and tighten to 60 ft. lbs. (81 Nm) for vehicles through 1988 or to 55 ft. lbs. (75 Nm) for 1989–93 vehicles.

➡ **When installing the steering gear, be sure that the intermediate shaft bottoms on the worm shaft, so that the pinch bolt passes through the undercut on the worm shaft. Check and/or adjust the alignment of the pitman arm-to-pitman shaft.**

12. Align and install the intermediate shaft coupling using the pinch bolt. Tighten the bolt to 30 ft. lbs. (41 Nm).

13. If not done already, align and install the pitman arm to the shaft. Refer to the procedure earlier in this section for details.

14. If applicable, install the coupling shield over the intermediate shaft-to-gear coupling.

15. Remove the jackstands and carefully lower the vehicle.

16. Connect the negative battery cable.

Power Steering Gear

The recirculating ball type power steering gear used on these vehicles is basically the same as the manual steering gear, except that it uses a hydraulic assist on the rack piston.

The power steering gear control valve directs the power steering fluid to either side of the rack piston, which rides up and down the worm shaft. The steering rack converts the hydraulic pressure into mechanical force. Should the vehicle loose the hydraulic pressure, it can still be controlled mechanically.

REMOVAL & INSTALLATION

1. Raise and support the front of the vehicle safely using jackstands.

2. For MFI-Turbo vehicles, drain the charge air cooler system and remove the charge air cooler radiator. For details, please refer to Section 3 of this manual.

3. Position a fluid catch pan under the power steering gear.

4. Disconnect the feed and return fluid hoses from the steering gear. Immediately cap or plug all openings to prevent system contamination or excessive fluid loss.

➡ **Be sure to plug the pressure hoses and the openings of the power steering pump to keep dirt out of the system.**

5. On late model vehicles (or if equipped) remove the intermediate shaft lower coupling shield.

6. Remove the intermediate shaft-to-steering gear bolt. Matchmark the intermediate shaft-to-power steering gear and separate the shaft from the gear.

7. Matchmark and remove the pitman arm from the gear pitman shaft. For details, please refer to the procedure earlier in this section.

8. Remove the power steering gear-to-frame bolts and washers, then carefully remove the steering gear from the vehicle.

To install:

9. Position the steering gear to the vehicle and secure by finger-tightening the fasteners. For some late model vehicles, the pitman arm must be connected to the gear while it is still removed from the vehicle or while it is partially installed and lowered for access. If necessary, align and install the pitman arm to the shaft at this time.

10. Torque the power steering gear-to-frame bolts to 55 ft. lbs. (75 Nm).

11. Align and install the intermediate shaft to the power steering, then secure using the pinch bolt.

12. If equipped, install the shield over the intermediate shaft lower coupling.

13. Remove the caps, then connect the feed and return hoses to the power steering gear. Refill the pump reservoir.

14. On MFI-Turbo vehicles, install the charge air cooler radiator.
15. Remove the jackstands and carefully lower the vehicle.
16. On MFI-Turbo vehicles, properly refill and bleed the charge air cooler system.
17. Properly bleed the power steering system.
18. Road test the vehicle.

Power Steering Pump

▶ See Figure 84

Two types of power steering pumps are commonly found on these vehicles; the submerged and the non-submerged types. The submerged pump has a housing and internal parts which are inside the reservoir and operate submerged in oil. The non-submerged pump functions the same as the submerged pump except the reservoir is separate from the housing and internal parts.

REMOVAL & INSTALLATION

Except MFI-Turbo

▶ See Figures 85, 86, 87 and 88

1. Position a fluid catch pan under the power steering pump.
2. Disconnect the feed and return hoses from the power steering pump, then drain the excess fluid into the catch pan.

➡ **On models equipped with a remote fluid reservoir, disconnect and plug the hose(s) in order to prevent system contamination or excessive fluid loss.**

3. Remove the drive belt from the pulley.
4. Install a puller tool such as J-25034, or equivalent onto the power steering pump pulley. While holding the pilot bolt, turn the tool nut counterclockwise in order to press the drive pulley from the pump.

➡ **When installing the puller tool onto the power steering pump pulley, be sure that the pilot bolt bottoms in the pump shaft by turning the head of the pilot bolt.**

5. Remove the power steering pump-to-bracket bolts and, if applicable, the rear brace, then remove the pump from the vehicle.

To install:
6. Position the pump to the vehicle and secure using the retaining bolts and, if equipped, the rear brace.
7. Use a pulley installer such as J-25033 or equivalent to press the drive pulley onto the power steering pump. While holding the pilot bolt, turn the tool nut clockwise in order to press the drive pulley onto the pump.

➡ **When positioning the installer tool onto the power steering pump pulley, be sure that the pilot bolt bottoms in the pump shaft by turning the head of the pilot bolt.**

8. Properly install the drive belt and, if applicable, adjust the tension.

➡ **Be sure to secure any hoses which may get in the way or rub other components.**

9. Remove the caps, then connect the feed and return hoses to the pump.
10. Properly refill and bleed the power steering system.
11. Test drive the vehicle.

MFI-Turbo

1. Disconnect the negative battery cable, then remove the air cleaner and duct.
2. Remove the upper fan shroud screws and shroud.
3. Loosen the fan nuts, then remove the serpentine drive belt.
4. Remove the fan-to-water pump pulley nuts, then remove the fan and pulley assembly.
5. Install J-25034-B to the steering pump pulley. Make sure the pilot bolt bottoms in the pump shaft by turning the nut to top of pilot bolt. Hold the pilot bolt and turn the nut counterclockwise in order to drive the pulley from the shaft.
6. Raise and support the front of the vehicle safely using jackstands.
7. Remove the left wheel, then remove the left wheelhousing panel screws and the panel.
8. Position a drain pan below the pump assembly, then remove the bolt from the hose bracket.
9. Disconnect the return and pressure hoses from the pump. Immediately cap or plug all openings to prevent excessive fluid loss or system contamination.
10. Remove the bolts from the rear bracket, at the alternator.
11. From underhood, remove the pump and rear bracket. If necessary, remove the nuts and separate the pump from the bracket.
   To install:
12. If separated, install the rear bracket to the pump and tighten the retaining nuts to 37 ft. lbs. (50 Nm).

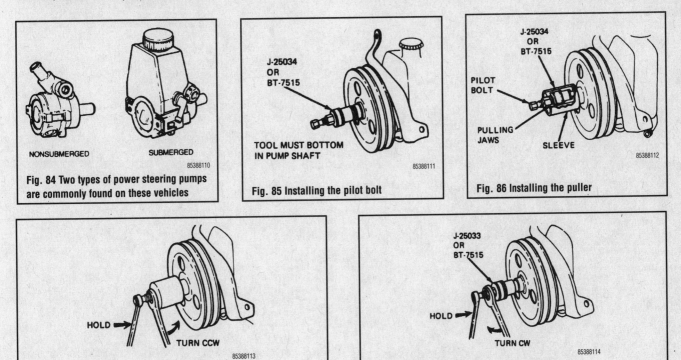

NONSUBMERGED   **SUBMERGED**
85388110

Fig. 84 Two types of power steering pumps are commonly found on these vehicles

J-25034 OR BT-7515

TOOL MUST BOTTOM IN PUMP SHAFT
85388111

Fig. 85 Installing the pilot bolt

J-25034 OR BT-7515

PILOT BOLT

PULLING JAWS   SLEEVE
85388112

Fig. 86 Installing the puller

HOLD   TURN CCW
85388113

Fig. 87 Removing the power steering pump pulley

J-25033 OR BT-7515

HOLD   TURN CW
85388114

Fig. 88 Installing the power steering pump pulley

13. Install the pump and rear bracket assembly to the vehicle.

14. Install the bolts to the rear bracket, at the alternator, then tighten to 37 ft. lbs. (50 Nm).

15. From under the vehicle, remove the caps or plugs, then connect the pressure and return hoses to the pump. Tighten the fittings to 20 ft. lbs. (27 Nm).

16. Install the retaining bolt to the hose bracket.

17. Install the left wheelhousing panel and secure using the screws, then install the left wheel.

18. Remove the jackstands and carefully lower the vehicle.

19. Install the pulley to the pump using J-225033-B or an equivalent tool. First, place the pulley on the pump shaft, then install the tool, making sure the pilot bolt bottoms in the pump shaft by turning nut to top of pilot bolt. Hold the pilot bolt and turn the nut clockwise in order to drive the pulley into position.

20. Install the fan and pulley assembly, then tighten the pulley nuts to 18 ft. lbs. (24 Nm).

21. Install the serpentine drive belt.

22. Install the upper fan shroud, then tighten the retainers to 89 inch lbs. (10 Nm).

23. Install the air cleaner and duct.

24. Connect the negative battery cable, then properly refill and bleed the power steering system.

SYSTEM BLEEDING

1. Add fluid to the reservoir until the proper level is reached, then allow the fluid to settle for at least 2 minutes. Start the engine and let it run for a few seconds, then turn it off and check if the level has changed. Repeat this until the level remains constant.

2. Raise and support the front of the vehicle safely using jackstands under the frame to the wheels are free to turn.

3. Start and run the engine, then slowly turn the wheels in both directions (lightly hitting the stops) several times.

4. Stop the engine and check the fluid level. If necessary, add power steering fluid to obtain the level indicated on the reservoir.

➡**Maintain the fluid level just above the internal pump casting. Fluid with air in it will have a light tan or milky appearance. This air must be eliminated from the fluid before normal steering action can be obtained.**

5. Remove the jackstands and carefully lower the vehicle.

6. Start and run the engine while turning the wheel slowly from stop to stop.

7. Stop the engine and check the fluid level. If necessary, add fluid in order to obtain the proper indicated level.

8. If the fluid is extremely foamy, allow the vehicle to stand for a few minutes, then repeat the procedure through this step.

9. Road test the vehicle to make sure the steering functions normally and is free from noise.

10. Allow the vehicle to stand for 2–3 hours, then recheck the power steering fluid.

TORQUE SPECIFICATIONS

Component	U.S.	Metric
Ball joints		
Service replacement retainers	17 ft. lbs.	23 Nm
Stud nut		
2WD		
Upper		
1982–86	65 ft. lbs.	90 Nm
1987–93	61 ft. lbs.	83 Nm
Lower stud nut		
1982–88	90 ft. lbs.	120 Nm
1989–93	83 ft. lbs.	113 Nm
4WD (upper/lower) stud nut	70 ft. lbs.	95 Nm
Control arm bumper retainer	20 ft. lbs.	27 Nm
Idler arm		
Frame bolts	60 ft. lbs.	82 Nm
Relay rod nut		
2WD	35 ft. lbs.	47 Nm
4WD	60 ft. lbs.	81 Nm
Leaf spring		
U-bolts (using 2 passes of a diagonal sequence)		
1st pass	18 ft. lbs.	25 Nm
2nd pass	85 ft. lbs.	115 Nm
Front and rear spring mounting fasteners		
1982–88	88 ft. lbs.	120 Nm
1989–93	92 ft. lbs.	125 Nm
Lower control arm		
2WD		
Pivot bolt jam nuts		
Front nut 1982–92	94 ft. lbs.	127 Nm
Rear nut 1982–92 and both nuts 1993	67 ft. lbs.	91 Nm
4WD		
Bolts		
1982–92 if threaded into a fitting	148 ft. lbs.	200 Nm
Nuts (with the suspension at normal trim height)		
1982–92	92 ft. lbs.	125 Nm
1993	70 ft. lbs.	95 Nm
Pitman arm		
Pitman shaft nut	185 ft. lbs.	250 Nm
Relay rod nut	60 ft. lbs.	82 Nm
Shock absorber		
Front		
2WD		
Upper nut	100 inch lbs.	11 Nm
Lower bolts	20 ft. lbs.	27 Nm
4WD (upper/lower)	54 ft. lbs.	73 Nm
Rear		
Upper retainer		
1982–88	15 ft. lbs.	20 Nm
1989–93	17 ft. lbs.	23 Nm
Lower retainer		
1982–88	50 ft. lbs.	70 Nm
1989–93	47 ft. lbs.	64 Nm
Stabilizer bar		
2WD		
Bracket bolts	24 ft. lbs.	33 Nm
Link bolts	13 ft. lbs.	17 Nm

TORQUE SPECIFICATIONS

Component	U.S.	Metric
Stabilizer bar		
4WD		
Bar clamp-to-control arm bolts	24 ft. lbs.	33 Nm
Frame clamp retaining bolts/nuts	35 ft. lbs.	48 Nm
Steering column		
Column-to-intermediate shaft joint nut/bolt		
1982–92	26 ft. lbs.	35 Nm
1993	45 ft. lbs.	62 Nm
Floor/toe retainers	120 inch lbs.	13 Nm
Column bracket-to-column bolts	17 ft. lbs.	22 Nm
Column bracket-to-instrument panel		
1982–93	22 ft. lbs.	30 Nm
Steering damper		
Frame bracket bolt/nut	26 ft. lbs.	35 Nm
Relay rod bolt/nut tighten	45 ft. lbs.	62 Nm
Steering gear		
Except manual 1982–88	55 ft. lbs.	75 Nm
Manual 1982–88	60 ft. lbs.	81 Nm
Intermediate shaft-to-gear pinch bolt	30 ft. lbs.	41 Nm
Steering linkage installer tools		
J-29193 (12mm) or J29194 (14mm)	40 ft. lbs.	54 Nm
Steering wheel retaining nut	30 ft. lbs.	40 Nm
Tie rod		
Adjustment clamp bolt	14 ft. lbs.	19 Nm
Tie rod end retaining nuts	35 ft. lbs.	47 Nm
Torsion bar		
1983–91		
Nuts (or bolts from below the frame)	26 ft. lbs.	35 Nm
Top center retainer bolt	25 ft. lbs.	35 Nm
1992–93		
Insulator mounting retainer bolts	26 ft. lbs.	35 Nm
Nuts	25 ft. lbs.	34 Nm
Upper control arm		
2WD		
Pivot shaft/bushing nuts		
1982–86 (with weight on suspension)	65 ft. lbs.	88 Nm
1987	85 ft. lbs.	115 Nm
Control arm-to-frame bolts		
1982–86	45 ft. lbs.	60 Nm
1987–93	65 ft. lbs.	88 Nm
4WD (cam end nuts)		
Wheel lug nuts		
1982–91		
Except MFI-Turbo		
Steel wheels	73 ft. lbs.	100 Nm
Aluminum alloy wheels	90 ft. lbs.	120 Nm
MFI-Turbo wheels	100 ft. lbs.	140 Nm
1992 wheels	90 ft. lbs.	120 Nm
1993 wheels	95 ft. lbs.	130 Nm

8844RT5A

9

BRAKES

BRAKE OPERATING SYSTEM

Adjustments

FRONT DISC BRAKES

Disc brakes are not adjustable. They are, in effect, self adjusting during normal operation. For details on how the disc brakes operate, please refer to the operating principles found earlier in this section.

REAR DRUM BRAKES

▶ See Figure 1

Normal adjustments of the rear drum brakes are automatic and are made during the reverse applications of the brakes. The following procedure should be used ONLY if the linings have been replaced.

1. Raise and support the rear of the vehicle safely using jackstands.
2. Using a punch and a hammer on the rear of the backing plates, knock out the lanced metal areas near the starwheel assemblies on each plate. The metal areas may already have been removed and covered with rubber adjustment plugs, if so remove the plugs by grasping and pulling with a pair of pliers.

➡**After knocking out the lanced metal areas from the backing plate, the wheels must be removed and all of the metal pieces discarded, then the wheels should be reinstalled for adjustment.**

3. Insert a suitable brake adjustment tool such as J-4735 or equivalent, into the breaking plate slots and engage the lowest possible tooth on the starwheel. Move the end of the brake tool downward to move the starwheel upward and expand the adjusting screw. Repeat this operation until the wheels can JUST be turned by hand. This is a position immediately before the brakes lock.

➡**The brake drag should be equal at both wheels.**

4. Back off the adjusting screws 24 notches (clicks). By the time you have backed off the adjustment 12 clicks, the brakes should have no drag. If a heavy drag is still present, the parking brake cable is likely in need of adjustment.
5. Make sure both sides of the brakes are properly adjusted. When backing off the brakes on the other side, the adjusting lever must be backed off the same number of turns to prevent side-to-side brake pull.
6. After the brakes are adjusted, install a rubber hole cover into each of the the backing plate slots. To complete the brake adjustment operation, make several stops while backing the truck to fully equalize the adjustment.
7. Road test the vehicle.

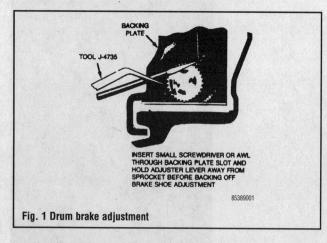

Fig. 1 Drum brake adjustment

BRAKE PEDAL TRAVEL

▶ See Figure 2

The brake pedal travel is the distance the pedal moves toward the floor from the fully released position. On most vehicles covered by this manual it is not adjustable, but checking the distance will give an indication of system condi-

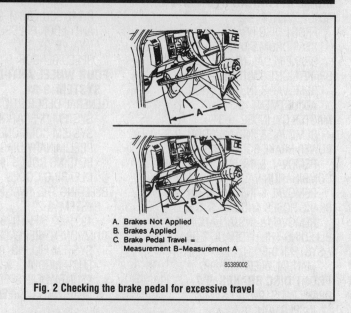

A. Brakes Not Applied
B. Brakes Applied
C. Brake Pedal Travel = Measurement B-Measurement A

Fig. 2 Checking the brake pedal for excessive travel

tion. Inspection should be made using 100 lbs. (445 N) of pressure on the brake pedal, when the brake system is Cold. On power brake equipped vehicles, be sure to pump the brakes at least 5 times to remove vacuum from the booster before making the check.

To check the travel, first measure the distance from the top of the released pedal to the bottom of the steering wheel, then depress the pedal (using 100 lbs. of force) and re-measure the distance. The difference between the 2 measurements (pedal travel) should be approximately 4¾ in. (120mm) for manual brakes or 2½ in. (61mm) for power brakes.

If the pedal travel is excessive, check the pedal and the hydraulic brake system for wear or damage and repair, as necessary. If no damage can be found on early model vehicles adjustment may be possible. Check the pedal pushrod for an adjuster nut. If equipped with an adjustable pushrod and no damage or wear was found in the brake system, adjust the travel as follows:

1. From under the dash, remove the pushrod-to-pedal clevis pin and separate the pushrod from the brake pedal.
2. Loosen the pushrod adjuster locknut, then adjust the pushrod.
3. After the correct travel is established, reverse the removal procedure and check for proper operation.

Brake Light Switch

A brake light switch is mounted to the pedal bracket on all vehicles covered by this manual. The purpose of the switch is to illuminate the brake lights whenever the pedal is depressed, therefore proper operation and adjustment is critical to safe vehicle operation. All switches are normally mounted using an interference clip. The clip holds ribs located on the switch's neck. The ribbed switch is self-adjusting when installed properly.

REMOVAL & INSTALLATION

▶ See Figure 3

1. Disconnect the negative battery cable.
2. Disengage the vacuum and/or electrical connector(s) from the switch.

➡**Some brake light switches may be combined with the cruise control release switch, therefore may contain a vacuum hose or an additional electrical connector. If so, be sure to tag all hoses/wiring before disconnecting in order to assure proper installation.**

3. Grasp the switch and withdraw it from the clip. If necessary the clip can be removed from the pedal bracket as well. Some clips are designed with lock tangs and may be pivoted in order to pull them from the bracket. On these, you may twist the switch and retainer clip together and withdraw them as an assembly. Other clips are also an interference fit and must be squeezed and withdrawn.

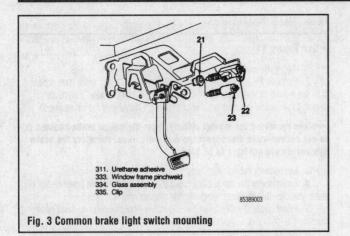

311. Urethane adhesive
333. Window frame pinchweld
334. Glass assembly
335. Clip

85389003

Fig. 3 Common brake light switch mounting

To install:

4. If removed, install the retainer to the pedal bracket.

5. With the pedal depressed so it will not interfere, insert and fully seat the switch into the clip on the pedal bracket.

6. In order to adjust the switch, grasp the pedal and pull it fully back against the stop. While pulling the pedal backwards, a clicking sound should be heard as the switch is pushed backwards in the clip until it is in the proper position. Make sure the switch plunger is seated when the pedal is released and that the plunger fully extends as the pedal is depressed. Check the switch operation and adjust again, if necessary.

7. Engage the vacuum line and/or electrical connector(s) to the switch.

8. Connect the negative battery cable.

9. Verify proper switch operation.

ADJUSTMENT

Most vehicles covered by this manual utilize a self-adjusting brake light switch which is mounted to an interference clip on the pedal bracket. If adjustment becomes necessary on interference clip switches, check to be sure the retaining clip and switch ribs are not worn or damaged, then replace, if necessary. If no damage is found, adjust the switch:

1. Depress the brake pedal and press the brake light switch inward until it seats firmly against the clip.

➡**As the switch is being pushed into the clip, audible clicks can be heard.**

2. Release the brake pedal, then pull it back against the pedal stop until the audible clicks can no longer be heard. The clicks indicate that the switch is moving into position in the clip for proper adjustment.

3. Verify that the switch operates properly when the pedal is depressed and released.

Master Cylinder

REMOVAL & INSTALLATION

◗ **See Figures 4 thru 10**

1. Apply the parking brakes and block the drive wheels.

2. Use a line wrench to loosen and disconnect the hydraulic lines from the master cylinder. Immediately plug the lines to prevent system contamination or excessive fluid loss.

3. If equipped with non-power brakes, disconnect the pushrod from the brake pedal.

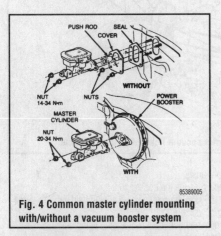

85389005

Fig. 4 Common master cylinder mounting with/without a vacuum booster system

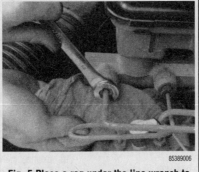

85389006

Fig. 5 Place a rag under the line wrench to help minimize spillage when disconnecting the brake lines

85389007

Fig. 6 Once the line nut is loosened, carefully pull the fitting outward (note the homemade drain pan)

85389008

Fig. 7 Once the lines are disconnected and plugged, loosen and remove the cylinder retaining nuts . . .

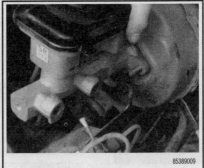

85389009

Fig. 8 . . . then, reposition the combination valve bracket so the master cylinder may be removed

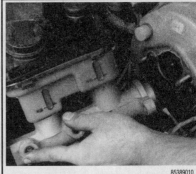

85389010

Fig. 9 Carefully pull the master cylinder from the mounting studs

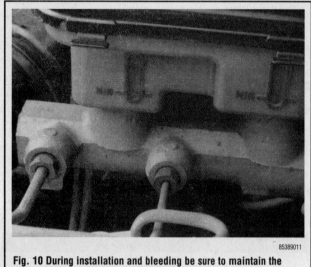

Fig. 10 During installation and bleeding be sure to maintain the proper brake fluid levels in the reservoir

4. Remove the master cylinder attachment nuts, then separate the combination valve/bracket from the master cylinder.

5. Remove the master cylinder and, as equipped, the gasket and/or rubber boot from the vehicle.

To install:

6. In order to ease installation, bench bleed the master cylinder before installation:

a. Plug the master cylinder outlet ports. This can be done using rubber or plastic plugs or, more effectively, using a single length of brake line with appropriately sized flares/flare nuts on each end.

b. Mount the cylinder in a soft-jawed vise with the front end tilted slightly downward.

c. Fill the reservoir with clean brake fluid, then use a tool with a smooth rounded end (such as a wooden dowel or pencil eraser) to stroke the primary piston about 1 in. (25mm) several times. As air is bled from the cylinder, the primary piston will no longer travel the full distance.

d. Reposition the master cylinder in the vise with the front end tilted slightly up, then continue stroking the primary piston to further bleed air.

e. Reposition the master cylinder so it is level, then loosen the plugs one at a time and push the piston into the bore forcing air from the cylinder. DO NOT allow the piston to return with the plugs loosened or air will be drawn back into the master cylinder.

f. Make sure the plugs are tightly sealed, then check and refill the reservoir.

7. Position the master cylinder to the cowl or brake booster (as applicable), then reposition the combination valve bracket over the studs.

8. Install the master cylinder/combination valve bracket retaining nuts and tighten as follows:

a. Vehicles through 1993 except MFI-Turbo—20 ft. lbs. (27 Nm).

b. MFI-Turbo—13 ft. lbs. (17 Nm).

9. Working on one line at a time, remove the plugs and quickly connect the brake lines to the master cylinder. Tighten each of the line nuts to 20 ft. lbs. (27 Nm).

➡**If equipped with manual brakes, be sure to reconnect the pushrod to the brake pedal.**

10. Refill the master cylinder with clean brake fluid, then properly bleed the hydraulic brake system and check the brake pedal travel.

11. When all service is finished, remove the blocks from the drive wheels.

Power Brake Booster

The power brake booster is a tandem vacuum suspended unit. Some early models may be equipped with a single or dual function vacuum switch which activates a brake warning light should low booster vacuum be present. Under normal operation, vacuum is present on both sides of the diaphragms. When the brakes are applied, atmospheric air is admitted to one side of the diaphragms to provide power assistance.

REMOVAL & INSTALLATION

▶ **See Figure 11**

1. Apply the parking brake and block the drive wheels.

2. Remove the master cylinder-to-power brake booster nuts, then reposition the master cylinder and combination valve out of the way; if necessary, support the master cylinder on a wire to prevent damaging the brake lines.

➡**When removing the master cylinder from the power brake booster, it is not necessary to disconnect the hydraulic lines, therefore the brake system should not have to be bled.**

3. Disconnect the vacuum hose from the power brake booster.

4. From under the dash, disconnect the pushrod from the brake pedal. On most vehicles this involves removing the retainer and washer.

5. From under the dash, remove the power brake booster-to-cowl retaining nuts.

6. Back under the hood, remove the power brake booster and the gasket from the cowl.

To install:

7. Position the booster to the cowl using a new gasket.

8. Install the booster retaining nuts and tighten to 15 ft. lbs. (20 Nm) for vehicles through 1988, or to 16 ft. lbs. (22 Nm) for 1989–93 vehicles.

9. Connect the pedal pushrod and install the washer or switch and the retainer.

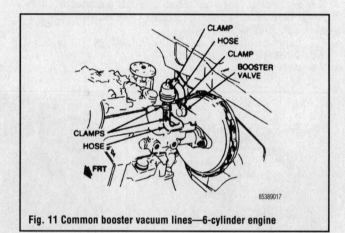

Fig. 11 Common booster vacuum lines—6-cylinder engine

10. Connect the vacuum hose.

11. For 1992–93 vehicles, gauge the booster rod:

a. Apply 25 in. Hg (85 kPa) of vacuum using a hand held vacuum pump or apply maximum engine vacuum.

b. Check the maximum and minimum rod lengths using J-37839 or an equivalent pushrod height gauge.

c. If the piston is not within limits, install a service adjustable piston rod and adjust it to the correct length.

12. Reposition the master cylinder and combination valve bracket to the booster studs, then secure using the retaining nuts. For details, please refer to the master cylinder procedure located earlier in this section.

13. Start and run the engine, then check for proper booster operation.

Combination Valve

The combination valve is located in the engine compartment, directly under the master cylinder. It is usually mounted to a bracket which shares the master cylinder mounting studs on the brake booster. The valve consists of three sections: the metering valve, the warning switch and the proportioning valve.

The metering section limits the pressure to the front disc brakes until a predetermined front input pressure is reached. The specific pressure is enough to overcome the rear shoe retractor springs. Under 3 psi (20 kPa) on vehicles through 1991 or under 30 psi (200 kPa) on 1992–93 vehicles, there are no restrictions of the inlet pressures; this way pressures are allowed to equalize during the no brake period.

The proportioning section controls the outlet pressure to the rear brakes after a predetermined rear input pressure has been reached; this feature is provided for vehicles with light loads, to help prevent rear wheel lock-up. The by-pass feature of this valve assures full system pressure to the rear brakes in the event of a front brake system malfunction. Also, full front pressure is retained if the rear system malfunctions.

The pressure differential warning switch is designed to constantly compare the front and the rear brake pressures; if one circuit should malfunction, the warning light (on the dash) will turn On. The valve and switch are designed to lock in the warning position once the malfunction has occurred. The only way the light can be turned Off is to repair the malfunction and apply a brake line force of 450 psi (3100 kPa).

REMOVAL & INSTALLATION

1. Disconnect the negative battery cable.
2. Disconnect the hydraulic lines from the combination valve one at a time. Immediately plug all openings to prevent system contamination or excessive fluid loss.
3. Disengage the electrical connector from the combination valve pressure switch.
4. If equipped with Rear Wheel Anti-Lock (RWAL) brakes, disengage the RWAL pressure valve connector.
5. On most vehicles, remove the master cylinder/combination valve-to-bracket retaining nuts, then remove the valve from the vehicle. On some early model vehicles the combination valve may be removed from the bracket by removing the retaining bolt. If desired, remove the bolt and valve leaving the bracket and master cylinder secured to the booster.
6. If used, remove the RWAL pressure valve.

➡**The combination valve is not repairable and must be replaced as a complete assembly.**

To install:
7. If applicable, install the RWAL pressure valve.

cracking or scraping; such damage can create a weak spot in the hose and it could fail under pressure.

Any time the lines are removed or disconnected, extreme cleanliness must be observed. Clean all joints and connections before disassembly (use a stiff bristle brush and clean brake fluid); be sure to plug the lines and ports as soon as they are opened. New lines and hoses should be flushed clean with brake fluid before installation to remove any contamination.

REMOVAL & INSTALLATION

▶ **See Figures 12, 13, 14 and 15**

1. Disconnect the negative battery cable.
2. Raise and safely support the vehicle on jackstands.
3. Remove any wheel and tire assemblies necessary for access to the particular line you are removing.
4. Thoroughly clean the surrounding area at the joints to be disconnected.
5. Place a suitable catch pan under the joint to be disconnected.
6. Using two wrenches (one to hold the joint and one to turn the fitting), disconnect the hose or line to be replaced.
7. Disconnect the other end of the line or hose, moving the drain pan if necessary. Always use a back-up wrench to avoid damaging the fitting.
8. Disconnect any retaining clips or brackets holding the line and remove the line from the vehicle.

➡**If the brake system is to remain open for more time than it takes to swap lines, tape or plug each remaining clip and port to keep contaminants out and fluid in.**

To install:
9. Install the new line or hose, starting with the end farthest from the master cylinder. Connect the other end, then confirm that both fittings are correctly threaded and turn smoothly using finger pressure. Make sure the new line will not rub against any other part. Brake lines must be at least 1/2 in. (13mm) from

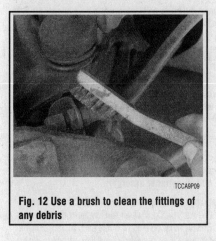

Fig. 12 Use a brush to clean the fittings of any debris

TCCA9P09

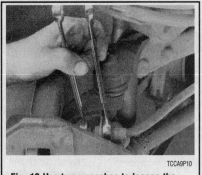

Fig. 13 Use two wrenches to loosen the fitting. If available, use flare nut type wrenches

TCCA9P10

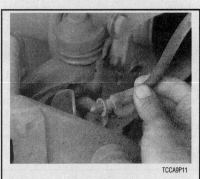

Fig. 14 Any gaskets/crush washers should be replaced with new ones during installation

TCCA9P11

8. Install the combination valve and bracket assembly, then install and tighten the master cylinder/valve bracket retaining nuts to specification. For details, please refer to the master cylinder procedure located earlier in this section. If on early model vehicles only the valve was removed from the bracket, install the valve using the retaining bolt and tighten to 12 ft. lbs. (17 Nm).
9. If used, engage the RWAL pressure valve connector.
10. Engage the pressure switch electrical connector.
11. Remove the caps (one at a time) and connect the brake lines to the combination valve, then tighten the fittings.
12. Check and refill the master cylinder reservoir, then properly bleed the hydraulic brake system.

Brake Hoses and Lines

Metal lines and rubber brake hoses should be checked frequently for leaks and external damage. Metal lines are particularly prone to crushing and kinking under the vehicle. Any such deformation can restrict the proper flow of fluid and therefore impair braking at the wheels. Rubber hoses should be checked for

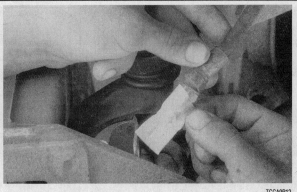

Fig. 15 Tape or plug the line to prevent contamination

TCCA9P12

the steering column and other moving parts. Any protective shielding or insulators must be reinstalled in the original location.

✳✳ WARNING

Make sure the hose is NOT kinked or touching any part of the frame or suspension after installation. These conditions may cause the hose to fail prematurely.

10. Using two wrenches as before, tighten each fitting.
11. Install any retaining clips or brackets on the lines.
12. If removed, install the wheel and tire assemblies, then carefully lower the vehicle to the ground.
13. Refill the brake master cylinder reservoir with clean, fresh brake fluid, meeting DOT 3 specifications. Properly bleed the brake system.
14. Connect the negative battery cable.

Bleeding the Hydraulic Brake System

The hydraulic brake system must be bled any time one of the lines is disconnected or any time air enters the system. If a point in the system, such as a wheel cylinder or caliper brake line is the only point which was opened, the bleeder screws down stream in the hydraulic system are the only ones which must be bled. If however, the master cylinder fittings are opened, or if the reservoir level drops sufficiently that air is drawn into the system, air must be bled from the entire hydraulic system. If the brake pedal feels spongy upon application, and goes almost to the floor but regains height when pumped, air has entered the system. It must be bled out. If no fittings were recently opened for service, check for leaks that would have allowed the entry of air and repair them before attempting to bleed the system.

As a general rule, once the master cylinder (and the brake pressure modulator valve or combination valve on ABS systems) is bled, the remainder of the hydraulic system should be bled starting at the furthest wheel from the master cylinder and working towards the nearest wheel. Therefore, the correct bleeding sequence is: master cylinder, modulator or combination valve (ABS only), right rear wheel cylinder, left rear, right front caliper and left front. Most master cylinder assemblies on these vehicles are NOT equipped with bleeder valves, therefore air must be bled from the cylinders using the front brake pipe connections.

✳✳ CAUTION

If the vehicle has rear wheel or 4 wheel anti-lock braking, do not use this procedure without first reading the information on ABS system bleeding found later in this section. Improper service procedures on Anti-Lock Braking Systems (ABS) can cause serious personal injury. Refer to the ABS service procedures.

MANUAL BLEEDING

▶ See Figures 16, 17, 18 and 19

For those of us who are not fortunate enough to have access to a power bleeding, the manual brake bleeding procedure will quite adequately remove air from the hydraulic system. The major difference between the pressure and manual bleeding procedures is that the manual method takes more time and will require help from an assistant. One person must depress the brake pedal, while another opens and closes the bleeder screws.

➡In addition to a length of clear neoprene bleeder hose, bleeder wrenches and a clear bleeder bottle (old glass jar or drink bottle will suffice), bleeding late-model ABS systems may also require the use of one or more relatively inexpensive combination valve pressure bleeding tools (which are used to depress one or more valves in order to allow component/system bleeding). To fully bleed the late model ABS systems, a scan tool should also be used to run the system through functional tests.

1. Clean the top of the master cylinder, remove the cover and fill the reservoirs with clean fluid. To prevent squirting fluid, and possibly damaging painted surfaces, install the cover during the procedure, but be sure to frequently check and top off the reservoirs with fresh fluid.

✳✳ CAUTION

Never reuse brake fluid which has been bled from the system.

2. The master cylinder must be bled first if it is suspected to contain air. If the master cylinder was removed and bench bled before installation it must still be bled, but it should take less time and effort. Bleed the master cylinder as follows:
   a. Position a container under the master cylinder to catch the brake fluid.

✳✳ WARNING

Do not allow brake fluid to spill on or come in contact with the vehicle's finish as it will remove the paint. In case of a spill, immediately flush the area with water.

   b. Loosen the front brake line at the master cylinder and allow the fluid to flow from the front port.
   c. Have a friend depress the brake pedal slowly and hold (air and/or fluid should be expelled from the loose fitting). Tighten the line, then release the brake pedal and wait 15 seconds. Loosen the fitting and repeat until all air is removed from the master cylinder bore.
   d. When finished, tighten the line fitting to 20 ft. lbs. (27 Nm).
   e. Repeat the sequence at the master cylinder rear pipe fitting.

➡During the bleeding procedure, make sure your assistant does NOT release the brake pedal while a fitting is loosened or while a bleeder screw is opening. Air will be drawn back into the system.

3. Check and refill the master cylinder reservoir.

➡Remember, if the reservoir is allowed to empty of fluid during the procedure, air will be drawn into the system and bleeding procedure must be restarted at the master cylinder assembly.

4. On late model ABS equipped vehicles, perform the special ABS procedures as described later in this section. On 4 wheel ABS systems the Brake Pressure Modulator Valve (BPMV) must be bled (if it has been replaced or if it

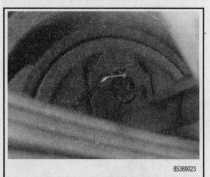
Fig. 16 Position a bleeder wrench over the wheel cylinder bleeder screw (rear wheels)

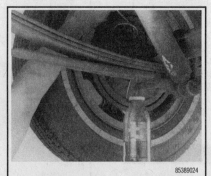
Fig. 17 Attach a clear plastic hose to the screw and submerge the other end in clean brake fluid

Fig. 18 Rubber caps are often used to keep dirt and moisture away from the system (caliper bleeder shown)

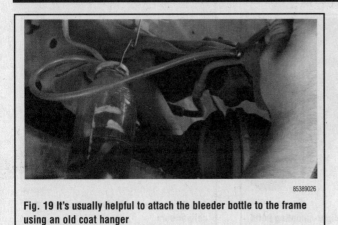
Fig. 19 It's usually helpful to attach the bleeder bottle to the frame using an old coat hanger

is suspected to contain air) and on most Rear Wheel Anti-Lock (RWAL) systems the combination valve must be held open. In both cases, special combination valve depressor tools should be used during bleeding and a scan tool must be used for ABS function tests.

5. If a single line or fitting was the only hydraulic line disconnected, then only the caliper(s) or wheel cylinder(s) affected by that line must be bled. If the master cylinder required bleeding, then all calipers and wheel cylinders must be bled in the proper sequence:

   a. Right rear

b. Left rear
c. Right front
d. Left front

6. Bleed the individual calipers or wheel cylinders as follows:

   a. Place a suitable wrench over the bleeder screw and attach a clear plastic hose over the screw end. Be sure the hose is seated snugly on the screw or you may be squirted with brake fluid.

➡**Be very careful when bleeding wheel cylinders and brake calipers. The bleeder screws often rust in position and may easily break off if forced. Installing a new bleeder screw will often require removal of the component and may include overhaul or replacement of the wheel cylinder/caliper. To help prevent the possibility of breaking a bleeder screw, spray it with some penetrating oil before attempting to loosen it.**

   b. Submerge the other end of the tube in a transparent container of clean brake fluid.

   c. Loosen the bleed screw, then have a friend apply the brake pedal slowly and hold. Tighten the bleed screw to 62 inch lbs. (7 Nm), release the brake pedal and wait 15 seconds. Repeat the sequence (including the 15 second pause) until all air is expelled from the caliper or cylinder.

   d. Tighten the bleed screw to 62 inch lbs. (7 Nm) when finished.

7. Check the pedal for a hard feeling with the engine not running. If the pedal is soft, repeat the bleeding procedure until a firm pedal is obtained.

8. If the brake warning light is on, depress the brake pedal firmly. If there is no air in the system, the light will go out.

9. After bleeding, make sure that a firm pedal is achieved before attempting to move the vehicle.

FRONT DISC BRAKES

✳✳ CAUTION

Brake shoes contain asbestos, which has been determined to be a cancer causing agent. Never clean the brake surfaces with compressed air! Avoid inhaling any dust from any brake surface! When cleaning brake surfaces, use a commercially available brake cleaning fluid.

Brake Pads

INSPECTION

▶ **See Figures 20 and 21**

Brake pads should be inspected once a year or at 7,500 miles, whichever occurs first. Check both ends of the outboard pad, looking in at each end of the caliper; then check the lining thickness of the inboard pad, looking down through the inspection hole. On riveted pads, the lining should be more than 1/32 in. (0.8mm) thick above the rivet (so that the lining is thicker than the metal backing in most cases) in order to prevent the rivet from scoring the rotor. On bonded brake pads, a minimum lining thickness of 1/32 in. (0.8mm) above the

backing plate should be used to determine necessary replacement intervals. Keep in mind that any applicable state inspection standards that are more stringent take precedence. All four front pads MUST be replaced as a set if one shows excessive wear.

➡**All models should be equipped with a wear indicator that makes a noise when the linings have worn to a degree where replacement is necessary. The spring clip is an integral part of the inboard pad and lining. When the brake pad reaches a certain degree of wear, the clip will contact the rotor and produce a warning noise.**

REMOVAL & INSTALLATION

▶ **See Figures 22 thru 33**

➡**The following procedure requires the use of a C-clamp and channel lock pliers.**

1. If the fluid reservoir is full, siphon off about 2/3 of the brake fluid from the master cylinder reservoirs in order to prevent the possibility of spillage when the caliper pistons are bottomed. A common kitchen turkey baster may also be used to remove brake fluid, but make sure the tool is clean before inserting it in the reservoir.

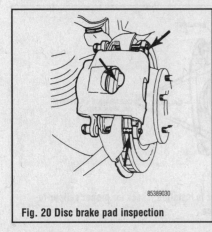
Fig. 20 Disc brake pad inspection

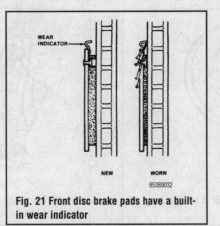
Fig. 21 Front disc brake pads have a built-in wear indicator

Fig. 22 Use a C-clamp to bottom the piston (this provides clearance for new pad installation)

Fig. 23 Loosen the caliper mounting bolts/pins

Fig. 24 Remove the caliper mounting bolts

Fig. 25 Remove the outboard pad from the caliper ears

Fig. 26 Remove the inboard pad from the caliper piston

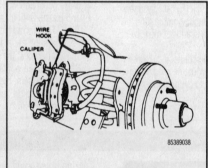

Fig. 27 While working on the brakes, support the caliper to prevent damage to the brake line

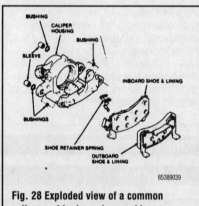

Fig. 28 Exploded view of a common caliper and brake pad assembly

Fig. 29 The spring clip must be properly installed on the inboard pad

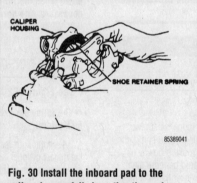

Fig. 30 Install the inboard pad to the caliper by carefully inserting the spring clip in the piston

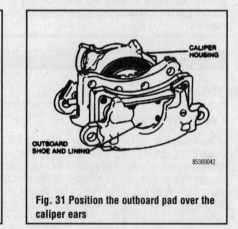

Fig. 31 Position the outboard pad over the caliper ears

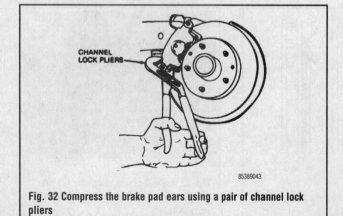

Fig. 32 Compress the brake pad ears using a pair of channel lock pliers

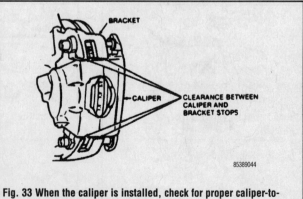

Fig. 33 When the caliper is installed, check for proper caliper-to-knuckle bracket clearance

❋❋ CAUTION

The insertion of thicker replacement pads will push the piston back into its bore and will cause a full master cylinder reservoir to overflow, possibly causing paint damage. In addition to siphoning off fluid, keep the reservoir cover on during pad replacement.

2. Raise and support the front of the vehicle safely using jackstands.
3. Remove the front tire and wheel assemblies.

➡**Replacing the pads on just one wheel may cause uneven braking; always replace the pads on both wheels.**

4. Install a C-clamp on the caliper so that the solid frame side of the clamp rests against the back of the caliper and the driving screw end rests against the metal part (center backing plate) of the outboard pad.
5. Tighten the clamp until the caliper moves sufficiently to bottom the piston in its bore, then remove the clamp.
6. Remove the two Allen head caliper mounting bolts from the back of the caliper.
7. Remove the caliper from the mounting bracket and support from the vehicle's suspension using a coat hanger or length of wire. DO NOT allow the brake line to support the caliper's weight and be sure the line is not otherwise kinked or damaged.
8. Remove the inboard and outboard pads from the caliper.
9. Remove the inboard pad spring clip from the piston or pad. Remove the spring clip carefully as it must be reused upon installation of the new pads.
10. Remove the bolt ear sleeves and rubber bushings for cleaning, inspection and lubrication.

To install:
11. Check the inside of the caliper for leakage and the condition of the piston dust boot. If necessary, remove the caliper and overhaul or replace it.
12. Lubricate the sleeves and bushings using a suitable silicone lubricant, then install them.
13. Make sure the piston is fully bottomed in the caliper providing clearance for the new brake pads. If the piston is not compressed, install the old inboard pad and use the C-clamp on the pad and back on the caliper to bottom the piston. BE CAREFUL not to pinch and damage the piston boot.
14. Install the spring clip to the inboard pad, then install the pad to the caliper.

➡**Make sure that the wear sensor is facing in the proper direction. On most vehicles it should face toward the rear of the caliper.**

15. Place the outboard pad in the caliper with its top ears over the caliper ears and the bottom tab engaged in the caliper cutout.
16. Place the caliper over the disc, lining up the hole in the caliper ears with the holes in the mounting bracket. Make sure that the brake hose is not twisted or kinked.
17. Carefully insert the mounting bolts through the bracket and caliper (bushing and sleeves), then tighten to 37 ft. lbs. (50 Nm).
18. Pump the brake pedal a few times to seat the linings against the rotors.
19. Use a pair of channel lock pliers to compress the pad ears so no clearance exists between the pad ears and the caliper.
20. Check the clearance between the caliper and steering knuckle. Clearance at each end of the caliper should be measured individually and the results added together. Clearance should not exceed 0.010–0.024 in. (0.026–0.60mm).
21. Install the wheels, then remove the jackstands and carefully lower the vehicle.
22. Check and refill the master cylinder reservoirs with brake fluid.

❋❋ CAUTION

DO NOT attempt to move the vehicle until a firm brake pedal is obtained.

23. Pump the brake pedal to make sure that it is firm. If necessary, bleed the brakes.

Brake Caliper

REMOVAL & INSTALLATION

▶ **See Figures 22, 23, 24, 32 and 33**

1. If the fluid reservoir is full, siphon off about ⅔ of the brake fluid from the master cylinder reservoirs in order to prevent the possibility of spillage when the caliper pistons are bottomed. A common kitchen turkey baster may also be used to remove brake fluid, but make sure the tool is clean before inserting it in the reservoir.
2. Raise and support the front of the vehicle safely using jackstands.
3. Remove the front tire and wheel assemblies.
4. If the brake pads are being replaced (and the caliper is NOT being overhauled), install a C-clamp on the caliper so that the solid frame side of the clamp rests against the back of the caliper and the driving screw end rests against the metal part (center backing plate) of the outboard pad. Tighten the clamp until the caliper moves sufficiently to bottom the piston in its bore, then remove the clamp.
5. Remove the two Allen head caliper mounting bolts from the back of the caliper. If the caliper is not being completely remove from the vehicle, remove it from the mounting bracket and support it from the suspension using a coat hanger or length of wire. DO NOT allow the hose to be stretched, twisted, kinked or otherwise damaged.
6. If the caliper is being completely removed from the vehicle, disconnect the flexible brake hose-to-caliper banjo-bolt, discard the pressure fitting washers (they must be replaced with new ones during assembly), then remove the brake caliper from the vehicle and place it on a work bench.
7. To inspect the caliper assembly, perform the following procedures:
   a. Check the inside of the caliper assembly for pitting or scoring. If heavy scoring or pitting is present, caliper replacement is recommended.
   b. Check the mounting bolts and sleeves for signs of corrosion; if necessary, replace the bolts.

➡**If the mounting bolts have signs of corrosion, DO NOT attempt to polish away the corrosion. Instead the bolts must be replaced to assure proper caliper sliding and prevent the possibility of brake drag or locking.**

To install:
8. Lubricate and position the caliper bushings and sleeves. Apply Delco® silicone lube or equivalent to lubricate the mounting bolts.
9. With both pads installed to the caliper, place the caliper over the disc, lining up the hole in the caliper ears with the holes in the mounting bracket.
10. If the caliper was completely removed, install the flexible hose to the caliper and secure using the banjo bolt and new washers. Make sure that the brake hose is not twisted or kinked, then tighten the bolt to 32 ft. lbs. (44 Nm).
11. Carefully insert the mounting bolts through the bracket and caliper (bushing and sleeves), then tighten to 37 ft. lbs. (50 Nm).
12. Pump the brake pedal a few times to seat the linings against the rotors.
13. Use a pair of channel lock pliers to compress the pad ears so no clearance exists between the pad ears and the caliper.
14. Check the clearance between the caliper and steering knuckle. Clearance at each end of the caliper should be measured individually and the results added together. Clearance should not exceed 0.010–0.024 in. (0.026–0.60mm).
15. Install the wheels, then remove the jackstands and carefully lower the vehicle.
16. Check and refill the master cylinder reservoirs with brake fluid.

❋❋ CAUTION

DO NOT attempt to move the vehicle until a firm brake pedal is obtained.

17. Properly bleed the hydraulic brake system. If only a caliper fitting was disconnected, bleeding of the entire system should not be required. Bleed air from the system at the caliper that was disconnected. Check the system for proper operation. If air remains in the system, bleeding at all points in the system may be required.

Caliper

OVERHAUL

▶ **See Figures 34 thru 39**

➡Some vehicles may be equipped dual piston calipers. The procedure to overhaul the caliper is essentially the same with the exception of multiple pistons, O-rings and dust boots.

1. Remove the caliper from the vehicle and place on a clean workbench.

✳✳ CAUTION

NEVER place your fingers in front of the pistons in an attempt to catch or protect the pistons when applying compressed air. This could result in personal injury!

➡Depending upon the vehicle, there are two different ways to remove the piston from the caliper. Refer to the brake pad replacement procedure to make sure you have the correct procedure for your vehicle.

2. The first method is as follows:
   a. Stuff a shop towel or a block of wood into the caliper to catch the piston.
   b. Remove the caliper piston using compressed air applied into the caliper inlet hole. Inspect the piston for scoring, nicks, corrosion and/or worn or damaged chrome plating. The piston must be replaced if any of these conditions are found.

3. For the second method, you must rotate the piston to retract it from the caliper.

4. If equipped, remove the anti-rattle clip.

5. Use a prytool to remove the caliper boot, being careful not to scratch the housing bore.

6. Remove the piston seals from the groove in the caliper bore.

7. Carefully loosen the brake bleeder valve cap and valve from the caliper housing.

8. Inspect the caliper bores, pistons and mounting threads for scoring or excessive wear.

9. Use crocus cloth to polish out light corrosion from the piston and bore.

10. Clean all parts with denatured alcohol and dry with compressed air.

To assemble:

11. Lubricate and install the bleeder valve and cap.

12. Install the new seals into the caliper bore grooves, making sure they are not twisted.

13. Lubricate the piston bore.

14. Install the pistons and boots into the bores of the calipers and push to the bottom of the bores.

15. Use a suitable driving tool to seat the boots in the housing.

16. Install the caliper in the vehicle.

17. Install the wheel and tire assembly, then carefully lower the vehicle.

18. Properly bleed the brake system.

Brake Disc (Rotor)

INSPECTION

▶ **See Figure 40**

Check the disc brake rotor for scoring, cracks or other damage. Rotor run-out should be measured while the rotor is installed, while rotor thickness/thickness variation may be checked with the rotor installed or removed. Use a dial gauge to check rotor run-out. Check the rotor thickness to make sure it is greater than minimum thickness and check for thickness variations using a caliper micrometer.

1. Raise and support the front of the vehicle safely using jackstands.

2. Remove the front wheels.

3. Visually inspect the rotor for cracks, excessive scoring or other damage. A light scoring of the surface which does not exceed 0.06 in. (1.5mm) in depth is normal and should not be considered detrimental to brake operation.

TCCA9P01

Fig. 34 For some types of calipers, use compressed air to drive the piston out of the caliper, but make sure to keep your fingers clear

TCCA9P02

Fig. 35 Withdraw the piston from the caliper bore

TCCSA9P04

Fig. 36 Use a prytool to carefully pry around the edge of the boot . . .

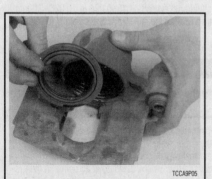

TCCA9P05

Fig. 37 . . . then remove the boot from the caliper housing, taking care not to score or damage the bore

TCCA9P06

Fig. 38 Use extreme caution when removing the piston seal; DO NOT scratch the caliper bore

TCCA9P07

Fig. 39 Use the proper size driving tool and a mallet to properly seal the boots in the caliper housing

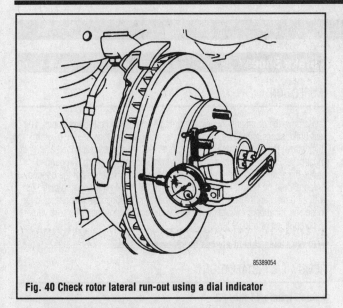

Fig. 40 Check rotor lateral run-out using a dial indicator

➡Before attempting to check rotor run-out on 2wd vehicles, make sure the wheel bearings are properly adjusted. On all vehicles, the bearings must be in good condition and not contain excessive play.

4. Check the disc for excessive run-out using a dial indicator:

a. Position and secure a dial indicator so that the button contacts the disc about 1 in. (25.4mm) from the outer edge. Set the dial indicator to zero.

b. Rotate the disc one complete revolution. The lateral run-out reading should not exceed 0.004 in. (0.1mm) on vehicles through 1992 or 0.003 in. (0.08mm) for 1993 vehicles. If the reading is excessive, recondition or replace the disc.

5. Check the disc minimum thickness and the disc parallelism (thickness variation):

a. Use a micrometer to check the disc thickness at 4 locations around the disc. Make sure the measuring point is at the same distance from the edge at all locations.

b. The thickness should be greater than the minimum specification (which is normally cast onto the disc) and should not vary more than 0.0005 in. (0.013mm). If the variations are excessive, recondition or replace the disc. A disc which is smaller than the discard dimension MUST be replaced for safety.

REMOVAL & INSTALLATION

2WD Model

1. Raise and support the front of the vehicle safely using jackstands.
2. Remove the tire and wheel assembly.
3. Remove the brake caliper mounting bolts and carefully remove the caliper (along with the brake pads) from the rotor. Do not disconnect the brake line; instead wire the caliper out of the way with the line still connected.

➡Once the rotor is removed from the vehicle the wheel bearings may be cleaned and repacked or the bearings and races may be replaced. For more information, please refer to the wheel bearing procedures in Section 1 of this manual.

4. Carefully pry out the grease cap, then remove the cotter pin, spindle nut, and washer. Remove the hub, being careful not to drop the outer wheel bearings. As the hub is pulled forward, the outer wheel bearings will often fall forward and they may easily be removed at this time.

To install:

5. Carefully install the wheel hub over the spindle.
6. Using your hands, firmly press the outer bearing into the hub.
7. Loosely install the spindle washer and nut, but do not install the cotter pin or dust cap at this time.
8. Install the brake caliper.
9. Install the tire and wheel assembly.
10. Properly adjust the wheel bearings:

a. Spin the wheel forward by hand and tighten the nut to 12 ft. lbs. (16 Nm) in order to fully seat the bearings and remove any burrs from the threads.

b. Back off the nut until it is just loose, then finger-tighten the nut.

c. Loosen the nut ¼–½ turn until either hole in the spindle lines up with a slot in the nut, then install a new cotter pin. This may appear to be too loose, but it is the correct adjustment.

d. Proper adjustment creates 0.001–0.005 in. (0.025–0.127mm) end-play.

11. Install the dust cap.
12. Install the wheel/hub cover, then remove the supports and carefully lower the vehicle.

4WD Model

▶ **See Figures 41, 42 and 43**

1. Raise and support the front of the truck safely using jackstands under the frame.
2. Remove the tire and wheel assembly.
3. Remove the brake caliper mounting bolts and carefully remove the caliper (along with the brake pads) from the rotor. Do not disconnect the brake line; instead wire the caliper out of the way with the line still connected.
4. If equipped, remove the lockwashers from the hub studs in order to free the rotor.
5. Remove the brake disc (rotor) from the wheel hub.

To install:

6. Inspect the disc for nicks, scores and/or damage, then replace if necessary.
7. Install the disc over the wheel hub studs.
8. If used, install the lockwashers over the studs.
9. Install the brake caliper and pads. For details, please refer to the caliper procedure located earlier in this section.
10. Install the tire and wheel assembly.
11. Remove the jackstands and carefully lower the vehicle. DO NOT attempt to move the vehicle unless a firm brake pedal is felt.

Fig. 41 The brake disc is easily removed once the tire and wheel is out of the way

Fig. 42 If equipped, remove the lockwashers from the hub studs

Fig. 43 Remove the rotor by pulling it of the hub studs

REAR DRUM BRAKES

❊❊ CAUTION

Brake shoes contain asbestos, which has been determined to be a cancer causing agent. Never clean the brake surfaces with compressed air! Avoid inhaling any dust from any brake surface! When cleaning brake surfaces, use a commercially available brake cleaning fluid.

Brake Drums

REMOVAL & INSTALLATION

1. Raise and support the rear of the vehicle safely using jackstands.
2. Remove the rear tire and wheel assemblies.
3. Matchmark the drum to the hub or hub studs for installation purposes.
4. Pull the brake drum from the hub studs. It may by necessary to gently tap the rear edges of the drum using a rubber mallet to start it off the studs.
5. If the drum will not come off past the shoes, it will be necessary to retract the adjusting screw. Remove the access hole cover from the backing plate and turn the adjuster to retract the linings away from the drum.

To install:

➥The rear wheel bearings are not adjustable, they are serviced by replacement ONLY. If necessary to replace the rear wheel bearings, please refer to the axle shaft, bearing and seal, removal and installation procedures located in Section 7 of this manual.

6. If removed, install a rubber adjustment hole cover before reinstalling the drum.
7. Install the drum in the same position on the hub as removed.
8. Install the rear tire and wheel assemblies.
9. Remove the jackstands and carefully lower the vehicle.

INSPECTION

Clean all grease, brake fluid, and other contaminants from the brake drum using brake cleaner. Visually check the drum for scoring, cracks, or other damage and replace, if necessary.

Check the drum inner diameter using a brake shoe clearance gauge. There are 2 important specifications when discussing rear drum diameters. The refinish diameter is the maximum diameter to which the drum may be machined. This diameter allows room for drum wear after is has been machined and is returned to service. The discard diameter is the point at which the drum becomes unsafe to use and must be discarded. NEVER refinish a drum to the discard diameter. If after refinishing the drum the diameter is within 0.030 in. (0.76mm) of the discard diameter, the drum MUST be replaced.

Brake Shoes

INSPECTION

Remove the drum and inspect the lining thickness of both brake shoes. The rear brake shoes should be replaced if the lining is less than 1/32 in. (0.8mm) thick above the rivet (so that the lining is thicker than the metal shoe backing in most cases) in order to prevent the rivet from scoring the drum. On bonded shoes the same specification should be used and the thickness of the bonded lining should be 1/32 in. (0.8mm) thick above the metal shoe backing plate. As with all brake service, keep in mind that local regulations take precedence over these specifications. Always check with your local authorities to be sure you are in compliance with local laws.

➥**Brake shoes should always be replaced in sets.**

REMOVAL & INSTALLATION

▶ **See Figures 44 thru 62**

1. Raise and support the rear of the vehicle safely using jackstands.
2. Remove the rear wheels.
3. Matchmark and remove the brake drums.
4. Remove the shoe return springs and disconnect the actuator link (the link may be removed at this time), then remove the shoe guide from the stud at the top of the backing plate.

➥**Special brake spring tools are available from the auto supply stores, which will ease the removal and installation of the return springs and the shoe hold-down spring and anchor pin.**

5. Remove the shoe hold-down springs and pins.
6. Remove the actuator lever, pivot and return spring.
7. If not done earlier, remove the actuator link.
8. Remove the parking brake strut and strut spring, then remove the parking brake lever from the shoe (it may be easier to wait until the shoe is being removed to separate the lever).
9. Remove the brake shoes, the adjuster screw assembly and the adjuster spring.
10. Clean and inspect all of the brake parts.
11. Check the wheel cylinders for seal condition and leaking.
12. Inspect the axle seal for leakage and replace, if necessary.

To install:

13. Inspect the replacement shoes for nicks or burrs, lightly lubricate the backing plate contact points, the brake cable, the levers and adjusting screws with a white lithium brake grease.
14. Make sure that the right and left hand adjusting screws are not mixed. You can prevent this by working on one side at a time. This will also provide you with a reference for reassembly, just keep in mind that the assembly on one side of the vehicle is the mirror image of the assembly on

Fig. 44 Use an evaporative spray brake cleaner to remove brake dust from the components

Fig. 45 Use a brake tool to release the return springs

Fig. 46 When the first spring is released, pivot it and remove it from the shoe

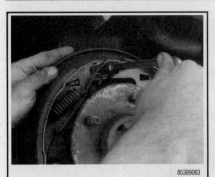

Fig. 47 Usually the easiest way to release the other return spring is to free the actuator link

Fig. 48 When the link us pulled back the tension is relieved from the spring and it can be removed

Fig. 49 If you want, the actuator link can be removed at this time

Fig. 50 Remove the shoe guide from the stud at the top of the backing plate

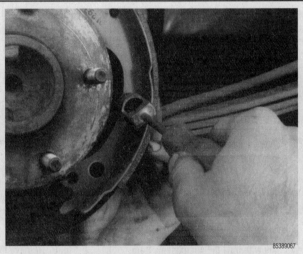

Fig. 52 Use the brake tool to compress the hold-down spring and twist the plate to free the pin

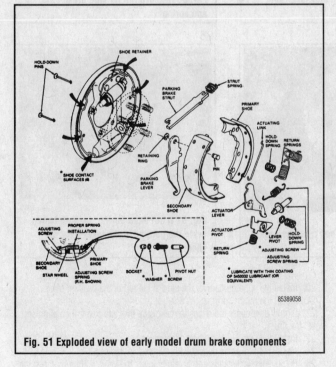

Fig. 51 Exploded view of early model drum brake components

Fig. 53 With the pin and slot (on top of spring plate) aligned, separate the hold-down spring and pin

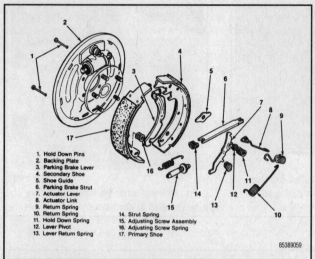

1. Hold Down Pins
2. Backing Plate
3. Parking Brake Lever
4. Secondary Shoe
5. Shoe Guide
6. Parking Brake Strut
7. Actuator Lever
8. Actuator Link
9. Return Spring
10. Return Spring
11. Hold Down Spring
12. Lever Pivot
13. Lever Return Spring
14. Strut Spring
15. Adjusting Screw Assembly
16. Adjusting Screw Spring
17. Primary Shoe

85389059

Fig. 54 Exploded view of the late model drum brake components used on most vehicles covered by this manual

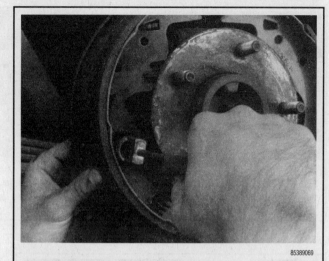

85389069

Fig. 55 Use the brake tool to remove the hold-down spring and pin from the other shoe

85389070

Fig. 56 Again, once the pin is released you may withdraw the components from the backing plate

85389071

Fig. 57 Remove the actuator lever and return spring

85389072

Fig. 58 Remove the parking brake strut and spring

85389073

Fig. 59 You may wish to remove the adjuster screw at this time (to avoid dropping when the shoes are removed)

85389074

Fig. 60 Remove the shoes from the backing plate

85389075

Fig. 61 If not done earlier, be sure to separate the parking brake lever from the shoe

the other side. The star wheel should be nearest to the secondary shoe when correctly installed.

15. Install the adjusting screw assembly and spring to both shoes, then position the shoes to the backing plate.

16. Install the parking brake lever to the secondary shoe.

17. Install the strut spring to the parking brake strut, then position the strut.

18. Install the actuator lever, lever pivot and the link. Install the lever return spring.

19. Install the shoe hold-down pins and springs.

20. Install the shoe guide over the stud at the top of the backing plate.

21. Install the return springs.

22. Lightly sandpaper the shoes to make sure they are clean, then align and install the drum.

23. Install the rear tire and wheel assemblies.

24. Adjust the brakes as described previously in this section.

25. Remove the jackstands and carefully lower the vehicle, then road test the vehicle.

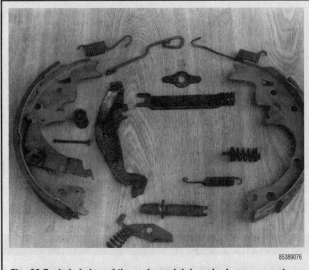

Fig. 62 Exploded view of the early model drum brake components

Wheel Cylinders

REMOVAL & INSTALLATION

▶ See Figures 63, 64, 65 and 66

1. Raise and support the rear of the vehicle safely using jackstands.
2. Remove the tire and wheel assembly.
3. Matchmark and remove the brake drum for access to the wheel cylinder assembly.

➡In most cases, the wheel cylinders may be removed from the backing plate without completely removing the brake shoes and related components, however completely removing the shoes will make the operation MUCH easier. If the shoes are not completely removed, some of the upper springs must be removed in order to allow the shoes to spread and provide the necessary clearance for wheel cylinder removal.

4. Remove the brake shoes or disconnect them sufficiently for wheel cylinder clearance.
5. Clean away all dirt, crud and foreign material from around wheel cylinder. It is important that dirt be kept away from the brake line when the cylinder is disconnected.
6. Disconnect the inlet tube line from the back of the wheel cylinder. Immediately plug or cap the line to prevent system contamination or excessive fluid loss.

➡Wheel cylinders are retained to the rear of the brake backing plate by two types of fasteners. One type uses a round retainer with locking clips while the other simply uses two bolts threaded into the wheel cylinder body.

7. To remove the round retainer type cylinders, insert two awls or pins into the access slots between the wheel cylinder pilot and the retainer locking tabs. Bend both tabs away simultaneously. The wheel cylinder can be removed, as the retainer is released.
8. To remove the bolted wheel cylinders, loosen and remove the bolts from the back side of the backing plate, then remove the wheel cylinder assembly.

To install:

9. For round retainer type wheel cylinders, position the cylinder and hold it in place with a wooden block between the cylinder and the axle flange. Install the new retainer clip, using a 1⅛ in. 12-point socket and socket extension (to help preserve your fingers). The socket is used to assure that the retainer seats evenly.

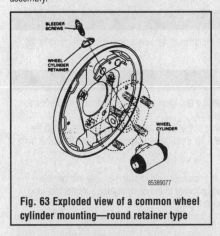

Fig. 63 Exploded view of a common wheel cylinder mounting—round retainer type

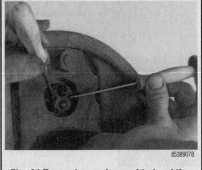

Fig. 64 Two awls may be used to bend the retainer stubs, releasing the wheel cylinder

Fig. 65 Once the cylinder is free of the backing plate, it can be removed from the vehicle

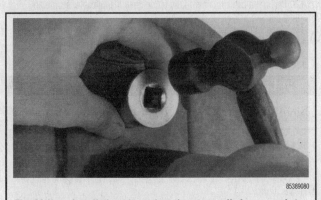

Fig. 66 Upon installation of round retainer type cylinders, a socket should be used to seat the retainer

10. For bolt type wheel cylinders, position the cylinder, then install the retaining bolts and tighten to 115 inch lbs. (13 Nm).
11. Remove the cap or plug, then connect and secure the hydraulic inlet line.
12. Assemble the remaining brake components which were removed.
13. Align and install the brake drum, then install the tire and wheel assembly.
14. Bleed the wheel cylinder and adjust the brakes (if necessary).
15. Remove the jackstands and carefully lower the vehicle.

OVERHAUL

▶ See Figures 67, 68 and 69

Wheel cylinder overhaul kits may be available, but often at little or no savings over a reconditioned wheel cylinder. It often makes sense with these components to substitute a new or reconditioned part instead of attempting an overhaul.

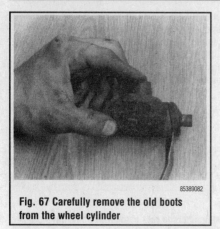

Fig. 67 Carefully remove the old boots from the wheel cylinder

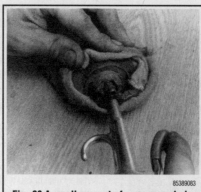

Fig. 68 A small amount of compressed air may be used to free the inner components

Fig. 69 Exploded view of the wheel cylinder assembly

If no replacement is available, or you would prefer to overhaul your wheel cylinders, the following procedure may be used. When rebuilding and installing wheel cylinders, avoid getting any contaminants into the system. Always install clean, new, high-quality brake fluid. If dirty or improper fluid has been used, it will be necessary to drain the entire system, flush the system with proper brake fluid, replace all rubber components, refill, and bleed the system.

1. Remove the wheel cylinder from the vehicle.
2. First remove and discard the old rubber boots, then withdraw the pistons. Piston cylinders are equipped with seals and a spring assembly, all located behind the pistons in the cylinder bore.
3. Remove the remaining inner components seals and spring assembly. Compressed air may be useful in removing these components. If no compressed air is available, be VERY careful not to score the wheel cylinder bore when removing parts from it. Discard all components for which replacements were supplied in the rebuild kit.
4. Wash the cylinder and metal parts in denatured alcohol or clean brake fluid.

✳✳ CAUTION

Never use a mineral-based solvent such as gasoline, kerosene, or paint thinner for cleaning purposes. These solvents will swell rubber components and quickly deteriorate them.

5. Allow the parts to air dry or use compressed air. Do not use rags for cleaning since lint will remain in the cylinder bore.
6. Inspect the piston and replace it if it shows scratches.
7. Lubricate the cylinder bore and seals using clean brake fluid.
8. Position the spring assembly.
9. Install the inner seals then the pistons.
10. Insert the new boots into the counterbores by hand. Do not lubricate the boots.
11. Install the wheel cylinder to the vehicle.

Wheel Bearings

Refer to the Section 7 of this manual for service procedures relating to the rear axle shaft and bearings.

PARKING BRAKE

All vehicles covered by this manual are equipped with a foot operated ratchet type parking brake. A cable connects this pedal to an equalizer which controls tension on the 2 rear cables that are attached to the brake shoe levers. Adjustment is made at the equalizer.

Front Cable

REMOVAL & INSTALLATION

♦ **See Figures 70, 71 and 72**

1. Raise and support the front of the vehicle safely using jackstands.

➡**The parking brake equalizer threads will often rust in service making adjustment or removal difficult. If necessary, spray a penetrating lubricant on the nut and equalizer threads, then allow time for the lubricant to work.**

2. Under the left-center of the vehicle, loosen the nut on the cable equalizer assembly.
3. Separate the front cable from the equalizer.
4. If applicable, remove the front-cable retaining bolts and clips.
5. Bend or squeeze the frame retainer fingers and release the cable from the frame.

➡**On some models, it may be necessary to remove the dash trim panels to gain access to the brake pedal.**

6. If necessary for access, remove the lower trim panel from the left side of the dash.

7. Release the cowl retainer and grommet, then disconnect the front cable from the parking pedal assembly.
8. Attach a length of wire to the cable, then carefully pull it through the cowl leaving the wire in place for installation purposes. Remove the cable from the vehicle.
To install:
9. Use the wire left in the cowl opening to pull the cable into position.
10. Seat the retainer and grommet to the cowl, making sure the retaining fingers are completely through the hole.
11. Attach the cable to the lever, then if removed for access, install the lower trim panel.
12. Install the cable retainer to the frame, then if applicable, secure any retaining clips.
13. Connect the cable to the equalizer, then properly adjust the parking brake. For details, please refer to the procedure located later in this section.
14. Remove the jackstands and carefully lower the vehicle.

Rear Cables

REMOVAL & INSTALLATION

♦ **See Figures 73, 74 and 75**

1. Raise and support the rear of the vehicle safely using jackstands.
2. Remove the rear tire and wheel assembly, the matchmark and remove the brake drum.

➡**The parking brake equalizer threads will often rust in service making adjustment or removal difficult. If necessary, spray a penetrating lubri-**

Fig. 70 On this truck, the equalizer is just behind and to the side of the transfer case

Fig. 71 To loosen, hold the adjuster rod from turning while you turn the nut using a box wrench

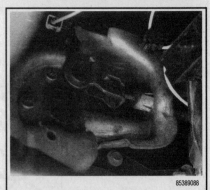

Fig. 72 The cable is usually attached to the lever using a button retainer

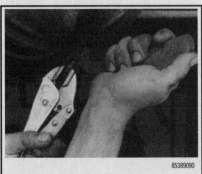

Fig. 73 A pair of vise grips are handy when disconnecting the cable from the shoe lever

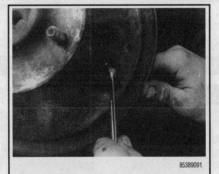

Fig. 74 To release the cable retainer, position a box wrench over the retainer in order to squeeze the fingers

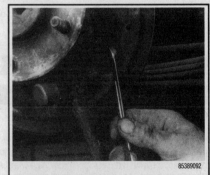

Fig. 75 Gently tap on the wrench with a hammer to free the cable and retainer from the backing plate

cant on the nut and equalizer threads, then allow time for the lubricant to work.

3. Under the left-center of the vehicle, loosen the nut on the cable equalizer assembly.

4. Separate the cable from the equalizer.

5. If equipped, release the rear cable retainer from the frame rail.

6. Remove the brake shoes and disconnect the parking brake cable from the shoe lever.

7. Remove the cable retainer from the backing plate by squeezing all of the retainer fingers and pulling the cable/retainer out of the plate. One easy way of accomplishing this is to position a box wrench (which is slightly smaller than the cable retainer) over the retainer to squeeze the fingers, then gently tap the wrench with a hammer to free the cable.

8. If equipped, remove the cable bolt and clip from the frame.

9. Remove the cable from the vehicle.

To install:

10. Position the cable under the vehicle and insert it through the brake backing plate. Seat the retainer on the plate making sure all of the fingers are locked in position. Route the cable and, if equipped, secure the frame retainer in the same manner.

11. Install the brake shoes, attaching the cable to the parking brake lever.

12. When installing the cable, attach it to the brake shoe lever and assemble the brakes. Before installing the drums, pull the cable by hand and watch the parking brake action for smooth operation.

13. Align and install the brake drum, then install the tire and wheel assembly.

14. If equipped, install the retaining clip and bolt. Tighten the bolt to 13 ft. lbs. (17 Nm).

15. Properly adjust the parking brake cable. For details, please refer to the procedure located later in this section.

16. Remove the jackstands and carefully lower the vehicle.

ADJUSTMENT

▶ **See Figures 76 and 77**

The parking brake cables MUST be adjusted any time one of the cables have been disconnected or replaced. Another indication of a need for cable adjustment is if under heavy foot pressure the pedal travel is less than 9 ratchet clicks or more than 13. Remember that the brake shoes must be properly adjusted before attempting to adjust the parking brake cable.

➡**Before adjusting the parking brakes, check the condition of the brake shoes and components; replace any necessary parts.**

1. Block the front wheels.

2. Raise and support the rear of the vehicle safely using jackstands.

➡**The parking brake equalizer threads will often rust in service making adjustment or removal difficult. If necessary, spray a penetrating lubricant on the nut and equalizer threads, then allow time for the lubricant to work.**

3. Under the left-center of the vehicle, loosen the nut on the cable equalizer assembly.

4. Set the parking brake pedal to the appropriate number of clicks:
   a. On 2wd models from 1982–84— set the pedal on the 8th click
   b. On 2wd models from 1985–93— set the pedal on the 2nd click.
   c. On 4wd models from 1983–84— set the pedal on the 10th click.
   d. On 4wd models from 1985–93— set the pedal on the 3rd click.

5. Tighten the cable equalizer nut until the rear wheel cannot be turned forward by hand without excessive force.

6. Loosen the equalizer nut until there is just moderate drag when the rear wheels are rotated forward.

7. Release the parking brake and verify that there is NO brake drag in either direction.

8. If equipped, tighten the equalizer locknut.

9. Remove the jackstands and carefully lower the vehicle.

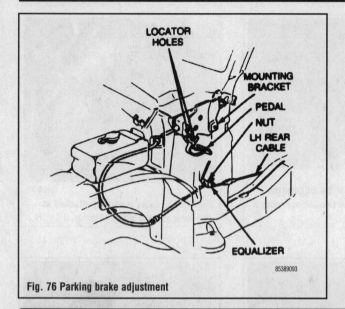

Fig. 76 Parking brake adjustment

85389093

Fig. 77 Be careful when attempting to turn the equalizer nut, rusted threads may release without warning, be sure to lubricate the threads

85389094

REAR WHEEL ANTI-LOCK (RWAL) SYSTEM

General Description

▶ See Figures 78 and 79

The RWAL system was introduced to the S/T series trucks as standard equipment in 1989. It may be found on all 1989 and later trucks covered by this manual (except the MFI-Turbo equipped with the 4 wheel ABS system). The system is particularly useful because of the wide variations of loading the vehicle may experience. Preventing rear wheel lock-up often makes the difference in controlling the vehicle during hard or sudden stops.

Found on both 2wd and 4wd vehicles, the RWAL system is designed to regulate rear hydraulic brake line pressure, preventing rear wheel lock-up during hard braking. On most 4wd vehicles, the system is deactivated when operating in four wheel drive. In this case the braking system acts as a normal hydraulic system. Pressure regulation is managed by the control valve, located under the master cylinder. The control valve is capable of holding, increasing or decreasing brake line pressure based on electrical commands from the Electronic Brake Control Module (EBCM), originally known as the RWAL Electronic Control Unit (ECU).

The control valve holds pressure when the control module energizes the isolation solenoid. This isolates the rear hydraulic circuit and prevents fluid from entering or leaving, therefore holding constant at a given pressure. Pressure is decreased when the module keeps the isolation solenoid energized and then energizes a dump solenoid which allows fluid from the rear hydraulic circuit to enter an accumulator, thereby reducing pressure and preventing wheel lockup. Pressure may be increased (though never over the driver's input) when both the isolation and dump solenoids are de-energized allowing the rear hydraulic circuit to function normally from full master cylinder pressure.

The RWAL ECU/EBCM is a separate and dedicated microcomputer mounted next to the master cylinder; it is not to be confused with the engine management computers also found in these vehicles. The ECU/EBCM receives signals from the speed sensor. The speed sensor sends its signals to the Vehicle Speed Sensor (VSS) buffer (previously known as the Digital Ratio Adapter Controller or DRAC) usually found within the instrument cluster. The buffer translates the sensor signal into a form usable by the computer module. The brake control module reads this signal and commands the control valve to function.

The RWAL system is connected to the BRAKE warning lamp on the instrument cluster. A RWAL self-check and a bulb test are performed every time the ignition switch is turned to **ON**. The BRAKE warning lamp should illuminate for about 2 seconds and then go off. Problems within the RWAL system will be indicated by the BRAKE warning lamp remaining illuminated after this initial test period.

If a fault is detected within the system, the control module will assign a diagnostic fault code and store the code in memory. The code may be read to aid in diagnosis, much in the same way codes are used in the engine emission control systems used by these vehicles.

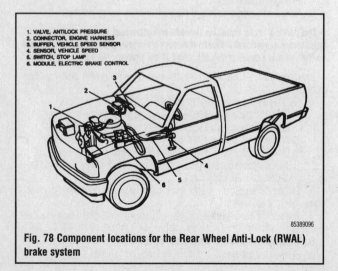

1. VALVE, ANTILOCK PRESSURE
2. CONNECTOR, ENGINE HARNESS
3. BUFFER, VEHICLE SPEED SENSOR
4. SENSOR, VEHICLE SPEED
5. SWITCH, STOP LAMP
6. MODULE, ELECTRIC BRAKE CONTROL

85389096

Fig. 78 Component locations for the Rear Wheel Anti-Lock (RWAL) brake system

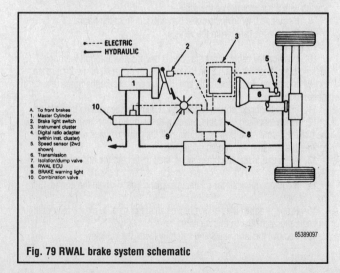

- - - - ELECTRIC
——— HYDRAULIC

A. To front brakes
1. Master Cylinder
2. Brake light switch
3. Instrument cluster
4. Digital ratio adapter (within inst. cluster)
5. Speed sensor (2wd shown)
6. Transmission
7. Isolation/dump valve
8. RWAL ECU
9. BRAKE warning light
10. Combination valve

85389097

Fig. 79 RWAL brake system schematic

SYSTEM COMPONENTS

No component of the RWAL system can be disassembled or repaired. Should the control module, control valve containing the isolation/dump valves or the speed sensor fail, each failed component must be replaced as an assembly. If the axle ratio or tire size is changed on the vehicle, the VSS buffer must be replaced with one of the appropriate calibration.

CIRCUIT MAINTENANCE

All electrical connections must be kept clean and tight. Make certain that all connectors are properly seated and all of the sealing rings on weather–proof connectors are in place. The low current and/or voltage found in some circuits require that every connection be the best possible. Special tools are required for servicing the GM Weather–Pack and Metric–Pack connectors. Use terminal remover tool J–28742 or equivalent for Weather–Pack and J–35689-A or equivalent for Metric–Pack connectors.

If removal of a terminal is attempted with a regular pick, there is a good chance the terminal will be bent or deformed. Once damaged, these connectors cannot be straightened.

Use care when probing the connections or replacing terminals; it is possible to short between adjacent terminals, causing component damage. Always use jumper wires between circuit connectors for testing circuits; never probe through weather–proof seals on connectors.

Oxidation or terminal misalignment may be hidden by the connector shell. When diagnosing open or intermittent circuits, wiggling the wire harness at the connector or component may reveal or correct the condition. When the location of the fault is identified, the connector should be separated and the problem connected. Never disconnect a harness connector with the ignition **ON**.

➡When working with the RWAL ECU/EBCM connectors, do not touch the connections or pins with the fingers. Do not allow the connectors or pins to contact brake fluid; internal damage to the RWAL ECU/EBCM may occur.

SYSTEM PRECAUTIONS

• Certain components within the RWAL system are not intended to be serviced or repaired. Only those components with removal & Installation procedures should be serviced. DO NOT ATTEMPT to disassemble or overhaul RWAL system components.

• Do not use rubber hoses or other parts not specifically specified for the RWAL system. When using repair kits, replace all parts included in the kit. Partial or incorrect repair may lead to functional problems.

• Lubricate rubber parts with clean, fresh brake fluid to ease assembly. Do not use lubricated shop air to clean parts; damage to rubber components may result.

• Use only brake fluid from an unopened container. Use of suspect or contaminated brake fluid can reduce system performance and/or durability.

• A clean repair area is essential. Perform repairs after components have been thoroughly cleaned; use only denatured alcohol to clean components. Do not allow components to come into contact with any substance containing mineral oil; this includes used shop rags.

• The RWAL ECU/EBCM is a microprocessor similar to other computer units in the vehicle. Insure that the ignition switch is **OFF** before removing or installing controller harnesses. Avoid static electricity discharge at or near the controller.

• Never disengage any electrical connection with the ignition switch **ON** unless instructed to do so in a test.

• Always wear a grounded wrist strap when servicing any control module or component labeled with a Electrostatic Discharge (ESD) symbol.

• Avoid touching module connector pins.

• Leave new components and modules in the shipping package until ready to install them.

• To avoid static discharge, always touch a vehicle ground after sliding across a vehicle seat or walking across carpeted or vinyl floors.

• Never allow welding cables to lie on, near or across any vehicle electrical wiring.

• Do not allow extension cords for power tools or droplights to lie on, near or across any vehicle electrical wiring.

PRELIMINARY DIAGNOSIS

Before reading trouble codes, perform the Diagnostic Circuit Check (1989–91 vehicles) or Function Test (1992–93 vehicles) according to the appropriate charts for your truck. The charts are located earlier in this section. This test will aid in separating RWAL system problems from common problems in the hydraulic brake system. The diagnostic circuit check will direct the reading of trouble codes as necessary.

DO NOT ground the brake trouble code terminal of the ALDL/DLC if the BRAKE lamp is not on indicating a stored trouble code. Attempting to activate trouble code read out with the BRAKE lamp off may set a false Code 9. This will turn the BRAKE lamp ON and disable the anti-lock brake system.

READING CODES

▶ **See Figures 80 and 81**

The computer control module (ECU/EBCM) will assign a code to the first fault found in the system. If there is more than 1 fault, only the first recognized code will the stored and transmitted.

Trouble codes may be read either though the use of Tech 1® or equivalent scan tool or by connecting a jumper wire from pin H on the ALDL/DLC to pin A. If the jumper method is used, the fault code will be displayed through the flashing of the BRAKE warning lamp on the dash. The terminals must be connected for about 20 seconds before the display begins. The display will begin with 1 long flash followed by shorter ones—count the long flash as part of the display.

➡Sometimes the first display sequence will be inaccurate or short; subsequent displays will be accurate.

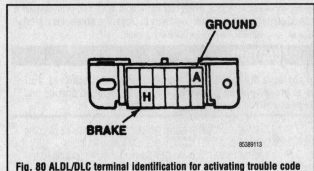

Fig. 80 ALDL/DLC terminal identification for activating trouble code read out

CODE	SYSTEM PROBLEM
CODE 1	Electronic control unit malfunction
CODE 2	Open isolation valve or faulty ECU
CODE 3	Open dump valve or faulty ECU
CODE 4	Grounded antilock valve switch
CODE 5	Excessive actuations of dump valve during an antilock stop
CODE 6	Erratic speed signal
CODE 7	Shorted isolation valve or faulty ECU
CODE 8	Shorted dump valve or faulty ECU
CODE 9	Open circuit to the speed signal
CODE 10	Brake lamp switch circuit
CODE 11	Electronic control unit malfunction
CODE 12	Electronic control unit malfunction
CODE 13	Electronic control unit malfunction
CODE 14	Electronic control unit malfunction
CODE 15	Electronic control unit malfunction

Fig. 81 Possible RWAL trouble codes—ECU malfunction DOES NOT necessarily mean the module must be replaced, consult a reputable repair shop to be sure

If using a hand scanner, note if a soft code is stored, only the last recognized code will be retained and displayed on the scanner. Soft fault Codes 6, 9 and 10 (vehicles through 1993) can only be read with a scan tool. On some models, Codes 1, 11 and 12 will not read on the scan tool and must be read using the jumper wire method.

➡**Never ground terminal H of the ALDL to terminal A if the BRAKE warning lamp is not lit. Doing so will usually set a false code 9 and illuminate the BRAKE warning lamp. With the brake lamp on, the RWAL system will be disabled.**

CLEARING CODES

Stored trouble codes must be cleared with the ignition switch **OFF**. NEVER attempt to clear codes while the ignition switch is in the **ON** position or the computer module will likely be destroyed. Remove the ECMB fuse for at least 5 seconds, then reinstall the fuse.

Bleeding the RWAL Brake System

On RWAL systems through 1992 the brake system may be bled in the usual manner with no special procedures. On 1993 vehicles a few steps (listed below) should be added to the bleeding sequence in order to ease the procedure and assure all air is removed from the system. If you have access to the additional tools required, you may use these extra steps on all RWAL vehicles to assure proper bleeding.

The use of a power bleeder is recommended, but the system may also be bled manually. If a power bleeder is used, it must be of the diaphragm type and provide isolation of the fluid from air and moisture.

Do not pump the pedal rapidly when bleeding; this can make the circuits very difficult to bleed. Instead, press the brake pedal slowly 1 time and hold it down while bleeding takes place. Tighten the bleeder screw, release the pedal and wait 15 seconds before repeating the sequence. Because of the length of the brake lines and other factors, it may take 10 or more repetitions of the sequence to bleed each line properly. When necessary to bleed all 4 wheels, the correct order is right rear, left rear, right front and left front.

✳✳ CAUTION

Do not move the vehicle until a firm brake pedal is achieved. Failure to properly bleed the system may cause impaired braking and the possibility of injury and/or property damage

On all 1993 RWAL vehicles, or earlier vehicles if desired, use the bleeding procedure found earlier in this section, with the following additions:

1. Make sure the ignition is in the **OFF** position to prevent setting false trouble codes.
2. After properly bleeding the master cylinder, install J-39177 or an equivalent combination valve depressor tool to the combination valve. This tool is used to hold the internal valve open allowing the entire system to be completely bled.

➡**This tool is relatively inexpensive and should be available from various aftermarket companies. Although a homemade tool may suffice, DO NOT attempt to fabricate a homemade tool unless you are CERTAIN it will not damage the valve by over-extension.**

3. Recheck the master cylinder fluid level and add, as necessary.
4. Bleed the wheel cylinders as described earlier in this section.
5. Attach the Tech 1® or an equivalent scan tool, then perform 3 RWAL function tests.
6. Re-bleed the rear wheel cylinders.
7. Check for a firm brake pedal, if necessary repeat the entire bleeding procedure.
8. Once you are finished, be sure to remove the combination valve depressor tool.

Component Replacement

SYSTEM FILLING

The master cylinder is filled in the usual manner with no special procedures being necessary. Only DOT 3 brake fluid must be used; silicone or DOT 5 fluid is specifically prohibited. Do not use any fluid which contains a petroleum base; these fluids will cause swelling and distortion of the rubber parts within the system. Do not use old or contaminated brake fluid.

RWAL ECU/EBCM

The Electronic Brake Control Module (EBCM), formerly known as the RWAL Electronic Control Unit (ECU), is a non-serviceable unit. It must be replaced when diagnosis indicates it is faulty. Because it is expensive and normally non-returnable, be absolutely sure the module is at fault before replacement.

1. Turn the ignition switch **OFF**. The switch MUST be **OFF** whenever you are connecting/disconnecting power from the module. Failure to do this may destroy the computer.
2. Disengage the wiring harness connector(s) from the computer control module.
3. Grasp the module and remove it by pulling toward the front of the vehicle. If necessary, gently pry the tab at the rear of the module while pulling.

➡**Do not touch the electrical connectors or pins; do not allow them to contact brake fluid. If contaminated with brake fluid, clean them with water followed by isopropyl alcohol.**

To install:
4. Install the computer module by aligning it and carefully sliding it into the bracket until the tab locks into the hole.
5. Engage the wiring harness connector(s) to the module.
6. Turn the ignition **ON**, then verify proper system operation.

ANTI-LOCK PRESSURE CONTROL VALVE

The Anti-Lock Pressure Valve (APV), formerly known as the isolation/dump or control valve assembly is not serviceable. The entire component must be replaced as an assembly should a malfunction be confirmed.

1. Turn the ignition switch **OFF**. The switch MUST be **OFF** whenever you are connecting/disconnecting power from the module (as will done later in this procedure). Failure to do this may destroy the computer.
2. Disconnect the brake line fittings at the valve, then immediately cap or plug all openings to prevent system contamination or excessive fluid loss. Remember to protect the surrounding paintwork from damage by fluid spillage.
3. Disengage the bottom connector from the RWAL ECU/EBCM. At NO time should you allow the APV to hang by the wiring.

➡**Do not touch the electrical connectors or pins; do not allow them to contact brake fluid. If contaminated with brake fluid, clean them with water followed by isopropyl alcohol.**

4. Remove the bolts holding the valve to the bracket.
5. Remove the valve from the vehicle.
To install:
6. Place the valve in position and install the retaining bolts. Tighten the bolts to 21 ft. lbs. (29 Nm).
7. Engage the electrical connector to the RWAL ECU/EBCM.

➡**Before engaging the electrical connector, double check to be sure there is NO brake fluid on the terminals or the control module may be damaged. If necessary, clean the terminals with water, followed by denatured alcohol.**

8. Remove the caps or plugs, then install the brake lines and tighten the fittings to 18 ft. lbs. (24 Nm)
9. Properly bleed the RWAL hydraulic brake system at all 4 wheels.

SPEED SENSOR

▸ See Figure 82

The speed sensor is not serviceable and must replaced if malfunctioning. The sensor is usually located in the left rear of the transmission case on 2wd vehicles and on the transfer case of 4wd vehicles.

The speed sensor may be tested with an ohmmeter; the correct resistance is normally 900–2000 ohms. To remove the speed sensor:
1. Raise and support the vehicle safely using jackstands.

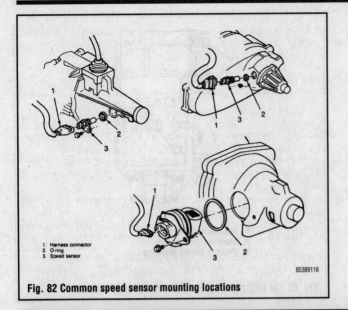

1. Harness connector
2. O-ring
3. Speed sensor

85389116

Fig. 82 Common speed sensor mounting locations

2. Disengage the electrical connector from the speed sensor.
3. If used, remove the sensor retaining bolt.
4. Remove the speed sensor; have a container handy to catch transmission fluid when the sensor is removed.

➡**If equipped with the 4L60-E automatic transmission, use J-38417 or an equivalent speed sensor remover/installer tool whenever the sensor is serviced.**

5. Recover the O-ring used to seal the sensor; inspect it for damage or deterioration.

To install:
6. When installing, coat the new O-ring with a thin film of transmission fluid.
7. Install the O-ring and speed sensor.
8. If a retaining bolt is used, tighten the bolt to 97 inch lbs. (11 Nm) in automatic transmissions or 107 inch lbs. (12 Nm) for manual transmissions.
9. If the sensor is a screw-in unit tighten it to 32 ft. lbs. (43 Nm).
10. Engage the wire harness to the sensor.
11. Remove the jackstands and carefully lower the vehicle.

FOUR WHEEL ANTI-LOCK (4WAL) SYSTEM

General Description

The four wheel anti-lock brake system was first used on these trucks on the 1991–92 MFI-Turbo Syclone. The 4 wheel anti-lock system is designed to reduce brake lock-up during severe brake application. The basic function of each system is similar to the RWAL system described earlier in this manual, the major difference simply being that the 4 wheel system monitors and controls wheel spin/lockup on the front wheels as well as the rear.

Instead of the APV (control valve) used on RWAL systems, the 4WAL system utilizes a Electro-Hydraulic Control Unit (EHCU) module. The EHCU module is located on the left fender, near the master cylinder. The module contains two types of valves, and controls the hydraulic pressure within the brake lines. The system also uses 4 wheel speed sensors (one located at each wheel).

SYSTEM OPERATION

In a severe brake application, the EHCU valve will, depending on the circumstance: allow pressure to increase within the system, maintain (isolate) the pressure within the system, or release existing pressure through the dump valves into the accumulators.

The EHCU valve operates by receiving signals from the speed sensors, located at each wheel, and from the brake lamp switch. The speed sensors connect directly to the EHCU valve through a multi-pin connector.

The system is connected to the ANTILOCK warning lamp on the dashboard. The warning lamp will illuminate for about 2 seconds every time the vehicle is started as a lamp check. The warning lamp will illuminate if the computer detects a problem within the anti-lock system during vehicle operation. If the warning light comes on when the vehicle is started and does not go out, or if the light comes on and remains on during vehicle operation, trouble has been detected by the computer module.

SYSTEM COMPONENTS

EHCU Module

The EHCU module is mounted near the master cylinder and combination valve assemblies on the left fender. The module contains two types of valves. Isolation valves maintain pressure to each front wheel separately and the rear wheels combined. These valves are controlled by a microprocessor in the EHCU module. The module is not serviceable and must be replaced if malfunctioning. The module is also the sight for the only additional attention required to properly bleed the 4WAL hydraulic system.

Front Wheel Speed Sensors

On most 2 and 4wd vehicles covered by this manual, the front wheel speed sensors are permanently mounted to the brake rotor splash shield which must be replaced as an assembly should the sensor fail. On 4wd vehicles, the hub and bearing assembly must be removed.

The front wheel speed sensors operate with the help of sensor tone wheels. The tone wheels are metal rings equipped with teeth on their outer diameter. The AC voltage is produced as the teeth come into and leave alignment with the sensor. The tone wheels are attached to the front hub and bearing assembly on 4wd vehicles.

A properly operating speed sensor should have a resistance value of 900–2000 ω.

Rear Wheel Speed Sensors

The rear wheel speed sensors on the 1991–92 MFI-Turbo vehicles are held in position by 2 bolts at each rear wheel. The brake drum and primary brake shoe must be removed for access.

PRELIMINARY DIAGNOSIS

System diagnosis begins with the Diagnostic Circuit Check or Function Test, depending on the application. Please refer to the charts located earlier in this section. If the chart is used correctly, it will aid in elimination of simple, non-system problems such as blown fuses, failed bulbs or non-ABS related brake failures. The chart will prompt the reading of codes at the proper point in the diagnosis.

➡**Some of the diagnostic or repair procedures refer to the performance of a Function Test. This test is performed with the scan tool; it operates all components of the EHCU and checks their function. The test cannot be performed without the scan tool.**

READING CODES

▶ **See Figures 83 and 84**

Stored trouble codes may be transmitted through the flashing of the ANTILOCK dash warning lamp. On these vehicles, the system may be placed in diagnostic mode using a jumper wire, however, the use of the Tech 1®® scan tool or its equivalent is highly recommended.

On vehicles where flash-diagnosis is possible, trouble code read out may be started using a jumper wire to connect Terminal H on the ALDL/DLC (diagnostic

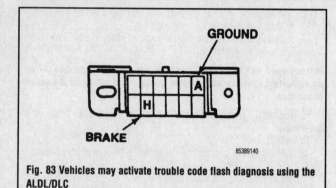

Fig. 83 Vehicles may activate trouble code flash diagnosis using the ALDL/DLC

connector located under the instrument panel—refer to self-diagnostics in Section 4 of this manual for more information) to either body ground or to terminal A (internal ground). The terminals must be connected for a few seconds before the code will transmit. Observe the ANTILOCK light on the dash and count the flashes in groups: a group of 4 flashes, a pause and a group of 3 flashes indicates Code 43.

Remember that trouble codes cannot specify the exact cause of the problem, but may only relate which circuit is affected by the problem. Before replacing any component, be sure that it is the cause of the problem, especially when dealing with a control module fault. Control modules are quite expensive and are usually not returnable.

```
Code 21—Right Front Speed Sensor or Circuit Open
Code 22—Missing Right Front Speed Signal
Code 23—Erratic Right Front Speed Sensor
Code 25—Left Front Speed Sensor or Circuit Open
Code 26—Missing Left Front Speed Signal
Code 27—Erratic Front Speed Sensor
Code 28—Erratic Speed Sensor Signal
Code 29—Simultaneous Drop-Out Of All Four Sensors
Code 31—Right Rear Speed Sensor or Circuit Open
Code 32—Missing Right Rear Speed Signal
Code 33—Erratic Right Rear Speed Sensor
Code 35—Left Rear Speed Sensor or Circuit Open
Code 36—Missing Left Rear Speed Signal
Code 37—Erratic Left Rear Speed Sensor
Code 38—Wheel Speed Sensor Error
Codes 41 Through 66 and 71 Through 74—4WAL Control Unit
Code 67—Open Motor Circuit or Shorted ECHU Output
Code 68—Locked Motor or Shorted Motor Circuit
Codes 68, 43, 44, 47, 48, 53, and 54 Simultaneously—Loss of Power or Ground
Code 81—Brake Switch Circuit Shorted or Open
Code 86—Shorted Antilock Warning Lamp
Code 88—Shorted Brake Warning Lamp
```

Fig. 84 Diagnostic trouble codes—1991–92 MFI-Turbo

CLEARING CODES

Stored codes may be erased with the hand scanner if available or, using a jumper wire:

1. If a hand scanner is available, use it to erase the computer module code memory.

2. Codes may be cleared without a scan tool as follows:

   a. Turn the ignition switch **ON** but do not start the engine.

   b. Use a jumper wire to ground ALDL/DLC terminal H to terminal A for 2 seconds.

   c. Remove the jumper wire for 1 second.

   d. Repeat the grounding for 2 more seconds.

3. When the trouble codes are cleared, the ANTILOCK and BRAKE lamps should both illuminate and then extinguish.

Bleeding the 4WAL Brake System

▶ See Figures 85 and 86

The EHCU module is the one component which adds to the complexity of bleeding the 4WAL brake systems. For the most part the system is bled in the same manner as the non-ABS vehicles. Refer to the procedure earlier in this

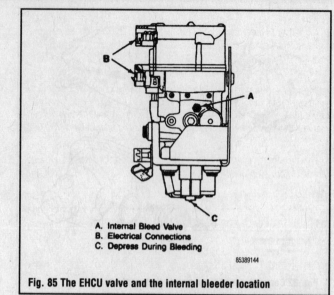

A. Internal Bleed Valve
B. Electrical Connections
C. Depress During Bleeding

Fig. 85 The EHCU valve and the internal bleeder location

section for details. But because of the EHCU's complex internal valving additional steps are necessary if the unit has been replaced or if it is suspected to contain air. These bleeding steps are NOT necessary if the only connection/fitting(s) opened were downstream of the unit. These steps may or may not be necessary after master cylinder replacement. If in doubt (or without the necessary special tools) thoroughly bleed the system and see if a firm brake pedal can be obtained, if not, the EHCU must be bled as well.

As with the RWAL brake system, the use of a power bleeder is recommended, but the system may also be bled manually. If a power bleeder is used, it must be of the diaphragm type and provide isolation of the fluid from air and moisture.

Do not pump the pedal rapidly when bleeding; this can make the circuits very difficult to bleed. Instead, press the brake pedal slowly 1 time and hold it down while bleeding takes place. Tighten the bleeder screw, release the pedal and wait 15 seconds before repeating the sequence. Because of the length of the brake lines and other factors, it may take 10 or more repetitions of the sequence to bleed each line properly. When necessary to bleed all 4 wheels, the correct order is right rear, left rear, right front and left front.

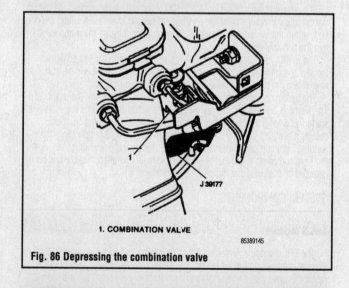

1. COMBINATION VALVE

Fig. 86 Depressing the combination valve

✳ CAUTION

Do not move the vehicle until a firm brake pedal is achieved. Failure to properly bleed the system may cause impaired braking and the possibility of injury and/or property damage

If the EHCU requires bleeding, the following procedure may be used to free all trapped air from the component. Three combination valve depressor tools and a scan tool are required. The combination valve depressor tools are used to hold the internal passages (combination valve and EHCU bleed accumulator bleed stems open allowing the entire system to be completely bled.

➡**The combination valve tools are relatively inexpensive and should be available from various aftermarket companies. Although a homemade tool may suffice, DO NOT attempt to fabricate a homemade tool unless you are CERTAIN it will not damage the valve/bleed stem by over-extension.**

Finally, remember to always bleed the 4WAL brake system with the ignition **OFF** to prevent setting false trouble codes.

1991–92 MFI-TURBO

The EHCU used on the 1991–92 MFI-Turbo is equipped with the internal bleeders AND a pair of external bleeder screws. These external bleeders look like normal brake bleeders and are found on top of the unit. Like any bleeder screw, they MUST remain closed when the unit is not pressurized.

The Internal Bleed Valves on either side of the unit must be opened ¼–½ turn before bleeding begins. These valves open internal passages within the unit. The valve located on the left side (nearest the fender) is used for the rear brake section, while the valve on the right (nearest the engine) is used for the front brakes. Actual bleeding is performed at the two bleeders on the top of the EHCU module. The bleeders must not be opened when the system is not pressurized. The ignition switch must be **OFF** or false trouble codes may be set.

1. Make sure the ignition is in the **OFF** position to prevent setting false trouble codes.
2. Open the internal bleed valves ¼–½ turn each.
3. Install J–35856 or equivalent combination valve depressor tool on the left accumulator bleed stem of the EHCU. Install one tool on the right bleed stem and install the third tool on the combination valve (rear).
4. Inspect the fluid level in the master cylinder, filling if needed.
5. Have an assistant slowly depress the brake pedal and hold it down.
6. Open the left bleeder on top of the unit. Allow fluid to flow until no air is seen or until the brake pedal bottoms.
7. Close the left bleeder, then have your assistant release the pedal slowly and wait 15 seconds.
8. Repeat these steps starting with depressing the brake pedal (including the 15 second pause), until no air is seen in the fluid.
9. Tighten the left internal bleed valve to 60 inch lbs. (7 Nm).
10. Bleed air from the right bleeder screw on top of the EHCU in the same manner as the left screw.
11. When bleeding of the right port is complete, tighten the right internal bleed valve to 60 inch lbs. (7 Nm).
12. Remove the 3 special combination valve tools.
13. Check the master cylinder fluid level, refilling as necessary.
14. Bleed the individual brake circuits at each wheel. Again, please refer to the hydraulic brake bleeding procedure located earlier in this section.
15. Switch the ignition **ON** and use the hand scanner tool to perform 3 function tests on the system.
16. Evaluate the brake pedal feel and repeat the bleeding procedure if it is not firm.
17. Carefully test drive the vehicle at moderate speeds; check for proper pedal feel and brake operation. If any problem is noted in feel or function, repeat the entire bleeding procedure.

Component Replacement

SYSTEM FILLING

The master cylinder reservoirs must be kept properly filled to prevent air from entering the system. No special filling procedures are required because of the anti-lock system.

When adding fluid, use only DOT 3 fluid; the use of DOT 5 or silicone fluids is specifically prohibited. Use of improper or contaminated fluid may cause the fluid to boil or cause the rubber components in the system to deteriorate. Never use any fluid with a petroleum base or any fluid which has been exposed to water or moisture.

EHCU MODULE

The EHCU module is not serviceable and must never be disassembled or repaired. If tests indicate the unit is faulty, the entire assembly must be replaced.

1. Tag and disconnect the brake lines from the bottom of the combination valve. Plug the openings to prevent brake system contamination or excessive fluid loss.
2. Detach the combination valve electrical connector.
3. Tag and disconnect the brake lines from the EHCU. Immediately cap or plug all openings to prevent system contamination or excessive fluid loss.
4. Tag and disengage the electrical connectors from the EHCU.
5. Unfasten the retainers holding the EHCU upper bracket to the lower bracket and vehicle. Remove the upper bracket and hydraulic unit as an assembly.
6. If necessary, once they are removed from the vehicle, separate the bracket from the EHCU.

To install:
7. If removed, assemble the EHCU to its bracket. Install the retainers and tighten to 60 inch lbs. (7 Nm). Be careful as overtightening these bolts can cause excessive noise transfer during system operation.
8. Install the assembly into the vehicle, then tighten the retainers to 33 ft. lbs. (45 Nm).
9. Engage the electrical connectors as tagged during removal. Make certain each is squarely seated and secure.
10. Remove the caps or plugs, then connect the brake lines to their original locations, as tagged during removal. Tighten the fittings to 16 ft. lbs. (25 Nm).
11. Attach the electrical connector to the combination valve, then unplug and attach the brake lines to the bottom of the combination valve. Tighten the brake line fittings to 15 ft. lbs. (20 Nm).
12. Properly bleed the hydraulic brake system, including the EHCU module.

FRONT WHEEL SPEED SENSORS

▶ **See Figure 87**

1. Raise and support the front of the vehicle safely using jackstands.
2. Remove the tire and wheel assembly.
3. Remove the brake caliper from the mounting bracket and support aside from the suspension using a coat hanger or wire. Make sure the brake line is not stretched, kinked or otherwise damaged. The line should NEVER support the weight of the caliper.
4. Remove the brake rotor/disc (please refer to the procedure earlier in this section), then remove the hub and bearing assembly. For details on hub and bearing removal, please refer to the steering knuckle procedure in Section 8 of this manual.
5. Disengage the sensor wiring connector.
6. Disconnect the sensor wire from the clip(s) on the upper control arm.

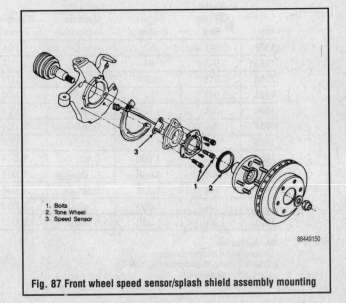

1. Bolts
2. Tone Wheel
3. Speed Sensor

88449150

Fig. 87 Front wheel speed sensor/splash shield assembly mounting

On most vehicles this will involve removing the retaining bolt/nut in order to free the clip, then separating the wire from the clip.

7. Remove the splash shield retaining bolts, then remove the shield and sensor assembly.

To install:

8. Mount the sensor and splash shield assembly to the steering knuckle. Install the retaining bolts and tighten them to 11 ft. lbs. (15 Nm).

9. Connect the wiring to the clip(s) on the upper control arm. Check the wiring for correct routing. If removed, install and tighten the clip retaining bolt/nuts, refer to the illustrations for locations and torque specifications. The wiring on some vehicles/components may be marked at the appropriate clip mounting position, look for a paint stripe on the sensor wire.

10. Engage the wiring connector.
11. Install the hub and bearing assembly.
12. Install the brake rotor (disc).
13. Remove the support, then reposition and secure brake caliper.
14. Install the tire and wheel assembly.
15. Remove the jackstands and carefully lower the vehicle.

REAR WHEEL SPEED SENSORS

▶ See Figures 88 and 89

1. Raise and support the rear of the vehicle safely using jackstands.
2. Remove the tire and wheel assembly.
3. Matchmark and remove the brake drum.
4. Remove the primary brake shoe. For details, please refer to the brake shoe procedure located earlier in this section.
5. Disengage the sensor wiring at the connector.
6. Remove the sensor wire from the rear axle clips.
7. Unfasten the 2 bolts holding the sensor to the brake backing plate, then remove the sensor by carefully tracking the wire through the hole in the backing plate.

To install:

8. Route the wire through the hole in the backing plate and fit the sensor into position.
9. Install the retaining bolts and tighten to 26 ft. lbs. (35 Nm).
10. Secure the sensor wire within the rear axle clips.
11. Engage the sensor wiring to the harness connector.
12. Install the primary brake shoe.
13. Align and install the brake drum.
14. Install the tire and wheel assembly, then remove the jackstands and carefully lower the vehicle.

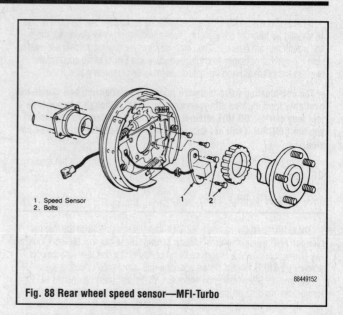

1. Speed Sensor
2. Bolts

88449152

Fig. 88 Rear wheel speed sensor—MFI-Turbo

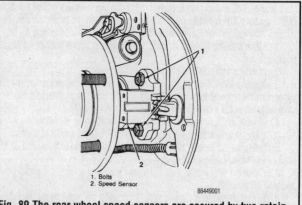

1. Bolts
2. Speed Sensor

88449001

Fig. 89 The rear wheel speed sensors are secured by two retaining bolts

BRAKE SPECIFICATIONS
All measurements in inches unless noted.

Year	Master Cylinder Bore	Brake Disc			Brake Drum Diameter			Minimum Lining Thickness	
		Original Thickness	Minimum Thickness	Maximum Runout	Original Inside Diameter	Max. Wear Limit	Maximum Machine Diameter	Front	Rear
1982	0.945 ①	NA	0.965 ②	0.004	9.45	9.59	9.56	1/32	1/32
1983	0.945 ①	NA	0.965 ②	0.004	9.45	9.59	9.56	1/32	1/32
1984	0.945 ①	NA	0.965 ②	0.004	9.45	9.59	9.56	1/32	1/32
1985	0.945 ①	NA	0.965 ②	0.004	9.45	9.59	9.56	1/32	1/32
1986	NA	1.030	0.965 ③	0.004	9.50	9.59	9.56	1/32	1/32
1987	NA	1.030	0.965 ③	0.004	9.50	9.59	9.56	1/32	1/32
1988	NA	1.030	0.965 ③	0.004	9.50	9.59	9.56	1/32	1/32
1989	NA	1.030	0.965 ③	0.004	9.50	9.59	9.56	1/32	1/32
1990	NA	1.030	0.965 ③	0.004	9.50	9.59	9.56	1/32	1/32
1991	NA	1.030	0.965 ③	0.004	9.50	9.59	9.56	1/32	1/32
1992	NA	1.030	0.965 ③	0.004	9.50	9.59	9.56	1/32	1/32
1993	NA	1.030	0.965 ③	0.003	9.50	9.59	9.56	1/32	1/32

NA—Not available
① Specification is piston diameter
② Specification is discard thickness, DO NOT machine rotor past 0.978
③ Specification is discard thickness, DO NOT machine rotor past 0.980

10

BODY

EXTERIOR

Hood

REMOVAL & INSTALLATION

▶ See Figures 1 and 2

➡**To prevent damage to your vehicle an assistant should be used when attempting to remove or install the hood.**

1. Raise and support the hood, then place protective covers on the fenders.
2. If equipped, disengage the electrical wiring connector from the underhood light.
3. Using a scribing tool or permanent marker, matchmark the area around the hinges to make the installation easier.
4. Support the hood and remove the hinge-to-hood bolts.
5. Remove the hood from the truck.
6. Installation is the reverse of removal. Tighten the hood mounting securely, but do not exceed 18 ft. lbs. (25 Nm).
7. If necessary, adjust the hinges or the bump stops in order to achieve proper hood alignment.

ALIGNMENT

Align the hood so that the gaps between all of the components are equal; it must be flush with the fender and the cowl vent grille. Center the hood in the opening between the fenders, the cowl and the radiator grille. If it is difficult to center the hood or if the hood appears to be out of square, the front end sheet metal may need to be adjusted.

Most of the hood adjustment is achieved through the hinge-bolts, though on some vehicles adjustment may also be obtained through repositioning the striker and/or through the used of bump stops.

Tailgate

REMOVAL & INSTALLATION

▶ See Figures 3, 4 and 5

1. Lower and support the tailgate on a table, pair of saw-horses or an equivalent support. In fact, a willing friend will do here as well, and is usually better company than a table.
2. Remove the left and right-side tailgate-to-fender striker bolts.

➡**On most early model (and some late model) vehicles the striker does not have to be removed, the support link may be slotted for removal from the striker assembly. If so, the support link must usually be bent at the joint in the opposite way from normal extension/installation (normal motion when the tailgate is lowered or raised). In other words, pull up on the middle of the link while partially raising the tailgate. The larger portion of the retaining slot may then be slid over the head of the pivot and removed.**

Fig. 1 Matchmark the hood to the hinges in order to simplify installation

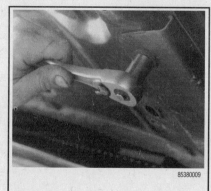

Fig. 2 Hold the hood securely while loosening the mounting bolts

Fig. 3 Some early model tailgates may be disconnected from the striker without removing any retaining bolts

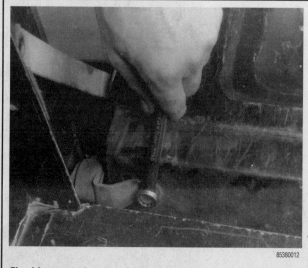

Fig. 4 Loosen and remove the hinge bolts, then remove the tailgate

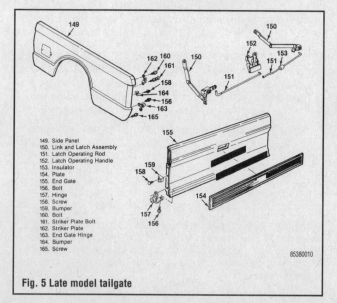

149. Side Panel
150. Link and Latch Assembly
151. Latch Operating Rod
152. Latch Operating Handle
153. Insulator
154. Plate
155. End Gate
156. Bolt
157. Hinge
158. Screw
159. Bumper
160. Bolt
161. Striker Plate Bolt
162. Striker Plate
163. End Gate Hinge
164. Bumper
165. Screw

Fig. 5 Late model tailgate

Fig. 6 To remove the grille, loosen and remove the retainers

Fig. 7 On some early models it may be necessary to remove the headlight bezels or shared bezel retainers for grille removal

Fig. 8 Once the retainers are removed, the grille may be separated from the radiator support

3. Remove the left and right-side tailgate side hinge bolts, then remove the tailgate from the truck.

4. To install, reverse the removal procedures. Torque the tailgate hinge bolts and the striker-to-fender bolts (as applicable) to 20 ft. lbs. (27 Nm).

5. Check for proper tailgate operation.

ALIGNMENT

Align the tailgate so the gaps between all of the components are equal; it must be flush with the fenders. Center the tailgate in the opening between the fenders by adjusting the hinges and/or the striker bolts.

Grille

REMOVAL & INSTALLATION

▶ **See Figures 6, 7 and 8**

1. On early model vehicles with separate grille and headlight bezels, check the sides of the grille to see if any retainers are hidden below or shared with the bezel. If necessary, remove the headlight bezels for access. If there are shared retainers it may be possible to remove only one of the bezels and the shared retainer(s) from the opposite bezel.

2. Loosen and remove the grille-to-fender and grille-to-radiator support retainers.

3. On late model vehicles with composite grille/headlight bezels, pull the grille forward sufficiently and disengage any necessary wiring (such as side marker wiring and bulb sockets).

4. Remove the grille from the vehicle.

5. Installation is the reverse of removal. Be careful not to overtighten any of the fasteners as the grille, bezel and fasteners are all easily damaged. Most fasteners should be tightened to no more than 12 inch lbs. (1.4 Nm).

Outside Mirrors

➡**A damaged mirror glass face may be replaced by placing a large piece or multiple strips of tape over the glass then breaking the mirror face. Adhesive back mirror faces should be available for most applications.**

Removal of outside mirrors is easily accomplished on most vehicles covered in this manual by removing the attaching screws from the anchoring plate and removing the mirror. On some late model vehicles the bolts (studs in this case) are not accessible from the outside and the door trim panel and water deflector must be removed in order to access the retaining nuts. Once the mirror housing is free it may be removed from the door, but make sure there is no power window option or the wiring harness must first be disengaged.

➡**The water deflector is secured by a strip of adhesive between the deflector and door, as well as waterproof sealing tape. Upon installation, make sure a good seal is achieved to keep water from entering into the body. If necessary, use strip caulking as a sealant between the deflector and door.**

Antenna

REMOVAL & INSTALLATION

▶ **See Figure 9**

1. Disconnect the negative battery cable.
2. Remove the mast retaining nut, mast and bezel.
3. Disconnect the antenna cable from the receiver cable.
4. Remove the screw and star washer attaching the antenna to the fender.
5. Remove the antenna.

➡**When installing the antenna to the fender make sure the retaining nut is tight. A loose antenna or one that does not make good contact at the fender can cause radio interference.**

6. Installation is the reverse of removal.

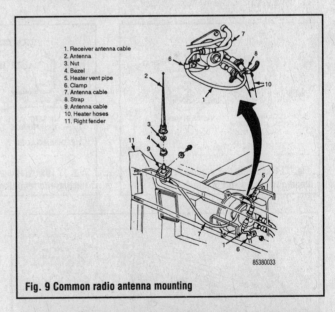

1. Receiver antenna cable
2. Antenna
3. Nut
4. Bezel
5. Heater vent pipe
6. Clamp
7. Antenna cable
8. Strap
9. Antenna cable
10. Heater hoses
11. Right fender

Fig. 9 Common radio antenna mounting

Spare Tire Carrier

REPLACEMENT

1. Raise and support the vehicle safely using jackstands for access.
2. Lower the spare tire and remove it.
3. Remove the cotter pin and bolts attaching the spare tire hoist to the frame.
4. Remove the spare tire hoist.
5. Installation is the reverse of removal. Tighten bolts to 11 ft. lbs. (15 Nm).

INTERIOR

Door Trim Panel

REMOVAL & INSTALLATION

▶ See Figures 10 and 11

➡The following procedure requires the use of the Trim Pad Removal tool No. J-24595 (early models), J-21104 (late models) or equivalent, and the Window Regulator Clip Removal tool No. J-9886-01 or equivalent.

1. Remove the door pillar/garnish molding.
2. Unless equipped with power windows, use a window regulator clip removal tool such as J-9886-01 or equivalent, to remove the window regulator clip and separate the handle from the door.
3. If necessary, remove the door handle bezel-to-door screws and the bezel.
4. Remove the armrest-to-door screws and the armrest.
5. If equipped with power windows, remove/disengage the switch.
6. Using a suitable trim pad removal tool, remove the nylon fasteners from their seats.
7. Installation is the reverse of removal.

Door Locks

REMOVAL & INSTALLATION

▶ See Figures 12, 13, 14, 15 and 16

Door Lock Assembly

1. Remove the door trim panel. For details, please refer to the procedure located earlier in this section.
2. If necessary, remove the water deflector.

➡The water deflector is secured by a strip of adhesive between the deflector and door, as well as waterproof sealing tape. Upon installation, make sure a good seal is achieved to keep water from entering into the body. If necessary, use strip caulking as a sealant between the deflector and door.

3. Remove the lock rods from the inner door handle housing.
4. Remove the outside handle lock rod from the lock assembly.

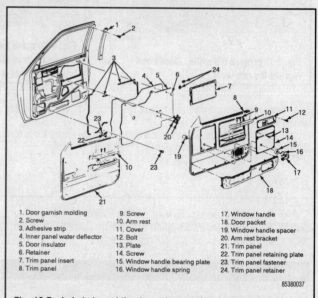

1. Door garnish molding	9. Screw	17. Window handle
2. Screw	10. Arm rest	18. Door packet
3. Adhesive strip	11. Cover	19. Window handle spacer
4. Inner panel water deflector	12. Bolt	20. Arm rest bracket
5. Door insulator	13. Plate	21. Trim panel
6. Retainer	14. Screw	22. Trim panel retaining plate
7. Trim panel insert	15. Window handle bearing plate	23. Trim panel fastener
8. Trim panel	16. Window handle spring	24. Trim panel retainer

85380037

Fig. 10 Exploded view of the door trim panel and related components—early model shown (late model similar)

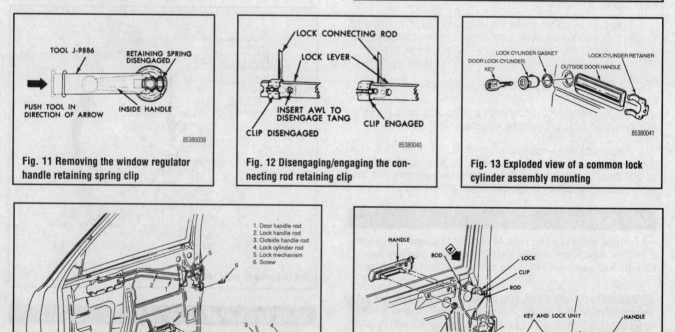

Fig. 11 Removing the window regulator handle retaining spring clip

Fig. 12 Disengaging/engaging the connecting rod retaining clip

Fig. 13 Exploded view of a common lock cylinder assembly mounting

Fig. 14 View of a common door lock assembly and components

Fig. 15 Exploded view of the early model outside door handle/lock assembly

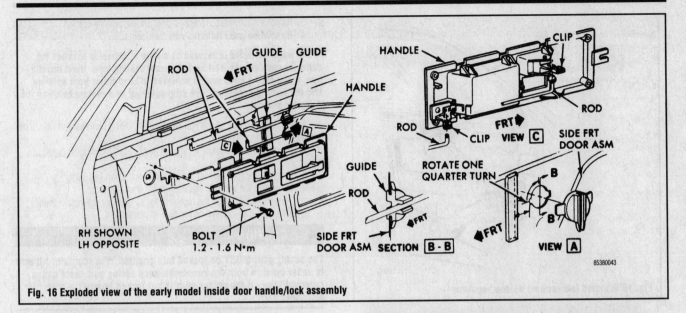

Fig. 16 Exploded view of the early model inside door handle/lock assembly

5. Remove the lock cylinder rod from the lock cylinder.

6. Remove the lock assembly-to-door retaining screws, then remove the assembly from the door.

7. Installation is the reverse of removal. Be sure to check the operation of the lock assembly before installing the door water deflector (if equipped) and trim panel.

Lock Cylinder Assembly

1. Remove the door trim panel. For details, please refer to the procedure located earlier in this section.

2. For early model vehicles, remove the armrest bracket-to-door screws and the bracket from the door.

3. Remove the water deflector (if equipped) and roll up the window.

➡The water deflector is secured by a strip of adhesive between the deflector and door, as well as waterproof sealing tape. Upon installation, make sure a good seal is achieved to keep water from entering into the body. If necessary, use strip caulking as a sealant between the deflector and door.

4. Disconnect the actuator rod from the lock cylinder.

➡On some late model vehicles, it may be easier to remove the lock cylinder retainer, then disconnect the linkage.

5. Remove the lock cylinder-to-door retainer, then remove the lock cylinder and seal from the door.

6. Installation is the reverse of removal. Check the operation of the lock cylinder before installing the water deflector (if equipped) and the door trim panel.

Door Glass and Regulator

REMOVAL & INSTALLATION

▶ See Figures 17, 18 and 19

❊❊ CAUTION

Always wear heavy gloves when handling glass to minimize the risk of injury.

Door Glass

1. Remove the door trim panel. For details, please refer to the procedure located earlier in this section.

2. Remove the armrest bracket-to-door screws and the bracket.

3. Remove the water deflector from the door.

➡The water deflector is secured by a strip of adhesive between the deflector and door, as well as waterproof sealing tape. Upon installation, make sure a good seal is achieved to keep water from entering into the body. If necessary, use strip caulking as a sealant between the deflector and door.

4. Lower the window until it and the sash channel can be seen in the door panel opening, then remove the sash assembly-to-window bolts.

5. Remove the sash assembly and the window from the door.

➡On some late model vehicles it may be necessary to remove the sash assembly, then cut the clips from the glass in order to remove the glass from the door. If this is done, new clips must be installed on the glass before it is lowered into the door and rotated into the run channel.

6. Installation is the reverse of removal. Check for proper window operation before installing the water deflector and trim panel.

Door Regulator

1. Remove the door trim panel. For details, please refer to the procedure earlier in this section.

2. Remove the armrest bracket-to-door screws and the bracket.

3. Remove the water deflector from the door.

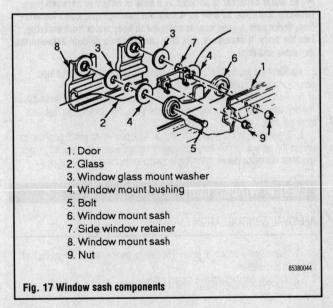

1. Door
2. Glass
3. Window glass mount washer
4. Window mount bushing
5. Bolt
6. Window mount sash
7. Side window retainer
8. Window mount sash
9. Nut

Fig. 17 Window sash components

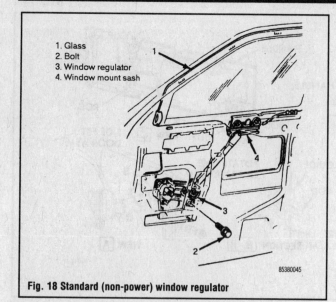

1. Glass
2. Bolt
3. Window regulator
4. Window mount sash

Fig. 18 Standard (non-power) window regulator

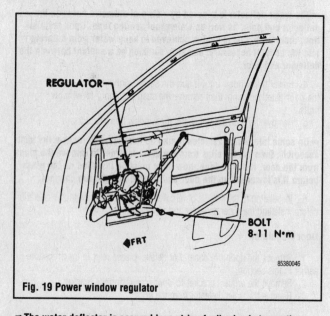

REGULATOR

←FRT

BOLT
8-11 N•m

Fig. 19 Power window regulator

➡The water deflector is secured by a strip of adhesive between the deflector and door, as well as waterproof sealing tape. Upon installation, make sure a good seal is achieved to keep water from entering into the body. If necessary, use strip caulking as a sealant between the deflector and door.

4. Raise the window to the Full Up position. Using cloth backed tape, securely tape the glass to the door frame.

5. Remove the regulator-to-door bolts or rivets (as applicable) and separate the regulator lift arm roller from the window sash, then remove the regulator from the door.

6. Installation is the reverse of removal. Use new rivets (when applicable) unless the service kit contains replacement bolts. Be sure to check for proper regulator operation before installing the water deflector and trim panel.

Electric Window Motor

REMOVAL & INSTALLATION

1. Remove the door trim panel. For details, please refer to the procedure earlier in this section.

2. Disconnect the negative battery cable.

3. Remove the armrest bracket-to-door screws and the bracket.

4. Remove the water deflector from the door.

➡The water deflector is secured by a strip of adhesive between the deflector and door, as well as waterproof sealing tape. Upon installation, make sure a good seal is achieved to keep water from entering into the body. If necessary, use strip caulking as a sealant between the deflector and door.

5. Raise the window to the Full Up position. Using cloth backed tape, tape the glass to the door frame.

6. Disengage the electrical wiring connector from the window regulator motor.

7. Separate the regulator lift arm roller from the window sash.

8. To remove the window regulator motor from the door:

a. Drill a hole through the regulator sector gear and backplate, then install a bolt/nut to lock the sector gear in position.

✳✳ CAUTION

The sector gear MUST be locked into position. The regulator lift arm is under tension from the counterbalance spring and could cause personal injury if the sector gear is not locked before the motor is disconnected.

b. Using a $\frac{3}{16}$ in. (5mm) drill bit, drill out the motor-to-door rivets.

c. Remove the motor from the door.

To install:

9. Position the motor to the regulator, then secure using $\frac{3}{16}$ in. (4.8mm) rivets.

10. After the motor is riveted to the door, remove the nut/bolt from the sector gear.

11. Install the regulator lift arm roller to the window mount sash.

12. The balance of installation is the reverse of removal. It is usually wise to check operation of the system before installing the water deflector and trim panel.

Windshield and Fixed Glass

REMOVAL & INSTALLATION

If your windshield, or other fixed window, is cracked or chipped, you may decide to replace it with a new one yourself. However, there are two main reasons why replacement windshields and other window glass should be installed only by a professional automotive glass technician: safety and cost.

The most important reason a professional should install automotive glass is for safety. The glass in the vehicle, especially the windshield, is designed with safety in mind in case of a collision. The windshield is specially manufactured from two panes of specially-tempered glass with a thin layer of transparent plastic between them. This construction allows the glass to "give" in the event that a part of your body hits the windshield during the collision, and prevents the glass from shattering, which could cause lacerations, blinding and other harm to passengers of the vehicle. The other fixed windows are designed to be tempered so that if they break during a collision, they shatter in such a way that there are no large pointed glass pieces. The professional automotive glass technician knows how to install the glass in a vehicle so that it will function optimally during a collision. Without the proper experience, knowledge and tools, installing a piece of automotive glass yourself could lead to additional harm if an accident should ever occur.

Cost is also a factor when deciding to install automotive glass yourself. Performing this could cost you much more than a professional may charge for the same job. Since the windshield is designed to break under stress, an often life saving characteristic, windshields tend to break VERY easily when an inexperienced person attempts to install one. Do-it-yourselfers buying two, three or even four windshields from a salvage yard because they have broken them during installation are common stories. Also, since the automotive glass is designed to prevent the outside elements from entering your vehicle, improper installation can lead to water and air leaks. Annoying whining noises at highway speeds from air leaks or inside body panel rusting from water leaks can add to your stress level and subtract from your wallet. After buying two or three windshields, installing them and ending up with a leak that produces a noise while driving and water damage during rainstorms, the cost of having a professional do it correctly the first time may be much more alluring. We here at Chilton, therefore, advise that you have a professional automotive glass technician service any broken glass on your vehicle.

WINDSHIELD CHIP REPAIR

▶ **See Figures 20 and 21**

➡**Check with your state and local authorities on the laws for state safety inspection. Some states or municipalities may not allow chip repair as a viable option for correcting stone damage to your windshield.**

Although severely cracked or damaged windshields must be replaced, there is something that you can do to prolong or even prevent the need for replacement of a chipped windshield. There are many companies which offer windshield chip repair products, such as Loctite's® Bullseye™ windshield repair kit. These kits usually consist of a syringe, pedestal and a sealing adhesive. The syringe is mounted on the pedestal and is used to create a vacuum which pulls the plastic layer against the glass. This helps make the chip transparent. The adhesive is then injected which seals the chip and helps to prevent further stress cracks from developing

➡**Always follow the specific manufacturer's instructions.**

Inside Rear View Mirror

REPLACEMENT

▶ **See Figure 22**

1. Determine the location of the rear view mirror and using a wax pencil, draw a centerline on the outside of the glass from the roof panel to the windshield base.
2. Draw a line intersecting the centerline approximately 23 1/8 in. (587mm) from the base of the glass. The base of the support will be located at the intersection of these lines.
3. Clean the inside glass within 3 in. (76mm) of the intersecting lines. Using a glass cleaning solution rub the area until completely dry. Reclean with a towel saturated with alcohol.
4. Sand the bonding surface of the rear view mirror support with 320 grit sandpaper. Remove all traces of the factory adhesive if reusing the old support. Wipe the mirror support with alcohol and allow to dry.

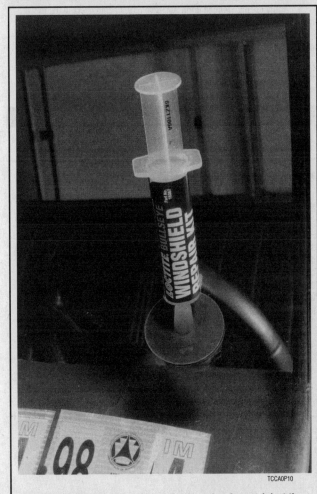
Fig. 21 Most kits us a self-stick applicator and syringe to inject the adhesive into the chip or crack

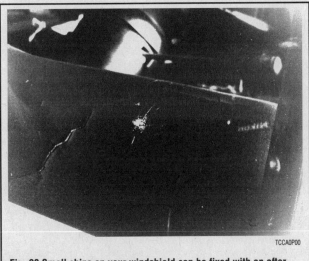
Fig. 20 Small chips on your windshield can be fixed with an aftermarket repair kit, such as the one from Loctite®

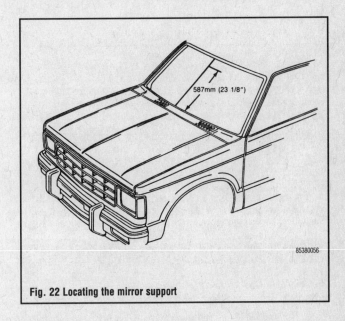
Fig. 22 Locating the mirror support

5. Apply Loctite® Minute Bond Adhesive 312, or equivalent to the mirror support bonding surfaces.

6. Place the bottom of the support at the premarked line. The rounded edge of the support should face upward.

7. Press the support against the glass for 30–60 seconds with a steady pressure. Allow the adhesive to dry 5 minutes before cleaning.

8. Clean all traces of adhesive and wax from the windshield with alcohol.

Seats

REMOVAL & INSTALLATION

◆ **See Figures 23 and 24**

Most vehicles covered by this manual are equipped with bench seats. Removal of the bench seat assembly is a relatively simple process. Locate and remove the retainers (usually nuts), then carefully lift the seat from the brackets.

Some vehicles (such as the MFI-Turbo and some other later model trucks) may be equipped with manual or power bucket seats. Removal of a bucket seat is also a relatively simple process, once you find the retainers. On some vehicles you will have to remove the lower trim panels which are used to hide the brackets. Also, power seats will have one or more electrical wiring connectors which must be disengaged before attempting to remove the seat. Once the fasteners are removed and any wiring has been disconnected, lift the bucket seat from the brackets.

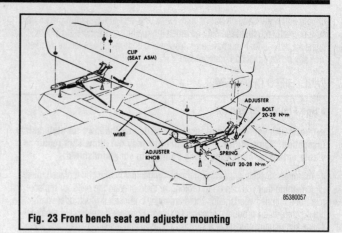

Fig. 23 Front bench seat and adjuster mounting

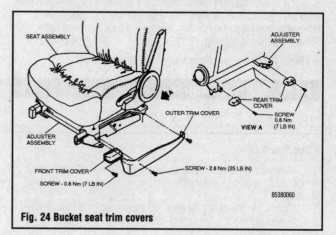

Fig. 24 Bucket seat trim covers

GLOSSARY

AIR/FUEL RATIO: The ratio of air-to-gasoline by weight in the fuel mixture drawn into the engine.

AIR INJECTION: One method of reducing harmful exhaust emissions by injecting air into each of the exhaust ports of an engine. The fresh air entering the hot exhaust manifold causes any remaining fuel to be burned before it can exit the tailpipe.

ALTERNATOR: A device used for converting mechanical energy into electrical energy.

AMMETER: An instrument, calibrated in amperes, used to measure the flow of an electrical current in a circuit. Ammeters are always connected in series with the circuit being tested.

AMPERE: The rate of flow of electrical current present when one volt of electrical pressure is applied against one ohm of electrical resistance.

ANALOG COMPUTER: Any microprocessor that uses similar (analogous) electrical signals to make its calculations.

ARMATURE: A laminated, soft iron core wrapped by a wire that converts electrical energy to mechanical energy as in a motor or relay. When rotated in a magnetic field, it changes mechanical energy into electrical energy as in a generator.

ATMOSPHERIC PRESSURE: The pressure on the Earth's surface caused by the weight of the air in the atmosphere. At sea level, this pressure is 14.7 psi at 32°F (101 kPa at 0°C).

ATOMIZATION: The breaking down of a liquid into a fine mist that can be suspended in air.

AXIAL PLAY: Movement parallel to a shaft or bearing bore.

BACKFIRE: The sudden combustion of gases in the intake or exhaust system that results in a loud explosion.

BACKLASH: The clearance or play between two parts, such as meshed gears.

BACKPRESSURE: Restrictions in the exhaust system that slow the exit of exhaust gases from the combustion chamber.

BAKELITE: A heat resistant, plastic insulator material commonly used in printed circuit boards and transistorized components.

BALL BEARING: A bearing made up of hardened inner and outer races between which hardened steel balls roll.

BALLAST RESISTOR: A resistor in the primary ignition circuit that lowers voltage after the engine is started to reduce wear on ignition components.

BEARING: A friction reducing, supportive device usually located between a stationary part and a moving part.

BIMETAL TEMPERATURE SENSOR: Any sensor or switch made of two dissimilar types of metal that bend when heated or cooled due to the different expansion rates of the alloys. These types of sensors usually function as an on/off switch.

BLOWBY: Combustion gases, composed of water vapor and unburned fuel, that leak past the piston rings into the crankcase during normal engine operation. These gases are removed by the PCV system to prevent the buildup of harmful acids in the crankcase.

BRAKE PAD: A brake shoe and lining assembly used with disc brakes.

BRAKE SHOE: The backing for the brake lining. The term is, however, usually applied to the assembly of the brake backing and lining.

BUSHING: A liner, usually removable, for a bearing; an anti-friction liner used in place of a bearing.

CALIPER: A hydraulically activated device in a disc brake system, which is mounted straddling the brake rotor (disc). The caliper contains at least one piston and two brake pads. Hydraulic pressure on the piston(s) forces the pads against the rotor.

CAMSHAFT: A shaft in the engine on which are the lobes (cams) which operate the valves. The camshaft is driven by the crankshaft, via a belt, chain or gears, at one half the crankshaft speed.

CAPACITOR: A device which stores an electrical charge.

CARBON MONOXIDE (CO): A colorless, odorless gas given off as a normal byproduct of combustion. It is poisonous and extremely dangerous in confined areas, building up slowly to toxic levels without warning if adequate ventilation is not available.

CARBURETOR: A device, usually mounted on the intake manifold of an engine, which mixes the air and fuel in the proper proportion to allow even combustion.

CATALYTIC CONVERTER: A device installed in the exhaust system, like a muffler, that converts harmful byproducts of combustion into carbon dioxide and water vapor by means of a heat-producing chemical reaction.

CENTRIFUGAL ADVANCE: A mechanical method of advancing the spark timing by using flyweights in the distributor that react to centrifugal force generated by the distributor shaft rotation.

CHECK VALVE: Any one-way valve installed to permit the flow of air, fuel or vacuum in one direction only.

CHOKE: A device, usually a moveable valve, placed in the intake path of a carburetor to restrict the flow of air.

CIRCUIT: Any unbroken path through which an electrical current can flow. Also used to describe fuel flow in some instances.

CIRCUIT BREAKER: A switch which protects an electrical circuit from overload by opening the circuit when the current flow exceeds a predetermined level. Some circuit breakers must be reset manually, while most reset automatically.

COIL (IGNITION): A transformer in the ignition circuit which steps up the voltage provided to the spark plugs.

COMBINATION MANIFOLD: An assembly which includes both the intake and exhaust manifolds in one casting.

COMBINATION VALVE: A device used in some fuel systems that routes fuel vapors to a charcoal storage canister instead of venting them into the atmosphere. The valve relieves fuel tank pressure and allows fresh air into the tank as the fuel level drops to prevent a vapor lock situation.

COMPRESSION RATIO: The comparison of the total volume of the cylinder and combustion chamber with the piston at BDC and the piston at TDC.

CONDENSER: 1. An electrical device which acts to store an electrical charge, preventing voltage surges. 2. A radiator-like device in the air conditioning system in which refrigerant gas condenses into a liquid, giving off heat.

CONDUCTOR: Any material through which an electrical current can be transmitted easily.

CONTINUITY: Continuous or complete circuit. Can be checked with an ohmmeter.

COUNTERSHAFT: An intermediate shaft which is rotated by a mainshaft and transmits, in turn, that rotation to a working part.

CRANKCASE: The lower part of an engine in which the crankshaft and related parts operate.

CRANKSHAFT: The main driving shaft of an engine which receives reciprocating motion from the pistons and converts it to rotary motion.

CYLINDER: In an engine, the round hole in the engine block in which the piston(s) ride.

CYLINDER BLOCK: The main structural member of an engine in which is found the cylinders, crankshaft and other principal parts.

CYLINDER HEAD: The detachable portion of the engine, usually fastened to the top of the cylinder block and containing all or most of the combustion chambers. On overhead valve engines, it contains the valves and their operating parts. On overhead cam engines, it contains the camshaft as well.

DEAD CENTER: The extreme top or bottom of the piston stroke.

DETONATION: An unwanted explosion of the air/fuel mixture in the combustion chamber caused by excess heat and compression, advanced timing, or an overly lean mixture. Also referred to as "ping".

DIAPHRAGM: A thin, flexible wall separating two cavities, such as in a vacuum advance unit.

DIESELING: A condition in which hot spots in the combustion chamber cause the engine to run on after the key is turned off.

DIFFERENTIAL: A geared assembly which allows the transmission of motion between drive axles, giving one axle the ability to turn faster than the other.

DIODE: An electrical device that will allow current to flow in one direction only.

DISC BRAKE: A hydraulic braking assembly consisting of a brake disc, or rotor, mounted on an axle, and a caliper assembly containing, usually two brake pads which are activated by hydraulic pressure. The pads are forced against the sides of the disc, creating friction which slows the vehicle.

DISTRIBUTOR: A mechanically driven device on an engine which is responsible for electrically firing the spark plug at a predetermined point of the piston stroke.

DOWEL PIN: A pin, inserted in mating holes in two different parts allowing those parts to maintain a fixed relationship.

DRUM BRAKE: A braking system which consists of two brake shoes and one or two wheel cylinders, mounted on a fixed backing plate, and a brake drum, mounted on an axle, which revolves around the assembly.

DWELL: The rate, measured in degrees of shaft rotation, at which an electrical circuit cycles on and off.

ELECTRONIC CONTROL UNIT (ECU): Ignition module, module, amplifier or igniter. See Module for definition.

ELECTRONIC IGNITION: A system in which the timing and firing of the spark plugs is controlled by an electronic control unit, usually called a module. These systems have no points or condenser.

END-PLAY: The measured amount of axial movement in a shaft.

ENGINE: A device that converts heat into mechanical energy.

EXHAUST MANIFOLD: A set of cast passages or pipes which conduct exhaust gases from the engine.

FEELER GAUGE: A blade, usually metal, or precisely predetermined thickness, used to measure the clearance between two parts.

FIRING ORDER: The order in which combustion occurs in the cylinders of an engine. Also the order in which spark is distributed to the plugs by the distributor.

FLOODING: The presence of too much fuel in the intake manifold and combustion chamber which prevents the air/fuel mixture from firing, thereby causing a no-start situation.

FLYWHEEL: A disc shaped part bolted to the rear end of the crankshaft. Around the outer perimeter is affixed the ring gear. The starter drive engages the ring gear, turning the flywheel, which rotates the crankshaft, imparting the initial starting motion to the engine.

FOOT POUND (ft. lbs. or sometimes, ft.lb.): The amount of energy or work needed to raise an item weighing one pound, a distance of one foot.

FUSE: A protective device in a circuit which prevents circuit overload by breaking the circuit when a specific amperage is present. The device is constructed around a strip or wire of a lower amperage rating than the circuit it is designed to protect. When an amperage higher than that stamped on the fuse is present in the circuit, the strip or wire melts, opening the circuit.

GEAR RATIO: The ratio between the number of teeth on meshing gears.

GENERATOR: A device which converts mechanical energy into electrical energy.

HEAT RANGE: The measure of a spark plug's ability to dissipate heat from its firing end. The higher the heat range, the hotter the plug fires.

HUB: The center part of a wheel or gear.

HYDROCARBON (HC): Any chemical compound made up of hydrogen and carbon. A major pollutant formed by the engine as a byproduct of combustion.

HYDROMETER: An instrument used to measure the specific gravity of a solution.

INCH POUND (inch lbs.; sometimes in.lb. or in. lbs.): One twelfth of a foot pound.

INDUCTION: A means of transferring electrical energy in the form of a magnetic field. Principle used in the ignition coil to increase voltage.

INJECTOR: A device which receives metered fuel under relatively low pressure and is activated to inject the fuel into the engine under relatively high pressure at a predetermined time.

INPUT SHAFT: The shaft to which torque is applied, usually carrying the driving gear or gears.

INTAKE MANIFOLD: A casting of passages or pipes used to conduct air or a fuel/air mixture to the cylinders.

JOURNAL: The bearing surface within which a shaft operates.

KEY: A small block usually fitted in a notch between a shaft and a hub to prevent slippage of the two parts.

MANIFOLD: A casting of passages or set of pipes which connect the cylinders to an inlet or outlet source.

MANIFOLD VACUUM: Low pressure in an engine intake manifold formed just below the throttle plates. Manifold vacuum is highest at idle and drops under acceleration.

MASTER CYLINDER: The primary fluid pressurizing device in a hydraulic system. In automotive use, it is found in brake and hydraulic clutch systems and is pedal activated, either directly or, in a power brake system, through the power booster.

MODULE: Electronic control unit, amplifier or igniter of solid state or integrated design which controls the current flow in the ignition primary circuit based on input from the pick-up coil. When the module opens the primary circuit, high secondary voltage is induced in the coil.

NEEDLE BEARING: A bearing which consists of a number (usually a large number) of long, thin rollers.

OHM: (Ω) The unit used to measure the resistance of conductor-to-electrical flow. One ohm is the amount of resistance that limits current flow to one ampere in a circuit with one volt of pressure.

OHMMETER: An instrument used for measuring the resistance, in ohms, in an electrical circuit.

OUTPUT SHAFT: The shaft which transmits torque from a device, such as a transmission.

OVERDRIVE: A gear assembly which produces more shaft revolutions than that transmitted to it.

OVERHEAD CAMSHAFT (OHC): An engine configuration in which the camshaft is mounted on top of the cylinder head and operates the valve either directly or by means of rocker arms.

OVERHEAD VALVE (OHV): An engine configuration in which all of the valves are located in the cylinder head and the camshaft is located in the cylinder block. The camshaft operates the valves via lifters and pushrods.

OXIDES OF NITROGEN (NOx): Chemical compounds of nitrogen produced as a byproduct of combustion. They combine with hydrocarbons to produce smog.

OXYGEN SENSOR: Use with the feedback system to sense the presence of oxygen in the exhaust gas and signal the computer which can reference the voltage signal to an air/fuel ratio.

PINION: The smaller of two meshing gears.

PISTON RING: An open-ended ring with fits into a groove on the outer diameter of the piston. Its chief function is to form a seal between the piston and cylinder wall. Most automotive pistons have three rings: two for compression sealing; one for oil sealing.

PRELOAD: A predetermined load placed on a bearing during assembly or by adjustment.

PRIMARY CIRCUIT: the low voltage side of the ignition system which consists of the ignition switch, ballast resistor or resistance wire, bypass, coil, electronic control unit and pick-up coil as well as the connecting wires and harnesses.

PRESS FIT: The mating of two parts under pressure, due to the inner diameter of one being smaller than the outer diameter of the other, or vice versa; an interference fit.

RACE: The surface on the inner or outer ring of a bearing on which the balls, needles or rollers move.

REGULATOR: A device which maintains the amperage and/or voltage levels of a circuit at predetermined values.

RELAY: A switch which automatically opens and/or closes a circuit.

RESISTANCE: The opposition to the flow of current through a circuit or electrical device, and is measured in ohms. Resistance is equal to the voltage divided by the amperage.

RESISTOR: A device, usually made of wire, which offers a preset amount of resistance in an electrical circuit.

RING GEAR: The name given to a ring-shaped gear attached to a differential case, or affixed to a flywheel or as part of a planetary gear set.

ROLLER BEARING: A bearing made up of hardened inner and outer races between which hardened steel rollers move.

ROTOR: 1. The disc-shaped part of a disc brake assembly, upon which the brake pads bear; also called, brake disc. 2. The device mounted atop the distributor shaft, which passes current to the distributor cap tower contacts.

SECONDARY CIRCUIT: The high voltage side of the ignition system, usually above 20,000 volts. The secondary includes the ignition coil, coil wire, distributor cap and rotor, spark plug wires and spark plugs.

SENDING UNIT: A mechanical, electrical, hydraulic or electro-magnetic device which transmits information to a gauge.

SENSOR: Any device designed to measure engine operating conditions or ambient pressures and temperatures. Usually electronic in nature and designed to send a voltage signal to an on-board computer, some sensors may operate as a simple on/off switch or they may provide a variable voltage signal (like a potentiometer) as conditions or measured parameters change.

SHIM: Spacers of precise, predetermined thickness used between parts to establish a proper working relationship.

SLAVE CYLINDER: In automotive use, a device in the hydraulic clutch system which is activated by hydraulic force, disengaging the clutch.

SOLENOID: A coil used to produce a magnetic field, the effect of which is to produce work.

SPARK PLUG: A device screwed into the combustion chamber of a spark ignition engine. The basic construction is a conductive core inside of a ceramic insulator, mounted in an outer conductive base. An electrical charge from the spark plug wire travels along the conductive core and jumps a preset air gap to a grounding point or points at the end of the conductive base. The resultant spark ignites the fuel/air mixture in the combustion chamber.

SPLINES: Ridges machined or cast onto the outer diameter of a shaft or inner diameter of a bore to enable parts to mate without rotation.

TACHOMETER: A device used to measure the rotary speed of an engine, shaft, gear, etc., usually in rotations per minute.

THERMOSTAT: A valve, located in the cooling system of an engine, which is closed when cold and opens gradually in response to engine heating, controlling the temperature of the coolant and rate of coolant flow.

TOP DEAD CENTER (TDC): The point at which the piston reaches the top of its travel on the compression stroke.

TORQUE: The twisting force applied to an object.

TORQUE CONVERTER: A turbine used to transmit power from a driving member to a driven member via hydraulic action, providing changes in drive ratio and torque. In automotive use, it links the driveplate at the rear of the engine to the automatic transmission.

TRANSDUCER: A device used to change a force into an electrical signal.

TRANSISTOR: A semi-conductor component which can be actuated by a small voltage to perform an electrical switching function.

TUNE-UP: A regular maintenance function, usually associated with the replacement and adjustment of parts and components in the electrical and fuel systems of a vehicle for the purpose of attaining optimum performance.

TURBOCHARGER: An exhaust driven pump which compresses intake air and forces it into the combustion chambers at higher than atmospheric pressures. The increased air pressure allows more fuel to be burned and results in increased horsepower being produced.

VACUUM ADVANCE: A device which advances the ignition timing in response to increased engine vacuum.

VACUUM GAUGE: An instrument used to measure the presence of vacuum in a chamber.

VALVE: A device which control the pressure, direction of flow or rate of flow of a liquid or gas.

VALVE CLEARANCE: The measured gap between the end of the valve stem and the rocker arm, cam lobe or follower that activates the valve.

VISCOSITY: The rating of a liquid's internal resistance to flow.

VOLTMETER: An instrument used for measuring electrical force in units called volts. Voltmeters are always connected parallel with the circuit being tested.

WHEEL CYLINDER: Found in the automotive drum brake assembly, it is a device, actuated by hydraulic pressure, which, through internal pistons, pushes the brake shoes outward against the drums.

MASTER

INDEX